THE BEST OF BASEBALL DIGEST

The Best of

Baseball Digest

THE GREATEST PLAYERS,
THE GREATEST GAMES,
THE GREATEST WRITERS
FROM BASEBALL'S MOST
EXCITING YEARS

EDITED WITH AN
INTRODUCTION BY

JOHN KUENSTER

 IVAN R. DEE, CHICAGO

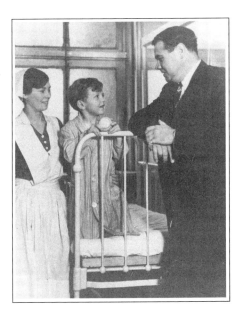

www.ivanrdee.com

Library of Congress Cataloging-in-Publication Data:
Kuenster, John.
  The best of baseball digest / John Kuenster.
     p. cm.
  Includes index.
  ISBN 1-56663-655-8 (cloth : alk. paper)
  1. Baseball—United States—History. 2. Baseball—United
States—Miscellanea. I. Baseball digest. II. Title.
  GV863.A1K845 2006
  797.357—dc22   2005020683

To all fans who enjoy the game and savor its history

as their life journey lengthens

Contents

Introduction

Capturing the allure of baseball in a few words might be like catching a butterfly in flight without a net. It can be done, but it isn't easy.

Perhaps the legendary manager Casey Stengel and the equally legendary baseball writer Red Smith can help us out.

"I've had many years that I was not so successful as a ballplayer," Stengel once said, "as it was a game of skill."

"Ninety feet between bases," Smith wrote, "is perhaps as close as man has ever come to perfection."

Two simple statements, but they both touch on the core of a game that has engrossed millions of fans, young and old, generation after generation, since the nineteenth century.

Baseball at the major league level undeniably requires, as Stengel intimated, special skills for a player to excel in hitting, pitching, fielding, and base running. And, as Smith suggested so adroitly, its measurements between bases—as well as from the pitcher's mound to home plate—sharpen competition to its finest edge.

But of course there are other factors that add to the game's magnetism. A player doesn't have to be a huge physical specimen to be a winner. Willie Keeler stood only five feet, four and a half inches tall, and he was elected to the Hall of Fame. So was Joe Morgan, who reaches five feet seven.

There's also the fact that the game is played mostly in warm-weather months, a time of relaxation for many of its followers. It features rich green playing surfaces and fan-friendly ballparks. It embraces both long-time continuity in its basic rules and unpredictability in any single game—regular season, playoff, or World Series. As Yogi Berra might add about the surprises that can happen: "It ain't over till it's over."

Finally, baseball's generally leisurely pace allows spectators, especially between innings and during pitching changes, to talk among themselves, dissecting a manager's moves, griping about an umpire's call, celebrating a hometown hero.

Baseball has cultivated deep literary roots, and mention of the game can be found in many of the most highly acclaimed works of American writers, including the novels of F. Scott Fitzgerald and Ernest Hemingway. In *The Great Gatsby*, Fitzgerald quotes his central character in describing a third man to an associate: "He's a gambler." Gatsby hesitated, and then added cooly, "He's the man who fixed the World Series back in 1919."

In *The Old Man and the Sea*, Hemingway writes about Santiago, the Cuban fisherman who endures an agonizing battle with a giant marlin far out in the Gulf Stream. Before he heads out to sea, he says: "The Yankees cannot lose. Have faith in the Yankees, my son. Think of the great DiMaggio. I would like to take the great DiMaggio fishing."

Fitzgerald's book was published in 1925, Hemingway's in 1952, indicating how the interest in baseball spans eras, from the Jazz Age to the conforming Eisenhower Years to the current time of awesome technology that offers cell phones and Mars explorations.

Through its appeal to the masses, the game has become thoroughly embedded in American culture and along the way has stimulated a vast amount of literature that explores its players and teams, its "joys of victory and agonies of defeat," its tragedies, its unexpected outcomes, and its sometimes wacky humor.

Since its founding in 1942, *Baseball Digest* has continuously published articles about the game's history, including such dark episodes as the 1919 Black Sox scandal and such bright moments as Jackie Robinson's courageous demeanor in breaking down racial barriers in 1947.

In assembling material for this book, however, there's been no intent to cover every important event or personality or twist of capricious fate that has enriched the sport since its beginning. Rather, we have aimed to provide a few dashes of literary seasoning in a convenient collection, hoping to bring a little enjoyment and enlightenment to younger readers while arousing the favorite memories of older fans.

As the founding publisher and editor of *Baseball Digest*, Herb Simons set standards that enabled the magazine to grow into a welcomed source of information for serious as well as casual fans. A meticulous craftsman when it came to fashioning a story line or compiling statistics, Simons died in 1968 at the age of 60 after a brief illness. Since 1928 he had been a baseball writer for the *Chicago Journal* and its successor, the *Chicago Daily*

Times. At his passing he held membership card No. 12 in the Baseball Writers Association of America, attesting to his seniority among the nation's chroniclers of the game.

Because he launched *Baseball Digest* in the midst of World War II, Simons faced serious challenges in making a go of his enterprise. The government was directing all its resources and energies to the war effort, and earlier in 1942 there were doubts that the major leagues would be allowed to play that year's season. But President Franklin D. Roosevelt came to the rescue, telling Baseball Commissioner Kenesaw Mountain Landis, "I honestly feel it would be best for the country to keep baseball going."

Still, plans were set in motion for the rationing of vital commodities, including gasoline, and the government was ready to clamp down on the availability of newsprint that Simons needed for his magazine. At first he also had to rely solely on newsstand sales for survival, a roll-of-the-dice venture for him since he was operating with limited capital.

Here's what was happening in 1942: In January, not long after Pearl Harbor, Bob Feller reported for navy duty at Norfolk, Virginia. In March, after first being asked to take a pay cut, Joe DiMaggio signed a contract with the Yankees for $43,750. And in the same month Jackie Robinson worked out for White Sox manager Jimmy Dykes during spring training in Pasadena, California, but no offer was made to assign him to a minor league affiliate.

In May, lights were turned on at Ebbets Field and the Polo Grounds in a test to see if they might reveal focal points for German submarines prowling the Atlantic Ocean off New York City. Later on, the Dodgers and Giants were asked as a precaution to cancel their remaining night games.

Also in May, Ted Williams was sworn into the navy, but he remained with the Red Sox while awaiting his call to report for active duty.

When *Baseball Digest* made its debut in August, Elmer Valo, a Czech-born outfielder with the Philadelphia A's, was pictured on its first cover, a black-and-white creation with a red logo centered on a white baseball. It sold for fifteen cents.

During those weeks in August, Rogers Hornsby, seven-time National League batting champion, entered the Hall of Fame alone. Shortstop Phil Rizzuto and second baseman Joe Gordon executed seven double plays, an American League record, as the Yankees beat the Philadelphia A's, 11-2. And Babe Ruth, 47, and Walter Johnson, 56, briefly returned to the playing field to help raise money for the Army-Navy Relief Fund before 69,136 fans at Yankee Stadium. Ruth hit one of Johnson's pitches into the lower right-field stands for a home run, and after his last at-bat he circled the bases, tipping his cap to the admiring crowd.

As the years passed, *Baseball Digest* gradually increased its circulation, attracting readers from throughout the country. Today it has subscribers living in such distant lands as Japan, Australia, England, France, and Venezuela.

The lifetime of the magazine has paralleled some of the greatest years in the game's history, with covers in the late 1940s, 1950s, and 1960s featuring such Hall of Fame players as DiMaggio, Williams, Feller, Stan Musial, Robin Roberts, Yogi Berra, Whitey Ford, Willie Mays, Mickey Mantle, and Al Kaline. In the 1970s, 1980s, and 1990s, a similar pattern unfolded with such Cooperstown-bound stars as Johnny Bench, Hank Aaron, Reggie Jackson, George Brett, and Ozzie Smith gracing the magazine's covers.

Inside were articles describing the details of some of the special confrontations in baseball history, told from the divergent viewpoints of winners and losers.

In 1951, for example, Andy Pafko of the Dodgers was playing left field in the Polo Grounds when Bobby Thomson hit his "Shot Heard 'Round the World" to win the National League pennant for the Giants. The home run sailed over Pafko's head near the 315-foot marker. Pafko later admitted, "That made me part of a famous trivia question, 'Who was the left fielder who watched Thomson's homer go over the wall?'"

Bill Skowron was playing first base for the Yankees in 1960 when he saw Bill Mazeroski's home run fly out of Forbes Field to win the World Series for Pittsburgh. "When I saw that ball going out," Skowron recalled, "I thought, 'There goes $3,000 over the fence.' That was the difference between the winners' and losers' share in that Series."

Long after he had pitched the only perfect game in World Series history, beating the Dodgers 2-0 in 1956, Don Larsen told *Baseball Digest*, "I didn't even know I was going to pitch in that game until I saw the ball in my locker. I threw mostly fastballs, with some sliders and a few curves. I never had such good control in all my life as I had in that game. That was the secret to my success."

In the 2001 World Series, won by the Diamondbacks over the Yankees in the ninth inning of Game 7, Luis Gonzalez, with the bases loaded, produced the decisive hit against reliever Mariano Rivera by punching a looping ball over Derek Jeter's head to give Arizona a 3-2 victory. Gonzalez had hit 57 homers that season, but he played it smart against Rivera: he choked up on his bat.

"To be honest," he said, "that was the first time I choked up all year. I knew the infield was playing in, and I didn't have to hit it hard."

Through the years *Baseball Digest* has covered them all, winners and losers, Hall of Famers and benchwarmers, nice guys and scoundrels. It has helped readers relive such moments as:

• Willie Mays's superb catch of Vic Wertz's long drive at the Polo Grounds in the 1954 World Series.

• Sandy Amoros robbing Yogi Berra of an extra-base hit that preserved a 2-0 victory for the Brooklyn Dodgers and Johnny Podres in Game 7 of the 1955 World Series.

• Roger Maris slamming his 61st home run off Boston's Tracy Stallard on the final day of the 1961 season, and having to be forced back out of the Yankees dugout by teammates to acknowledge the cheers of the crowd.

• Hank Aaron breaking Babe Ruth's career home run record against Al Downing of the Dodgers in 1974.

• Reggie Jackson hitting three home runs on three swings in Game 6 of the 1977 World Series.

• Kirk Gibson, limping on an injured leg, blasting a home run against Dennis Eckersley on a 3-and-2 pitch to give the Dodgers a 5-4 win over the A's in Game 1 of the 1988 World Series.

• Cal Ripken surpassing Lou Gehrig's long-held record by playing in his 2,131st consecutive game in 1995.

In addition to its articles on players and events, *Baseball Digest* has accumulated a number of distinctions since its birth. It was pioneer in publishing annual rookie reports by all major league clubs, a custom that began in the early 1950s. It launched a popular series entitled "The Game I'll Never Forget," told by the game's leading performers to the prolific writer George Vass. It compiles an annual necrology of former players, managers, executives, and umpires. It continues to feature a regular column on baseball rules. And it introduced a forum for readers— "The Fans Speak Out"—an appetizing section of some twenty-five letters and responses in each issue. The thousands of letters received over the years reveal the tremendous pull baseball has on young and old, doctors, lawyers, merchants, chiefs, blue-collar workers, and, let us not forget, women.

Readers frequently request copies of box scores of the first major league game they saw as kids, usually with a father or uncle or friend. They ask for interpretation of the rules. They have their say on the banning of Pete Rose, or the fairness of Hall of Fame elections, or bad decisions by umpires, or the use of steroids by players, or the employment of a designated hitter in one league and not in the other.

They offer suggestions on how to improve the game. They express criticism as well as thanks, with words of appreciation coming from researchers, from students and teachers, from members of the armed forces overseas, and even from men in prison.

While we have not included any of these letters in this book, perhaps a few random samples can demonstrate how people love to express themselves about baseball:

"I was watching a game last season, and a play was made where the umpire's call was obviously wrong and proven so by the instant replay on TV.

"Why can't each manager have the opportunity to have three close plays reviewed per game in order to have the right calls made?

"Let's leave the balls and strikes alone, just the plays on the field. I think getting the right calls made is fair, not only to the players but to the fans as well."

—Donna Welch, Hooksett, N.H.

"Regarding the recent item in *Baseball Digest* about nicknames for major league players, one for Roberto Clemente was not mentioned.

"Roberto was called 'Mome' by anybody who knew him during his amateur years with the Juncos Mules team in Puerto Rico, first as a shortstop and later as a center fielder.

"The nickname was originated by his sister, but has no special meaning."

—Luis Soltero, San Juan, P.R.

"As an avid baseball fan, I have noticed over the last few years an obvious decline in baseball uniform standards. Players wear pants that stretch down to the top of their shoes.

"What happened to the leg stirrups that were worn previously? Leg stirrups added color to the uniform, and gave a continuity of appearance to all teams.

"Will blue jeans and sneakers be next?"

—John E. Simpson, Manitou Springs, Colo.

"My dad took me to Philadelphia on June 29, 1938, for a doubleheader between the New York Giants and Phillies. The Giants won both of those games.

"The next day, the same two teams played in the last game ever in the Baker Bowl before the Phillies moved to Shibe Park. Could you please print the box score of that last game in Baker Bowl?"

—Charles Marsh, Allentown, Pa.

"In a recent issue, a letter-writer complained about the emphasis that has been placed on the long ball these days, and I couldn't agree more. He also said Barry Bonds was boring, and I'm with him on that, too.

"Give me bunts, base stealing, and sacrifices over clobbering home runs."

—Bev Gepp, Golf Coast, Australia

"I would like to see the pitching mound raised back to fifteen inches. I am tired of all these games with scores like 11-9, and all the home runs. I want to see guys get struck out, and have a real nail-biter of a game, won in the late innings."

—Robert Wyble, Butler, N.J.

"If it can be proven that all of the recent home run records were set by players who were on steroids, then those records should be erased by Major League Baseball.

"Accepting such records is the epitome of disrespect to Hank Aaron, Babe Ruth, Roger Maris and many former great players who hit the ball with God-given natural ability."

—Charles W. Finkbeiner, Richmond, Va.

Most of the letters received by *Baseball Digest* now arrive by e-mail, as do many manuscripts. Up-to-date research can be quickly accomplished via websites and fax machines. Page-making is done by computer. These are technical improvements that Herb Simons never enjoyed. In his time, typewriters were the essential tools of the trade, as well as a pair of scissors and a bottle of glue to paste up galleys on layout sheets.

Writers in his day filed their reports and feature stories to their newspapers via Western Union teletype. They were allowed to smoke in the press box—which they commanded—and could enjoy a free drink, or two or three, in the media room after action on the field had ended. This refreshing privilege occasionally involved engrossing conversations with people like Casey Stengel and Bill Veeck, who didn't mind indulging during these gatherings.

With the death of Simons in October 1968, the future of *Baseball Digest* was momentarily in doubt. Jerome Holtzman, then a baseball writer for the *Chicago Sun-Times* who later became Major League Baseball's official historian, held things together for a few issues until Norman Jacobs purchased the magazine early in 1969 and became its new publisher.

In search of an editor, Jacobs sought the advice of Bob Elson, a veteran broadcaster who had announced games for the White Sox and Cubs for thirty-eight years, beginning in 1929 and continuing, with time out for service in the navy, through 1970.

"Do you know of a baseball writer who can do the job?" Jacobs asked.

"Why don't you call Kuenster?" Elson said. "He's got a bunch of kids and probably could use the money because he lost enough of it to me playing gin rummy."

While Elson was exaggerating about the amount of money I lost to him in marathon card games during our travels with the White Sox, I have to admit I beat him only once in gin rummy. That momentous triumph

occurred on a stormy flight from Baltimore to Chicago when I was a baseball beat writer for the *Chicago Daily News*. Elson hated to fly in bad
weather, and evidently he hadn't been able to concentrate on blitzing me.

When Jacobs invited me to lunch, he asked if I wanted the job. After fifteen seconds of profound reflection, I said yes and became editor of *Baseball Digest*. At that moment there were about ten days remaining to the
copy deadline for the May 1969 issue.

With only one article on holdover from the preceding issue, it was a
stressful race to meet the deadline, but the sprint was won. There have
been no similar close calls since.

My years in covering the White Sox and Cubs during the 1950s and
1960s paid dividends in the following decades since I knew many of the
contributors to the magazine and was able to ask for their help and suggestions. Writers like Jack Lang in New York, Bob Broeg in St. Louis, John
Steadman in Baltimore, Joe Falls in Detroit, Furman Bisher in Atlanta, Earl
Lawson in Cincinnati, Les Biederman in Pittsburgh, Allen Lewis in
Philadelphia, and Jerome Holtzman in Chicago frequently provided stories they thought were suitable for publication. Their volunteer support
made my job much easier. So did that of many freelance authors whose
words revealed their love for the game.

The work of producing the magazine, however, has not been without
its numerous crises, including the unpleasantries of a paper mill strike, a
printing plant that went bankrupt, a trucking walkout, and soaring costs
of paper, postage, and distribution. The Baseball Players Association strike
that forced owners to cancel the 1994 World Series made many of our
readers mad as hell and ready to cancel their subscriptions. A typical reaction regarding the players' strike came from a physician in Texas who
called our office in anger.

"Is *Baseball Digest* subsidized by Major League Baseball?" he asked.

"No," I said, "we're an independent operation."

"Good," responded the doctor, "otherwise I would've dropped my sub-
scription."

In piecing together the selections in this book, I could see in my mind's
eye the many authors who have written with insight about the game and
its participants:

Red Smith, bent over his typewriter in the press box at Yankee Stadium,
struggling to get the precise lead for his story.

John Carmichael, listening to Casey Stengel during one of his dugout
monologues without taking a note, and turning out a column the next day
quoting Stengel word for word—which was no mean trick.

Jim Murray, nationally syndicated columnist for the *Los Angeles Times*,
sitting in a godforsaken spot far from the action on the field during a

World Series game without murmuring a word of complaint about his seating assignment.

James T. Farrell, author of the famed Studs Lonigan trilogy, slightly inebriated and attired in rumpled clothes that looked like he had slept in them, enjoying baseball talk in the Pink Poodle press room after watching the Cubs in Wrigley Field.

Wendell Smith, during a pre-season stopover in Macon, Georgia, sadly but graciously declining an invitation to join other Chicago baseball scribes for a dinner in a local restaurant because the color of his skin was different from theirs, and he knew he wouldn't be served.

Jerome Holtzman, keeping a careful set of statistics in a large notebook in the 1960s, recording performances of major league relief pitchers, an endeavor that eventually led to the creation of the save statistic.

Arthur Daley, the *New York Times* Pulitzer Prize–winner, always using a legal-size pad of lined paper to scribble the notes from his interviews.

Ed Prell of the *Chicago Tribune*, chomping on a cigar as he typed out his game story, and denying an insinuation that his discarded stogie caused a fire that burned down the Memphis Chicks' old wooden ballpark when the White Sox visited there for an exhibition many springs ago.

These writers and others enlivened the contents of *Baseball Digest* from its earliest years, but so have many freelance authors whose work reveals their emotional attachment to the game.

In this book, for example, Sister Mary Barbara Browne, C.S.C., tells how she became a baseball fanatic when she was young, watching the San Francisco Seals at old Recreation Park. Frank L. Ryan relates how baseball bridged a gap of silence between him and his father during the 1930s. Dr. Stephen D. Boren describes the healing powers of baseball trivia that helped relax some of his patients. Jon Beatty Fish recounts how he savored baseball memories while serving in Vietnam. And John Deedy writes with relish about the day he collected Babe Ruth's autograph.

Since *Baseball Digest* first spun from the presses, the basics of the game itself have remained unchanged in the major leagues with the exception of the introduction of the designated hitter rule in 1973. But the number of teams has increased from sixteen to thirty; integration, spearheaded by Jackie Robinson and Larry Doby, has triumphed; regular season schedules have jumped from 154 to 162 games; division and league playoffs are now part of the post-season; the American and National League presidential jobs have been abolished; umpiring staffs of the two leagues have been merged; artificial turf and indoor stadiums have been added to the mix; new parks with all kinds of amenities have popped up around the country; interleague games count in the standings; and rosters have gained a decided international touch with the inclusion of many Hispanic and Japanese players.

Fans who have been eyewitnesses to baseball history carry treasured memories with them for a long time. They remember the heart-rending farewell speech in 1939 by Lou Gehrig; Roberto Clemente's tremendous range in right field; the rifle arms of Carl Furillo and Al Kaline; the daring base running of Rickey Henderson; the braggadocio of Dizzy Dean; the towering home runs of Mickey Mantle; the gifted glove work of Ozzie Smith and Luis Aparicio at shortstop; the playing savvy of Derek Jeter; the leaping catches of Jim Edmonds in center field; the gifted performances of Johnny Bench and Ivan Rodriguez behind the plate; the durability of pitchers like Warren Spahn, Nolan Ryan, Roger Clemens, and Greg Maddux.

As you browse through the following pages, you may enter your personal "field of dreams" through memories you have stored away—from the days when you first became enamored with the game to the autumn of 2004 when those tenacious characters in Boston finally won a World Series for the Red Sox nation after eighty-six years of frustration, and on to the fall of 2005 when the Chicago White Sox made an equally exciting run to a world championship after 88 years of denial.

—JOHN KUENSTER

THE BEST OF BASEBALL DIGEST

Baseball's Best Batters

BY BILLY EVANS

I shall never forget the day that I heard Wee Willie Keeler expound his now-famous batting theory: "Hit 'em where they ain't!" That was in 1906, the year I made my big league debut. We were sitting on the bench of the New York Highlanders, now better known as the Yankees, awaiting game time. Mark Roth, then a baseball writer on the *New York Globe*, had come down to the bench to interview Keeler on the art of hitting.

The day before, Keeler, who was on the way out at the time, having passed his peak, had made five hits in a row. Two of them were bunts that he beat out; another was a drag bunt that the pitcher, first baseman, and second baseman chased, with the latter finally reaching the ball but finding no one covering first. The other two hits were flyballs that dropped between the shortstop and left fielder, although the outfielder seemed to be playing almost directly back of the shortstop.

"What have you to say to the kids of America on how to become a great hitter?" asked Roth.

"Hit 'em where they ain't," replied Keeler.

"I understand," said Roth, "but you must explain to the youngsters how you manage to hit 'em where they ain't."

"Just do it," was Keeler's answer.

It is questionable if the game ever produced a hitter just like Keeler. He had no power. The outfielders knew it and played in close. In reality, when Keeler came to bat there were seven infielders, all set to stop him. Yet he always batted better than .300.

Despite all the defenses set up to stop him, Keeler, with his uncanny ability to place the ball out of reach of the opposition, baffled all attempts to stop him. Hitting was a science with Keeler. He was one of the originators of so-called "place-hitting," so gauging his batting stroke, according to the pitch, that the ball would fall where no one was playing.

It is my conviction that all the great hitters past and present are born not made. Over nearly 40 years in baseball, 22 in the role of big league umpire in which I have called balls and strikes on these great hitters who made baseball history, I have reached the decision that hitting is a gift. You either have it or you don't. It is seldom, if ever, acquired. I have asked many of the great hitters to explain just how they did it, but invariably their answers were just as illuminating as the favored reply of Wee Willie Keeler to all such questions: "Hit 'em where they ain't."

Unquestionably, timing is the greatest asset of all the outstanding batsmen. Timing at the bat is a combination of a number of things. There must be perfect rhythm between the stride and the swing. If either is a trifle late, the coordination between brain, muscle, feet, and arms is lacking.

If there ever was a greater all-around baseball player than Ty Cobb, I have yet to see him. Babe Ruth had more power, Tris Speaker was a greater fielder, Joe DiMaggio has a better arm, but none possessed the all-around finesse of the Georgia Peach. Cobb did everything well.

Well do I recall a reply that Cobb made to me years ago when sitting on the bench with him. I asked how he analyzed batting slumps, which every now and then overtook even him.

"It's hard to explain why they happen," Ty replied. "It's even more difficult to offer a solution as to how to come out of a batting slump. Illness and injuries often cause a batter to fall into a slump. Illness destroys some of his physical resistance, causing him to press in an effort to make up for the lack of that little extra zip in his swing. Injuries to either arms or legs often cause a player to lose his timing, simply because in favoring the injury he throws himself off stride. When a slump is directly attributable to temporary physical defects, a return to normal invariably gets the batter back in stride.

"In a great many cases, however, worry is the start of a slump. When I went into a slump, I tried my best to keep from worrying. I tried to think of the many lucky hits I had gotten to balance a lot of the hard-hit balls that were going directly into the hands of some fielder. I always determined not to press."

Cobb had fewer batting slumps than most of them. And I have always felt the reason was that Cobb had great confidence in his ability, knew that batting slumps were merely temporary and that if he continued in the routine way he would emerge without any great handicap. Yet I also always felt that Cobb's spread grip, which he affected most of the time, was his greatest asset in keeping him out of slumps. I have never seen a great hitter who had better control of his bat at all times than Cobb.

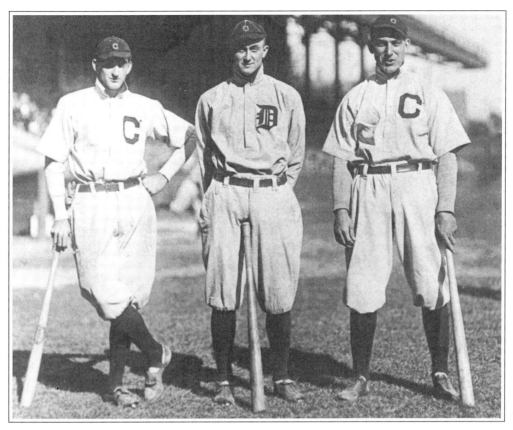

Among the greatest hitters chosen by Hall of Fame umpire Billy Evans were, left to right, Joe Jackson, Ty Cobb and Nap Lajoie. Their career batting averages were .356, .366 and .338 respectively.

In any discussion of the great hitters of the game, you have to come quickly to Babe Ruth, the greatest distance hitter of them all. When the sagacious Ed Barrow, who, more than any other man, made the New York Yankees what they are today, decided that Ruth would have more value every day playing in the outfield rather than taking his pitching turn every fourth day, I seriously doubted the wisdom of the move.

As the best left-handed pitcher of his pitching era, Ruth every now and then would make you gasp at the distance he would drive some pitch to his liking. However, he was often a strikeout victim, and there was a serious question in my mind whether Ruth, because of his penchant for striking out, wouldn't be a bust as an everyday hitter. However, Barrow saw possibilities in Ruth that others couldn't see. For a time he took considerable criticism as Ruth continued to strike out a couple of times in most every game—sometimes more. But Barrow never wavered in his belief in Ruth, and it wasn't long before Ruth began to definitely justify his opinion.

Babe Ruth was a do-or-don't batter—always shooting the works. He called on no tricks to get his base hits. They were manufactured through the medium of sheer power. Every now and then, more for the humor of the situation, he would lay down a bunt and beat it out, to his great satisfaction. Reaching first base he would shake with laughter, at the same time deriding the opposition.

Ruth, greatest slugger of all time, could be pitched to but there had better be no slip in the procedure. The smart pitchers—those with a limited amount of natural stuff—caused Ruth more trouble than pitchers who had plenty. Such type pitchers worked on Ruth, seldom gave him the ball he liked best to hit—the fast one—and kept trying to make him swing at the ball they wanted him to, rather than the one he liked to hit. As a result Babe often struck out; on the other hand, pitching smart to Ruth, meaning just missing the plate, caused him to get a lot of bases on balls, in addition to the many intentional passes he received.

Lou Gehrig, who followed Ruth in the Yankee batting order for many years, was in some respects as great a hitter as Ruth.

There was a rhythm to Gehrig's swing that made you feel there was no excuse for him not hitting every pitch. The start of the swing by Gehrig and Ruth was entirely different. Ruth was fidgety and seemingly nervous. His bat would move back and forth on his shoulder awaiting the pitch. His feet were close together, ready for the lunge into the ball that meant the kill. Gehrig, on the other hand, used an open stance of perhaps a foot. His bat rested quietly on his shoulder as the pitcher prepared to deliver the ball. When the delivery was started Gehrig slowly lifted the bat from his shoulder and assumed an almost defiant attitude. When the pitch neared the plate he took a short step and a rhythmic swing that made for almost as great power as Ruth, although their styles were definitely different.

Gehrig was much harder to pitch to than Ruth. He murdered the change of pace and slow curve that Ruth disliked.

Ruth, because of his lunge, was unable to control his bat as could Gehrig from his flat stance. Gehrig was never off balance and always able to adapt his swing and timing to the slow ball and speed ball.

The greatest difference between Ruth and Gehrig, however, was not so much of a mechanical nature as it was in temperament. Ruth oozed color, while Gehrig had none. Ruth's every move was that of the showman, while Gehrig was the well-oiled machine, the robot that wasted no effort but moved constantly in the same perfect groove. When Ruth hit a home run he let you know that he was just as delighted over the happening as his most loyal rooter. By the time he reached first he was in tune with everything. The crowd seemed to sense his enthusiasm and became a part of it. His every step as he circled the bases was wildly cheered. He would repeatedly doff his cap to the crowd in a manner that increased the applause.

The four batters we have discussed—Cobb, Ruth, Gehrig, and Keeler—were left-handers. So let's consider two of the greatest hitters ever produced by the National League—Hans Wagner and Rogers Hornsby, both right-handers.

Wagner did all of his hitting against the dead ball and before the abolition of trick deliveries. I believe it is conservative to say that had Wagner hit against the lively ball now in use, his average over his career of 21 years would have been closer to .350 than the .328 figure he amassed.

Honus was very bowlegged and had unusually long arms. His style at the plate was rather grotesque because of his bowlegs and long arms, but he had no weakness as far as I could judge and I never heard a pitcher argue that he had. He had a remarkable eye and seldom hit at bad balls.

Unquestionably in the field and at the bat, Wagner was the most awkward "graceful" performer in all the history of the game.

Rogers Hornsby, one of the greatest right-handed hitters of all time, on the other hand, exemplified motion. At the plate, he was the modern Adonis of the game. He had a perfect physique. His stride and swing were in keeping with his physique—models of grace and precision. In some ways the style of Hornsby was as unique as that of Wagner. Certainly it was more unorthodox, though not to Hornsby.

Hornsby stood in the extreme rear of the batter's box. It appeared that the smart pitcher could keep the ball low and on the outside, particularly the curveball, and make a sucker of Hornsby. A lot of smart pitchers had such a notion during the early years of Hornsby's career, but soon found their strategy a boomerang.

I once remarked to Hornsby that his style seemed definitely contrary to all mechanics of the game. He smiled and replied:

"On the contrary, Billy, my style enables me to meet all the different pitches. The toughest pitch for any batter is the 'tight' pitch—high or low and inside. My position takes the dynamite out of the tight pitch, and to hit the low pitch on the outside, curve or fastball, you take a full stride in the direction of the plate as the pitch is started, which brings you pretty much on a line with the plate and enables you to either push the ball to right field or drive it for distance—depending on the power you put behind the effort. I have always felt that my style at the plate immediately created a hazard for the smart pitcher by practically eliminating his having a chance to pitch to your stance and make you hit the ball that he wants you to hit."

Billy Evans umpired in the American League from 1906 to 1927. He started at age 22, youngest umpire in major league history.

Tris Speaker, the last word in center-fielding, was not far behind in his activities at the plate. Speaker was another of the rhythm hitters. His stance was just about the opposite of Hornsby. He used a spread stance lined up with home plate, rather than being three or four feet back of it like Hornsby. Speaker took no devastating swing but had a perfectly timed follow-through, like a golfer. His swing stressed timing and the follow-through. Ordinarily he didn't go for distance but in a pinch, when an extra-base hit was needed, Speaker could slip his grip to the bottom of the bat and swing from the ground.

The career of Eddie Collins covers 25 years as a big league star, more than any of the other great hitters of the game. Ty Cobb, who played one year less than Eddie, ranks second. Collins was not a power hitter. He was in the same class as Keeler and George Sisler, who might be termed the brain hitters of the game.

Collins, unlike many of the other outstanding left-handed hitters, was not a pull-hitter. A great majority of Collins' hits went to left field, line drives over the shortstop's head, or sizzling grounders just between the third baseman and shortstop.

Collins was a difficult man to strike out. He had a keen eye. He was a fine bunter, got away from the plate quickly, and beat out many a bunt or dragged ball for a well-earned base hit. Next to Cobb, Collins was the best base-runner in the history of the American League. When it came to laying down a perfect sacrifice with runners on, there was no one in the game who could compare with Collins.

Of all the modern hitters, George Sisler, who over a period of 16 years in the majors turned in a .340 batting average, bore the closest resemblance to Willie Keeler. Sisler, a left-handed hitter, was faster than Keeler and used his speed to better advantage than any of the other stars with the exception of Cobb. Sisler always had his eye on the play of the rival infield. If it was playing deep, he was quick to take advantage of the bunt and the drag to get base hits. He would poke bad pitches just over the infield, to the consternation of the opposition, the pitcher in particular.

Larry Lajoie, great right-handed hitter of the old school, was the good-to-look-at hitter. There was an aloof nonchalance in the manner in which Lajoie stepped into the batter's box that ordinarily would have caused the pitcher to become careless had not Lajoie's fame as a hitter made him feared by all. Larry's theory was to hit the pitch to the field to which it should go. He was definitely a straightaway hitter whose chief thought was to get proper timing and thereby make correct contact.

To my way of thinking, there never was a greater hitter than Joe Jackson. A left-handed hitter, Joe stood well back of the plate, keeping his feet fairly close together, and as the ball approached him, took a slow, even stride, and started the swing of the bat in unison with the stride. No hitter had more perfect coordination than Jackson. He could have hit fourth on my all-time team of great hitters of the game.

That brings us to the two great hitters of modern times, Joe DiMaggio of the Yankees and Ted Williams of the Red Sox. The styles of these two batsmen are entirely different. Of all the great hitters, past and present, DiMaggio, the greatest present-day right-hander, uses the most open stance of all. He is the only power hitter who ever swung from a flat-footed position.

Ted Williams, in contrast to DiMaggio, is a bundle of nerves. He seems to bubble over with enthusiasm for his work from the time he leaves the bench until he reaches the batter's box. Getting into the box, he goes through a dozen acrobatic maneuvers. It seems that he will never be ready for the pitch, but American League twirlers will testify to the contrary. He laughs at his own antics when he misses a healthy swing. He grins with satisfaction when he connects for the base hit. He is the big kid all over and, like Babe Ruth, wins his audience early. I have always felt that Williams, the greatest of today's left-handed hitters, is the nearest approach in every way that baseball has had to Ruth.

Editor's Note: In 1973, Billy Evans became the third umpire to be elected to the Baseball Hall of Fame.

[1942]

Ty Cobb Thrived on Fierce Opposition

BY BOB FRENCH

Ty Cobb has been out of baseball so long it is difficult to get the right slant on the achievements of this remarkable athlete. In some instances the legendary feature is at work and exaggeration creeps in until one is inclined to doubt the testimony. On the other hand, fierce opponents of Cobb in his playing days still come up from time to time with some criticism of his efforts and refuse to give him credit for what he really did. Cobb was no sweet-tempered pal of other players back in his halcyon days, and some of them haven't yet forgiven him.

Fred Haney, manager of the Toledo Mud Hens, is one of the best sources of unprejudiced Cobb history. Fred was closely associated with Cobb for six years and studied without prejudice the amazing career of the Georgian both as player and manager at Detroit. Haney appreciated Cobb's outstanding ability as a player and his tremendous mental qualifications, but at the same time he wasn't blind to his eccentricities.

"Cobb was the first man who really put psychology into baseball," said Haney. "He knew how to spur himself and his players to a mental pitch which would help his side; he also knew how to worry the opposition until it lost some of its efficiency. He worked along entirely original lines.

"There probably have been players in the game who had as much natural ability and as good a physique as Cobb; there may also have been some—although I doubt it—who could think as fast. But there certainly never was another athlete who combined Cobb's ability and his smartness—or even came close."

Cobb was the perfect example of an athlete who thrived on the fiercest sort of opposition. The tougher the other fellows were, the better Cobb played baseball. But merely the taunts of spectators and the attacks of opposing players weren't enough to suit him. He actually would battle with himself, Haney says, in order to fan the flames of competition in his own breast.

"It was a study watching Cobb on the bench as his turn to bat approached," Haney went on. "It could easily be seen from his facial expression that he was lashing himself into that fighting mood which made him feel that nobody on earth, and especially no pitcher, could stop him. In his baseball he instinctively centered on the fellows who gave him the most trouble, gradually found out how to circumvent them, and finally had them utterly licked and pushed into the background so far as he was concerned.

"When he first broke into the American League, Doc White, the great southpaw pitcher of the Chicago White Sox, had Cobb completely stymied. Tyrus could hardly get a foul ball off White, and many believed that as soon as other pitchers learned White's knack of fooling Cobb, the fiery young man would be chased out of the league.

"Exactly the opposite happened. Cobb centered on White. He studied him as he studied no other player. Pretty soon Cobb was hitting White, and soon after that he was murdering the Chicago star. Baseball history will show that when Cobb really reached his stride, White was his easiest victim.

Ty Cobb slides hard into third base as Jimmy Austin of the New York Highlanders swipes at him with a too-late tag.

"The same thing with his many fistfights. Cobb was no great battler in his early days as a player. But he was willing to fight anybody and he took one beating after another. The climax came when he got into a wordy war with a well-known and husky umpire. Cobb invited the umpire to meet him under the stands after the game. The umpire was more than willing. The two got together and Cobb just about got his head knocked off.

"That winter Cobb hired a boxing instructor and took him to his winter home in Georgia. Ty worked all winter with the gloves. When the next season rolled around, he could hardly wait until that umpire appeared in a Detroit series. The big day came at last. Cobb rushed up to the umpire after the first game of the series. 'I still think you're all the things I called you last fall,' shouted Cobb, 'and I dare you to meet me under the stands again.' The umpire gladly complied and this time Cobb just about murdered the umpire."

The place where they really went after Cobb was in New York. The instant he came on the field there the crowd would be on him and, thus encouraged, the Yankees would center on him with terrific energy and venom.

"And if Cobb had played all his games in New York," Haney said, "he would have had a lifetime batting average of .750 and would have stolen about 200 bases a season. The instant Ty came on the field and the abuse started, he began to boil and steam, and by the time the game started he was simply invincible. The Tigers loved to play in New York; the rest of them could take it easy and Cobb would win the games all by himself."

It is a fact that Connie Mack, who had great ball clubs in Philadelphia when Cobb was tearing things apart, used to caution his players to let Cobb strictly alone. Connie believed that if Cobb were not antagonized he would be easier to handle.

"Let him sleep, if he will," said the wise old Connie. "If you get him riled up he'll annihilate us."

Once when Haney was battling for a job with the Tigers, he discovered he could read the signs of Steve O'Neill, catching for Cleveland. Haney went to Cobb and suggested that he be allowed to work on the coaching lines and flash information to Detroit hitters on curveballs and fast ones. But Cobb was not enthusiastic.

"You probably could do it all right, Fred," said Cobb, "but it won't help much. I know just about every ball a pitcher is going to throw to us without looking for the signs and I've tried to wise up our fellows, but they don't seem to profit by it."

Haney must have indicated he didn't believe Cobb was clairvoyant, so Tyrus said: "Come over to the bench when the game starts: I'll show you something."

As the game began Cobb sat on the edge of the dugout and made no effort to get the catcher's signs. He admitted he couldn't call the first pitch, but after it was made, a fastball and a strike, he used that for his first information and correctly told in advance what the pitcher was going to throw for *twenty-six consecutive* pitches. He missed on the *twenty-seventh*.

[1942]

Baseball in Paris, 1918

BY HEYWOOD BROUN

The day after the Americans marched into Paris one of the French newspapers referred to the doughboys as "Roman Caesars clad in khaki." The city set itself to liking the soldiers and everything American and succeeded admirably. Even the taxicab drivers refrained from overcharging Americans very much. Schoolchildren studied the history of America and "The Star-Spangled Banner." There were pictures of President Wilson and General Pershing in many shops and some had framed translations of the President's message to Congress. In fact, so eager were the French to take America to their hearts that they even made desperate efforts to acquire a working knowledge of baseball.

Excelsior, an illustrated French daily, carried an action picture taken during a game played between American ambulance drivers just outside of Paris. The picture was entitled: "A player goes to catch the ball, which has been missed by the catcher," and underneath ran the following explanation: "We have given in our number of yesterday the rules of baseball, the American National game, of which a game, which is perhaps the first ever played in France, took place yesterday at Colombes between the soldiers of the American ambulances. Here is an aspect of the game. The pitcher, or thrower of balls, whom one sees in the distance, has sent the ball. The catcher, or *attrapeur,* who should restrike the ball with his wooden club, has missed it, and a player placed behind him has seized it in its flight."

The next day *L'Intransigeant* undertook the even more hazardous task of explaining American baseball slang. During the parade on the Fourth of July, some Americans had greeted the doughboys with shouts of "ataboy." A French journalist heard and was puzzled. He returned to his office and looked in English dictionaries and various works of reference without enlightenment. Several English friends were unable to help him, and an American who had lived in Paris for 30 years was equally at sea.

But the reporter worked it out all by himself, and the next day he wrote: "Parisians have been puzzled by the phrase 'ataboy' which Americans are prone to employ in moments of stress and emotion. The phrase is undoubtedly a contraction of 'at her boy' and may be closely approximated by *au travail, garcon.*" The writer followed with a brief history of the friendly relations of France and America and paid a glowing tribute to the memory of Lafayette.

The high tide in the American conquest of Paris came one afternoon in July. I got out of a taxicab in front of the American headquarters in the Rue Constantine and found that a big crowd had gathered in the Esplanade des Invalides. Now and again the crowd would give ground to make room for an American soldier running at top speed. One of them stood almost at the entrance of the courtyard of "Invalides." His back was turned toward the tomb of Napoleon, and he was knocking out flies in the direction of the Seine.

Unfortunately it was a bit far to the river, and no baseball has yet been knocked into that stream. It was a new experience for Napoleon, though. He has heard rifles and machine guns and other loud reports in the streets of Paris, but for the first time there came to his ears the loud sharp crack of a bat swung against a baseball. Since he could not see from out of the tomb, the noise may have worried the emperor. Perhaps he thought it was the British winning new battles on other cricket fields. But again he might not worry about that now. He might hop up on one toe as a French caricaturist pictured him and cry: *"Vive l'Angleterre!"*

One of the men in the crowd that watched the batting practice was a French soldier headed back to the front. At any rate he had his steel helmet on and his equipment was on his back. His stripes showed that he had been in the war three years, and he had the Croix de Guerre with two palms and the Medaille Militaire. His interest in the game grew so high at last that he put down his pack and his helmet and joined the outfielders. The second or third ball hit came in his direction. He ran about in a short circle under the descending ball, and at the last moment he thrust both hands in front of his face. The ball came between them and hit him in the nose, knocking him down.

His nose was a little bloody, but he was up in an instant grinning. He left the field to pick up his trench hat and his equipment. The Americans shouted to him to come back. He understood the drift of their invitation, but he shook his head. *"C'est dangereux,"* he said, and started for the station to catch his train for the front.

[1943]

How Connie Mack Passed Up Babe Ruth

BY RED SMITH

You'd think that after 81 years, he'd be starting to lose the hop on his high hard one. At least, after these ever so many seasons you wouldn't expect Connie Mack to come up with many more surprises.

Yet, when the crowd gathered in the Shibe Park tower for the annual ceremony of a birthday interview, he wound up and pitched a fast one right down the middle. He was rambling along through the years, talking of great pitchers of the past and retelling the story of how he signed Christy Mathewson in 1901 but lost him to the Giants.

"Outside of Mathewson," he was asked, "and more recent stars like Red Rolfe and Jim Tabor, were there any of the great ones whom you almost had but didn't land?"

Connie considered that a moment. "No," he said slowly, "I don't think so. Fellows like Cobb and Alexander—I never had a chance to get them."

He went on then, talking about great players, and the conversation got around to some of those for whom he paid important money—Lefty Grove, who cost $100,500; George Earnshaw, whom everyone figured as a $30,000 buy, but who actually cost $85,000; and Joe Boley, $65,000.

The ever-dapper Connie Mack, right, with another famous manager, John McGraw of the New York Giants. Mack managed the Philadelphia A's for 50 years, 1901–1950, winning eight pennants and five World Series.

In those days Connie was pretty thick with Jack Dunn, the Baltimore owner, and they were buying and selling players right and left.

"That's right," the Old Man recalled. "I remember when Jack—it must have been about 1914—offered me two pitchers, Ruth and Ernie Shore, and told me to take 'em for nothing. I said no."

There was a horrified silence. Then someone said weakly:

"You don't mean Babe Ruth?"

Connie smiled faintly.

"Yes. Oh, I didn't turn him down because I didn't think he was good. He was already a star in Baltimore, although I believe Shore's record was even better than Babe's down there.

"But Jack didn't have any money in those days and we didn't either. I remember I told him, 'No, you keep those fellows, Jack, and sell 'em where you can get some money. You can use it as well as I.

"Well, sir, he finally sold them to Boston and I think he let the two of 'em go for something like $6,000."

It was the first time this story was told, and it aroused some fascinating speculation. Suppose Ruth had come to the Athletics in 1914, just as one of Connie's great teams was breaking up, and had played for Philadelphia through the years leading up to the championship days of 1929–31. It would have changed the whole American League history.

Connie chatted on. He mentioned some of the famous bargains he has made in the player market—Jimmie Foxx, whom he got for $2,000; Home Run Baker, $500; Chief Bender, who cost $100; and Eddie Collins and Eddie Plank, who came free.

Viewing the increasing popularity of the knuckleball, Connie recalls earlier days when one freak pitch after another came into vogue—the forkball, the shine ball of Eddie Cicotte, the spitter, the "mud ball."

"Back in the '90s," the Old Man said, "there weren't any trick deliveries. Just the fastball and curve. Not even the half-speed ball. The change of pace was one of the last to come in.

"Not all pitchers need a change, although most of 'em think they do because the other fellow has it. Earnshaw never used to slow up until he saw Al Crowder getting by with slow stuff and he tried to imitate him. The result was he began having a lot of trouble late in 1930.

"Ed Collins asked me to speak to George about it, but I wouldn't. I said, 'I know what's wrong, but let him come to me.' And finally George did come up to this office. I asked him to promise that he wouldn't throw a single thing but the fast one and the curve in the World Series with the Cardinals.

"Well, on his first start he kept his word for about six innings. Then he threw a slow one up to Frank Frisch. Frank really slugged it, on a line to Mule Haas. Earnshaw looked over at me and waved me down, like this, as if to say, 'I know, I know, you're right and I won't do it again.'"

Somebody mentioned prospects for 1944 and the old eyes brightened. "Of course," Connie said, "we never know who we might lose, but we're going to have almost entirely a new team. There'll be Radcliff behind Siebert at first and Joe Rullo at second and—"

He was off in full cry, looking forward once again.

[1944]

'34 Series Win, "A Big Day in My Life"

BY DIZZY DEAN AS TOLD TO
JOHN P. CARMICHAEL

I just wish my arm was like it was nine-ten years ago. . . . I'd have me a picnic in this league. When I came up, every club had three-four .300 hitters who really could powder that ball. Now? Shucks! I'd breeze home any day.

I never forget Frank Frisch the day I beat Detroit, 11–0, in the last game of the World Series in 1934. We're in the clubhouse, see, celebratin' and I got a rubber tiger, all blown up, and I'm twistin' his tail and hollerin' like the rest and Frisch came by and stopped and you know what he said?

"Anybody with your stuff should have won 40 games this year instead of a measly 30," he said. "You loaf, that's the trouble. Thirty games! You ought to be 'shamed of yourself." Imagine that, and me just winning the Series for him; ol' Diz out there pitchin' outta turn, too, don't forget that. He wanted me to pitch, although he'd said Bill Hallahan was gonna work the last game. But he came to me the night before and he asked: "Diz, you wanna be the greatest man in baseball?" I told him I already was, but he didn't even hear me I guess, 'cause he went on: "You pitch that game to-morrow and you'll be tops." I just told him: "Gimme that ball tomorrow and your troubles are over." He wanted me to pitch. I knew that. Hell, I was afraid he would let Hallahan start.

That was a big day in my life, I admit it. First World Series and all the ex-citement and everybody wild, and two trucks goin' up and down the streets, one playin' "Hold That Tiger" and the other tootlin' the "St. Louis Blues." I saw Babe Ruth and got his autograph, by jingo, and 'taint everybody pitches in a big series and gets Babe's name on a ball, too. I liked that ol' Frisch, he was a helluva guy, but he worried all the time. He had nothin' to fret about with ol' Diz out there. You know we was leadin' 11-0 in the ninth with one out and he sent four pitchers down in the bullpen to warm up.

So help me, I thought they must be gettin' ready for the 1935 season. Eleven-nothing I got 'em and that Billy Rogell on base and Hank Green-berg came up. I already struck him out twice, no trouble 'tall, and when he came up in that ninth I hollered over to the Tiger bench. I said: "What, no pinch hitter?" and Hank looked at me like he'd a liked to break one of them sticks over my head, but hell, he was my meat. He was easy.

You know what that Frisch did? I put two fastballs right past the letters on that Greenberg uniform and when he missed the second one I hadda laugh. I put my glove up to my face to keep from laughin' right in his face, he looked so funny, and before I could throw any more Frisch came out. He was mad. He said: "Cut out the foolin', we got a lot at stake," and I just stood there and looked at him like he must be outta his mind . . . me leadin' 11-0, with one out in the last of the ninth. Just then Leo Durocher came in from short and he said: "Aw, what the hell, Frank, let the guy have his fun. What's the matter with you?" Well, you know what Frisch told me? "Yeah . . . ," he said, "you lose this guy and you're through." Eleven-nothing . . . I can't get over that yet. He was gonna pull me.

That Greenberg couldn't a hit that next pitch if he'd a started to swing when I wound up. Gonna pull me. He didn't even see it, and the next guy

Dizzy Dean helped tame the Tigers in the 1934 World Series, winning the first and seventh games.

was Owen and he forced Rogell and the whole thing was over. Them Tigers weren't bad; they gave us a good battle, but they were just pussy cats with me. I don't like to brag a lot, because folks think I'm a big lunkhead or somethin', but when I had my fastball, before I broke my toe [in 1937] and couldn't throw it any more, nobody hit me . . . much. You know what I did one day? I pitched a game in Boston and never took a sign or never threw nothin' but fastballs. A whole game, Bill De-Lancey was catchin'. I told Al Spohrer, the Braves' catcher, before the game that he could tell everybody I was gonna do that, too. I beat 'em 10-0 or 13-0 . . . some score like that. Just wound up and fogged that ball over.

I'll tell you another day in Boston I got a helluva kick. Remember seein' a big fat guy around with me a lot? Well, he was Johnny Perkins and he worked in a nightclub around St. Louis and he made this trip with us. He made me a bet I wouldn't strike out Vince DiMaggio the first time he came up. I did and when I went back to the bench I made motions to Perk I'd double the bet the next time. I struck him out again and I put everything back on a third bet and I fanned him three straight times. Then Perkins wanted to make it all or nothin' so I took 'im and when DiMaggio came up again he lifted a pop foul back of the plate. I thought Ogrodowski was gonna catch it and I ran and hollered: "Let it go, let it go." He couldn't get the ball anyway, as it turned out, 'cause it hit the screen, but I'd a bumped him sure as hell if he'd a got under it. I wanted to win that bet. I struck DiMaggio out on the next pitch . . . four straight times.

That game I beat Pittsburgh in 1938 [September 27; Dean had been traded to the Cubs before the '38 season started] was just about as big a day as I ever remember. I never had nothin'. I wasn't even supposed to pitch. I was on the inactive list or somethin' and Gabby Hartnett came in the clubhouse that day and you know he twirls that big seegar around in that red face of his (I like ol' Gabby, even if I did call him a pickle-puss in Wichita which he was because he bawled me out right in front of all the players and people a-gazin' at me and fined me $100) and he said: "Dean, you're the pitcher," and I said, "Fine," but I thought he was kiddin' and then Larry French and Herman and them said: "He ain't foolin', Diz . . . you're pitchin'." My God I couldn't break a pane of glass and I knew it, but I pitched.

They finally had to get me outta there in the ninth and I was leadin' 2-0, and Bill Lee went in and the first pitch he made was a wild one and a run scored, but he hung on and they didn't score again and, boy, I felt like a million. Ol' Diz saved many a game for Cardinal pitchers in his day and here was a guy who saved one for me and I told him, I said, "Lee, you're a great man," and he was a helluva guy and a swell pitcher. I always liked old Gabby, but he shouldn't have yelled at me in front of all those people in Wichita. They was a-gazin' at me like I was a freak and I don't stand for bein' shown up by nobody. The fine was all right. . . . I didn't get in until 20 minutes to two and we had a midnight deadline . . . but he could-a told me on the quiet.

[1945]

When Goslin Edged Me Out for the Batting Title

BY HEINIE MANUSH AS TOLD TO
JOHN P. CARMICHAEL

I suppose I should remember the day I won the American League batting championship, the last day of the season in 1926, and I do. I beat out Babe Ruth and that was a great afternoon but, after all, he was playing in St. Louis and I was in Detroit. We weren't on the same field like that closing day two years later when "Goose" Goslin and I went down to the final game to see who won. Yeah, he won, but that isn't all of it.

I was with the Browns then, hitting third, and "Goose" was with Washington, also hitting third. We were playing each other in St. Louis, and going into the game he was hitting .379 and I had .377 and a fraction. At least that's what the newspapermen told me before the "kickoff." He'd only made about 170 hits all season to 239 for me, but he hadn't played as many games and he was up there most of the year and I had to hit over .400 the last three weeks to even get close. But there we were. Sam Jones started for them and George Blaeholder was our pitcher.

Before the series opened Dan Howley, our manager, asked me if I wanted him to throw left-handers at them, because "Goose," like myself,

Heinie Manush hit .378 with the St. Louis Browns in 1928.

was a southpaw hitter. I told him no. "But I wish you'd do one thing," I asked him. "Play Oscar Melillo at second."

We'd been playing a kid named Brannon . . . a fair hitter, but not much of a fielder, and I figured I'd like Oscar out there to play "Goose" back on the grass. I'll say one thing . . . that Melillo made a couple of plays in the first two games that cut at least two hits off Goslin's total.

You see, "Goose" was a dead pull hitter while I hit more or less straightaway, and I recall in that series Lu Blue, our first baseman, played way back even when they had a man on the bag if Goslin was up. Later on, when "Goose" and I both were with Washington, I followed him in the batting order and I used to get a lot of hits because sometimes the other outfield, which would swing way around when he was up, would forget to move back again when I got to the plate and I'd level one into left. Used to drive Al Simmons crazy with those pokes.

But, anyway, this particular day Washington was up first and "Goose" lifted one into short right field. Earl McNeely, Frank McGowan and Melillo all went after it, but the ball fell among 'em for a double. McGowan was playing right and he roomed with me all season and he felt terrible. He came into the bench moaning: "Should have had it, 'Hein' . . . it was my ball."

Well, Goslin was batting 1.000 then and, if I'm not wrong, I got out my first trip, so he had the jump on me, especially with two points to start. One of the Washington players told me afterward that Goslin, after that hit, had suggested to Jones that he keep walking me and that Sam refused. "No sir," he told "Goose," the way I got it. "I'm going to stop him if I can, but he's entitled to a chance to hit under the circumstances." Anyway, that's what I was told. The game went on and, of course, I was out in left field. I was watching for Goslin to come up the second time.

All of a sudden I looked up and saw Sam Rice starting out from the dugout with a bat in his hand and it was Goose's turn. For a second I just stood still and then I let out a yell and began running in. I don't know what might have happened, because I was mad, thinkin' what they were gonna do to protect his average. I was going to stop the game, I know that, and raise a fuss with the umpires and maybe Goslin and I would have wound up in a fight, but before I got there Rice had gone back and "Goose" came out swinging two bats. Somebody—maybe "Bucky" Harris—must have decided to make him play it out. I know he didn't hit, and the next time I got to the dish I singled and we were all even so far.

Ol' Sam [Jones] was pretty good that day and the hit I got was a "slicer" over short. As it turned out he licked us, 9-1, and gave only seven hits. They got a one-run lead on us, but Blaeholder was doing all right himself and got the "Goose" out a second time, so I picked up a little on him. Then came the fifth or sixth inning, whichever it was, and Goslin poled one right onto that ol' roof and they got four runs all told. He had nicked a foul off the end of his bat the previous pitch and the ball had glanced off the roof of our dugout, barely away from our third baseman's hands. I thought to myself out there by the left field stands: "He'll probably

Leon "Goose" Goslin batted .379 for the Washington Senators in 1928 to lead the American League.

blast one now," and he did. The boys said later he must have guessed another outside pitch because he stepped right into it and "Goose" could get his bat around fast.

Howley sent in a left-hander named Wiltse to get things under control again and he did, but "Goose" was two for four by this time and the Senators were slapping him on the back when he hit the bench and I knew that nothin' but a big rally by our side, which would let me get an extra turn or two at bat, could help. Maybe if we would have had Wiltse in there the whole game, he would have stopped Goslin cold, because he got him out in the seventh or eighth to make him stand two for five for the nine innings, but that's second-guessing and besides, I popped up myself on a soft, sidearm curve in the sixth, so I had nothing to kick about. I still can see Harris, at third that day, circling under it and I thought: "Even if he drops the ball, it doesn't mean a thing."

I got a triple in the ninth to make me batting .500 for the day while Goslin had hit .400, so as things turned out, I gained a point on him, but that was just enough to lose. Howley and the boys tried to cheer me up by saying the official records wouldn't be out until December and maybe I was tied or something, but I found out Eddie Eynon, the Washington secretary, had the figures all tabbed before game-time and knew that "Goose" had made it, .379 to my .378.

When we got in the clubhouse McGowan came over and he was feeling pretty bad because if he'd caught that one in the first inning Goslin would have had one for five and I'd a won, .378 to .377, but I didn't let him say anything. What the heck, you do or you don't in baseball and I've missed a few myself in my days and that's part of the game. But at least it was the closest finish in American League history, as far as I know, and there was something about the two of us, in the same park on the same day, battling it out, that made it a great afternoon, even if I had to lose. "Goose" and I played on a pennant team for Washington five years later, but neither of us ever mentioned that game in St. Louis.

Editor's Note: Henry "Heinie" Manush was elected to the Hall of Fame in 1964 after a 17-year career in the majors (1922–1939) finishing with a .330 lifetime batting average. Leon "Goose" Goslin, elected to the Hall of Fame in 1968, played 18 years in the majors (1921–1938) and owned a .316 career batting average.

[1946]

You Can't Kill the Umpire

BY GEORGE BARR

More times than I've hoisted my right thumb into the air and declared a runner out I've said (always to myself, of course), "This is no business for a guy who wants to stay sane. I'm going to quit." That's what I've said, and mostly because umpires are the most abused of the men who hustle around a diamond during the baseball season.

Why, I've been bombarded with enough pop bottles to supply the soft-drink concessions at the Polo Grounds for the next twenty years. I've been escorted through half a dozen angry crowds by a cordon of cops with nightsticks at the ready. I've faced swarms of abusive women waiting at the gates after so-called "Ladies' Day." And I've had to step into a wild and woolly welter of players' flying fists to try to settle a dispute more often than I like to remember.

If I had a nickel—even a penny—for every time some fan yelled, "Kill the umpire!" I could buy every team in the National League today and still have enough left for a fair-sized string of farm clubs.

But, oddly enough, neither the players nor the fans have ever succeeded in putting me six feet under the sod. It took three extra-inning games in a row—starting with that record-breaking nineteen-inning, 0-0 tie between the Dodgers and the Reds at Brooklyn last September—to get me off the diamond. And even after that I'm back behind the plate and on the bases again this season for my sixteenth year in the National League.

In other words, you *can't* kill the umpire, no matter how hard you try.

There was, for instance, what I always think of as the wildest afternoon in baseball, the day the great Dizzy Dean pulled a balk and I, somehow, escaped with all my teeth, my scalp, and every bone in one piece.

Diz, as you will recall, thought baseball was invented for Dizzy Dean, and Dizzy Dean was born for baseball. But that morning—it was May 19, 1937—I had received an official letter from National League headquarters ordering me to enforce Rule 27, which stated, "With a runner on first or second base, the pitcher must face the batsman with both hands holding the ball in front of him. If he raises his arms above his head or out in front, he must return to a natural pitcher's position and stop before starting his delivery of the ball to the batsman." And the letter added, "Don't warn the pitchers. Call a balk."

Put yourself in my place. It was a real pitchers' duel. Carl Hubbell vs. Dizzy. Besides, it was Ladies' Day and the park was jammed to the gates, packed with people who were looking for plenty of baseball thrills. They got 'em.

I did everything I could to assure enforcement of the rule. I talked to Sam Breadon, St. Louis owner, and he said he would tell Frankie Frisch, then the Cards' manager, about it. Later, before the game started, I warned Frank personally. On my way to home plate I passed Dizzy, who was warming up.

"Dizzy, don't forget to come to a stop when there are runners on base."

Diz said okay.

The game was one of those naturals, a real out-and-out hurlers' duel. Twice during the game, when the Giants had men on base, I told Mickey Owen, behind the plate for the Cards, to go out and warn Dizzy about the balk.

Then, in the sixth inning, the lid blew off. The Cards were leading, 1-0, and the Giants were at bat. Burgess Whitehead singled. I told Mickey to go out to the mound again and warn Dean, and he did. Carl Hubbell, the next man up, sacrificed Whitehead to second. Up came Dick Bartell.

Diz took his stretch and—despite all the warnings—didn't come to a stop. Bartell slugged away and poled out a fly to deep short, which Leo Durocher, then the Card shortstop, snagged with his back to the infield. But, in the meantime, I had thrown up my arms and started yelling, "That is a balk, that is a balk," automatically making the ball dead and advancing Whitehead to third.

Every Card in the dugout swarmed on the field and denied that Dizzy had committed a balk. For ten minutes the argument raged, until I finally was able to restore order. Unfortunately, that was only the beginning.

Bartell, still entitled to a wallop at the ball because Diz's balk had made his fly dead, slammed out a short fly to center. Pepper Martin raced in. Nine times out of ten he would have caught such a ball. But this was the tenth, and he dropped it and kicked it. Whitehead scored.

Two more hits and a misjudged fly gave the Giants four runs.

The tension was terrific. Dizzy was tossing them close to the batters. Every player on the field, in the dugout, or in the bullpens was as ready to swing a fist as he was a bat. In the ninth, the whole thing blew up like a Fourth of July fireworks display.

Jim Ripple of the Giants came to bat and placed a neat bunt down the first base line. The Cards' second baseman came in fast for it, and tossed to Johnny Mize on first. Dean, meanwhile, rushed in to cover the bag, and bumped Ripple, knocking him to the ground.

The field looked like a combination of a department-store sale of nylons for twenty-two cents and a newsreel of Russian youth giving a mass display of boxing and wrestling. The dugouts belched out players faster than a machine gun pumping bullets. There were at least ten different and assorted scraps going on about the field. Right in front of me, the two catchers, Mickey Owen and Gus Mancuso, were testing their headlocks on each other. They were the only ones I could see close up. I tossed them out of the game.

When order was restored, some fifteen minutes later, Don Gutteridge was displaying a beautiful shiner.

Frankie Frisch came up to me, fire in his eyes. "What about Ott?" he demanded. "Well, what about Ott?" I replied. "He hit Gutteridge," said Frisch. I told him I hadn't seen it.

Frisch boiled over. "No, but you could see the balk," he stormed.

That took another five minutes before Leo the Lip charged in. "What about Luque?"

"Yeah, what about Luque?" I asked.

"He hit Gutteridge," said Durocher.

By this time it was getting a bit tiresome.

Jess Haines, Cards pitcher, had his two cents' worth to put in. "What about Chiozza?" he wanted to know.

"Here we go again," I thought.

"He hit Gutteridge," claimed Haines.

I was strongly tempted to telephone the coroner. If everyone was right, Gutteridge needed a death certificate rather than a steak for his eye.

The end of the game—the Giants won, 4-1—didn't end the argument. Fans surrounded the umpires' dressing room; police had to drive them away. All evening there were phone calls and telegrams to my hotel room, some raising Cain, some complimenting me on my stand. I finally had to tell the operator to say I was out for the rest of the night.

Murdering the umpire as a milder form of sport has, at times, assumed serious proportions. When you figure that a plate umpire makes an average of 300 decisions a game you begin to realize that someone in the stands or on the field is going to be sore about something. Sometimes you don't even know why they're mad.

Down in Waco, Texas, before I started working in the National League, a particularly irate fan almost got me one day. The ballparks weren't so well patrolled or fenced in as they are in the majors. I was crossing the park after the game when an automobile came roaring across the lot headed straight for me. I dodged. So did the car. I swivel-hipped like a halfback in the other direction. The auto charged after me. Somehow I managed to evade it. The driver came to a stop with a screeching of brakes, leaped out of the car with a blacksmith's big hammer in his hand, and started for me.

Luckily, I had a head start. I sprinted across the street to a service station, where a bystander offered to take me to my hotel in his car. But police arrived and took care of my would-be slayer at that moment.

So far I've managed to escape injury in this seasonal contest for my health and well-being, but there were two occasions when I wished I had been batboy instead of umpire. The ladies—bless 'em—when they became baseball fans made the Faithful of Brooklyn look like a flock of sissies. To them, every close decision against their team became a matter of personal insult, to be avenged only by violence on the person of the poor guy who called the play.

I was on the bases one day in Philly and had to call a close one at second. Manager Doc Prothro protested the decision, and the fans—it was Ladies' Day—backed him up.

In fact, I don't remember when I've taken a worse tongue-lashing than that day. It continued for the rest of the game.

After changing clothes following the game, I left the dressing room before Charlie Moran, my partner, and ran smack into a crowd of angry women, flourishing umbrellas and demanding, "Where's Barr?"

[1947]

Pitchers Are Sissies Now

BY KID NICHOLS AS TOLD TO SAM MOLEN

A big league pitcher who wins twenty games today becomes the toast of the baseball world and is given a fat raise in pay. In my day—the nineties—if you won only twenty games the club owner would say, "You didn't do so good this year—we are going to cut your salary next season."

Strange Happenings at the Old Ball Park

By MALCOLM WELLS

He steps out of the box.

And now the league-leading hitter is on deck.

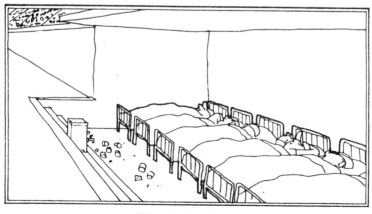

The side is retired.

Every so often a young sportswriter stumbles onto my record as a pitcher for the Boston Nationals, when I won thirty or more games for seven consecutive years, from 1891 through 1897. Always they ask the same question: "Why aren't there more thirty-game winners today?"

One reason is that modern-day clubs carry too many pitchers, which prevents the hurlers from working enough to bring out the best that is in them. The old-time clubs carried three pitchers; today they have ten. Whereas we were required to work forty or fifty full games in a season, present-day pitchers winning twenty games are considered top-notchers; and their baseball lifetime is no longer than it was in the old days.

Cy Young, a contemporary of mine, pitched 751 complete games, averaging 34.1 complete games per season for each of his twenty-two years in the majors; which is slightly terrific when you allow for the lean years coming and fading in the big show. Young's average is more complete games than any pitcher in the last twenty-five years has hurled in his best season. In one season, 1884, Charley Radbourne, pitching for Providence in the National League, won sixty games. In 1908, Ed Walsh won forty games for the Chicago White Sox.

Remember Joe McGinnity? When Joe was pitching for the New York Giants in 1903, he hurled 434 innings in fifty-five games and in forty-four of those games, went the entire nine innings. And Jack Chesbro? He pitched forty-eight complete games for the 1904 New York Yankees.

When Ace Adams established a modern major league record by working in seventy games for the Giants in 1943, I had to laugh. Adams hurled only 140 innings and won only eleven games. Had he pitched all those innings in succession, he would have hurled only sixteen complete games.

Sometimes we pitched every other day. Twice I pitched three days in succession and went the distance in each game. It was during my 1892 season with Boston. On August 23, we played a doubleheader with St. Louis in Kansas City. I pitched one game, winning, 5 to 3. August 24, we played another double-header with St. Louis in St. Louis. I pitched one game and won, 3 to 1. August 25, we played Louisville in Louisville. I pitched, winning, 6 to 1.

Pitching wasn't the only job pitchers had in the nineties. The day after we had pitched a game it was our duty to stand at the gate, and afterwards to count the tickets. I remember counting 30,000 tickets one day at the Polo Grounds in New York. That was a tougher assignment than pitching a full nine innings. Occasionally, when we weren't pitching, we played the outfield.

Modern-day pitchers spend half their time trying to develop and master tricky deliveries. The record book shows that I struck out 1,820 National League batters, an average of more than 130 for each of my fourteen seasons under the big tent. Yet, I had no fancy curves. Speed, change of pace and control are all any pitcher needs—if he masters them.

And did you ever hear of Amos Rusie, Cy Young, Radbourne or Mathewson having an elbow operation for the removal of chipped bone? Such operations were unheard of until recent years. If the arm got sore, we went out and pitched until the soreness left—we had to, or we would have been dropped from the team. Nothing short of a broken leg could have kept us out of uniform.

We worked hard, but I wouldn't say we were overworked. During my twelve years with Boston, I took part in 517 games, averaging 27.3 wins per season. My pitching days were thought to be over in 1904 when I took over the management of the St. Louis Cardinals; but while managing the team, I also pitched thirty-six games, winning twenty-one.

If I was overworked, it didn't affect my arm. I spent seventeen years in organized ball, far above the average of present-day hurlers.

The game of baseball hasn't changed much in the past fifty years, but the players have a different philosophy toward the game. They want to make a lot of money and retire. I played the game at a time when the league had a salary ceiling of $2,400—the fabulous salaries later to be drawn by Ruth, Greenberg, Newsom and Feller were undreamed of. We played for the love of the game: there were few holdouts. We wanted to pitch every day to win more games than the other guy—not for the money, but for the glory of winning.

It's different today.

Editor's Note: Elected to the Hall of Fame in 1949, Kid Nichols won 360 games and lost 203 during his major league career from 1890 through 1906.

[1948]

Joe Jackson, Finest Natural Hitter of Them All

BY ARTHUR DALEY

Who was Shoeless Joe Jackson?

Well, this is what Ty Cobb once told me about him. "The finest natural hitter in the history of the game," said the Georgia Peach, "was Shoeless Joe Jackson. He was batting against spitballs, shine balls, emery balls and all the other trick deliveries now outlawed. He never figured anything out or studied anything with the same scientific approach I gave it. He just swung. If he'd have had my knowledge of the intricacies of the batting art, his averages would have been truly phenomenal."

Babe Ruth said of him, "I copied Jackson's batting style because I thought he was the greatest hitter I had ever seen. I still think the same way." Tris Speaker declared: "I can't ever remember him being in a batting slump. His swing was so perfect that there was little chance of it getting disorganized. He was the greatest natural hitter who ever lived."

Shoeless Joe probably was the most gifted ball player ever to swing a bat. He came out of the Carolina hills, unable to read or write. But he was poetry itself at the plate. His lifetime average was .356 and one year, his freshman year no less, he hit a cool .408. Ironically enough, he didn't even win the batting championship that season because Cobb surpassed him with his magnificent .420.

But fate was unkind to him. Or perhaps he just didn't know any better. He became involved in the Black Sox scandal of 1919 and was forever barred from baseball. In fact, one of the most immortal of all sports lines evolved from that scandal. As the Shoeless One emerged from the hearing chambers a tear-stained little newsboy accosted him with the unforgettable phrase: "Say it ain't so, Joe." And Joe could merely hang his head in shame.

There are some who insist even today that Jackson, illiterate and none too bright, merely was an innocent dupe of the city slickers who engineered the coup. It is probably true to a great extent. It's also probably true he never received a penny of the bribe. There's still no getting away from the fact that Shoeless Joe, who supposedly was helping to throw the World Series to the Reds, wound up as the leading hitter on both teams with an average of .375.

It may be truth or it may be legend, but the story is that Jackson was playing barefoot in the outfield among rocks, glass and stubble in his pre–major league days. In the fourth inning he announced that he was quitting.

"Are the rocks and glass cutting your feet?" he was asked. "Naw," responded the Shoeless One. "It ain't that. But they's fuzzin' up the ball and I can't throw it." He was Shoeless Joe Jackson from that day onward.

Connie Mack had him first, and Connie brought him north with the second-stringers and saw him hit a ball in Louisville that he insists to this very day was the longest ball he ever saw hit. But Joe was getting restless. One night on the way north Connie noticed Jackson gazing wistfully at some milk cans with red destination labels on them at a railroad siding.

"I wish you'd put a red tag on me," he told Connie. The boy was getting increasingly homesick. He jumped the team at the next stop. So Connie sent Socks Seybold after him with orders to bring him back alive. Socks

"Shoeless Joe" Jackson was a smooth-swinging, left-handed batter who played in the majors from 1908 through 1920. An illiterate from South Carolina, he hit .408 in his first full major league season with the Cleveland Indians, but lost the American League batting title to Ty Cobb who posted a .420 mark. Jackson was traded to the White Sox in 1915 and hit .382 at age 33 in 1920, his last year with Chicago.

corralled Jackson, put him in a berth and awakened to find his quarry had disappeared in the night. Since Mr. Mack had a surplus of outfielders then, he sold him to Cleveland. Later Jackson went to the White Sox and sudden oblivion.

Although Joe had no weakness as a hitter, John Picus Quinn once held a theory that Jackson couldn't hit a low curveball on the inside. News of this got to Shoeless Joe and it worried him. Before he next faced Quinn he practiced for a couple of hours at hitting that kind of delivery. Quinn's first pitch was a low curve ball on the inside. Jackson hit it over the screen in right field, a feat previously accomplished only by Wahoo Sam Crawford.

One day at the Polo Grounds a crack pitcher, whose name has been forgotten, really fooled him with a wicked toss that broke so sharply downward it was about to strike the plate. But it never got the chance. Jackson golfed it high over the stands and into Manhattan Oval outside the ballpark. He hit Walter Johnson as though he owned him, using a half-swing to overcome the terrific Johnson speed. He was just doing what came naturally.

Al Schacht tells a tale about Jackson. When the Clown Prince of Baseball was pitching for Washington as a rookie, Clark Griffith discussed the hitters with him. He skipped all the White Sox but Jackson. "Never a fastball, Albert," warned the Old Fox. But with two men on base in the opening round, and Jackson at bat, the catcher signaled for a fastball. Rookie Schacht was caught on the horns of a dilemma, not knowing what order to obey.

He threw a fastball. Two sounds ensued, the bat striking the ball and the ball striking the fence. Schacht came out of there fast as Griff upbraided him with these words: "Albert, I thought you were a smart pitcher. But if you will take a look in the mirror, you will see the dumbest pitcher who ever lived." Albert gulped hard and snapped back. "Mr. Griffith," he said, "it just struck me that there must be a lot of dumb pitchers in this league because Jackson is only batting .390."

Oh, well, that's who Shoeless Joe Jackson was, young man. He probably was the greatest of them all, but his records have been expunged from the books and he never will reach Cooperstown's Hall of Fame. He is baseball's most tragic figure by far.

[1949]

The Messiest No-Hitter

BY RED SMITH

The Yankees had won the first two World Series games easily, but the Dodgers expunged Bobo Newsom early in the third and Hugh Casey arrived in time to preserve the last fragment of Brooklyn's lead. So New York was ahead, two games to one, on the afternoon of October 3, 1947, when Bill Bevens started pitching against Harry Taylor.

Something very, very peculiar happened that day in Ebbets Field. There'd been other World Series pitchers who fell only this far short of no-hit games—Claude Passeau and Monte Pearson and Burleigh Grimes and a raft of others. But they all were sharp. They'd really been pitching. Big, moon-faced Bevens was coming up with the flabbiest, messiest no-hitter imaginable. In eight innings he walked eight batters, one of whom scored on an infield out. But in eight innings there wasn't a Brooklyn hit.

In the ninth inning, two more Dodgers walked. The first was Carl Furillo, and Al Gionfriddo went in to run for him. With two out and Pete Reiser at bat, Gionfriddo stole second. Reiser, lame and unable to play in the outfield, was a pinch batter. He had taken a baleful cut at Bevens' first pitch, missed, and almost fell when his weight came down on his bad leg. He seemed scarcely able to stand, let alone get a hit.

But first base was open and Bucky Harris had more respect for Reiser than for the unwritten law against putting the winning run on base. (The Yankees led, 2-1, with one more putout needed.) The manager instructed Bevens to walk Reiser purposely. Eddie Miksis went in as a runner.

Cookie Lavagetto, batting for Ed Stanky, hit the right field wall for two bases and the ball game. Gionfriddo and Miksis fled home, the score was 3-2, and the World Series was all square.

There are some things it is impossible to forget. Things like the scene that developed when the unbelieving crowd at last came to realize what had happened. Lavagetto, running in from second base, had met Bevens near the mound and flung an arm about the pitcher's shoulder and they hustled toward the dugout together.

Two or three civilians in the formal attire of Brooklyn fans—checkered shirts with the tail hanging out of the pants, tennis shoes, no hat or tie—were bearing down on Lavagetto, leading the hungrily howling mob. The other Dodgers were running for Lavagetto, too, along with a half-dozen ushers. And there were three cops in the group, but they weren't holding off the crowd; they were scrambling over one another to get at Cookie, to claw at him and pummel his back or, at least, touch the hem of his playsuit.

Afterward, for upward of half an hour, a knot of fans lingered in the right field corner, worshiping the spot on the wall where Lavagetto's line drive had struck.

It was, maybe, the most memorable of all World Series scenes.

And now Bevens is gone from New York. The Yankees have sold him to the White Sox on a trial basis. Lavagetto is gone, too, of course. The greatest Brooklyn hero of the Series didn't even last in the majors until the next season. The Dodgers shipped him down to Oakland. For that matter, Reiser's gone, too, and Gionfriddo and Stanky.

After Bevens' one-hitter—"It wasn't, really; we got eleven hits," Burt Shotton argued that night, counting the ten bases on balls as singles—after that game, Bevens pitched two and two-thirds innings in the same Series and that was his end with the Yankees.

He had a sore shoulder last season and the Yanks sent him to Newark, where he worked only eight innings. He is one of those guys who can't pitch except for the world championship. There've been others before him. There was a time when Marius Russo did almost no summer work for the Yankees, seldom showing up on the mound except to beat some National League club in the autumn. Assorted ailments used to keep Monte Pearson largely idle between World Series, too, and, of course, there was the classic case of Howard Ehmke, who rested up all one summer to strike out thirteen Cubs in the fall.

Bevens is so unlucky he couldn't even get a break when he was sold. Frank Lane, general manager of the White Sox, wanted big headlines on the deal so he announced it for release in the roomy Sunday papers. A Kansas City radio station broke the release date, so the story came out a day ahead of schedule and got only a few paragraphs in the crowded Saturday papers.

It was like what happened to Lou Gehrig, who would have basked in a much brighter glare of publicity than he did if almost all of his career hadn't been thrown in the spacious shadow of Babe Ruth.

One day Lou hit four home runs in consecutive times at bat in one game. Even that wasn't enough to get him top billing. Biggest headlines read: "John McGraw Dies."

[1949]

My Greatest Thrill as a Player

BY CASEY STENGEL AS TOLD TO
JOHN P. CARMICHAEL

I joined the Brooklyn Dodgers for my first crack at the big leagues in 1912, and the things that happened to me in that first game on September 17 that year make it the greatest of 'em all for me as a player.

I'd gone two and a half years to dental school and saved up $150 for another year's tuition plus instruments. I was playing in Montgomery, Alabama, when I got the offer to join Brooklyn.

The fabulous Kid Elberfield, just back from the majors, told me, "Forget about being a dentist . . . you're good enough so you'll never come back. Get yourself a decent grip and forget about the money."

So I laid out $18 for the bag, and there I was in New York. A cab driver showed me a cheap hotel on Forty-seventh Street, and I spent that first evening walking a block or two and then hustling back to the lobby for fear I'd get lost.

By midnight I'd made it as far as Forty-second Street, and back, and I went to bed. Next morning I started for the park. Brooklyn played at Fifth Avenue and Third then, and I reported to the gateman there. He waved me toward the clubhouse and called after me, "You better be good."

I'll never forget walking into the locker room. There was a crap game going on in one corner. The only fellow who paid any attention to me was Zack Wheat. He introduced me around. Nobody shook hands. Some grunted. A few said hello.

I walked over to the game and decided maybe I ought to get in good with the boys by participating in the sport, so I fished out $20 and asked if I could shoot.

Somebody said, "Sure." And somebody handed me the dice. I rolled 'em out. A hand reached for my twenty and a voice said, "Craps, busher." And I never even got the bones back. I was about to reach for more money when I felt a tap on my shoulder. I looked around and there was manager Bill Dahlen.

"Are you a crapshooter or a ballplayer, kid?" he asked. I told him I was a player, and he said, "Well, get into a suit and on that field while you still have carfare."

I hustled, believe me, and I've never touched dice since, either. I got to the bench and just sat there. I knew better than to pick up a bat and go to the plate.

Elberfield told me what happened to rookies who tried that. Finally, Dahlen came over and said, "Let's see you chase a few," and I ran like the devil for the outfield.

Casey Stengel played in the outfield for five clubs during his major league career from 1912 to 1925. A left-handed batter and thrower, he became a manager later in his career, piloting the Yankees to ten American League pennants. He was elected to the Hall of Fame as a manager in 1966.

Behind the fence was a big building with fire escapes all down one side, and guys in shirtsleeves were parked on the steps, passing around pails of beer and getting set for the game.

I never expected to play, but just as the umpires came out Dahlen told me to "get in center." Hub Northen, the regular center fielder, had been sick, and I guess they decided they might as well get me over with quick.

My first time at bat we had a man on first, and Dahlen gave me the bunt sign. The pitch wasn't good and I let it go by.

Claude Hendrix, the league's leading pitcher, was working for Pittsburgh, and George Gibson was catching.

Hendrix threw another, and I singled to right center. When I got back to the bench after the inning, Dahlen stopped me. "Didn't you see the bunt sign?" he asked.

I told him yes, but that down South we had the privilege of switching on the next pitch if we wanted to.

"I don't want you to carry too much responsibility, kid," he said, "so I'll run the team, and that way all you'll have to worry about is fielding and hitting." My ears were red when I got to center field.

Up on the fire escape the boys were having drinks on my hit, and I could hear them speaking real favorably of me. I heard somebody holler, and it was Wheat telling me to move back.

Hans Wagner was at the plate. He larruped one, and I went way back and grabbed it. In the dugout Wheat said, "Play deeper for him."

I thought of the catch I'd made and said to myself, "I can grab anything he can hit."

Two innings later he came up again, and Wheat waved me back, but I wouldn't go. And wham! Old Hans peeled one off.

The ball went by me like a BB shot, and he was roosting on third when I caught up with it. Wheat just looked at me as much as to say, "You'll learn."

I got three more hits, all singles, right in a row. The first time Hendrix had fed me a fastball, figurin' why waste his best pitch, a spitter, on a busher.

He was pretty mad by the time I combed two blows off his spitter and another off his hook. Once when I was on first, Dahlen gave me the steal sign, and away I went.

I beat Gibson's throw, and Wagner just stood there, looking down at me. Never said a word.

I stole two bases, and when I came up the fifth time we'd knocked Hendrix out and a left-hander was pitching for the Bucs.

Pittsburgh manager Fred Clarke hollered at me, "All right, phenom, let's see you cross over." I was cocky enough to do it.

I stepped across the plate and stood hitting right-handed, and darned if I didn't get a base on balls.

"You hit fourth tomorrow," said Dahlen after the game. Those words were like music to my ears. Why, the big leagues were no different than any place else!

Editor's Note: Stengel spent his entire major league playing career in the National League as an outfielder for Brooklyn, Pittsburgh, Philadelphia, New York, and Boston from 1912 to 1925. He was in three World Series, 1916 with the Dodgers, and in 1922 and 1923 with the New York Giants. In the 1923 Series he hit two homers—one inside the park—to win as many games, on October 10 and 12, against the Yankees. Stengel posted a .284 lifetime batting average in the majors but hit .393 in his three World Series appearances.

[1950]

Grover Alexander Shatters a Myth About '26 World Series

BY GERRY HERN

In his own mild way, a man whose face is so white his freckles look like pennies shattered a sports myth during the World Series in the Yankees' Series headquarters in New York. The man was Grover Cleveland Alexander, an almost forgotten figure in the game of baseball. His pitching prowess was great. Old-timers still refer to sharp corners on railroads as "Alexanders." In 1915 he won thirty-one games and lost ten with the phenomenal earned run average of 1.22. He is one of the all-time greats of baseball. But much of his skill is lost in the memory of his most renowned performance, at the tag end of his baseball career, when he won a world championship for the St. Louis Cardinals.

Grover Cleveland Alexander won 373 games in a long career that began in 1911 and ended in 1930. He pitched 16 shutouts in 1916 for the Phillies, a one-season record that still stands. In 1938 he was elected to the Hall of Fame.

That was in the World Series of 1926, eleven years after Pete Alexander's carrying of the Philadelphia Phillies to the pennant. Alexander became a historic figure mostly because of the circumstances surrounding his condition when called in from the bullpen to pitch to Tony Lazzeri with the bases crowded. Alex, who had pitched the previous day, struck out the Yankee star on four pitches and all next season the out-of-town fans sang "Does Your Mother Know You're Out, Lazzeri?" every time Tony came to bat on the road.

The great story behind Alex's pitching that day has always been that, having won his game the previous day, he had celebrated extensively and arrived at the ballpark bullpen just in time to fall asleep to ease his aching head. And it has always been believed that Alex pitched slowly to Lazzeri because he was trying to focus his eyes well enough to establish the location of home plate. Through the pink haze, the story went, visibility was not good.

Alex was asked during his recent New York visit if he had been rolling the hoop the night before he gave the classic relief pitching performance.

He looked out of the pale blue eyes that have seen as much personal misfortune and human failure as a normal man could stand, and said, "I don't want to spoil anyone's story, but I was cold sober that night. There were plenty of other nights before and since that I have not been sober, although I have been cold, but the night before I struck Lazzeri out, I was as sober as a judge should be.

"Let me tell you what happened: I was leaving the locker room after the game and Hornsby came over and slapped me on the back. He said, 'You were great today and I suppose you want to celebrate. But don't do it. I may need you tomorrow.' And as sure as I'm sitting here I went back to my room at the Hotel Ansonia that night and didn't leave it—and I didn't celebrate either.

"I didn't expect to work that day because Jess Haines was going good. He had great stuff but all of a sudden he got in trouble. Hornsby telephoned the bullpen. He asked who was ready. They told him two or three pitchers were ready. Then Hornsby said, 'I don't care about them. I want

Alex.' Whoever was handling the bullpen phone said, 'He isn't ready. Hasn't even warmed up yet.'

"'I don't care. Send him anyway,' said Hornsby.

"So in I walked to that game without even taking off my sweater. I was cold but if Hornsby needed me, I was ready to pitch. That's what they were paying me for. I knew how to pitch to Lazzeri, and he knew I did. The umpire let me throw eight warm-up pitches and I just lobbed the last two. I didn't need them."

The man was asked what he used on Lazzeri.

"Nothing but this," he said, putting down the fork and bringing up his right hand over his shoulder.

"Just this one," he went on, whipping his arm down and snapping his wrist.

"O-o-o-w, that hurts now. Right here in the forearm, but it didn't then. Not that day. The first one was a strike, the second a ball. Then I threw him a low curveball that he missed. I knew then I had him and he did, too.

"Look, move this dish over here. Let that be home plate and this knife will be the batter's box. This salt shaker is Lazzeri, a tough guy at the plate. Give him anything good and he'd drive you out of the park. I have him on the count of one and two and he figures I'll waste one.

"Bob O'Farrell, who was catching me, didn't even bother giving a sign. He knew the pitch that was coming up. Look, I started it out here like this. Right at the salt shaker. That's Lazzeri, mind you, and he's looking to be brushed back but he also figures I'm going to curve him. At least he knows I'm not going to try to throw a fastball past him. I wasn't crazy. He murdered fastball pitching.

"That curve I threw started out here, as I told you, right at Lazzeri. He stood there. As I said, he was a tough guy. The ball started breaking about ten feet in front of the plate and swish! just like that it went out. He missed it by two feet."

Alex hasn't been too kind to himself through the years, and the luck he has known has been mostly bad. The side of his head is taped from a recent operation on his ear and he is completely broke, but no one can ever take away from him that moment in Yankee Stadium when he saved the St. Louis Cardinals from losing a World Series. The record books carry the stories of the tremendous season-long pitching marks he set, like winning thirty-one games in 1915, thirty-three in 1916 and thirty in 1917 and the earned run average of 1.53 for the two games he pitched in the 1915 World Series against the Boston Red Sox.

Those figures will be buried in the record books. The one thing for which Alex is famous is the story that he struck out Lazzeri while peering through bloodshot eyes after a night of revelry in which he didn't even sleep. That's the story you hear about him. Alex says it isn't true, but as he says, "Why spoil a good story?"

[1951]

Ed Walsh Fanned the "Big Three" on Nine Pitches

BY JIMMY CANNON

The old man is tall and fiercely proud of what he did in his youth, which is beyond the horizon of this generation's memory. It is as though Ed Walsh, who won forty games in 1908, edited the errors of men whose recollections were damaged by senility. Walsh narrates the acts of his genuine greatness as though they happened recently.

There is no fraudulent modesty to soil his opinions, and he appreciates the worth of his accomplishments. At seventy, Walsh seems to have a separate identity from himself as a young athlete. The old man stands aloof from the boy in ruthless examination and finds him marvelous and appealing.

We sat together at the fete commemorating the seventy-fifth year of the National League's existence. The old man, unimpaired by time, spoke above the snarling concert of a jazz band and the tumult of men drinking in drifting groups. The spitball, made tricky by moisture and falling in unbelievable dips, was his pitch.

Ty Cobb, softened by the years, stood talking to Willard Marshall, the Boston Braves outfielder.

"I never had any trouble with Ty," Walsh said. "He'd hit me. I'd stop him. He was the greatest."

"Was Babe Ruth better?" a guy at the table asked.

"No, no," the old man protested. "Ruth was a great pitcher when he was in it. Hitting the home runs he had it. But the greatest was Mister Ty Cobb. That's Mister Baseball for me."

On a summer's day in Philadelphia forty years ago, Walsh struck out Stuffy McInnis, Eddie Collins and Home Run Baker on nine pitched balls.

"Not a foul," Walsh said. "I went in to relieve with the bases filled and none out in the ninth. Came off the bench. They didn't even get a foul off me. I won forty games and pitched a no-hitter and pitched and won two doubleheaders. But striking those three out on nine balls with the bases drunk. . . ."

The old man looked around the table. They listened respectfully but Walsh appeared disappointed. It was the type of pause a professional orator uses when he anticipates applause.

"I almost duplicated it," Walsh said. "In St. Louis I went in under the same circumstances. The bases drunk . . . the ninth inning . . . no one out. I struck out George Stover . . . Bunny Brief and Bobby Wallace. They didn't get a foul either. But it took me ten balls. Billy Evans was umpiring behind the plate. Know what he told me afterwards? He said he missed the one he called a ball. Billy's here. Ask him if you doubt me."

The modern pitcher who throws at a man's head infuriates Walsh.

"We never hit a man in the head," said Walsh. "We might hit him in the calf of the leg and he'd be out for a few days. But the head never."

"Big Ed" Walsh relied on a spitball and fastball to deny American League batters. He pitched from 1904 to 1917, and in 1908 won 40 games while working 464 innings for the White Sox. In 1946 he was elected to the Hall of Fame.

The old man, whose top salary was $6,000 a year, turned to me and laughed. "What would they give you now for winning forty games?" he asked unexpectedly. "What would they pay me now? Ted Williams is the greatest hitter in the country right now. I'd get him, though. I'd get Joe DiMaggio. They all have weaknesses: all of them. I'd find their weakness and pitch to that. When they'd find out how to hit that pitch I'd give them another. They'd have to learn to hit me."

The old man looked at the parliament of great ball players gathered in the room for the N.L. shindig.

"I'll give you the team," Walsh said. "Put it down. This is the cream. They couldn't beat this. Jimmy Collins on third base . . . Hans Wagner at shortstop. Eddie Collins must be at second, Joe Jackson in left, Ruth in right and Mister Ty Cobb in center. Lou Gehrig at first and Bill Dickey is the greatest catcher I've ever seen. You have to have Walter Johnson and Cy Young. You know who else? Rube Waddell. If Rube had've stopped drinking you would have seen records like you've never seen. The utilities would be Tris Speaker, Nap Lajoie and George Sisler."

I asked him who should manage such a team.

"John McGraw," the old man said. "I come from a family of singers. I made a hit with him when I sung a couple of Irish songs at one of his banquets. He was a man who had a banquet on his birthday. But not for that. But because he was the greatest manager."

The old man glared around the table. No one challenged him.

[1951]

Fighting Billy Martin

BY CHARLES DEXTER

For two years Billy Martin was just a name on the New York Yankees' roster. Then in mid-May this year Jerry Coleman reentered the armed services and the kid from West Berkeley became the Stengeleers' regular second baseman.

At precisely 1:25 p.m. on May 24 Billy was tossing a baseball back of third base at Fenway Park, Boston. On the diamond where the Red Sox were taking infield practice, Jim Piersall chattered loudly between grounders batted in his direction. "Busher!" yelled Piersall as he went into the hole back of third base. "You'd be back in the bushes, Martin, if you didn't sit in Stengel's lap! Showboat! Busher!"

"Shut up, you French hot dog!" shouted Martin.

"Busher . . . I can lick you with one hand tied behind my back!"

"I'll buy that," Billy cried. "Any time . . . any place!"

"See you under the stands in three minutes!"

As the Sox quit the field Billy dashed toward the runway beside the home team's dugout. "Hey, kid," Piersall said to the Red Sox bat boy, "hold my cap. I've got a job to do!"

Billy's cap was on his head as he darted down the steps, turning to confront the Sox rookie. He shot a left to the jaw, crossed with a right. Piersall tried a jab, failed to connect and then went into a clinch. "Okay, if you want to wrestle," Billy panted. He grabbed Piersall's shirt, ripping it. Older heads stepped between the young pugilists. Ellis Kinder used two hands to push their heads apart. Coach Bill Dickey bodily carried Martin toward the steps. The bout was over, Billy the technical victor.

"Sure, we rode Piersall when the Sox played at the Stadium a couple of weeks before," said Billy afterwards. "But I didn't ride him more than anyone else. He was talking about me all the time that day in Boston, standing with the batboy, making cracks. That's all right, but when he called me a busher in front of the whole Yank team and then challenged me, I had to fight.

"I don't know what it is, maybe my hot blood, but when someone pushes me against a wall I get mad. And when I get mad I can fight like blazes. You see, I was born and grew up in West Berkeley, California. Berkeley's a college town, but West Berkeley's where the factories are. Somehow the kids all liked to fight.

"Someone'd say, 'So-and-so says he can lick you,' and you'd say, 'Like heck he can!' and you'd go off and find so-and-so and give him a licking. I must have been in a hundred fights when I was a kid and only lost one. That time I was fighting a bigger fellow—I was always fighting bigger fellows. I was licking him when he pushed me against an automobile and I fell down.

"I was getting up when someone stopped the fight. I guess you'd call that getting beat.

"I used to fight around the playground and there was a gym in town where I went. The instructor there gave me a few lessons in boxing. But I was never a boxer. I just had a hard punch and that was enough to win in our gang.

"My stepfather and I used to clean out the aisles and around the altar at St. Ambrose's Church. Pop wouldn't take any pay for it so the Father sent me to a charity camp that summer at St. Mary's.

"There was a big affair one day and a hundred of us kids were walking across a field. I was with my roomie when some other kid bumped into him and a fight started. My roomie licked the other kid.

"The next day the other kid's roomie challenged me. He said I'd jumped his pal. I couldn't take that, so I said, 'I'll fight you anywhere . . .'

"Someone said, 'You better be careful. He's been in the Golden Gloves.'

"I said, 'I'll lick him anyhow.' And I did! The gang was so excited they set up a fight for us in the St. Mary's college gym, right inside a regular ring. An older man was referee and they had a timekeeper to hit the gong. They didn't need a timekeeper. There was about a hundred in the other kid's corner and only my roomie in mine, but after he hit me once, I got mad. I began to swing and knocked him down ten times. His pals stopped the fight before the first round was over. I was champion of that camp, all right."

If Billy Martin weren't a slick little ball player he might be contesting Ray Robinson for the world's middleweight title. Billy is of Italian ancestry, one of five children ranging in ages from eleven to thirty-three. His mother, the former Joan Salvini, was born in San Francisco. His stepfather, Jack Downey, is a Berkeleyite, living across the Bay.

"Yes, we were real poor," he says. "My stepfather is a wonderful guy. He tried hard to get work when I was a kid and couldn't and went on WPA. He worked as a truck driver until a few years ago when he got arthritis. My brother Frank was the Frank Pesano who played professional ball for Fort Smith, Arkansas, some years ago. He was a fastball pitcher and might have made it if he hadn't come up with a sore arm.

"Frank taught me a lot about baseball. But I had to go to work when I was fifteen to help support the family. I was assistant director of the playground one summer and worked as a laborer in a steel factory.

"Augie Galan lived about four blocks from us on Seventh Street. Augie would come down to the playground every day during the fall and winter. He taught me a lot about baseball. I started in as a pitcher when I was twelve or thirteen, learning how to pitch from Frank. By fifteen I was a third baseman and shortstop. We had some fine sandlot teams around West Berkeley, Legion teams and so on. We got into competition for the All-Star Sandlot team that went east to play for the world's championship.

"That June in 1946—school was not over yet for the year—the ACAL or Alameda County Athletic League All-Stars were picked from all the sandlot clubs in the vicinity. I made the team and went to Oakland for the local finals.

"That's where Casey Stengel first saw me. He was managing the Oaks and was a judge that day. And was I terrible! I made two errors at shortstop. I hit the ball hard, but I got no hits. Casey and the other judges picked a big, hard-hitting outfielder, Babe Van Heiut, as the candidate for the national All-Stars. I got second place but that didn't mean anything but honorable mention.

"Then Red Adams, trainer for the Oaks, kept telling Casey he ought to call me in for a workout. Casey looked me over at the Oaks' park and sure enough, I got a contract with the Class C Idaho Falls team in the Pioneer League.

"I never got a chance there. Service guys were coming back and they got first shot at infield jobs. The next spring I went to spring training with Oakland and was sent to Phoenix in the Arizona-Texas League.

"That was my best year. Arkie Biggs was our manager. He played me every day and I led the league in batting with .392 and in most everything else, hits, doubles, RBIs, putouts, assists—and even errors, fifty-five.

"That September I was called up to Oakland. It was great playing for Casey and it still is great. He knows how to handle ball players. He's got the psychology angle down to a T.

"In 1948 I fought it out with Merrill Combs for the shortstop job and lost. Then Johnny Lodigiani got hurt playing second base and I had about three months at that spot. One day Schnozz Lombardi threw into the dirt trying to catch a runner stealing. I dove for the ball, tagged the guy but his spikes ripped my kneecap. That was all, brother! I was out for the rest of the season.

Billy Martin was engaged in many on-field battles during his career. He is shown on the far right after exchanging punches with Clint Courtney in a game with the St. Louis Browns at Yankee Stadium on July 12, 1952. Martin had put a hard tag on Courtney at second base, and Courtney came up swinging. Casey Stengel, No. 37, went to Martin's rescue, attempting to restrain an upset umpire.

"Casey went up to the Yankees in 1949 and I played under Charlie Dressen. The Oaks won the pennant, their first in twenty-one years, and I led the league in fielding at shortstop, playing in 172 games. I was teamed with Artie Wilson at short and we had a sweet double-play combination, thanks to Cookie Lavagetto, who taught me a lot about that kind of stuff.

"Cookie worked me afternoons, teaching me not to backhand thrown balls and how to get in front of the runner for the throw to first. He helped me, too, in batting. Kids get overanxious and bite at fastballs, and they had some real fast pitchers in the Coast League. Cookie taught me how to hit curves.

"And playing every day is the only way to learn—which I did. I'd been playing with men ten to fifteen years older and had to find out my own faults and correct them. I worked hard to make myself a better player. I kept asking questions and getting wiser, and by the end of the season four clubs in each major league were after me.

"I almost had a choice of picking my own club. Brick Laws, who owns the Oaks, advised me to go to the Yankees because they were a first-place team. And I wanted to go there because Casey was the manager.

"As it happened, I wasted the whole year of 1950 on the Yankee bench. Sure, I made money, the World Series money. But I'd hit .360 in that year's spring training, playing regular second base. And I only made one error. I was in the lineup Opening Day and started the second game, but then Jerry Coleman went in. If I hadn't played that useless month in 1946 with Idaho Falls I could have been kept another year at Oakland. That would have been better for me, for I'd have played every day.

"After the World Series in 1950 I married Elaine Berndt, whom I'd gone to junior high with. Then I was called by the army. I was sent to Camp Ord, where I only played one game of ball. Two months after I was in I went to the CO and asked him to send an allotment to my parents and the two younger kids, Pat and Joan. 'You can't do that,' he says. 'You don't earn enough.' He looked at a table of figures and said, 'I'd have to make you a Captain to pay all that money to your folks. Under regulations, I'll have to discharge you as a hardship case.'

"And so in May last year, I was back with the Yanks. More benchwarming . . . it's no wonder I got in the habit of jockeying the other teams, yelling at them. I had to do something with my time! The Yanks started to call me 'Arcaro' because I jocked so much. That's how I happened to jockey Piersall and got him red-eyed. . . ."

It took Billy a week to get into the hang of regular play following Jerry Coleman's departure. During that week the Yankees lost ground in the pennant race. But soon the angular, dark-haired boy from Berkeley began to bang hits and execute smooth fielding plays. Yankee pitchers, supported by a sound defense, hurled low-hit victories.

Said Casey Stengel: "We had the best second baseman in baseball out there, Jerry Coleman. He's graceful and pretty to watch. Billy Martin looks like nothing at all, but he's got the makings, too. He's awkward because he's built that way but he has baseball intelligence. He knows what the next play is likely to be and when something unexpected happens he thinks fast.

"The kid fits in nice with Rizzuto on the double play. He can go back for a ball fast and accurately. I'm amazed the way he runs bases on that leg he broke in spring training. He takes wonderful care of himself—I watched him testing out the leg day after day, like a puppy dog that's busted a bone, feeling the ground, stamping on it, making sure he could run.

"And how about his scoring from first on a single against the White Sox? You can't beat that, on a leg busted in two places three months before. He can hit, too. He gets distance, pound for pound. And he has spirit. A Brown runner tried to knock the ball out of his hand on a baseline tag with a double play coming up. You didn't see him drop it. That's fighting baseball."

Says Billy: "I don't hate Jim Piersall. But I couldn't help picking up his challenge. When I played basketball in school I was the smallest kid on the court. When a big guy tried to shoot and I was guarding him, I'd climb up his back. He'd toss me off, then look at me, see how small I was and then rough me up. I had to defend myself, didn't I? I'd fight back. You had to do that in our neighborhood or you'd have been run out of town. . . ."

[1952]

Roy Campanella's Tricks Behind the Plate

BY CHARLES DEXTER

When Roy Campanella went on a batting rampage this spring, Brooklyn fans woke up to the fact that they had been taking him for granted. Whenever he went to bat they set up that special kind of cheer reserved for the super-slugger, the Ruthian cheer, a mixture of awe, anticipation and high hopes for a blast out of the lot.

It was pretty difficult to realize that Campy, age 31-plus, has been playing professional ball longer than all but a half-dozen or so major leaguers and that while most of the others (save Enos Slaughter of the Cards) are used only as part-timers, Campy is not only a regular but one who is indignant when he is asked to take a day off.

He had just taken his first day off of the 1953 season and was reporting at Ebbets Field the following day when someone asked him why. "'Twasn't none of my doing," he said. "I'm all right. I'm in perfect condition—"

"But how do you keep yourself in perfect condition?" someone asked.

"Work!" snorted Campy. "That's all . . . work!"

Of course there's more to it than that: Campy is the most relaxed player in the game. He enjoys life to the full, worries about nothing. He's his natural self at all times. At the Dodgers' spring training camp in Havana in 1947 Campy was breaking in as first-string receiver for the Montreal Royals. The Royals were playing the Dodgers and a reporter picked a box seat behind the Royals' bench to watch Campy. After an inning in which the Dodgers were retired in order, Campy returned to the bench. He was a newcomer to the Royals. One might have expected any rookie to have bided his time before taking charge.

But Campy began to talk from the moment he neared the bench. He paced up and down, addressing his mates. "Toughest batter they got is that Stanky," he said. "Best thing to do with him is to put it right down the middle. Got to watch how that Lavagetto shifts his feet—he'll hit to right on you." He addressed the pitcher: "Keep an eye on Reese—he's got the best jump I ever saw. I'll take care of him if he tries to steal. And about

With the Brooklyn Dodgers, Roy Campanella won National League MVP Awards in 1951, 1953 and 1955, but his career was cut short by a tragic auto accident in 1958 that left him a quadriplegic. In 1969 he was elected to the Hall of Fame.

Jackie—" He roved up and down, chuckling, stimulating the Royals, the perfect picture of a vet who was a rookie.

"Sure, I remember that day," Campy said as he sat on a stool before his locker. "But the game I remember best is the one in 1948 when I broke in with the Dodgers. Rex Barney started at the Polo Grounds and Bruce Edwards was catching, and then in the seventh or eighth Hugh Casey went in and I was told to catch. I didn't do anything. I got no hits. But that was the red letter game for me . . . in the big leagues, that was it!"

Back in 1936, when Campy was 15, he was signed to a $60-a-month contract with the Baltimore Elite Giants of the National Negro League. He'd actually earned his first $5 as a professional one year earlier on the Bachrach Giants in Philadelphia. He had a hero then—Josh Gibson, the peerless catcher of the Homestead Grays. "They talk about home runs," says Campy today. "Mantle's made a long one or two or three and Larry Doby and Luke Easter. They say Ruth and Gehrig and Foxx could clout 'em 500 feet, but the longest one I ever saw was hit by Josh at Yankee Stadium in 1937. It went so far up into the bleachers it almost went out of the lot." Campy chuckled. "I hit a pretty good one myself off Brazle last year in St. Louis. They say Mantle hit one right over the bleacher roof, and Bill Dickey did it in the 1943 World Series, they tell. But I sent one right over the roof and almost in center field."

Campy makes catching look so easy that almost anyone ought to do it as well as he. He squats behind the plate like any sturdy man sitting in a swivel chair. He handles pitchers so faultlessly that wild pitches look like sinkers when they hit the turf. He seems to amble after foul pops, never hurrying but always getting them. He throws to second base with no waste motion and with uncanny accuracy. He never seems to hurry, never wastes an unnecessary step.

"The day after Gibson hit that home run in 1937," he says, "I met him on the field. 'I been watchin' you, Kid,' he says. 'You don't need any lessons in catching, but if you want to work out with me the next morning we're both around, I'll give you a few pointers.'"

From Gibson Campy learned the art of relaxation. "He taught me how to lay my right hand against my right thigh, giving signs to pitchers from that angle, so they can't be stolen by base runners. He showed me how to raise my mitt quick, right after giving the sign so the pitcher'll have a target for as long as possible. That helps his control.

"There's another trick about holding the target. I keep the mitt in position, but just as soon as the pitcher begins his delivery I snap up to an erect position so I can be free and easy going after wild pitches. Maybe that's why not so many bad balls get by me.

"Now, when there are runners on base, it makes no difference whether I think they're going to steal or not—I always cock my arm to throw just as soon as I get the ball. That's a warning to the runner I'm good and ready to throw. And in case he is stealing, cocking the arm saves a fraction of a second and helps me get the ball down to the base that much quicker.

"Josh also taught me a lot about picking runners off base. The 'arm-cock' helps, of course. But there's a special way of throwing, too. If it's a pickoff I aim for the bag and I guess I've been playing so long I don't have to aim much—it's sort of automatic. But when I get a man in a rundown I don't aim for the bag, I aim for him. He's got to stay inside the baseline, anyhow, and if he sees the ball's coming straight at him he'll duck or side-step and lose a step. My infielder's got to be alert—it's his job to be at the bag or on the basepath ready to grab the ball."

In the thousands of games Campy has played, one stands out above all others. It wasn't one in which he hit a jackpot homer or went "5 for 5" or nursed a pitcher into a no-hitter. It's a game in which he pulled a pickoff play which set the baseball world buzzing.

"I'll never forget that one," he says. "The Yanks were playing us the fourth game of the 1949 Series. They had Rizzuto on third in the first inning and Tommy Henrich on second. And Yogi Berra grounds to Eddie Miksis, who's playing third for us.

"Well, Rizzuto is trapped off third and the rundown begins. I get the ball and aim it at him and he steps out of the baseline and the umpire calls him out. And then, out of the corner of my eye, I see Henrich standing a couple of feet off second, watching the play.

"Tommy was a smart guy, no one to fool, but I took a chance he was saying to himself, 'Heck, that's too bad,' so without moving my body I whip a throw to Robby, who's covering second. Man, that was it! Henrich's out without knowing what happened to him. . . ."

As for foul pops, they're sugar candy to Campy. Long experience gives him that sixth sense of knowing in which direction the ball is going. "Catchers who lose fouls make the mistake of taking their eye off the ball," he says. "They're afraid of running into something. I never blink an eye when I'm after a fly. I keep my eye on it until it's either in my mitt or fallen into the stands. I know my teammates will yell to me if it looks like I'm going to crash. And I catch the ball like I'm an infielder, hand and mitt joined. None of that fancy one-hand stuff or keeping my hands apart. All I care about is getting the ball and hanging onto it."

Campy scoffs at the notion that his batting surge of this spring was due to a change in his stance. He has never given much thought to his style at the plate, wielding the stick in the manner which is most comfortable and natural to him. He was blasting homers for the Elite Giants in 1937 and going 7 for 7 in a game between Monterrey and Tampico in the Mexican League in 1942, the same as the big league record set by another catcher, Wilbert Robinson of the famous old Baltimore Orioles, in 1892. Back in 1948 Branch Rickey sent Campy to St. Paul in May. When he returned to the Dodgers on July 2 he struck two homers to lick the Giants in his first game and was hitting .465 on July 18. In 1951 he crashed 33 circuit clouts, his high as a Dodger.

Campy strikes a philosophic pose in explaining why he is often the terror of the league at bat. "The ball comes in and I hit it. When I've got enough wood behind it, it goes safe. When I haven't, it's an out. When I meet it on the nose, it goes places."

In the Dodger clubhouse Campy is teacher, pal and hero. His locker is at the end of a row near the canteen of portly Senator John Griffin of the weird hats and good humor. It is a natural gathering place for members of the squad who drop down for a coke and persiflage. Campy takes youngsters under his wing. "Did all right on that double play yesterday, Jim," he tells Junior Gilliam. "But you could've been wrong, going fancy with an underhand throw and posing like an acrobat." He's a hero to the pitchers. "I suppose you went down to the street corner and told all the boys about it, Billy," he'll say to Bill Loes after the young right-hander has pitched a shutout. Loes wanders over to find out why so-and-so hit his curve. Preacher Roe avers that Campy can read his mind when they team up for a game. "He and I know the batters so well I don't even have to look at his signs," says Preach.

Campy can't pick out one of the thousands of games he's played or seen as the greatest. But he does recall the play he thinks was "a miracle." It happened in 1952, just before Willie Mays went into the army. The Giants were playing the Dodgers at Ebbets Field and "that doggone Mays is away over in right center when Bobby Morgan's at bat. Bobby crosses him up with a drive to left center. Didn't seem no chance of Willie's getting the ball and I'm counting up the runs for us when all of a sudden I see him zooming out of nowhere, diving like a seal going after a fish and then tumbling over and over. And when he picks himself up the ball's in his hand."

In a fatherly way Campy keeps an eye on young Negro players. Gilliam is his special pet, for Junior is on the Dodgers. But he closely watches Jim Pendleton and Bill Bruton of the Braves, both of whom he regards as future stars. As for pitchers, he doesn't hesitate when asked to name the fastest: "Newk . . . that man can throw, and he'll be back throwing for us next year," he says of big Don Newcombe. The cleverest? "Roe, of course. No one smarter." Not even Satchel Paige? Campy batted against the venerable Satch as long ago as 1937. "He never did shut me out completely," he says. "I got a single off him . . . once, I think."

[1953]

Jocko Conlan: "Umpires Must Have Command and Respect"

BY ROBERT CROMIE

Sometimes infuriated National Leaguers ask umpire John "Jocko" Conlan if he ever was thrown out of a ball game when he played center field for the Chicago White Sox 20 years ago. Jocko, an honest fellow, admits he was.

The questioner then asks why, and Jocko has a pat answer: "For doing what you're doing now," he snaps, waving the offender toward the showers.

Conlan, a native Chicagoan whose square-cut Irish face is so unmistakably Irish that Jimmy Cannon, a New York sportswriter, invariably greets him with "Here comes the Rose of Tralee!", has a working theory about his profession and pursues that theory come hell, high water or Leo Durocher.

"You must have *command* and you must have *respect*," says Jocko firmly. "Without either, a man's not a good umpire. I don't care if the ball players don't love me; I just want respect."

And Jocko gets it.

Conlan has had his share of brushes with both players and fans since Ford Frick, then National League president, bought his contract from the American Association in 1941, and always manages to emerge without losing stature.

In Brooklyn, seven or eight years ago, Jocko was the focal point of an outburst by Flatbush fanatics which could have had tragic results.

"Bragan, probably the slowest runner in the National League, was on first base for Brooklyn," Jocko says, "and Pete Reiser, the fastest man in baseball, was at bat. With the Cubs leading, 2-1, and two out, Reiser hit a potential three-bagger and was out sliding into third on a close play. But Bragan hadn't crossed home plate. He was still about five steps away when Reiser went out, and I hollered that the run didn't count.

"Manager Leo Durocher ran out and called me a real bad name, then kicked dirt on my pants. That's embarrassing, and that was the only time I ever lost my head umpiring. I pulled off my mask and followed him back to the dugout, asking him to take a punch at me. He didn't, and I chased him. Then I ordered the run off the scoreboard.

"Now, in Brooklyn, when they put up a run, that's theirs, and the beer bottles came down. There must have been 200 of them. Charlie Grimm, who was managing the Cubs, came out to where I stood at home plate, facing the stands, and said: 'Get out to second base, you stubborn Irishman, or you'll be killed.' I told him: 'Get out of here or you'll be with Durocher.'

"Then about 500 policemen came out of nowhere and the throwing stopped. But the papers next day said the stand Jocko Conlan took (I don't mean I defied 'em; I just wanted to watch those bottles, see?) helped quiet the crowd as much as the police.

"Well, the chief of detectives came to see me in the dressing room after the game and said he'd have a couple of policemen take me to the subway. But I told him that would cause more trouble than ever.

"It was August, and I came out wearing a light tan tropical suit, a tan straw hat, and brown and white shoes. There were about 5,000 people waiting for the umpire, but not one of them knew me. They were looking for a guy in a blue suit."

Frankie Frisch, one of Jocko's best friends off the diamond, also was the man he used to toss off the premises most frequently. But Frisch, although he always made the same unprintable suggestion each time he was given his eviction notice, never held a grudge and invariably showed up the next day with a smile and a cheery greeting.

"One time it started to mist in Brooklyn about the third inning, with the Pirates a run behind," Jocko recalls. "Frankie, then manager of the Pirates, kept arguing that the game should be called.

"'You haven't got guts enough to call it,' he said. 'All my players will get pneumonia.'

"I said: 'What's the matter? Haven't you got guts enough to play it?'

"Three or four photographers came up during the argument, and one had a raincoat and umbrella. When I turned to start the fourth inning, Frisch had borrowed the umbrella and was in the coaching box with it over his head.

"I gave him a dandy wave, and said, 'Take it with you!'

"He asked: 'What's the matter, can't a guy have a little fun?'

"'Have all you want to,' I told him, 'but not at *my* expense!'"

In a 1961 game between the Dodgers and Pirates, Jocko Conlan is kicked in the shins by Leo Durocher, then a Dodger coach, who was disputing a foul ball call by Conlan. The umpire promptly retaliated with a kick of his own and ejected Durocher from the game. The catcher is Hal Smith of the Pirates.

Frisch gave Jocko a textbook decision to make in 1944. Let Conlan tell it:

"The Pirates were playing the Cubs and Frisch was coaching at third base. Ed Stanky was the Chicago third baseman and Frankie Zak was on first base for the Pirates, with Jim Russell at the plate. Russell hit a long drive and, as Zak came around third, Stanky gave him the hip. It was a muddy day, and Zak slid halfway to the Cubs' bench. Frisch started yelling, 'Obstruction! What is it?' I said, 'He scores.'

"Now here came the ball from right field, and, just as Russell came sliding in, Frisch made a terrific slide for third base from the coaching box, and Stanky tagged Frisch. I said: 'You're safe (to Russell), and you're out, Frisch—out of the game!' All he said was:

"'How do you like that? Here, I make the best slide I've made in 15 years, and I get put out of the ball game. So long.'"

John Bertrand Conlan was born December 6, 1902, on Chicago's south side, where he attended All Saints Parochial School, was a White Sox batboy, and finally entered semipro baseball with the famous Pyotts. Jocko was a center fielder and threw and batted left-handed.

In 1923 he went to Wichita, then was sold to Rochester in the International League, where he played four seasons for the late great George Stallings. Jocko broke a leg in 1926, the same day he was to have been sold to Cincinnati for $18,000 and three players.

The deal was off, and Jocko was traded to Newark, where he played in 1927-28-29. A year later he went to Toledo, where he played two years, and, after a year's layoff, Jocko wound up his playing career with the White Sox, with whom he played in 1934 and 1935 and hit .249 and .286, respectively.

Jocko was fast, averaging 30 or 35 stolen bases a year (one year he stole 52 with Wichita), and, "it isn't nice for me to say it, but I always was a good center fielder."

If Emmett "Red" Ormsby hadn't been overcome by the heat in St. Louis 20 years ago, it is quite possible that Conlan never would have become a big league umpire. But Ormsby's inability to work the second game of a White Sox–St. Louis doubleheader left Harry Geisel in need of assistance, and Jocko, then the White Sox center fielder, and a St. Louis player were chosen.

That game passed without incident, but the next day it was different. The Sox were trailing late in the contest and Jocko again was assisting Geisel. Luke Appling hit a long drive to the outfield and began racing around the bases. Jocko, still in Chicago uniform, was keeping pace beside him, shouting such sterling advice as "Get that trunk off your back! Run! Run!"

Appling hit the dirt at third and the play was very close, but Jocko called him out. Manager Jimmy Dykes, considerably chagrined at seeing a promising rally end, began to chide Jocko, but Appling took the heat off by agreeing with the call.

The next season Conlan umpired in the New York–Pennsylvania league, a recommendation from Will Harridge, American League president, helping him get the job, and from there he went to the American Association, whence Frick grabbed him for the National League.

Conlan says umpiring was difficult at first because "I just walked out cold, didn't even know how to hold a mask. Much as I thought I knew about baseball, I didn't know much about umpiring, and no one else does either till he puts on that mask. You have to learn positions and angles. How to watch the strike zone and where to stand."

Umpire Bill Klem used to say he never made a wrong decision in his life. Conlan is a bit more conservative. What Jocko says is that he never *admitted* missing one.

"If you know in your heart that you called one wrong," he goes on, "you just try to call the next one right. Never 'even up.' That just makes two wrong decisions instead of one. It's a funny thing. Ball players do something wrong and nobody boos. We call one play wrong and 40,000 people scream at us. If a player hurts his little finger on the field, they rush him off for X-rays and the crowd is sympathetic. When an umpire is hurt, the crowd cheers.

"Most players," Jocko continues, "wouldn't have enough nerve to be umpires. They're used to cheers and couldn't take the razzing."

Jocko has been hurt several times while calling 'em from behind the plate. Twice he's suffered broken collarbones but finished the games, and in Brooklyn in 1950 a foul tip fractured his larynx and it was feared he might never talk again, a fate worse than death for an Irishman. He then designed a special chest protector, which covers his throat.

"The fans love it when a foul ball hits your protector and goes 'BOOM!'" Jocko says. "They think you're hurt."

Conlan sat down one day and figured out that only about two men on each major league team, including managers and coaches, give the umpires any trouble, and it's always the same two. He thinks second base is the toughest spot for an umpire because of the problems posed by steals, the start of double plays, pickoffs, and other action. Some umpires think the so-called "half-strike" is one of the most difficult things to call, but Jocko has a simple solution for that.

"I never call a half-strike a strike unless the ball is in the strike zone. A batter is entitled to a swing."

Conlan says players used to curse him when he first came into the league, but the practice has become unfashionable.

"I don't mind a little cussing on the field as long as it isn't directed at me," he explains. "From the time I put on an umpire's uniform, I never cursed a ball player, and I won't let them curse me, for the simple reason that I'm none of those things they call me. Leo Durocher hasn't cursed me in nine years. He got chased every time he did, a dozen times at least."

Conlan, who played under Casey Stengel at Toledo, has a wealth of Casey stories. One concerns the time Stengel dressed for a game while holding a clubhouse meeting, then walked out of the dressing room without his pants. Conlan, walking beside him, tried to prevent Casey from noticing his bow legs, clad only in wild lavender shorts. The effort failed when a couple of feminine fans tittered as Casey walked by.

There also is another yarn involving the playful Frankie Frisch which Jocko delights to tell. The scene is the Polo Grounds, with the temperature hovering around 100 degrees.

"About the third inning Frisch [then manager of the Pirates] comes in from the third base coaching box, and says, 'Jocko, put me out of the game.' I asked him what for.

"'I can't stand this heat,' said Frankie, 'and I can't stand those .220 hitters I got. I want to go home and sit by my petunias.'"

Jocko did not oblige.

[1955]

How the Braves Lost Out in Signing Willie Mays

BY SAM LEVY

This is a story about the great Willie Mays, a story probably never printed before. It was related by Louis Perini, president of the Milwaukee Braves, on a two-hour cruise aboard his yacht, the *Bontina*.

In 1949, Harry Jenkins, then head of the Braves' growing farm system, asked Perini, "What's your policy on Negro ball players?"

Jackie Robinson, first Negro to play in the majors, then was starring with Brooklyn.

"We want them by all means, if they have ability," said Perini. "I would suggest that we get young ones and develop them."

"I've found one," Jenkins told Perini. "He's going to be the rage in baseball in a few years. I'll bet on it."

"Who is he?" asked Perini.

"He's a boy of 15. Mays—Willie Mays is his name," said Jenkins. "He's playing with the Birmingham Barons of the Negro League. We've offered the Barons $7,500 for him. The price is O.K., the Barons tell me. Willie must stay in high school, however, for three more years. Mr. Perini, this boy is going to be great! I've seen him play. I've never seen anything like him before."

"Every time I saw Jenkins after that, he immediately started to rave about Willie Mays," continued Perini. "Once, at a National League meeting, I sat next to Horace Stoneham [owner of the New York Giants]. Horace asked Happy Chandler, then the baseball commissioner: 'If we give the Birmingham Barons $10,000 for a player, will that make him a bonus baby?'

"'No,' replied Chandler. 'In fairness to the Barons' owner and others, I'd like to see all clubs in the future reimburse the owners for these boys. Too many players are being signed and owners are not being paid. I've heard about your transaction with Birmingham. By the way, what's the name of your phenom with the Barons?'

"'Mays—Willie Mays,' said Stoneham. 'He's going to be the greatest of them all.'

"Well, I almost fell off my chair when I heard Horace say 'Mays.' I turned to Stoneham and said, 'Horace, Mays is our player.'

"'He *was* your player, Lou,' replied Stoneham. 'You didn't want to meet the price—$10,000. I did. He's mine, Lou.'"

Perini returned to Boston a few days later. He called in Jenkins.

"Harry, I'm disturbed," Perini told Jenkins. "Every time I've seen you for the last three or four years you've always greeted me about this kid

Mays. I've just returned from a league meeting in New York. Horace Stoneham told me that he had signed this boy for $10,000. How come you let him get away for only $2,500? I thought you had the deal all sewed up for $7,500. What happened? How did the Giants get him?"

Jenkins had an excuse.

"I sent two of our scouts to watch Mays play just before he was graduated from high school," he told Perini. "Both reported that he wasn't worth more than $7,500."

"But you yourself had such great faith in this boy," Perini said dejectedly. "If you thought he was worth $7,500, then surely he must have been worth another $2,500. You raved for four years. Harry, we have paid bonuses, big bonuses, to boys in the last few years. Here where we have a chance to get a really great player, you let him get away."

Willie Mays, pictured in 1969, holding the ball he hit for his 600th career homer against San Diego Padres rookie pitcher Mike Corkins. In 1949, Mays was scouted by the Boston Braves when he was with the Negro League Birmingham Barons, but he signed with the New York Giants who outbid the Braves.

About two years later, Perini attended a Braves-Giants game in the Polo Grounds, New York.

"It was a tie game going into the ninth," Perini recalled. "Bob Elliott had reached third. One was out. Our next batter hit a fly to deep center. 'This is it,' I told a friend who was next to me. 'It's a cinch.'

"Elliott tagged up after the fly and headed for the plate," continued Perini. "Well, he was out by about ten feet. I hadn't paid too much attention to the Giants' center fielder until Elliott was caught at home. Then I asked, 'Who threw that ball?' When everyone around me yelled, 'Mays, Mays—Willie Mays,' I almost got sick. It was hard for me to believe that the boy we thought one day would be in center field for the Braves was already started on the road to fame."

Jack Schwarz, a member of the Giants' farm staff, admits that his club got Mays accidentally.

"We sent a scout to watch a player named Perry. Eddie Montague, who was assigned to trail him, called us and said, 'Perry won't do.' Montague added, however, 'But Birmingham has the best young player I have ever seen, a boy named Mays.'

"We checked on Mays' contract in the Negro League and found that the Braves had made an offer of $7,500, but that we could get him for $10,000 straight, no strings attached. We made the deal."

Jenkins later married an Australian shoe heiress, a member of one of the wealthiest families in the land down under. He resigned as head of the Braves farm system to move to Australia after his marriage. He visits the States occasionally and is expected to vacation here this summer. He may have an opportunity to watch Willie Mays, the boy he allowed to slip away from the Braves for $2,500.

[1955]

For All-Around Skill, "You Should Have Seen Old Hans"

BY FRANCIS STANN

In the course of his 50 years in baseball, which included that period from 1920 to 1945 when he made the Yankees what they are today, Edward G. Barrow developed one unshakable conviction: the late Honus Wagner was the greatest ballplayer of all time.

As he put it in his own words:

"Babe Ruth was the game's greatest personality, and its greatest home-run hitter. Ty Cobb was the greatest of all hitters . . . though I have always had a tremendous admiration for Larry Lajoie and consider him only a step behind Cobb as the greatest batsman of all.

"But there is no question that Wagner was the greatest all-round ballplayer who ever lived."

Barrow, builder of the Yankees, essentially was an American Leaguer and had been Ruth's man. It was he who converted Ruth from a great pitcher into a greater hitter. But Barrow it was who more or less discovered Wagner. That is, he talked Honus into playing ball for a living. So he had a rooting interest in each man, and if he says Wagner was the greater—and greatest—it must be assumed Barrow was speaking impartially.

Certainly John McGraw was impartial toward Wagner, Ruth, and Cobb, and the late leader of the Giants had agreed with Barrow.

Hans could play all the infield positions and the outfield with equal facility, so the early historians agree. As a matter of record, Wagner was a big-leaguer for six years before manager Fred Clarke of the Pirates made him a permanent shortstop. He wasn't any teenager when he began in pro ball—Honus was about 29 at the time.

Honus Wagner shown in 1917 at age 43 when he finally yielded his shortstop position to a rookie in the final season of his Hall of Fame career with the Pirates. In his prime he combined offensive and defensive skills and was noted for his large, strong hands and powerful arm. "The only way to get a ball past Honus is to hit it eight feet over his head," John McGraw once said.

This is a late date to begin a shortstopping career so outstanding that whenever qualified baseball men pick all-time teams they arbitrarily choose Wagner at short and go on to some other position.

Back in 1939, sitting on the porch of a small inn at Cooperstown, some of the Hall of Fame old-timers were chewing the fat with some newspapermen, who were asking for their versions of all-time players. Larry Lajoie said:

"You know, except for Ruth and Cobb, there's only one other man, Wagner, who is unanimous. People quibble over the pitchers, catchers, first basemen, and so forth, but never about those three."

"I can think of a lot of other great shortstops," said a reporter, "so Wagner must have been good."

Walter Johnson was there. "You weren't born when Wagner was at his best," he said. "There wasn't anything he couldn't do—hit, run, and field. I'm glad he stayed on his side of the fence [the National League]."

The reporter, who had known Wagner slightly because of his connection with Pittsburgh as a coach, said, "I wonder how he could run so fast on those bowlegs. I never saw such bowlegs."

"Find any old catcher, infielder, or outfielder who had to throw out Wagner and ask him," Lajoie advised. "He'll tell you if he could run."

The record books tell the story—not only of how Wagner could run but do everything else—as eloquently as any human voice. During his 21-year career, Honus' feats bordered on the incredible. Seventeen straight seasons he batted .300 or better, and he was over 40 years of age before he dropped below that figure. Between 1900 and 1911, he led the National League in hitting eight times, four times in succession. Defensively his skill is so well remembered by old-timers that whenever praise is heaped upon a Travis Jackson or a Marty Marion, they merely smile and say:

"But you should have seen old Hans."

Only three players in history stole more bases than Wagner, they being Cobb, Max Carey, and Billy Hamilton, the latter excluded from "modern" baseball. Hans averaged better than 55 stolen bases per season over one stretch of five years and finished with 720.

Until a couple of years or so ago, Wagner was the oldest man in uniform. He was frankly a pensioner, although listed as a Pirate coach, but he survived many a manager and even a change of ownership.

Because he was Hans Wagner, that's why.

[1956]

How to Stay Alive on Second Base

BY NELLIE FOX AS TOLD TO MILTON RICHMAN

Have you ever been hit by a car just as you stepped off the curb? I know exactly how it feels because it happens to me practically every day during the summer. Not that I'm ever hit by an auto, but I get knocked over time after time by some of the burliest base-runners in the American League, and take it from me, there can't be much difference.

My job is playing second base for the White Sox, and even though I wouldn't trade it for a seat in the Senate, it's as risky as directing traffic at State and Madison Streets in downtown Chicago.

The runners who fly into me trying to break up a double play aren't dropping around for pink tea. Those steel spikes can cut like a butcher slicing a side of beef.

My future as a big league second baseman depends on my ability to avoid the 101 different hazards at my position. When I first broke into the majors nine years ago, I was only 19 and green as grass. I remember asking a veteran the best way to stay in one piece out there at second base.

"Kid," he said, "it's simple. All you need is the nerve of a tightrope walker, the guts of a burglar, and the grace of an adagio dancer."

Since then I've found that a little luck doesn't hurt, either, but there are days when nothing helps.

Take that day last year when Hank Bauer of the Yankees crashed into me. Bauer hit me so hard coming into second that the newspapers built it up as an all-out feud between the White Sox and Yankees. Actually, Bauer was merely insisting that as a runner he was entitled to the basepath. Me? My teeth were loosened up a bit, but I considered it all in a day's work.

If you've ever seen me play you know darn well I don't get by on my brawn. Standing on my toes I'm only 5 feet 8½ inches, and the last time I got on a scale I weighed 157 pounds. Minnie Minoso, one of my teammates, calls me Li'l Bit. But don't get me wrong, I'm not looking for any sympathy.

When I pick up my glove and head out for second base, I know what I'm getting into. I can show you spike scars on my legs where runners left their calling cards. You come to expect that.

But playing second base has its rewards, too. It gives you the satisfying feeling of being right in the middle of the action. People always ask me what it feels like to click off one of those real quick double plays. Well, picture this if you can:

There are a couple of men on base, and the ball is hit to either third or short. You race for second base, and the ball and the runner both come at you from different directions. That's the time I like to get my business over with fast and get out of the runner's way in a hurry. Moving on instinct and generally without looking, I brush second base with my right foot—that leaves me in a better position to throw. Then I pivot—sometimes leap-frogging over the runner at the same time—and fire the ball to the first baseman.

There's no use worrying about the onrushing runner or his spikes, because if a second baseman does this, he's a dead duck. What's more, he gets the reputation for being "gun shy," and it spreads around the league quicker than a prairie fire.

Naturally, there are ways for a second baseman to protect himself. On the throw to first base, for example, we generally aim the ball right at the runner. It's the only way to make the runner duck and slide into the bag instead of having him come into you full tilt. What happens when the runner doesn't duck? Dizzy Dean didn't in the fourth game of the 1934 World Series between the Cardinals and Tigers. He was hit on the head with the ball and had to be carried off the field.

That leap-frog stunt is another handy maneuver. It's the best way of avoiding the runner's spikes and getting rid of the ball at the same time.

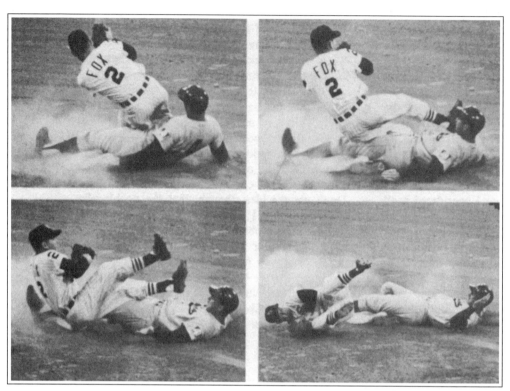

Little Nellie Fox is upended in action at second base by big Bob Allison in a game between the White Sox and Twins in 1961. Fox was taking a throw from center fielder Jim Landis in an effort to prevent Allison from getting a double.

Then there's a trick called "cheating." That takes some finesse. To cheat on a double play, you catch the ball from the third baseman or shortstop with your foot off the bag instead of on it, as the rules specify. Then you make your throw to first just as if everything is according to Hoyle. Several second basemen in the majors cheat. Frankly, so did I. But Bill McKinley, the umpire, caught me twice against the Red Sox, so I can't get away with it anymore.

Don't get the idea, though, that the double play is the only thing I have on my mind. There are plenty of other problems. When the other team has a man on first, for instance, and we know they're going to bunt, our first baseman charges the plate, and I have to run over and cover his position. It can become confusing.

A play exactly like that helped shorten the career of second baseman Davey Williams of the Giants two years ago. Jackie Robinson of the Dodgers bunted and Williams hustled over to cover first base. Williams had to reach in toward the infield for the throw and Robinson barreled into him on his "blind" side. Davey was out of action 11 days, and his back bothered him so much after the collision that he finally quit as an active player last year even though he was only 26 years old.

Pop flies look as if they're a cinch, too—from a seat in the grandstand. The average fan gets the idea that my seven-year-old daughter, Bonnie Ray, could catch any pop-up. But some of those cloud-scrapers have a habit of getting caught in the wind and blowing near the stands. Texas Leaguers can drive a second baseman crazy, too. They're the balls that somehow manage to fall safely between the infield and the outfield.

Jim Busby, who used to play center field for the White Sox but is now with Cleveland, came tearing in on a pop fly one day while I was dashing out trying for the same ball. I thought the roof caved in on me when we rammed together. My ribs hurt me for two weeks. Busby was luckier; he only sprained his thumb. And with all that, the ball dropped between us for a hit.

Maybe it's pure coincidence, but I always seem to get some lumps from the Yankees. Bob Cerv flattened me just a few weeks ago. And it was a Yankee player, Johnny Lindell, who hit me so hard in 1949 that repercussions were heard in the American League office.

At that time I was playing for the Philadelphia Athletics. Lindell was on first and Joe DiMaggio on second. We had a chance to make a double play but Lindell took care of that and me at the same time. When I came to, I was lying out in left field. DiMaggio scored from second, and Lindell rambled on to third.

Soon afterward, there was an official announcement from the American League office that henceforth a runner coming from first base would have to slide at second base, not at the second baseman! But when a runner is charging down my way, I don't have time to get out the rule book and read it to him.

Actually, they call third base the "hot corner" in baseball. That's because so many hot grounders are hit in that vicinity. But there isn't a third baseman in the big leagues who wouldn't tell you that more action takes place at second.

Maybe my dad knew all that in 1944 when he took me from our home in St. Thomas, Pennsylvania, to meet Connie Mack, manager of the A's.

"Mr. Mack," Dad said, "my boy can play second base."

Pop must have been a convincing talker because I was only 16 years old and weighed 140 pounds. Anyway, I was given a tryout and sent to Lancaster, Pennsylvania, in the Class B Inter-State League. My contract called for only $125 a month but I was tickled to death.

Matter of fact, I still am, because I think I have the best job in the world. Dangerous? Sure! But that just adds to the excitement.

Whenever I leave my house for the ballpark, my wife, Joanne, always says, "Good luck." There are days when I need it.

[1956]

Did Buck Weaver Get a Raw Deal?

BY JAMES T. FARRELL

Shortly after noon on a day in January 1956, a slender man of 64 years of age was walking along West 71st Street on the South Side of Chicago, on his way to see an income tax consultant. He began to crumble and clutched a picket fence. A passing motorist saw the stricken man, stopped his automobile and rushed to give what aid he could. But before he could be reached, the old man dropped dead on the sidewalk. A small crowd collected. The police were called. The body was taken to a hospital and there it was said that the man had died of natural causes.

The next day the obituary page of the *New York Times* carried, over a seven-paragraph story, the following head:

Buck Weaver of 1919 'Black Sox' Dead;
3rd Baseman One of 8 Barred from Game

For years, Buck Weaver had been a baseball legend. Now and then I would ask a baseball fan:

"Do you remember Buck Weaver?"

Generally, I would be answered:

"Do I remember Buck Weaver? He was one of the greatest third basemen who ever lived. He got a raw deal."

Fans in American League towns, and especially in Chicago where he played with the White Sox from 1912 to 1920, thought of him with sympathy and affection. As is well known, Weaver was one of the eight White Sox players suspended by the late Charles A. Comiskey, White Sox owner, late in the 1920 season on the grounds that they had allegedly thrown the 1919 World Series to the Cincinnati Reds.

The evidence against Weaver has always been vague and unclear. It was charged that he had been approached by Eddie Cicotte, a pitcher and one of the eight "Black Sox," and asked to participate in the Series fix. Also, it was alleged that he had been present when the conspiracy was discussed by the involved players, and, hence, he knew of the plot but did not talk.

Since Weaver's death, Chick Gandil, White Sox first baseman in the 1919 Series, granted an interview in which he declared that Weaver attended a meeting of the guilty players. Gandil further asserted that Weaver wanted to collect the money from the gamblers immediately. But Weaver is dead now and cannot speak any more.

There were also other rumors and stories. One is that Buck refused to take a lie detector test. Another is that Weaver, after the 1919 Series, is supposed to have gone hunting with a teammate of previous years. Buck seemed troubled and not at all himself. Finally, he is rumored to have broken down and told the story of the "fix" but also to have insisted that he had done nothing himself to throw the games.

If this story is true, then Buck had what is termed "guilty knowledge." But his distress while hunting is easily understandable. His knowledge, then, could only have left him in a moral quandary, faced with the risk of being a squealer and possibly a goat. For had he told on his teammates, he could not have been certain that he would have been believed.

During Buck's playing days, it seems that there was considerable talk of thrown games among players and in baseball circles. In *McGraw of the Giants,* Frank Graham writes that Hal Chase's manager in Cincinnati, Christy Mathewson, charged Chase with not having given his best efforts to the club in 1918. Graham declares that Mathewson meant throwing games.

Chase was tried, but Mathewson was in France and ignored cables requesting a deposition. The testimony of other players was inconclusive, and Chase was exonerated.

But there are other stories about the Mathewson-Chase incident which, to my mind, have not been printed. Mathewson is reported to have been advised by a baseball writer that if charges of crookedness were made against Chase and not proven, Chase could sue and collect heavy damages.

For this reason, it is believed that Chase was exonerated. In 1919, Chase was first baseman for John McGraw's New York Giants, and Mathewson, returned from France, signed up as a coach. Frank Graham comments on this strange coincidence: "Chase grinned inscrutably when he heard" that Mathewson was to be a coach. Toward the end of the 1919 season, Chase dropped away from the Giants. So did Heinie Zimmerman, the third baseman. When the Black Sox scandal broke, Chase never denied allegations of crookedness made against him, but Heinie Zimmerman did. At all events, both players were let out of baseball in such a manner that they could not sue. And Mathewson did not press the charges against Hal Chase to the point where he was out on a limb.

Buck Weaver knew only baseball. The code by which he grew up cast scorn and opprobrium on a squealer. He must have heard tales and rumors of other thrown games prior to 1919. These, if there was such—as seems to have been the case—were not reported. What should a player like Weaver have done? And had he told of the "fix," could he have felt safe in his own career? There could have been the word of seven against one.

With Buck dead after having suffered for years because of his disbarment from organized baseball, I most certainly do not want to accuse him. But there was a cloud over him and the evidence suggests that he probably knew. Withal, his failure to report this "guilty knowledge" is more than understandable. And he well could not have known what to do.

Up to his death, Weaver consistently maintained his innocence. He and the other players were indicted by a Cook County Grand Jury in the early twenties. As I have suggested, the legal evidence against Buck was so insubstantial that Judge Hugo Friend wanted to dismiss the indictment against him. Lawyers for the other indicted players feared that if this were done, the defense of their clients would be damaged. Weaver agreed, therefore, to stand trial. The Judge consented to this but also declared that, were Weaver to be found guilty by the jury, he would overrule the verdict. All of the defendants were acquitted. Weaver periodically applied for reinstatement in organized baseball, but his efforts all were in vain. Two baseball commissioners, the late Judge Kenesaw Landis and Governor Happy Chandler, rejected his appeals to clear his name and to be reinstated in organized baseball. He had wanted to do this before he died. Many fans supported him in this effort.

One Chicago sportswriter remarked to me while Buck was still living:

"The two players I have sympathy for are Weaver and Joe Jackson. They were brought up in an environment where you were not supposed to squeal. What could they have done? Jackson once talked to me about it. He said: 'I was just a dope!' And Weaver—I'd like to see him clear himself. If baseball would clear him, it wouldn't hurt baseball."

And an old-time ball player and teammate of Buck's remarked: "I'm in Buck's corner."

In the fall of 1954, I went to Chicago to interview Buck Weaver and to get him to tell his story in his own words. After some difficulty, I located him through his old and loyal friend, Marty Bleeker, a tavern keeper on the South Side of Chicago who is a familiar and popular figure among Chicago's baseball old-timers. Buck came to see me in my room at the Morrison Hotel.

He was a thin, pale, gray man in his sixties. He dressed on the sporty side, and there were small red blotches on his face. He smiled easily and readily. During his playing days he was always smiling and kidding on the field. Buck's smile as well as his great playing ability made him one of the most popular White Sox players of his time at Comiskey Park.

In answer to the contention that he should have talked about the alleged conspiracy, he told me:

"Landis wanted me to tell him something that I didn't know. I can't accuse you and it comes back on you and I am . . . a goof. That makes sense to me. I didn't have any evidence."

He went on to say:

"All I did in that Series was field 1.000 and I hit something like .336. [He hit .334, with five of his 11 hits in 34 times at bat being for extra bases, one triple and four doubles.] I'd have hit .600 if I had any luck. There wasn't a

Buck Weaver, seated second from left, with other White Sox players indicted for conspiring to defraud the public by fixing the outcome of the 1919 World Series against the Cincinnati Reds. The players are seen here with their attorneys (standing in the rear) during their 1921 trial in Chicago. Seated, left to right, are Joe Jackson, Weaver, Eddie Cicotte, Swede Risberg, Lefty Williams and Chick Gandil. Although the six players, in addition to Happy Felch and Fred McMullin who are not pictured, were acquitted, Commissioner Kenesaw Landis banned them all from baseball.

game that they didn't spear one or two line drives. But that's the breaks. In the court session, it lasted a month . . . all I can say is the only thing we got left in the world is our judges and our jurors. I was acquitted in court."

He spoke of his visits to the office of the late Judge Landis.

"He was a funny man. I'd come in. He'd say, 'Sit down, sit down!' He had that big box on his desk full of tobacco. He knew I chewed tobacco, too. He'd give me a chew of tobacco. I appealed I don't know how many times, maybe half a dozen times. But he never did tell me to my face. He said he'd send me a letter."

According to the *Chicago Tribune*, Landis, in his decision rejecting Weaver's appeal, wrote:

"I regret that it was not possible for me to arrive at any other conclusion than that set forth in the previous decision that your own admissions and actions in the circumstances forbid your reinstatement.

"You testify that preceding the World Series, Cicotte, your team's leading pitcher that season, asked you if you wanted 'to get in on something—fix the World Series,' and you replied: 'You are crazy; that can't be done.'"

When Weaver was disbarred, he had one more year to play on a three-year contract. He filed suit for breach of contract. The case was finally settled out of court.

"I sent a letter to Frick [present Commissioner Ford Frick]. It says Mr. Comiskey settled for my 1921 contract. That shows that they're wrong and I'm right. But still they paid it and I can't do nothin' about it."

He was disappointed that he received no answer from Frick.

"I never threw a ball game in my life," he said with passion and a ring of sincerity. "All I knew was win. That's all I know."

And several times he repeated:

"I can't do nothin' about it."

Weaver believed that if he were to have had his name cleared, he might have become a scout, or else helped kids learn the game. He prided himself on having discovered Nick Etten who played on one Yankee world's championship team. Following his disbarment, he played semipro ball with the Duffy Florals in Chicago and was rarely seen at social events where sports people gather. Almost every day, during the off-racing season, he went to a saloon near Sixty-third Street and Cottage Grove Avenue and in the back room played pinochle with some cronies. He did not drink. He had no children of his own but raised two children of relatives. In recent years his wife was ailing and he took care of her and was usually home with her almost every evening. All he wanted from life was to support and care for Mrs. Weaver, see his cronies and clear his name. About the latter he was pessimistic and at times, when he talked to me, bitterness came into his voice.

But about the game of baseball itself, he felt love, not bitterness. He talked of baseball enthusiastically and with a sharp and clear baseball intelligence. Baseball was a way of life to him as well as a profession. He lived the game and thought of it on and off the field. And because of his feeling for the game, the mark against him hurt.

"Even a murderer," he said, "serves his sentence and is let out. I got life."

Speaking of the game, he said:

"What are the qualifications you must have to be a ball player? You got to run. You got to throw. You got to hit. You got to field. You got to think. If you can't meet all of these qualifications, you ain't a 100 percent ball player."

He was not only a fans' player but he was also something of a ball player's player. And many who saw Weaver play between 1912 and 1920 would readily agree that he met all of these qualifications. In his last few years especially, he had developed into a highly polished big leaguer. Lean and of medium height, he almost invariably had the dirtiest uniform of any player on the team. When he broke in with the White Sox in 1912, he was an erratic shortstop. He would throw many balls away. Fans even spoke of his daily error, and for a while some of them nicknamed him "Error-a-Day Weaver." Buck said that he couldn't explain why this was so. Once he was shifted to third, he rarely made a wild throw. When he broke into the American League, he was a weak hitter. In his first year he batted .224 in 147 games. But when he became a switch hitter his average picked up and in his last season, 1920, he hit .333 in 151 games.

"I couldn't hit 'em high. I couldn't hit 'em low. I couldn't hit," he said, speaking of his early years in the American League.

During one off-season he was visiting Oscar Vitt, the Detroit Tiger third baseman, at the latter's cabin in California. Buck was chopping wood. He noticed that when he chopped left-handed, he always hit the groove in the wood; when he swung the axe right-handed, he missed the groove. This led to his decision to bat left-handed.

"But I didn't start swinging right away," Buck explained. "First I just stood up at the plate like this." He illustrated his stance with his feet close together. "I let them pitch to me. Then I practiced taking one step forward like this. Then I practiced my swing like this. I didn't try to hit the ball. I just wanted to get my swing and my confidence. Then I practiced getting away, runnin'. I got my confidence that way. And then I knew I could hit anything. I'd have the ball always comin' in to me. If a left-hander was pitching, I'd bat right-handed where my power was. The ball would still be comin' in to me. All of them pitches would be comin' in."

Fans may still remember how Buck often played a shorter third base than most of his contemporaries.

"I didn't know nothin' about the National League. I didn't play in it. But I knew the American League. You take this situation. There's a man on first. There's a man on second. There's a man on third. I'm playing third, right on the line with the base. I know the speed of each of them runners. I know how fast the batter can run. I know the speed of the ball. So I get the ball. I know what to do just like that. If I played back a few feet, I'd be licked on a dragging bunt. And I could get the hard ones, too, where I played."

Buck stood up and showed me how he could pick up a bunt with both hands and without bending his knees.

Following his death, the Associated Press reported comments of Ty Cobb on Weaver as a third baseman. Calling him "the greatest third base-man I ever saw," Cobb also remarked:

"Weaver was one third baseman I didn't try to bunt against. I was sup-posed to be a fast man getting to first base but I knew better than to lay one down in Weaver's direction. There was no chance of beating out a bunt to him. He'd throw you out every time.

"Buck just wasn't the type to be in a crooked deal like that and certainly there wasn't anything wrong with the way he played in the 1919 Series."

"One year," Buck also said in our interview, "a baseball writer asked me why I played shortstop in 15 feet closer than he thought I ought to. I explained it to him this way. 'I'll play where I stand. You play 15 feet behind me. I won't make more than one or two errors than you make. And I'll have a chance to get runners out. You see it in the assists.'"

Speaking of players of the past and the present, he asked:

"Who's a shortstop today?"

"Phil Rizzuto was."

"I'll give you that. But in our day, who was the shortstop for the Red Sox? Everett Scott. And who did the Yankees have? Roger Peckinpaugh. And the Tigers had Donie Bush. Who did Cleveland have? Ray Chapman. Who did the Athletics have? Jack Barry. Do you have shortstops like that now?"

He spoke of the salaries today as compared with salaries in his day. Perhaps there was a touch of bitterness here. He began with the White Sox for $1,800, and in 1920 his salary was $7,200.

He recalled some of his rival stars. "I was playing in a game in St. Louis in 1917. George Sisler hit one along the ground. I run in and scoop it up. But I don't throw this ball. I hold it. There were ten perforations in it, one, two, three, four, ten perforations. I ran to the umpire and said he had better look at Sisler's bat. He had driven nails in it and filed them down."

And Ty Cobb.

"That was a fellow, that Cobb. And they say he was a dirty player. That baseline belongs to the runner. Take Baker. He was a little bit slow. A man is coming in. He jumps high for the ball and comes down on that line and it belongs to the runner. So what happens? He gets spiked. When I went up for one and came down, I spread my legs and I didn't get spiked. To me Cobb was not dirty.

"And I used to hit the ball with nothin' and two on me. Some batters need three strikes to hit. I could hit with one. Here's why I do it. When the pitcher has nothing and two on you, you know he's going to waste one. The infielders know it. So what do they do? They relax. So I have nothin' and two on me and the infielders are relaxed. They throw it outside or inside, but what difference does it make? I'd hit it and be off and the infielders were relaxed. They'd ask me how come I done a thing like that. I'd say, 'I don't know why I done it. I must have been a goof.'"

Weaver was born in Pennsylvania in 1890. His father was a laborer in the iron works. Back in 1909 he was playing semipro ball. A team of barnstorming major leaguers, managed by Charlie Dooin, then manager of the Philadelphia Phillies, played against Buck's team. And a scout named Kennedy came to watch the games.

"I didn't know nothin' from nothin'. Kennedy, the scout from Philadelphia, saw me and he asked me to sign a contract for $125 a month. *$125 a month!* Why I never seen that much money."

During the winter, Kennedy shifted from Philadelphia to Cleveland and hence Weaver signed a Cleveland contract. But he heard nothing about his contract when the 1910 season opened. Two or three weeks went by and he had not received word. He wrote a letter to the National Commission and was mailed a check for $62.50.

"Boy was that money!"

He was sent to play at Northampton, Massachusetts. Suddenly he discovered that when a batted ball was two feet away from him, he would lose sight of it. He told his manager about this, and he was never able to understand how this happened to him. His manager told him he was through. He thought he was through. He was released and went to Philadelphia to see Dooin. He saw a game on a Saturday afternoon, the first big league game he ever saw. "When I seen them fellows hit and run, I said, 'Hell, I can't play.'"

He spoke with Dooin and then was offered a contract to play with Park, Pennsylvania, for $175 a month. He played in the outfield and ran in on line drives. The fans hollered for him to be put in the infield. Dooin had the choice of taking Weaver or a pitcher and he passed up Buck. But Ted Sullivan, White Sox scout, bought Weaver for $750. In 1911 he was sent to play with San Francisco in the Pacific Coast League.

"I didn't get nowhere in spring practice. They had Oscar Vitt playing third base. I'm a goof. I didn't know nothin' from nothin'. Oscar was sick. He would field a few balls and call it a day. So I practiced. I didn't know they considered Vitt the best third baseman in the league. I said to myself, 'Brother, I can take your job.'

"I sat on the bench for about three weeks. One day the center fielder got hurt. The manager says to me, 'Georgie, can you play the outfield?' I told him, 'I can play any place.'

"A ball was hit just over the infield. I run. I keep running and make the catch right here off the ground." Buck stood up and illustrated. "And then I come to bat and swing. The ball sails and hits the fence. I make a two-base hit. The next time I bat, I hit the fence again. See, I got the breaks. But after that, I told myself, 'Georgie, my boy, now you're in.'"

He reported to the White Sox at Waco the next spring.

"When I joined the Sox, I didn't know Kid Gleason from the man in the moon. That's how green I was."

Gleason hit grounders to him. He missed one and chased it and called to Gleason to hit them harder. Gleason slammed the ball at him and every time he missed, he called for Gleason to hit the grounders still harder. In later years he and Gleason laughed over this incident.

He spoke warmly and admiringly of Gleason as a man who was for the ball players. He remembered other players of his day with affection and friendliness.

"We had a kid on our team," he also said, "a third baseman named Fred McMullin. He comes to me one day and says to me, 'Buck, can't you get sick for a couple of days?' He was dying to get into a ball game. So I made myself indisposed for a couple of days to let him play. Then I went back in there myself."

At the end of a long interview, he flashed at me his own winning smile. But there was something wounded and sad in Buck's smile. Buck wanted his reinstatement, but he felt that nothing could be done about it.

When we rode down in the hotel elevator, I suggested seeing him again for dinner, but he refused, saying that he always spent the evening with his wife.

"You know," he added, "she was a good hairpin."

Ironically, there was an old-timers' dinner held in Chicago on the evening of that same day when Weaver died in the street.

Two of his old White Sox teammates, Red Faber and Ray Schalk, were present. According to David Condon, Chicago sportswriter, both were visibly shaken. Faber said:

"I played baseball with Weaver, and I played cards with him, and I found him as honest as could be. No one can ever be certain about 1919, I guess. Weaver was a wonderful competitor, a fellow who played baseball because he loved it. Buck Weaver and Lena Blackburne were two I knew who never wanted to leave the field, not even in practice."

And Ray Schalk, who generally refuses to talk about the thrown World Series, remarked, as he often has done on other occasions:

"That incident caused Weaver the tortures of hell."

And an old-time baseball fan, who, like myself, used to see Buck play when we were boys, wrote me a few days later:

"Last Thursday evening on my way home from work I stopped at 79th Street and Emerald Avenue at the undertaker's chapel where Buck Weaver was laid out. It was about 6:00 p.m. No one was there at the time except the undertaker's assistant. Though Buck was not a Catholic and the chapel is used mostly by non-Catholics, nevertheless they had kneelers by the coffin. I knelt down and said a few prayers for him. Contrary to some places it did not seem cold to me. He looked, outside of thinning gray hair and that is all, like he could get right up and don a uniform and play third base for the Sox again. I don't think he was more than five pounds heavier than when he was playing ball. It sure was a shame to see him go from this world without getting his name cleared."

Many baseball fans had similar feelings when he passed away.

Like many others who saw him spear hot ones at third with graceful ease, who cheered and watched him, this writer also considers himself as one of those who was in Buck Weaver's corner. And now, on reflection, I have a hunch that when Buck said to me, "Landis wanted me to tell him something that I didn't know. I can't accuse you and it comes back on you and I am . . . a goof. That makes sense to me. I didn't have any evidence," he was telling his real story. I suspect that he did not know what to do. And because of a moral dilemma he suffered a life-long torment. Could he have accused? And had he, would he have been a "goof"?

Now, it is all over and long ago. But Buck Weaver was a great ball player and very likeable. He was caught in a net of circumstances as are many characters in tragic novels. For to him, baseball was a way of life, and his disbarment was a supreme defeat.

"Those fellows suffered hell," Ray Schalk often says.

Buck did.

[1957]

That Called Homer? It Never Happened!

BY HERBERT SIMONS

This is the 25th anniversary of a historic baseball event that never happened.

I know. I was there. I saw it never happen.

It was 25 years ago this World Series that Babe Ruth, standing at home plate before 50,000 hooting fans in Chicago's Wrigley Field, gestured with an upraised hand a moment before golfing a terrific line drive over the center-field fence for what has been called the most storied home run of all time.

Legend has it that the great Babe "called his shot" by finger-pointing to the precise spot he would homer to on Charlie Root's next pitch.

He didn't.

He didn't—in spite of what you may have read or heard, in spite of what you may have seen in the movies or on television.

True, the Babe did gesture with his right hand in that third game of the 1932 World Series, in which the Yankees whipped the Cubs four straight, and he gestured not only once, but twice—but he wasn't "calling his shot."

Not according to the memory and records of this eyewitness, who, as the baseball expert assigned to do the "lead" story of each game of that World Series for the *Chicago Times*, had a vantage seat in the center of the main press box, slung from under the second deck right back of home plate, less than 150 feet from the Babe.

Not according to such an authoritative observer as Warren Brown, whose columns for the *Chicago American* continually reflect his 35 years covering top sport assignments.

Not according to Gordon Cobbledick, able sports editor of the *Cleveland Plain Dealer* and a 30-year veteran on the big league beat.

And not according to scores of other veteran reporters to whom we have talked and whose from-the-scene writings we have researched in the task of setting the legend at rest for you and for ourselves.

Cobbledick wrote recently: "The story has no basis in truth, but that hasn't impeded its circulation. It has become part of the Babe Ruth saga. Persons who were present at Wrigley Field that afternoon and saw no such gesture have heard it and read it so many times that they are now convinced they have witnessed the making of history. Now *they* are telling it, with embellishments limited only by their own inventiveness."

Damon Runyon was one of the truly great reporters of all time, one with an inherent flair for the dramatic. Yet you can't find a mention of the pointing incident in his story of the game in the next morning's *New York American*—and his story, starting on the front page, ran *two and one-half* columns long!

You won't find a mention of it in the story in the same issue of the *American* by Bill Slocum, another great baseball writer of the era, and his story ran one column and a half.

You can't even get Joe McCarthy, who managed the Babe and the other Yankees in that Series, to say the Babe "called his shot." I know that, too. I tried. At Cooperstown, a few weeks ago. It was the morning McCarthy was enshrined in the Hall of Fame, and we were there to help pay tribute to an old friend whom we had covered in his pre-Yankee managerial days with the Cubs.

"By the way, Joe, what is your version of that Babe Ruth 'called homer?'" we asked during what to then had been a pleasant reunion.

Old Marse Joe bristled.

"I'm not going to say he didn't do it," he snapped, obviously quite agitated by the question. "Maybe I didn't see it—maybe I was looking the other way."

"Come now," we chided, "you don't mean to say that with your team at bat in the World Series, the score tied, and nobody on base, you weren't watching the plate."

"No," said Joe, uneasily, "but maybe I was looking here or there. Anyway, I'm not going to say he didn't do it."

As Shakespeare would have phrased it, "Methinks my manager doth protest too much."

As the psychologists would phrase it, the fact that McCarthy became so emotional would indicate he wasn't revealing his true feeling, probably because he didn't want to be a party to destroying the legend.

Most significant, of course, is that McCarthy didn't say, "Sure, he did it—I saw it," or "I didn't see it myself; I happened to look away for a moment, but a lot of the fellows on the bench said they saw it."

For years now, Charlie Root has been having to answer the question, too, the last time (or probably not the last time, at that) when we saw old Chinski in New York this summer when the Milwaukee Braves, for whom Root is now the pitching coach, were at the Polo Grounds.

Having heard Root's heated denials through the years that Ruth never called the shot or anything like it, we didn't bother to ask him if it *did* happen. We merely said we were bringing up *that* subject again.

"You know," said Root, with a forced smile, "I'm better known for that—for something that never happened—than for the things that did happen."

[The "things that did happen" made Root one of the outstanding right-handers of all time. From 1926 through 1941, he won 201 games for the Cubs, including a 26-win season in 1927.]

"Did you ever talk to Babe about his version of the incident?" we asked.

"No," said Root, "because I never heard the story until years later. The only time I talked to the Babe after that game was before batting practice the next day. He was up at the plate and I walked over and was looking at the bat he was using and asked him if that was the bat he had hit it with, and he said 'yes' and handed it to me to feel.

"It was heavy—about 50 ounces I would say, and it was dark, a sort of hickory color; in fact, I think the wood was hickory.

"You know I had two strikes on him on fastballs right down the middle, belt high, in that fifth inning. Then I threw him a change-up curve, intending to waste it to get him off-stride. It wasn't a foot off the ground and it was three or four inches off the outside of the plate, certainly not a good pitch to hit, but that was the one he smacked. So I asked him how he happened to hit such a pitch.

"'I just guessed with you,' he told me.

"And that's all that was said," Root recalled. "You know me well enough, Herb, to know that if I had thought he had tried to show me up, I'd have knocked him right on his tail."

He would have, too.

The Cub hurlers of that era, Guy Bush, Pat Malone, Jakie May, and Root in particular, weren't at all bashful about setting any batter, even a Ruth, on his ear or any other portion of his anatomy.

In fact, the Babe did get it in his first time at bat the day after he had hit the legendary homer, but not because of the homer or by Root. Guy Bush, red-necked because of the Babe's and other Yankees' reference to his dark complexion in the raucous jockeying that earmarked the Series, almost maimed the Babe with an inside fastball that caught him on his right arm in the fourth and last game of the affair.

Next day, in the *New York World-Telegram,* Dan Daniel, now national president of the Baseball Writers Association, wrote: "Had there been a fifth game today, the Babe would have been forced to the side-lines. For in the first inning yesterday Bush struck the Babe with a fastball. The arm swelled at once and the pain was terrific, the Babe explained today. But he did not even tell McCarthy and played through. When the Babe was mobbed after the game, the arm pained so much he could not sign a single ball or autograph a scorecard." [The Babe, though he threw as well as batted left-handed, wrote with his right hand.]

Since the Babe didn't "call his shot," just what was the significance of his gestures? For a better understanding, let's review the setting. The Yankees, in McCarthy's second year at their helm, won their way into the Series in a breeze—their 107 victories giving them a 13-game bulge over Connie Mack's Athletics, whom they succeeded on the American League throne. The Cubs, lagging behind Pittsburgh until Charlie Grimm replaced Rogers Hornsby as manager on August 2, came on with a furious stretch drive to win by four games.

A big factor in the Cubs' resurgence was Mark Koenig, the Yankees' own star shortstop of their 1926-27-28 champions. Salvaged from the minors in late season, he sparked the Cubs' stretch rush. He played in only 33 games but was a spectacular figure in most of them. However, in the pre-Series meeting to divvy their share of the forthcoming players' pool, the Cubs placed the emphasis on Koenig's length of time with the club, rather than what he had accomplished in it. They voted him only a half-share.

The Yankees considered this unfair treatment of an old pal. The "cheapskate" theme became a featured part of their bench jockeying. Roast riders still rode high in that era. It wasn't until quite a few years later that the yearly edict from the Commissioner's office "to be little gentlemen—or else" turned the Series into the dignified, sedate affair it now is.

Both clubs were "on" each other unmercifully as the Yankees took the first two games in New York, 12-6 and 5-2. When the Series was resumed in Chicago Saturday, a crowd of 49,986 jammed Wrigley Field and also the temporary stands built outside the park in the streets back of the left- and right-field bleachers.

"The fans simply would not believe how severely or decisively their champions had been manhandled by the mighty Yankees in the East,"

A famous painting by Robert Thom depicts Babe Ruth pointing to center field before hitting a homer in that direction during Game 3 of the 1932 World Series against the Cubs. According to Woody English, who was playing third base at the time, Ruth was pointing more to the Cubs' dugout, letting the Chicago players know he still had one strike left against pitcher Charlie Root. "If he had pointed to the outfield," Root later insisted, "I would've knocked him right on his tail with the next pitch."

wrote John Drebinger, then and now an outstanding baseball writer for the *New York Times*. "The fans roared their approval of every good play made by the Cubs. They playfully tossed bright yellow lemons at Babe Ruth and booed him thoroughly, even when he homered in his first time at bat.

"And they howled with glee as Ruth failed in a heroic attempt to make a shoestring catch of Billy Jurges' low liner to left in the fourth inning (a double that enabled the Cubs to tie the score at 4-4). Good-naturedly the Babe doffed his cap to acknowledge the adverse plaudits."

"As the Babe moved toward the plate with one out in the fifth inning, swinging three bats over his shoulders, a concerted shout of derision broke out in the stands," wrote Richards Vidmer in the *New York Herald Tribune*. "There was a bellowing of boos, hisses, and jeers. There were cries of encouragement for the pitcher, and from the Cubs' dugout came a storm of abuse leveled at the Babe.

"But Ruth grinned in the face of the hostile greeting. He laughed back at the Cubs and took his place supremely confident. A strike whistled over the plate and joyous outcries filled the air, but the Babe held up one finger as though to say, 'That's only one, though. Just wait.'

"Another strike—and the stands rocked with delight. The Chicago players hurled their laughter at the great man, but Ruth held up two fingers and still grinned, the supershowman. On the next pitch, the Babe swung. There was a resounding report like the explosion of a gun. Straight for the fence the ball soared on a line, clearing the farthest corner of the barrier, 436 feet from home plate.

"Before Ruth left the plate and started his swing around the bases, he paused to laugh at the Chicago players, suddenly silent in their dugout. As he rounded first he flung a remark at Grimm; as he turned second he tossed a jest at Billy Herman and his shoulders shook with satisfaction as he trotted in."

Beautiful descriptive writing—but notice not one word about a "called shot."

In the *New York Times* Drebinger recounted: "Ruth signaled with his fingers after every pitch to let the spectators know exactly how the situation stood."

On the day after the Series ended, the *New York World-Telegram*, which had no Sunday edition in which to run follow-up stories on the Saturday "Ruth game," printed six full columns of World Series comment by such competent observers as Joe Williams, Tom Meany, and Dan Daniel—but in all six columns there was nary a word of a "called homer."

Warren Brown once recalled: "The Babe indicated he had one strike . . . the big one . . . left. The vituperative Cub bench knew what he meant. Cub catcher Gabby Hartnett, in the Babe's immediate vicinity, heard Ruth growl that this is what he meant. Ruth, for a long while, had no other version, nor was any other sought from him.

"Only recently, in a very authoritative volume, I read that Ruth *deliberately* took two strikes before pointing in the direction to which he was going to hit that home run!"

The first mention in print of a "called homer" that considerable research could find was made by Bill Corum and Tom Meany simultaneously three days after the game. In a column on "Men of the Series" for the *New York Journal*, Bill Corum wrote of Ruth:

"Words fail me. When he stood up there at the bat before 50,000 persons calling the balls and strikes with gestures for the benefit of the Cubs in the dugout and then, with two strikes on him, pointed out where he was going to hit the next one and hit it there, I gave up. The fellow is not human."

On the same day Meany, in the *New York World-Telegram*, noted:

"Babe's interviewer then interrupted to point out the hole in which Babe put himself Saturday when he pointed out the spot in which he intended hitting his homer and asked the Great Man if he realized how ridiculous he would have appeared if he struck out.

"'I never thought of it,' said the Great Man, which is the tipoff on the Babe. He simply had his mind made up to hit a home run and he did."

Fifteen years later, Meany elaborated on the incident in his book, *Babe Ruth,* calling it "the most defiant, and the most debated, gesture in World Series history."

"Root threw a called strike past the Babe and the Cub bench let the big fellow have it. Babe, holding the bat in one hand, held up the index finger of the other, to signify it was indeed a strike. Root threw another called strike. Ruth held up two fingers and the Cub bench howled in derision.

"It was then the big fellow made what many believe to be the beau geste of his entire career. He pointed in the direction of dead center field. Some say it was merely a gesture toward Root, others that he was just letting the Cub bench know that he still had the big one left. Ruth himself has changed his version a couple of times, but the reaction of most of those who saw him point his finger toward center field is that he was calling his shot.

"Late that winter, at a dinner at the New York Athletic Club, Ruth declared that calling his shot against Root was the biggest thrill he ever had in baseball. As time went on, however, there was a general move to discount the big fellow's gesture and in the general debate which followed, Babe himself grew confused and wasn't certain whether he had picked out a spot in the bleachers to park the ball, was merely pointing to the outfield or was signaling that he still had one swing to go."

Let the confusion end now. What a few romantically interpreted as "pointing" was merely a sweep of his hand as he brought it down from his "that's-only-two-strikes" gesture.

If Ruth had done the pointing act—one that was dramatic enough to have lived in legend for a quarter of a century—why didn't such top-rank observers as Damon Runyon, Warren Brown, Gordon Cobbledick, Dan Daniel, John Drebinger, Dick Vidmer, or many, many others even mention it, yet alone feature it?

Why doesn't Joe McCarthy say Ruth did it?

Why wasn't Ruth sure himself whether he did or not?

The answer is obvious.

It never happened.

I know.

I was there.

I saw it never happen.

Editor's Note: Here's how Herbert Simons telegraphed the details of Babe Ruth's legendary homer from the Wrigley Field press box to the *Chicago Times* a few minutes after it happened:

"Root pushed a strike past Ruth. The crowd roared. Good-naturedly the Babe lifted his right forefinger so that all could see. Only one strike, he indicated. Another called strike and another razzing roar from the crowd. The Babe good-naturedly stuck up two fingers. And if there was a fan in the crowd who couldn't appreciate the full significance of this 'I've got a big one left' motion, it certainly dawned on him on the next pitch. Ruth took his stance, and the ball took a 440-foot ride to the center-field flag-pole, a liner unequaled in the history of Wrigley Field."

[1957]

The Mickey Mantle I Know

BY MERLYN MANTLE AS TOLD TO CHRISTY MUNRO

I met Mickey Mantle for the first time after a high school football game in Commerce, Oklahoma, in 1949. He didn't say a word. I guess that's why I remembered him afterwards. I thought it was so odd.

Right then (in my mind, anyway), I was more a celebrity than he was, for I was drum majorette of the Picher High School band and a soloist at the First Baptist Church of Picher, and I'd sung at nearby army camps. Mickey had been graduated from Commerce High School that spring and was working as an electrician in the local lead and zinc mines, where his father was a ground boss.

I had never heard of Mickey, although Picher is only three miles from Commerce, and he had been playing baseball around those parts since he was five years old, from peewee leagues to pro ball. He'd even been signed by the New York Yankees at the time of his graduation. But I, like most of the other folks then in Oklahoma, was strictly a football fan. I knew so little about baseball that, on one of our early dates, I asked Mickey how many time-outs they could have during an inning.

The Wednesday after I met him Mickey came over to Picher for a date with a girl friend of mine named Levanda, a twirler in the band. My sister was going out with a friend of Mickey's and I also had a date, so all six of us drove out in the country.

The other boys horsed around and kidded, but Mickey still didn't talk. However, two or three times, I caught him looking at me and grinning.

And I must say, if I sound a little prejudiced, he has a grin that does things to a girl. I also noted how neat he looked. I rather hoped I had made an impression.

The next day I did get a telephone call, when I was working in the principal's office during a free period. But it wasn't Mickey. It was my sister Pat's boy friend, saying that Mickey Mantle wanted a date with me. I almost said: "Tell John Alden to speak for himself." Then I remembered his smile, and relented. The next Saturday night Mickey and I went to a show. After just two more dates, he asked me to go steady, which back home is like being engaged. I was pretty surprised, especially when I found out that he had decided I was the girl for him from the first time he saw me. But my mother was astonished. She told somebody: "I don't know how Merlyn" (I was named after my two grandmothers, Murl and Louise) "and Mickey ever got acquainted. Neither of them ever says a word."

As a matter of fact, compared to him, I'm a chatterbox. When somebody asks him a question and he doesn't answer at all, just lets it hang, I can't bear it. I speak up and answer for him. The same way on the telephone. He'll hang up without a word if it's a strange voice, but I get dragged into the weirdest conversations with strangers, just because I try to answer for my husband. However, both of us are reserved, and after almost six years of marriage and two sons, Mickey and I are still getting acquainted. The nice part about that is we're happier and get along better all the time.

The only thing that I object to is that, between baseball, and the many demands it makes on *his* time, and the children, and the many demands they make on *me*, we don't have enough chances to be alone together.

Mickey is still a shy and silent person, and sometimes not the easiest one in the world to live with. He has been put out of baseball games only twice in his major league career, for talking back to umpires. This may make him popular with umpires, but it is rough on a wife. I can't let off steam and fight with him because he just keeps still. He won't argue back.

Early in my married life, I learned not to talk at breakfast. We've never had a maid until this year, when I hired one in Florida during spring training to help with the children, and they liked her so well I brought her North. But for a while I was afraid I wouldn't be able to keep May, because she was such an ardent Yankee fan that she couldn't resist talking to "Mr. Mick" while he ate breakfast.

Our children are still pretty young. Mickey was four in April and Davy won't be two until December. But they have learned to step lively and ask no questions when their daddy comes home tired, with his legs aching, from the ballpark. Mickey is much better at discipline than I am, and the children adore him, so that all they need is one sharp word from him and they behave. Mommy isn't so effective, I'm afraid. Maybe it's because they're so used to me. The only time they see much of their father during baseball season is when they are watching the Yankees on television.

Young Mick has a habit of pointing to the numbers on the television dial and identifying them with the numbers the Yankees wear: 7 for his father, 8 for Yogi, 9 for Hank Bauer and so on. Early this season some of us Yankee baseball widows were talking—about baseball and our children, as usual—and Mrs. Bauer said her boy's favorite was Yogi Berra, not his dad. Then Mrs. Joe Collins said her son liked Mickey best. I told them I thought Young Mickey rooted harder for Billy Martin, Mickey's Yankee roommate (it was just before Billy was traded to Kansas City), than he did for his father. Whereupon my elder son spoke up: "I like my daddy better than anybody in the world." And I guess he does.

When Daddy is in a slump, or the Yankees lose—and the two often go together—the children have learned to leave him alone. He sits glued to a chair, watching TV, a dark cloud around his head. His hay fever, always a nuisance, seems worse during a slump. Mostly, I leave him alone, too. But when, after playing a day game, he comes back to the house and sits in front of the TV, brooding and watching the Dodgers play at night . . . well, I'm not so well disciplined as the kids. I get mad and turn the set off.

Because Mickey doesn't say much, people don't realize how much he notices. He often buys cashmere sweaters and even dresses for me, as surprises. He always gets the right size, which is quite a trick, for normally I wear junior sizes 5 or 7, and he also gets me things that are more becoming than the ones I pick out myself. I wouldn't dare buy clothes for him, except sports shirts.

For Christmas the year Davy was born, Mickey bought me a beautiful light brown mink stole in Oklahoma City and had it sent down to Commerce by express on Christmas Eve. But he wouldn't let me show it to our friends and neighbors back home, for fear they might think he was getting big-headed, buying mink.

Back home during the winter on Saturday nights, when the men play poker and the girls sit around talking children, I sometimes overhear Mickey telling stories about the funny things that have happened during the baseball season, stories that are new to me. He loves a good story on himself—and even better, one on me. But he doesn't talk much in mixed company. He relaxes best with other men, especially the old friends with whom he hunts and fishes during the winter. He also has made good friends on the team, men like Yogi Berra and Billy Martin and Whitey Ford.

It was hard for me to understand, when we first started going together, why he said so firmly that we couldn't get married until he had made good with the Yankees. But all his life, from the time he was about as big as our Mickey, my husband has been trained for just one thing—to play baseball. I'll never forget last year, when he got home on Christmas Eve from the tour he had made with Bob Hope of army camps in Alaska. He saw all the presents I had put out for the children and said: "I can't remember ever having any toys but baseballs and bats."

Both Mickey's dad and his grandfather were crazy about baseball and I guess they decided when Mickey was born that he was going to be a major leaguer. As my husband says, the only recreation they had in Commerce was baseball, and they felt being a big-time star was almost equivalent to being President of the United States. They taught Mickey to be a switch hitter, his grandpa throwing to him right-handed, and his dad left-handed. When he was just a little fellow, they would have him out in the back yard af-

Mickey Mantle broke in with the Yankees in 1951 as a somewhat shy 19-year-old Oklahoman who could hit with power from both sides of the plate. He led the American League in homers four times, won three MVP Awards and played in 12 World Series before retiring after the 1968 season.

ternoons taking batting practice until it got dark. Of course, that is largely why he is where he is today, and Mickey is fully aware of the debt he owes them both. Grandpa died in 1935; I never knew him. But I got to know his dad during Mickey's first year with the Yankees.

I had just graduated from high school and was working in the bank at Picher during the summer. I was still Mickey's girl, but both of us were dating other people. Then Mickey got into a slump. The Yankees sent him back to Kansas City, which just about broke his heart. Mickey admitted he even cried when he heard the news. Kansas City was about 150 miles from Commerce, but Dad and Mother Mantle drove over there often to see Mickey play and keep up his morale. They sometimes took me along, too.

When Mickey made good in Kansas City and the Yankees recalled him, Dad Mantle was even more thrilled than Mickey. He got a group together to go to see Mickey play in the World Series in New York: Mickey's uncle, and his uncle's brother-in-law, and a couple of other men. He was more excited than my Young Mick gets at Christmas time; this was something he had been waiting for all his life.

But in the second game, Mickey, who was playing in right field, tripped on one of the drains in the outfield and tore all the ligaments in his right knee. They had to carry him off the field on a stretcher. I can imagine how Dad Mantle must have felt. He hurried to the clubhouse and went down to Lenox Hill Hospital with Mickey. But as Dad Mantle tried to help Mickey out of the cab, poor Dad collapsed.

He had been sick for some months, losing weight and complaining of backaches, but he had insisted it was nothing. The doctors at Lenox Hill, however, found out he was in the last stages of cancer, and told Mickey his father couldn't live more than six months. At the time, Mickey was only 19, but he realized he had to grow up and take care of his mother and his three younger brothers and sisters.

Dad Mantle came home shortly after the Series was over, but Mickey had to stay in the hospital about a month. When he got home, he asked me to marry him as soon as possible. On December 23, 1951, we were married in my house in Picher.

Mickey had had his twentieth birthday that October. I was 20 the next January 28. We rented a little furnished house in Miami, Oklahoma, which is close to both Picher and Commerce, and saw a lot of both of our families. In March we went to St. Petersburg, Florida, for spring training. It was the first time I had ever been away from home.

Mickey was under tremendous pressure. He wanted to make good, both for himself and for his dad. He also had financial reasons. He had been voted a full share of the World Series money and had used it to pay the mortgage on the family's house. But he was now the sole support of two families and he was aware of his responsibilities. Dad Mantle died in May. There was a night game with the Indians and Mickey played because he knew his father would have wanted it. Then we went home to the funeral.

I never saw Mickey cry about his father until years afterwards, when they made a television show of Mickey's career and it came to the part where the doctors told Mickey about his father. I think Mickey still thinks of his father often and wishes that he might have lived to see some of the baseball honors his son has received. I wish, too, that he could see our children, especially Young Mick when he gets out in our back yard and, copying all his father's mannerisms, even pretending to knock the dirt out of his spikes, hits a "home run."

Mickey and I were very young that first year, very inexperienced, and both of us were spoiled. I was lonesome and homesick. I had given up a music scholarship to Miami Junior College, in Oklahoma, to marry

Mickey, and I must admit I occasionally felt twinges of regret when I had to settle down to housework.

We lived for about a month at the Concourse Plaza Hotel in the Bronx. There was a movie theater nearby, and I had so little to do that every time the show changed, I went. Most of the other Yankee wives had children and, although I went to most of the games and sat with them, I was shy about making friends. After Mickey's father died, we moved into a furnished apartment. I was so lonesome when he had to go out of town with the team that my mother came from Oklahoma to stay with me for a while. But she was even more nervous in New York than I was. Every time we went out, we seemed to see some kind of street fight. On the subways, she thought that the people were staring at us—planning to rob us or worse.

Mickey had to get used to his bride's cooking, which was no minor hurdle. He enjoys eating and is particular about the way food is prepared. In those days, when he came home hungry from the ballpark, I would innocently serve up limp cold cuts and potato salad from the delicatessen. He wouldn't say anything, but in the morning, when I started to make breakfast, I would discover that the icebox was bare. He had gotten up in the middle of the night and eaten everything in it, down to the last orange or grape.

Then I would make the mistake the next night of suggesting: "Let's eat out." He was worn out, his legs hurt, and he would have to get dressed and take me out to a restaurant, where he couldn't enjoy his dinner because people recognized him and stared.

Finally we rented our spare bedroom to Billy Martin and his former wife Lois. The money helped and Lois could cook. But that was still the hottest summer in my memory. We used to sit in the living room in our bathing suits watching TV.

I also had my first experience with baseball fans. Mickey used to come home from the park followed by a string of boys and girls. Sometimes their kidding wasn't so good-natured, especially if he'd had a bad day. If he didn't stop to sign autographs, they threw ink at him. Several good shirts and jackets were ruined, and we couldn't afford that. His Fan Club, girls around 14 years old, used to settle for hanging around me if they couldn't find Mickey. When I did my daily marketing, I was followed down the street and into stores by a group of little girls wearing jackets with "Mickey Mantle" on their backs.

Now that we have children, the Fan Club has lost interest in us. But I still get letters from teenagers, offering to baby-sit for nothing. And we still have funny experiences with fans—and some not so funny. Once, while we were living in Commerce, a stranger called long-distance to tell Mickey he had smashed up his car, and would we please send money so he could buy a new one? Another day after a game at Yankee Stadium, a female autograph hunter grabbed Mickey's wristwatch, and tore his arm quite painfully with her daggerlike fingernails.

Last summer, when we were living in Glen Rock, New Jersey, and Mickey was having a good year, we had such avalanches of autograph hunters that traffic was stalled around our house after games. We live in River Edge this year, for which I'm sure our Glen Rock neighbors are grateful. Our telephone is now unlisted, and the police are very nice about keeping traffic moving past our house on the days Mickey is home.

I used to answer his fan mail, before I was so busy. Now one of Mickey's twin brothers does most of it, with help from some secretaries in the Yankee organization. But the lovelorn girls—and older women, too—don't seem to get discouraged. If they only knew that Mickey seldom reads any letters, even the ones from home! We do all our communicating on long-distance telephone.

Of course, many nice things happen to us, thanks to baseball. Mickey had the beautiful big diamond from the belt which he won as the "athlete of the year" mounted for me, and I wear it as my engagement ring. I've met some very nice girls, Yankee wives. A contingent of Yankees live over in New Jersey—including the Skowrons, the Sturdivants, the Berras, the Slaughters, the Darrell Johnsons; we wives keep each other company when the team is on the road. Mickey and I don't get into New York often. But I was human enough to get a kick out of being able to get tickets to *My Fair Lady* on short notice, and at regular prices, when we wanted to take friends from Oklahoma. I also can't help being flattered when a sales person in a New York store gets excited when she finds out who I am. But I don't do too much shopping in New York. The stores at home look out for dresses for me, in my size. And frankly, I don't spend the kind of money for a dress—$150 and $200—that the New York saleswomen expect me to, when they find out I am Mrs. Mickey Mantle.

It's true that Mickey's salary is large. But we are in a high income tax bracket. Also, baseball is precarious. I try not to think about it, but Mickey's legs are vulnerable. He has osteomyelitis in his left ankle, which made him 4F, and his right knee has been operated on and the cartilage removed. Any minute of any game, he might be injured and never able to play again.

Right now, little Mickey wants to be a ball player like his father. He is old enough to get proper training from Mickey, but Mickey thinks that if Young Mick doesn't show signs of being an outstanding player, he should definitely train for some other career. I agree. But I'll go one step further. I think that even if Young Mick is going to be a very good baseball player, it would be smart if he also had a second profession, just in case.

We have set up funds for the children, and we have a part interest in a motel in Joplin, Missouri, with our good friends, the Harold Youngmans. We own a seven-room house in Commerce, which is already too small, with our growing family. We talk about buying a ranch. Mickey's granddad was a farmer and butcher, and Mickey lived on a farm when he was small and thinks he would like the life. But, frankly, I wouldn't be too sure of him as a handyman. Last winter the screen was still on our front door in January. Finally I got my dad to come over and put in a piece of glass.

So far as I am concerned, I would settle for Mickey's quitting when he finishes ten years of baseball in the majors, which will be after the 1960 season. But if Mickey's legs hold out, I don't think he will stop that soon. There is nothing else he was ever trained for, and nothing he loves to do as much.

[1957]

The Most Exciting Team Ever

BY JIMMY CANNON

There was never a more exciting ball club than the St. Louis Cardinals when Frankie Frisch managed them in the mid-'30's. Guys who played on that team became Cardinals forever. It didn't matter where they were traded. They always go back in reverie. Sitting with Leo Durocher, a guy would think he had never managed the Dodgers and the Giants once the conversation turns to the Cardinals.

"We fought among ourselves," Durocher said, "but we stuck together if anyone picked on us. I remember one afternoon a ball was hit over my head. I must have run four miles but I couldn't get to it. Joe Medwick was in left and he didn't come in as fast as he should. Dizzy Dean was pitching and the hit cost him a couple of runs. He was sizzling when we came in to the bench.

"He sat there, making cracks about Medwick not hustling. And then he announced he was going to punch Joe in the nose. Diz got up and his brother Paul got up with him. They started walking toward him. Joe ran to the rack and grabbed a bat. He shook it at the Deans and told them if they took another step he would separate them forever. They stopped.

"The next time Dizzy's pitching, Joe hit a home run with the bases loaded. He was mean. Real mean. He went to the fountain and took a big drink of water. He walked down the bench and stopped right in front of Diz. He spit the water all over Dizzy's shoes. Then he said, 'Let's see you hold this lead, you so-and-so.' That's the kind of ball club we were.

Four members of the 1934 St. Louis Cardinals celebrate after winning Game 6 of the World Series against the Detroit Tigers. Included, left to right, are Dizzy Dean, his brother Paul, manager Frank Frisch and catcher Bill Delancey. Known as "The Gashouse Gang," the Cardinals that year also featured such colorful players as Pepper Martin at third, Leo Durocher at short, Rip Collins at first, and Joe Medwick in left. They beat the Tigers, 11-0, in Game 7 of the Series.

"We had Frisch crazy. You know how mad he used to get. He'd be hollering and raging and we'd be fighting among ourselves. Poor Bill Delancey. What a catcher he was. And he died so young. He was just a kid but he was like the rest of us. One day Frisch is bawling us out because we blew a lead and Delancey says to him, 'Why don't you go in the clubhouse and let us alone? If you'd shut up, maybe we'd win a game.' Can you imagine a kid saying that to a manager? I thought Frank would drop dead. But stuff like that was going on all the time.

"There was a fight every day. We were fighting with each other or the other ball club. I remember once Diz threw at Jimmy Ripple. He took his cap off. The cap's in the air and Ripple's down. Both benches charged out on the field. Twenty-five Giants and 25 Cardinals. We're going to it and I see Carl Hubbell's still in the dugout. He's the only ball player on either club not in the scrimmage. He looked at me and said, 'I don't get paid for fighting. I'm paid to pitch.' I guess he didn't have to fight. If he was paid for pitching, he certainly earned his pay.

"What a town that Chicago was. Every time we went in there, there was a battle. They had some nice kids pitching for them then . . . Pat Malone . . . Guy Bush . . . Charlie Root. I was a lousy .230 hitter and Malone'd get sore at me if I took a good swing.

"Just swinging good burned him up. I remember once I missed a strike. He walked halfway down to the plate and said, 'You're swinging too hard. I got to teach you a lesson.' So he hit me just for swinging too hard. I couldn't hit him so I needled him—he'd hit me. That was the only way I ever got on first base with him.

"It's changed. The whole thing's changed. Can you imagine announcing you were going to hit a guy? Burleigh Grimes was as mean as you could get. He pitched that spitball off his toes. He'd stand on his toes and hit you right on top of the head with it. He knew you were going to duck, so he threw that spitter so it would break down on top of your head. The color isn't there any more.

"The Yankees were different. They were great, but they didn't fight like Cards. I mean in '28 and '29 when I was with the Yankees. What a ball club that was. We were a couple of games behind the A's in '28. I needed that World Series money to bail me out of my hotel. I hated the A's. They were taking my money, I figured, but it didn't worry Babe Ruth. He sat on the bench and before the game he told the A's, 'Tonight you're nothing. You're never getting into the Series. Forget about spending that money.' We beat them a couple of games and that was it.

"The Babe loved pressure. He enjoyed it. It could never get too tough for him—but what a club that was. The leadoff man was Earle Combs, hitting .330. A leadoff man. People used to say he couldn't throw. He didn't have to throw, the way he got them—and Bob Meusel, people said he was lazy, didn't run. He'd take one step where the average guy took three or four. He was running all right, but he didn't look like it. What a chance I had with a club like that!

"You know how I got into the National League? I was getting $6,000 and I wanted $7,000. Ed Barrow was sitting at his desk. He just looked up and said, 'Six.' That's all he said. 'Six.' I began to tell him how much I needed the raise and how I earned it.

"The office was on Forty-second Street then. Barrow turned in his chair and looked out the window while I was talking. I got mad. I yelled, 'Go to hell.' He turned around. He said, 'What did you say?' I said, 'You heard me,' and walked out the door. He heard me all right. The next day I was out of the league. The next day I was with Cincinnati."

[1958]

What It Takes to Be a Winning Pitcher

BY ROGER KAHN

In those rich, winy days when his stomach is at peace and his Yankees are winning, Casey Stengel patiently lectures all comers on a spectrum of topics that ranges from day games to night games. A few seasons back, an experienced Yankee relief pitcher named Johnny Sain tranquilized both the Stengel stomach and the American League with slow curve balls but at the same time troubled most of the reporters traveling with the Yankees by his deep and unbroken silence. Sain was a strapping, patently shrewd man from Arkansas, but he bore no message for the outside world save "Hiya."

"Now I can see where some of you fellers would like the feller to say more, because it would help you in your work," Stengel announced in the Yankee Stadium press room late one evening, "but the way he is, which you know, shouldn't bother you. He don't say much, but it don't matter, because when he's out there on the mound there ain't nobody he can talk to. Out there, he's all alone."

With meaning so triumphant over syntax, it was a Stengelism of genuine purity and depth. More than ever before, the pitcher has become the solitary craftsman of baseball. Against the trend toward home run worship, amid grandstand cries for more and more hitting, he must go an utterly solitary way. There is no such thing as group pitching. It is strictly a one-man job.

The pitcher stands there and, as he considers, action on the field suspends. The game waits for the working of his arm, but now he is working with his head. What does the batter, tensely crouched some 60 feet away, least like to hit? What did he throw this batter last week and last month? What stuff was working well when the pitcher warmed up? What is the batter expecting? Questions and answers run so quickly through the pitcher's mind that he scarcely hears the infield chatter behind him.

It isn't always this way, of course, but with all the great pitchers of our time, with such men as Early Wynn and Warren Spahn, for example, the process of thought and the physical act of throwing are mingled in a single complex whole. Some young pitchers, full of endurance and strength, can survive for a time merely by throwing hard and accurately. Some specialists, like, say, Hoyt Wilhelm, Baltimore's knuckleball expert, can survive with a single baffling delivery. But almost any pitcher who wants to work profitably past the age of 30, when his fastball starts to slow down, must possess the ability to think. No other job on the field makes the same curious requirement.

It is a matter of environment rather than heredity. These are infinitely difficult days for pitchers, and the ones who have not learned to adapt themselves stand no more chance than a Dodger official in Brooklyn. Gradually, over almost four decades, pitchers have been stripped of armor and of weapons. The mind alone is safe from the assault that has been leveled against the solitary craft.

In the innocent era before 1920, a pitcher could apply saliva to the baseball and throw spitballs, a delivery that broke sharply while placing minimal strain upon the arm. Furthermore, wet or dry, the baseball felt soggy. The ball was so dead that most batters went to their graves without ever hitting a 400-foot drive. Then, about the time Warren Harding entered the White House, baseball officials outlawed the spitter and introduced the lively ball. The rule makers haven't bothered pitchers since, for fear of revolution.

But soon after World War II, pitchers were again victimized, this time by the avarice of club owners. Reasoning that home runs meant box office, owners erected fences or built grandstands on what had previously been virgin outfield. The inevitable conclusion has been reached in Los Angeles, where the left field screen is only 250 feet away, a condition that gives even infielders claustrophobia.

Finally, pitchers insist that umpires have recently redefined the strike zone. Once any pitch crossing home plate between the knees and the shoulders was called a strike. Now the upper limit is the armpits and, in the words of Early Wynn, who enjoys small jokes after work, "The darn thing's shrunk like a cheap shirt in a Chinese laundry." The difference between shoulder and armpit may seem minute, but the high inside fastball is a classic clutch pitch. With current umpiring, the late Walter Johnson's best high, hard strike would be no more than "ball one."

How have pitchers done against this attack of nearly four decades? At first, understandably, they were shell-shocked, but lately they have been doing magnificently. Between 1920, the first year of the lively ball, and 1938, nobody ever led the major leagues in batting with an average of less than .350. Meanwhile, slugging records were broken regularly.

Then, after World War II, pitching made its comeback. In the last ten years an average of less than .350 has led the majors exactly six times. The rumble of home runs remains with us, but it shows only that there are limits even to the ingenuity of men who handle things radioactive, such as present-day baseballs.

To some extent, credit for shrinking batting averages must go to managers who have come to use relief pitchers with remarkable skill. Certainly, night games bother batters since there is some loss of visibility. But most praise for the current pitching revival belongs to baseball's persecuted minority, the pitchers themselves.

"You have to learn a helluva lot to make it now," says Whitey Ford, the tough little left-hander from New York City who has been the Yankees' ace. "First, you got to forget your high school curve and learn a curve that breaks just a couple of feet from the plate. Then you have to learn a changeup and maybe a screwball. Then you have to learn to control them and your fastball—not just over the plate, but to a spot, like high inside or low outside. Finally, you got to figure out when to use what. When you figure it, you're a big league pitcher."

Warren Spahn, the Milwaukee Braves' superb left-hander, who has won more than 250 major league games, is the leading exponent of the intellectual approach to pitching. Spahn brings total recall to his work and can remember innings, pitch by pitch, for years.

Spahn also brought considerable foresightedness to his career. As a rookie, he possessed a good fastball and an overhand curve, a taxing pitch which breaks not laterally but downward. He quickly added a changeup, or slow ball, and then began to teach himself a screwball. As his curve lost some effectiveness, the screwball took up the slack. Then, two years ago, he mastered the slider, a fast pitch with a small, sliding break on the end, that looks like his waning fastball until it bends.

Since he seldom throws the curve any more and relies only lightly on the fastball, Spahn last year was a completely different pitcher from the Spahn of 1947 in all respects but one: he was a 20-game winner both times.

Even his motion, a flowing swirl of arms and legs that begins with a high kick, is an extension of Spahn's cerebral approach. Sometimes he takes an inch or two off the kick, on the theory that this may be just sufficient to upset a batter's timing. "The one thing that bothers me," he says, "is that you can't really be consistent. A ballet dancer studies a pirouette and, after a while, can do it exactly the same way all the time. Why can't it be that way with pitching, throw the same pitch the same way every time?" It is a rhetorical question, and Spahn shrugs.

Early Wynn, the 39-year-old star of the Chicago White Sox, like Spahn, has passed the 250 mark in victories, but Wynn relies more on psychology than on pure intellect. Although bright, Wynn was born with a low brow, and in manhood he has perfected a disturbing glower. "Why, he looks just the way I always imagined Simon Legree," exclaimed a spectator once, as he sat with binoculars trained on Wynn. It was a comparison that filled Wynn with delight. He throws at batters' chins fairly frequently and relishes his reputation for meanness.

"I was pitching to my boy," Wynn said not long ago. "He's 17 and he's grown pretty big. He lined a couple of my best curves against the left field fence in Chicago."

"What did you do?" someone asked.

"What do you think I did?" Wynn returned. "I knocked the boy down with a fastball."

Actually, Wynn is neither sadistic nor mean. He is only a man making a living. "If I really wanted to hurt somebody," he remarked once, as the mask of Legree dropped away, "I'd stick it in his ribs. A batter can't move his body as quick as he moves his head."

Wynn chooses the role of blackguard because batters who are worried about a beanball may settle for their health rather than for a base hit on any given time at bat. Wynn gets them out with knuckleballs, sliders, curves and fastball strikes, a more than adequate assortment. But it is his glower that gives him the extra edge.

With Lew Burdette, who is a perfect complement to Spahn on Milwaukee's staff, the margin comes from a mystery pitch. Despite current rules, perhaps a half-dozen major league pitchers still throw occasional spitballs. Umpires insist that detection is difficult, but batters admit to no such problem. To a man, they maintain that Burdette falls back on the spitter for critical pitches.

Burdette says simply, "If the hitters want to worry about the wet one, let 'em. I ain't here to ease their minds." On the mound he often goes through the motions of moistening the ball and, whether he cheats or not, the fact that he works to worry batters is a significant aspect of his effectiveness.

Johnny Antonelli, the San Francisco Giants' skillful left-hander, won a $60,000 bonus contract 11 years ago for a powerful fastball and a sharp curve. He still uses both, but before Antonelli could win consistently in the majors, he had to add a trick pitch, a unique change of pace that drifts away from right-handed batters.

Billy Pierce of the Chicago White Sox and Herb Score of the Cleveland Indians are outstanding examples of current pitchers who succeed chiefly with the traditional assortment of fastball, curve and straight changeup. Score, incidentally, responded courageously after a line drive almost blinded him in 1957. He was back pitching the following year. But he and Pierce have yet to respond to the challenge that will be posed when their fastballs begin to fade and they must develop extra pitches and extra guile.

A pitcher who does not develop special tactics, who does not constantly improve his skills, is in for serious trouble. As a young pitcher, Robin Roberts of the Philadelphia Phils possessed a fine fastball, a good curve and splendid control. With just the fastball and the curve in 1952, he won 28 games and lost only seven. Last year, at 31, Roberts had lost a little of his speed but was still pitching as he always had. He won 17 and lost 14. This year he is trying to adjust his style.

In the dead-ball days, Roberts might have gone an unchanging way for most of his career. In each lineup then, there were only two or three home run hitters, and after concentrating on them the pitcher could let up as long as there was no one on base. There is no let-up now, when even the opposing pitcher can reach the seats, and the upshot is a troubling little cycle.

Under existing conditions, pitching arms lose their zip more rapidly than they once did, and the first pitch that shows this is the fastball. As batters cheerily attest, the not-so-fast ball, thrown frequently, becomes the perfect home run ball. The slipping pitcher then drives himself to throw harder, which in turn takes still more out of his arm.

Against this trend, joining the wisdom of such great veterans as Wynn and Spahn with the body of pitchers at large, are the new institution of the pitching coach and the old institution of the underground.

For the most part, managers tried to be their own pitching coaches until recently. Now the position is recognized as a full-time job, and such men as Jim Turner of the Yankees and Whitlow Wyatt of the Braves are hired exclusively to tutor pitchers.

The underground is simply an informal pitchers' union, dedicated to sharing knowledge that might hamper batters. No one outside knows precisely how the underground works. There are rules against ball players fraternizing, which make pitchers reluctant to admit they talk to rival pitchers in hotel rooms, or over beers, or under the stands, or possibly by long-distance telephone. But the underground remains vital and seems to have become international.

A few years ago, when the Giants went to Japan, they brought along Dusty Rhodes, their best pinch hitter and a man who could slug everything but a change-of-pace. From Nagasaki to Tokyo, Rhodes was thrown an unvarying pattern of slow balls. "If I ever went to the North Pole to hit," he said after the tour ended, "there'd be some darn Eskimo pitcher up there getting ready to throw me change-ups."

In some quarters, there is a theory that intelligent catchers are really the men behind intelligent pitchers, and that the pitching revival began behind the plate. But, in practice, the catcher only suggests each pitch with his finger signals; the pitcher can veto the suggestion simply by shaking his head. Young pitchers may allow catchers to think for them, but the old pros never do.

Before each game, pitcher and catcher discuss what lies ahead and, in the course of catching a pitcher every fourth day for years, catchers learn to anticipate tactics. A veteran pitcher becomes comfortable with the catcher who knows him best, since thinking then follows a common outline, but it is a matter of comfort, not necessity.

A batter can thrive on muscle, eyesight and reflexes. Outsized gloves have reduced most fielding plays to exercises in mechanics. The pitcher alone cannot reach his full measure without intellect and acuity, as well as body. He stands by himself, the pitcher, alone in the middle of a crowd, but this is where good pitchers like to stand. For their craft—like the very act of thinking—at its finest is a solitary pursuit.

[1959]

What Players Thought When Under Pressure

BY JOHN KUENSTER

What does a ball player think of when he's under pressure . . . when his hit will clinch a pennant or win a World Series . . . when his pitch will undo or save a perfect no-hitter?

In covering the American and National League beats in recent years, we've had a chance to talk to players involved in some rather dramatic situations that put a high premium on their skill, courage and determination.

We selected six particularly exciting games over the last decade and used them as a focal point to find out what the star performers actually *did* think of when destiny beckoned.

Their admissions—some of them revealed here for the first time—provide an interesting insight into human behavior in time of stress.

October 1, 1950—Robin Roberts retires two Dodger hitters with bases filled in ninth inning as Philadelphia Phillies clinch pennant on final day of National League season.

"*I was scared.* The score was tied, 1-1, in the bottom of the ninth at Ebbets Field and the Dodgers had the bases filled, with only one out. If they scored, a playoff would have been necessary to settle the championship.

"Carl Furillo and Gil Hodges, two tough hitters, were coming up. I was scared because I was thinking of all the things that could go wrong—a freak hop of the ball, an error, a bad pitch.

"I was determined, but on edge, tense. At one time we held a seven-game lead on the Dodgers and now they were breathing down our necks. I was going to fire away with the best I had.

"Furillo hit the first pitch, a high fastball. He popped up. I got behind on Hodges, and then got him to fly out, also on a fastball.

"That took the pressure off and we went on to win the game on Dick Sisler's three-run homer in the tenth inning.

"When I think back about that game, it seems more dramatic than when I was going through it. Maybe, at the time, if I thought too much about what the game meant to us, I might not have done so well."

October 3, 1951—Bobby Thomson slams three-run ninth-inning homer at the Polo Grounds to provide Giants with 5-4 comeback victory over Dodgers in final game of pennant playoff series.

"We were trailing the Dodgers, 4-2, with one out and two runners on base in the last of the ninth. *I was never more thankful* that I had a chance to get up and hit.

"In the eighth inning Don Newcombe had blown us down so easily, it didn't look like we'd have a chance. But, now, as Ralph Branca emerged from the bullpen in center field to replace Newcombe, it dawned on me we might win it after all. I was tickled.

"Before I got in the batter's box, all I thought about was hitting the ball. *I got mad at myself.* I said to myself, 'Get in there, you so-and-so, and bear down. Watch the ball, wait for it. Don't swing at a bad pitch.'

"I guess my anger was a way of disciplining my anxiety, forcing me to concentrate on the pitch, making me be selective.

"I let Branca's first pitch go by, then swung at the second, a high fastball. It was up where I could see it and I pulled it into the left field stands, about 30 feet fair. I wasn't mad any more. I was floating on a cloud."

October 9, 1956—Don Larsen of New York Yankees pitches first perfect, as well as first no-hit, no-run, game in World Series history, retiring 27 Dodgers in a row to post 2-0 triumph.

"I knew I had a no-hitter going for me in the seventh inning, but I didn't think too much about it until then. When the Dodgers came to bat in the ninth inning, I was so weak in the knees, I thought I was going to faint.

"*I had been nervous* since the seventh inning. Before we went out on the field in the ninth, Yogi Berra hit me on the seat of the pants and said, 'Go out there and let's get the first batter.'

"When Furillo came up to lead off, the thing I wanted to do more than anything else in my life was to get out of the ninth inning. *I mumbled a little prayer.* I said, 'Please help me get through this.'

"I got Furillo on a mild fly, Roy Campanella on a slow roller to Billy Martin, and pinch-hitter Dale Mitchell on a called third strike.

"Just before I threw the last pitch to Mitchell, I said to myself, 'Well, here goes nothing.'

"Looking back on that ninth inning, I can say every one of those three batters looked like Ted Williams to me."

June 27, 1958—Billy Pierce of Chicago White Sox comes within one out of pitching perfect no-hitter against Washington Senators, his bid ruined by an opposite-field double.

"It was a warm, muggy night at Comiskey Park. My curve ball was breaking real good and I was getting my fastball where I wanted it.

"For eight and two-thirds innings I didn't allow a Washington runner to reach first. From the fifth inning on I had thrown exactly nine pitches each inning, so I wasn't tired.

"Now I had one more batter to go. Ed FitzGerald, a right-handed pinch hitter, was up. We had a 3-0 lead, so there wasn't much at stake except that no-hitter.

"I knew I had a perfect game going from the third inning on. When I saw FitzGerald in the box, there was only one thought on my mind: keep the ball down and away.

"I figured he was a good fastball hitter, so I threw him a curve—about where I wanted—but he got the end of his bat on it and slammed the ball down the first base line, fair by two feet. I struck out the next batter, Albie Pearson, on three pitches and that was the game.

"Since then, I've thought more about that game than when I actually pitched it. *I was concentrating so hard* on keeping the ball down and away from FitzGerald, I can't say I had any emotion one way or another."

May 26, 1959—Harvey Haddix of Pittsburgh Pirates pitches perfect ball for 12 innings, only to lose to Milwaukee Braves, 1-0, in thirteenth inning.

"I reached a peak in the ninth inning. I wanted that no-hitter. It had always been my ambition to do something like that.

"After the ninth inning I was concentrating on trying to keep the Braves from scoring, but I felt more pressure on me in the ninth than at any other time. I think *I got a little bit angry.*

"I don't know exactly what I got mad at . . . maybe just at myself in trying to finish something that is very difficult. After I struck out Lew Burdette, the 27th batter to face me, the thing uppermost in my mind was to hope our guys would get me a run or two.

"I knew I had a no-hitter all the time, but I didn't know I had a perfect game. I thought I might have walked a man somewhere along the line.

"In the 13th inning an error, walk and Joe Adcock's double scoring Felix Mantilla turned the game into just another loss. But it hurt a little more."

October 13, 1960—Bill Mazeroski blasts Ralph Terry's fastball over left field wall at Forbes Field in deciding game of World Series to give Pirates title, 10-9.

Bill Mazeroski heads for the plate after hitting his home run off Ralph Terry of the Yankees to win the 1960 World Series for the Pirates. In recalling his thoughts in facing Terry, he remarked, "I kept saying to myself, 'Don't overswing. Just meet the ball.'"

"When we trotted off the field for our turn at bat in the ninth, I was thinking, 'I'd like to hit a home run and win it all.'

"The time before, in the seventh inning, I had gone for the long ball and I overswung. I grounded into a double play. This time I kept saying to myself, 'Don't overswing. Just meet the ball.'

"I thought I'd be more nervous this time, but I wasn't a bit. I wanted a homer, but I didn't want to overswing. *I was guessing* all the way.

"As Terry wound up, I was saying to myself, 'Fastball! Fastball!' That's what I wanted.

"The first one was a high slider. The next one was down a little, but still high—a fastball right into my power.

"A moment after I hit that ball, a shiver ran down my back. We always felt we could pull it out—even after the Yankees tied it up in the ninth—but I didn't think I'd be the guy to do it."

[1961]

The Spitter That Lost the World Series

BY HERBERT SIMONS

The legal spitter has won a lot of World Series games; an illegal spitter has lost at least one.

Using the damp delivery, Cleveland's Stan Coveleski defeated the Dodgers three times in the 1920 Series, holding them to two runs in 27 innings. In the 1917 Series the White Sox' Red Faber, also a saliva server, beat the Giants three times in four starts.

Burleigh Grimes, last of the special spitball licensees given lifetime dispensation when the pitch was outlawed in 1920, beat the Athletics in behalf of the Cards twice in 1931. Dick Rudolph of the 1914 Braves and Phil Douglas of the 1921 Giants also won two World Series games with the wet ones.

The last spitball ever to be thrown *legally* in a World Series was to the Yankees' Frankie Crosetti in the ninth inning of the fourth game of the 1932 Classic at Chicago. The one who threw it was Grimes, who had used it for a World Series win for the 1920 Dodgers as well as for his two Series triumphs for the 1931 Cardinals.

But Grimes wasn't the author of the last spitter ever to appear in a World Series, not by a good many dewdrops. Claude Passeau did a pretty good job of dishing up some moist ones in holding the Tigers to one hit, a single by Rudy York, for a 3-0 shutout in the third game of the 1945 doings at Detroit. Ol' "Pass" as much as admitted it to us on the train back to Chicago that night. And the late Hugh Casey, also by his own admission, put the wet on one in what may have been the deciding pitch of the 1941 Series.

The Dodgers were playing the Yankees that year. The latter, regaining the American League pennant, won in their patented runaway. The Dodgers, winning their first flag in 21 years, beat out the Cardinals by two and one-half games in a furious stretch drive.

The first three games of the Series that year were bitterly contested. Each was decided by a run. The Yankees won the first and third games, the Dodgers the second. Scoring pairs of runs off Atley Donald in the fourth and fifth innings, the Dodgers overcame an early 3-0 Yankee lead in the fourth game and entered the ninth inning ahead, 4-3.

Hugh Casey, the Dodgers' ace reliever who had pitched scoreless ball from the fifth inning, when he had been rushed in to quell a Yankee uprising, easily retired the Yankees' leadoff and No. 2 batters, Johnny Sturm and Red Rolfe, to open the ninth and had a three-and-two count on Tommy Henrich.

Within one strike of victory, Casey loaded up and poured in a wet one for the kill. Henrich swung and missed for the third strike, a strikeout that apparently ended the game with a Dodger victory and the Series tied up at two games each.

But the pitch swerved erratically and catcher Mickey Owen, who was no more expecting it than was Henrich, saw it skit away from and right by his glove for an error as Henrich reached first.

"They caught lightning in a bottle," was Durocher's comment on the play to us in the clubhouse afterwards.

The ball eludes Dodger catcher Mickey Owen as Tommy Henrich breaks for first after striking out in Game 4 of the 1941 World Series at Ebbets Field. Hugh Casey, seen coming off the mound, later admitted the pitch to Henrich was a spitter.

If it were lightning, the thunder certainly followed. The opening was all the Yankees needed. Joe DiMaggio whistled a single into left. Charlie Keller, on a two-strike, no-ball count, doubled off the right field wall, scoring Henrich and DiMaggio, and the Yankees went on from there for four runs and a 7-4 victory.

All after "three outs"!

Instead of the Series being tied up, two games each, the Yankees were ahead, three games to one. Next day the disheartened Dodgers were easy 3-1 victims and the thing was over.

Until Casey, quite a few years later, admitted moistening up the fatal pitch, Owen wore goat's horns—still does in some quarters, in fact.

But he didn't have to wait until they found horns specially suitable for such a happenstance. Old-timers recalled that his unhappiness was an exact duplicate of the performance of Detroit's Charles Schmidt in the first game of the 1907 World Series with the Cubs when, in the ninth inning, he let the game-ending strike on Del Howard get away after Wild Bill Donovan had struck out the pinch hitter.

On that error Harry Steinfeldt bounded in with the tying run and there was no scoring in three extra frames, the game being called at 3-3 at the end of the twelfth inning because of darkness.

So in 1941 history once again was written with carbon paper—wet carbon paper, to be sure.

[1961]

The Case of the Nervous Batter

BY LEONARD KOPPETT

"I'll tell you one I've never seen before or since," said Al Lopez in his cozy new clubhouse office at Comiskey Park. "I tell this story a lot but maybe you've never heard it."

It happened, the White Sox manager went on, in 1945. He was catching for the Pirates. They were playing the Giants in Pittsburgh.

"Mel Ott was managing then, from right field, and you remember how he used to complain whenever any rhubarb would come up," said Al. "Our manager was Frankie Frisch, and he was a screwball, too. Ernie Lombardi— you remember how big and lumbering he was, and this was at the end of his career—was catching for the Giants.

"They were leading us, 9-7, or something like that, in the last of the ninth. Rip Sewell was pitching for us, and remember, he was a pretty good hitter. We had a kid on the club named Art Cuccurullo [pronounced *Koo-koo-rullo*], a left-handed pitcher and a very nervous, jittery type of kid."

In the ninth the Pirates got a man on and Lopez batted with two out. He got on also, putting the tying runs on base. Frisch sent Cuccurullo up to hit for Sewell, much to Sewell's visible disgust, and the nervous youngster had to be told three times to go up to the plate.

Harry Feldman, who used to throw a big, down-breaking curve, was on the mound for the Giants. His first pitch was a great big hook which came inside, ankle-high to the batter—who simply lifted his hind leg out of the way.

"Just as if he were stepping out of a puddle," described Lopez, laughing at the recollection, "and, of course, the ball went past Lombardi, too. But it went over to the side, near the Giant dugout, hit at a funny angle, came around the wall in back of the plate, hit something else, and finally wound up on the other side near our dugout."

Everybody started running—Lombardi, slowly and painfully, after the elusive ball; the man from second; Lopez from first.

And Cuccurullo from home.

Two men scored and Kookie wound up sliding into third.

Lombardi, having retrieved the ball, complained to umpire Beans Reardon.

"That ball hit him on the foot," Ernie claimed. That, of course, would mean only bases loaded, with the two runners prevented from scoring.

"It did not, Ernie," said Reardon.

"It went right past him. Now don't argue, or you'll have Ott in from right field and you know how long that argument is going to take."

"Well, I still think it hit him," insisted Lombardi.

Sure enough, here came Ott. "What's going on?" he demanded. "The pitch hit him, I think," Lombardi told Ottie.

"It didn't," said Reardon firmly. "Now let's get on with the game."

"If it didn't hit him," asked Ott, "what's he doing on third base?"

"What's he where?" yelled Reardon, doing a double take. He looked at third. "I thought that was Lopez. I don't know what he's doing there, but we'll find out."

Throwing aside his mask, Reardon marched out to third base.

"What's the matter with you?" he scolded Kookie, the nervous one. "What in the world did you run for?"

"I don't know, Beansie," confessed Kookie. "I just saw everybody start running—so I ran. I guess I got excited."

"Well, calm down," roared Reardon, "and come on back and finish hitting."

Lopez doesn't remember how the game finally came out.

"I'll tell you one that happened to me," said Wally Moses, the Yankee coach, "when I was playing with the White Sox. I was on third base with two out in the last half of the tenth inning of a tie game. Don Kolloway was the batter.

"I stole home. The pitch came in close but I slid under it and the umpire called me safe which would end the ball game with us winning.

"But Kolloway was hollering that the pitch hit him—and the umpire let him have his way. 'O.K.,' he said, 'it hit you.' And he sent me back to third base and Kolloway to first. The next man flied out and there we were playing the eleventh inning instead of in the clubhouse with a victory.

"We finally did win the game in the twelfth," Moses concluded, "but I don't have to tell you how mad Jimmy Dykes was about that one. He was our manager and I'm sure he's never forgotten it."

Dykes never has, and his memory of the scene is even more vivid. You must picture Moses, just getting up from his slide; Kolloway, holding his hat and arguing; the umpire, his mask off listening; and Dykes, just arrived at the plate. The dialogue went:

Kolloway: "It hit me."

Dykes: "Shut up."

Kolloway: "It hit me, it hit me!"

Dykes: "SHUT UP, shut up!!!"

[1962]

Hornsby's Five Fabulous Years

BY TOM MEANY

An earnest man, Al Spohrer attempted the impossible in the summer of 1929. He tried to talk Rogers Hornsby out of a base hit. Catching for the last-place Boston Braves against the first-place Chicago Cubs at Wrigley Field, Spohrer reached a decision which had been reached in advance of him by many another, and older, head. The decision was that Hornsby couldn't be kept from hitting by ordinary means.

Spohrer, who had been a teammate of Hornsby the year before at Boston, knew of the Rajah's fanatic devotion to steaks. Rogers was the original beef eater, and in whatever town he landed—and he landed in several before he was through—he was always on the prowl for a place that served steaks better than any other place in that particular town.

The thought struck Al that if he could get Hornsby talking about his hobby it might take his mind off his hitting. Or, rather, off the Boston pitching, which Hornsby was finding as appetizing as any steak.

"Say, Rog," began Spohrer conversationally when Hornsby came to bat for the third time, "my wife has discovered a butcher in Boston who sells the finest steaks anyone ever ate."

"That so?" said Hornsby with polite interest.

"Strike one!" bawled the umpire.

"Not only that, Rog," continued Al, really warming to his task, "but my wife can cook steaks better than anybody I know. Grace really has a knack for broiling 'em."

"That sounds good," commented Rogers.

"Strike two!" was the umpire's contribution to the conversation.

"What Grace and I thought," enthused Spohrer, "was that maybe on the next trip up to Boston, you'd come over to the house for dinner some night and try one."

"Crack!" That wasn't the umpire but the bat. The ball disappeared over the left field wall of Wrigley Field and Hornsby began a slow trot around the bases. When he completed the circuit and put his spikes into the rubber of home plate, he turned to face the chagrined Spohrer.

"What night shall we make it, Al?" Hornsby asked.

The story of Spohrer and Hornsby has been told so often that it has attained the status of a baseball legend and, like so many legends, it may be apocryphal. The chances are, however, it is true, but true or not, it serves as a perfect example of the fierce concentration Hornsby was able to put in his task of hitting a baseball. Nothing, not even conversation about a succulent steak, could cause any deviation from the course he plotted.

To Hornsby, who died early in 1963 at the age of 66, there was only one way to play baseball and that was by giving it one's full and undivided attention. It was the being-all and end-all of his existence. Many years after the dinner invitation, extended to him by Spohrer, Hornsby was sipping a Coke at the bar of the old Auditorium Hotel in Chicago, talking with Bill McCullough, a New York sportswriter who was doing publicity in Chicago that fall.

It was a Saturday evening and the abstemious Hornsby was idly turning the pages of the final sports extra of the *Chicago Daily News*. The date was November 13, 1937, and the front page was filled with reports of the Army–Notre Dame game in New York. There were stories on Wisconsin-Purdue, Northwestern-Minnesota, Illinois–Ohio State, Michigan-Pennsylvania, Pitt-Nebraska—even one on Chicago and Beloit. There were photos and charts, color stories and play-by-play.

The sports section ran eight pages and was a truly magnificent compilation of the day's doings on the gridiron. As Hornsby looked up one column and down another for some item about baseball without success, he finally put the paper aside.

"Lord, Bill," said Rog to McCullough, "there's *nothing* in the sports pages these days, is there?"

There was always an air of mystery to Hornsby, an air of mystery to his personal comings-and-goings and an air of mystery to his departure from one club to another.

When Hornsby joined the Giants in the spring of 1927, after being traded from the Cardinals when he had brought St. Louis the first of many pennants, Ferdie Schupp, who had been with Rogers on the Cardinals, was questioned as to what manner of man Hornsby might be.

"Nobody knows," answered Schupp honestly. "He never talks to anybody. He just goes out and plays second base, and when the game is over he comes into the clubhouse, takes off his uniform, takes a shower and gets dressed, without saying a word. Then he leaves the clubhouse and nobody knows where he goes."

Hornsby didn't deliberately cultivate this air of mystery. He wasn't precisely anti-social. It might be more accurate to regard him in the light of a self-sufficient man. He needed nobody to lean on, any more than he needed anybody to help him up at the plate. It was this trait that led directly to his many tactless remarks. Rog always spoke his mind—and his mind wasn't always complimentary.

Just as nobody knew what Hornsby did between games, neither did anybody know why Hornsby went from club to club. When he was traded by the Cards to the Giants, the civic repercussions in St. Louis were greater than in any city, any time, after the trading of a star ball player.

Hornsby was traded from the Cards because he wanted a three-year contract at $50,000 to be playing manager, a job he had held for a year and one-half without any pay increase. Why he was traded from the Giants to the Braves, after one season, nobody knows to this day. He was traded from the Braves to the Cubs after one season because Judge Emil Fuchs, the owner of the Braves, needed the cash that Hornsby would bring, which turned out to be $120,000, although it was announced as $200,000 when the deal was made. And there is no known reason for the Cubs suddenly releasing Hornsby as player-manager in the middle of the 1932 season.

The opinion here always has been that Hornsby was hurt more by being traded from the Cardinals to the Giants than by any other single factor in his turbulent career. When he went to the Giants he was a player apart. He had been a manager, and he never went back to mingle with the rank and file again. John McGraw gave him privileges no other Giant player ever had—or ever was to have again. Hornsby neither flaunted nor abused these privileges, but it kept him from being one of the gang.

Hornsby, as has been intimated, always said what he thought and he always spoke for publication. There was no off-the-record stuff with Rog. If you asked his opinion, he gave it and he didn't care whether you printed it or not. It was all one with Hornsby.

When Hornsby reported to the Giants in the spring of 1927, McGraw was absent frequently from the Sarasota camp. He left the club in charge of Rogers. Fred Lindstrom, the third baseman, and Hornsby had an argument over the proper way to make the double play.

Hornsby wanted Lindy to fire the ball to him at second as quickly as possible. (Some said this was to save his own arm, so he wouldn't have to hurry to complete the relay to first base.) Lindstrom said that McGraw always instructed his players to make sure of getting the "head man" on double plays. In other words, McGraw wanted the force-out at second to be certain, preferring to get only one rather than to miss both because the throw to second base was hurried.

"If that's the way the Old Man wants it," snapped Hornsby, "do it that way when he's in charge. When I'm in charge, do it my way."

Lindy, like Hornsby, also could be outspoken. He told Hornsby that once he laid his bat down he was no bargain, and not to get all puffed up with his own importance.

"I'm not arguing with you. I'm telling you," declared Hornsby. "You'll do as I say. And keep your mouth shut."

Hornsby paused for a moment to look at the other Giants. "And that goes for the rest of you," he barked. It did, too. Whenever McGraw left Hornsby in charge—and he did it several times, not only that spring but during the summer when the club was fighting for the pennant—Hornsby always took charge literally.

Awkward as was his position with the Giants, it was even more so the following season when he was traded to Boston. McGraw fled to Cuba when the trade was made and never did answer any questions about it. With the Braves, Hornsby joined a slaphappy club with a thoroughly confused front office and a manager named Jack Slattery, who had been a college baseball coach the year before.

Visiting newspapermen came to Hornsby for interviews in the spring. They knew Hornsby and they didn't know Slattery. There were rumors that Slattery wouldn't even last long enough as manager to get the club home from spring training. As a matter of fact, Jack mightn't have opened the season had the Boston papers not lined up solidly behind him.

At Miami, a writer traveling with the Dodgers accosted Hornsby in the hotel dining room.

"They tell me," opened the writer, "that this club has a chance for the first division."

"These humpty-dumpties?" snorted Hornsby in honest disgust. "The first division? With what?"

When Slattery finally was let out, Hornsby at first refused to take over the managership. He felt that baseball would feel he had undermined Slattery. As a matter of fact, Slattery was doomed from the start because he never had a ball club. Fuchs argued sufficiently to make Rogers assume the managership, and the Braves played the last two-thirds of the season under Hornsby, no better or no worse than they had played under Slattery.

Hornsby felt a genuine fondness for Judge Fuchs and he advised Fuchs to sell him that winter for what he would bring on the open market. It was then that he went to the Cubs, back to the playing ranks again under Joe McCarthy. Hornsby helped McCarthy win his first pennant in 1929 and at the end of the following season succeeded McCarthy as manager.

Once again Rogers was on the spot, but he had no more to do with McCarthy leaving the Cubs than he had to do with Slattery leaving the Braves.

After the dismal showing of the Cubs in the 1929 World Series, the club was receiving second-guesses in carload lots. And McCarthy, one of the greatest managers the game ever knew, was not one to take second-guessing from the front office.

Hornsby lasted a season and one-half as Cub manager and was released outright, August 2, 1932. He left behind him a club that won the pennant under Charlie Grimm. There was no logical reason for Rog being let out by the Cubs. He was riding the players hard, but he felt that they needed it, that they had the best club and weren't putting out. His con-

Rogers Hornsby was an average-fielding second baseman, but he ranks as one of baseball's greatest right-handed hitters. A native of Texas, he batted .358 in his 23-year career that started in 1915 and ended in 1937. In a five-year stretch with the Cardinals, 1921 through 1925, he hit .397, .401, .384, .424 and .403.

tention was borne out when the club won for Grimm. Maybe he should have used sugar instead of vinegar but nobody had ever sugared up Hornsby. In fact, nobody ever had to.

In view of Hornsby's magnificent achievements as a batter, it may come as a surprise to learn that he was purchased by the Cardinals because that astute scout, Bob Connery, saw fielding greatness in the skinny kid who was playing shortstop for Denison, Texas, in the Class D Western Association.

Hornsby was a perfectly coordinated athlete. He had long, loose arms, sure hands and was a strong thrower. He always maintained that his fielding would have been good enough to keep him in the major leagues even if he had been only an ordinary hitter. Rog's batting was so sensational that his fielding skill, which he maintained even when shifted from short to second, was overlooked. Hornsby had only one fault as a fielder—he had trouble with pop flies. He had one of the great double-play arms of any second baseman in history, throwing straight across his chest with no perceptible shifting of his feet.

Another generally forgotten item about Hornsby is that he came up to the Cardinals as a choke-hitter who batted from a crouch, which may explain his .277 average with Denison. It was Connery and Miller Huggins who got him to adopt the stance he later made famous, standing well back in the box, farther from the plate than any ranking hitter ever did.

Hornsby stood with his feet close together and took a tremendous stride, stepping up to meet the ball. "It was impossible to hit me with a pitched ball," said Rogers, "because I always was moving with the pitch."

Because of this stance Hornsby could, and did, hit to all fields. I remember him beating Dutch Ruether with a home run into the right field stands, close to the foul line, at Sportsman's Park one August Sunday in 1924. The score was tied and Hornsby was the leadoff batter for the Cards in the ninth.

Hornsby's stance had a lot of imitators, most of them unsuccessful. It is believed by batting theorists that only a batter who takes a stance with his feet close together, and thus is in a position to hit into the opposite field, can ever achieve the magic .400 figure. The only exception to the rule was Ted Williams, who batted over .400 in 1941 without hitting to the opposite field very often. Hornsby hit over .400 on three different occasions.

Probably Hornsby was the most devastating hitter baseball ever has seen through the five seasons of 1921, 1922, 1923, 1924 and 1925. Rog's averages for those seasons, respectively and respectfully, were .397, .401, .384, .424 and .403. In those five consecutive seasons the Rajah went to bat 2,679 times and rapped out no fewer than 1,078 base hits. His overall average for the five-year period was .402.

There is no question that the lively ball helped Hornsby. His average jumped from .318 in 1919 to .370 in 1920. And once his average went up, it stayed up until he was through. The fact that Rogers was aided by the lively ball is no reflection upon his hitting skill. The other batters of his time were hitting at the same rabbit ball but Hornsby was outhitting them by so far that he led the National League for six consecutive seasons.

Hornsby had been gone from Boston a decade before Casey Stengel went there to manage, but the magic of Hornsby's name lived on. Braves Field had the reputation of being one of the most difficult parks in the National League for hitters. The prevailing wind was always from the east and swept from the mound to the plate.

One of Stengel's players, in a woeful slump, came back to the dugout, flung his bat from him in disgust and started to revile the ball park, its architecture and its prevailing wind.

"How the hell can they expect anybody to hit up here?" he wanted to know. "The wind is always with the pitcher. Nobody can hit up here."

"All I know," answered Stengel mildly, "is that Hornsby played here one whole season and batted .387."

Although Hornsby generally was not regarded as a great manager, he was a great and inspiring leader for the Cardinals when he won the pennant in 1926 and then upset the vaunted Yankees in the World Series that fall. The general charge against Hornsby was that he was impatient with young players, that things came too easily for him, that he couldn't understand others not acquiring the skills that were natural to him.

That may be so, but anybody who ever conversed with the Rajah will admit that Hornsby always made sense when he spoke about baseball. And he rarely spoke about anything else. For all of his reputation as a horse player, Rogers never talked about the ponies. He just bet 'em.

Hornsby never went to the movies during the baseball season, rarely read and never attempted to read on a train. He had incredibly clear, blue eyes and, even when past fifty, he never needed glasses to aid his vision.

Baseball was his abiding passion, and his refusal to do anything that might possibly subject his eyes to strain was only part of his devotion to the game. In the sere and yellow of his career, Hornsby went into the bushes to manage at Baltimore . . . Oklahoma City . . . Chattanooga . . . Fort Worth . . . wherever there was baseball, there was Hornsby if there was room for him.

Hornsby took over the managership of Oklahoma City in the Texas League in June 1940. A month or so later, I happened to run across him down there and he told me of the lecture he had given his club when he took over. It is worth retelling, for it is illustrative of his baseball credo.

"I never smoked or drank in my life," began Hornsby to his squad, almost in a Billy Sunday manner. "And you fellows'd be smart if you'd cut out drinking or smoking while you're playing ball. I'm not saying this merely because I don't drink or smoke but merely because it's the best way to keep your legs and wind in shape.

"Don't kid yourselves about baseball. There's only one place to play it—the big leagues. And the idea is to get to the big leagues as quickly as you can and stay there as long as you can. And, if you're in shape you've got a better chance to get up there and stay up there.

"Anybody who is content to dub around in the minors is a sucker. If you haven't got a chance to make the majors, get out of baseball and go into business or learn a trade while you're still young enough."

It was, to anyone who knew Hornsby, a typical Hornsby talk. One of the Texas sportswriters asked Rogers what did a kid need the most if he was to become a successful ball player.

"What does a kid need the most to become a successful ball player?" repeated the forthright Rajah. "That's a cinch—ability."

In a word, Hornsby summed up his philosophy of life. During his 23 years in the majors, the Rajah saw time and again that the race is always to the swift. Baseball pays off only in the major leagues and pays off only on ability. Those who have it, thought Hornsby, should protect its longevity to the utmost. When he spoke of the evils of drink or the dangers of nicotine, Hornsby was speaking not as a moralist but as the realist he always was.

[1963]

How Early Wynn Made DiMaggio Quit

BY ART ROSENBAUM

In an informal mood, recalling the physical aches and pains of being a Yankee, Joe DiMaggio recently revealed for the first time the details of (and the man responsible for) his decision to quit baseball after 13 seasons.

"Early Wynn did it," Joe explained, at the same time providing another indication of the acumen that helped Wynn become one of the 14 pitchers ever to win 300 games.

"He found out I was no longer able to hit the high inside fastball. After I broke my left collarbone I wasn't able to bring my left arm around high enough to be ready for the tight pitch. If I say so myself, in my younger days I could murder the high inside hummer. Usually I'd drive it to deep center, or maybe right-center. In those days a pitcher wouldn't dare to deliberately throw it there, because he knew there was a good chance I'd pickle it.

"I didn't tell anybody, not even our trainer, that I couldn't come all the way around. I just hoped I could keep the secret. As I said, I knew pitchers wouldn't throw high and inside to me on purpose. Well, Wynn threw one and then another and another. I couldn't just stand there, and he saw my grinding swing. I tell you, it didn't take more than a week for the word to get around the American League. They all had me pegged, and I was dead.

"It was my last season."

Though the shoulder was the break that killed Joe, it was the least painful of his problems. He was, in a phrase, the Mickey Mantle of his day. Beautiful but fragile.

Any year that Joe was able to open the season was something of a miracle. He was bought originally as "distressed merchandise" from the old San Francisco Seals because of weakened cartilage in his knee, jammed while he was stepping into an automobile. "The doctors didn't operate much on knees in 1935," he said. "Our doctor said I was young enough then to heal by myself. To this day the knee hurts when I turn too much."

Bone spurs in the heel area lost him many playing days. At the time the DiMag heel was the cause of national concern. Diagrams of the jagged edges were published on front pages along with maps of Europe, where border governments were feeling another kind of heel.

Later, DiMag suffered from leg burns, ulcers, arthritis, and once a wracking pain across the left chest that cardiograms couldn't diagnose and fortunately turned up as a plain old torn muscle.

"My worst day in baseball," Joe continued, "was in my next to last season when some of the fellows weren't hitting. Casey Stengel decided to put

Hank Bauer in center field and me at first base. They asked me if I minded playing first—an old man's job, anyway, they said—because they had to get more hitting strength spread around the team.

"So I agreed. I worked out for a week at the position, learning the plays and handling hard grounders. Then I was ready. That day I handled 13 chances. Once I started to field a ball that the second baseman should have gobbled up easily. I fouled up what could have been a triple play.

"One day was enough. Then they asked me if I minded playing center field again and I told them I didn't mind. No one could ever convince me first is an old man's haven. For me, center field was heaven. But I'll tell you this. For me, center field was a must, because that one day at first caved in my knee and ruined an entire season of hitting. I wanted to retire at the end of the year, but I was persuaded to stay on another season.

A selective hitter, Joe DiMaggio never struck out more than 39 times in a season during his 13 years with the Yankees, reaching that high mark as a rookie in 1936. In seven seasons, he recorded more home runs than strikeouts.

"Here's what happened: I was swinging as well as ever, I thought, but all of a sudden everything would pop up. I never looked up at so much sky in my life as I did the next few months. I finally realized that every time I swung, that left knee would buckle and I'd hit under the pitch. Yes, that one day at first helped start me toward the end of my career.

"It worked out O.K. for us, though, because right after that Johnny Mize began to hit the stuffings out of the ball and we won the pennant."

DiMag admires and envies Stan Musial and Early Wynn for their baseball longevity. He rooted for Wynn to pitch his 300th victory in major league ball, even though Wynn was the smart pitcher who ran him out of baseball.

"If it wasn't Wynn, it would have been someone else," Joe reflected. "Looking back on all those days I spent in the whirlpool and the doc's office, I think I was the luckiest guy alive to have been a Yankee for 13 seasons."

[1963]

The Lingering Shadow of the Iron Man

BY AL HIRSHBERG

"Twenty-five years—is it that long?" Joe DiMaggio tugged at his cap and looked off into space. We were standing near first base at the New York Yankees' spring-training camp in Fort Lauderdale, Florida, where DiMaggio was helping out as a special coach. I had just asked him about Lou Gehrig.

A legend in his lifetime, Gehrig ran up a record streak of playing in 2,130 straight games before he was stricken with amyotrophic lateral sclerosis, a rare disease that eventually killed him.

Lou Gehrig played his last full season with the Yankees in 1938, when Joe DiMaggio was baseball's brightest young star.

"It doesn't seem like 25 years," DiMaggio mused. "The time goes by so fast. I remember now—1938. They called it a bad year for Lou, but anyone else would have gladly settled for it. He was close to hitting .300 and had nearly 30 home runs, but that wasn't up to his usual pace. And he got only four singles in the World Series."

DiMaggio ducked a flying baseball and we moved out of range. Then he said, "None of us thought there was anything seriously wrong. Lou wasn't a kid anymore, and he hadn't missed a game in 14 years.

"He figured to slow up. Then he came back for spring training in 1939."

The Yankee Clipper shook his head. "Poor Lou," he said. "He couldn't hit a loud foul. He stood up there once in batting practice and missed 19 straight swings—all on good fastballs that he ordinarily would have smacked into the next county. Still, we didn't really suspect anything. His timing was way off, but the older you are, the longer it takes to get that back in the spring.

"Then we noticed he was having trouble catching thrown balls at first base," DiMaggio said. "Lou had never been a great fielder, but he was good enough to get by. But now he sometimes didn't move his hands up fast enough to protect himself. A ball would go right through them and bounce off his chest. Then one day in Houston, while we were barnstorming north, he fell down the dugout steps."

DiMaggio shook his head again. "Say," he said, "what was the name of that disease he had?"

"Technically, it is called amyotrophic lateral sclerosis," I said. "But I guess almost everybody, including medical men, calls it Lou Gehrig's disease now."

"Funny," DiMaggio said. "Here was the most powerful hitter I ever saw—and one of the greatest ball players of all time—and he's more famous for what killed him than for what he did when he was alive. I wonder if they're working on it; it's so rare. Lou was the only one I ever knew who had it."

Amyotrophic lateral sclerosis is indeed rare.

At that time it was announced that the ailment was a form of polio. Since then it has been determined that amyotrophic lateral sclerosis has nothing to do with polio. Later there were attempts to prove that it had some relationship to multiple sclerosis, but it has nothing to do with that, either. The only similarity is in the name.

"Amyotrophic lateral sclerosis, sometimes called Lou Gehrig's disease, or motor-system disease, has characteristics all its own," says a Boston medical specialist. "It is a progressive, degenerative disease of the nerve cells in the spinal cord, and it is not related to anything else. But, while we can't yet prevent or cure it, at least we now know what goes on.

"When it hits, it usually affects people in their forties," the doctor added. "The nerve cells of the spine harden and thicken, the muscles begin to atrophy, and there is increasing inability of various parts of the body to function. The earliest symptoms are failure to coordinate properly, and this becomes more serious as time goes on. Death comes in two to three years."

Gehrig was apparently a bit younger than the average victim of the disease. He was a few weeks short of his thirty-sixth birthday in June 1939, when his case was first diagnosed at the Mayo Clinic in Rochester, Minnesota. Gehrig died on June 2, 1941, two years later almost to the day. He would have been 38 on June 19.

While, as Joe DiMaggio pointed out, Gehrig's fame today seems to rest more on the manner of his death than on the achievements of his life, he ranks among the greatest sluggers that baseball has ever known. Because of his illness and imminent death, Gehrig was voted into the game's Hall of Fame by special election in 1939. Ordinarily, players have to wait until five years after their retirement. If Gehrig had lived, he would have walked in the moment he became eligible for the honor.

His fantastic streak of consecutive games, a record that probably will never be broken, was just one of his claims to immortality. Only Babe Ruth drove in more runs than Gehrig, and only Ruth, Ty Cobb and Stan Musial scored more.

For years Gehrig was the American League's undisputed leader in runs batted in. He led the league five times, and his record of 184 RBI in 1931 has never been matched. Only one man, National Leaguer Hack Wilson, ever knocked in more runs than Gehrig did in a single season. Wilson, of the Chicago Cubs, drove in 191 runs in 1930, but he was a one-year wonder who did nothing before or after to merit attention.

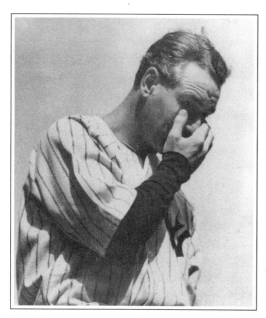

Lou Gehrig wipes a tear from his eye as he is honored at Yankee Stadium on July 4, 1939, following his retirement as an active player because of amyotrophic lateral sclerosis, known today as Lou Gehrig's disease.

Although he lived in the shadow of Babe Ruth for nearly ten years, Gehrig was one of baseball's greatest home run hitters. He was the first man in modern times to hit four in one game, and he was one of the few to hit three in a game three different times. He was baseball's home run king twice, its leading batter once, and he was voted the American League's Most Valuable Player in 1927 and 1936.

Roger Maris and Mickey Mantle notwithstanding, Gehrig formed with Ruth the most fearsome one-two punch in the history of baseball. These two left-handed sluggers, with Ruth batting third and Gehrig fourth, ripped apart both American and National League pitching staffs. Their peak year was 1927, when Ruth hit 60 homers and Gehrig hit 47. A year later they led the Yankees to a murderous four-straight World Series victory over the St. Louis Cardinals. Ruth batted .625 and Gehrig batted .545 in that Series, and four of Gehrig's six hits were home runs.

The two were close friends until the winter of 1934, when they got into a bitter argument during an exhibition trip to the Orient. From that time until 1939—after Gehrig's disease became apparent—they rarely spoke to each other.

Gehrig's illness and premature death, although a crushing blow to his many fans, was particularly tragic for his parents—who had already lost their other children. One of four youngsters, Henry Louis Gehrig was born in the Yorkville section of New York City, June 19, 1903. He was educated in the city's public schools and entered Columbia University in 1921, but stayed only through his sophomore year. He signed with the Yankees after his father, a skilled mechanic, lost his job.

Gehrig reported to the ball club in June 1923, but spent most of that season at Hartford, where he hit 24 home runs in 59 games. After he had another great year in the Eastern League in 1924, the Yankees brought the 22-year-old up permanently for the 1925 season.

Gehrig sat on the bench for about six weeks. On June 1, Wally Pipp, the regular first baseman, reported with a headache, and manager Miller Huggins sent Lou in to replace him. Pipp might as well have stood in bed, because he never got his job back.

For the next 14 years—despite a broken thumb, a broken rib, a broken toe, a twisted back, innumerable colds, and frequent attacks of lumbago—Gehrig didn't miss a ball game.

This was a fantastic achievement even in those years, when there was little or no night baseball, far less traveling than today, and a shorter schedule—154 games instead of 162 that are played now. In Gehrig's time, only seven or eight men played in every game of the season, and few did it two seasons in a row, much less 14.

Eventually, Gehrig broke Everett Scott's record of 1,307 consecutive games and then went on to put his own record out of reach of everyone. The only time the streak was really in danger came after Gehrig suffered a painful head injury. But Joe McCarthy, the Yankees' manager, sent him up in the leadoff spot, then ordered him back to his hotel. The next day Lou was back to normal again.

A quiet, shy man, Gehrig disliked the spotlight into which he was constantly thrown. He and his roommate, catcher Bill Dickey, were inseparable on the road, and they and their wives were always together when the team was at home. Both men were bridge enthusiasts. On trains and in hotels, they played for years as partners against George Selkirk and Johnny Murphy.

"I first met Gehrig in 1932," says Selkirk. "But it wasn't until a couple of years later that I really got friendly with him. Although sometimes moody, he was a great guy who would do anything for people he liked. And he was a marvelous bridge player—a real student of the game."

Frank Crosetti, first the shortstop and later the Yankees' third base coach, remembers Gehrig with deep affection. "He did something for me I'll never forget," says Crosetti. "When I first broke in, I was so scared I didn't dare open my mouth. One day just before the season started, we went to New Haven for an exhibition game with Yale. I had such a cold I could hardly breathe, and Lou was having trouble with his back. McCarthy let us both off early, so I sat in the locker room, waiting to go back to New York with the ball club.

"'Don't sit around here all afternoon,' Lou said. 'You'll get pneumonia. Come on back to my house.' So one of the greatest hitters in the business drove a scared rookie back to his home in Westchester for the night, and made a friend for life. That's the way he was."

Although Gehrig wasn't quite up to par during the 1938 season, there seemed nothing wrong with him physically. He spent the winter at his home in New Rochelle, ice skating with his wife, Eleanor, almost every day. When he reported to the club for spring training in 1939, Gehrig appeared to be in excellent shape.

His clumsiness at the plate and first base was obvious to everyone, but not until he fell down the dugout steps in Houston was there any real concern for his health. Even then, McCarthy refrained from broaching the subject. Lou's streak was still going, and the Yankees' manager had decided to let him continue to play until he requested relief himself.

One day, just before the season opened, Eleanor noticed that Lou stepped off a curb feeling his way like a blind man, then she recalled that during the winter he had often fallen on the ice, although he was an excellent skater. She begged him to have a physical checkup, but he insisted that there was nothing wrong.

When the Yankees opened the 1939 season at Washington, Gehrig was still at first base. But in the first eight games of the year he had only four singles and one run batted in, and the Yankees lost two games because easy grounders went right through his legs.

Then one day, with Johnny Murphy pitching, somebody hit a routine grounder right at him. Picking the ball up, he flipped it to Murphy, who came over to cover first, and the runner was out. Murphy, Dickey, and the Yanks' second baseman, Joe Gordon, all slapped Gehrig on the back and told him what a great play he had made. But Lou wasn't fooled. He knew his mates were congratulating him for a simple maneuver that he had performed hundreds of times before.

The next day, May 2, he went to McCarthy and said, "Better put Babe Dahlgren on first. I'm not doing the club any good out there."

He went to the Mayo Clinic a few weeks later, then phoned his wife and cheerfully told her that he had a 50-50 chance to live. Eleanor wasn't fooled, either. She had already been given the medical report, and she knew that her husband was doomed.

Gehrig rejoined the ball club and traveled as long as he could. As team captain, he took the lineups out to the plate umpire before each game, but his step was slower, and he had more trouble holding the card in his hand with each passing day.

July 4, 1939, was designated "Lou Gehrig Day," and more than 62,000 fans went to Yankee Stadium to honor him. It was there that Babe Ruth came out to the plate, threw his arms around his old friend, and tearfully broke a silence of five years. And it was there that Gehrig, dying and almost surely aware of it, murmured over the microphone his heartfelt thanks and added a sentence remembered from that day to this as a classic of simple courage: "I'm the luckiest man in the world."

Gehrig's physical deterioration was rapid after that, and soon he could not walk without help. On January 1, 1940, Mayor Fiorello H. LaGuardia of New York appointed him a city parole commissioner. Lou and Eleanor moved to Riverdale so that he could be closer to his office, and for some time he went to work every day.

But before the year was over, he couldn't even do that. By late autumn he was in a wheelchair. He continued to play bridge but had trouble holding the cards. Eleanor had to feed him, light his cigarettes, and write letters for him.

In late May 1941, Selkirk, accompanied by Tommy Henrich, went to see Gehrig at his Riverdale apartment. Lou, once a powerful 205-pounder, was down to 90 pounds and had trouble speaking, but he grinned a greeting.

"I'll be all right," he said cheerfully. "The doctor told me this thing has to run its course before I'll start building up again."

In recalling it, Selkirk said, "But he knew. He just didn't want to worry Eleanor."

A week later Lou Gehrig, one of the greatest men baseball has ever known, was gone.

[1963]

The First Baseman Who Outpitched Walter Johnson

BY GEORGE SISLER AS TOLD TO LYALL SMITH

Every American kid has a baseball idol. Mine was Walter Johnson, the "Big Train." Come to think about it, Walter still is my idea of the real ball player. He was graceful. He had rhythm, and when he heaved that ball in to the plate he threw with his whole body just so easy-like that you'd think the ball was flowing off his arm and hand.

I was just a husky kid in Akron (Ohio) High School back around 1910–11 when Johnson began making a name for himself with the Senators, and I was so crazy about the man that I'd read every line and keep every picture of him I could get my hands on.

Naturally, admiring Johnson as I did, I decided to be a pitcher, and even though I wound up as a first baseman my biggest day in baseball was a hot muggy afternoon in St. Louis when I pitched against him and beat him. Never knew that, did you? Most fans don't. But it's right. Me, a kid just out of the University of Michigan, beat the great Walter Johnson. It was on August 29, 1915, my first year as a ball player, the first time I ever was in a game against the man who I thought was the greatest pitcher in the world.

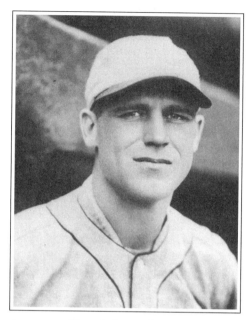

An outstanding pitcher at the University of Michigan, George Sisler made it to the Hall of Fame as a graceful first baseman and lifetime .340 hitter. In 1915, however, he went to the mound for the St. Louis Browns and outdueled his idol, Walter Johnson, 2-1. Once again, in 1916, he beat Johnson 1-0, shutting down the Washington Senators on six hits.

I guess I was a pretty fair pitcher myself at Central High in Akron. I had a strong left arm and I could throw them in there all day long and never have an ache or pain.

Anyway, I got a lot of publicity in my last year in high school, and when I was still a student I signed up one day to play with Akron.

I had no idea when I signed that contract I was stepping into a rumpus that went on and on until it finally involved the National Baseball Commission and the owners of two big league clubs.

I was only 17 years old when I wrote my name on the slip of paper that made me property of Akron, a club in the Ohio-Pennsylvania League and a farm club of Columbus in the American Association. After I signed it I got scared and didn't even tell my dad or anybody 'cause I knew my folks wanted me to go on to college and I figured they'd be sore if they knew I wanted to be a ball player.

In a way, that's what saved me, I guess. For by not telling my dad, he never had a chance to O.K. my signature and in that way the contract didn't hold. The way it worked out, Akron sold me to Columbus and Columbus sold me to Pittsburgh and all the time I was still in high school and hadn't even reported to the team I signed with—wasn't even legally signed, the way it turned out.

They wanted me to join the club when I was graduated from high school, but I was all set to go to Michigan so I said "no" and went up to Ann Arbor. Well, to make a long story short the story came out in the open there, and when the whole thing was over I had been made a free agent by the old National Commission and signed up with Branch Rickey who at that time was manager of the St. Louis Browns.

I pitched three years of varsity ball up at Michigan and when I was graduated on June 10, 1915, Rickey wired me to join the Browns in Chicago. Now all this time I was up at school I still had my sights set on Walter Johnson. When he pitched his 56 consecutive scoreless innings in 1912 I was as proud as though I'd done it myself. After all, I felt as though I had adopted him. He was my hero. He won 36 games and lost only seven in 1913, and he came back the next season to win 28 more and lose 18. He was really getting the headlines in those days, and I was keeping all of them in my scrapbook.

Well, then I left Michigan in 1915 and came down to Chicago where I officially became a professional ball player. I hit town one morning and that same day we were getting beat pretty bad, so Rickey called me over to the dugout.

"George," he said, "I know you just got in town and that you don't know any of the players and you're probably tired and nervous. But I want to see what you have in that left arm of yours. Let's see what you can do in these last three innings."

I gulped hard a couple of times, muttered something that sounded like "thanks" and went out and pitched those last three innings. Did pretty good, too. I gave up one hit, but the White Sox didn't get any runs so I figured that I was all right.

Next day, though, I was out warming up and meeting more of the Browns when Rickey came over to me. He was carrying a first baseman's glove. "Here," he said. "Put this on and get over there on first base."

Well, nothing much happened between the time I joined the club in June until along about the last part of August. Rickey would pitch me one day, stick me in the outfield the next and then put me over on first the next three or four. I was hitting pretty good, and by the time we got back to St. Louis the sportswriters were saying some nice things about me.

They were saying it chiefly because of my hitting. I'd only won two-three games up to then. I still remember the first one. I beat Cleveland and struck out nine men. Some clothing store gave me a pair of white flannels for winning and I was right proud of them. Didn't even wear them for a long time, figured they were too fancy.

As I was saying, we got back to St. Louis late in August. Early one week I picked up a paper and saw that a St. Louis writer, Billy Murphy, had written a story about Washington coming to town the following Sunday and that Walter Johnson was going to pitch.

I was still a Johnson fan and I guess Murphy knew it, for when I got about halfway through the story I found out that he had me pitching against Johnson on the big day, Sunday, August 29.

That was the first I knew about it and I figured it was the first Manager Rickey knew about it, for here it was only Tuesday and Murphy had the pitchers all lined up for the following Sunday.

Well, he knew what he was talking about, because after the Saturday game Rickey stuck his head in the locker room and told me I was going to pitch against Johnson the next day. I went back to my hotel that night but I couldn't eat. I was really nervous. I went to bed but I couldn't sleep.

At 4 a.m. I was tossing and rolling around and finally got up and just sat there, waiting for daylight and the big game.

I managed to stick it out, got some breakfast in me and was out at Sportsman's Park before the gates opened. It was one of those typical August days in St. Louis, and when game-time finally rolled around it was so hot that the sweat ran down your face even when you were standing in the shadow of the stands.

All the time I was warming up I'd steal a look over at Johnson in the Washington bullpen. When he'd stretch way out and throw in a fastball I'd try to do the same.

Well, the game finally started and I tried to be calm. First man to face me was Dan Moeller, Washington's left fielder. I didn't waste any time and stuck three fast ones in there to strike him out. Eddie Foster was up next and he singled to right field. Clyde Milan singled to right center and I was really scared. I could see Mr. Rickey leaning out of the dugout watching me real close, so I kept them high to Hank Shanks and got him to fly out to Tilly Walker in center field. He hit it back pretty far though and Foster, a fast man, started out for third base. Walker made a perfect peg into the infield but Johnny Lavan, our shortstop, fumbled the relay and Foster kept right on going to score. That was all they got in that inning, but I wasn't feeling too sure when I came in to the bench. I figured we weren't going to get many runs off Johnson, and I knew I couldn't be giving up many myself.

Then Johnson went out to face us and I really got a thrill out of watching him pitch. He struck out the first two Brownies and made Del Pratt fly to short center. Then I had to go out again and I got by all right. In the second inning, Walker led off with a single to center field and Baby Doll Jacobson dumped a bunt in front of the plate. Rip Williams, Washington catcher, scooped it up and threw it ten feet over the first baseman's head. Walker already was around second and he came in and scored while the Baby Doll reached third.

I think I actually felt sorry for Johnson. I knew just how he felt because after all, the same thing had happened to me in the first inning. Del Howard was next up for us and he singled Jacobson home to give us two runs and give me a 2-1 lead.

Well, that was all the scoring for the day, although I gave up five more hits over the route. Johnson got one in the first of the fifth, a blooper over second. I was up in the last of the same inning and I'll be darned if I didn't get the same kind. So he and I were even up anyway. We each hit one man, too.

There wasn't much more to the game. Only one man reached third on me after the first inning and only two got that far on Johnson.

When I got the last man out in the first of the ninth and went off the field, I looked down at the Washington bench hoping to get another look at Johnson. But he already had ducked down to the locker room.

I don't know what I expected to do if I had seen him. For a minute I thought maybe I'd go over and shake his hand and tell him that I was sorry I beat him, but I guess that was just the silly idea of a kid who had just come face to face with his idol and beaten him.

[1965]

Eddie Cicotte: "I Did Wrong But I Paid for It"

BY JOE FALLS

The yellow brick house sets in maybe 300 feet from the road, concealed in front by a dozen tall pines. They left the porch light on but it didn't help much.

The dirt road in off Seven Mile was dark, and it was impossible to read the name on the mailbox.

He's hiding. He's still hiding from the world.

Frankly, I didn't know what to expect. I'd heard about Ed Cicotte, read about the infamous Black Sox scandal, but I'd never met the man, and a sudden feeling of apprehension came over me as I drove up the dark, narrow road.

I'd looked up his birthdate . . . it was June 19, 1884. That made him 81. I also looked up his record: 213 wins, 147 losses.

He was a 29-game winner in 1919 and a 21-game winner in 1920. After that, nothing. Not even an asterisk. He'd been banned from baseball for his part in the scandal.

What if he won't talk to me? What will I say? What will he say? How can I ask him?

Ed Cicotte was 35 years old when the Chicago White Sox were charged with throwing the 1919 World Series to the Cincinnati Reds. He was one of eight players banished from the game by Commissioner Kenesaw Mountain Landis.

They'd been acquitted of criminal charges by a Cook County jury in 1921, yet Landis made the ban stick. He said: "Regardless of the verdict, no player who throws a ball game, no player who entertains proposals or promises to throw a game, no player who sits in a conference with a bunch of crooked players and gamblers where the ways and means of throwing games are discussed, and does not promptly tell his club about it, will ever again play professional baseball."

Ed Cicotte had lost the first and third games of the Series. Frederick G. Lieb, in his book *The Story of the World Series,* wrote:

"Even the most rabid fans could scarcely believe their eyes when Cincinnati won the opener in a 9-1 breeze. Cicotte, the 29-game winner, was belted out in a five-run Red fourth and reports drifted out of some hot words between Cicotte and Cracker Schalk in which the Chicago catcher accused Cicotte of repeatedly crossing his signals. Reporters also remembered how gamblers had made the Reds strong favorites before the game. . . .

"According to other reports, the conspiring players realized that a defeat such as Cicotte's first one looked bad, and Eddie allegedly said, 'We've got to be smarter and think of our next year's contract.'

"Cicotte gave a much better account of himself in the third game, yet he lost, 2-0, and managed to bungle things when Cincinnati scored its two runs in the fifth. . . .

"With one out, Duncan tapped to the pitcher's box for what should have been an easy out. But Cicotte threw without steadying himself, and his wild throw hit the grandstand as Duncan pulled up at second. Larry Kopf then hit a short single to left, on which Duncan reached third. Jackson fielded the ball cleanly and threw to the plate as Duncan had rounded the base by some 15 feet.

"But instead of letting the ball go through, Cicotte stabbed his glove at it and deflected it from its course. Duncan scored standing up; Kopf reached second, from where he came home on Neale's single. . . ."

I pressed the doorbell and caught my breath.

What if he can't talk? Or can't remember?

The door opened.

"Mr. Cicotte?" I said hesitantly. "Yes," he said.

"I'm Joe Falls of the *Free Press.*" "Oh, yes," he said brightly. "Won't you come in?"

He gripped my hand . . . gripped it like a vise . . . and in that precise instant I relaxed.

He was dressed in a plaid shirt, blue denims and tan shoes. His hair was white and his eyes seemed to twinkle behind his spectacles.

He introduced me to his daughter and to his granddaughter—a red-headed doll of three—and for five minutes we chatted about nothing.

I asked him about the Tigers and, yes, he said he still followed the game, although he didn't think much "of this rubber ball they're playing with nowadays."

We talked of Ty Cobb. They were roommates in Augusta and he told me how he came to recommend him to the Tigers.

We talked about Babe Ruth. He told me how the Babe never hit a home run off him.

"I used to talk him out of it," he chuckled. "I'd say to Schalk, 'Who's that big bum up there?' and my, you should have heard the Babe. 'Why, you pea souper,' he used to say. . . . He'd get so mad he couldn't swing."

It went on like this for maybe a half-hour. I began to feel a little ashamed. I knew why I was there and he did, too.

Finally, I said: "Ed, does anyone ever come around and ask about the Black Sox thing?"

He smiled. It was a very familiar smile to him.

"Yes, they come around," he said. "From time to time they come around."

"What do you tell them?"

He sat forward on the edge of his chair. The smile was gone. He looked straight at me.

Eddie Cicotte was the leading pitcher for the White Sox in 1919 when he had a 29-7 won-lost record and a 1.82 ERA while completing 30 of his 35 starts.

"I admit I did wrong, but I've paid for it," he said in a soft, even voice. "I've paid for it for the past 46 years.

"Sure, they asked me about being a crooked ball player. But I've become calloused to it. I figure if I was crooked in baseball, they were crooked in something else.

"I don't know of anyone who ever went through life without making a mistake. Everybody who has ever lived has committed sins of his own.

"I've tried to make up for it by living as clean a life as I could. I'm proud of the way I've lived and I think my family is, too.

"That's all I think about, my family. I think they're proud of me—I know they are. I know they look up to me. And my friends, they feel the same way . . ."

His daughter came into the room with a small bronzed trophy and handed it to him.

"Here," he said, "look at this. The Old-Timers' Association gave it to me."

It was a plain trophy, showing a batter and catcher. The inscription read: "To Ed Cicotte. Old-Time Baseball Players' Association."

Those were the only words. It didn't say what the trophy meant, what it stood for. It didn't have to.

"They've invited me to every gathering," said Cicotte.

Cicotte spends these twilight years raising strawberries on the five and one-half acre farm behind his house. He's not as active as he used to be but he still runs his tractor the year round, tilling the soil in summer and clearing his neighbors' driveways in the winter.

He spends much of his spare time answering letters from youngsters all over the country.

"I still get two or three letters a week," he said, his face lighting up in delight. "I answer every one of them—every one."

"Do they ask you about the Black Sox?"

"Some of them do," he said.

"What do you tell them?"

"I tell them I made a mistake and I'm sorry for it. I try to tell them not to let anyone push them the wrong way."

He is proudest of the letter he got from a lad in Germany.

"All he wanted was my autograph," he said. "Imagine that, all the way from Germany."

The hour was growing late and Ed Cicotte was on his feet again calling for his daughter.

"Virginia, give Mr. Falls some strawberries for his youngsters. He's got five kids and they like strawberries."

We shook hands again as we reached the door.

"Listen, now," he said, "if you need more strawberries or more news, you know where to come. This door is always open."

As I went down the steps, I waved good-bye to the man in the plaid shirt, the blue denim pants and the tan shoes, but what I noticed for the first time were his socks.

They were white.

[1966]

My Double No-Hit Game

BY JIM VAUGHN

There hasn't been another game in history like the one I'm going to talk about. It was between the Cubs and the Cincinnati Reds at Chicago's Weeghman Park, May 2, 1917—it wasn't until two years later that the park became known as Wrigley Field.

The attendance that day was only about 3,500, but since then at least 10,000 people and maybe more have told me they saw that game.

It was the game where neither Fred Toney nor I allowed a hit for nine innings, but I lost out in the tenth. There didn't seem to be very much unusual about the game as it went along. I was just taking care of each batter as he came up there, that was all. And I didn't even notice what Toney was doing.

As a matter of fact, I never even spoke to Toney in the entire game.

We never spoke to a player on another team on the field—there was none of this glad-handing and hello business. Why, if anyone on the other club ever spoke pleasantly to me, I thought he was framing on me. I didn't want 'em to speak to me at all.

I'd always given Toney's team, Cincinnati, a fit, so this day they laid for

James "Hippo" Vaughn was a 6-4, 215-pound left-hander who won 23 games for the Cubs in 1917. His opponent in the no-hit contest, Fred Toney, a right-hander, won 24 games for the Reds that year.

me. One feature that seldom has been mentioned is the fact that there wasn't a left-handed hitter in the Reds' lineup that day. They even took Edd Roush out of there to give 'em another right-handed hitter and an all-right-handed lineup.

Another feature is this—after I'd got the first two men out in the first inning, Greasy Neale came up and hit a little looping fly just back of second base. The second baseman could have gotten it easy, but Cy Williams came in from center and made the catch. That was the only ball hit out of the infield off me until the tenth inning.

Well, while we were at bat in the eighth inning, I was sitting on the bench, right at the end nearest the clubhouse. One of the fellows at the other end said: "Come on, let's get a run off this guy." Another one chimed in: "Run, heck: we haven't even got a hit off 'im!" "Well," another chap chimed in, "they haven't got a hit off Vaughn, either."

Well, I figured: "If this is a no-hitter and only one more inning to go, I'm going to give it everything I've got to get through that inning." And with the last three men in the batting order coming up, I really intended to get past them. I got Manny Cueto on a line fly to Charley Deal at third, and I got a third strike past Pat Kuhn. Then that big Toney came to bat.

Remember how he used to hit—with that powerful, stiff-armed swing? Well, I gave him everything I had on that first pitch—and was careful to keep it inside. He took that big swing and missed. It looked like he might have hit it a mile, but he missed it with the handle of his bat.

He missed the second one. And I made up my mind to give him everything I had on the next one. I pitched—he missed—and I'll never forget the great cheer that went up. But Toney went out and set us down, too, and we went into the tenth inning. I knew I was tired, but I felt that I still had my stuff.

Gus Getz, the first man up, hit a pop fly which our catcher, Art Wilson, got in front of the plate. Then came the first hit of the game. Larry Kopf hit one into right center for a single. But Greasy Neale hit an easy fly to Williams in center and Hal Chase hit a fly out that way. It was a hard hit ball, but not a line drive, and it was right at Williams. He got both hands on it—and dropped it. Any outfielder ordinarily would catch it easy. It was just a plain muff. Kopf got to third on that one, and Chase stole second.

There's been a lot of discussion about the play that came up next— the one that lost the ball game. Indian Jim Thorpe, the famous old football player who was trying to make good in baseball, was at bat and he sent a swinging bunt toward third. I knew the minute it was hit that I couldn't get Thorpe at first. He was fast as a racehorse. So I went over to the line, fielded the ball, and scooped it toward the plate. Kopf, running in, was right behind me and he stopped when he saw me make the play to the plate. I didn't see him, or I could have just turned around and tagged him out.

Now, some of the writers said that Wilson didn't expect the play. The truth is that Art just went paralyzed—just stood there with his hands at his sides staring at me. The ball hit him square on the chest protector—I'll never forget—it seemed to roll around there for a moment—and then dropped to the ground. The instant Kopf saw it drop, he streaked for the plate. But Wilson still stood there, paralyzed. I looked over my shoulder and saw Chase round third and start in, too. So I said to Art:

"Are you going to let him score, too?"

He woke up, grabbed the ball and tagged Chase out easily. But it was too late, the one big deciding run was in. Wilson cried like a baby after the game. He grabbed my hand and said: "I just went out on you, Jim—I just went tight."

In the clubhouse afterward everybody was pretty sore. Charley Weeghman, the boss, stuck his head in the door and yelled:

"You're all a bunch of ——s." But I wasn't sore. I'd just lost another ball game, that's all.

[1966]

Jim Gilliam Recalls Tough Times in the Negro Leagues

BY JOHN WIEBUSCH

The bus was old and orange and dirty and the driver would hit a hole in the road and all the seats would shake. A voice would come from somewhere in the darkness saying, "Hey, man, take it easy," and the driver would look up in the mirror and see nothing and say, "Ain't me built these roads."

The bus would move on through New Jersey and the driver would turn to the kid who sat by the front door with his back to the window and he would yawn and say, "Son, Newark has some mighty fine women. Mighty fine indeed." The kid would nod and listen.

The driver would hum and sing softly, and the only other sound was the turning of the wheels. The kid fought to stay awake and he would look out the front window. "Ain't no fun, really," the driver would say. "You got the fun playing ball and I got to drive the bus." The kid would nod and the driver would continue. "You're a lucky boy, know that? You in the big time now."

"Big time," the kid would repeat, and the driver would grin and say, "You say hello to Josh next time you see him. Tell him Amos from 78th Street says hello."

And then they would be in Newark and the kid would be the first one off the bus and the first one in his room in the dollar-a-day hotel. He would look at the New York papers and he would read about the Giants and the Dodgers and the Yankees.

James Malcomb Gilliam, Jr., would fall asleep and think that he would never be there in that white world where the black man swept the locker room and said, "Yes, sir," when he was spoken to.

It is 23 years away, the bus ride through New Jersey from Baltimore to Newark, and the kid is a man with kids of his own. There is James Malcomb Gilliam III in college and his father talking about how he left high school after the 10th grade. There is a rookie outfielder who bats left-handed saying, "Hey Junior, teach me how to hit the ball to left field," and the patient coach sighing and saying, "That's what I've been trying to teach you all spring." There is a boy in a Cardinals T-shirt, with an autograph book holding out a pencil and saying, "You a player?" And the lean man of 40 years bending down and saying, "Nowadays I just watch, son."

Later he sits in the chill of the lobby with the jukebox roaring and Ray Charles singing about "All the lonely people" and you know what it must have been like. No, you *think* you know what it must have been like. Only the man they call "Junior" and "Jim" really knows.

A versatile player, Jim Gilliam broke in with the Brooklyn Dodgers in 1953 and stayed with the club when it moved to Los Angeles. He finished his career in 1966 after playing in seven World Series. He was a switch-hitter and performed in 1,046 games at second base, 761 at third, and 224 in the outfield.

"I'm one of the lucky ones," he says. "I was born at the right time."

It is Stevie Wonder in the background now.

Junior looks up and his soft brown eyes gaze across the table. "I'm lucky," he says, "because I got a chance. Ever hear of Josh Gibson? If they came to Josh Gibson today and he were 17 years old they would have a blank spot on the contract and they'd say, 'Fill the amount in.' That's how good Josh Gibson was."

You have heard of Josh Gibson. As strong as Babe Ruth, they said, and the greatest catcher who ever lived. Only he was black.

"How about Tommy Butts and Willie Wells? Tommy played for our team, the Baltimore Elite (he pronounces it, E-light) Giants, and Willie played for the Newark Eagles. They would be playing shortstop for any team around now. And Jonas Gaines, a left-handed pitcher who threw smoke. A great one. There were a hundred others that I know of."

It is Aretha Franklin's turn now, and Junior taps his fingers.

"See why I'm lucky? Most of them are dead. Most of them never got a chance. They were making $275 a month like me. And you know what? They never thought it would happen. They never thought a black man would play in the white leagues. Most of them were happy doing what they were doing—playing baseball and making a buck."

He was 15 when he quit school to play baseball. The man from the Nashville team in the Southern League—the Southern Negro League—liked the way he handled himself around second base and gave him a job. He made $125 a month for two years.

He was 17 when they sent him to the National League—the National Negro League—and he watched the men—black men—he had heard about while he sat on the bench with the Elite Giants of Baltimore.

He was 18 when he became a regular, and since he was the youngest they called him "Junior." He played with the team for five seasons. There were a thousand bus rides and a thousand ghetto hotels and ballparks where the black man could sit right behind the first base dugout and not have to go to the bleachers.

He was 21 when a scout from the Brooklyn Dodgers saw him play. He was back in Nashville that winter when he heard that the Dodgers had purchased him and pitcher Joe Black from the Elite Giants for $11,500.

He played two years at Montreal, where Jackie Robinson had been, and he went to Brooklyn, where Jackie Robinson was, in 1953. He has been a Dodger ever since.

"I think of the old days often," he says. "I think of the games we played at Bugle Field in Baltimore and how rough it was then. I think of the guys who made it—the Roy Campanellas, the Monte Irvins, the Larry Dobys, the Willie Mayses . . . the Junior Gilliams."

"Then I think of Josh Gibson and the others. And Satchel Paige and the barnstorming days and the guys who played for the New York Black Yankees and the Washington Homestead Grays."

Someone has played Ray Charles again, and Junior Gilliam talks about what it is like, the satisfaction of being a coach, and about how he thinks all the time about becoming a manager someday. He talks about his four children and his wife and about playing golf and shooting pool. He talks about what the good life is like.

And you know that Amos from 78th Street would be prouder than hell of the kid who only nodded and listened.

[1969]

How Casey Stengel Got His Nickname

BY JOHN KUENSTER

Major league managers have always had to live with a certain amount of stress, whether their clubs are in the thick of an ulcer-popping pennant race or merely struggling to keep from being trampled by more talented opponents.

The pressures that bear in on the managers originate from several sources: the writers, the fans, the ownership, and the players themselves.

A manager does his thing—on stage—before the eyes of critics who like to make a habit of second guessing the man even though they seldom have as much information on a given situation on the field as he has.

There was always fun to be had when Casey Stengel and Bill Veeck were around. Here, on the occasion of his 70th birthday, Casey pretends to blow out sparklers on top of a cake at old Comiskey Park on July 30, 1959.

The fact that his rationale and behavior are continually subjected to public examination does little to soothe a manager's nerves.

Neither does the habitual percentage of players who can disrupt a team with their delusions of grandeur or their lack of self-discipline.

If professional men in other fields had to operate under conditions similar to those confronting major league managers, half of them would be sent away to the funny farm before the end of the season.

Baseball managers, if nothing else, must learn to co-exist with frustration. How they have done this through the years varies with their capacity for punishment.

After a disappointing or outrageous defeat they have reacted in any number of ways.

Freddie Hutchinson would smash things in the clubhouse.

Eddie Stanky would pace back and forth in the outfield, monotonously swinging a bat.

Al Lopez would keep it all inside.

Casey Stengel would tell stories and perhaps join the writers for a drink or two.

One of my most vivid impressions of what defeat can do to a manager involved Al Lopez in 1964 when the White Sox lost the American League pennant to the Yankees by one game.

Early in the season, Lopez knew the Sox had a chance to win it all and, with a little luck, might do it. Well, one night, the Sox bungled away a game to the Senators in Washington. The game was gone, never to be retrieved, and Lopez knew just how much it might cost his club in the long run. A championship team is never supposed to let a second-division club off the hook.

After the game I went down to the Sox dressing room to chat with Lopez.

He sat behind a desk, strumming his fingers methodically on the desk top. He answered a few questions, and then said:

"I'm not going to let this game kill me."

And the point of the story is that he meant it!

Casey Stengel, of course, had the marvelous faculty of talking away his frustrations and hostilities. He would spin his listeners dizzy with eloquent non sequiturs which would leave novices on the beat scratching their heads trying to figure out what the man was talking about.

It brings to mind the day Casey was visiting Wrigley Field in Chicago as manager of the New York Mets. On the bench before game time, a reporter decided he would do a story on Stengel rather than on the Mets, who were rather horrendous at the time.

"How," the reporter asked Stengel, "did you get the name of Casey?" It was a seemingly innocent query, one that might lead to an interesting story, whether it was fact or fiction.

Before Stengel took three breaths, he sounded as though he was going to lead his listeners on a non-stop tour through baseball history.

"When I first lived in Kansas City," Casey began, "they used to have big yards in the back of the houses. They never had any playgrounds, well, they had one, but that was the only one, and we used to play in these yards, and we'd blow up the football and throw it around, and get barrel staves and stick it up there, and try to throw a basketball through it.

"Now, in those days, I was young and short, and they called me 'Dutch.' My father's name was Stengel, my mother's Jordan and my middle name is Dillon. He was a judge. My mother called me by my first name which is Charles.

"The best thing I know I got into baseball in 1910 when I started at Kankakee in the Northern Association, and the league blows up on July 4th and I'm out of a job. I used to come up by the electric lines, and it'd take half the night.

"I knew a young girl in New York once who never got to New Jersey, but after I got to Kankakee, they'd ask me 'You from K.C.?' and I'd say, 'Yes.'

"Here's the thing. They had to change my name. They'd say, he's from K.C., and they'd say 'Hey, K.C.!' so the writers commenced to use the name Casey.

"In 1911 I went to Aurora in the Wisconsin-Illinois League, and they put my name in the box score which I thought was terrific, and I was drafted by Brooklyn for $300 or $400.

"The Cubs didn't want me because they had too many outfielders, so I went to Montgomery in the Southern League, and when I come up to the big leagues, they don't know me by 'Dutch.'

"I didn't hit home runs then. I had a lousy year striking out, and maybe the bat is too heavy, and later, what's his name, DeWolf Hopper, the vaudeville fella, used to recite that poem, 'The mighty Casey strikes out,' and I'd go on stage and listen to it.

"Now, after I corrected that, they started calling me 'Home Run Casey,' and Damon Runyon and all those guys had me nicked.

"I still get letters from folks, oh, about 70 or so, and they address me as 'Dutch' Stengel. Half the people in Kansas City still call me 'Dutch,' and so does Bill Powell who went to Central High School with me there and afterwards he became an actor.

"And, that's how I got the name Casey," concluded Stengel who spotted the umpires waiting impatiently for him to bring his lineup card to home plate.

Stengel stepped smartly out of the dugout with card in hand. A couple of his listeners remained in the dugout, dazedly trying to fathom what he said.

"The closest I can figure it," commented Jack Rosenberg who works with the WGN television crew in Chicago, "is that he got the name Casey somewhere between the barrel staves and Brooklyn."

[1969]

Drysdale Put His Brand on the Hitters and the Game

BY JIM MURRAY

Everywhere you looked were stoves, dogs, automobiles, paintings, plaques, stereo tapes, trays, color television, clothes, a saddle, a ranch wagon. He looked like a one-man Sears, Roebuck warehouse.

But Donald Scott Drysdale didn't get his windfall by knowing any geography except the strike zone; any history except the score and how many

Don Drysdale, left, with Dodger manager Walt Alston after the big right-hander struck out 11 Twins in a 7-2 victory over Minnesota in Game 4 of the 1965 World Series. Right-handed batters didn't relish hitting against Drysdale whose pitches seemed to be coming at them from third base.

outs, and whether the batter liked the ball high and tight or out over the plate. Donald didn't know the lives of the saints but he knew the weaknesses of the cleanup hitters.

There are certain prerequisites for being given a "day" in baseball, such as the one they gave Drysdale last season. It's like getting a bank loan. First of all, you have to prove you don't need it. Second, you have to be in good standing with the resident management. Sandy Koufax, for example, was handing out gifts at this one, not reaching out for them.

But, in the case of Big D, I would have to say he earned every icebox. Two more sidearm fastballs and he wouldn't be able to reach up for those gifts.

Some days they give a "day" for some outfielder who has been with the club for 20 years and doesn't even have corns. A traffic cop gets more exercise. But Big D fogged in more than 20,000 pitches, all with something on them—sometimes something that many suspected was illegal.

Some pitchers throw out of a crouch, others straight overhand, some are underhanded. Big D threw out of a rage. You had the feeling that guy up there with the bat had just made a nasty remark to his mother, or threw a brick through his church window, or voted Communist. Don would be shaking with rage when they gave him the ball. Early in his career, Don used to content himself with knocking the bat out of the hands of the batters. Later, he found that vice versa was just as satisfactory.

Off the field, he was like a big collie dog who had just been sent to fetch his slippers. On it, he was Mr. Hyde. I wouldn't be surprised if a rocking chair and house slippers were in that pile of loot, tagged "Compliments of the National League Hitters." They would have taken a collection 10 years ago to retire Big D.

In the first place, there were those long arms. If he had let his fingernails grow, you had the feeling Don could have *handed* the ball to the catcher. He almost had to pull his fingers out of the way of the swinging bat. And in the second place, the pitch seemed to be thrown at you by the third-base coach. In the third place, the ball was as heavy as a cannon shot. Your fingers tingled for days if you fouled one off the fists on a cold night. Big Don struck out 2,486 batters in his day and you had to feel some of them heaved a sigh of relief.

You see, only one pitcher in the long history of the game ever hit more batters than Don—Walter Johnson. And there was some reason to believe Walter Johnson was wild.

Don never maimed anybody. He hit 152 batters. All of them are walking around safe and sound today. Don hit you where you would heal. It would take the batter several days to rub the "Warren Giles, President of the National League" off his back, but it would take several weeks before he would dig in against Big D again.

Don threw six straight shutouts in 1968. He won 85 games in one four-year stretch, and the Dodgers won two world championships and got in a playoff for another pennant in that stretch. In those four years, they didn't score as many runs as the 1927 Yankees of that time. That's a condition that is a cross between poison ivy and a belt of hot branding irons around your stomach. And he never missed a turn.

With all due respect to Don Larsen's perfect game, Don Drysdale pitched the two best World Series games I ever saw. He beat the Yankees, 1-0, in one; he lost to Baltimore, 1-0, in the other. That's the way the Dodger hitters were.

You hit this Drysdale in self-defense. Either you hit the ball or it hit you. Batters used to suspect Don put something on the ball that belonged on a scalp, that he was really Don "Wetsdale." But what was on a Drysdale pitch was venom.

You'll see lots of batters swagger up to the plate during the regular season. They'll be up against a lot of kids who won't take the position Drysdale did that anyone who leaned out over home plate was claim-jumping.

If Big D were out there, they'd have to be pushed out of the dugout like a guy making his first parachute jump. The game is going to be a lot more polite now with Big D gone.

That sound you hear will be 152 guys jumping on pitches that used to jump on them. But I can remember when they used to flinch even when Don was warming up on the sidelines.

Editor's Note: In 14 years with the Brooklyn and Los Angeles Dodgers, Don Drysadale won 209 games, lost 166 and pitched 49 shutouts from 1956 through 1969. Elected to the Hall of Fame in 1984, he died at age 56 in 1993.

[1970]

Rudy York's Letter to His Son

BY FURMAN BISHER

In the obituary, near the bottom where the surviving offspring of Rudy York were enumerated, there was the line I was looking for. It said simply, ". . . a son, Joe, a Presbyterian minister preparing for foreign missionary service."

So he has become the Rev. Joe Wilburn York. A few years ago he worked in a sheet metal plant. A few years before that he had tried baseball, but it never took, and Joe Wilburn had the good sense to go looking for something that satisfied the soul.

Apparently he found it, something that surely must have satisfied also the soul of his daddy, who died this year of cancer in a hospital at Rome, Georgia. Rudy York once had another ambition for Joe. It was bent almost as much in the direction of correcting some of the father-first baseman's mistakes as he played his game as it was toward achievement for Joe.

Rudy York spent 13 years in the American League, most of them as a first baseman. The Detroit Tiger management tried everything but sorcery to find a position he could play that he wouldn't render unplayable for the man who followed him. Finally, after four seasons of experiment at catching, outfielding, third-basing, and others, and leaving the impression that as a defensive player he would have made one helluva boxer, he was finally "hidden" at first base.

Rudy York, left, pictured with Hall of Famer Hank Greenberg. York played for the Tigers from 1934 through 1945, and in 1943 led the American League in home runs with 34 and RBI with 118. He did some catching but was primarily a first baseman.

There he settled. There he performed, if not spectacularly, at least satisfactorily until a letter arrived from Connie Mack in January 1949, telling him he was unemployed.

"So there I was, washed up at 35."

That's one of the plaintive lines from his own personal story, "A Letter to My Son." Joe Wilburn was the son. He had the arm. He had the style. He had the bat at the age of 17 that seemed to indicate he could play in the big leagues. Rudy figured there was a better way of doing it than he had done.

"I made enough mistakes for both of us," he said, and he warned his young man of the temptations and the pitfalls of life in the big leagues.

Rudy's story was an honest one. He had his bouts with a variety of problems and became an authority on the bullets that Joe Wilburn should dodge. He allowed himself this hedge, that being part Cherokee, he was a target for exaggeration.

"Any time an Indian puts on a baseball uniform," he said, "he becomes about six times as much of a character as any other player."

Rudy began his story with the end. "You were only 12 years old and it couldn't have made much of an impression on you when the mailman delivered my release from the Philadelphia Athletics in January 1949.

"I wasn't surprised. I knew it was coming, for after you've played in only 31 games and hit .157, you know you're not scaring the pitchers any more and you know you're over the hill."

From that point on, what Rudy York said to Joe Wilburn could be condensed into a code for major league living. You can pick out some pungent pieces of advice and compose a Six Commandments for the ball player.

"Leave that liquor alone (I can tell you it never helped anybody)."

"Don't be a clubhouse lawyer (that has ruined as many good ball players as booze has)."

"Be sure not to forget the folks back home. I never did put much into making friends back home. . . . They were glad to claim me and brag about me when I was hitting home runs. . . . When I was in trouble, I was just an Indian from the mill village."

"Ball players have to be twice as careful about their behavior away from their work as anybody else."

"When you start making money, invest it (the only place I ever put mine was a checking account, and that made it too easy to get to)."

"Don't be short-sighted (remember there's a future after you're through playing)."

Those were despairing times for York. He had a career record of 277 homers, including 18 in one month (August 1937) to set a major league mark. He had played in two World Series, 1940 and 1946, getting key hits in both. He had made over $250,000 playing baseball, in lumps of $40,000 a season in his days of glory. He had come home to Cartersville to a $150-a-month job as a fire-fighter for the state forestry commission.

It was sort of an ironic turn in his life. During his playing days, York had been a rather careless smoker and he left a string of scorched hotel rooms from Boston to St. Louis. It was said of him that he led the league in arson.

Later he found his way back to the major leagues as a batting instructor and a coach, and I think that in those seasons he found himself a certain degree of peace that had escaped him. Joe Wilburn must have become a pleasure to him, that the son should have chosen a life of helping others rather than assaulting pitchers, and would not have to call upon his father's book of warning.

"I've had my picture on breakfast cereal signs as big as a house. I've had kids mob me for my autograph. I've heard thousands cheering for me. . . . I've been rich. It was a great life, but now I miss it.

"That's the reason I'm writing this to you. . . . I don't want you to have to write a letter to your son about the mistakes you've made. (signed) Your Dad."

The Rev. Joe Wilburn York apparently has made certain of that. He chose to live his example rather than write of his regrets.

[1970]

What Baseball Needs Is a Little More Hostility

BY JOE McGUFF

Rocky Bridges, the California Angels' first base coach, was sitting alone in a corner of the dugout. He seemed to be principally engaged in chewing tobacco and observing the Royals' batting practice, but as it developed Rocky was also meditating on the changing scene in baseball.

His thought for the day had to do with what he regards as an alarming trend toward gentlemanly conduct and courteous speech in the present-day player.

In years past the bench jockey was as much a part of the baseball scene as four balls and three strikes. No one was safe from his venomous tongue and caustic wit. No subject was sacred, including race and religion.

"They really had some beauties around in the days when I broke in with the Dodgers," Bridges said. "Every club had one or two guys who could really cut you up. I don't know what some of these players today would do if they had to take what the players did then.

"Players today are sensitive about everything. Back in the days when I broke in, the bench jockeys would never let up if they found they could agitate you.

"The year I came up Charlie Dressen was managing the Dodgers and Leo Durocher was managing the Giants. The Giants had two catchers hurt, and Sal Yvars was the only catcher they had left. He was a red-neck player anyway, and so we started getting on him. We figured if he got mad enough he might try to start a fight and get thrown out of the game.

"We called him everything you could think of. Finally he rips off the mask and comes charging over to our dugout to fight. Durocher comes running right after him, grabs him and pulls him back to the plate.

"The umpire calls the next pitch a ball. Yvars is still fuming, so now he gets mad at the umpire. Durocher has to come out again to keep him from getting kicked out. Durocher was in and out of that dugout all day trying to keep Yvars in the game.

"There was one game where Dressen got seats for a bunch of his friends behind the Giant dugout. Back in the days when Durocher was playing, someone had accused him of stealing a watch. Well, all of Dressen's friends have watches and every time Leo sticks his head out of the dugout they're waving them at him."

Pete Reiser, another former Dodger and also a member of the Angel coaching staff, joined Bridges on the bench and was drawn into the conversation.

"One of the funniest incidents I ever saw involved Claude Passeau, the old Cub pitcher," Reiser said. "I was playing for the Dodgers and Durocher was managing the club at that time. We had been on Passeau pretty good, and finally someone called him a gutless S.O.B.

"He came storming over to our bench and shouted, 'The guy who called me that doesn't have guts enough to step out here.'

"No one on our bench said anything. Finally Durocher turned to Joe Gallagher and told him to go up and pinch hit. Gallagher had been horsing around somewhere and hadn't noticed what was going on. He grabbed a bat, came out of the dugout, and Passeau hit him right on the jaw.

"Gallagher was the most surprised guy in the park. Passeau hit him a second time and finally Gallagher, who weighed about 240, grabbed him and said, 'What's the matter? Have you gone crazy or something?'

"You don't hear any real jockeying anymore. Everyone is nice and polite. You can't argue with the umpires anymore. You say one word to them and they throw you out. If a pitcher throws close to a hitter, it's $50.

"I remember one time we're playing and Frankie Frisch is on the coaching lines. It's starting to rain and Frisch wants the umpires to call the game, but they won't do it. He goes in and gets an umbrella and pulls his pants up over his knees. He walked up and down the lines that way for a couple of innings. He finally got tired of it and quit. If you did that today the umpires would run you right out for showing them up."

Reiser calls Johnny Allen the meanest pitcher he ever saw when it came to knocking down hitters. Allen had his best years at Cleveland but finished up in the National League.

"Allen ruined Frank McCormick as a hitter," Reiser said. "McCormick had been a good hitter for Cincinnati but then Allen started knocking him down. Then the other pitchers started doing it and Frank never was the same hitter after that.

"In one game he knocked him down three straight times. Bill McKechnie was managing Cincinnati and he also coached third base. He started getting on Allen. Johnny yelled at him, 'Just because you have gray hair doesn't mean you can't come out here.'

"McKechnie started out to the mound and the whole Cincinnati bench came running out. Allen held up his hand and said, 'I'll take you one at a time. Who's going to be first?' Nobody wanted any part of him, either.

"The next time McCormick came to bat, Allen hit him right in the ribs.

"I'll never forget one time we were playing the Cubs and Clyde McCullough got knocked down. Jimmy Wilson was managing the Cubs, and he called to McCullough to bunt down the first base line so the pitcher would be forced to cover.

"Dolph Camilli was playing first. He was the strongest man I've ever seen in baseball. Instead of the pitcher fielding that ball, Camilli comes in and takes it and the pitcher covers first. Camilli grabs the ball, hits McCullough with one of those swinging tags and knocks McCullough right on his back.

"When McCullough finally gets up, he goes back to the dugout and tells Wilson, 'Hey, Jimmy. You can forget about those fancy plays.'"

[1970]

Home Run Record a Bitter Memory for Roger Maris

BY IRA BERKOW

Roger Maris holds a special place in American sports. He performed the unprecedented feat of hitting 61 home runs in a single big league season, and has never been forgiven for it.

To many persons in Gainesville, Florida, Roger Maris is now just another beer salesman. But to many sports fans across the country, Maris is at best an enigma, at worst an object of scorn and, in fact, an iconoclast of sorts.

He retired from baseball two years ago, at the relatively youthful age of 33, and became, with his brother Rudy, the full-time Budweiser beer distributor in Gainesville and nearby Ocala. He weighs 225 pounds, about 20 pounds more than he did in 1961 when he broke the revered Babe Ruth's legendary record of 60 homers, and which inflicted upon Maris as much pain as it brought pleasure.

"If I ever had to have good memories about my baseball career," he said recently, "they probably had to be before 1961."

Few men have had to withstand the withering pressure of publicity that Maris did in 1961 and after, and few men were as ill-suited to endure it.

"It would've been a helluva lot more fun to play the game under one mask, and then leave the park wearing another mask. Some guys loved the life of celebrity, like Pepi [Joe Pepitone]. Some of 'em would have walked down Fifth Avenue in their Yankee uniforms if they could have. But all it brought me was headaches. You can't eat glamour."

Maris now seems content, relaxed and happy. His hair is still cropped in a crewcut, his pale eyes are candid and kindly, his dark tie is unfashionably thin, his socks are unfashionably white, his belly is ample and his neck and forearms are still as thick as a slugger's.

"I don't read the papers much," he said, "too busy. Rudy and I drive to the brewery in Jacksonville, we go into the taverns and supermarkets and other outlets to see how our Bud stock is, how it's placed on the shelves.

I'm usually out of the house by 8 o'clock in the morning, and sometimes I don't get home until 1 o'clock in the morning.

"My customers don't talk baseball much. They used to. But now they'll ask how I think the Cardinals will do or something, but that's all. I never look at the standings. Not at all."

He was asked what he thought of the Yankees' winning surge earlier this year.

"The Yankees?" he asked, smiling. "Did I ever play for the Yankees?" Then, seriously, he asked what division they're in. He did not know.

He has little fond recall for his seven years (1960–66) as a Yankee.

Although he says it is all in the past, "finished and done," his voice betrays a resentment to what he refers to as the "Yankee organization." For one thing, he felt the Yankees did not want him to break Babe Ruth's record. (For much of '61, Maris stayed just a couple of homers ahead of Mickey Mantle as both pursued the ghost of Babe Ruth.)

"They favored Mickey to break it," said Maris. "I was never the fair-haired boy over there. When I'd get hurt, they thought I could still play. When Mickey or Tom Tresh or someone got hurt, they'd let 'em rest.

"I'll never forget the 1965 season. I injured my right hand on about May 18. Ralph Houk, the general manager then, said I should keep trying to play. Finally, with about two weeks left in the season, I went up to his office and told him I wanted permission to go home to take care of my hand, and I said if he didn't give me the O.K., then I'd go anyway.

"Then he said to me, and I'll never forget it, Houk said, 'Rog, I might as well level with you, you need an operation on that hand.' Now what do you think?"

Maris also felt that many writers did not want him to break the record.

"They tried to make me into the mold of Babe Ruth, and I didn't want to fit anyone's mold. I'm Roger Maris. And a lot of the older writers didn't think anyone should break Babe Ruth's record.

"Some of the younger writers felt they could make a reputation at my expense. So I was called surly. Yet I'd stay and answer their questions, sometimes the same questions as new writers came over to my locker, for two or three hours after a game.

"If I had that to do over again, I wouldn't say a word until all the writers were there. Then I'd talk for 15 minutes, and quit."

The controversial asterisk was considered by then Baseball Commissioner Ford Frick to be placed alongside Roger Maris' name in the record book after the 1961 season. Maris had hit 61 homers in a 162-game schedule, Babe Ruth had hit 60 in a 154-game schedule.

"I didn't make the schedule," Maris said, "and do you know any other records that have been broken since the 162-game schedule that have an

Roger Maris connects on his 61st home run on October 1, 1961. During his pursuit of Babe Ruth's record, Maris had a difficult time dealing with the pressure of the chase.

asterisk? I don't. Frick should have said that all records made during the new schedule would have an asterisk, and he should have said it before the season—if he should have said it at all. But he considered the asterisk when I had about 50 homers and it looked like I'd break the record.

"But I understand—and this is only what sportswriters have told me—that when Frick was a New York sportswriter, he was a big drinking buddy of Babe Ruth's.

"But when they say 154 games, which 154 games are they talking about? The first 154, the middle 154, the last 154? If it's the first 154, then I'd still have tied Ruth, because I didn't hit my first homer until the 11th game. If it was the last 154 games or the middle 154, then I'd have broken the record anyway."

If he had it all to do over again, would he have wanted to break the record?

"I was a professional baseball player," he said, "and when I was out on the field I gave everything I had. No one ever worked harder than me. Baseball was my life then. If there was a record in the way of my doing my best, then the record had to fall. So what's to regret? The fact is, no one ever had as good a season as I did in 1961."

Is there anything he would have done differently during his baseball career?

"Yes," he said. "I would have been more careful not to jeopardize my health. Every day my body tells me I used to be a baseball player. I can't sleep on my stomach because my rib cage is so tender. It got that way because of how I'd bust up double plays. But that's the way I was taught to play baseball, in the minors, by Jo-Jo White.

"And my knees hurt if I just brush against them. That's from banging into outfield walls. And I still don't have any feel in the ring finger and little finger of my right hand, from when I broke my hand in '65."

Maris announced plans to retire from baseball after the 1966 season. Then the Yankees traded him to the St. Louis Cardinals. He played two more years for them. (It was Cardinal owner August Busch who helped establish Maris in his present business.)

"With the Yankees," said Maris, "I was booed for 81 games at home, and for 81 games on the road. You say it doesn't affect you, but it does, finally. All that stopped when I went to the National League. Oh, I got booed the first series at Shea Stadium against the Mets, but the booing stopped after that.

"I knew it would be different in St. Louis on Opening Day in '67. The team was paraded around the field in open convertibles. My name was announced and the people cheered. After those seven years in New York, I felt that, hell, there is some good left around here yet."

But no longer was he a long-ball pull-hitter, because of his injured hand. "I couldn't tell anyone because then the pitchers would know—and they found out soon enough. But I became a guy who tried to punch the ball over the third baseman's head.

"Finally, I couldn't stand to play anymore. I'd had my fill of it. The game itself was enjoyable, but the traveling was the big factor. It's not the kind of life for a family man. . . . It's all in what you like."

Maris now has six children, ranging in age from four to 12.

Roger Jr., 11, and Kevin, 9, play in the local Little League. "I haven't encouraged them to play, and I haven't stopped them," he said. "They haven't asked for my help, and so I haven't done nothin' with either one. Better they play the way they want to."

Would he want to return to baseball, as a coach or manager?

"I don't say I'd never want to, but right now I like it down here in this small town, and I'll let the other guys do it up there. It's fun to sit back and watch.

"You know, but I was happy my first year in New York, in 1960, before the writers used the poison pen. But now, when I think about the good times, I think that I was just as happy my first game in the big leagues, in 1957 with Cleveland, as I ever was.

"I remember we played the White Sox, and Billy Pierce was pitching against us. They beat us 2-1, I think. But I got most of our hits. I went three-for-five. We only got five hits altogether.

"I remember that a couple days later I got my first major league homer, up in Detroit. It was with the bases loaded. I don't think many guys can say that their first big league homer was with the bases loaded. But don't print that, it might sound like bragging.

"But the 61 homers? I don't think much about that. It's in the past. And I'm too busy now, anyway. Maybe it'll become important to me when I'm 65 or 70. Maybe then I'll think about it, and enjoy it."

[1970]

Tragic Pitch Recalled by Carl Mays

BY JACK MURPHY

Carl Mays, who specialized in submarine-style fastballs, threw the fatal pitch that struck Ray Chapman in the head in a 1920 game against the Indians. Nicknamed "Sub," Mays won 26 games for the Yankees that year.

He is best remembered as the man who threw the pitch that killed Ray Chapman some 50 years ago. His name is Carl W. Mays. He will be 80 on his next birthday, and he deserves better from history than he has received.

The death of Chapman gave him the kind of notoriety that tends to eclipse his accomplishments during the period 1915–29. He was a 20-game winner in both the American and National Leagues, he is one of 62 pitchers in a century of baseball with 200 or more victories, and his earned run average (2.92) places him 14th among his peers.

Mays, you might conclude, is a fellow who belongs in the Baseball Hall of Fame. Yet the veterans committee of the Baseball Writers Association of America recently voted to enshrine six old-timers, including Rube Marquard and Chick Hafey, and Mays was not among them.

That was another disappointment for the old submarine pitcher in his twilight years, and he doesn't try to conceal it.

"I think I belong," he says. "I know I earned it. They took in Marquard this year and that's fine with me. He was a great pitcher. But I deserve it, too. I won seven more games than Rube and I lost 51 less than he did. What's wrong with me?"

It was August 17, 1920, when Ray Chapman crumpled after being struck by one of Mays' submarine fastballs. He died later in a hospital and there was speculation the tragedy would shatter Mays. Ban Johnson, the league president, predicted Mays would never throw another pitch.

He did, though. He pitched in turn and did his job so effectively he won 26 games for the New York Yankees that year. The following season, 1921, his record was 27-9.

A half century later Mays freely discusses his role in the death of Chapman because he feels no guilt or remorse. Mays is a young 79. He looks 60 and his only concessions to age are a cane for his arthritis-ridden legs and a tendency to shout.

But he's spry enough that he still does bird and deer hunting in the country around his home in Dayville, Oregon, pop. 174, and he goes south each winter to San Diego to assist his nephew, Jerry Bartow, the baseball coach at Hoover High School. Three afternoons each week he does the thing he loves best—teach baseball to young people who are eager to listen and learn.

If they ask, he'll tell them about Ty Cobb ("the greatest and the meanest ballplayer who ever lived"), Babe Ruth (his roommate for 13 years), and Ray Chapman, the only ballplayer ever killed by a pitch.

"I don't mind discussing it," he says, "it's not on my conscience. It wasn't my fault."

He reconstructs the scene. "Chapman was the fastest base runner in the league, he could fly. He liked to push the ball toward second or down the first base line and run. I had to guard against this, of course.

A shortstop and right-handed batter, Ray Chapman, 29, was in his ninth season with Cleveland when he became the first major league player to die of an injury on the field. His place at short was taken by future Hall of Famer Joe Sewell, and the Indians went on to win the American League pennant.

"I knew that Chapman had to shift his feet in order to get into position to push the ball. I saw him doing this—I was looking up at him because I was an underhand pitcher, my hand almost scraped the ground—and I threw my fastball high and tight so he would pop up.

"Chapman ran into the ball. If he had stayed in the batter's box, it would have missed him by a foot."

Mays summoned strength to continue his career. "I fooled them. I went out and pitched the rest of the year. Why should I let it ruin the rest of my life? I had a wife and two children and they had to eat. I had to make a living. I had to provide for them."

The tragedy of Ray Chapman aside, Carl William Mays was a pitcher to remember. Five times he won 20 or more games, and when he quit after the 1929 season he had a career total of 208 victories and 126 defeats.

Later Duffy Lewis was to say of him: "Carl Mays wasn't very popular, but when nobody else could win Carl could. He was a great stopper."

"I had a good sinking fastball—what they call a slider now—and it broke in on either right or left-handers. I pitched inside to everybody."

Harry Hooper, voted into the Hall of Fame this year, remembers Mays: "Carl had an odd disposition but he was a great pitcher and I have a warm regard for him."

When Mays retired as an active player he served for 20 years as a scout with the Cleveland and Milwaukee clubs, and that part of his life gave him great pleasure. He likes young people, he enjoys their company. His son, Carl Jr., is senior vice-president of the U.S. National Bank of Oregon, and you can see the pride in the face of the elder Mays when he shows you the clipping.

He'll also roll up a trouser leg and show you a long, ugly scar—a souvenir from the spikes of Ty Cobb. He got it while covering first. Cobb laughed at the bloody wound.

"The next time you cover the bag," he told Mays, "I'll take the skin off the other leg." That was baseball in the time of Carl Mays. They didn't hit one of his pitches out of the ballpark until August of his third season in the big leagues. A pitcher, Reb Russell, was the first. Mays was humiliated.

"I couldn't eat that night. I thought I was through. A pitcher had done that to me. It was awful."

That was 1917. Poor Carl. He only lasted 12 more seasons.

[1971]

Baseball—A Bridge Between Two Silences

BY FRANK L. RYAN

Major league baseball is in full swing again, and the game jostles my memory into sharp recall of my father.

Father-son relationships are delicate affairs, poised perpetually on the brink of small and large clashes of will and temperament. This is something that modern youth thinks it has discovered and to which it has given the solemn title, "the generation gap."

In reality, today's youth are merely reflecting, perhaps in an exceptionally conscious way, what history records as an inevitable consequence of the existence of fathers and sons.

My own relationship with my father suggested what history proves. It was a relationship that was not only delicate but painful. I spent my adolescence in the depression years, the 1930s, and the warmth and vitality that ideally exists between father and son were thwarted both by the times and by the temperament of my father, which even in better times might have been sorely tested.

My father drank heavily in that desperate way in which some frequently unemployed men drank in those desperate days, and the drinking and the oppressive presence of idleness drove him often into deep silences that I answered with silences of my own. But there was one bridge between us during the 1930s, and I've always hoped that in the last years, when we were unable to close the gaps of our silences, he remembered our mutual love for baseball.

If my father took to drink as a grim solace for unemployment, he turned to baseball in the same spirit in which a monk turned to a cloister— for its own sake. I use the comparison in earnest. To him, attendance at a ball game was an experience detached from any local economic or civic interest. I don't think he ever cared who won a game, and it wasn't until years after we stopped going to games that I fully realized why he didn't care.

He saw baseball as a kind of synchronization of opposing forces, not a battle between the invaders and the local heroes. If a defensive player made a brilliant play, my father attributed it not only to that player's ability but also to the pressure exerted by an offensive player.

If an outfielder crashed into a wall, for example, and yet made the catch, it was because a hitter was capable of driving a ball against the fence. He saw games this way, and that's why he was indifferent to who won.

I remember being at a Giants-Braves game in Boston with him when Bill Terry, then managing the Giants and playing part-time, put himself into the game as a pinch-hitter with the bases loaded and tripled off some remote spot on the center field wall. It was one of those acts of almost supreme self-confidence that you expected of Terry, and though the Braves lost, my father was tremendously pleased. What was important to him was not that the Braves lost the game but that they had forced Terry to a challenge which he had accepted and handled beautifully.

And I remember another game, this time between the Cardinals and the Braves, in which a Cardinal hitter—I think it was Frankie Frisch— batting right-handed with men on base, hit a vicious drive foul and almost out of the park. This so alarmed the Braves manager that he brought in a right-hander to pitch and Frisch simply switched to the left side of the plate and hit another vicious drive, this time fair and out of the park. It was another moment of tremendous pleasure for my father, another case of challenge, confrontation, and fulfillment. Years later, when I had acquired intellectual pretensions, I wondered what his response would have been had I suggested that baseball was a kind of ballet to him. He probably would have expressed amused tolerance since part of his detachment was the conviction that baseball as a human activity was unique and invited no disturbing comparisons.

I have come to admire this detachment. In this our day of fierce competition and emphasis on champions and championships, the detached view seems to have vanished.

Some of my father's detachment got through to me. I have not yet abandoned his idea that you went to the park for an afternoon of baseball and not just for the game. The game was the big thing, of course, but it was also the culmination of an afternoon of something closely approaching ritual. We always left home early enough to be in the park, either Fenway Park or Braves Field, about an hour before the game was to begin. I think if you love baseball you must do that. If you don't, you miss the gradual unfolding of the rituals. The first thing was the initial glimpse of the field. After the hot, summer streets and the cool, steel-smelling shade under the stands I was always surprised by the greenness of the grass and the sense of concentration of brightness within the enclosure of the park.

Usually there was only a little activity on the field, perhaps an infielder getting some practice on ground balls to his left or right, or a couple of players jogging around the outfield. After a while the batting practice would get under way and my father thought this a rare treat because you could watch different kinds of great hitters like Hack Wilson and Paul Waner take 20 or 30 cuts, sometimes calling for special pitches and hitting them off or over the fences or, in the case of Waner, spraying them all over the field.

Another pre-game ritual that had great fascination was the pitchers of the day warming up. You could lose a great deal of satisfaction in missing that.

Lefty Grove, for instance, was something to watch. It used to take Lefty quite a while to warm up. At the start, he would merely toss the ball lazily to his catcher—I think it was usually Moe Berg, the bullpen catcher. After a few minutes, Lefty had a rhythm going and you sensed that you were watching a great pitching machine getting under way. It was best to keep one eye on him from the beginning so that you had something to which you could compare the ending when he was firing them into Berg not quickly but with great concentration, as though he were already facing hitters. When he was finishing you could see Berg pulling his glove back to take some of the force out of the pitch, and then a split-second later you could hear the smack of the ball in the mitt.

My father taught me to watch all this ritual-like activity so that the beginning of the game would not be abrupt, something that gave the appearance of just having been decided upon.

As a result, I got some long looks at the great hitters and fielders of those days—Mel Ott, Babe Herman, Lou Gehrig, Bill Rogell, Chuck Klein, Charlie Gehringer, and many others. And it seemed that they had a special ease and grace in those moments, probably the reason why my father enjoyed that time so much. The grace was important to him. He never thought of baseball as a complex game and said that if the game was as complex as some writers and commentators thought it to be, there would be no grace to it.

It was the gracefully competent whom he admired most, though both of us admired Pepper Martin who did things on the bases and at third that were tributes to his enthusiasm but alien to grace. My father had seen many of the great players who had had their peak years before 1925 or thereabouts—Ty Cobb, Joe Wood, Nap Lajoie, Eddie Collins—but the one he admired most was a player named Hobe Ferris. Whenever he wanted to give a player the highest of praise he compared him to Ferris, and there were only three whom he thought to be as graceful: Joe Judge, the Washington first baseman; Kiki Cuyler, the Cincinnati outfielder; and Pie Traynor, the Pittsburgh third baseman. We saw our last game together early in July 1938. I'm glad now that it was a fine game, a pitcher's battle between the Phillies and the Bees (formerly the Braves), which the Bees won.

It is customary in these days when reminiscing about one's father to make him sound like the one in *Life with Father*, a combination of Charlie Chaplin, W. C. Fields, with a touch of God. My father was not like that. To me his life was tragic, made so by a complex combination of social events and personal temperament. Baseball did not help him find an escape from either the panic or anxiety of the Depression, and the panacea he did turn to was worse than the ailment.

But baseball did provide a bridge, temporary and fragile to be sure, whereon we could meet for a few moments. It seems almost romantic to call those moments imperishable, and yet here I am remembering them again and speculating, with just the smallest tremor of apprehension, on whether or not the bridges that I have so carefully built between my sons and me will prove as enduring.

[1971]

Mental Blunders Are Part of the Game

BY EDWARD PRELL

Baseball lore is bulging with thrilling incidents, mostly on the plus side, except for a few back-sliding things like Fred Merkle neglecting to touch second base on a New York Giants teammate's single which eventually brought a Cub pennant in 1908. . . . And Mickey Owen's passed ball that cost the Brooklyn Dodgers their 1941 World Series with the New York Yankees. . . . A few flubs like that.

However, the game has also been marked by many tactical blunders committed by managers and players alike. These blunders form an interesting litany of human frailty, and have shook up such experienced baseball people as Leo Durocher and Paul Richards at least once or twice in their careers.

Durocher unabashedly recites his devastating goof.

"This was in Pittsburgh's old Forbes Field and my Giants were tied with the Pirates, who had the bases loaded with two out in the ninth inning," Leo said with a grimace.

"I called in Hoyt Wilhelm from the bullpen. His first pitch sailed behind the batter, but my catcher made a great save. The second one was way off the target. And after Wilhelm's next pitch was almost a wild one, I jumped up and yelled to Freddy Fitzsimmons, my pitching coach:

"'Get him out of there!'

"I don't recall the name of the pitcher we called in from the bullpen as Wilhelm started that slow walk off the field. My new man started tossing practice pitches.

"So here came toward our dugout the plate umpire, my old pal, Jocko Conlan.

"'You can't do that!' Jocko yelled in his high-pitched voice.

"'Yeah, I know it now,' I said, peeking out from the towel I'd thrown over my head to hide my shame.

"I had completely forgotten that a pitcher, starter or reliever, must face at least one batter. Wilhelm had gone only three-fourths of the way. I sent a benchwarmer on the double to the clubhouse, where Hoyt already was stripped to his shorts. So he put on his baseball clothes and returned to the mound.

"His first pitch missed the strike zone and a Pirate walked home with the winning run. It wasn't any comfort to me that the Pirates also had been unaware a pitching change couldn't be made. And I've always thought, too, that Jocko was a trifle slower on the trigger than usual!"

In 1942, Lou Boudreau, later to become a Hall of Famer, was the 24-year-old shortstop-manager of the Cleveland Indians. One day he was sniffling from a cold but still felt strong enough to flash signals from the bench.

"Our sign for the double steal was putting a towel to the face," says Lou. "Pat Seerey, sometimes called Fat Pat, who couldn't beat his sister in a foot race, was on second base. Our guy on first, whose name I can't recall, never set any speed records, either.

"Well, my nose was dripping and I picked up a towel, blowing my nose. First thing I saw, Seerey was huffing and puffing toward third base and his other accomplice was resolutely plodding toward second base. Both were thrown out for a double play.

"I turned to one of my coaches, Oscar "Spinach" Melillo, and barked, 'Whatever made you put on a deal like that with those truck horses on the bases?' He reminded me I had been the guilty party.

"After the game, Bill Veeck, then the Indians' owner, asked me to explain my strategy and I 'fessed up.

"'Next time you have to blow your nose, go into the runway, out of sight,' Bill suggested.

"Incidentally, we also blew the game!"

Joe Cronin, president of the American League, confesses his biggest mistake in baseball stemmed from a violation of the manager's code of strategy.

"When I was managing the Boston Red Sox we were playing the Chicago White Sox in old Comiskey Park," recounts Cronin. "We went into the ninth inning with a two-run lead. The White Sox put the tying runs on third and second with two out. Their next hitter was Luke Appling, who had won two American League batting championships. Following Luke in the batting order was Oris Hockett.

"Now, to whom would you rather pitch—Luke Appling or Oris Hockett?

"Even though I knew it was a cardinal sin for a manager to deliberately put the winning run on base, I ordered Appling walked.

"A few seconds later Tex Hughson was the losing pitcher and I was a raving maniac. Oris Hockett had cleared the bases with a triple!"

It was the second game of the 1917 World Series between John McGraw's Giants and Pants Rowland's White Sox in Comiskey Park—October 7, a Sunday. Urban "Red" Faber, who was to win three times as the Sox won in six games for Chicago's last World Series triumph, was making his debut in the big show.

This is the record book's account of Chicago's fifth inning in that second game:

With one out, the Giants' Art Fletcher booted Buck Weaver's grounder. Buck took second on Ray Schalk's infield out. Faber singled to right, Weaver holding third, but Faber slid into second base on the throw to the plate. Faber tried to steal third with Weaver occupying the bag, Heinie Zimmerman tagging him after taking the throw from catcher Bill Rariden.

"Well," recites the lively 82-year-old Faber, "I can't argue with that play-by-play, but I can fill you in on some details.

"When I went into second base I figured Weaver had scored. I dusted off my pants, and when I saw the Giants' pitcher, Pol Perritt, winding up, I took off for third base.

"Gosh blame [Red's pet expression], was I surprised, as I came down the baseline, to see Weaver scooting back to third. 'Where do you think you're going?' Buck growled.

"'Back to pitch,' I told him."

The White Sox won, 7 to 2. Faber lost to Ferdie Schupp in the fourth game, won the fifth in relief, and the sixth to complete the conquest with a route-going job.

Fred Lindstrom, a boy wonder third baseman with the New York Giants and star with the champion Cubs of 1935, was back in the old Polo Grounds in 1936, but as a left fielder for the Brooklyn Dodgers against his original team.

"The Giants and Dodgers had a tremendous rivalry in New York, just as they now have in California," said Lindstrom. "Van Lingle Mungo, the fireballing and pugnacious right hander, was our pitcher, and we led in a freewheeling battle, 8 to 6, when the Giants came up in the ninth. Our manager was Casey Stengel.

"Eventually, the inning reached the point where the bases were filled and two were out. Travis Jackson hit a high pop fly into left field—remember, it was only 280 feet from the plate to the wall. The sun came right over the top of Coogan's Bluff in the late afternoon, hitting you smack in the eyes, making left field indeed hazardous.

"When Jackson connected, I flipped down my sunglasses and charged in. I didn't notice that our shortstop, James 'Lord' Jordan—he had elevated the prestige of sweaty ball players by marrying a Romanian countess—also was zeroing in on the ball. I think I had yelled that I'd take it. But maybe not.

"Anyway, just as the ball settled into his glove I crashed into him. The ball popped out and rolled away. We both sprawled and my sunglasses were knocked off. By the time our second baseman, or maybe the center fielder, retrieved the ball, it was too late. All three base runners had scored. In that split-second, I had turned an 8 to 6 victory into a 9 to 8 defeat!

"Not a word was said in the clubhouse. For once, even Stengel was speechless. I had never felt so badly in my baseball life. I think we all sensed—even the hot-tempered Mungo—that this was the time for not only a moment of silence but to forget it into eternity!"

Did Paul Richards ever get mixed up in his thinking and do a mental flip-flop? Richards, as manager of the White Sox and Baltimore Orioles, was rated one of the sharpest tacticians ever, though his teams never won a pennant.

"My biggest goof," Paul acknowledges, "came in 1950 when I was managing Seattle in the Pacific Coast League. Remember Jim Wilson, who later pitched for the White Sox? Now, in this season of '50, he was our man against Fred Haney's Hollywood Stars on their field.

Strange Happenings at the Old Ball Park

By MALCOLM WELLS

He hammered it over the right field fence.

He gets a visit from the bench.

The pitching coach pays a visit to the mound.

"Jim had won 16 straight games. After this game with the Stars, his next start would be in Seattle, and if that winning streak were still alive we'd draw at least 12,000 when he went after No. 18.

"So now it's the seventh inning against Haney's team. Wilson is leading, 2 to 1. My thought then was that he would not lose this game if I could help it. I was thinking about that return to Seattle with the record intact. I told Skinny Brown, my star reliever, to get ready; if the Stars got that tying run on base, he was coming in. That way Wilson couldn't possibly lose.

"Wilson cut down the Stars until two were out in the ninth. Then our shortstop, John Albright, kicked an easy ground ball. Now the tying run was on base and it was time for me to act to make it certain Wilson would arrive in Seattle with the streak alive.

"Here came Skinny Brown from the bullpen. Then I made the mistake of trying to think. Heck, I told myself, Wilson has pitched a great game and was in trouble through no fault of his. I must say I had the thought, too, that I might be criticized for yanking him. So I waved Skinny back to the bullpen.

"So—Frank Kelleher smashed Wilson's first pitch for a game-winning homer. End of streak and also the glorious homecoming to Seattle.

"Moral to all managers: When you make up your mind, go through with it no matter if it 'hair-lips' all of Ellis County, of which my home town Waxahachie, Texas, is the county seat!"

Mayo Smith will be the first to admit that even the manager of the 1968 world champion Detroit Tigers has made a mistake or two along the way. "I've pulled more than my share of rocks," he said after what he considered was a proper pause. "I can't think of a more shocking boo-boo to my ego than what happened when I was playing in 1941 for Buffalo in the International League.

"Steve O'Neill was our manager, and we were playing the old Montreal Royals in Buffalo. It was the eighth inning and I hit a triple to drive in the tying run. I felt great—you might say exhilarated—as I slid into third.

"Don Ross, the Montreal third baseman, told me, 'Hey, get off the bag and let me dust it off.'

"I obligingly stepped off and—bingo he tagged me in the ribs with the ball. And did those home fans start hooting!

"What did Manager O'Neill say? Nothing. I don't think he knew, either, that Ross had the ball in this unusual version of the old hidden ball trick.

"Yes, we lost in extra innings. But the bitter lesson served me well. After that I always knew where the ball was, even though, sometimes, as a batter, I couldn't hit it!"

Pete Reiser, more than one smart man has testified, would have landed among the greatest except for a flaming competitive spirit which compelled him to crash into outfield walls to the detriment of his career as a Dodger.

Pete's moment of embarrassment on the playing field came in 1940, his rookie season in Brooklyn's cozy Ebbets Field. The cast of characters: Hilda, the notorious cowbell-wielding fan; Reiser, the kid center fielder; Leo Durocher, the Dodgers' manager; Larry MacPhail, the Dodgers' president; pitchers Whitlow Wyatt and Hugh Casey.

"We were pretty far out in front," says Reiser, "when Hilda yelled down to me while we were in the field. She tossed a wadded-up piece of paper. 'Give this to Leo,' she commanded.

"When the inning was over and as I came toward our dugout, I spoke to MacPhail, who was sitting in a nearby box. Leo was within earshot and I told him, 'Here's a note for you.'

"I noticed that Durocher had a puzzled look. Next inning, when Wyatt got into mild trouble, Durocher hastily called in Casey, our star reliever. Casey didn't have it that day. Because of a wide lead, we held on to win.

"After it was all over, Leo shouted to me, 'Don't you, or anyone else, ever bring me a note from MacPhail.'

"'But, Mr. Durocher,' I protested, 'that wasn't from Mr. MacPhail.'

"'Then who in hell gave it to you?' he inquired.

"'Hilda,' I answered.

"I hadn't read her crumpled message. Long afterward, when I'd made it with Leo and the Dodgers, I asked him about that note.

"'It said that Wyatt was losing his stuff and to get Casey ready,' Durocher laughed. 'I've heard of front-office interference, but how about me listening to that crazy dame with the cowbell!'"

In 1954, the first full season for Ernie Banks with the Cubs, the team one day was playing the Pittsburgh Pirates and the score was tied in the seventh inning.

"The Pirates had a runner on third base and our infield was drawn in for a play at the plate," is the way Banks sketches the scene. "Jim Greengrass was the batter. I was playing shortstop. Gene Baker was our second baseman and over at first base was Dee Fondy.

"Greengrass grounded the ball sharply to me. I threw it to Baker, who recovered from surprise just in time to stab the ball and flip it to Fondy at first base to nick Greengrass. The Pittsburgh runner on third also was so surprised that he failed to break for the plate.

"Baker, my roomie, had kidded me before on occasions when I made the wrong play, just to keep me loose. But this time he really scolded me because I hadn't thrown the ball to Fondy for the automatic out.

"'Ernie, you gotta do a little thinking out there on the field,' he said. 'That was the dumbest play I ever saw, even if it didn't cost us a run. Why did you do it?'"

"'I just knew you'd have a better idea than me on what to do,' was my weak answer."

Floyd (Babe) Herman is remembered more as one of baseball's screw-balls than as the great outfielder-slugger whose stories are legion. Once he was hit on the head while moving toward a fly ball. And he's the goat in one of baseball's most remembered goof-ups.

He came on the stage with the bases filled, so the story goes.

Hank DeBerry was on third, Dazzy Vance was on second, and Chick Fewster was hit by a pitch, so the bases were jammed for Herman. He drove a hit into right field, scoring DeBerry. Vance, fearing the ball might be caught, held up at third. Fewster flew around second and headed for third. Herman, figuring he had knocked a real extra-baser, raced toward third, too. All three wound up in the vicinity of third base.

"So I was a no-no in the outfield and on the bases if they want it to be that way," Babe agrees. "But that traffic at third base was not my biggest rock. It was leaving the Dodgers. Yes, I know I was traded, but I actually *left* them.

"I had hit .313 in 1931 with the Dodgers. That wasn't much in those days and considerably below my .393 of the year before. I had been Wilbert Robinson's fair-haired boy, but now he was gone and Max Carey was the manager. A fellow named Frank York was the Dodgers' president. We made a verbal deal for 1932 and he called me in to sign. When he said it was for $1,000 less than we had agreed on, I backed away.

"Next thing I knew, I got a call from Dan Howley, manager of the Cincinnati Reds.

"'You're a Big Red now,' he said. 'Okay, I've been called worse than that,' I told him.

"'I don't mean you're a Communist,' he said. 'You're now with the Cincinnati Reds, a baseball team.'

"So I played with the Reds in 1932. Sid Weil, the owner, was in financial trouble, and I guess I was his most valuable piece of property. He invited me to choose between going to the Cubs or the Giants.

"I wanted to play on a pennant winner, so I chose the Cubs, who had won in 1932. Know who finished first in 1933? The Giants, helped along by a new pitcher named Roy Parmelee, who joined Carl Hubbell, Hal Schumacher and Fred Fitzsimmons. That was another boo-boo.

"Why was leaving the Dodgers my biggest mistake? I'm sure my lifetime batting average would have been 15 or 20 points higher had I stayed in Brooklyn with those friendly fences. I hit only .289 with the Cubs in '33. It was tough to see the ball because of the sea of white shirts in the center field bleachers. I batted .304 for the Cubs in 1934. Next year the Cubs won, but by then I was with the Pirates."

Don Gutteridge, one-time manager of the White Sox as successor to Al Lopez, was a speed boy in his playing days, most of them with the Cardinals. Don also had played with the Red Sox before they traded him to the Pirates just before the 1948 race started.

"On this day early in the season we were playing the Reds," Gutteridge recounts. "Clyde Kluttz, our slow-footed catcher, doubled in the late innings and Billy Meyer, the manager, told me to run for him.

"As I jumped out of the dugout, I heard Billy tell the players: 'Watch this fellow. You'll learn something. He's one of the best base runners in the business.'

"Lanky Ewell Blackwell was pitching for the Reds. With Meyer's praise still ringing in my ears, I took a couple of extra steps off the bag. First thing I knew, Blackwell had whirled and Bobby Adams, the second baseman, was tagging me out."

Joe DiMaggio was known as the perfect player, but he didn't have to ponder long to come up with his most painful *faux pas*.

"We were playing the Tigers in Yankee Stadium," says the Hall of Famer. "Hank Greenberg was at the plate and Rudy York was on first base. Hank blasted one a country mile, and I brushed against the Col. Jake Ruppert monument in deep center as I leaped for a one-handed catch.

"Sixty thousand fans were cheering like mad and the 'Great DiMag' stood there taking bows. Next thing I knew, Frankie Crosetti, our shortstop, was racing toward me, frantically waving his arms. Then I came to my senses. Frankie wanted the ball. By this time York, sometimes accused of running in the same place, and who had rounded second base, was digging back toward first.

"I fired the ball to Crosetti. His hurried throw hit Rudy. The ball bounced away, Rudy wound up on second base, and Frankie was charged with an error on what should have been a simple double play! It was my most red-faced moment in baseball—a thrill gone completely sour."

[1971]

When the Cardinals Ended the Yankee Dynasty

BY TIM McCARVER AS TOLD TO ALLEN LEWIS

They always say your first pennant and World Series is the one you remember most. I'll have to agree with that. I played on three pennant-winners and in three World Series with the St. Louis Cardinals, but the first will always stand out in my memory.

Tim McCarver argues with plate umpire Bill McKinley in the second game of the 1964 World Series between the Cardinals and Yankees in St. Louis. McCarver disputed McKinley's call on a pitch by Bob Gibson, which the umpire said hit Joe Pepitone. The Cardinals won the Series in seven games.

There are other reasons for that in addition to the fact that 1964 was the first. That's partly because of the way we won the National League pennant that year, and because we beat the New York Yankees, who were still regarded as something special by almost all ball players in those days, in the World Series.

Then, too, I played better in that Series than in the other two. And it's easy to pick out the fifth game in that Series because I hit a homer in the 10th inning to win it.

The pennant race that year was really unusual. It looked like the Cardinals were out of it in August. I think we were nine games out in the middle of August when Bing Devine was fired as general manager.

That made it sort of look as if the front office figured we were finished, and we were 11 games behind with three clubs ahead of us with just six weeks left.

But we won eight straight games and the Cincinnati Reds won nine in a row, while the Phillies, who looked like a cinch with two weeks to go, were losing 10 straight.

We beat the Phillies three in a row in the last week to take over first place, but we almost blew it by losing on Friday and Saturday to the New York Mets at home.

We went into Sunday's final game knowing we had to win to have a chance at the pennant. If we lost and the Reds won, they would have it clinched. If we lost and the Phillies beat the Reds, we'd end in a three-way tie.

Well, we didn't play very well, but we managed to beat the Mets and the Phillies shut out the Reds, so we were in the Series.

This was only my second full season in the big leagues and I was only 22, so being in a Series that soon meant a lot.

I was lucky to do well in the Series. I caught all seven games and wound up the leading hitter, batting .478.

We split the first two games of the Series in St. Louis, then broke even in the first two in Yankee Stadium. We felt we would win the Series for sure if we could go back home with a 3-2 lead, and that's why the fifth game was so important. It would give us a big edge.

The Yankees had Mel Stottlemyre going for them against Bob Gibson, and he had beaten Gibby in the second game. Still, we always felt confident whenever Bob pitched.

Both pitchers were sharp. We took advantage of a couple of bad plays by the Yankees to score two runs in the fifth inning. First, a pop fly that should have been caught fell safely in short left for a hit with one out, and then Bobby Richardson, who hardly ever made an error, booted a double-play ball, Lou Brock singled in a run and Bill White hit into a force with a grounder to second for the other. The Yankees argued they had doubled White on the play, and it was close.

We still had a 2-0 lead going into the ninth, and Gibby then made a big play that probably saved the game for us.

Mickey Mantle reached first on an error and after the next hitter struck out, Joe Pepitone hit a shot off Gibby's right thigh. The ball bounced away to his right and he made a super play, getting the ball and throwing Pepi out at first on a close play, very close.

Tom Tresh then hit one out in deep right center. If Pepi had been safe, the Yankees would have won it right there in the ninth.

That's how one play really decided the Series. If they had won that game they'd have won the Series since they beat us in the sixth game.

Pete Mikkelsen, who had relieved in the eighth, was still in there when White walked to start the 10th. Ken Boyer tried to sacrifice but beat out his first bunt of the year with one to the right side.

Then we got another break. Dick Groat missed a bunt attempt and Elston Howard threw down to second and Bill was trapped. He broke for third and made it when Phil Linz threw a one-hopper to third.

Groat then hit into a force and I hit a homer into the right stands on a 3-2 pitch, and that was it. The Yankees won the sixth game and we won the seventh.

That was the end of the Yankee dynasty.

[1972]

When a Midget Batted as a Major Leaguer

BY BOB BROEG

Bud Blattner, the former big league infielder now broadcasting for the Kansas City Royals, remembers how puckish Bill Veeck first got the notion to use a midget in a major league ball game.

This was 1951 when Veeck, who had worked wonders at Cleveland, was finding that even Merlin the magician couldn't bestir the Browns out of last place or their fans out of their atrophy and apathy.

"If only we could just get the first man on base in an inning," moaned Veeck to Browns broadcaster Blattner as they drove back to St. Louis from a speaking trip.

Just then the burrheaded baseball pixy with the corrugated forehead brightened. The next thing Blattner knew, Veeck had in his office a 3-foot-7, 65-pound Chicago stunt man named Eddie Gaedel.

"And furthermore," the P. T. Barnum of baseball admonished the midget, "if you so much as swing that bat at the plate, I'll kill you. No, I won't, but I can get the job done cut-rate because you wouldn't be hard to hide."

Back there on August 19, 1951, celebrating the American League's golden anniversary season, Veeck pulled out all the stops to please a crowd of 20,299, which was mighty good for a ball club that was in last place, 37 games behind co-leaders Cleveland and New York.

Fans were given birthday cake, ice cream and other souvenirs when they entered the park. Between games of a doubleheader with Detroit—sure, the Browns lost the first one—an eight-piece band paraded in Gay '90s attire, antique cars and cycles circled the running track at Sportsman's Park.

A juggler juggled at first base. Trampolinists somersaulted at second. Hand-balancers pyramided at third.

A four-piece Brownie band paraded onto the diamond with Satchel Paige on the drums, Al Widmar playing the bull fiddle, Ed Redys with an accordion and Johnny Berardino, now the movie actor, manipulating the maracas.

Aerial bombs exploded, sending miniature flags floating onto the field. Then popping out of a papier-mache cake and wielding a miniature bat came a cute little fellow dressed in a Browns uniform.

The midget, of course. The crowd laughed then and gasped in surprise a half-inning into the second game when field announcer Bernie Ebert intoned over the P.A.:

"For the Browns, No. 1/8, Eddie Gaedel, now batting for Frank Saucier." Three of the four principals are dead, meaning umpire Ed Hurley, catcher Bob Swift and the midget himself. The pitcher on that memorable occasion, Bob Cain, flew from Cleveland to Chicago for Gaedel's funeral 10 years ago. Class, yes. They were all pros. Hurley insisted on seeing the contract manager Zack Taylor brandished when beckoned from the dugout, but the red-necked Irish umpire took it calmly. So did the Detroit battery.

Three feet, seven inches tall and weighing 65 pounds, Eddie Gaedel made history when at the age of 26 he batted for the St. Louis Browns in a game against the Tigers at Sportsman's Park on August 19, 1951. He walked on four pitches by Detroit hurler Bob Cain, and then was removed for a pinch runner. A feisty character, Gaedel was the only midget to appear in a big league game.

Swift couldn't make up his mind whether to try to take the pitches sitting down, but finally decided he'd kneel. Cain wanted to pitch underhanded but, no, the catcher said he'd have to do it correctly. And with Gaedel crouching as coached by Veeck, the pitcher walked the smallest baseball batter ever on four pitches.

Cain actually laughed as Gaedel trotted down to first base. The pitcher could afford to be charitable. The Browns loaded the bases, but, as usual, they didn't score and, also as usual, lost.

Gaedel, replaced by Jim Delsing, reached up to give his pinch-runner an encouraging pat on the rump and retired amid cheers.

Later, after showering, the midget was in the pressbox. I propped him on the ledge so I could watch the game and interview him, too.

"For a minute," he said, "I felt like Babe Ruth."

I told him that he was now what I wished I'd become.

"What's that?" he asked.

A former big leaguer.

Eddie Gaedel's chest suddenly puffed with pride. Two nights later, filled to his half-pint gills just about the time stuff-shirted, high-collared American League president Will Harridge was expunging Edwin F. Gaedel from the official records, the little man was arrested in Cincinnati—for abusing a cop.

[1972]

The Making of a Baseball Fanatic

BY SISTER MARY BARBARA BROWNE, C.S.C.

Where does that special species known as the baseball "nut" grow? Recently I strolled past a beautifully grassed school lot where a group of Little Leaguers—Giants and Dodgers, decked out in appropriate uniforms—were playing. An announcer blared each player's name, the crowd roared, and the future star stepped to the plate. This is how the "nut" gets his start in an affluent society today; but the real ones flourished in the city streets and sandlots forty years ago.

I first became aware of the "national pastime" when we lived behind old Recreation Park in San Francisco. In its place today stands a used-car lot, but in 1929 the park housed the now defunct San Francisco Seals. We lived in a lower flat right behind the wooden structure. In the vacant lot between the flats and the park, many of the kids of the neighborhood gathered, especially on game days. We delighted in knocking out knotholes in the wooden wall of the park in order to get a one-eyed view of home plate. Even the young Joe DiMaggio had his knothole so that he could watch his brother Vince—whom he was later to replace and go on to eclipse in fame—play for the San Francisco Seals.

At one time you'd have thought a machine gun had peppered the wall. Then the management decided to fill up the holes with cement—but never underestimate the power of the baseball "nut," no matter what his age. Suffice it to say, we were at our holes next day. How did we dissolve this cement? Let's just say it's a secret held sacred by all kids who run the streets of the asphalt jungle and play the game by their own rules.

Many a future major leaguer stood at home plate and hit balls to his loyal fans outside the hallowed walls of the "Old Rec." When Frankie Crosetti or Gussie Suhr were at the plate, we yelled and screamed for a trophy—and many times they obliged. We weren't always satisfied to be banished to a vacant lot, however. Sans money or tickets, we devised a way to get into the park. After the seventh inning, the ticket windows closed, but a wary gatekeeper guarded the entrance.

Now, for a gang of boys and girls who wanted to get into the ballpark, he was fair game. Since kids can scamper like rabbits, more often than not we got past the watchman. Naturally, he made a show of trying to stop us, but once we got past him, he paid little heed. His resistance was only token for he loved the neighborhood gang who lived by their wits and not pennies jingling in their pockets.

After the game we lined up outside the locker room doors waiting for our favorites to emerge. Those ball players were kind to the kids—maybe because they remembered when they were in our position, or they just understood our love of baseball. I can't recall anyone of them refusing to sign our grubby little notebooks. If only I could find that tablet that had the scrawls of such Seal greats as Frankie Crosetti, Vince DiMaggio, and Gussie Suhr, but it has long since been lost along with other childhood treasures. What a collector's item it would be today.

Then one day the awful news came—they were going to tear down Recreation Park and build Seals Stadium at Sixteenth and Bryant Streets. For the neighborhood gang something else was torn down with the park. Our favorites were moving away—we'd never be so close again. There would be no knotholes in the concrete walls of Seals' Stadium; no locker room door would open onto the street. Oh, yes, we could get to the new park by streetcar, or more likely by hiking fifteen blocks uphill. Yet it was never the same.

Loving the Seals the way we did, we followed them to their new home, which yielded its share of memories. During the summers of my high school years, I spent several afternoons a week when the Seals played, at the ballpark, for each weekday was "Ladies' Day." For a while my sister went with me, but she gave that up because she said I disgraced her with my yelling and screaming for the home team, but what else does a baseball "nut" do?

I recall one night when our whole family went to a rather crucial game. As far as I know this was the first and last time my mother ever attended a baseball game. I don't remember whom the Seals were playing, but I vividly recall the bottom of the ninth when the Seals came from behind to win the game. We screamed, yelled, and hollered and did everything else sports fans do when the home team wins. What makes this night so memorable is that in the excitement, my father threw his new Panama straw hat in the air—and it never came back. I don't think Mom ever forgave him for that. The lost hat is still a favorite family anecdote.

Then there was Lefty O'Doul, the peppery manager of the Seals. Now, there isn't a manager or fan in baseball who agrees with the decision of the

The DiMaggio brothers, Vince, Joe and Dom, left to right, all played for the San Francisco Seals in the 1930s before moving up to the majors.

umpire, unless, of course, the judgment is in favor of the home team. After a particularly exasperating call that irritated Lefty beyond endurance, he took out a large white handkerchief and waved it. Naturally, that was the signal for the fans. The stands looked like Mrs. Murphy's backyard on laundry day. I don't know for sure, but I assume the umpire banished Lefty to the locker room for the remainder of the contest; however, after that, a waving mass of white handkerchiefs greeted every unpopular decision by an umpire—one of Lefty's legacies to the lore of the game. I guess that's strictly minor league stuff because I don't see such manifestation of emotions today.

As for the players I remember, Joe DiMaggio has to be the greatest. My most treasured memory is his throw from center field to get the runner out at the plate. I know you don't believe it, but I saw it. Of course, he was one of the greatest batters of all time. Long before he went to the Yankees, we dubbed him "deadpan" because no matter whether he struck out or hit a homer, his expression never changed. Joe DiMaggio belongs to San Francisco as much as the cable car, Fisherman's Wharf, or Coit Tower. His name is as synonymous with San Francisco as St. Francis. To most of us who grew up in the late 1920s and early 1930s, he symbolizes the "local boy makes good" in the big city of New York.

Perhaps I remember DiMaggio so vividly because the year I became a nun, he went to the Yankees—1936. I amused all my friends in the Novitiate by dating my entrance with DiMaggio's departure from "Baghdad by the Bay." When a person enters religious life, he talks of things and persons given up. When I said the hardest thing for me to leave behind was baseball games, I was eyed as a "nut" of some kind. I'm not sure that anyone understood, but when you have baseballs for red corpuscles, you don't give up the game without a constriction of the blood vessels.

Years later I returned to California and the Bay Area only to find that my favorite team, the Seals, had been ousted by some team known as the New York Giants who played in Seals Stadium. I didn't even get interested in the now San Francisco Giants until they moved into Candlestick Park—and then not because they were a baseball team, but because the name of the park intrigued me. I think it's the most imaginative name for any ballpark in the majors.

Then the "nut" that had lain dormant for years began to respond to the names of Willie Mays, Juan Marichal, Willie McCovey, et al. When I visited my family in San Francisco the talk revolved around the Giants. The fever started, mounted, and has never abated. My poor mom still hates the game because during the season, a game is on TV and every member of the family has a radio plug in his ear, or else both TV and radio blare at the same time.

After so many years of not attending ball games, I looked forward with keen interest to my first visit to Candlestick Park. I'll never forget the first view—it was like coming home. I don't expect anyone but a baseball "nut" to understand how I felt, how I yelled, how I enjoyed the game. As the game progressed and we talked—a baseball crowd is just one big happy family—one young man (I always seem to sit beside a man who can't resist "the brotherhood" and after half a pack becomes talkative) asked, "How do you know so much about baseball?"

I looked at him, young and enthusiastic. He probably knew his baseball via the Little League route. I said, "I grew up behind old Recreation Park in San Francisco." Right there the generation gap became a chasm. Certainly he'd heard of Seals Stadium, but the "Old Rec" meant nothing to him.

His noncommittal "Oh" demonstrated how young he was and how old I am.

However, an old-timer heard my answer and I had found a kindred spirit. Between pitches we swapped stories that could only have been known by knothole watchers. We bemoaned the fact that baseball would never be the same. But time takes its toll and now my allegiance is firmly rooted in the rise and fall of the Giants' fortunes. It's the home team that nurtures the growth of the "nut."

When the team is winning a divisional pennant as the Giants did in 1971, the joy of the baseball "nut" almost causes him to crack. He lives and dies on every pitch, especially when the contender is breathing down the team's neck as the Dodgers did in the September home stretch.

Although the 1972 season spelled disaster for the Giants' hopes because of dubious trades and serious injuries, Giant fans still followed their favorites as they slipped steadily to fifth place. What happened to the baseball "nut" then? Did he give up? Of course not. Baseball "nuts" never crack. They just smile broadly and say, "Wait'll next year."

[1973]

The Jackie Robinson I Knew

BY WENDELL SMITH

The Jackie Robinson I knew was a man around whom the winds of controversy swirled and blew during most of his spectacular lifetime.

From his boyhood days in Pasadena, California, throughout his adulthood, he was a constant source of worry and agitation to those who resented his black aggressiveness. They declared he was too "pushy, wanted too much too soon."

But nobody could tell him that and smother his quest for racial equality in American life.

I first met Jackie Robinson in 1945. He was playing shortstop for the Kansas City Monarchs of the Negro American League. He believed then that he was a player of major league quality and was determined to break the barrier that had been erected to keep black players out.

His determination was easily discernible that season, two years before he reached his goal. As sports editor of *The Pittsburgh Courier,* I was taking Jackie and two other black players, Sam Jethroe of the Cleveland Buckeyes and Marvin Williams of the Philadelphia Stars, to Boston for what ostensibly was a tryout with the Boston Red Sox.

We got to talking about this tryout—which turned out to be nothing more than a gesture—and Jackie said grimly, "I don't know what's going to come of this but if it means that the Negro player is a step closer to the major leagues then I'm all for it. I'll do my best to help make this project a success."

We were on a train going from New York, where the players had met me, to Boston.

The following day we went to Fenway Park. The Red Sox had not returned from spring training camp. Instead they went directly to New York where they were to open the season against the Yankees.

Jackie Robinson and Branch Rickey, upper left, in 1946 as Robinson signed a professional contract with the Dodgers organization. Robinson, upper right, played first base, second base and the outfield during his 10-year major league career. Jackie, lower right, is congratulated by Stan Musial after Robinson's first All-Star homer in 1952 game. Robinson, lower left, was elected to the Hall of Fame in 1962.

Duffy Lewis, the old-time Boston star, was looking over a group of sandlot and high school prospects. Robinson and the two other black players joined them. Jackie and his two colleagues were impressive, to say the least.

Afterward, Duffy Lewis said good-bye and assured the players, "You'll hear from us."

On the way back to New York, Robinson said, "We probably won't hear from him, but it may have put a crack in the dike."

It did. I stopped off in Brooklyn while Robinson and the other two players returned to their respective teams in Negro baseball. Branch Rickey of the Dodgers expressed an interest immediately and from that point on had scouts tailing Robinson, Jethroe and Williams.

Jackie didn't know it but he was on his way to the majors then. Instead of Boston, however, he was to end up in Brooklyn.

In the spring of 1946 I accompanied Robinson and a pitcher, John Wright, to Sanford, Florida, the training site of the Montreal Royals, No. 1 Brooklyn farm club.

This event, which Rickey called "the great experiment," was the big training camp story that year. With Robinson and Wright in camp, Montreal, a minor league club, received more publicity than most big league teams.

The press paid more attention to Robinson because he was better known than Wright. Jackie had been an all-around star at UCLA. When World War II came he went into the service and became a first lieutenant.

Controversy followed him there. He became embroiled with some MPs because, according to Robinson, they had roughed up a Negro woman passenger on a bus trip while trying to force her to sit in the back.

Jackie was almost court martialed for that incident. Only the intervention of Joe Louis, then stationed at Fort Riley, Kansas, saved Jackie from a long sentence. Louis appealed to Washington in Jackie's behalf and the matter was dropped.

During those spring training days in Florida, the townspeople in Sanford resented Jackie's presence in the camp. Controversy flared again when a spokesman for the chamber of commerce came to me and advised us to get out of town immediately.

When I told Jackie, he balked, saying he wasn't going to leave. Controversy again. I called Branch Rickey at his hotel and told him the problem. "Get Robinson out of this town immediately," he said. "We can't have any racial trouble now." We left with Robinson grumbling and protesting.

Robinson was making his Montreal bid as a shortstop. The regular shortstop was a French-Canadian and popular in the northland. When that was pointed out, Jackie said, "I don't care what he is, I intend to beat him out of the job because I believe I am better than he is." Controversy again. The French press fired its guns at Jackie for his "cockiness."

Wherever he went Jackie was in the midst of a racial controversy. After his first year at Montreal, where he was a sensation, and it became apparent that he was a cinch to play with the Dodgers, Dixie Walker asked to be traded. Even before that, during spring training in 1947, some Dodger players signed a petition against his eventual presence on the team.

And after the season started the St. Louis Cardinals threatened to strike rather than play against him.

He had a feud with manager Leo Durocher and never hesitated to shower an opposing pitcher he thought was throwing at him with a volley of obscenities. When he slid into Roy Smalley of the Cubs at Wrigley Field, they almost came to blows.

But through all this Jackie Robinson was always himself. He never backed down from a fight, never quit agitating for equality. He demanded respect, too. Those who tangled with him always admitted afterward that he was a man's man, a person who would not compromise his convictions.

In fact, in his last public appearance, with death just around the corner, he was still fighting for his people and equality. During the 1972 World Series, he threw out the first ball and thanked baseball for all it had done for him.

His final words were controversial. "I won't be satisfied," he told the capacity crowd and millions on television, "until I look over at the coach's box at third base and see a black manager there."

As I sat there and listened and watched, I just knew that Jackie Robinson was going to say something like that.

Editor's Note: Former baseball writer Wendell Smith was instrumental in helping Jackie Robinson get his start in the majors.

[1973]

Roberto Clemente Was a Sensitive Superstar

BY MILTON RICHMAN

Roberto Clemente was like most baseball players, a little boy inside. Sometimes he was moody . . . petulant . . . complaining . . . and openly antagonistic. But other times he was the warmest, softest, most compassionate human being you could ever hope to meet.

You had to be around him a while to see both sides. I've seen him when he'd rail up at a newsman's perfectly innocent question, and as a guest at

Roberto Clemente shown with his family in 1971 when he was honored at Shea Stadium in New York. With him are his wife, Vera, and three sons, from left, Enrique, Roberto and Luis. The ceremony was designated "Roberto Clemente Night." The following year on December 31, Clemente was killed in a plane crash as he and four companions were flying supplies from San Juan, Puerto Rico, to earthquake victims in Nicaragua.

his home in Rio Piedras, Puerto Rico, as well as on other occasions, I've seen him when he was one of the most hospitable, helpful and cooperative individuals ever to wear a major league uniform.

Roberto Clemente was a superstar, and he knew it, but that still didn't keep him from being extremely self-conscious about the fact. Particularly outside the environs he knew best—baseball parks.

He didn't go for public celebrations.

Maybe it was because he didn't want to show too much of the real Roberto Clemente to the general public. In that way, he was a private person.

When all the rest of the Pittsburgh Pirates were dousing themselves with champagne after knocking over the Baltimore Orioles in the final game of the 1971 World Series, Clemente purposely passed up most of the hi-jinks, much the same way he had after the Pirates had clinched the National League pennant two weeks earlier.

"That's OK for some of the younger fellows," said Clemente, when they asked him why he wasn't participating.

Yet on the plane back to Pittsburgh from Baltimore an episode took place that never got into any newspaper.

"My wife, Karen, and I were on the plane, and Roberto suddenly came over and embraced me," remembers Steve Blass, who beat the Orioles in the deciding contest.

"That was a very personal thing with me," says Blass. "I could feel the true warmth of the man."

Dave Giusti, the Pirates' reliever, remembers something else.

"I recall a game in Houston," he says. "I hadn't gone six innings in three years, and I finally went six in this one. Bobby made a point of coming over to me. It was the way he approached me, and the way he said what he did. You could tell he was sincere."

Roberto Clemente was paid very well by the Pirates, his salary climbing above the $135,000 level, but he wanted one thing even more than he wanted money, and that was recognition.

I remember him showing me a particular bat at his home in Rio Piedras.

"See this," he said, picking up the thick-handled bat. "This is the bat I used when we won the world championship in 1960. I think I should've won the MVP that year, but I didn't get it. Not because I didn't deserve it, but because of 'political' reasons."

Despite this tremendous desire for the recognition he felt was due him, Clemente, before his tragic death at age 38 last December 31, wasn't that serious he couldn't laugh at himself.

He was sensitive about repeated charges he wouldn't play at times because he said he was ailing, yet he sat in a corner of the Pirates' clubhouse and laughed heartily one day when one of the club doctors came in and made a ritual of examining a life-sized statue of him some of his teammates had obtained and placed on the training table.

Roberto Clemente later complained there weren't enough writers following him around as he was approaching his 3,000-hit milestone last season, yet laughed louder than anybody else when some of the Pirate players dug up a picture of all major leaguers ever to achieve 3,000 hits, Clemente included, and pasted it in their lavatory.

Clemente's 3,000th hit was his last in regular National League play in 1972. After the accomplishment he announced he would not play in the last three regular season games.

"I'm glad it's over," he said at the time. "Now I can get some rest."

Clemente rested for the National League playoffs against the Cincinnati Reds, which Pittsburgh lost in five games. He had four hits in 17 at bats for a .235 average.

Asked if he was glad the 3,000th hit was a line drive, he said, "I was just glad to get the hit, period. I give this hit to the fans of Pittsburgh and to the people of Puerto Rico."

He said that he had been embarrassed by the standing ovation.

"I fool bashful when I get a big ovation. I am really shy and so is my family. I never was a big shot and I never will be a big shot."

Clemente was asked if the hit was his most satisfying moment in 18 years in the majors.

"The World Series was more satisfying, because we won," he said.

The Pirates won the World Series in 1960 against the New York Yankees and in 1971 against the Baltimore Orioles, both in seven games. He hit .310 in 1960 and was the outstanding player in 1971 with a .414 average. Clemente hit safely in all 14 Series games in which he played.

Clemente compiled a .317 lifetime batting average while winning four National League batting titles. He batted over .300 13 times. His highest average was .357 in 1967. Last season he hit .312 in 102 games.

He won the National League's Most Valuable Player award in 1966 and was selected for the All-Star Game 12 times.

Perhaps because of his all-out play, Clemente missed many games during his career because of a myriad of injuries that went beyond conventional bumps and bruises.

This past season he was stricken with tendinitis of the ankles shortly after recovering from an intestinal virus which took more than 10 pounds off his 5-foot-11, 182-pound frame.

In previous seasons he had been afflicted with everything from malaria and bone chips to food poisoning and insomnia.

This all led to an image of Clemente as baseball's leading hypochondriac, an image he claimed had been fostered by baseball writers.

Clemente criticized writers for allegedly refusing to accept top Latin players as the equals of other stars.

Yet he was nearly always patient and pleasant with writers, just as he was to countless autograph seekers—even the ones who interrupted him in restaurants.

Roberto Clemente gave much to baseball.

He will be missed by all who knew him—as a man and as an extremely gifted player.

[1973]

The Day I Got My 3,000th Hit

BY STAN MUSIAL AS TOLD TO GEORGE VASS

I went into the 1958 season only 43 hits short of 3,000, and there was no doubt I would make No. 3,000 without any trouble. The way I had hit in 1957 (.351) it was clear I had two or three more years to go although I was 37 years old.

At the time, only seven players in major league history had gotten 3,000 or more hits. The last one to do it had been Paul Waner of the Pittsburgh Pirates, one of my boyhood heroes.

All through spring training of 1958 the reporters asked me to set a date when I thought I would get No. 3,000. I couldn't do that, of course, but I estimated to myself it would be sometime in late May.

Things went even better than I could have hoped for. I got off to a great start, hitting close to .500 going into early May. On May 11 we beat the Chicago Cubs twice in St. Louis, coming from behind each time in the ninth inning, and I got five hits.

That gave me 2,998 hits, and that night we closed down the restaurant Biggie Garagnani and I owned to hold a private party in anticipation of my 3,000th hit.

Stan Musial, left, collected his 3,000th career hit, a double, against the Cubs in 1958 when Cardinal manager Fred Hutchinson, right, sent him into a game at Wrigley Field as a pinch-hitter.

Our next series was against the Cubs in Chicago, and with two games there it looked like I might get the 3,000th hit on the road. That's not quite the way I wanted it. I would rather have gotten it at home, before the Cardinal fans in St. Louis.

Just in case I did get No. 3,000 in Chicago my wife, Lil, and several friends came along to Chicago for the Cubs series, which opened Monday, May 12. I got a double in the first game, which left me just one hit away.

After the game, just talking with Terry Moore, one of our coaches, I said, "You know, I hope we win tomorrow but I'd like to walk four times and save the big one for St. Louis."

Terry must have said something to manager Fred Hutchinson because later Hutch called me on the phone in my hotel room. He told me he was going to use me only as a pinch-hitter if he needed me. Otherwise, he'd try to save the "big one" for St. Louis.

"I just hate to see the guy get the big one here before 3,000 or 4,000 fans when his home fans can have the chance a day later," Hutch told the newspapermen.

So I figured that if everything went well the next day I could sit this one out and get No. 3,000 in St. Louis.

When the game against the Cubs started on Tuesday, May 13, I was sitting on the bench in the right field bullpen at Wrigley Field, soaking up the sun. I stayed there five innings but things didn't work out the way I hoped. We were behind 3-1 going into the sixth.

We got a runner on second base with a man out when Hutch sent word. He wanted me to pinch hit.

There were only 6,000 people in Wrigley Field that day, but they made a lot of noise when I walked up to the plate.

Moe Drabowsky was pitching for the Cubs, and he had been going pretty good until Gene Green got to second base for us with one out in the sixth. The next hitter was our pitcher Sam Jones, so Hutch sent me up to hit for him.

Drabowsky's first pitch was wide—a ball. I got a piece of the next two pitches and fouled them off. Then another wide pitch. It was 2-2 and I fouled off the fifth pitch.

Drabowsky's next pitch was a breaking ball outside. I got good wood on it and the ball went down the left field line. I saw right away that Moose Moryn, the Cub left fielder, didn't have a chance on it. I never broke stride before I pulled up at second base with a double.

That was hit No. 3,000.

Umpire Frank Dascoli retrieved the ball and gave it to me. Then Hutch came over from the dugout to stick out his hand and offer me his congratulations. He took me out for a pinch runner.

I left the field and stopped only to kiss my wife, who was sitting behind the Cardinal dugout, before I went into the clubhouse.

The game was still going on out on the field but all the press and photographers were mobbing me in the clubhouse. The radio was on so we could keep track of the score. Finally we won 5-3 and it made the day perfect, especially since it was our sixth straight win.

Hutch came into the clubhouse and—can you imagine—apologized for having had to use me as a pinch-hitter.

"I'm sorry," he said. "I know you wanted to get it in St. Louis, but I needed you."

I wasn't sorry. It was a hit that counted for something, helping to win a game, whether it was the 3,000th hit or not.

I'll never forget the train trip back to St. Louis after the game on the Illinois Central Railroad. There were crowds of fans at several stops along the way. At Clinton, Illinois, they were chanting, "We want Stan, we want Stan," when we pulled in. There was another crowd waiting at Springfield.

And when we finally got to St. Louis, which must have been about midnight, there were more than 1,000 people there, too. I had to make a little speech.

That game in Chicago was one I'll never forget, and even if I'd rather had the hit in St. Louis, just getting it anywhere was a tremendous moment in my life.

[1973]

The Day Cleveland Went Wild
BY LOU BOUDREAU AS TOLD TO IRV HAAG

My old boss, Bill Veeck, wrote in his book, *Veeck as in Wreck,* there was absolutely no doubt in his mind that Cleveland would beat Boston in our sudden-death playoff for the 1948 American League pennant.

I sure wish he'd told me that before the game.

I was far from bursting with confidence, let me tell you. And, I didn't have more than a few hours' sleep—reporters were everywhere trying to outscoop each other.

For one thing, I refused to tell anybody who would be my starting pitcher. Our ballclub knew it would be Gene Bearden, but they, too, kept it a secret, thank heavens.

So many thoughts kept racing through my mind, I wished the game would get started so at least I could concentrate on playing ball and managing. I'd got to Fenway Park early as usual—it was my habit to tape my ankles before every game.

I can't even remember doing it that day, maybe because I was second-guessing myself a thousand times. Even thinking about the money to be won or lost—up to $7,000 for the World Series winners—made me edgy.

Finally, out on the field, I saw Bearden. He looked well rested, anyway. Our plan had worked out okay. Instead of the press pestering him, they hounded Bob Feller, Bob Lemon, Satchel Paige and my other pitchers, never dreaming my knuckleballer would start.

After all, Bearden had been spectacular on Saturday, beating the Tigers 8-0 for his 19th win of the year. That clinched at least a tie for the pennant. We could have been "in" on Sunday before our home fans except for those fired-up Tigers. Over 75,000 turned out to see us wrap up the pennant. But instead, Hal Newhouser had a great day and caught Feller on an off day and they whipped us, 7-1.

While we were disappointing our rooters, Boston was knocking off the Yankees, 10-5. Since Sunday was the last day of the season, the Red Sox and Indians both finished with 96 wins, 58 losses.

So here we were in Boston. Forcing myself to appear unworried, I had told the press we just came to Boston a day early, meaning, of course, to face the Braves, National League champs, in the Series. I wondered if I'd have to eat my words.

Across the way, I spotted Joe McCarthy, Boston manager. I knew how badly he wanted this game—it was his first year with the Red Sox. And you know the kind of record he had with the Yankees, six pennants in seven years (1937 through 1943).

He had a surprise up his sleeve, too. Instead of going with lefty Mel Parnell (15-8) as most of us figured, he named right-hander Denny Galehouse. Joe's strategy made sense. Galehouse had held us to only two hits in eight and two-thirds innings about mid-summer.

That made me ask myself if maybe I was pushing my luck too far by expecting Bearden to come through again for us.

The sight of Ted Williams didn't do much to calm me down, either. He was leading the league in hitting at about .365, had 25 homers, 44 doubles, and 127 RBIs. What worried me most was—he was hot. He'd gone six for eight to lead the Sox in three straight wins over the Yanks to force this playoff.

Then, I looked out at the "Green Monster," Fenway's giant 37-foot left field wall that, with its screen on top, rises about 60 feet. How inviting to a visiting team. It looks as if you could pop one out as easy as pie. It fools a lot of hitters into going for the wall, only to pop up or hit into the dirt.

Still, my strategy was based on the hope we could pepper that wall and get a few runs on the board. That's why I wanted as many right-handed batters in our lineup as possible. I even put Allie Clark at first base instead of my regular first baseman, left-handed swinger Eddie Robinson.

To put it mildly, both Veeck and Hank Greenberg strongly disagreed with my move. I must admit, they had a point. Eddie had belted 16 homers and had 83 RBI. (In fact, counting the playoff game, our infield alone accounted for 432 runs. Second baseman Joe Gordon had 32 homers, 124 RBI, Ken Keltner at third had 31 homers and 119 RBI, and I chipped in with 18 homers and batted in 106 runs.)

I wasn't kidding myself, McCarthy's team was loaded with power, too. Besides Williams, he could send up guys like Vern Stephens (29 HR), Dom DiMaggio with 185 hits, including 40 doubles, Billy Goodman hitting .310, and Bobby Doerr with 27 homers.

Knowing how Veeck and Greenberg felt about my substituting for Robinson, I would have only myself to blame if we blew it. If only the

American League did what the National League had done—make it a three-game playoff!

Maybe that would have been just as nerve-wracking, I don't know. One thing's for sure, some great competitors got us to the playoff and I certainly didn't want to let them down. Feller, for example. He started off with a rocky year, but in the stretch he was just great and wound up winning 19 games for us. Satchel Paige with six wins out of seven. What a help *he* was! Bob Lemon, 20-14. Sam Zoldak, picked up by Veeck during the season for relief insurance, 11 wins.

Then there was our other great rookie, Larry Doby, who not only hit .301 but also contributed 14 homers, 9 triples, and 23 doubles. And Jim Hegan behind the plate. He had his greatest season ever. Despite his .248 batting average, he had 14 homers, 21 doubles, and 6 triples, and he was valuable in handling our pitchers.

Winning pitcher Gene Bearden, left, shortstop Lou Boudreau, center, and third baseman Ken Keltner rejoice after the Indians beat the Red Sox, 8-3, in a one-game playoff on October 4, 1948, to capture Cleveland's first American League pennant since 1920.

I sure didn't want to let down the fans of Cleveland, either—we'd set an all-time attendance record, thanks to Veeck's wild and zany promotions. I thought the game would never start, but when it did, about the only thing that eased my mind was the fact I was also playing. If I'd been a bench manager, I would've been climbing the dugout walls.

There wasn't much conversation on either side. The tension was so thick, even their fine catcher, Birdie Tebbetts, usually a chatterbox, was quiet.

A crowd of 33,957 fans had elbowed into Fenway, and the game started out tamely enough. Galehouse retired our slugging left fielder, Dale Mitchell (.336), and Clark, our utility man.

I was up next. All I had on my mind was to do what I told my ballplayers to do—aim for that wall. Luckily, I got pretty good wood on the two-one pitch and just cleared the left field screen. It wasn't a booming homer by any means, but I was mighty happy to accept it!

The way the Sox started off in their half of the first didn't chase any of the butterflies in my stomach. We got Dom DiMaggio, but then Johnny Pesky came up. I had a hunch and signaled my right fielder, Bob Kennedy, to move over and play Pesky to pull. Johnny ripped one down the right field line, but Kennedy was in a position to hold him to a double.

Williams stepped in and something told me to look for one up the middle. Fortunately, that's where Ted put it and I robbed him of a hit. We couldn't stop Stephens, though. He singled to drive in Pesky with the tying run. It remained 1-1 until the fourth.

Leading off, I singled, Gordon also singled and I stopped at second. As Keltner was stepping into the batter's box, I had my first big decision of the day to make. Even though Ken was a power hitter, should I have him lay one down, hopefully to surprise the Sox? Or should I have him swing away? Doby was on deck. If we got the runners to second and third, a hit by Larry meant one run for sure, and probably two.

Anyway, I gambled, signaling for Keltner to hit away. Ken made me look like a genius. He parked the ball over the left field wall—and we were out front, 4-1. After that, McCarthy wasted no time. He pulled Galehouse and brought in Ellis Kinder.

Doby greeted him with a double. I had Kennedy sacrifice Larry to third, and he scored as Stephens was throwing out Hegan, making it 5-1.

Later, I found out that after Ken hit his homer, folks listening to their radios in downtown Cleveland went wild, tearing up all kinds of paper and cardboard for confetti to throw on the streets below from office buildings. And, one driver started honking—soon, almost everybody was blasting away on his car horn.

Sure, I felt a lot more secure with that lead but also remembered how many other times I'd seen big leads disappear like magic at Fenway. The Sox made good use of that wall, too—you never had enough runs, it seemed.

That's why I was especially happy to add another run in the fifth. Actually, Kinder had me fooled on the pitch but I recovered in time to put another one over the wall—I was pulling everything that day. It wasn't much of a blast, either, but it counted.

Meanwhile, Bearden was holding the Sox in check. At the finish, he'd yielded only six hits and no more than one to each hitter. Doerr hit a two-run homer in the sixth to end Boston's scoring for the day. We added a run in the eighth and ninth; one when Williams dropped Bearden's high fly, allowing Hegan to score from second; another on singles by Kennedy, myself, a wild pitch and double play.

What a performance by Bearden! He allowed only two hits in the last seven innings. Making it even more outstanding, the two runs he gave up in the sixth were unearned when Gordon couldn't handle Williams' high fly. Gene struck out the dangerous Stephens for what should have been the third out.

Then came the greatest moment of the most memorable game in my career. My last time up, the fans gave me a standing ovation. I'd never experienced anything quite like it. Here they'd seen their beloved Red Sox almost certain to lose, barring a miracle, and they give *me* a standing ovation! I've never felt so gratified in my life. I'm sure it lasted only a few seconds but to me it was like hours of sweet, sweet music.

You can't play major league baseball for almost 15 years without piling up a lot of wonderful memories. Like the time I was fortunate enough to lead off the 1942 All-Star game at the Polo Grounds with a homer off Mort Cooper.

The game of July 17, 1941 at Cleveland when Ken Keltner made two sensational plays to rob Joe DiMaggio of base hits as Joe's 56-game hitting streak finally ended. And, as long as somebody had to be the last to throw Joe out, I'm happy it was me. DiMag hit a double-play ball to short in his final at bat and that was it.

If Ken hadn't outdone himself that night, DiMaggio's record might have been 73 consecutive games instead. The Yankee Clipper hit safely in his next 16 games after our Indians stopped him.

But, no sense trying to kid anybody. That pennant playoff game on October 4, 1948, was the most unforgettable and satisfying moment of my baseball career.

[1973]

Andy Seminick Once Decimated the Giants' Infield

BY RICHIE ASHBURN

When the Phils' first baseman Willie Montanez and ex-Phil Joe Lis got into a fight earlier this spring, I couldn't help but chuckle a bit. Most fights in baseball don't amount to much. Usually there's a lot of pushing and shoving but not many good punches are thrown. Most injuries come from being stepped on or from wrestling matches.

Even the brawl between the Phillies and the Montreal Expos a couple of years ago didn't produce much in the way of fighting. This brawl, brought on by Steve Carlton's beaning of Tim Foli, involved a lot of players and lasted a long time, but the only serious casualty was the Montreal manager, Gene Mauch. He was injured because half the Phillies team piled on top of him when Mauch fell to the ground. Two years after that skirmish, Mauch still doesn't have full use of his left arm.

Baseball players as fighters are usually pretty good baseball players. I haven't seen any good fighters in baseball. I've seen a lot of tough guys who could be good fighters, but they never got involved in fights for a simple reason: Who wants to fight a guy who knows how to fight?

I've seen guys who thought they were fighters. The late Don Hoak was one of those. He got into a lot of fights but to my knowledge never won one. In fact, his fight record was so bad the players used to call him "canvas-back" and accused him of having "eat at Joe's" written on the bottom of his shoes.

Billy Martin, the Texas Rangers' manager, is supposed to be a tough bird and maybe he is. I only saw him in one fight. When I played with the Cubs we had a fight with Cincinnati. Martin was an infielder with the Reds, and he and pitcher Jim Brewer of the Cubs had some words between the mound and home plate. It appeared that words would be the extent of the action and Brewer turned to walk away. Martin hit him then and broke the bone near the eye socket. Brewer never saw the punch and always claimed Martin hit him with a sneak punch.

I played with one guy who I know was tough and I know he could fight. I'm referring to a tough Russian, former Phils catcher Andy Seminick. If all Russians are as tough as Andy, then I'm going to start buying Russian war bonds. Andy, by nature, was an easygoing guy, and I can't think of a person who didn't get along with him. But you never wanted to get him riled up. I saw that happen one day and it was a frightening scene. It happened in the early 1950s.

The New York Giants were in town. They came into Philadelphia with a pretty good ball club—after Andy got through with them they were a shambles. The Giant second baseman, Eddie Stanky, started the whole thing.

The first time Andy came to bat in the game, Stanky got behind the pitcher and started jumping up and down and waving his arms. He did this in order to distract Andy when the pitcher threw the ball, and this can obviously be very dangerous to the hitter when you can't concentrate on seeing the ball. (Incidentally, Stanky's antics caused a rule change that now prohibits such gesturing.)

Andy got on base anyway and a ground ball later, Stanky was taken out of action by a crunching football block at second base. The Giants' first mistake in the game was having Stanky jump up and down. Their second mistake was letting Seminick get on base for the second time in the game.

Andy's second slide into second base knocked Giant shortstop Bill Rigney almost into left field. Rigney took offense at this and took a swing at Andy. One more swing later, this one by Seminick, Bill Rigney was taken off the field on a stretcher. Now the Giants had lost their second baseman and shortstop.

However, Andy wasn't through yet. He was still on second base.

Somebody hit a long fly ball to the outfield and Seminick tagged at second so he could try to make third base. It looked like it would be a close play. The Giant third baseman, Henry Thompson, was standing at third waiting for the ball to come to him. The ball did come to him but unfortunately for Henry, Andy got there at the same time.

I was never a Giant fan but I felt just a pang of remorse for Henry Thompson. Andy turned him every way but loose—all you could see was arms and legs and a few teeth (they were Henry's) and sure enough, Henry left the game on a stretcher.

Giant manager Leo Durocher was beside himself. Andy had just wiped out three-fourths of a very fine infield and he was still on third base, kinda pawing the ground and snorting like a wounded bull. Leo appealed to the umpires to take Andy out of the game—the Giants were fighting for a pennant and Leo didn't want to blow the whole season because of Andy Seminick.

I've never seen the umpires do too many favors for Leo Durocher, but I think even they felt sorry for him this day. They didn't throw Andy out of the game—they gently asked him to leave. As I said, Andy, by nature, was a gentle man. He didn't have a beef against the umpires, so he left peacefully.

[1974]

I Remember the Polo Grounds

BY JACK LANG

It has been more than a decade since the New York Mets played their last game at the Polo Grounds in New York City but it will be many, many more decades before the millions of fans who witnessed games there and the thousands of players who trod the lush green turf will forget the old horseshoe park that stood in the shadow of Coogan's Bluff.

The Polo Grounds, when it finally fell victim to the wreckers' iron ball in 1964, not only was the oldest major league ballpark in America, it also was unique.

Gene Mack drew this sketch of the Polo Grounds, home of many memorable events in baseball history.

Boston's Fenway Park has its famed Green Monster for a wall in left; old Yankee Stadium had the short porch in right; Crosley Field had its terraced outfield and Wrigley Field still maintains its ivy-covered walls.

But no other ballpark ever had the "Chinese Home Run" [Editor's Note: except for the Los Angeles Coliseum, which was used temporarily by the Dodgers after they left Brooklyn]. No other ballpark had a right field foul line of 259 feet and a left field line of 280. In no other park in America was it possible to hit a routine fly ball to either left or right fields and have it nick an upper grandstand that jutted out and become an automatic home run while an outfielder stood helpless under the ball. "Hit the façade," was the umpire's cry as he waved the batter around the bases.

And in no other ballpark in America was a fan ever shot to death in a bizarre, real-life reenactment of the famed *Death on the Diamond* movie.

That tragic event took place prior to a July 4th doubleheader between the Giants and Dodgers in the late 1940s when baseball's greatest rivalry was at its peak.

I recall police rushing to the aid of the fan in the left center grandstand and finding him dead on arrival. The first reaction of the gendarmes was to clear the park.

"We may have a nut in the park," said one lieutenant.

Chub Feeney, then a veep with the Giants and now the National League president, pleaded that the games go on. The Giants didn't want to lose that 50,000 gate.

"Okay," the lieutenant replied almost comically, "but if one more guy gets killed, we're clearing the park."

The shot, it later developed, came from atop an apartment house roof high on Coogan's Bluff. A man in his twenties had found a rusty rifle, fired it out over the bluff and the bullet traveled almost a quarter of a mile before piercing the forehead of the innocent fan in the left field seats. It was a million to one shot.

There was another shot more than 10 years later that was forever to be known in baseball as "The Shot Heard 'Round the World." It was, of course, Bobby Thomson's dramatic ninth-inning home run off Ralph Branca in the third and deciding playoff game that gave the Giants the victory and the 1951 National League pennant.

It was the climax of a tremendous stretch drive by the Giants that began in mid-August when they were 13½ games behind the Dodgers. They wound up tied for the pennant on the final day, and the three-game playoff series followed.

To this day old Brooklyn fans will argue that Charlie Dressen brought in the wrong relief pitcher, that Clem Labine, who had pitched a 10-0 shutout the previous day, could surely get the final outs when Don Newcombe faltered.

While it may be one of the most dramatic home runs ever hit, it was also one missed by many of the sportswriters covering the playoffs. When the Dodgers went into the bottom of the ninth with a 4-1 lead, most of us afternoon paper writers began the long trek from the press box behind home plate to the Dodger clubhouse in left field. We were in the clubhouse getting the final inning on the radio when Thomson connected.

Ironically, the writers didn't even hear Russ Hodges' famed description of the shot . . . shouting "The Giants win the pennant! The Giants win the pennant! The Giants win the pennant!" The radio in the Dodger clubhouse was tuned into the broadcast of their own announcers, Red Barber and Connie Desmond. There was a quick signoff by Barber that day.

I made my first trip to the Polo Grounds on Memorial Day, 1937. I was the guest of my sister and brother-in-law, and when we arrived at the park around noon, the only seats still vacant were in the far reaches of left field. I spent the afternoon talking to a fan in the bleachers, the two of us separated only by a screen. My neighbor had paid half what my brother-in-law shelled out for our "grandstand" seats.

The crowd that day was to set a record. There were 60,747 jammed into the old park for a holiday doubleheader between the Giants and Dodgers.

It constituted the largest National League crowd in New York history up to that time.

And the fans—especially the loyal Brooklyn rooters—were not to be denied a thrill of thrills. In the opening game, with the great Carl Hubbell on the mound for the Giants, the Dodgers knocked King Carl out in the fourth inning and ended his 24-game, two-season winning streak. With unheralded Freddie Frankouse pitching for them, the Brooks rolled to an easy 10-3 victory.

Between games, Babe Ruth, by then retired, approached home plate and presented Hubbell with a gold watch, emblematic of his selection as the National League's Most Valuable Player the previous year.

Cheered by the fans, Hubbell accepted the watch and said: "Defeat had to come some time. A fella can't keep winning every game. I'm glad the pressure is off."

Before the day was over, it was the Dodger fans who were saddened. In the second game, Buddy Hassett, their first baseman and leading hitter, was hit on the wrist by a pitch and suffered a fracture that sidelined him for a few weeks. Thus a streak and a wrist were broken in one day.

The Polo Grounds was opened in 1889 and was built specifically for the New York Giants and for baseball. History shows that polo was never played there, but the name was given the new park because that was the name of the park the Giants had formerly occupied downtown.

Like most old parks, history permeated every nook and corner of the Polo Grounds. But few moments have lived on in baseball lore as vividly as some of those that occurred at the odd-shaped stadium on the banks of the Harlem River.

It was at the PG, as they called it, that Fred Merkle was guilty of his famous "boner" on September 23, 1908, . . . a mistake that eventually gave the Cubs a pennant over the Giants.

Merkle was on first base for the Giants with two out in the bottom of the ninth when Al Bridwell singled to center and Moose McCormick scored from third with what Merkle thought was the winning run.

But the alert Johnny Evers of the Cubs, after seeing that Merkle didn't bother to go to second, called for the ball from the outfield, stepped on second where umpire Hank O'Day ruled a force play that ended the inning.

The turmoil on the field when the fans ran all over it prevented continuation of the game into extra innings, and it had to be replayed in its entirety on October 8. The Cubs won that day and also won the pennant.

Perhaps the greatest individual feat in All-Star game history and one of the most electrifying strikeout streaks of all time took place at the Polo Grounds in the 1934 All-Star game when Hubbell, at his peak, struck out Babe Ruth, Lou Gehrig and Jimmie Foxx with two men on base in the first inning, and then fanned Al Simmons and Joe Cronin to open the second. Five of the American League's outstanding sluggers in succession!

One year earlier Hubbell had pitched one of the greatest single games in history when he worked a full 18 innings to defeat Tex Carlton and Jesse Haines of the Cardinals, 1-0. In the second game, LeRoy ParmeLee edged Dizzy Dean in another 1-0 game in regulation time.

The Polo Grounds was, of course, Willie Mays' first playpen, and how he roamed that spacious outfield. His back-to-the-plate catch on Vic Wertz in the first game of the 1954 World Series and his return throw to the infield has been hailed as one of the greatest defensive plays ever. That series also made famous Dusty Rhodes, a deluxe pinch hitter who took advantage of the short right field foul line.

Rhodes went to the plate six times as a pinch hitter, had four hits, including two homers, drove in seven runs and batted .667.

Rhodes' three-run homer in the ninth won the first game and was a typical Polo Grounds homer—right down the line about 260 feet into the lower deck. These cheapie homers are what caused fans years ago to refer to them as "Chinese Homers."

In the second game of the Series, Dusty drove in two runs, one with a single and the other with another PG homer—this one ticking the façade of the upper deck in right as Wally Westlake waited in vain for the ball to come down.

There are many memories of the Polo Grounds with its strange dimensions and all those intense contests between the Dodgers and Giants. It was there that Carl Furillo won a batting championship for Brooklyn when he was unable to play the last few weeks of the '53 season after someone stepped on his hand and broke it during a melee between the outfielder and the entire Giant bench.

It was there also that Rex Barney pitched a no-hitter in the rain in 1948. And the place where little Mel Ott, right foot cocked high, hit so many of his 511 homers.

It was also the scene where the Mets were born—stillborn, people said for years—in 1962 and where they lost 105 home games in two years. It was there that banners first flourished in ballparks—only after newspapermen pleaded with club press to let the kids parade around after the brass first tried to eject them.

I attended or covered games at the Polo Grounds for more than a quarter of a century and I will always treasure the memory of having been the official scorer for the last game ever played there. Two years after the Mets moved to brand new Shea Stadium, a high-rise apartment stood in the old ballpark's place.

[1975]

And Their Catchers Weren't Too Good, Either!

BY HAROLD ROSENTHAL

In their first undistinguished year of origin (1962), the New York Mets lost 120 games and used seven catchers. You could get rich betting the most ardent fan he couldn't name half this number.

The first man drafted by the Mets in the expansion was Hobie Landrith, made available by the Cincinnati Reds. The Mets' idea was to get a good catcher before anything else because that's what you need more than anything else. Hobie was little but durable, and Hobie—pronounced with a long "o"—was his real name. That is, he was durable until he came to the Mets.

Once in an exhibition game in St. Petersburg, Florida, at Al Lang Field, there suddenly was a commotion around home plate which shivered the crowd back to awareness. Landrith was on the ground and they were trying to slip his mask off. It developed that a backswing had nailed him on the side of the head . . . a rare occurrence where the end of the swung bat hits the catcher.

Catchers know instinctively how close they can get without being hit. After ten years of playing, Landrith had to become a Met to learn that his micro-measurements could be off by that vital fraction.

A couple of weeks later when the Mets went over to Orlando to play the Senators, Landrith was back in business behind the plate. He didn't stay there long. Another backswing got him. "God," he exclaimed, "ten years without being hit and now twice in a month."

Landrith lasted until mid-summer when he went to the Baltimore Orioles in part payment for first baseman Marv Throneberry. Throneberry was another story that won't be gone into here.

Then there was Clarence Choo-Choo Coleman, and I forget where the Mets got him. Casey Stengel liked him because of his low stance. "He catches them on his belly like a snake," said the old man. Couldn't hit, though, and there was a certain spareness in his vocabulary. Someone made the mistake of interviewing him on TV between games of a doubleheader and nothing happened. Finally in desperation, the announcer asked, "Choo-Choo, what sport do you like best?" "Tennis," said Choo-Choo. "Tennis? Where would you have played tennis?" "High school," said Choo-Choo. End of interview.

At the end of that first lamentable season, and to get ready for another equally as inept, the players were asked to provide the club with their home phone numbers. Choo-Choo gave his Daytona Beach number to the road secretary.

During the winter there was occasion to get in touch with him. The face of the secretary placing the call was something to see. "This is the number of the Daytona Beach city hall?" she said in a semi-quaver while trying to contact Coleman.

And then there was Chris Cannizzaro, a tense young man drafted out of the Cards' organization. Stengel, never much on names, called him "Canzoneri." There had been a lightweight boxing champion, Tony Canzoneri, about thirty years earlier.

Cannizzaro was a graceful performer behind the plate although you had to bat him seventh or eighth because of his threadbare hitting. Came that inevitable afternoon when Cannizzaro let a low pitch get past him and it cost the Mets a ball game against the Giants they thought had been won.

It seemed to shock Stengel well beyond its importance in the general aura of ineptitude surrounding the Mets. Someone asked him why he was taking it so badly?

"Jeez," rasped Stengel, "they told me he couldn't hit but they forget to tell me he couldn't catch neither."

But there were other catchers that incredible first year, people like Joe Pignatano, the ex-Dodger, who was to stay as a coach for Gil Hodges and pick up a World Series check seven years later; Joe Ginsberg, acquired as a possible attraction for Jewish fans (Jewish fans or not, he was cut before the season began); another Jewish catcher, Norm Sherry, picked up late from the Dodgers (two Jewish catchers on one club in a single season is a major league record); and Harry Chiti, who came from Cleveland in the funniest trade made anywhere that year. That is "funny" as in boffo, not as in peculiar.

Chiti was a big, slow-moving left-handed hitter, and someone told George Weiss, who had brought his talent-sniffing abilities with him when he came from the Yankees, that Chiti would hit, given the chance. And with a fifteen-foot wall only 257 feet away in the old Polo Grounds, man, get that Chiti.

Chiti got his chance to hit. His .195 effort indicated that you can't win 'em all. So he was sent down to Jacksonville, a Mets farm club, where he stuck around until September 1. That was the deadline for the delivery to Cleveland of the "player to be named later." Three guesses as to who it was.

The best hitter the Mets had that first year was Frank Thomas, a third baseman–outfielder acquired from Milwaukee in a big deal. Thomas hit 34 homers. A dozen years later it's still a Met record.

Thomas, like the Chiti trade, was funny; but not as in hah hah. Someone had tagged him with the nickname "Big Donkey." Sometimes he gloried in it, laughing it up, sometimes he resented it. You just had to be sure you picked the right day.

Thomas' biggest moment was not seen by roaring thousands in the Polo Grounds, nor by millions on TV. It came during a warmup before a game with the San Francisco Giants at that aging ballpark, which was to become a housing development only a few years later.

Thomas was standing around the batting cage hooting down some of the Giants' pitchers who were throwing batting practice. "Can't you throw any harder than that?" he'd demand. "I could catch you barehanded."

Willie Mays, jumping to the defense of his lesser-salaried teammates, came through with a brilliant retort. "Shut up, Thomas," he exclaimed.

"And you, too, Mays," Thomas retorted. "I can catch anything *you* throw barehanded."

"For how much?" demanded Mays. "For anything you wanna bet," responded Thomas.

"For ten bucks," says Mays. "You got it," said Thomas.

So while the field crew wheeled away the batting cage, Mays strode to the mound, ball clenched in his right fist. Thomas took up his position behind home plate, wearing nothing but his bare hands and an owlish look.

"Y'still wanna do it?" shouted Mays, trying to figure out why someone would want to get himself crippled.

Thomas answered in the affirmative.

Mays wound up. The arm whipped back, and the few newspapermen, who were in on the whole thing from the first exchange, cringed. The ball would go right through Thomas approximately in the vicinity of his belt buckle.

Mays let go. In whizzed the throw.

Thomas put his two hands in front of him to meet the throw just over the plate. On contact, he whipped his hands *with the ball,* to his left. The force of the throw took his clenched hands and the ball back somewhere behind his shoulder blade, but he held on.

Still unsmiling he called, "Okay, Mays, pay me."

Mays' eyes bugged. Then he glared at Thomas. He made a derogatory comment, turned on his heel and made for the dugout.

That's how it was with the Mets in 1962.

[1975]

The Love Story of a Baseball Legend

BY BRAD WILLSON

There was a piece on the Associated Press wire that struck a memory nerve. It told about a museum being opened in Newcomerstown, Ohio, named after Cy Young, the winningest pitcher in the history of baseball.

He's the man in whose name each year the outstanding pitcher is honored with the Cy Young Award.

It's been 85 years since Denton True Young, 23 years old, trudged out of the southern Ohio hills to write one of the greatest chapters in the game's annals.

The rawboned farm boy won 511 and lost 316 games during a 22-year career in the big leagues. He pitched three no-hit games in the bigs.

At 44, Cy called it a career after losing 1-0 to a rookie named Grover Cleveland Alexander. Along the way, he'd struck out 2,803 batters.

You can't help but wonder what kind of fantastic wages Cy Young would have commanded on today's market. He never earned more than $3,500 a year in his glory-filled days.

The reason the piece about the newly opened museum gave pause to reflect was linked to an interview I had with Cy a few years before his death.

He had been chopping wood on the little farm where he lived near Peoli, Ohio (population 30 or so). I'd driven down from Columbus in March 1947 to talk to Cy and take some pictures of the grand old man.

More poignant than his diamond accomplishments was the tender and enduring love story he confided, late one spring afternoon as we sat over a beer in the Elks Club with his longtime friend John Benedum.

"I got home with more than $1,000 out of that first year's pay. And when I got home with more money in one lump than anyone in these hills had ever seen, I married the girl on the next farm," he recalled.

That was Robba Miller, nicknamed "Bobby"—his one and only girlfriend.

"For almost a quarter of a century," the old gentleman went on, "Bobby and I walked hand in hand through baseball. Then we came home and moved into the old farmhouse I had inherited from my grandparents who raised me.

"Bobby loved flowers and she had our yard filled with them."

They had been married 44 years when Bobby died in 1934.

"Somehow I didn't want to live in the old farmhouse anymore," Cy said.

Benedum and the visitor sat in the long silence before Cy took a deep breath and picked up the thread of his story.

The next year Cy moved into a hilltop home owned by Mr. and Mrs. Benedum.

"From up there on the porch, I can look down on the little churchyard where Bobby is buried. I'll just stay there, waiting for the day I can join her."

It was a long wait—21 years. He died at 88 of a heart attack. He was sitting in the big armchair at a bedroom dormer window where he could see the little churchyard and the grave with the flowers and sprigs of pussywillow he placed there daily.

Pictured in a Cleveland uniform near the end of his career, Cy Young recorded the most wins, 511, and most losses, 316, in major league history. He pitched from 1890 through 1911, retiring at age 44.

Later, during services in the Peoli Methodist Church cemetery, Mrs. Benedum would recall:

"He was 88 when he died and he lived his love story for 65 of them. In the 21 years since Bobby died, he always spoke of her as if she were in the next room. He was a wonderful gentleman."

Another story confided that lazy afternoon in the cool lounge at the Elks Club concerned the time he was approached by gamblers before he pitched and won two games in the 1903 World Series between Pittsburgh and Boston.

Cy had lost the first game, 7-3 (four errors by Boston), in this first "modern day" World Series. The weather caused the Series to last 13 days. Cy pitched three games.

"These two fellows came up on the field before the game—I was over in a quiet corner—and first talked about the game and the Series in general."

(In those days it wasn't unusual for fans to approach a player and chat with him before the game.)

One of the men said, "Young, we represent some operators who have a proposition for you."

"Proposition?" said Young.

"Well, a suggestion. If you ease up a little in this game, there will be a neat $20,000 in it for you."

Sitting there in the Elks Club so many years later, Cy's jaw hardened as he described his quiet reply.

"I told them fellows, 'If you value your money you'd best bet on me. I'm going in there and win this game.'" He turned his back on them and walked to the dressing room.

Cy said he just didn't think it was worth mentioning to anyone at the time.

Cy was Boston's winning pitcher, 11-2, turning back Pittsburgh with six hits. He pitched again two days later and Boston won, 7-3. Big Bill Dinneen shut out Pittsburgh 3-0 in the next and final game as Boston won the Series five games to three.

In 1937, Cy Young was inducted into baseball's Hall of Fame. He was serving as sergeant of arms in the Ohio Senate at the time.

The story came over the wires that Denton Tecumseh Young had made the Hall of Fame.

"That's not my name, but I think I'm the fellow they mean," drawled old Cy.

He explained his real name was Denton True Young. The "Tecumseh" came because his teammates always called him "The Chief."

Cy won more than 20 games during 16 of his 22 big league seasons. Five times he won 30 or more.

The legend says the Cy nickname came during his first trial in a little ballpark in Canton, Ohio.

The farm boy's fastball got away from the catcher several times and splintered the wooden backstop. Somebody said "looks like a cyclone hit it." From then on he was Cy Young.

But he was best remembered by the home folks in Peoli as a tall, rather awkward guy with Bobby always at his side.

[1975]

Ernie Banks, Baseball's Ambassador of Goodwill

BY JOHN KUENSTER

There is only one time we can remember Ernie Banks getting mad. Really mad. Yet somehow he managed to contain his anger. The occasion was a game against the San Francisco Giants many years ago at Wrigley Field. Jack Sanford, a hard-throwing right-handed pitcher for the Giants, had zinged Banks in the shoulder blade with a fastball.

When we visited the Cubs' training room later to investigate how bad Ernie was hurt, he was lying on Doc Al Scheuneman's rubbing table. A mean-looking lump, the size of a small lemon, had ballooned on his back where he had been struck by the ball.

As other writers gathered around Banks, somebody suggested that Sanford had intentionally hit Banks. No one in the room disagreed with the opinion.

Banks in those days was practically the Cubs' entire franchise. He had been voted the National League's Most Valuable Player in 1958 and 1959, and had developed into a premier home run hitter and a feared RBI producer.

Ernie held his tongue as the writers tried to get him to say something nasty about Sanford.

Finally, a reporter said, "Ernie, are you gonna get even? You gonna retaliate?"

Banks looked at his interrogator and smiled. "I'm going to get even with my bat."

Banks' brief statement of retaliation did not mean he was going to commit mayhem on Sanford physically. But he was going to "even up" by using his bat and creaming, to the best of his ability, whatever pitches Sanford had to offer in the future.

The incident is a minor one in Banks' long career with the Cubs, yet it gives you a measure of the man. Ernie's productive career, which stretched from 1953 to 1971, included league home run crowns in 1958 (47) and 1960 (41), RBI titles in 1958 (129) and 1959 (143), and fielding championships at shortstop in 1960 and 1961 and at first base in 1969.

When his legs finally gave out at the end of the 1971 season, he had accumulated 512 major league homers, had played in 2,528 games, had been on 14 National League All-Star teams, and had become one of Chicago's most popular baseball figures.

His popularity was so great that writer Jim Enright tagged him "Mr. Cub," a label that has stayed with him to this day.

On August 8, Ernie Banks will be enshrined in the Baseball Hall of Fame at Cooperstown, New York, an honor he richly deserves, not only because of his distinguished record as a player but also for a quality that endears him to the fans: he loves baseball, pure and simple. He gave to the game as much as it had given him by constantly expounding on its virtues, by patiently signing thousands upon thousands of autographs for kids, by continually making himself available to the public for talks on baseball, and by his refusal to knock a teammate or foe.

"Is this guy for real?" an incredulous writer once asked us. And we had to respond, "You better believe it."

That's not to say Banks is a candidate for sainthood, but certainly in all the years he has been associated with baseball, he has been good for the game and has added a little sunshine to the lives of many people.

Banks had his share of disappointments as a player. As a major leaguer for 19 seasons, he never had the thrill of appearing in a World Series. That was a big frustration for him. And we remember 1962 when an All-Star game was played in Wrigley Field. The National League team got its ears knocked off by the American League, 9-4. When Banks came trotting back into the dressing room after the game, you could sense his embarrassment. There, in his own home park, before his fellow Chicagoans, his team had been humiliated.

Always a fan favorite at Wrigley Field, Banks greets a group of "Country Cousins" from Lowell, Indiana, before a game against the Phillies in August 1958. Ernie never considered himself a crusader like Jackie Robinson, but his contributions to racial harmony were immense.

"We got Tiger-ed up," said Ernie. He didn't make the admission facetiously. He was serious. He had wanted his team to win, badly. But it didn't.

Then there was the time in the early 1960s when the Cubs' management decided Banks could no longer cut it at shortstop, and told him he was going to be switched to first base. We sat with him in the backyard of his south side home in Chicago when he had a couple of days off to rest an injured knee. He knew what was in store for him, and he was discouraged, down on himself because he was being shifted from a key defensive position to one that traditionally is considered "old folks' home" in baseball.

It took most of the afternoon for him mentally and emotionally to accept the change that was ordered. But not once did he utter a word against management for its decision.

Banks had some excellent years as a fielder. In 1959 at shortstop he committed only 12 errors in 790 chances. In 1969, at first base he committed only four miscues in 1,506 chances. He never had super range, but what balls he got to, he handled with skill and dispatch.

The stories of his long-ball hitting are legend, and too numerous to mention here. But in one season, 1955, he hit five grand slammers. Four times he hit three homers in a single game. Five times he collected more than 40 homers in a season, and 13 times he hit 20 or more round trippers.

Ernie was a wrist hitter, held his bat up high, nervously wriggled his top thumb, and could take a low or high pitch "downtown" with seemingly effortless ease.

While Banks was something special on the field, a natural hitter and good fielder, he had to surmount personal challenges in the world outside of baseball. And he succeeded. He had humble beginnings in Dallas, Texas. He was one of 11 children and had only a high school education. Yet he trained himself to be a polished public speaker who could express himself when the need arose. And he did so many, little, good things for people that went unnoticed by the general public. We remember one particularly poignant visit to a rehabilitation center in Chicago. He went there to visit a quadriplegic who had been maimed in an accident. The quadriplegic was a baseball fan. After his visit with the young man and as Ernie was leaving, a nurse said quietly, "Thank you, Mr. Banks. I think you gave him a reason for living."

That's the kind of impact Banks has had on many people. He never considered himself a Jackie Robinson type, but in his own way he broke down barriers and hatreds that poisoned and corroded the mind.

Some years ago, Ernie was emcee at the baseball writers' dinner in Chicago, and before the dinner we visited the room where the speakers were gathering. Banks greeted us at the door, and memories of those fun years, on the field for him and on the baseball beat for me, came rushing back.

Banks broke into a big grin and started to sing: "Those were the days, my friend, we thought they'd never end . . . but they did."

And then, "Mr. Cub" erupted in a hearty laugh.

[1977]

Curt Flood: Baseball's Forgotten Pioneer

BY MURRAY CHASS

The smallish black man in a pale yellow shirt and brown-and-white striped slacks walked into the lobby of the Edgewater Hyatt House in Oakland, California, one day last fall, and Lou Piniella stood next to him without showing any sign of recognition. Mickey Rivers and Elrod Hendricks passed him in a corridor of the motel and did not know him. Billy Martin came out of his room, and the smallish black man stopped.

"Mr. Martin," he said to the Yankee manager, "I'd love to shake your hand."

Martin eyed him tentatively, figuring this was another bothersome fan, the kind of thing baseball personalities always get in hotels and restaurants and on the street. Then, after a moment, the black man said, "I'm Curt Flood."

Curt Flood played center field for the St. Louis Cardinals for 12 years and compiled a .293 batting average. Then the Cardinals traded him to the Philadelphia Phillies, but he wound up in court instead of the Phillies' uniform. He challenged baseball's reserve rules that bound a player to a team for life, he lost and he was forgotten.

He fled to the island of Majorca, off the Mediterranean coast of Spain, to get away from everything. He ran a bar there, the Rustic Inn, for five years and now he is back in the city where he grew up, and he is forgotten.

No, his face didn't jolt anyone's memory that day at the motel, but it is said that any player out of baseball for five years is forgotten. Still, the name—Curt Flood—and the person should not be forgotten by anyone playing baseball today.

Most directly because of Andy Messersmith and Dave McNally, baseball players are beginning to make thousands and hundreds of thousands, perhaps millions of dollars more than they have made before and ever hoped to make. But seven years ago, Curt Flood, boldly and at great sacrifice to his own career and future, pioneered an effort to gain some freedom for himself and his fellow players, an effort that now has reached fruition, affecting even the other professional sports.

And today, while baseball's Messersmiths and Morgans and Seavers are earning $200,000 and more, Curt Flood is earning nothing. With no job and no income, Curt Flood is living in an apartment in Oakland, next to his 80-year-old mother. Only many people wouldn't call it living; it's more like existing.

Flood, now 38 and five years removed from his last attempt to play baseball, seems to be hiding from the outside world, a man prevented by his own pride from letting people know what his life is really like. Some months ago he suffered a fractured skull that nearly ended his life. He fell down some stairs, he said, after having "a couple of beers too many." Others, though, are not so certain his fall, wherever it happened, was an accident.

"They gave me a brain scan," Flood said, "and they found nothing."

Flood laughed at his own joke. At least he could still joke and laugh, although sometimes the laughs came too easily, as if they were masking some deeper, less humorous feelings. Flood is a proud man who once made $100,000 for playing baseball when not everyone was making $100,000, and he is not about to admit to the world that life no longer is a

A stellar outfielder and member of three Cardinal pennant-winners in 1964, 1967 and 1968, Curt Flood was a front-runner in the battle to gain free agency for major league players.

$100,000 romp through the woods on a Sunday afternoon in autumn.

"The ability just to get up and do nothing is a delight for me," said Flood, who returned to this country more than a year ago. "I can't afford to do it, but I'm going to do it anyway. I live well enough. It's a little difficult to find a job for a used center fielder. You can't look in the want ads and find a job like that."

Flood, still looking fit at 5 feet 9 inches and about 165 pounds, scoffed at the idea that anyone in baseball would hire him, if, indeed, he wanted to be hired at all. But toward the end of the long, rambling conversation, he was resigning himself to taking a baseball job if he could find what he wanted.

During the afternoon he also recalled his legal battle with baseball, the way he was treated that prompted the suit and the total lack of interest his fellow players showed in his lonely legal challenge to the millionaires who ran the game. But Flood in no way begrudges today's players the money they're earning; they deserve it all, he said. At the same time, he has come to understand the way the owners think and feel and why they so determinedly deserve to control their employees.

Not unexpectedly, he also played down the importance of the suit he began after his trade to the Phillies late in 1969.

"The things that I did, I did for me," he said. "I did that because I thought they were right. I thought I should have some control over what happened to my life. I played for 12 years in St. Louis, we won the pennant three times, made a lot of money, built a new stadium for them and you know what they did to me? If I had worked for the Pacific Gas and Electric Co. for 12 years, they'd have given me a watch, a nice gold watch, and I'd probably still have it. But they said, we just traded you for Richie Allen. And the guy hung up. It was just the shabby way that these executives have of handling men. We had contributed so much to St. Louis, and to get a kick in the butt like that. I don't think I deserved it that way.

"What I did then is relative today only because it happens that other people have benefited by it, and that's cool," Flood said. "These guys are making more money and deservedly so. They're the show. They're it. They're making money because they work hard. Don't you tell me one minute that Catfish Hunter doesn't work his butt off. I know he does and he's the show. People come out and see the Bird, Mark Fidrych of Detroit. Every time this guy goes on he draws 50,000 people. Well, why not get paid for it? You could put World War II in that damn stadium right there and you couldn't draw 30,000 people.

"So what happened five years ago is significant in only one respect, that it gave the ballplayer a chance to think what am I worth, what is my talent worth? Do I have to spend the rest of my life in servitude to this one person? Can he juggle my life any way he wants to? Now these guys are getting what they're worth and that's cool."

Players being as selfish as anyone else, they don't stand around giving credit to Flood or Messersmith or anyone else for what they have reaped. That doesn't bother Flood, but what did gnaw at him for a long time was the total lack of moral support (financial support he had from the players association) he received from his fellow players.

"I spent six weeks in New York during the trial," he said, wisps of cigarette smoke curling toward the ceiling, "and not one player came to see what was going on. All right, I had all the news media there; that was cool. There were ex-baseball players who came and said how they got ripped off. But not one baseball player who was playing at the time came just to see— I didn't want them to testify—just to see what was going on because it involved them so dramatically. But no one came just to sit and say, 'Hey, this is pretty important. It concerns me and my wife and my kids and, if they ever play baseball, their kids.'"

And so Flood lost the case that reached the United States Supreme Court. He disappeared in Majorca and now he has reappeared—but not really. He isn't a recluse, but he apparently is not far from it. His friends and family would like him to emerge from the prison he has built around himself "and be more of a human being than just sitting around and winding up like a vegetable."

[1977]

Luck Had a Role in My Perfect No-Hitter

BY SANDY KOUFAX AS TOLD TO GEORGE VASS

I wouldn't say it was the most memorable game of my career, though it certainly was one of them.

It possibly was Bob Hendley's most memorable game because I doubt if he ever pitched a better one for the Cubs. With any sort of luck Hendley would have won that game, but as so often happens to a pitcher, he was working on a day when his team couldn't score a run.

It's been often said that pitching a no-hitter involves a lot of luck because everything has to go right for you. Anything can happen to break it up. A pop fly can land between three fielders, none of whom can quite reach it. A grounder can take a hop or find a hole in the infield.

As for a perfect game, that's even more of an accident, if you can compare degrees of such things. It's unthinkable. It just happens.

It happened to me in 1965 (September 9). I pitched a perfect game against the Cubs for the fourth no-hitter of my career, something no pitcher had ever done before.

Hendley gave up one hit, and that was a blooper. Ironically, it had nothing to do with the run that scored.

I think I had more than 20 wins at that point of the season [21-7 for the Los Angeles Dodgers], but I'd lost my last three starts. We just weren't getting too many runs when the Cubs came into L.A. for one game, a strange bit of scheduling.

The Cubs were down in the standings, but they had a good hitting team. They had real power with Ron Santo, Ernie Banks, Billy Williams, Harvey Kuenn and some others.

At the start of the game I didn't have anything special, just average stuff. The fastball didn't have the zip it sometimes did, the curveball didn't break sharply. But as the game went on my fastball really came alive. It began to pop as good as it had all season.

The Cubs were going down 1-2-3 inning after inning, but we weren't having much better luck against Hendley. He was getting the side out, too, with his sinker working and our batters beating it into the ground.

In the fifth inning we got a run but it was without a hit, and it was typical of the way we'd been scoring all year. We got a break and took advantage of it.

Lou Johnson walked and Ron Fairly moved him to second with a sacrifice bunt. The way the game was going, a run looked pretty big at that point, so Johnson decided to try and steal third, from where he might be able to score on a sacrifice fly or a ball hit to the right side of the infield.

When Johnson slid into third, catcher Chris Krug's throw sailed into left field, down the line. Johnson picked himself up and scored on the error.

I can't say I felt terrible about Hendley getting a bad break like that while pitching so well. I was hoping we'd get six more runs and put the game away.

We weren't about to. As it turned out, we were lucky even to get a hit. It didn't come until the seventh inning. Johnson blooped a pop fly down

Sandy Koufax holds baseballs marked with zeroes, symbolizing his four no-hitters, the last of which was a perfect, 1-0 victory over the Cubs on September 9, 1965, at Dodger Stadium.

the right field line and it landed for a double. That was the only thing that kept Hendley from pitching a losing no-hitter while I was pitching the perfect game.

I don't remember any exceptional fielding plays early in the game, and there really weren't many opportunities for them. I was striking out a lot of Cubs, especially after my fastball came around.

I had good control, too. I was consistently ahead of the hitters, until Williams came to bat in the seventh inning with two out. I fell behind 3-0.

I didn't try to finesse him. I couldn't afford to. If I walked Williams, Santo was next up and he could hit the ball out of the park, and that 1-0 lead would be gone. I challenged Williams. I threw the ball as hard as I could down the pike and got him to end the inning.

So that was seven complete innings, but nobody on either bench said anything about a no-hitter. Usually the team in the other dugout will let you know, hoping to shake you up, to break your concentration. But nobody in the Chicago dugout said anything, or if they did I didn't hear it.

The eighth inning I was throwing as hard as I ever had, not thinking *so* much about the perfect game as about the 1-0 lead, which could disappear with one swing of the bat.

I struck out Santo to start the eighth and then the next two batters.

The first two batters in the ninth struck out, and then it came down to the last man, Kuenn, pinch-hitting for Hendley.

I gave him everything I had. Three fastballs, right down the pike. The third one ended the game, my 14th strikeout.

A perfect game for me, and disappointment for Hendley, who'd given up just one hit. I sympathized with him, up to a point, and only after we'd won.

[1977]

Why the Red Sox Hate the Yankees

BY RAY FITZGERALD

Strike a medal for Harry Frazee. Write him a sonnet, sing him a love song, build a statue on the Boston Common to his memory.

Frazee was the Red Sox owner who sold George Herman Ruth to the Yankees for $125,000 prior to the 1920 season.

And with that one moment of inspired madness, Frazee struck the spark that has flamed into the longest and most passionate rivalry in professional sport.

There are those who will dissent, who will cite the Dodgers and the Giants, but that subway surliness went flat when the teams moved from Ebbets Field and the Polo Grounds to Chavez Ravine and Candlestick Park.

No, from the day Frazee sold Babe Ruth, the Red Sox and the Yankees have been the Hatfields and McCoys of American sports.

The Red Sox fan may admit to grudging admiration for such immortals as Joe DiMaggio and Mickey Mantle, but otherwise he has a raging, all-consuming hatred for the Yankee uniform.

He sees it as a symbol of arrogance, smugness, pomposity, and greed, the ultimate in big-city con.

And the true Yankee fan, though he might concede that Ted Williams could hit a little, and might admire Carl Yastrzemski (mostly because Yaz grew up on Long Island), looks upon the Red Sox as whiners, nit-pickers, overrated players suffering from an immense inferiority complex, in short, the very epitome of everything contained in the term "bush league."

The dividing line in this love-hate relationship, thinks Red Sox public relations chief Bill Crowley, is Waterbury, Connecticut.

"East Waterbury," says Crowley, "is Red Sox territory. West Waterbury belongs to the Yankees."

Red Sox fans pour down Interstate 95 to the Stadium. Transplanted Bostonians come out of their New York apartments and their homes in Jersey to root for their team.

And when the Yankees visit Fenway, look out. New York collegians from Brandeis, MIT, Boston University, Suffolk, Tufts, Northeastern, and Boston College hear the siren call and head like lemmings for the bleachers.

Sometimes at Fenway on a spring night, you can't tell which is the home team. In both Boston and New York, emotions run high.

Which brings me to the fights. Ah, the fights.

On Memorial Day, 1938, the biggest crowd in Stadium history—81,841—turned out to watch Joe McCarthy and the Yankees beat Joe Cronin and the Red Sox in a double-header.

But the games were the least of the long day. The highlight was a fight between playing manager Cronin and Yankee outfielder Alvin "Jake" Powell.

Tell us about it, Joe.

"Archie McKain, a little lefty, was pitching for us. He threw a high curve close to Powell. Hell, if the ball had hit him it wouldn't have hurt.

"Powell came out toward McKain and made some threatening gestures. I thought he was overreacting, so I came in from shortstop.

"There were some words and we started punching and rolling around, and Cal Hubbard, the umpire, threw us both out.

"In those days the visiting team had to go through the Yankee dugout to get to its locker room. As I went down the runway, Powell began popping off some more. It was dark, a lot of beer barrels around, but we squared off again.

"The trouble was, this was enemy territory. I was surrounded by Yankees. They started to gang up on me, but then Hubbard showed up. He was a big guy, a former All-American football player and a pro, and he must have thought the odds were against the Irish kid. He tossed me one way and Powell the other, and that was the end of the fight."

In the last week of the dramatic pennant race in 1949, the Yanks and the Red Sox were tied at 6-6 going into the ninth.

Johnny Pesky was on third and Bobby Doerr laid down a surprise bunt. Tell us about it, Johnny.

"Tommy Henrich at first base fielded the ball and threw home. I'd have been out by 20 feet but Ralph Houk missed the tag. I got a corner of the plate with my slide, and Bill Grieve, the umpire, called me safe.

"All hell broke loose. Casey Stengel and Houk charged Grieve, and they wound up getting fined $150 each. The big beef was from Cliff Mapes, the outfielder. He told Grieve he had no guts and that he must have had a bet on the game to make such a terrible call.

"Mapes had to apologize and it cost him $200."

In 1952, Red Sox rookie Jim Piersall, on his way to a nervous breakdown, screamed insults at Billy Martin. Suddenly the high-strung Martin broke toward the Red Sox dugout and battled Piersall in the runway. The only casualty was Yankee coach Bill Dickey, hurt when he tried to restrain Martin.

In 1967 at Yankee Stadium, Jim Lonborg plunked pitcher Thad Tillotson on the back with a fastball, one of 19 men Lonnie hit that remarkable season.

As Tillotson walked slowly toward first, he made a move toward Lonborg, and the melee was on. Players poured off the benches and out of the bullpens. Rico Petrocelli battled Joe Pepitone, and Rico's brother, a special stadium policeman, raced onto the field to protect his brother.

Muscular Reggie Smith lifted Tillotson high into the air, squeezed him and then dropped the pitcher to the ground like a crushed grape.

On August 1, 1973, Gene Michael of the Yanks missed a squeeze bunt, but Thurman Munson on third kept coming. He crashed into catcher Carlton Fisk and both came up swinging.

So did Michael, on the possible assumption that the missed bunt was only one swing, therefore he was entitled to two more. Fisk came out of the scrap with a bruised eye, courtesy of Munson, and a scratched face, compliments of Michael.

And there was the 1976 brawl at the Stadium, which began when the Yankees' Lou Piniella slid into Fisk. The two began fighting and soon everyone joined in the fun.

Pitcher Bill Lee said something nasty to Graig Nettles, and the next thing he knew he was at the bottom of a big pile. Lee hurt his arm so badly he was of little use the rest of the season.

When the Yankees next came to Fenway Park, the customers turned their wrath on center fielder Mickey Rivers, whom they'd picked out on television clips as the villain of the Stadium fight.

In a disgusting display of non-sportsmanship, bleacherites threw ball bearings, golf balls, and cherry bombs at the beleaguered Rivers, who wore a batting helmet in the outfield for protection.

But brawls alone don't make this rivalry special.

"We just played hard against each other," says Pesky. "The Yankees had a third baseman named Billy Johnson, strong guy. He trampled little Roy Partee at home plate once. I mean, he flattened him.

"Partee didn't say anything. Two months later the same situation arose. Here came the ball and Partee dipped his shoulder as Johnson bulled in. He flipped Billy tail over teakettle. Billy just got up and dusted himself off and went to the bench. He accepted it.

"In Pesky's rookie year, Joe DiMaggio slid hard into second, knocking the kid for a loop.

"A while later, we're ahead 5-0, Joe's on first and there's a hot two-hopper to Doerr. He flipped it to me and I took my sweet time with my throw. It hit Joe right on the chin. Like I say, we all played hard."

Joe Dugan is 79 years old now and has lost a step from the days when he roomed with Babe Ruth's suitcase on the Yankees. But Dugan is still quick of wit and sharp of memory, and recalls the day the Stadium opened.

April 19, 1923 it was, with the Red Sox as opponents, and Dugan drove in the first run in a 4-1 victory.

Jumpin' Joe then scored on the building's first homer, hit, naturally, by the man Dugan always refers to as "The Big Fella."

The largest crowd in baseball up to that time, 74,200, attended that inaugural. Twenty-five thousand were turned away.

There was one other incident of passing interest. In the fifth inning, Babe Ruth dropped a fly ball. As Dugan pointed out, if it had been a scotch and soda, he'd have held onto it.

Though the rivalry certainly continues to sizzle today, it was hot in the late 1930s and perhaps reached its peak in those seasons immediately preceding and following World War II.

"All you'd hear and read about," said Pesky, "were the great Yanks, the great Yanks. All they were supposed to do would be throw their gloves on the field to beat you. Well, we played 'em tough."

In 1941, when Joe DiMaggio hit in an astounding 56 straight games, bandleader Les Brown made a smash recording called "Joltin' Joe DiMaggio" (Joe, Joe DiMaggio . . . we want you on our side).

This was answered in Boston by two lines of doggerel that went like this:
"He's better than his brother Joe . . .
"Do-mi-nic DiMaggio."

"The Yankees were always the top dog," says Dom, now a successful businessman in the Boston area. "We always felt we had as much talent. They'd come up here and we'd knock 'em around, but of course, their lineup was perfect for the Stadium."

On June 28, 29, and 30 in 1949, Joe D. put on one of the most dramatic hitting displays ever seen at Fenway. Out all season because of a bone spur

Carlton Fisk squares off against Thurman Munson in one of the brawls that has spiced the rivalry between the Red Sox and Yankees.

on his heel, Joe started his first game on the 28th and won it with a homer off Mickey McDermott.

He hit two more homers the next day, with the second being the game winner, and polished off his performance with a three-run homer off Earl Johnson to win the third game.

"Oh, how it hurt losing those three," says Dom, "but I was happy and proud as hell for Joe."

Dom's 34-game hitting streak, the longest in Red Sox history, ended that year when he lined out to—who else?—his brother at Fenway in his last at bat.

And always in those years, as a sub-theme to the team rivalry, was the comparison between Joe DiMaggio and Ted Williams—easy does it Joe, the great all-round ballplayer, and flamboyant Ted, the magnificent cruncher of a baseball.

"If Joe had played with Boston and Ted with New York," says Dom, "they'd have each been in the perfect park and each would have broken Ruth's home run record."

Says ex-Yankee Gil McDougald: "If Ted had played half his games at the Stadium, he'd have hit 75 to 80 homers a year."

In three seasons, Williams lost out to Yankees in the balloting for the Most Valuable Player award, which only made Red Sox fans more certain than ever that New York had only to snap its fingers to make the rest of baseball jump.

In 1941, Ted hit .406, but that was DiMag's streak season, so he was named MVP. The next year, Williams led both leagues in batting (.356), in runs batted in (137) and in home runs (36), but Yankee second baseman Joe Gordon beat him by 21 points in the MVP voting.

In 1947, Williams once more won the Triple Crown, but DiMaggio was elected MVP by one vote, the issue being decided when a writer with a grudge against the volatile Williams failed to put him in the top ten.

The rivalry has been filled with the strange and the wonderful and the offbeat.

Lou Gehrig knocked himself out chasing a foul in 1926 and Ruth had to finish the game at first base. In 1930, and again in '33, Ruth, though he hadn't pitched all season, started the last game of the year and both times beat the Red Sox.

In 1950, a year Rizzuto was the Most Valuable Player, he received a letter saying that if he showed up that night at Fenway he would be shot.

"Two policemen were assigned to me," said Rizzuto, "but nothing happened. Stengel wanted Billy Martin to switch uniforms with me. He said if we were going to lose anybody, let it be Billy instead of me."

The Red Sox found out that Rizzuto got all queasy when confronted with insects and other crawly creatures, and so they would brighten a quiet ball game by stuffing dead mice and sparrows into the shortstop's glove.

Consider, for a moment, the second game of a doubleheader at Fenway on Sunday, September 3, 1939. A 6:30 p.m. blue-law curfew is in effect, so when the Yankees get ahead by scoring two runs in the eighth, they are anxious to complete the inning and make the two runs official.

Therefore they seek to put themselves out. George Selkirk and Gordon stroll nonchalantly toward home and are tagged out, reluctantly, by catcher Johnny Peacock.

However, manager Cronin, not wanting the inning to end, orders his pitchers to hand out some intentional walks. Pop bottles and other debris pour down on the field, and umpire Hubbard forfeits the game to the Yankees, only to be overruled by the league office five days later. The game is rescheduled but never played, because of rain.

In 1951, Allie Reynolds pitched his dropped-foul-ball no-hitter against the Red Sox. With two out in the ninth, Williams hit a mile-high foul that was dropped by Yogi Berra.

"Don't worry, Yogi, we'll get him again," yelled Reynolds.

"Cronin was in the press box," recalls former *Boston Globe* writer Bob Holbrook, "and he said, 'Hit the next sonofabitch into the upper deck.'"

But Williams didn't. He hit another high foul and this time Yogi held on to it.

Want some names? Roger Maris hits his 61st home run against Tracy Stallard of the Red Sox in 1961 at Yankee Stadium.

Rookie Ted Bowsfield beats the Yankees three straight times in 1958 and is forever afterward referred to by Stengel as "that fella what throws them ground balls."

A second baseman named Marlon Coughtry is recalled from the minors at the tag end of the year, and in the last game of the season chases Mantle back to first base as the winning run crosses the plate. It is Marlon Coughtry's last game in the major leagues.

Joe Page, just another pitcher on the Yankee staff, has walked a couple of men and is three and nothing on Rudy York. One more ball and he is on his way to the minor league farm at Newark.

But Page fights back to strike out York and goes on to become the best relief pitcher in baseball.

Billy Rohr, a skinny left-hander, makes his major league debut in 1967, and with one out in the ninth has a no-hitter at the Stadium.

Tom Tresh slams a drive to deep left, a sure triple, but Carl Yastrzemski makes a spectacular catch. However, Old Folks Elston Howard then breaks up the no-hitter and for the next month is the recipient of much hate mail, postmarked Boston.

And the ultimate irony is that by the end of the season, Howard has been traded and is catching for the Red Sox in the World Series, while Rohr has faded to the minors.

Mel Parnell is leading the Yankees, 9-0, going into the eighth on opening day of 1950. A breeze. Final score, 15-10, Yankees.

Rich McKinney is brought over from the White Sox to play third base for the Yanks and on April 11, 1972, makes four errors that account for nine Red Sox runs.

The teams play a twi-night doubleheader at the Stadium on August 22, 1967, that lasts eight hours and 27 minutes.

Ruth comes to town on August 12, 1934, to play his last game in Boston as a Yankee, and the largest crowd of all time at Fenway, 41,766, jams the park. The outfield is roped off, there are 24 doubles in the twinbill and Al Zarilla of the Red Sox injures his leg diving into the crowd in the outfield.

And there are the last two games of 1949 at the Stadium, with the Red Sox needing only one victory to capture the pennant.

Ellis Kinder, though he has allowed only two hits, is behind to the Yanks, 1-0 going into the eighth, and so is lifted for a pinch hitter.

New York scores four more runs in the last of the eighth, and so a Red Sox rally in the ninth, which would have been good enough for a win if Kinder had stayed in there, falls short, setting up some mammoth second-guessing.

"That was the lowest point in my baseball career," says Joe Cronin. "Mr. Yawkey and I were struck dumb for an hour after the game."

What is little remembered is that in the ninth, after Doerr's two-run triple over a limping Joe DiMaggio, Joe called time out and removed himself from the game.

Over the years, the Yankees have won 856 games and the Red Sox 685 (excluding this season).

It's been The Big Apple vs. The Beantown. Fun City vs. The Athens of America. Huge, vast Yankee Stadium vs. funny little Fenway Park.

"Hey, Thurman Munson's a shoemaker behind the plate."

"Yeah, well up a tree with Bill Lee." Oh, what a lovely war.

[1977]

Stealing Home Is Not for the Faint of Heart

BY MELVIN DURSLAG

Just because Rod Carew has hit .300 nine years in a row, people have developed the notion that this man is something special.

It even is being said that Mr. Carew has won a niche for himself in the Hall of Fame.

When he makes his appearance at that shrine, the proclamation should be read that Carew was an uncommon batsman, but that he was being admitted for the damndest achievement in baseball.

By the summer of '77, he had stolen home 16 times.

You may try to minimize this accomplishment, but to those artists especially gifted at stealing bases, the theft of home 16 times is the Pulitzer Prize, the Nobel Prize, the Congressional Medal and the Triple Crown, all in one.

Stealing home is so inconceivable to a formidable base runner such as Davey Lopes that he refuses to acknowledge it is, even for professionals.

"That's for amateurs," says Lopes, with the disdain of a London jewel thief for one who swipes hubcaps. "I've never tried to steal home. Your only chance is if the pitcher's mind is in the next county."

In his distinguished career as a base gonif, Maury Wills attempted the theft of home only once, admitting candidly he was restrained by the fear of failing.

You won't find Lou Brock or Joe Morgan working that area, and even Mickey Rivers, rated a scattergun runner, as opposed to a scientist, won't try it very often.

But Carew not only has the will to try but is excited by the action.

"I started in 1969 when Billy Martin was managing the Twins," he recalls. "Runs were coming hard for us, and Billy told me not to be afraid to take a chance."

Since those attempting the theft of home do so unfailingly while the pitch is on the way to the plate, or while the pitcher is in motion, Carew began a study of those at the mound.

"I watched the way they held the ball in their glove, the way they held it in their hand and how they wound up," he says. "I tried to calculate how

Jackie Robinson steals home in Game 1 of the 1955 World Series at Yankee Stadium. Catcher Yogi Berra always claimed he tagged Robinson before Jackie's foot touched the plate.

much of a walking lead I could take on them. If it was big enough, I would surprise them by breaking for the plate."

Incredibly, Carew stole home seven times in 1969.

From that point forward, he has been under surveillance as much as known family heads of the Cosa Nostra.

"I can't think of anything more humiliating than losing a ball game to a guy who steals home on you," says Nolan Ryan, the California pitcher. "It happened to me one time against Kansas City. I had a 2-and-2 count on the hitter—and Amos Otis broke from third. The pitch was a ball and he slid in safe. I felt like a nickel."

Since Ryan comes from Alvin, Texas, and since it is well established that a stranger running a shell game can work a small town only once, Nolan is duly wary.

"When I see Carew on third," says Nolan, "I'll usually work from a stretch and we'll have our third baseman hold him close. You give up something when you do this. I lose the advantage of a windup and we leave a bigger hole at third for the batter."

But Nolan and other pitchers are quite willing to make that sacrifice when they think of the alternative.

"Does your batter know when you are going to break for home?" Carew was asked.

"I flash the sign," he answered. "But hitters don't always pick it up. Harmon Killebrew, for instance, missed it one time and swung as I headed for the plate. It gave me a terrible fright. I thought he was going to kill me."

It was a similar experience that discouraged Wills, the terror expanding when Frank Howard, the hitter, took an awesome swing and hit a liner foul that missed Maury by inches.

Trembling visibly, Wills related afterward that the ball zooming past his head looked as big as a casaba—and Howard's bat took on the dimensions of the Eiffel Tower.

Carew confides he never has felt a fear of failing, and the record gives him little reason for feeling otherwise.

In 19 attempts at this colossal undertaking, he has been caught only three times.

"When I start to feel I can't make it," says Rod, "I'll probably stop."

That, of course, will be a very happy day for pitchers, who may begrudge him four hits in every 10 at bats, but not nearly as much as they begrudge him the theft of home.

As Ryan says, this is the ultimate in degradation, and pitchers who are burned usually enter a lamasery.

[1977]

Lefty Gomez Enlivened the Game with Comedy

BY JERRY D. LEWIS

Driving up to northern California to see Lefty Gomez, you wonder whether time has changed the man who might have been the most genuine flake ever to play major league baseball. The suspicion arises because of a three-line filler item on the sports page. It says Vernon "Lefty" Gomez had just won a national organization's Good Guy Award.

True, he was a nice guy back in the days when you were a very young sportswriter in Manhattan and he was a star for the New York Yankees intent on proving that Broadway and Vernon Gomez was a marriage made in heaven. He was such a regular at every watering hole that John Lardner described his heritage as "one part Iberian and one part Hibernian, with just a dash of vermouth."

You park your car in front of Casa Gomez, a very attractive hillside villa in a small town some 25 miles north of San Francisco. It's close to El Camino Real, so even on this coast, he's not too far from the Main Stem.

Sportswriters today call the Phillies' Jay Johnstone a flake because he throws lighted firecrackers into his own team's dugout. They call the Tigers' Mark Fidrych a flake because he talks to the ball. Those young men are promising tyros, but they haven't established a track record entitling them to admission into the select company of Zanies, Inc.

Once inside the Gomez residence, it's immediately obvious that at 67 he still retains the leprechaun mind of the left-hander who advanced the art of flakiness from an avocation to a profession. You find him painting words on a small flat rock, hardly the way straight, right-handed folks spend their time.

It seems a neighbor's boy has been hospitalized and is very depressed. Lefty doesn't know the boy or his parents too well, but hearing about the youngster's depression is enough, because Gomez has waged a lifelong crusade against gloom. The words he's painted on the rock are:

Please turn me over.

Later, he turns the rock over and paints on the other side:

Thanks.

When he finishes, his wife, June, gift-wraps the rock and has it delivered to the hospital, leading one to suspect she might be a little left-handed, herself.

In that episode, you have the two vital necessities for an act of pure, inspired flakiness—originality and humor. They just come naturally to Gomez. During his brilliant career with the Yankees, when they were the Yankees of Ruth, Gehrig, DiMaggio, etc., Lefty lived up to the old show business axiom and always left everybody laughing—except the hitters who faced him. He never took life or himself too seriously, and he hasn't changed.

Accepting the Good Guy Award—which disproved the adage about where nice guys finish, from the collected sayings of that famous Chinese philosopher, Mao Tse Durocher—Lefty told the assembled guests:

"When Neil Armstrong first set foot on the moon, he and all the space scientists involved in the Apollo Project were puzzled by an unidentifiable white object. I knew immediately what it was.

"That was a home run ball hit off me by Jimmie Foxx in 1937."

For those who came in late, and don't recognize the name, Vernon "Lefty" Gomez was one of baseball's brightest (in every sense of that word) stars. From 1931 to 1938—eight seasons—he won 151 ball games, an average of almost 20 a year. In 1934, he led the American League in almost every statistic—26 wins against five losses, 2.33 earned run average, most strikeouts, most shutouts and most laughs per nine inning game.

All in all, his record was so brilliant he was a shoo-in to be voted into the Baseball Hall of Fame. When he was, he commented: "It's only fair. After all, I helped a lot of hitters get in."

Jimmie Foxx, who did hit a prodigious home run off Gomez in 1937—and in quite a few other years—hit a total of 534 homers during his 20-year career. Foxx was a strong, chunky, granite hard hunk of man. His strength was so startling Gomez once observed:

"Foxx wasn't scouted. He was trapped."

One day, after Jimmie had been purchased by the Red Sox when Tom Yawkey was trying to buy a pennant, Gomez was pitching against the Bostonians. Foxx came to bat with the bases loaded. Yankee catcher Bill Dickey signaled for Gomez' best pitch, a fastball. Lefty shook his head. Dickey signaled for a curveball. When Lefty again shook his head, the catcher called for a changeup. Once more, Gomez shook him off. Dickey called "time," and trotted to the mound.

"You've shaken me off on everything," he said. "What do you want to throw this guy?"

"Nothing," Lefty replied. "Let's wait a while. Maybe he'll get a phone call."

Gomez came up to the major leagues at the age of 18, after an incredible season with the San Francisco Seals in which he won everything but the Miss America crown. The Yankees paid the Seals $50,000 for the ultra-slim southpaw who stood 6-2 and weighed under 150 pounds.

"I was so skinny," Lefty reminds you, "that until I was 23, I never cast a shadow."

The Yankees would've been better off buying him by the carat. To give you an idea of how high a price that $50,000 was, consider that a few years later the Yankees bought another highly touted star from the Seals for half that much—an outfielder named Joe DiMaggio.

Gomez, the complete extrovert who could cement a close friendship in five minutes with the Abominable Snowman, and the shy DiMaggio, who regarded "hello" as an oration, roomed together for six years when the Yankees were on the road. They're still good friends, often playing against each other in celebrity golf tournaments in the San Francisco area.

Lefty was one of the very few who got close enough to DiMaggio to bring out Joe's dry, offbeat humor. One day in 1939, Hank Greenberg of the Detroit Tigers really tore into a fastball and drove it some 450 feet to deepest center field. DiMaggio turned at the crack of the bat and raced toward the flagpole in front of the bleachers.

"I had to take my eye off the ball three different times," Joe remembers, "to make sure I wasn't going to hit the fence or the flagpole. I finally caught it with my back to the plate. It was the best outfield play I ever made."

Jim Dawson, reporting the catch in the next day's *New York Times,* commented that by playing a shallow center field so he could catch "bloopers," and still have the grace and ability to go back on Greenberg's smash, DiMaggio would make big league fans forget Tris Speaker. Up to then, Speaker was regarded as baseball's all-time great center fielder.

In a subsequent game, with Gomez pitching, Rudy York hit two drives over DiMaggio's head for triples. After the second, Lefty asked Joe why he was playing Detroit's big slugger so shallow.

"Didn't you see the paper?" Joe asked, deadpan. "I'm going to make the fans forget Tris Speaker."

"Okay," Lefty told him. "Just be sure you don't make 'em forget Gomez."

One of those clumsy sluggers who could knock in about 100 runs a year with his bat and let in almost that many with his fielding, York was part Indian. Needling him one day, Lefty asked if it was true that he was three-quarters Cherokee and one-quarter first baseman.

Lefty picked up quite a few nicknames during his 12-year career in Yankee pinstripes. He got his first while heading for his initial training camp on the train from New York to St. Petersburg, Florida. When the Orange Blossom Special stopped at Washington, one of the passengers who came aboard was Albert Einstein.

A sportswriter asked the 18-year-old Gomez if he knew who Einstein was. "Sure," Gomez nodded, "he's an inventor—like me."

"What did you ever invent?" challenged the scribe.

"The revolving goldfish bowl. It keeps turning so the fish can see everything in the room without swimming all the time and wearing themselves out."

"You're goofy," the writer groaned, and from then on Lefty was Goofy Gomez, El Goofy, and, among others, the Gay Caballero.

Even as a raw rookie, Lefty refused to be awed by reputation or tradition. Sportsman's Park, the old stadium in St. Louis and the site of many historic moments in baseball history, was revered by some as a shrine. Actually it was a dingy, unswept, decaying arena, so when Lefty first hit the Mound City with the Yankees and a St. Louis sportswriter asked what he thought of the stadium, Lefty looked around and replied:

"They'd have to paint this place before they could condemn it."

He also had ready answers for umpires. One day, after Philadelphia slugger Al Simmons swung at two pitches and missed both, umpire Bill McGowan called "time." Walking to the mound, he told Lefty: "Simmons says you're throwing spitballs."

Lefty Gomez, left, with Red Ruffing seen here before pitching for the Yankees in the 1937 World Series against the New York Giants. Gomez won two starts and Ruffing one as the Yankees took the Series in five games. Both Gomez and Ruffing are in the Hall of Fame.

"Tell him," Lefty replied, "to hit it on the dry side."

His refusal to be daunted made Gomez seem to be a young man without nerves. Yankee manager Joe McCarthy started him in the second game of the 1932 World Series against the Chicago Cubs. Lefty calmly beat them, 5-2, shutting them out over the last six innings before a crowd that filled every cranny of Yankee Stadium.

He was human, though. Sitting in his sunswept back yard, he remembers that day very well. "I wasn't nervous while the game was on," he tells you. "As soon as it was over, I showered, got dressed and hopped into my car. I was driving downtown, going merrily along when, after about a mile, it suddenly hit me. I had won a World Series game! I started to shake all over, and had to stop and rest about ten minutes."

He was to get used to that feeling, rolling up the best pitching record in World Series history—six wins, no losses. Catfish Hunter was the only active pitcher threatening Lefty's undefeated record until Cincinnati bombed him in the 1976 sweep by the Reds.

Jim Murray of the *Los Angeles Times* asked Lefty a couple years ago if he thought the record would hold up.

"Well," he replied, "I don't think I'm gonna lose any."

"Don't give me all the credit, though," Lefty tells you. "I was on clubs with some pretty good men." Indeed he was. Nine, besides himself, have already gone into the Hall of Fame—Babe Ruth, Lou Gehrig, Joe DiMaggio, Earle Combs, Red Ruffing, Herb Pennock, Waite Hoyt, Bill Dickey and manager Joe McCarthy.

The roster of the '37 Yankees featured five of those Hall of Famers. Some New York sportswriters, looking for a new angle to write about, took to speculating that second baseman Tony Lazzeri was the backbone of the team. He was the smartest player in baseball, they wrote, a player who always did the right thing instinctively.

The club was breezing along in first place when suddenly, as will happen even to immortals, the team went into a slump. They lost a few games in a row and were starting to tighten up when up came Lefty's turn to pitch.

The situation called for a touch of Gomez to loosen them up. With a man on first base, the batter hit a one-bouncer back to Lefty. He gloved it, turned, saw shortstop Frank Crosetti approaching second base, and calmly threw the ball to Lazzeri, standing halfway between first and second. Lazzeri, startled, walked the ball to the mound. "What the hell did you do that for?" he growled, obviously edgy.

"I been reading about how you're the smartest ballplayer on this club, and I wanted to see what you'd do with that one," quipped Gomez.

Manager McCarthy asked Gomez the same question when he came up out of the dugout. "There are too many Italians on this team," Gomez told him with a straight face. "I saw Crosetti and Lazzeri and got confused."

For once, Gomez was topped. Pointing out to center field, McCarthy replied: "It's lucky you didn't see DiMaggio."

That and other Gomez pecadillos kept the Yankees loose and they went on to win the pennant easily. In that year's World Series, against the Giants, Gomez was pitching at the Polo Grounds when he pulled another stunt that demonstrated nobody was going to wrest the El Goofy title from him by default.

In a late inning, the Giants got a couple men on base. The great Giant slugger Mel Ott, who had already hit a Gomez fastball into the stands for a homer, came to the plate. Ott was the potential winning run. Gomez, a fanatic about aviation, called "time" and calmly delayed the World Series while he watched an intrepid pilot fly low over the ballpark. When he disappeared over the clock in center field, Lefty threw three fastballs for strikes.

Any keen observer could have spotted signs of Lefty's potential as a true flake even before he came up to the big leagues. "When I was a rookie in the minors, I watched all the good hitters as they went to the plate, and decided to copy their habits. Came my turn to bat, I swaggered toward the box. I pulled at my cap, then spit on my hands and wiped them on my pants. Then I lifted one foot and swung the bat to knock the dirt out of my cleats. I missed my shoe, cracked my ankle, and was in a hospital for a week."

Maybe he couldn't hit, but *mama mia,* could he pitch! He was chosen to start the very first All-Star game in 1933, and was the American League's starting pitcher in five of the first six All-Star shindigs. You don't get an honor like that on your clippings.

There were, of course, other great pitchers in the league during that period. Cleveland's Bobby Feller, for one. He had a blazing fastball that intimidated even the top sluggers because Bobby was a wee bit on the wild side.

One day Gomez was pitching against Feller in Cleveland. Late in the afternoon, huge black clouds rolled in from Lake Erie. It got darker and darker, and in those days ballparks had no lighting systems. The Yankees asked umpire Bill Summers to call "time" lest one of them, in those pre–batting helmet days, get skulled. Summers refused.

When Lefty's turn at bat arrived, he approached the plate slowly, holding one arm behind him. As he stepped into the batter's box, he held out what he'd been hiding: a lantern.

Summers got the point and called "time."

In 1939, Lefty suffered a back injury. Trying to help the Yankees win the pennant again, which they did, he altered his pitching motion to minimize the back pains, and came up with a sore arm. Though he hung on for another three years, his days of glory as a flame-throwing left-hander were over.

Even during those last few years, when he very understandably might have worried about his future and bemoaned his fate, Lefty took it upon himself to keep tensions on the club at a minimum.

Shortstop Phil Rizzuto's first game as a Yankee came on opening day of the 1941 season. Yankee Stadium was jammed. Gomez was the starting pitcher, and realized the rookie had never seen, no less played in front of 70,000 howling fans.

Before the first pitch, he waved Rizzuto in toward the mound. As Phil approached, Lefty asked: "Is your mother here?"

"Yeah, sure," Rizzuto said nervously. "Come on. Let's go."

"Wait a minute," Gomez told him. "Just stand here. She'll be proud of you. She'll think you're giving advice to the great Gomez."

Rizzuto laughed, turned and trotted back to his position, his rookie jitters abated. They didn't get him out of the lineup for another 13 years.

Three rooms at the Gomez home today are filled with autographed pictures, bats, balls, gloves and awards, plus mementos of June's stage career on

Broadway and photos of their seven grandchildren. Lefty is obviously a happy man. One reason may be that while he probably couldn't rip a Kleenex with his fastball, his mind is still as quick on the uptake as a hot rod.

Getting up to go after the afternoon of rapping about old times and old friends, you mention one of the current big league flakes, Mark Fidrych, and idly wonder if Lefty ever talked to the ball.

"Lots of times," he says.

"What did you say to it?" you ask.

"Go foul, you bastard, go foul!"

You're satisfied as you drive away. Time has not withered nor custom staled the talents of Vernon "Lefty" Gomez, baseball's vintage flake.

[1977]

Reggie's Moment Arrived in the '77 World Series

BY JOE McGUFF

At the time Reggie Jackson was seeking a new place of employment in baseball in 1976, he talked about the possibility of having a candy bar named after him if he played in New York, thereby following in the tradition of Babe Ruth.

Jackson's ego is better than his facts. Contrary to common belief, the Baby Ruth candy bar was not named after the baseball slugger. It was named after President Grover Cleveland's daughter, the first baby ever born in the White House. Jackson's critics have suggested that it would be more appropriate to have a hot dog named after him, but in this instance Reggie's ambitions proved to be much too modest.

In the sixth and decisive game of the 1977 World Series, Jackson hit home runs his last three times at bat and drove in five runs to enable the Yankees to defeat the Dodgers, 8-4. The Series came to an end at 10:44 p.m., and if a vote had been taken at that moment in New York the chances are excellent the natives would have been willing to rename the entire city after Reggie. They might even have thrown in Staten Island as a bonus.

"I'm not Joe DiMaggio," Jackson said in the champagne-soaked Yankee dressing room. "I'm not Babe Ruth. Those guys were great, great baseball players."

However, in this instance Jackson surpassed DiMaggio and entered his name in the record books along with that of Ruth, who is the only other player to hit three homers in a World Series game. The Babe did it twice, first in 1926 and again in 1928. The fact that baseball had gone almost half a century without witnessing such a performance attests to the magnitude of Jackson's accomplishment.

His first home run came in the fourth inning with Thurman Munson aboard and gave the Yankees a 4-3 lead. His second came in the fifth with Willie Randolph on base and made the score 7-3. For his encore Jackson walloped a Charlie Hough knuckleball into the unused seats in center field.

"It was a knuckleball low and away," said Tom Lasorda, the Dodger manager. "They say he hit it 475 feet. That's amazing."

The exact distance the ball traveled is a matter of guesswork, of course, but it was hit so high and so far that the only one who could have caught it was the Great Dodger in the Sky.

Each of the homers was hit on the first pitch. Jackson had four home runs in his last four official at bats. He homered in the eighth inning of the fifth game in Los Angeles and walked his first time up in the final game at Yankee Stadium.

There were other elements to the Yankee victory besides Jackson's home runs. Mike Torrez went all the way and pitched a nine-hitter to gain his second Series victory. Chris Chambliss accounted for two runs with a homer, and Lou Piniella drove in another run with a sacrifice fly. But when baseball fans replay the 1977 World Series in years to come it will be remembered as the Series where Reggie Jackson hit the home runs.

After going through the ritual of a post-game champagne dousing, Jackson stood in his locker with his father, Martinez, beside him while reporters crowded around him straining to catch his words.

Jackson talked about the fact that he thought of DiMaggio and Ruth when he hit his homers.

"DiMaggio is a living legend," Jackson said. "The Yankee Clipper. I know he has been pulling for me. He came over to the dugout tonight when he threw out the first ball."

Jackson was asked what would have happened if he had followed his father's trade and become a tailor.

"I'd have been super just like my dad," he laughed.

Jackson said that at times in the 1977 season, he wondered if he had made the right decision in joining the Yankees, where he became a center of controversy.

"There were times when I was disappointed and hurt and felt sorry for myself like anyone would," he said. "Someone up there is looking out for me. I'm not that good."

Ironically, Jackson was benched in the fifth game of the American League playoff series with the Royals and his place in right field was taken by Paul Blair. Jackson was upset, and there was speculation at the time

He struck out a lot and was a mediocre fielder, but Reggie Jackson was admittedly "the straw that stirred the drink" when he played for the Yankees. His three consecutive homers, each on the first pitch from three different Dodger hurlers, in Game 6 of the 1977 World Series, made great theater for eyewitnesses.

that, had the Yankees lost, the move might have cost Billy Martin his job as manager. Jackson went 1-for-6 in the first two games of the World Series, and Blair won the first game in the 12th inning with a single after being inserted for defensive purposes. In the last four games Jackson was 8-for-13.

"After the second game you could roll the ball up to the plate and I couldn't hit it," Jackson said.

He attributed his sudden turn-around to some advice from Fran Healy, the Yankees' No. 3 catcher, and at one point during his lengthy interview he called for Healy to join him.

Healy said Jackson's problem stemmed from the fact he was trying so hard to hit home runs that he was opening up his right shoulder and committing himself too soon. As a result he was not making contact often and when he did he had little power.

"A guy like Reggie is expected to hit home runs," said Healy, who played with the Royals from 1973–75 and part of 1976. "I studied him when I was at Kansas City and played against him. Reggie is like most guys. When you hit a home run you want to start driving the ball even more. When you swing harder you open up too fast and the bat has slowed down by the time you make contact.

"Reggie Jackson is an excellent hitter. I had been watching him and saw what he was doing. Reggie is the sort of player who, when you mention something, is willing to listen.

"In batting practice tonight he didn't pull off the ball one time. He really hit some long balls. One was almost up against the back wall.

"The Royals pitched Reggie inside in Kansas City and went away from him here. He's so strong that in this park you can jam him and he'll still hit the ball out. Paul Splittorff pitched him away the last game in Kansas City. Paul is a very smart pitcher. The Kansas City pitching is very underrated. Leonard is one of the finest young pitchers I've ever seen. Whitey Herzog is an excellent handler of pitchers. If anyone says he made bad moves that last game they don't know what they're talking about."

In addition to his total of five homers, Jackson also set records for the post-season classic by scoring ten runs and collecting 25 total bases, credentials enough for his being named the Most Valuable Player of the Series.

[1978]

Ted Williams Goes Back to Where It All Began

BY CHARLES MAHER

"Come on," said Ted Williams. "I'm taking you back to where it all started."

It was early morning at a resort 25 miles north of San Diego, California. Williams had flown in from Florida to film a segment of a syndicated TV show, "Greatest Sports Legends."

In the opening scene he and Tom Seaver, host of the show, were leaving the clubhouse at Rancho La Costa to start a half-hour drive to San Diego's Hoover High School. That's where it all started for Ted Williams. That's where professional baseball discovered him 40 years ago.

At 59 the Splendid Splinter still looked splendid enough, though hardly like a splinter. He was up to 245 pounds, more than 50 over his best playing weight, and most of the surplusage was situated at one of his favorite fastball elevations: belt high. But the face had weathered well and the voice still had that cocksure crackle.

The TV cast and crew headed south in several cars, one shared by Williams, Seaver, two members of the production company and a reporter. As they pulled away from La Costa, somebody mentioned Joe McCarthy, one of Williams' managers at Boston.

"Dear old guy," Williams said. "Got a broken hip now. But he's some kind of guy. Ninety years old! Always believed in drinking liquor instead of beer. He used to say, 'That beer will go to your legs.'

"I called him one day when I was managing at Washington. I'd get into a situation and sometimes call to ask him about it. I told him, 'You know, I'm gaining weight in this damn business. I get home and I eat and I eat and I eat.' It's kind of a nervous reaction, you know. And he said, 'You're lucky. When we lost I used to drink and drink and drink.' Oh, he couldn't stand it. Losing. It was the third year, I guess, he started to drink. But he quit."

In a moment, several decades passed. Williams was talking about one of today's players.

"You know," he said, "the least impressive guy I've seen hit in the National League, and he's a hell of a player but I don't like his style at all, is Garvey. Don't like his style any at all. He swings down at the ball. But he's stronger than hell."

"That's why he hits," Seaver said. "He takes this ball right here and hits it about four inches from his hands and gets a single over the second baseman."

"I'd pitch away from him," Williams said, "and then back him away and give him plenty of breaking stuff. You know, that guy is a dangerous son of a bitch."

Inevitably, somebody asked about Joe DiMaggio.

"I've always said he was the greatest player I saw," Williams said. "He did it smoothly with power and finesse. And I admire him now even more than I did as a player because he's conducting himself so great. He's a hell of a nice man. Great guy."

"Could DiMaggio run in the same class with Mays?" Seaver asked.

"No, I don't think he could run quite as spectacularly as Mays," Williams said. "But he could probably run from first to third as good. Well, not quite, but close. Mays was truly a great one. But DiMaggio was a better hitter. You could pitch to Mays. And then again you've got to give it to him. I was in about 12 All-Star games with Mays and every time he had to get on base he got on."

"Amazing man," Seaver said.

"But he wasn't near as good a hitter as DiMaggio," Williams said. "Not in my book."

Somebody mentioned Mickey Mantle and Seaver remembered he got to pitch against him in an All-Star game, late in Mantle's career, and struck him out with three fastballs. "It was sad," Seaver said, "but it was a beautiful experience for me."

"I'll bet the air flew," Williams said.

"Bet your ass," Seaver said. "And it was the same with two strikes and with no strikes and one strike, baby. He wasn't going to cut down his swing. He took his three hacks."

"That's what happens," Williams said disapprovingly. "See, they don't concede [by cutting down] with two strikes. That's the key. You got to concede with two strikes. Is this the school?"

This was the school.

"Altogether different-looking school than when I was here," Williams said. "The auditorium was over there."

The party proceeded to the baseball field. Ted Williams Field. They weren't ready to start shooting yet so Williams walked over to look at the football field. A television reporter grabbed him for an interview.

"You know," Williams said, "the reason I came to Hoover was because I thought I could make the team. It was smaller than San Diego High. There were only two high schools in San Diego and I lived right on the borderline. I got to Hoover and I was always glad I did because my high school days were enjoyable and will live forever with me, of course. It's just great to be back here today to see it."

Williams did seem to be enjoying himself. He is sometimes abrupt, often impatient. But he would be spending about six hours on location at the old school, doing some scenes several times, and there would be no displays of temperament.

Williams was back on the baseball field now, and they were ready to shoot. "Seven-oh-two," somebody said. "Take one."

Seaver (on camera): "You weren't a real big strong kid, were you?"

Ted Williams began his pro career with the San Diego Padres of the Pacific Coast League in 1936, shortly after he graduated from Hoover High School in San Diego. After the 1937 season, his contract was purchased by the Boston Red Sox.

Williams: "No. As a matter of fact, when I signed up to play for the San Diego Padres [of the Coast League] just out of high school, I remember the paper said that I was 6-foot-3½ and I weighed 147 pounds. No, I'm sorry. They said 155 pounds and I weighed 147. I said, 'Boy, if only I weighed 155.' But then I started coming up every year, 6, 8, 10 pounds."

Seaver: "Did you play left field here?"

Williams: "I was a pitcher here. You didn't know that?"

Seaver: "Were you any good?"

Williams: "Well, I want to tell you . . . I signed [with the Padres] as a pitcher-outfielder. *Pitcher*-outfielder."

Seaver: "Pitcher first, then outfielder?"

Williams: "Well, I'm not sure about that. But I did pitch a little in the Coast League, and I got knocked around a little. I had done some pinch-hitting and I got a few hits and before I knew it I was put in the outfield."

There was a break and then: "Seven-oh-two, apple. Take one."

Seaver: "The first time you got called up to the big leagues—you remember that?"

Williams: "Yes, and I was disappointed that I'd been sold to the Red Sox [by San Diego] because, you know, you heard about the Yankees, the Giants, Detroit. Those were big teams in those days. Boston was just on the build. I knew nothing about them, and Boston to me didn't seem the right place to go. And then I went to spring training that year in Sarasota, Florida, 1938. And I wasn't there very long. I happened to make a little remark to Joe Cronin, the manager, and he didn't particularly like that. I asked him if I was on the bus to go to Bradenton or Clearwater or something and he said, 'Look at the bulletin board and find out.' And I said, 'OK, sport,' and that didn't go over too good. But I wasn't destined to be a member of the team that year because they had a great outfield."

There were no classes at Hoover High the day Williams came back. But the baseball team made an appearance. The TV company needed extras. Otherwise there were few students around. But some of Williams' old school friends were there. And they were planning to round up more for a dinner party that evening.

"How about Boonie?" one asked.

"Boonie?" Williams said. "Ray Boone? Sure. Get him."

"Roll sound, please. Seven-oh-three. Take one."

Seaver: "Nineteen forty-one. Probably the most phenomenal year anyone has ever had in baseball."

Williams: "I have to think I had the league betwixt and between. They didn't know whether to pitch me high or low. They didn't know what to do. The league was made to order for me then. I knew the pitchers. I was stronger. I had more confidence. And, again, I had everybody in doubt. 'How do you pitch to this guy?' It took a long time for them to get a defense against me. And I had holes. Gee, I look back now. I had holes that I never had from '46 on when I was strictly a pull hitter and everybody ganging up on me [by shifting the infield]."

When they put the "Sports Legend" show together for distribution in spring, they'll work in film clips. So if Williams and Seaver are talking about 1941, the viewer will see footage from that season. Maybe from the last day. Williams remembered the Red Sox had a doubleheader with the A's that day. His average had fallen below .400. It had been 10 years since anybody hit that high. But the prospect of having another .400 hitter aroused less anticipation than it would today.

Williams: "At the time I didn't even feel the importance of it. Nevertheless . . . I wanted to hit .400."

Seaver: "What did you do in the first game?"

Williams: ". . . Well, the first time up I hit a line drive between first and second. And that relieved a lot of tension. I got 3-for-4 in that game and was well over .400."

Seaver: "You could have sat down."

Williams: "Yeah. But I really didn't even think about that. Joe asked me about it. Joe Cronin. And I told him I wanted to play. And then I got three more hits. Not a bad day."

He finished at .406. That was 37 years ago. Thousands have tried but no one has batted .400 since. The filming went from mid-morning to mid-afternoon and Roy Engle watched it all. Engle was graduated from Hoover a semester ahead of Williams. Then he played football at USC. He won three letters as a running back and was co-captain in 1940. After the war he was backfield coach at USC. Then he coached at what is now UC Santa Barbara and returned to Hoover High in 1953. He has been football coach there most of the time since but is going into retirement now.

"Ted and I just sort of grew up together," Engle told a reporter.

"What sort of kid was he?" the reporter asked.

"Well," Engle said, "just the kind you see out there now. Enthusiastic. He just loved to play baseball all the time. He had kind of a—well, I don't know if I should say he had a bad home life. He didn't have any home life. His dad was gone. His mother was probably the biggest fund-raiser the Salvation Army ever had, so she was busy, and Ted just kind of drifted between pillar and post. We used to play a game at University Heights."

"A playground?"

"Yeah. They used to have handball courts. It was kind of like that batting cage there only they had a wooden wall to hit the ball against. We played a baseball game where if you hit that middle bar and the other guy didn't catch it, you got a home run. And if you hit up there it was a triple and . . . we would play that game on holidays and weekends and in the summertime till we couldn't walk home, we'd be so exhausted. We were kind of playground bums, I guess you'd say. Ted was a kid who said he was going to be a big league baseball player, and that's about all Ted Williams ever thought about."

"When did he say it?"

"It wasn't that he was always saying it. But that's all he ever lived for. His actions told you. You can tell Ted is a pretty intelligent person. And yet when he went to high school, hell, classes didn't mean anything to him. He'd just do enough so he would be eligible to play baseball."

"What sort of guy was he temperamentally?"

"Well, I don't think he was quite as flamboyant as he is now. But I remember one time. We had sort of a short right-field fence here then and every time Ted came up they used to walk him. He threw his gear on the coach's desk one day and said, 'I'm not going to play anymore. All I do is walk. I'm not playing baseball to walk.' And he left. I've often wondered what would have happened if somebody hadn't gone and dragged him back. What a terrible thing that would have been. But he never got out of the gym, I don't think."

"Did the kids in school here then recognize he was going to be an extraordinary professional athlete?"

"Yes, I think so," Engle said. "At the time there weren't all these scouts around, watching everybody. I can't remember anybody being signed then. And yet here Ted goes right out of high school and plays for the Padres in Triple-A baseball."

"How about the kids here now? Is there a real awareness of who Ted Williams was?"

"Well, we had it in the bulletin. And I asked my class, 'Do you guys know who Ted Williams is?' And one student says, 'Yeah, he works for Sears.'" (Williams is chairman of the Sears sports advisory staff. His name appears on a line of recreational equipment.)

A life-size photograph of Williams, taken in his first season with the Red Sox, was once on display at the school. But it was removed during reconstruction and has lately been in a storage room. It was brought out, though, the day Williams returned.

The TV company broke for lunch in early afternoon and Williams sat in the third-base dugout, eating a McDonald's hamburger and drinking a Coke.

It was time to go back to work.

There were maybe a couple of dozen kids and adults watching the filming now. Out beyond right field, a bunch of kids were playing touch football, paying no heed to the TV production.

"Stand by, please. Roll sound. Seven-oh-eight. Take 2."

Seaver: "Ted, you got back [from the service] for part of the '53 season. You were not a young man . . ."

Williams: "I was happy the way I did the end of '53. Fifty-four, '55 and '56 I don't really remember what I did. But '57 was a hell of a year."

Seaver: "That was one of the incredible years of any professional athlete. You were 38 years old at the time, right? You hit what?"

Williams: "Well, I hit .388. And I was only six hits away that year from hitting .400 again."

Seaver: "If you could have run just a little bit you would have hit .400."

Williams: "Just a little bit better."

Seaver: "So you have that great year, hit .388, and now you get up to 1960 and you've got to start thinking about retirement."

Williams: "That's right. In 1960 I had a pretty good year. I ended up with 29 home runs and I ended up hitting .316. I didn't play second games of doubleheaders but I played all the rest."

Seaver: "Tell me about your last time at bat."

Williams: "Well, I'll tell you, that had to be . . . "

Seaver and Williams were walking away from the cameras, talking into vest microphones, and only the sound man could hear them. But Williams talked about it between scenes:

"It was so damn dark that day. Holy cripes, it was dark. It was a windy, wet, misty day. I got the count to 2-and-0 and the pitcher—Jack Fisher of Baltimore—threw a fastball, a beautiful ball to hit. And how I missed it— I don't know yet how I missed it. I know he thought he threw it by me. I still don't think he did. Anyway, he couldn't wait to get the sign and fire another one, you know, and there it was, in the same place."

And, in his last at-bat, Ted Williams touched them all.

Seaver: "After you were in retirement for a while you went back as manager of the Washington Senators and you were named manager of the year one year."

Williams: "Well, I don't know yet how I got involved with that, but a very persuasive fellow named Bob Short bought the Senators and I guess he influenced me enough to try my hand at it. It was quite an experience, managing a major league ball club. I certainly learned a lot of things managing that eluded me as a player. Those years had their ups and downs so far as emotional feelings were concerned, because, boy, when you lose as a manager you feel like pretty near everything is on your back. If I had it to do over again I'd probably do it, but I'll tell you I don't want any more of it."

They were starting to load up the cameras when Williams stepped into the batter's box to take a few swings against one of the Hoover High kids. It looked like the same old swing, replayed at about three-quarters speed.

On about the third or fourth pitch there was a sharp crack. The ball flew toward right field, cleared the high fence there and landed in a street maybe 350 feet from home plate. That ended a rather prolonged slump. Ted Williams hadn't hit a home run at Hoover High in 40 years.

[1978]

When Gabby Hartnett Hit His Homer in the Gloamin'

BY JOHN P. CARMICHAEL

Even as a boy of 12, Gabby Hartnett couldn't run. Almost every other kid in Millville, Massachusetts, where he grew up, could beat him. He wasn't built for speed. Once he singled off the right field wall in Brooklyn's Ebbets Field and was almost thrown out at first.

In his debut as a Cub, he was sent up to pinch-hit in St. Louis and belted one to left-center in old Sportsman's Park. As the ball caromed along the fence, Gabby fell down between first and second, got up and chugged all the way to third. "If it had been anybody else he'd have been out of the shower and dressed for the street," admitted the brawny Irishman.

So that was his cross, but he bore it lightly through all those years as a Cubs stalwart, and the red-faced catcher didn't even have to run at all when it came down to exploiting the greatest year, the greatest day, the greatest moment of his career at Wrigley Field on a late September day in 1938. It was the culmination of a lifetime of happiness for the erstwhile Mr. Cub. He won in a walk!

The Cubs had won pennants in 1929, 1932 and 1935, although losing the World Series to the A's, Yanks and Tigers in those years, and now they were in the thick of another race as the year drifted into July with the veteran Charlie Grimm in command. A Pirate team that had power but shaky pitching maintained a steady lead with the Cubs pressing, but began to waver just a bit. The veteran Dizzy Dean was bravely lending his fading arm to the cause.

Suddenly, on July 20 of '38, there came a moment of decision. Owner Phil Wrigley decided on a change of command to see if he could give the club a finishing kick, as he said afterwards, to take some of the pressure off Grimm. The new manager was destined to be Billy Jurges, the peerless shortstop. On short notice, Bill was summoned to the Wrigley offices and offered the job.

With scant hesitation, Jurges turned it down. He said he thought he had a lot of playing time left and didn't want to compromise it with trying to manage, too. Virtually in the same breath, Billy told Wrigley: "Hartnett is your man. He's been a Cub for 16 years. The fans love him. He's the only man right now who can take over and he deserves first consideration." Wrigley smiled and asked one more man: Grimm himself. He voted for Hartnett too, and the die was cast for the remaining ten weeks of the campaign. Nobody could foresee what a long, final stand that would be.

With Gabby at the helm, the protracted struggle continued, nip and tuck, prolonged by a strategic maneuver by the new manager which turned the pennant tide around. In mid-September the Cubs were playing the Dodgers a twin bill in Brooklyn and lost the first game, 4-2. But they were leading by two runs in the nightcap despite a steady rain and impending darkness. Suddenly, the Dodgers tied the score in the fifth.

The game had to be called, ending in a tie. The Cubs were 3½ games out at the time and were booked in Philly the next day, so they couldn't stay over and play the tie off. But Larry MacPhail, then Dodger boss,

Gabby Hartnett of the Cubs heads for the plate at Wrigley Field after hitting his famous "homer in the gloamin'" that helped edge the Pirates for the pennant on September 28, 1938.

wanted to play it at the end of the Cubs-Phillies series, when there was an open traveling date. Gabby said he'd think it over. The Cubs wanted to do it, because they figured they could win and keep picking up ground on the Pirates.

"It was a tough thing to decide," Hartnett always maintained afterwards, "but I had figured it out that we had to beat the Pirates those last three games to win, and I had to think of my pitchers. I had to argue with all the players . . . they wanted to go back to Ebbets Field and play off the rainout." Finally, Hartnett stuck his neck out and said no. It was a touchy decision, because the Cubs could just as easily go back to Brooklyn and lose the game. So Gabby took the chance.

What happened then was the Cubs sat for three days in Philadelphia and watched it rain. Pittsburgh, moving into Brooklyn, couldn't play there either and remained three and one-half games in front. Finally the sun came out in Philly and the Cubs won a pair, 4-0 and 2-1, with Bill Lee and Clay Bryant the winning hurlers. But the Pirates also beat the Dodgers twice. The next day the Cubs won another double-header in Philly and the Reds beat the Bucs. Now the margin was only two games.

So that hesitant choice of Hartnett's to pass up Brooklyn had borne luscious fruit and the Cubs came home having gained good ground. They beat the Cardinals two straight while the Pirates also won a game. Now the lead was only one and one-half games. Again Gabby bowed his neck by starting

Dean in the opener of the Pirates series. He always said later, "I didn't mind sticking my neck out, because I had faith in ol' Diz. I knew he had guts. He wouldn't quit, and I'd made up my mind that if Dean got into any trouble, I'd come and get him.

"Well, we got out in front on a triple by Rip Collins and a single by Jurges and for five innings Diz went great. Then I thought he began to tire, just a bit. He didn't seem to have much on the ball, even though he was getting such tough guys as the Waner brothers and Arky Vaughan out."

Dean got by the seventh and eighth, still wavering, and Hartnett started Lee warming up in the bullpen. Bill wasn't an extra-good relief pitcher, but he was the best pitcher the Cubs had and this was a spot for the best. So, in he came with two outs in the ninth, and the tying runs on third and second, and catcher Al Todd up. He fouled one off. The next pitch was a strike. Then Lee cut loose with a wild pitch and the man from third scored.

There might not have been a glory day for Gabby if Todd had driven the tying run in from third, but he didn't. He struck out, the Cubs won, 2-1, and awaited the morrow just a half-game out of first place.

This has been a rather detailed preamble leading up to the Cubs' quest of the Holy Grail, but it had been a long, long upward climb for Hartnett and one he never would make again. Once he was telling me: "I couldn't sleep. I'd sit down to a meal and see Paul and Lloyd Waner sitting on the steak. I'd think to myself: 'Oh if Dean was only the man of '34, I could stick him right back in.' I begged the Lord that night to please let us get four-five runs early and that I'd help Him take it from there. Then I'd doze off awhile."

But the big day dawned, as they inexorably do. This was destined to go down in history as one of those "D" Days that come along once in a lifetime for the lucky ones to watch or take part in. Little Bill Benswanger, the Pittsburgh owner, came along, pushing his way through an obstreperous crowd, trying to reach his seat and pausing to say: "You guys won't win this one. It just can't happen again." He had already built extra seats in Forbes Field back home for the World Series.

Then it was time to play, time for the countdown, time for doing or dying. It was an overcast afternoon, which posed a threat of possible curtailment.

A couple of errors aided the Cubs to a lone run in the second inning, but the Pirates went ahead with three in the sixth. The Cubs got away with a tie score in the bottom half, but once again the Bucs took a 5-3 lead in the top of the eighth. In the Cub half, Collins opened with a single and Jurges walked. Tony Lazzeri, the great Yankee second baseman of yesteryear, batted for Lee and doubled, scoring Collins. Stan Hack walked and Billy Herman scored Jurges with the tying run on a double.

The game might have ended then, with no last-ditch heroics, but Joe Marty, who had been sent in to run for Lazzeri, was thrown out at the plate, just before a double play ended the inning.

It was pretty dark by this time, and the umpires took stock of the situation. There were no lights to be turned on, so they agreed to go one more inning and then, if still tied, call the game and play a double-header the next afternoon. Charlie Root got the Pirates out in the ninth, and it was the last time around for the Cubs. Phil Cavarretta led off with a screamer to center that Lloyd Waner pulled down. Carl Reynolds grounded out, and up to the plate strode Hartnett, a Colossus of Rhodes in the twilight, unaware that a kindly fate was perched on his shoulder.

That's how Carl Hubbell, the Giant southpaw, used to view Gabby. "He was the toughest man I ever faced," said Carl. "Oh, I got him out my share of times, but he always scared me, just standing there, twisting sawdust out of a bat with his bare hands."

Hartnett swung once at a Mace Brown curve and missed. He got a piece of the next one, but fouled. Then came another outside curve and Gabby swung with everything he had in him.

"I got that feeling you get when the blood rushes to your head and you get dizzy," he always said. The ball soared outward and onward. In legend, it may still be going, but it really came down in the bleachers. Not everybody saw it in the gloaming, or knew where it landed. But Gabby claimed he did from the second he hit it.

There are a lot of stories told about this homer. But it was so real then that by the time Gabby turned second base, there were players and fans mobbing one another over behind third, waiting to escort Hartnett all the way home. He could hardly walk, let alone run, through the delirious fans. ("I was just carried along," he said). But he could see umpire George Barr standing at the plate, to make sure Gabby stepped on it.

So there's the story again. That home run broke the Pirates' backs as the Cubs took the next two games and the pennant. The immortal Hartnett had just walked with the gods, never to retrace his steps.

Epilogue: The Cubs lost the World Series to the Yankees in four straight, and that winter Hartnett traded Jurges to the New York Giants for Dick Bartell. So the man who might have been the manager of the Cubs instead of Gabby, had he wanted the job, now scouts for the Seattle Mariners and lives with his wife, Mary, maybe dreaming now and then of what might have been.

[1978]

The Bat: A Hitter's Most Prized, Pampered Possession

BY THOMAS BOSWELL

Ever since the first caveman picked up the first cudgel, went to his front door and smacked the first nosy saber-toothed tiger in the snout, mankind has known the atavistic power and pleasure of the bat.

From Robin Hood's quarterstaff to Paul Bunyan's axe, men of myth have loved the taper of a handle, the texture of wood grain, the centrifugal surge in the end of a whirling mass.

Axes and stout staves have dwindled in everyday use. Now that ancient inherited desire for thudding force, for an instrument that will deliver a satisfying blow, has descended to the baseball bat.

What familiar sensation in sports is so universal as the pursuit of the perfect bat—the Old Ash, the Lumber, the Good Wood? From the office softball game to the World Series, who settles for the first weapon out of the rack?

Few things feel so annoying as the wrong bat. If it is too short or light, the frail thing seems unworthy of us, almost an insult. If it is too long or heavy, however, it is the bat's fault, not our own lack of strength. "Unwieldy," we say.

"When a bat feels just right, the balance is so perfect that it almost feels weightless," said Baltimore star Ken Singleton. "I've looked all my life for a bat that felt as good as the broom handles I used to play stickball with as a kid in the Bronx.

"I never have."

Call it "My Soul Pole" like Baltimore's Al Bumbry, or "My Business Partner," as New York's Jay Johnstone does, the bat is the most pampered, coddled, protected and defended piece of equipment in baseball.

"If you wanna rumble, just touch my lumber," says Boston's George Scott.

Of all the inanimate objects in sports—the balls and boots, gloves and goals, helmets and harness—none is so intensely personal, so surrounded by lore as the ubiquitous Louisville Slugger.

Few things look so similar yet hold such vital, almost mysterious qualities as a barrel full of big league bats.

"Every one feels different, even two bats of the same model," said Yankee Roy White, one of the many players who swear they can tell if a stick is a half-ounce off specifications.

"I once went five-for-five with five different bats. I kept switching 'cause none of them felt just right. After I got to three-for-three, I said, 'Maybe I better keep switching.'"

Tommie Agee, former New York Met, once got the same notion on a grander scale, using 22 different bats on a 22-game hitting streak. "Worst hitting streak in history—23 hits in 22 days," related Singleton, then a Met. "Agee was actually in a slump, but he kept switching bats every day."

Some of the most infamous bats are unmarked or else have phony monikers. These are the outlaw breed.

"Sure, there are guys who will 'fix' a bat for you," says Yankee Graig Nettles. "When it comes back, it's like a Mafia hit gun . . . no serial numbers."

Four years ago, Nettles shattered his bat while hitting a routine fly ball against Detroit. Out of the demolished barrel bounced six ultra-resilient, ultra-illegal Super Balls.

"Bill Freehan was catching and he dashed all over the place collecting the evidence," said Nettles sheepishly, thinking of those tiny black toys that even children can whack over tall buildings bouncing around home plate.

"I guess Bill thought they'd put me before a firing squad."

Nettles, however, knew the rules. Illegal bat equals automatic out. Nothing more. "What the hell," said Nettles to Freehan, "I was out anyway."

Many a well-loved bat is not made entirely of wood. Ted Kluszewski, Cincinnati batting coach, was so strong that he embedded tenpenny nails in his bat barrel for contraband oomph.

Many a big leaguer has a "corked" bat or two for special occasions. Or maybe for every occasion.

"Cork a bat?" says Baltimore manager Earl Weaver. "Easiest thing in the world. Hollow out the barrel with a drill. Fill it with cork. Put the plug end back in and seal it with plastic wood. You can't spot a good job with a magnifying glass. You gotta saw 'em up to find anything."

But Weaver, of course, has never used one of the nefarious instruments?

"Never used one?" Weaver snorted. "I played on a team at New Orleans in the minors where every bat on the club was corked.

"I hit six homers that season . . . every one of 'em in the one month before they found us out.

"The umpires raided our clubhouse like they were the Untouchables. They destroyed the bats in public, right on the field.

"I wanted to cry."

Have the Orioles ever used corked bats?

"Never," said Weaver. "However, Norm Cash used to use one against us. We're sure of it.

"You can't yell 'Check his bat' every time a guy walks up to home plate. What's the umpire going to do? Carry a saw?

"If you're wrong once, then maybe they won't check him next time you cry 'Wolf.'

"But when Cash used to come up in crucial situations in the ninth, a bunch of us would all yell, 'Check his bat.'

"Norm would turn right around, walk straight back to the dugout and switch bats before anyone could touch it."

Last season, Kansas City's Hal McRae, who, along with ex-Royal John Mayberry, has long been accused of using bats that would float, had his Louisville Slugger confiscated by the umps. The authorities sawed the weapon into six pieces but found only sawdust.

"My favorite," says Nettles, "is a guy I knew in the minors who had a tube of mercury in the heart of his bat.

"Mercury's very heavy, so the tube was only partly filled. When he held the bat upright, it felt very light. But when he swung it, the centrifugal force of the mercury whipping out to the end of the bat made it swing like it weighed a ton."

What happened to Mr. Mercury?

"He never made the majors," grinned Nettles. "He had a great bat, but he couldn't hit the ball with it."

Even the universe of perfectly legal bats is far from prosaic.

Frankie Frisch hung his bats in a barn during the off-season to cure like hams.

Honus Wagner boiled his bat in creosote, while Home Run Baker never revealed the ingredients of his secret ointment.

Jimmy Frye, Baltimore batting coach and minor league batting champ, had a treatment worthy of a bush league great: Frye soaked his bats in motor oil.

Some players will even smash their favorite bat against anything in sight. "The more you crush the wood on the hitting surface, the tighter the grain," says Johnstone. "The best thing is to find a bat with a knot in the wood right in the sweet spot."

Ah, yes. Tight grain vs. wide grain. Every player has an opinion on which is better. Each has a different theory.

Regardless, when a player discovers the bat that was made in heaven for him, he guards it with his life.

"In five years I'm not sure I ever saw Ron Blomberg without his bat," exaggerates an ex-Yankee teammate. "In airplanes, hotel lobbies, I think he'd swing that thing when he was in the men's room."

"If I ever found the perfect bat," grins Johnstone, "I think I'd take it to bed with me."

Perhaps the most cherished of all bats was Jimmy Reese's ancient fungo.

Reese, a roommate of Babe Ruth and now a California coach, cut the barrel end of his fungo in half (lengthwise) so the bat was flat on one side, round on the other.

With this wand Reese could hit a fly, liner or grounder to any target inside a hundred yards. Balls thrown back to him, he would deflect with the flat side of the bat and catch harmlessly with his bare hand. Reese even "pitched" Angel batting practice by hitting fungos from the mound.

One year Reese tortured an overweight pitcher named Bill Edgerton, making him chase countless spring training fungoes that were inches beyond his straining reach.

"Edgerton left Reese's fungo in the whirlpool overnight," recalled Ray Miller, Oriole pitching coach.

"When we got to the clubhouse next morning, the thing had warped and flared out in all directions like some kind of weird flower. Jimmy just sat by the whirlpool and cried."

Ted Williams valued his bats so highly that he traveled to Louisville in the off-season, went to the factory and picked out the chunks of ash from which his splendid splinters would be dowled.

Williams' technique: drop the wood on concrete and listen for the sound.

From that day to this, a man's progress could be measured by his bats.

A busher settled for standard models. If he reached a big league training camp, his name was stamped on his bats in block letters.

When he reached the majors, the block letters turned to script, and H&B took his personal specifications. A star might get his own model number, like Reggie Jackson's recently christened RJ 288.

"I was a block-letter man," grins Baltimore's Weaver. "Still got it in the attic somewhere."

No bats, of course, compare to the bats of memory.

"It doesn't seem to me that the wood is as good as it was 30 years ago," says Weaver. "HB had a fire years ago, and I've always wondered if their best aged wood wasn't lost."

Singleton has a more unorthodox theory: "I think they've run out of good trees. Sometimes I go up to the plate with a bat that I'm sure God intended to be a chair leg."

Never say that to Brooks Robinson, the old Oriole who never met a bat he didn't like. "My garage is full of hundreds of 'em," Robinson says. "I got the last hit of my career with a bat that had hung over my mantel for 16 years.

"I took it down one night," said Robinson, giving that universal waggle of the hands that goes back to the Stone Age, "and I could feel the line drives still rattlin' around in it."

[1979]

Bob Uecker, Baseball's Rodney Dangerfield

BY BOB VERDI

It is a hopeless proposition. Bob Uecker tries to hide his emotions, but, always, bitterness gets the best of him. This syndrome is common among retired ballplayers during this crazed era of free agents, but in Uecker's case, the pain is acute.

"It tears me up," Mr. Baseball pouted one day earlier this season, moments before donning a chartreuse sports jacket for the telecast back to Milwaukee of the Brewers' game against the White Sox. "Here I am, a lousy announcer, when if I were just a little younger, I could be the object of a bidding war.

"I would play out my option, and 26 teams would be drooling. I'd probably have to take my phone off the hook. Can you imagine what the market would be for a defensive catcher who had a career lifetime average of .200? Modestly, I'd say I could command a salary of $150,000 as a backup playing 60 games. Of course, if the team I signed with was deep in catching and only needed me for 30 games, I'd be worth $200,000. Fewer games I played, less chance for me to screw things up.

"And that doesn't include all the money I could make on the side. I see Dave Kingman had a newspaper column in the *Chicago Tribune*. Well, I would do one, too. It would be strictly instructional, of course. Tips on how to put pine tar on bats, how to stay awake in the dugout during the game. Important stuff that youngsters who want to grow up like me would need to know."

Before Uecker was a hit on the "Tonight Show," he was, of course, a miss with several major league teams (the Braves, Cardinals and Phillies— 1962–67). After his best season—the one when he played the fewest games—he was awarded his best salary, $23,000. Nowadays, naturally, that is tip money.

"As much as I know that I was underpaid, though, that doesn't mean I didn't have a lot of thrills in baseball," admitted Uecker, getting sentimental now. "Probably the biggest was when I started my first game for the Braves right in my hometown of Milwaukee back in 1957. My folks, friends, everybody was there. And they were all cheering. Wasn't until the third inning that the manager pulled me aside in the dugout and said, 'Kid, you're doing good, except that up here in the big leagues, most of us wear our athletic supporter on the inside of our uniforms.'

"Then there was the time when I hit a grand slam off the Giants' Ron Herbel. The manager, Herman Franks, came out of their dugout to lift Herbel and he was carrying Herbel's suitcase. For some reason, other teams took me lightly. I remember one time I'm batting against the Dodgers in Milwaukee. They lead 2-1, it's the bottom of the ninth, bases loaded for us, two out, and the pitcher has a full count on me. I look over to the Dodgers dugout and they're all in street clothes. No respect.

"But the biggest thrill a ballplayer can have is when your son takes after you. That happened to me last summer. My Bobby was in his championship Little League game in Milwaukee. He's only 14, but he showed me something. Struck out three times and lost the game for his team when a ball went through his legs at third base.

"Parents were throwing things at our car and swearing at us as we left the

parking lot. Gosh, was I proud. A chip off the old block. I took Bobby for a big dinner that night. He was first named Sidney when we had him, but when I saw he had no coordination, we changed it to Bobby Jr.

"My other son, Steve, is a different story. He upsets me. He has talent. But he might be coming around. He went to Colorado skiing last winter and broke a leg. In time, he may become what I was. Sporting goods companies paid me to not endorse their products."

Just then, White Sox general manager Roland Hemond walked by and turned pale at the sight of Uecker talking to a reporter.

"Roland goes through life scared, you know," allowed Mr. Baseball. "He's had a fine career, but one thing nobody is aware of is that he was the guy to sign me to a first major league contract with the Braves. I can't imagine why he wouldn't be proud of that. Milwaukee signed me for a $3,000 bonus. That bothered my dad at the time, because he didn't have that kind of dough to lay out. Finally, he scraped it up and got me to leave home.

"In the end, though, the signing ceremony was one of the great athletic events in the city's history. The Braves officials took me to one of the finest restaurants. I had to have my dad with me for the occasion, but he was very nervous. He rolled down the window of the car after we were there ten minutes, and the hamburgers fell off the tray."

Being released was a traumatic experience for Uecker. Back for a second time with the Braves in 1968, he walked into the clubhouse at spring training and general manager Paul Richards kicked him out, saying no visitors were allowed. Then manager Lum Harris happened by and promised Uecker a job in the organization. Coaching second base.

"Look. I know I wasn't a great hitter," says Uecker, "but I had a theory about guys who batted .350. What did they have to look forward to? Me, I hit .180 with four RBIs every season, and they could always say I had a lot of potential. Baseball hasn't forgotten me, though. I go to Old Timers games now and I haven't lost a thing. I sit in the bullpen and let people throw junk at me. Just like old times.

"I'm a little surprised that Cooperstown hasn't gotten hold of me. I admit every year around Hall of Fame voting time, I get a little nervous. I sit by the phone waiting for the big call. I know it's coming. I'm out of the limelight now, my number's not unlisted anymore. It's in the book."

The transition to broadcasting baseball, either for the Brewers or ABC's Game of the Week, has not been easy for Uecker.

"Hardest thing I've ever had to do," he confesses. "There's a great temptation, being a former ballplayer, to be overly critical of the athletes on the field now. But I just have to catch myself sometimes. Not fair for me to expect these guys to do things the way I did them. Just not fair."

[1980]

How It Was in the Old Days
of Class "D" Baseball

BY BEN FANTON

When baseball contract time comes around and the six-figure amounts fly through the air like birds winging their way back north, it's tempting to think back to a time when your contract called for you to get paid $75 a month, a dollar a day for eating money when you were on the road, riding in an uncomfortable old bus that could and often did break down any time, and required you to hustle your butt off every day.

That was the world of Class "D" baseball the way it was played from 1942 to 1965 in Wellsville, New York, in the New York–Pennsylvania League, the oldest continually operating Class "D" league until being reclassified as class "A" in 1963.

In those days, minor league classifications were AAA, AA, A, B, C, and D. Class "D" was the lowest of the low, the bottom of the ladder. If you didn't hustle to make it there, there was nowhere else to go except back to the farm or the lunch-bucket league. And when you played baseball in

Wellsville, New York, just above the Pennsylvania border in the western part of the state, with its population of 5,800 making it the smallest town in professional baseball, you were indeed at the bottom rung looking up . . . way, way up.

For 23 summers hundreds of fresh-faced young men passed through Wellsville on their way to fame and fortune in the big leagues. Among them were Tony Conigliaro, George Scott, Charlie Silvera and Jerry Coleman.

Coleman, broadcaster, then manager, and now broadcaster for the San Diego Padres, recalls the summer he spent in Wellsville in 1942 with sincere fondness. "It was a great, great summer . . . the best I've ever had in baseball. After that, it became only a matter of winning and money became too important."

Fresh out of Lowell High in San Francisco in the summer of '42, Jerry had planned to go to USC on a baseball scholarship, but World War II came along and he decided to go to aviation school and join the service. Only 17 at the time, he had to wait until he was 18, so he made a decision to play baseball and somehow ended up in Wellsville, along with Charlie Silvera.

"That was my first trip out of California," Jerry recalls. "It took four days, two by train to Chicago and two more to Wellsville by car. I got into town at 1:30 a.m. and when we got out of the car, someone turned the lights off and that was it." To add to his inauspicious debut in the world of sports, Jerry went to the room that had been arranged for him at "Pop" Pickup's Hotel. "There was a wall fan on the wall. Someone turned it on, I proceeded to stick my finger in it and couldn't play ball for two weeks."

Coleman doesn't consider the $75 a month he was paid as being exploitative. "I rented a room for $2.50 a week and you could eat on a dollar a day back then." Although claiming to be scared to death of girls, he began dating a local attorney's daughter and remembers raiding her family's icebox a lot. "There sure wasn't much to do. There was a roller rink and one movie and that was it."

Charlie Silvera, former New York Yankees reserve catcher, now West Coast scout for the Braves, also recalls that summer with fondness: "1942 was the first year that Wellsville had a pro team and we were quite well treated by the people in the town. I remember the fans were both enthusiastic and hospitable. There were three of us who came to Wellsville from San Francisco at the same time . . . Jerry, Bob Cherry, who now owns a bar in Colorado, and me. Thinking back to that time, I can't help remembering how nice the people in Wellsville were to three young kids from California."

Typical of those who had their summer in the sun is Adam Warchal, now of Nanticoke, Pennsylvania, and also a member of the 1942 Wellsville Yankees. "After that summer, I got a broken bone in my ankle, and that

caused me to give up playing professionally," he recalls. "I went in the service for a couple of years, came home, got married, raised a family and
since have lived a wonderful but not spectacular life. I remember we traveled in a dilapidated bus to places like Lockport, Batavia, Jamestown,
Olean, Hornell and Hamilton, Ontario. We played night games, and immediately after the games we would shower and return to Wellsville to save
the management money. Because our pay was so skimpy, we didn't eat too
well or have any money left over. I got $75 a month then."

Perhaps illustrative of the hustle that was required is a story by Wellsville resident and longtime fan Paul Ryan: "I went down to a game in '42
one night. I remember it had been raining a lot that day and the field was
in bad shape. I looked out on the field and there was the groundskeeper
and two players out there working on the field, trying to get it in shape. The
two players were Charlie Silvera and Jerry Coleman: they had what it takes."

They had to have. "Professional sports can be a very cruel thing," relates
Ryan. "I watched a lot of these kids come through here over the years,
every one thinking they were going to make the big time. So few of them
did, and when they were through with baseball—or rather when baseball
was through with them—they didn't know how to do anything else. Just a
lot of wasted years."

On the lighter side, he observes that many of the players left town being very good pool players. "There wasn't a damn thing for those kids to
do during the day. Sure, they could go to the movie in the afternoon, but
once they'd seen it that was it for the week. They couldn't go swimming
. . . at least they weren't supposed to, so they'd hang around the poolroom
all afternoon. It probably wasn't much of a thrill for these kids, being in a
little town like Wellsville. They'd usually rent a room in a private home and
eat at the Marathon Restaurant, where the owner was a ball fan and would
let them run up a tab until payday. They had a deal at that restaurant
where the owner would give a free steak dinner to any player who hit a
home run. If there was a really good hitter, sometimes he'd save up the
steak dinner coupons and treat the entire team at the end of the season. It
wasn't all that difficult since there would only be fourteen or fifteen guys
on the roster.

"The managers had a really miserable job back then," Ryan continues.
"They weren't just managers. They were also the trainer, the clubhouse boy
and on top of everything else they had to drive the team bus. Most of them
were on the way down. Maybe they'd had a cup of coffee with a major
league team and had gotten to know someone in the front office. They'd
get a job with a team like Wellsville and get their retirement time in."

The financial pressures of running a professional baseball team in a
small town are recalled by Don Ludden, the last general manager before

the team pulled out in 1965. "We'd have rummage sales and special nights . . . anything we could think of. Before 1963, the major league teams we were affiliated with didn't help us out all that much. It did get better though. I think our last contract we had with Boston called for the local team to pay the first $100 of a player's salary and they'd pay the rest.

"We were always at odds with the major league team. We'd get a good player and they'd move him up to a better class of baseball. When the Yankees had the farm team here in the 1940s, there was one year when we had 75 players go through. It seemed like every train that came in would have two guys with suitcases getting on and two getting off. Finally some of the fans hung a sign on the gate of Tullar Field where we played that said, 'New York Yankee Experimental Station.'"

The local fans supported the team well, with probably the best attendance per capita of any team ever. In 1947, attendance for the 63 home games totaled 54,442, which meant that roughly one-fifth of the population was at Tullar Field on any given night during the season.

The fans lent their own color to the games. There was "Gravel Gertie," who had a loud and irritating voice that could be heard throughout the park at every game. She is also remembered for attacking, with an umbrella, an equally loud female fan who continually rang a cowbell during an away game at Wellsville's perennial rival in the league, Hornell. A witness to the event recalls that Wellsville was getting beat so badly that night that most of the Wellsville fans who'd driven over to Hornell for the game turned around and watched the fight between the two women, since there was far more action going on there than on the field. Another favorite was Paul Kneffler, who could have qualified as a professional heckler in any league for his ability to rattle visiting pitchers. He was, in fact, approached by representatives from nearby Olean to attend their games one year when they made the league playoffs and Wellsville didn't. Others included "Nasty Nate," who obtained fiendish pleasure by setting off long strings of firecrackers near the visitors' dugout and avoiding apprehension by the police, and a host of fans with animal names . . . "Wolf" Munro, "Rat" Farley, "Weasel" Weiman and "The Sacred Ox," so named because no one in town could ever recall his having done a day's work.

Real animals were often a factor at Tullar Field, with games frequently delayed because of the presence of a dog on the playing field. Team officials would try to chase the dog off the field, marveling all the while at how quickly a dog can make a turn and change directions. Local newspaperman Jim Hopkins recalls a game in 1948: "It was the strangest damn game I've ever seen. This left-hander named Lou Blackmore was pitching for Wellsville, and he pitched a no-hitter which he lost seven to three. I think he walked about 17 batters that night. He had a lot of speed and no control. I don't recall what inning it was, but it was sometime in the advanced stages of the game when a skunk wandered onto the field and started out toward the mound. Blackmore reacted exactly the way he shouldn't have and threw the baseball at it. Probably if he'd hit it, it would have created a stink, so to speak. Well, he missed the skunk and the guy I was sitting with said, 'I wasn't worried about him hitting the skunk, he hasn't been able to find home plate all night.'"

The fans were quick to vent their anger at the umpires, who sometimes found it necessary to barricade themselves in their tiny dressing room until help could be summoned. On one occasion, a group of irate fans turned the umpires' car over following a game. After righting it, the umpires, who had been scheduled to spend the night in Wellsville, wisely drove to a nearby town instead.

Professional baseball left Wellsville in 1965, a victim of increased costs and dwindling attendance, and will never make an appearance in a small town of that size again. The fans who remain know they lost something very special when it left, and they still miss it. Tullar Field is still there, used now by a local fast-pitch softball league. A few people usually sit there on a spring night and watch a bunch of aging players try to hold in their beer bellies and play this game that's so similar to baseball and yet so different. The players repeat their shouts of encouragement over and over again. "Honnowbabyhowyoushootnow!"

A bored group of stoned bikers sits on the bleachers and imitates them. "Honabobhowyoushoo!" and then they laugh and pass around a wine bottle in a paper bag.

The metallic clunk of an aluminum bat on a softball has replaced the sharp crack of wood on a baseball. But if you close your eyes and work at it, it's not difficult to imagine the scene years ago when so many young men gave it all the hustle they had for $75 a month, a dollar a day on the road for eating money, and a chance to ride in an old wreck of a bus and be called a ball player.

[1981]

Dad, How Come We Never Played Catch?

BY ANDY LINDSTROM

We never played catch together, my father and I.

You'd think he might have liked to toss a baseball around with his sons, because he was a very famous player in his time.

His picture was on bubble gum cards, sportswriters compared him to Cobb and Wagner and other demigods of our so-called national pastime, and eventually his plaque was hung in the Baseball Hall of Fame.

But by the time I came along, his career was over. One day in Brooklyn, 36 games into the National League season of 1936, he just quit. He walked off the field and never played again.

A teammate had bowled over him in pursuit of a routine fly ball. "If this is what I'm reduced to, I'm through," he said. He was only 30, a veteran of 13 major league seasons and one of the highest-paid players in the game.

But he no longer was the best.

It's still hard for me to understand how anyone simply can walk away from the game he loves. Especially someone with the talents of my father. Even in the apogee of my fourth decade, I live for the chance to kick a soccer ball around with my fellow has-beens.

But then, I will never be chosen to sit with the immortals—baseball or otherwise. And he was.

In his prime, he was fast and graceful, self-confident and brash. He could shoot clay pigeons out of the sky with a .22 rifle and watch a pitched baseball until he saw it strike his swinging bat.

It may be presumptuous to make the comparison, but he was an artist at baseball. He did with ease what the rest of us could not even comprehend. And it was a talent that never deserted him.

"It's the easiest thing in the world," I remember him telling a group of Northwestern University players one afternoon. He coached baseball at Northwestern for several years, even managing in 1957 to win the Wildcats' only Big 10 championship ever.

"You just keep your weight back until the ball is almost in the catcher's glove. Then flick it to right field behind the runner."

To the dismay of the team's star pitcher—who was throwing his hardest fastballs and trickiest curves—he drove pitch after pitch over second base between the outfielders as if the ball were on a tee.

There was a time, not many years ago, when he was invited to New York to play in an old-timers' game. White-haired and roundish in his borrowed uniform, he batted only once. But his hit was a slashing line drive off the left field wall. Then a pinch runner took his place.

Later, as we gathered around to congratulate him, he brushed us aside. "I should have hit it out," was all he would say. "The pitch was right down the pipe. I should have hit a homer."

I was too young ever to see my father play for the Giants and Cubs, the Pirates and Dodgers. I wasn't even born in 1924 when, at the age of 18, he was playing third base for the New York Giants and his high school class was just starting its senior year. I was only two in 1935 when he

Fred Lindstrom, pictured on the right as a member of the New York Giants, broke into the majors in 1924 as an 18-year-old. In a 13-year career he hit .311, played on the pennant-winning Giants in 1924 and Cubs in 1935, and was elected to the Hall of Fame in 1976 as a third baseman.

came out of the shadows of his career and led the Cubs on a 21-game tear and his second World Series.

"There was a bar on the way to Wrigley Field," my dad recalled a few years ago in one of the few glimpses into his life I ever had. I did know, however, what alcohol could do to him.

"Every day before the game, I stopped there for a whiskey and beer chaser. It got to be good luck, so I never missed. Then the Cubs traded me after we lost the Series."

Dad had dozens of stories he could have told about his years in the majors. Once or twice he hinted at scandals and fixes, at skeletons in the big-league closet. Once I asked him if we ever could sit down and record some of those events. But nothing came of it. Dad never trusted journalists—not even his own son.

I thought of those things at his funeral in suburban Chicago, just before a large man in a grey suit ushered us out of the room so he could screw down the casket cover.

He was 75, and his death was not unexpected after a series of ailments that left him weighing 127 pounds. He looked so small and frail in the fruitwood box my younger brother picked out, wearing a new black suit with his waxy-marble hands crossed on his chest.

And now my parents are buried together in a cemetery outside Chicago, next to his parents and two of his sisters. I was unable to arrive in time for my mother's wake, so I didn't really see her go.

But I made Dad's. I stood in that funeral parlor and said goodbye to a father I never played catch with. A father I really didn't see too often over the past 25 years.

The man who lay before me seemed such a far distance from the smooth-faced, almost movie-star-handsome man of his old photographs: Posing with his famous Giants' manager, John McGraw, and several men who looked like gangsters in a Havana nightclub. Signing autographs outside the Polo Grounds in a camel hair topcoat and two-toned patent leather shoes. Cavorting on a Sarasota beach with some local bathing beauties.

For several years he was the best. He was the darling of New York City's top people—politicians, socialites and gangland dons. And then, perhaps because of the applause or perhaps for other reasons, it came to a sudden end on a field in Brooklyn.

"I'm not earning my salary any more," he said simply. "I can't take the Dodgers' money when I have nothing to give in return."

Not too many fans remember him now. It has been a long time.

I found myself crying, almost out loud, at the funeral parlor, while a stoop-shouldered old man touched my elbow to tell me what a great baseball player my father had been.

Dad . . . how come we never played catch?

Editor's Note: Fred Lindstrom, who died at 75 in October 1981, was an 18-year-old rookie when Earl McNeely's bad-hop grounder bounced over his head at third base to give the Washingon Senators a 12-inning, 4-3 victory over the New York Giants in the seventh game of the 1924 World Series. Lindstrom went on to play 12 more seasons in the National League, finishing with a .311 career batting average, and was elected to the Hall of Fame in 1976. Andy Lindstrom, his son, wrote this article for the *Tallahassee Democrat*.

[1982]

Warren Spahn Names His Toughest Batting Foes

BY GEORGE WHITE

From 400 miles away, speaking via the wonders of Alexander Graham Bell's invention, came the strong, clear voice of a former idol of mine. It was Oklahoma rancher Warren Spahn, 61 years old now but in the days of my childhood the most magnificent left-hander to ever throw a curveball.

Twenty years in this business still hasn't completely strangled the boy in me. Baseball was my reason for being as a child, as it was to almost every boy who grew up in the 1940s and '50s before there were Space Invaders and Mork and Mindy and Kiss. In the days of my boyhood, I used to wonder at how great the name itself sounded—Warren Spahn, pronounced like "Spawn." It was almost as perfect a baseball name as my all-time No. 1 idol, Stan Musial. I wonder what happened to guys with great-sounding names like that. Today we have players with proper names like Carlton Fisk, Robin Yount, Steve Garvey, George Foster. No more Carl Erskines, Clem Labines, Sal Maglies, Warren Spahns or Stan Musials.

But I digress. The purpose of the phone call was to query rancher Spahn about the days when he was pitcher Spahn.

How, I wondered, did Spahn pitch to some of the top hitters of his era? Spahn's memory is as sharp today as his low curveball was back in the '50s.

• Willie Mays—"Willie will always have a special spot in my memory. He got his first major league hit off me and also his first home run, both in the same game.

"When he first came up he went though an awful slump, something like 0-for-22. They had just finished playing the Phillies, and Robin Roberts had said that he got him [Mays] out pretty easily with breaking pitches down and away from him. So I threw him a breaking ball down there, and I realized immediately that the scouting report must not have been the same for left-handed pitchers. He only hit that pitch as far away from home plate as a human can hit it. He only knocked down about four seats.

"I had to do a combination of things against him. I had to work him in and out, pitch inside to try to get his attention focused there, then try to slip something past him on the outside.

"Willie liked to extend his arms to hit, so you had to be really careful about where you threw it if you were going to work the outside corner. If you got it over the plate, you might as well just ask the umpire for a new ball. It was gone."

• Hank Aaron—"Of course he was my teammate with the Braves, so I never actually pitched against Hank. But I saw him bat hundreds of times.

"I saw him hit balls off his shoelaces. I saw him hit balls off the bill of his cap. A pitcher has to throw the ball someplace, but if he threw it somewhere inside the ballpark, Hank was a threat to hit it.

"I honestly don't know what I would have tried to do against Hank. He was one guy, though, who could hit a pitch you were trying to waste as easily as a ball you were trying to throw for a strike."

• Stan Musial—"I faced Stan probably more times than any other batter in the National League. And after all those years of pitching to him, I never did find any pattern that would get him out. He just stood there and waited for the ball to eventually cross the plate. Then he would hit it. If I had to draw a picture of Stan at the plate, and put a dot at every point

Warren Spahn, left, and Hank Aaron, then with the Milwaukee Braves, display the Cy Young and Most Valuable Player awards they won in 1957. Spahn was elected to the Hall of Fame in 1973; Aaron in 1982.

where Stan hit the ball off me, the whole strike zone would be painted black. He didn't care what the ball did before it got there, he just put his bat on it when it finally cut across the plate."

• Roberto Clemente—"He was another one of those people who played 'Thou Shalt Not Pass Me with a Fastball.' He had extremely good power to right-center field. I found out through trial and error that the best way I could pitch to him was down and away. Always keep the ball down. He was a super high-ball hitter.

"Most of the great hitters are high-ball hitters. They see the ball better up there. And all good hitters hit with their hands above the ball. For that reason, they were always getting the big part of the bat on the ball when it was up higher in the strike zone."

• Jackie Robinson—"Jackie was another high-ball hitter. Every time I threw a fastball, he hit it hard. I had extremely good luck with Jackie throwing him changeups. I would do just about anything to keep him off the bases. He was a hell of a base runner. He was one of the best ever at stealing home, too, so you could never relax even when he got around to third base. Most runners, once they finally get around to third, you can forget them and just concentrate on the batter. Not Jackie. You were constantly aware that he had the ability to steal home on you."

• Ernie Banks—"He played in Chicago with that relatively short left-center field fence, so I concentrated on keeping the ball away from Ernie so he couldn't pull it. I stayed away from him enough to try to get him fishing outside, commit himself early to the outside pitch, then try to strike him out by sneaking a fast one past him on the inside.

"He had absolutely no flaws in his swing. He and Aaron had amazingly quick wrists. You could have them fooled and off-balance, but they both had strong enough wrists that they could put the ball in fair play with nothing but their wrists. They could be completely off-balance and still hit the ball hard."

It is most ironic that the player who gave Spahn the most trouble wasn't Musial, wasn't Mays, wasn't Banks. The biggest worries, he said, were some of the guys who were strictly patsies to his other pitching pals.

"There were a couple of guys who hit me well who weren't good hitters," he recalls. "That's just one of the quirks of this game, that some batters just have perfect timing against certain pitchers.

"There was a guy who played at Pittsburgh named Curt Roberts and a guy at St. Louis named Joe Cunningham who gave me all kinds of problems.

"Cincinnati had a guy named Gordy Coleman. Now, the old Reds had all kinds of big hitters—Kluszewski, Frank Robinson, Gus Bell, Wally Post—all those guys, and the one guy I could never get out was Gordy Coleman. Right-handers would pitch, and that son of a gun would chase curveballs in the dirt, balls would bounce up there and he would swing at them. Then I would get out there and he would just grin and take pitches an inch off the plate. I would eventually get behind on him and have to come in with a strike, and he would just cream me. There must have been some reason he didn't like me."

[1982]

The Mellowing of Leo "The Lip" Durocher

BY RICHARD DOZER

Amid some priceless antiques and artifacts that turn Leo Durocher's overstuffed apartment in Palm Springs, California, into a sort of mini-museum, you can't help noticing a large glass bowl that seems just a little out of place.

It's filled with the Wrigley brand of sugarless chewing gum—probably a couple hundred packs of it.

"Help yourself, buddy," Leo barks in the familiar snarl-smile that was a trademark of his half-century in baseball. "The Wrigleys still send me a carton of gum every month or two from Chicago."

Leo Durocher hasn't worked for the Chicago Cubs for 10 years—fired as manager in mid-1972. He was succeeded by Whitey Lockman, first in a parade of successors that reached five before the financially strapped Wrigley heirs finally sold out in 1981.

But if the late Phil Wrigley hadn't yielded to media and fan pressure in Chicago, Durocher likely would have stayed with the Cubs as long as either of them lived. You could say they loved each other. And Wrigley's son Bill, divorced now from the baseball business, still has the same kind of family attachment to Leo.

Meanwhile, the Orbit gum keeps coming—a monument of sorts to a unique bond of loyalty. On the one hand: a club owner criticized all the way to the grave by Chicago's press. On the other: a controversial manager who built him a contender but failed to win in seven frustrating years of widely varying acceptance by the same fickle media.

I was part of that media, and for the better part of seven years (1966 to July 26, 1972) Leo showed us his every side.

He came on the Chicago scene boldly. From the start, there surfaced a sort of conditional friendliness from which the "right people" were largely exempt. He was an overnight smash with the columnists and TV people—his verbiage usually brash, often believable. His most memorable statement was his winter of '65 banquet appraisal of the Cubs that awaited his touch of genius.

"This is definitely not an eighth-place club," he promised.

Leo was right. The league added two teams that year, and his Cubs finished 10th!

A rare combination of fear and respect soon pervaded the players' view of Durocher. He could say anything and make it sound right. For him, discipline was easy. He played cards with some of his players, took their money more often than not.

These, of course, were Leo's later years in baseball—his second time around. Post–Happy Chandler, so to speak. Chandler, baseball commissioner of a generation gone by, had suspended him in 1947 for his association with unsavory characters, a rap Leo steadfastly denies to this day. Durocher managed the Giants at the time, and the incident left him with one of the few grudges he ever held.

The simple truth is that more people may dislike Leo now than are detested any longer by him. He has mellowed—even says he no longer has anything against Jocko Conlan, the fiery ex-umpire who, it may be assumed, has no plans to invite Leo to his home in Paradise Valley.

"I don't get mad at anybody anymore," Leo says almost softly.

He wears his newly intensified Christianity on his sleeve but insists it's not a "born-again" thing.

He said he had learned a lot in the last four years, a period of something he likens to an inner peace. It began between visits to Houston for heart surgery under the knife of Dr. Michael DeBakey, another of the celebrity "pals" Leo has collected along the way.

The most recent operation, in 1980, "was a tough one," Leo recalled. "Michael leveled with me the night before, came right in and sat on the side of my bed. 'Leo, I could lose you on the operating table,' he told me, but I didn't wait a second. 'Let's go,' I said. Best move I ever made. I feel great now.

"I stayed in the hospital 10 weeks. Had a lot of pain. After I got back to Palm Springs, I never left the apartment for four months."

Durocher lost considerable weight, but he has it all back, plus five pounds he says he doesn't need. "Michael wouldn't like it if he knew I was up to 180, but I'll get a little of that off," he said.

Leo is 77 and holding. He lives very well, making occasional speeches at attractive fees, collecting Social Security and—best of all—cashing in on baseball's maximum pension of $28,000 (plus change) per year. He takes brisk walks almost every morning, plays nine holes of golf on most of the days he doesn't, spends hours answering fan mail and religiously autographs old bubble gum cards—some of them worth big bucks.

"I answer everything. The only thing that gets me is when I'm sent something by registered mail. If I'm not home, then I've got to go all the way to the post office to get it."

When Chandler was elected to baseball's Hall of Fame last winter by the old-timers' committee, Leo's mail increased. "People were telling me I ought to be in there, too," he said.

He's careful not to knock the enshrinement of Chandler, the arch-enemy he's never forgiven for suspending him. But privately he is puzzled at Chandler's recent Cooperstown statement that Happy was more than a little responsible for Jackie Robinson's breaking baseball's color barrier.

"That was strictly Mr. [the late Branch] Rickey's doing," said Leo, who'll tell you also that Kenesaw Mountain Landis, Chandler's predecessor, once indicated to him that he had no objection to black players in the major leagues.

During one of Leo's visits to Commissioner Landis' Chicago office, the volatile shortstop got on a subject other than the behavioral problem that had dictated his "invitation."

Durocher recalled that he mentioned having played in an exhibition against Josh Gibson, the great Negro League catcher, and observed that even though Gibson had great talent he apparently was not welcome in the major leagues.

"Landis looked down at me with that glare of his and said, 'Bring me the man who says you can't have a colored player in the big leagues, and I'll take care of him real quick.'

"I believe to this day that Landis would have accepted the black player if an owner had signed one," Leo said.

"But I'll never knock the Hall of Fame. I make one statement. Everybody there belongs there."

How about those who aren't? That's another story. Leo knows he never will make Cooperstown on his playing achievements alone. His best batting average was .286 (for the '36 Cardinals), his lifetime mark only .241. He was regarded, however, as a superb defensive shortstop, later as a winning manager and for all of his 50 years in the game unquestionably a living character out of Damon Runyon.

After his retirement from baseball, Leo Durocher may have lost some of his abrasiveness, but in his active days he could be a stormy character on the field. Here he argues with umpire Tom Gorman during a 1961 game between the Dodgers and Phillies.

"It's a crime that Phil Rizzuto, Marty Marion, Pee Wee Reese and Country Slaughter aren't in the Hall of Fame—an absolute disgrace," he said. By more than coincidence, three of the above were shortstops, as was Leo, who discreetly declined to plead his own case.

"Sure, the Hall of Fame would be nice. My whole life has been baseball. But there's another door I'd like to see open to me," he said. "That's the one upstairs. I'll put that ahead of Cooperstown any day."

Lounging in an easy chair alongside an autographed picture of President and Mrs. Reagan ("To Leo with best wishes and warmest regards—Nancy and Ron"), Durocher remains in character. As always, he's just one reminiscence after another.

Now we move to his den. It's covered with pictures—one featuring Leo and "The Babe"; another a rare panoramic view of the Polo Grounds at the moment of Bobby Thomson's historic "shot heard 'round the world"

(Giants, circa 1951). The Cardinals' Gas House Gang is pictured—its starting lineup for the 1934 World Series bounding out of the dugout.

Beside Leo, they were Jack Rothrock, Rip Collins, Ducky Medwick, Frankie Frisch, Pepper Martin, Bill DeLancey, Ernie Orsatti and Dizzy Dean.

"I've got to take that picture down," Leo said with a trace of emotion. "I'm the only one in it who's still alive."

There is nothing of which Durocher is more proud than his association with Frank Sinatra, the superstar of crooners who lives only 10 minutes away from Leo's apartment near the entrance to Tamarisk Country Club. Above Leo's sofa hangs a 3 × 4 foot original oil painting by Leroy Nieman, given to him by Sinatra. It depicts Conlan tossing Durocher out of a Cubs game in 1966.

"I've been offered $20,000 for it, but I wouldn't take a million," Leo insists. He says he has another 500 pictures in a storeroom downstairs. "Don't have the room for 'em up here." There is room, however, for a collection of striking furniture—some of it modern, some antique and all obviously expensive. A three-tiered circular bookcase turns a full 360 degrees in sections. It's a priceless bauble that he and a wife (whom he doesn't identify) picked up at an auction many years ago.

Leo was between wives when he took the reins of the Cubs at Long Beach in 1966, the year the club spurned Arizona before returning in 1967 to train in the Valley ever since. His first wife, Grace, was running her own dress-manufacturing firm in St. Louis. His second, Hollywood star Laraine Day, remained on friendly terms with him ("We get along better now," he once said). He hadn't yet met his third, a divorced society matron named Lynne Walker Goldblatt, well known on Chicago's night scene.

Leo always did like pretty ladies. He treated them well. He dressed in expensive suits. He kept some red in what little hair he still had. He smelled good. Wherever he went, he was on stage. His escorts loved it, although Leo occasionally rebelled when the attention got too heavy in public places. Everybody knew him, and he didn't relish an overzealous handshake or being slapped on the back.

In his first spring with the Cubs, it came to Leo's attention that a teen pitcher named Lee Meyer, heir to a bottling fortune, was courting actress Mamie Van Doren. Leo began paying more attention to the youngster than his talent may have warranted. Meyer was making the gossip columns, as would anyone barely half the age of a celebrity fiancée.

On one occasion, after both Meyer and another rookie named Ken Holtzman pitched well in the same exhibition game, Leo started blurting superlatives. He held his thumb and forefinger a half inch apart and declared the two of them to be "that far short of Sandy Koufax right now."

It developed that Holtzman was. But Meyer never made it. He did marry Mamie, but his was a tragic story. They divorced, and not long after, Meyer perished in an auto accident.

Durocher proudly wears his World Series ring of 1954, the year his Giants swept the Indians. He was a coach with the Dodgers and thus earned another ring in 1963. "That one I gave to Frank," he said.

Two sets of golf clubs are stuffed into Leo's front closet—one given to him by Sinatra, the other by PGA champ Ray Floyd, who still has a locker with uniform No. 37 hanging inside it in the Cubs' Wrigley Field clubhouse. Floyd occasionally worked out with the Cubs during the Durocher years, and has done so since.

"When Raymond won the PGA this year, I sent him a wire that said, 'So you always wanted to be a ballplayer, huh?'"

Durocher (believe it or not, Jocko!) is suddenly campaigning for umpires and insists they ought to get higher salaries. "The integrity of the game is in their hands," he said.

One of those he most respected was the late Bill Klem, who chanced to be working the plate during an exhibition in Cleveland, where a 17-year-old phenom named Bob Feller was facing the Cardinals back in 1936.

"The kid didn't look at you when he pitched," Leo recalled. "I took two strikes, and I didn't see either one of them, so I started to walk back to the dugout. Klem hollered at me, 'You got one more!'

"I said, 'I've seen all I want. You take it.'"

[1983]

Where Have All the Bench Jockeys Gone?

BY MARK KRAM

Many long and storied years ago, when the Dodgers were still in Brooklyn and there were Giants in the Bronx, simplicity of purpose seemed to underscore the personality of the game. In that irretrievable time before Styrofoam-blown, futuristic stadiums, $300,000 utility infielders and the dubious wisdom of Howard ("Gene Mauch is a genius") Cosell, there were still places like the Polo Grounds and $7,500 was still a substantial salary and Red Barber still occupied a seat behind a microphone, if not a corner of our imagination.

Close your eyes, remember how unassuming, how lively it used to be. From Arkansas or Georgia, from behind gas pumps or tobacco fields, the Cobbs and Deans and Fellers embodied a reckless, primitive spirit that appears lacking in their more sophisticated descendants. While players today may turn to the *Wall Street Journal* and keep an anxious eye fixed on the economy of Japan, the players of yesteryear could care less. Uncomplicated creatures, they survived on tenacity and guile, a pinch of Red Man and a pair of sharp, dangerous spikes.

Courtesy prevails now, but never then. Dugouts used to boil with activity years ago, get as raucous as an exhibit of ill-natured, agitated cockatiels. Taunting the opposition (or jockeying) was considered accepted behavior, a component of attack. Often crude, viciously personal—for example, you were a natural target if you were of strong ethnic origin or your wife just ran off with the insurance agent—jockeying was intended to throw you off your game, dig at your concentration and thus gain for the successful practitioner a narrow, if not decided, psychological edge.

The bench jockey has gone the way of the three-fingered glove. Etiquette disallows such conduct from the contemporary player, and in a way it is as if something has been torn from the fabric of the game.

"Sure has, if that's the way you want to put it," says Jack Tighe, Detroit Tiger manager of 1957–58 and now a scout. "Used to be they attacked your ancestry, your family life and, if the color of your skin happened to be black, God help you. Now they go out, play nine innings and go home, but years ago there used to be wars. Some clubs used to keep players on the roster just because they were outstanding bench jockeys. The White Sox used to have one, a terrible nuisance. I can still see him sitting over there riding us, but his name, unfortunately, escapes me."

Others were more memorable. Eddie Stanky, for example, or Billy Martin. Also Dick Williams. Alvin Dark (before he discovered religion) and, of course, Leo Durocher. Tracing the pedigree back from there, consider, if you will, the Gashouse Gang or legends like Ty Cobb. Assuming managerial responsibility of the Tigers in 1921, Cobb regarded it as incumbent upon his position to do something to stop Babe Ruth and the Yankees. Applying index finger and thumb to nose, he greeted Ruth with a less than delicate salutation.

"Fellows," Cobb called out, "you all smell something? Seems to me there's a polecat around here."

Turning several shades of purple, Ruth replied in a torrent of expletives and stormed off; he had what were called "rabbit ears," an acute susceptibility to insult. His misshapen form was the source of endless amusement to rival dugouts, but the jokes used to get under his skin and occasionally subverted his performance. Johnny Rawlings, a frail Giants infielder, rode Ruth through the entire 1922 World Series. Ruth batted a woeful .118, the Yankees lost and the Babe stormed the Giants clubhouse looking for Rawlings. He was eventually restrained.

Compared with the taunting endured by Jackie Robinson and other black pioneers of the major leagues, the abuse Ruth encountered seems complimentary. Crossing the color line and joining the Brooklyn Dodgers in 1947, Robinson was vilified, both for what he was and what he stood for. Waves of hostility rolled from opposing dugouts. Under fierce pressure—to perform and to observe a strict code of conduct—Robinson tried to ignore the din, but it ate at him. Many years later he recalled what it was like, how there were times he tottered on the verge of collapse.

"The Philadelphia Phillies came to Ebbets Field for a three-game series," Robinson recalled in his autobiography. "I could scarcely believe my ears. Almost as if it had been synchronized by a master conductor, hate poured from the Philadelphia dugout: nigger this, nigger that, nigger go back to the jungle. Perhaps I should have been inured to this type of garbage, but I was in New York City and unprepared for this brand of barbarism from a Northern team that I had come to associate with the Deep South. What did they want from me?"

As unpardonable as the Robinson ordeal appears from a distance, of course, it does illustrate the nature of the game then. The major leagues were smaller in 1947 (there were only 16 teams) and the clubs were closer, profoundly proud, alert to intrusion. Rivalries were more pronounced then than now. Grudges hardened and brawls invariably erupted, triggered no doubt by a round of beanballs or, perhaps, the incessant, derisive epithets of a third-string second baseman. Managers such as Durocher and Casey Stengel always liked to keep a bench jockey or two by their sides.

"Stengel always liked a lot of chatter, let 'em know you're there," says Phil Rizzuto, former Yankee shortstop and now a broadcaster. "When I played years ago, it used to get mean. Dick Williams was mean. He would call out, as loud as can be, 'Stick one in his ear,' and believe me, it was no joke. [Eddie] Stanky was no shrinking violet either. He discovered a skeleton in your closet and that was the end. As I recall, he had a high, shrill voice that carried all over the field. Like Billy Martin. Billy was one of the best."

It is no surprise that Martin could dish it out; he certainly took enough of it. With those jug ears and that Naples nose, he was a frequent target. Like Stanky, for whom Durocher had sincere admiration, Martin was of slight build but had the heart of an elephant. Stengel loved him like a son, and Martin did all he could to please. He used to bait Jim Piersall relentlessly, and on one occasion, up at Fenway, one word led to another and Martin put his lights out.

"Billy was fearless," says former Yankee catcher Yogi Berra, now a Yank coach. "He took it and gave it back out. We all did then. You had to; that was the way the game was played then."

Martin remembers those days wistfully. With a can of Captain Black on his desk and drawing on one of his big U-shaped pipes, he strikes a professorial pose as he thinks back to how vivacious that time was.

"Competition for jobs on clubs then was fierce; you had to do something to earn your keep, make yourself valuable to the team," Martin recalls. "Players used to have more pride, more loyalty to the team than they have now. Now, since free agency, the pride, the loyalty is gone. Stengel liked to hear jockeying on the bench. He encouraged it, but his days are gone."

If the ghost of Cobb or Stengel showed up in a major league dugout these days, he would most certainly be appalled. What he would find, most likely, would be a row of polite professionals, so polite you would think they were engrossed in watching someone line up a six-foot putt. If there is chatter, it is meant to amuse, not distract; it is invariably the sort of repartee you hear between Joan Rivers and Mel Torme in a "Tonight Show" rerun. To wit:

Reggie Jackson is on first base and Jim Palmer is removed in the first inning of a game in California last year. As Palmer leaves the mound, Jackson calls out, "Hey, Palmer, I thought you were supposed to be the guy who was supposed to pitch until 45."

From the Orioles dugout, Ken Singleton answers, "He was. 7:45."

Well, you had to be there. Try this one. Shortstop Larry Bowa (when he was with Philadelphia) to Cincinnati shortstop Dave Concepcion:

"Elmer, yeah you, Elmer." Concepcion is, naturally, bewildered. "Me?"

Bowa: "Elmer, isn't your name Elmer? Every time I look at a Reds box score I see E Concepcion. I thought the E stood for Elmer."

What did you say the name of the second baseman was? Well, regardless of what or who he is, he probably has a college education, has done several hairspray commercials and is considering a career in politics. Ask him if knows what a bench jockey is and you will probably draw a blank. Or, he may ask, "How do you define it?"

"We used to do a lot of it at USC, and it used to get really vicious," says Yankee shortstop Roy Smalley. "In fact, we had one guy who used to carry around a book full of insults. In one section he had insults for fat guys, in another insults for skinny guys, and so on. But that was college; pros conduct themselves as pros."

Says Lou Piniella of the Yankees: "You see some teasing, but it never gets serious the way it used to get. Players today are better educated, more sensitive, conduct themselves as gentlemen. An athlete is no longer an athlete, he is a businessman. If there is jockeying, it is usually done in a teasing manner. Most of it is friendly."

Until several years ago, Piniella says, players from opposing teams seldom convened at the batting cage before games. Now it has come to re-

semble the cocktail hour at "21." Piniella is unsure if this fraternization between foes is healthy, but others, such as Texas manager Doug Rader, are
sure it can be damaging. Since taking over the Rangers, Rader has instituted a new rule: no fraternization before or during games.

"After the game they can do what they want," Rader says. "But before and
during games I don't want to see any of my players making sucky-face with
the opponents. It accomplishes nothing. Let 'em save it for after the game."

Imagine Martin trading restaurant advice with Stanky at second base.
Or Durocher inquiring into the condition of the greens at Pebble Beach.
Indeed, for better or worse, baseball has evolved. Expansion has exploded
upon the game, the player has been freed from the iron-servitude of the re-
serve clause, and team identity—the loyalty Martin spoke of—is no more.
Passion, alas, has been replaced by parsimony; the bench jockey is extinct.

"Used to be a different game," says Tiger manager Sparky Anderson.
"Used to be that if a pitcher had two strikes on you, he threw at you, no ifs,
ands or buts. And there were guys who knew how to take the second baseman out on the double play. Now it has become a family hour out there.
Used to be a guy would ride you, you would ride him back. Nobody rides
anybody anymore."

Except, of course, in limousines.

[1983]

Pennant Fever Revives Cub Trivia Quiz

BY MIKE ROYKO

Cub fans have suddenly become gripped by pennant fever. We're the only
fans in America who go crazy over a team that has lost 54 percent of its
games. [Editor's note: At the time Royko's quiz appeared in 1983, the Cubs
were 27-30 in the win-loss column, three games out of first place.]

In some cities, when a team loses 54 percent of its games the manager
is fired and the stands are empty. Here the fans begin calling the team
"Destiny's Darlings."

To bring a sense of historical perspective to this, I am again running my
annual Cub quiz.

The purpose of this quiz is to separate the mature Cub fan, who knows
it is his lot to suffer, from the young Cub fan who naively believes there is
hope.

If you get 50 percent correct, you are a real fan. If you get 100 percent,
you have wasted your life by stuffing your brain with drivel.

Strange Happenings at the Old Ball Park

By MALCOLM WELLS

He makes a shoestring catch.

The Red Sox 8 - 2 over the Jays.

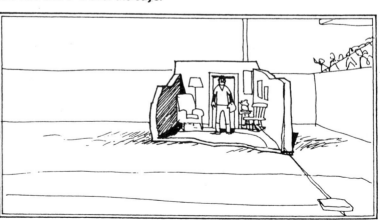

They gave him some room in right field.

The quiz:

Q. In 1960, the Cubs got a pitcher in a trade, and in his first game for us he pitched a no-hitter. Name this immortal.

A. He was the immortal Don Cardwell, who went on that season to win 9 and lose 16. Being a Cub, he wanted to make amends for his impressive start.

Q. What was the lifetime batting average of the immortal Max Zang?

A. He had no batting average, ninny. He was Gravel Gerty, the greatest beer vendor in Cub history. Actually, if they had put him in the lineup, he would have hit better than most Cubs.

Q. In 1958, Cub rookie Tony Taylor crossed himself and said a prayer every time he came to bat. What did the devout lad hit that year?

A. With the help of his prayers, he hit .235 and slammed six home runs. In contrast, drunken Hack Wilson had a hangover almost every time he came to bat in 1930, and the only things he crossed were his eyes. But he hit .356 with 56 homers. I mention that in case someone is trying to put together a training program for Little Leaguers.

Q. In 1950, the Cubs had the only full-time shortstop in baseball who was blessed with a deformed finger on his throwing hand. Who was he?

A. He was the immortal Roy Smalley, who led the league in the number of vendors struck by balls thrown toward first base.

Q. Quick, you have only five seconds to answer. Give me the first name of the immortal Slits.

A. He has no first name, dummy. He's what the immortal Leo Durocher said in a beer commercial: "Have another Slits, fellas."

Q. The Cubs once had a pitcher who said he could hypnotize his arm by talking to it. Who was the pitcher and what did he say to his arm?

A. It was the immortal Bill Faul. And what did he say to his arm? Maybe he said: "Hi, arm." Or "Do your stuff, arm." Or "Are you happy, arm?" How do I know what he said to his arm? Anybody who would talk to his arm is a nut. I only talk to my feet. "Hi, foot."

Q. In 1969, when the Cubs blew a pennant to the hated New York Mets, Ron Santo screamed at the Cub center fielder because he was goofing up. Who was this unfortunate young fellow?

A. The immortal Don Young. And if I ever see him I'll scream at him, too.

Q. During spring training in 1974, a Cub star revealed that his eyelid was stuck shut and that this would prevent him from playing on opening day. Who was the strangely afflicted athlete?

A. It was the immortal Jose Cardenal. But his eye miraculously snapped open before game time when the fans sang "Jose can you see . . ."

Q. During spring training in 1975, a Cub player said he was unable to sleep because a cricket had hidden in his room and was keeping him awake.

He said he probably wouldn't play on opening day because he was so exhausted. Who was this strangely tormented athlete?

A. Yeah, it was the immortal Jose Cardenal again. And again he overcame adversity and stepped into the opening-day lineup. How could the Cubs have traded a man with that kind of courage?

Q. *Name at least one Cub pitcher of the 1950s who wore a golden earring.*

A. The immortal Fernando Pedro Rodriguez. He didn't lose a game in 1958. But he didn't win any, either.

Q. *The Cubs had a pitcher who was born in Ozanna, Poland. Who was this immortal?*

A. Moe Drabowsky. Most experts still rate him as the best pitcher ever to come out of Ozanna, Poland. But the best hitter from that town was Slats Grobnik's father, Ziggy Grobnik, who once hit his wife 12 times without a miss.

Q. *Everyone used to laugh at the immortal Lennie Merullo because he made so many errors at shortstop. And they laughed at the way he hit. But in 1947, he led the Cubs in stolen bases. How many bases did he steal?*

A. Four. They laughed at him for that, too.

[1983]

Mental Discipline,
Key to Defensive Excellence

BY PETER GAMMONS

The years have clouded some of the details for Dwight Evans, like the inning and even the score. But not the play. It was the 11th inning of the sixth game of the 1975 World Series between the Red Sox and Cincinnati Reds, and Carlton Fisk had just lobbed the ball back to Dick Drago from the previous pitch.

"I remember, as the ball was hit, having that feeling that I'd gotten the perfect jump, or as close to perfect as I could ever get," Evans recalls. "It seemed to come together perfectly. The infielders had let me know what pitch Drago was throwing Joe Morgan. I knew the location because Carlton moved so much with every pitch behind the plate.

"It seemed as if my concentration right then was perfect, as if there was nothing else going on in the world but Drago pitching to Morgan. I had just been preparing myself by trying to anticipate, 'What's the worst thing that could happen?' Because of the pitch, I was geared for Morgan to pull, so my answer was: 'A line drive right over my head. My crashing into the stands.' So, mentally, I was prepared to break for the worst thing that could happen. As Morgan swung, it seemed as if I were already in motion.'"

Which is, of course, exactly what happened. Morgan pulled a line drive over Evans' head to the low fence in front of the right field stands. "I've never seen a right or left fielder break more quickly or perfectly for a ball directly over his head than Evans did on that ball, which is the toughest play one has to make in that position," Sparky Anderson still maintains. When Evans speared it crossing the warning track, crashed into the wall, spun and fired in towards first base to finish off the double play that saved Drago and the Red Sox in the 11th inning of that sixth game, Evans had taken his place in Series lore alongside Willie Mays in 1954, Harry Hooper in 1912 and Al Gionfriddo in 1947. As the American League's premier defensive right fielder over the last decade, he may have made better catches. But never one that was greater.

Pete Rose that October night marveled at what he considered "the ultimate jump" Evans got on Morgan's shot. "People say this guy or that guy gets a good jump on a ball because of his instincts," Evans says, "as if it's all something you're born with. Sure, some is physical—agility, quickness, things like that are physical. But as far as reacting to a batted ball—getting a jump—it's as much mental discipline as it is physical talent."

"The greatest players—Mays, Roberto Clemente, Joe DiMaggio—all had great instincts," says Oakland manager Steve Boros. "But all great instincts—whether it's getting a jump on the ball or running the bases, which is where instincts most clearly show up—involve great mental gymnastics. They anticipate the entire range of possibilities and their reactions to them, and they never see themselves failing in their reactions; their mental processes only deal in succeeding in every possible situation. Ron Santo once said to me, 'Defensive defensive players can't ever get a jump on a ball . . . you have to be an offensive defensive player.'"

Getting a jump on the ball. Ask Jerry Remy to define what it entails, and he answers "knowing the pitchers, total concentration and being able to react."

Ask Glenn Hoffman, and he relates a conversation he had with the Tigers' Alan Trammell, the finest defensive shortstop in the league, when Hoffman was having his problems readjusting to the position in 1981.

"What's the hardest thing about playing shortstop over the whole season?" Hoffman asked.

Trammell immediately responded, "Concentrating on every pitch in every game."

"Getting a jump on a ball is instinct, and instinct is the residue of concentration applied over a long period of time," Gene Mauch once said.

"Watch [Minnesota second baseman] John Castino do his work, and you'll see why he gets such a good jump on the ball that you'll swear he is breaking before the ball is hit."

"The people who say baseball is a boring game are the people who have never played it and don't know it," Remy says. "There's so much that goes into what may seem like a 'boring' defensive play. I have to concentrate as much in the field as I do at the plate. Some infielders—Rick Burleson, for example—cheat a lot, knowing the pitch and the hitter's tendencies and leaning as the ball is delivered. I try to do it more by positioning. But the same factors apply: If it's a right-handed hitter, how he's swinging the bat and how he reacts to each pitch. How a hitter is swinging the bat can change from series to series, really from game to game. One thing with this staff we have now is that they're easier to position behind because they throw strikes and are pretty consistent; it could be tough playing behind a guy like Nolan Ryan. When you're growing up, they always tell you that you have to make believe the ball's going to be hit to you on every pitch. It's true."

Hoffman went through a trying game early in the 1983 season because one of the Red Sox catchers had changed the signs, and the infielders weren't aware of it. "Knowing what a pitcher is throwing, where he's throwing it and how the hitter reacts to it 90 percent of the time goes into the break to the ball," says Hoffman. "It varies every night, and it often takes an inning to find out. In one game, for example, with Bruce Hurst pitching, a couple of balls got by me in the second inning—Hurst had struck out the side in the first—because I hadn't adjusted to the fact that he had such a good fastball that they couldn't pull it at all." And two plays that appeared routine later would have been hits in that second inning.

In the middle of the field—shortstop, second and center field—one sees the catcher's signs, the pitch and the swing unfurl. "It's a lot different at first and third," says Dave Stapleton. "I still can't get a jump on the ball at first. I can't know the location of the pitch or see it onto the bat. That's why two years ago, when I moved to short, it wasn't hard, because I'd been playing second. Last year, when I moved to first, I was lost. The only thing I can do at first is know when the pitcher's going to throw an off-speed pitch to a left-handed batter."

In important situations, Evans will get the pitches from the infielders, although he says, "Fisk moved so much behind the plate that he was easy to play with, because I always knew the location." The Yankees' great third baseman, Graig Nettles, leans toward the hole and tries to get the signs from his catcher, and after one of his magnificent diving catches across the foul line off Steve Garvey in the '81 World Series, he admitted that, having picked up Rick Cerone's sign for a changeup, he'd cheated and broken for the line before Garvey hit the ball.

"When you're in the outfield, you can go 140 pitches, sometimes even two or three games without any kind of difficult play," says Evans. "But you have to prepare, concentrate and anticipate on every pitch, and it's mentally wearing."

That is why there are fielding slumps as well as hitting slumps. "In hitting, when you're going well, every pitch looks as big as a beach ball. And when you're not, the ball seems so small you can't focus on it until it's on top of you," says Clete Boyer, the Athletics third base and infield coach who was regarded as one of the best defensive third basemen when he played for the Yankees in the '60s. "It's the same thing defensively. Players go through periods where they just can't focus on the ball."

Boyer, Hoffman and Evans all stress work habits. "It's not the number of fly balls you take," says Evans, "it's the way you take them to get yourself mentally prepared." When Hoffman was younger, both during the off-season when they'd work out together and with the Red Sox, he'd watch Burleson take ground balls "as he'd take them in a World Series game."

Boyer would go to his position before a game and take balls live off the bat "just to get my mind used to thinking that every pitch was going to be hit for a hard one-hopper to either side of me, because that's what I anticipated on every pitch in the game."

"Show me a player with great mental discipline, which can be as inherent as physical tools, and I'll show you a player with great instincts," Boros repeats. "Few things in this game just happen."

[1983]

Memories of a Tryout
with the New York Yankees

BY FRANK J. VESPE

A few years ago I was rummaging through my old room in my parents' house in Queens, New York, hoping to discover something left behind after I got married. Everything was still in its original place: junior high and high school diplomas on the wall, a letter received from Bobby Kennedy in the same dusty frame, numerous magazines and record albums scattered throughout the room and, of course, the twenty or so trophies I earned in high school and before.

Shaking my head, I realized they were only excellent dust collectors now. But were they?

Baseball was always my weakness. Living only a short subway ride from Yankee Stadium and a low line drive from Shea, I felt especially close to the game, wishing someday to play where Whitey, Mickey and Babe earned their keep. Staring at all those trophies, I felt 16 again preparing for the Sunday morning game.

While fantasizing in the full-length mirror like I was pitching in the seventh game of the World Series at Yankee Stadium and occasionally glancing at all those trophies as if a runner were on first, it came to me. Why not give it one last shot at the majors? Something a la Sylvester Stallone in "Rocky." Why not? Since I had always fantasized about playing for the Yankees, and after all, Whitey Ford *did* grow up in Astoria, I chose to write to the Yanks.

Being 26, married, a college graduate and employed as an account executive for a local cable television company, I really wasn't much like "Rocky." But the thought of giving it my best and knowing in later years I would have no regrets for my efforts seemed to justify the fifteen cents in postage.

My letter stated I had recently graduated college, and advised the club of the positions I had played. And, of course, I also asked for a tryout.

I mailed it on a Friday in early April to the attention of Minor League Operations. The response came a quick six days later. Wow! Never thought they would answer that fast or, for that matter, answer at all. Their response was a photocopy, a poor one in fact, advising me to fill in and return an enclosed questionnaire. They wanted to know the positions I played, the high school and college I attended with coaches' names, and my date of birth. The bottom of the page was a statement I was to sign relinquishing the Yankees of any liability if I became injured during the tryouts.

I'd sign anything to play at Yankee Stadium.

When I entered my birthdate, I remembered reading somewhere that teams will only allow tryouts for individuals not older than twenty-three. So instead of listing 1955 as my date of birth, my hand slipped and entered 1958. Big deal. I mailed it back the same day.

During the following weeks I was quite busy spending most of my nights at a local golf range where they had about ten batting cages. Twenty-five cents for five pitches. Don't ask me, or for that matter my wife, how many quarters I popped into those one-armed bandits.

Also at this time I began a daily routine of rigorous exercise, surely to get me in tip top shape for THE DAY with the Yankees. My wife's opinion at the time was, "Hey, why not? You never know."

On July 1, THE DAY, I woke up around 7:30 a.m. and almost immediately I had the radio on, listening for the day's weather report: mostly cloudy with a chance of afternoon thunderstorms.

At ten o'clock I ran across Queens Boulevard to a sporting goods shop for a new aluminum bat. I thought I'd rather be safe than sorry in swinging a lighter one than one somewhat heavier.

Back in my car, I headed out to the batting cages for one last warm-up. Once there, I threw in four dollars of quarters in the "Very Fast" machine, about 75–80 mph.

All my hits were real solid, close to 350 feet. When I left, I told one of the old-timers who was fixing the machines that I was trying out for the Yankees. His reply was, "If you hit them there as you did here, you got it made."

I felt confident after that.

Back in my apartment, I changed into my baseball pants I bought the week before for $4.99. A must in trying out for a major league team.

As I was proceeding over the Triboro Bridge at high noon, it started to drizzle. Thinking this might be my only chance to try out for the Yanks made me depressed. My frown turned to a smile as I noticed Yankee Stadium in the distance.

The drizzle stopped as I pulled into the parking lot directly across from the press gate. I walked from the parking lot to the press gate area, carrying my glove in one hand and my spikes and bat in the other. I had the feeling my fans would swarm all over me. Maybe I should have practiced my autograph? No such luck. No fans for miles, just about fifty other guys in uniforms with some enthusiastic mothers and a few friends for moral support. I think a lot of them felt this was their only way of getting into Yankee Stadium for free.

I looked at my watch; it was 12:30 sharp, the time the tryouts were supposed to begin. After twenty minutes, I asked one of the guys if he knew why there was a delay. He mentioned that the 9:30 tryouts had been delayed due to rain and we were waiting for their completion.

At 1:15 the press gate's metal door opened like the entrance to the Wizard of Oz's castle. Some guy in a Yankee uniform announced that players would be admitted first and all others would have to wait until we were signed in.

When it was my turn to be signed in, they asked for my name and the position I was trying out for. I hesitated and said pitcher and shortstop. The guy in the Yankee uniform who was about 28 and probably George Steinbrenner's nephew shook his head and said, "We have you listed for pitcher. Which one will it be, only *one*!" I hesitated again for at least a minute and finally mumbled, "Shortstop." After all, I did buy a new bat and planned to make sure I got use out of it.

I should have said pitcher.

Once signed in, I was handed a number that was to be pinned to the back of my shirt. Number 8, Yogi. We all marched to the inside men's room to change into whatever else we had to change into: spikes, protective cup and uniform if not already on. Putting on my spikes, I wondered if this was the same room many of my heroes used. Quickly I remembered it was the press gate, and most likely the likes of Frank Messer and company were the ones to frequent this place.

There were 35 or so guys cramped into that men's room. I was a little disappointed it wasn't the Yankee locker room, and I can distinctly remember how quiet it was. Put the same guys anywhere else and the noise would surely be deafening. The only sound anyone probably heard was his own heart beating at twice the normal rate.

Stepping onto the field, after carefully maneuvering up, over and around the lower box seats with spikes on, I reached a natural high. My whole perspective changed. Now I was a player looking into the seats. Walking over to the visitors' dugout, not the Yanks', I plopped my gear in one corner. Standing with one knee on the third step and the other on the lower, I scanned the infield and visualized the opposing team: Clete, Tony, Bobby, Joe and Elston.

Surrounding the mound were five or six guys in Yankee uniforms with clipboards in their hands. They reminded me of the policemen in the old silent movies: middle-aged, white hair and bouncing into each other trying to make an arrest.

Seemed quite funny at first. One guy had to be near my grandfather's age. Again I noticed the younger fellow who I thought had to be Steinbrenner's nephew in the group. They hovered around the mound as if discussing some major congressional issue. (They were probably discussing how to make this session as quick as possible.)

Within twenty minutes, everyone was in or near the dugout limbering up. The eldest scout came over and motioned for everyone to join him. "The first thing we'll do today, boys, is the sixty-yard dash," he said. At first I thought this was ridiculous because I'm sure George Herman Ruth would have finished last. "All pitchers go out to the left field bullpen while the others wait for your number to be called. Once called, go down the left field foul line and get ready for the dash," he continued.

While we all waited in left field for the dash, most of us ran along the warning track. All of a sudden, I found myself staring at the monuments in center field. I was star-struck. I must have stared at the Babe's plaque for at least three minutes.

Looking back towards home plate, I thought the distance didn't seem as far as I expected. Looking up at the 430 feet, I realized it was really farther than I expected.

The eldest scout finally called us all in to begin the dash. I was paired off with a guy named Richie from Brooklyn. He was 18 and had tried out two previous years. Good luck, kid. Numbers 8 and 46 echoed and we dug in for the race. "Get ready, GO!" screamed the scout. Dashing down the third base side, I imagined racing for the plate trying to beat out a throw from right field. Richie beat me by about five feet. The scout recorded our time like some secret agent. Walking past him, I tried to steal a peek, but he "ho-hummed" and turned away.

The next category was hitting, and I played shortstop for this. Most of the guys were quite mediocre in hitting the machine at 75 mph. The first guy up, one of the catchers, put one right over the left field fence and tagged the rest pretty good. (I found out later he played in the Seattle Mariner farm system.) There was another guy, a first baseman, who also popped one over the right field fence.

About 2:30, when it started to drizzle, half of us had not yet had our chance in the cage. The fifteen to twenty pitches per person quickly fell to maybe ten as I felt the scouts were rushing the tryouts. In addition, the worn balls being used, not brand new ones, were getting difficult to see and posed a threat to everyone. One line drive hit to the right side I didn't even see. This could have been corrected by turning the lights on.

All of a sudden, "Number 8, you're up next," rang out. My heart throbbed as I ran in from short. I swung a number of the bats the Yanks had supplied, but they were more for King Kong than myself. I settled for my new aluminum bat after swinging the sledgehammer provided in the on-deck circle.

Leaning on the batting cage with my bat in one hand and with the batting helmet on, I expected Phil Rizzuto to approach me with a few questions on how it feels to be a Yankee. No Rizzuto, only a scout with his logbook on the hitters.

It was finally my turn. Stepping into the batter's box, my heart rushed with excitement knowing such greats as the Babe, Mickey Mantle, Lou Gehrig and Roger Maris once stood where I was.

"Ready, son?" shouted the guy next to the machine as he produced a worn ball. I nodded and took my stance. The first two pitches were low and outside, and I smacked both to short. Next pitch I stroked to right center, maybe 350 feet. The following one was to left center, about the same distance. All of a sudden, "Two more son, that's it." Boy was I perturbed. Maybe they saw enough of me? Walking past the stone-faced scout, I smiled and expected a word of compliment. Only thing I got was "Number 51, you're up next."

About eight guys followed me in batting and we immediately went into fielding practice. Three guys went before me, including Richie, and two of them almost threw the ball into the first base seats. "Number 8" again rang out from home plate. I stepped into the place where Phil and a number of other greats once stood and felt all eyes upon me. The first shot to me was a low line drive which I unfortunately lost in the seats due to the darkness. It hit the palm of my glove and slipped through my legs. How embarrassing. I felt like hiding under a base. The next five grounders I fielded nicely and my throws were quite good. Right on the money. Once finished, I went to the dugout and joined Richie who was already taking off his spikes. "I guess that's about it," I said. Richie nodded and continued getting his things together.

After the catchers threw to second base, the guy who earlier popped one over the fence made about ten on-the-money throws to second. Then the eldest scout came over to announce who was to come back the following day for a scrimmage game. Four numbers were called out. No number 8. All the guys who popped the ball over the fences were called and one guy from Hunter College who played shortstop.

As the four candidates and scouts departed, I tried to break the silence in the dugout by saying, "There's always next year, guys." I didn't even get *one* acknowledgment. Not even "Drop dead!"

I wasn't surprised. I knew most of the guys had great expectations of making the Yankee farm team. It did briefly enter my mind.

I bid goodbye to Richie as his father waited in the box seats. We exchanged numbers and promised to call each other if we needed an extra shortshop in a local game. One guy with a videotape machine was still taking pictures of his brother on the field while I walked up through the box seats to leave.

Just before exiting the inside of the stadium, I turned around for a final look and saw the last scout disappearing into the Yankee dugout. I stared at the monuments in deep center field and for some reason found myself thinking, "It's better to have tried and lost than never to have tried at all."

[1984]

Hall of Famer Who Almost Didn't Make the Majors

BY WALTER M. LANGFORD

Although few people are aware of it, one of baseball's greatest pitchers almost never made it to the major leagues. In fact, it's quite possible he wouldn't have were it not for the Democratic National Convention in Houston in 1928. No, the convention didn't nominate this pitcher for a chance in the majors. Instead it nominated Alfred E. Smith, then Governor of New York, to be President of the United States. Smith, of course, never made it, but the pitcher who got to the big leagues as an indirect result of the convention made it big, real big. He was Hall of Famer Carl Hubbell.

Hubbell relates how he played a couple of years in a little Class D league in Oklahoma and when it folded he was picked up by Oklahoma City of the Western League. There he learned from an old pitcher named Lefty Thomas how to throw the sinker that soon came to be known as the screwball.

"Let me tell you how it came to be called that," says Hubbell. "When I got up to Oklahoma City, the owner bought an old minor league catcher. He'd been around baseball a long time, and I was warming up with him one day a little after he got there. I threw him a fastball and then a curve, and then I wound up and threw him a screwball. So he said, 'Throw that thing again.' I threw it again and he said, 'Well, that's the screwiest damn pitch I ever saw.' And it was the screwball after that.

"Before I go on, I want to establish something with you right now. I've heard a lot of old ball players talking about their recollections and tell great stories, and you know they're stretching things. But whatever I tell you, that's it. So that year I pitched for Oklahoma City and won 18 and lost nine or something like that, and immediately I was sold to Detroit. That was a surprise because most of the players out of the Class A Western League were sold to the International League, the American Association or the Pacific Coast League. You talk about somebody that was up in the clouds! I couldn't wait until the next spring when I'd go into training with Detroit.

"In 1926 we trained in Augusta, Georgia. Ty Cobb was the manager of the Tigers then. Of course, Ty never said a word to me at any time during training. George McBride was his guy to handle the newcomers and everything else. I started throwing the screwball and McBride said, 'What are you doing?' And I said, 'That's the screwball.' He replied, 'For Christ's sake, you're going to tear your arm up. Don't throw that.' Well, naturally, you're going to do what they say. If he'd said to stand on my head and throw I would have tried it. So I gave it up.

"But there was one thing I never figured out. I never pitched one inning of an exhibition game for Detroit in three years. Three years! I pitched batting practice a lot of the time, and they held on to me, farming me out every year.

"First they sent me to Toronto, where they were just opening a new stadium. They had a strong team with a bunch of old major leaguers and some younger guys. They put me in the bullpen and I never did start a game for them. But the Washington Senators, who had won the American League pennant a couple of years in a row and the World Series in 1924, stopped in Toronto for an exhibition game. We were in first place and the manager didn't want to break the rotation of his starting pitchers, so they threw me into the lion's den. I had been told not to use the screwball up there, but before the game I talked with Steve O'Neill, the old American League catcher who was with us in Toronto, and told him I'd just like to try the screwball. And he said sure.

"Well, we just wound up and beat Washington, 5-4. And I pitched the whole game. Then the Yankees with Babe Ruth and Lou Gehrig and all the others came into town for another exhibition, and they threw me in there again and we just wound up and beat them, 5-1. This is the truth. I had those box scores for a long time, and I just wish I had kept them. Wouldn't you have thought that those two games would have rung a bell somewhere up in Detroit?

"The next season Detroit optioned me out before spring training. The third year I went to training with them and didn't get into any ball games, and I was sent out to Beaumont in the Texas League. That was the only club that wanted me, I guess, after three years. And I didn't expect any scouts ever to come around, because they would think, 'Detroit had him for three years, and if he couldn't help them he sure isn't going to help us.'

"Right there is the only time that I questioned myself, you know, asking myself what in the world I was doing. After I had finished high school I worked two years in the oil fields, and the oil field companies in Oklahoma all had baseball teams. I could always go back to them and get a job. But I knew that if I did quit I'd blame myself for the rest of my life. So I said, 'Dammit, I'm going to stick it out some way or other and see if I can't possibly get a chance in the majors.'

"So we were in last place and Houston was in first place. I'm going to use the phrase 'it just so happened' so many times that you'll be sure I'm making it up. Anyway, the only scout the Giants had was Dick Kinsella, an old guy who was a politician in Illinois and lived in Springfield. He was a dear friend of John McGraw and about the same age. He'd go every time they heard about somebody in Triple A ball (it was only Double A then) and take a look at him.

"Dick Kinsella was a delegate to the Democratic National Convention in Houston in 1928. And it just so happened that Beaumont was playing in Houston, and it was 100 percent day baseball in those days. One afternoon there was nothing much going on in the convention and Kinsella said to himself, 'Hell, I'll just amble out to the ballpark and watch a ball game.' And again it so happened that I was pitching that day, against Bill Hallahan, a damn good pitcher.

"We got tied up in one out there and it was all even at 1-1 after nine innings, and I guess about the 11th inning we scored and won the game,

2-1. And from here on it's Dick Kinsella's story. I just read it in the paper because I didn't know anything about it until later.

"Kinsella hurried to a phone and called John McGraw. He said, 'I saw another Art Nehf today.' McGraw got all excited and asked who and where and was he available and everything else. Kinsella told him, 'Well, I don't know. He's been with Detroit for three years and they sent him down here to Beaumont, so he must be available.' McGraw told him, 'Forget about that damn convention. You get over there to Beaumont and find out about everything.'

"And the Giants bought me on July 16, 1928, and in three days or so I was on my way to join the Giants in Chicago. That's the truth, every bit of it. Nobody's going to believe it. You're the only person I ever told that to."

Asked if the screwball didn't put quite a strain on his arm, like a lot of people said it would, Carl responded this way: "The only thing it bothered was this. You see, my left arm is crooked. I never had an ache or pain in my shoulder, in a ligament or nothing. Just the calcium deposits in the elbow from all the pounding. Naturally, you feel it but you can still throw with a

Carl Hubbell, known as "The Meal Ticket" for the New York Giants, is pictured here wearing the National League jersey he donned for the inaugural All-Star game in 1933. He pitched his entire career, 1928–1943, for the Giants, winning 253 games. A left-hander, he threw a baffling screwball which he used to strike out five future Hall of Fame batters—Babe Ruth, Lou Gehrig, Jimmie Foxx, Al Simmons and Joe Cronin—in succession in the 1934 All-Star game.

bad elbow. But if anything happens in the shoulder area, you think you're going to keep on firing the ball, but you can't do it. And I never had an ache or a pain in my upper arm. Actually, my arm started crooking up in 1934, six years after I joined the Giants. And if I'd had it fixed then by a doctor like Bob Kurland I could have gone right on. Finally, a doctor in Memphis took the chips out. Pretty soon I was just half a pitcher. I'd win 11 or 12 games a year. That's all I could do."

Next Hubbell was asked to talk about John McGraw, his manager on the Giants until early in the 1932 season.

"I can tell you a lot about McGraw. This is something else I've never told. He's a legend in baseball, and a lot of people are going to say, 'Well, here's an old left-handed pitcher talking about a legend in baseball.' I'll tell you, he was something. He played that little Napoleon bit to the very hilt.

I mean that was his life. His life! He lived it. He must have dreamed it. The little Napoleon!

"I couldn't understand it. I didn't know what I was going to do. I'd had such a bad experience with Detroit and finally McGraw did give me a chance to pitch in the big leagues. And I appreciated that a hell of a lot.

"But he called every pitch, see, and every pitch was a breaking ball. It would be a curve ball or a screwball. The only pitcher he allowed to pitch his own game was Christy Mathewson. And the only reason for that was that he was the only college graduate pitching in the big leagues at that time. And so he let him pitch his own game and Christy won 30 or more games lots of years. But nobody else! Four years with him and I'm telling you it's a wonder my arm lasted as long as it did.

"When Babe Ruth came along, the salaries went up and the college players began coming in because now the teams could afford them. The Giants signed Frankie Frisch right out of Fordham. But McGraw did not change. He was the little Napoleon right straight on through. Why, Frisch quit and went home and told him what he could do with his ball club. That's when McGraw traded him for [Rogers] Hornsby.

"McGraw and Hornsby lasted together only one season. At the end of the year, Hornsby went to the Boston Braves. Burleigh Grimes, he quit, saying he'd never pitch another ball for him. And McGraw traded him in 1928 to Pittsburgh for Vic Aldridge. In the '28 season Grimes won 25 games for Pittsburgh while Aldridge won four and lost seven for McGraw.

"McGraw had Hack Wilson on the Giants and Hack was just running him crazy, so McGraw left him available in the draft and the Cubs drafted Hack for $7,500."

Carl Hubbell's 16 seasons with the New York Giants were dotted with spectacular pitching accomplishments, but of them all none is better remembered by the public than his feat of striking out Babe Ruth, Lou Gehrig, Jimmie Foxx, Al Simmons and Joe Cronin in succession in the 1934 All-Star game. Was it the screwball that did it?

"Yeah. That's the only thing I got over the plate. I didn't start off too good, for you get all pumped up waiting. Damn, you just want to get started. You wait around, and sit on the bench, and then walk up and down. And you finally get out there and naturally you have nervous energy built up, and you try to throw the ball harder than you usually do.

"Charlie Gehringer was the first hitter, and I got behind on him. Then I got one close enough that he singled to center. Then I walked Heinie Manush, the next batter. And now I had Ruth, Gehrig and Foxx coming up.

"Terry and Frisch and Traynor and Hartnett, all to be Hall of Famers later, gathered around me out at the mound, and none of them could help me a damn bit. But it did give me time to get control of my emotions and everything and to realize that I'd beat myself the way I was doing it. I knew I was going to have to start getting the ball over the plate and give myself a chance.

"I didn't expect to get out of it without some damage, but I did compose myself so that I knew what I was doing. And you know the rest. I got all five of them on strikes.

"Of course, All-Star games were new then and you got more worked up about them. And do you realize that those nine starters for the American League in 1934 all walked right into the Hall of Fame? There's never been anything like that since."

It can also be said that the All-Star games from then until now have produced lots of highlights but probably none so sensational as Hubbell's exploit in 1934. In fact, his whole career was characterized by a series of outstanding feats such as few pitchers have ever equaled.

On May 8, 1929, Hubbell threw an 11-0 no-hitter against the Pittsburgh Pirates. And on July 2, 1933, he pitched an 18-inning, 1-0 shutout against the St. Louis Cardinals. In both 1933 and 1936 he was the Most Valuable Player in the National League, the only pitcher in his league to be named MVP twice. (This was before the Cy Young Award for pitchers had been instituted.)

Starting in the year that John McGraw retired, Hubbell strung together five 20-game seasons in a row, winning a total of 115 and losing 50 in that span (1933–37). In 1933, ten of his 23 wins were shutouts and his ERA was a league-leading 1.66. During the '36 and '37 seasons he racked up the amazing total of 24 straight wins (his last 16 decisions in 1936 and his first eight in 1937). He pitched for the National League in five All-Star games between 1933 and 1940. He was the winning pitcher in '36 and gained a save in '40. In three World Series he won four games while losing two.

During his time with the New York Giants, Carl Hubbell was, almost without serious challenge, the dominant pitcher in the National League. But, remember, he almost didn't make it to the majors.

[1984]

The Mighty Mite Who Rarely Struck Out

BY WALTER M. LANGFORD

Tragedy stunned the baseball world on August 16, 1920. In a game at the Polo Grounds in New York, Yankee pitcher Carl Mays threw a ball that struck the Cleveland Indians' shortstop, Ray Chapman, in the head. This was, of course, decades before batting helmets came into use. Chapman suffered a double skull fracture and died the next day.

This fatal accident, the only one of its kind in major league history, was a terrible blow to the Cleveland team. Chapman, in his ninth big league season, was a sparkplug for the Indians, who had no suitable replacement. At the time of his death, Chapman was hitting .303 and was one of the top-rated shortstops in the American League.

For about three weeks the Indians used Harry Lunte at short. Harry's previous major league experience consisted of 26 games with Cleveland in 1919. He hit .195 that year and was batting only .197 as Chapman's replacement when he pulled a hamstring and went out of action.

In desperation, Tris Speaker, the Cleveland manager, called on a utility outfielder named Joe Evans to take over at shortstop until something else could be arranged.

Cleveland had a working agreement with the New Orleans Pelicans of the Southern Association, and at this juncture they brought up a 21-year-old Alabama lad barely three months out of college. His name was Joe Sewell, a mite of an athlete who stood five feet, six and a half inches tall.

Few players have entered the majors in a more dramatic situation. And very few with so little experience have ever made it so big once they got their chance. Joe batted .329 in the last 22 games of that 1920 season. With Sewell filling the vacuum at shortstop, Cleveland went on to win the pennant and then took the World Series, five games to two over the Brooklyn Dodgers.

Joe Sewell was no "sixty-day wonder." He played in the majors for 14 seasons (the last three with the New York Yankees) and hit over .300 in ten of those years. His career batting average of .312 places him 63rd among all the thousands of hitters in both major leagues. Besides the 1920 Series with the Indians, Joe also played with the winning Yankees in the 1932 Series clash with the Chicago Cubs. His career was crowned in 1977 with his induction into the Baseball Hall of Fame.

Let's allow Joe Sewell to tell us in his own words about his arrival in the big leagues:

"I signed a contract with the New Orleans Pelicans in the spring of 1920, after our season was over at the University of Alabama. I went to New Orleans and stayed with them part of the summer, until after Ray Chapman got killed.

"Now mind you, I had never seen a major league ball game. I didn't know anything about it. Well, they called me up to the office not long after Chapman had passed away. They said to me, 'Joe, how would you like to go to the major leagues?'

"'I don't want to go,' I said. 'I never saw a major league game. I don't know whether I could play up there or not.'

"At that moment Larry Gilbert, our center fielder, came in. Larry had played on the Boston Braves 'miracle team' of 1914. And he said to me, 'Joe you could play shortstop up there.' So Larry was the fellow who talked me into going to Cleveland.

"So I was brought up there, just in time to see the last of a four-game series in Cleveland with the Yankees. Babe Ruth hit two home runs that day. I remember sitting way down at one end of the bench and watching.

"Doc Johnston was playing first base for Cleveland and he got five base hits in five times up, and also stole home. Elmer Smith was in right field and he went to right center and jumped as high as he could and caught a line drive that was hit like a shot out of a cannon. Every time something happened, I'd scrunch down deeper and deeper on the bench. I said to myself, 'I ain't supposed to be up here.'

"So the next day, Tris Speaker came over to me in the clubhouse before we were dressing and said, 'Joe, you're playing shortstop today.' I said to myself, 'Oh, my God!' But there wasn't nothing for me to do but get ready.

"We were playing the Philadelphia Athletics and old Scott Perry was pitching. I'll never forget old Scott. Well, Tillie Walker was playing center field for them and the first time up, I hit a ball to left center like a shot. Old Tillie just coasted over there and got it.

"The next time up—I'll never forget it—old Scott threw me a little old curve. It came in on the outside of the plate and I hit that thing over the third baseman's head and away down there in the corner for three bases.

"Boy, I went around those bases just like I was flying. Not even my toes seemed to touch the ground. When I got to third base, I said to myself, 'Shucks, this ain't so tough up here.'"

It seems safe to say Cleveland would not have won the American League pennant in 1920 if Joe Sewell had not come along to plug the gap at shortstop. In the World Series, Joe was neither hero nor goat. He didn't hit much and made a few errors in the field, but still he contributed suitably to the Cleveland triumph.

Though the 1920 Series was not a memorable one in terms of competition, there was no lack of highlights and "firsts." For instance, Stan Coveleski, a spitballer, became the 8th of the 12 pitchers who have won three games in a single World Series as he allowed the Dodgers just five hits in each of his complete-game victories. And Elmer Smith of the Indians in the fifth game blasted a pitch over the right field fence and screen for the first grand slam in World Series history.

That same game witnessed two other Series firsts. Jim Bagby, the Cleveland pitcher, hit a three-run shot to become the first pitcher in Series history to hit a home run. And the most sensational was an unassisted triple play executed by the Indians' second baseman, Bill Wambsganss. With Dodger

In 7,132 at bats in a career that stretched from 1920 through 1933, little Joe Sewell struck out only 114 times, fewer whiffs than many hitters today amass in a single season. A shortstop/third baseman, Sewell stood five feet, six and a half inches tall and weighed about 155 pounds. He finished with a .312 batting average and in 1977 was elected to the Hall of Fame.

runners on first and second and no one out, the batter slashed a wicked liner toward right. Wambsganss leaped high to spear the ball, stepped on second for the second out and then tagged the runner coming from first to complete the triple play.

As soon as Joe Sewell had played a handful of games in the majors, it became apparent he didn't strike out much. But just how great a contact hitter he was came to light in 1925. In the four previous full seasons he had whiffed 17, 20, 12 and 13 times respectively. These yearly totals were rather eye-popping, but the baseball world hadn't really seen anything yet.

In 608 official trips to the plate during 155 games in 1925, Joe set a record which still stands by striking out exactly four times. Later he was to have two more four-strikeout seasons and even two years when he whiffed only three times, though he played fewer games in those seasons. In 1929, between May 17 and September 19, Joe Sewell went 115 consecutive games without striking out!

You can well imagine what a rare occasion it was when Joe struck out twice in one game, but it did happen. Willis Hudlin, a fine right-handed pitcher and a teammate of Sewell's with the Indians for five seasons, recalls one such occasion. "In one particular game," Willis remembers, "the White Sox had a left-handed pitcher named Pat Caraway, I think it was, and doggone if he didn't strike Joe out twice. Boy, that tore Joe up. And it made headlines all across the country."

In his 14-year career embracing 1,902 games and 7,132 official at bats, Sewell struck out a total of only 114 times, or about once in every 62 trips to the plate. These mind-boggling figures leave Joe so far ahead of all competitors in this respect that in truth it may be said he has no competitors. Of all of baseball's records, few seem more secure than those set by Joe Sewell as the hardest man to strike out.

For many years after he retired, Joe ranked third on the list of players who had appeared in the most consecutive games, behind Lou Gehrig's 2,130 straight games and Everett Scott's 1,307. Joe had a string of 1,103 games. Then in the early 1970s, Billy Williams inched ahead of Joe with 1,117. And at the end of the 1982 season, Steve Garvey also caught up with Joe and passed him. Sewell, however, would have had a string of nearly 1,700 games but for one mishap.

"I had played in 460 or so consecutive games," Joe relates, "and we were playing the St. Louis Browns in Cleveland. I hit a ball down to first base and the pitcher Vangilder came across to cover. I beat him to the bag, but he stepped on my heel with his front spike. They took four stitches. Well, the next day I couldn't walk and so I missed that ball game. We worked on the heel and soaked it in epsom salts and everything, and the following day I cut my shoe open a little and played. And then I went on to appear in 1,107 straight ball games."

Sewell played third base for the New York Yankees against the Chicago Cubs in the 1932 World Series, generally regarded as the Series that generated the most bitterness between the opposing teams.

Mark Koenig, who had played for several seasons with the Yankees, was picked up by the Cubs toward the end of the '32 season when their regular shortstop, Billy Jurges, was shot by a jealous female. Koenig was rather sensational for the rest of the season—he hit .353 and sparkled in the field. The common opinion was that the Cubs could not have won without him. But his teammates voted before the Series to give Koenig only one-half a share of the Series winnings.

The Yankees, led by Babe Ruth, heaped vituperation on the Cubs for what the Yankees considered a penny-pinching act toward the player who had assured the Cub pennant. New York won in four straight games, but the bitterness never subsided. It led to the enduring controversy over whether Babe Ruth "called" his shot as he pointed toward the center field seats before hitting the next pitch out there for what was to be his last Series home run. Although he was in the Yankee dugout at that time, Sewell believed that Ruth did indeed call his shot.

Sewell gets a kick out of the fact that one change was made in the baseball rules because of him. The incident occurred in a game when Joe was playing third for the Yankees against the White Sox. Lew Fonseca was batting for the Sox and Joe knew he had a trick bunt down the third base line that often worked for a hit. So Joe was on the lookout for the bunt and played up close. But when Lew took a strike, Joe moved back just one step, and as he did Fonseca dropped the ball down the third base line.

"The ball was rolling along just inside the foul line with pretty good momentum," recalls Joe. "Bill Dickey tried to catch up with the ball but couldn't, and I knew I had no chance to throw Lew out. The pitcher, Charlie Ruffing, came over to pick up the ball, but as he bent over I yelled, 'Let it roll.' And he did.

"I got out in front of that ball with my front spikes and scratched a trench across the foul line at a 45 degree angle. The ball hit that trench and rolled foul, and as soon as it did I grabbed it."

The umpire, Bill Dinneen, ruled it a foul ball and the livid Fonseca had to come back to the plate where he proceeded to strike out on the next pitch.

The next day during batting practice, Dinneen came on the field and called for Sewell. He told Joe, "You know that canyon you dug down the line and made the ball roll out? Well, that's against the rules today."

"What happened," explains Joe, "was that Dinneen had called the league president, Will Harridge, who decreed a temporary rule. And then the following summer, the rules committee put it in the rule book."

When asked about his best game in the majors, Joe pondered a bit and then spoke of a game one Sunday in 1933 when the Athletics came to New York and sent Lefty Grove out to the mound against the Yankees.

"A big crowd was on hand to see Ruth and Gehrig and Grove and the other big stars," Joe remembers. "I went to the plate five times that day against Grove and I got five hits, the last one a home run. When I got around to home plate, Ruth was there waiting to hit next, and he said, 'Well, kid—you know he called everybody kid—they all came out here today to see me hit a home run, and you pick me up.' I got a kick out of that."

Joe Sewell today is 85 years old, yet he still shows the zest and excitement of his playing days. A conversation with him leaves one with the unshakeable conviction that Joe got a kick out of nearly everything that happened to him in his illustrious career in the majors. And to think that it was all triggered by baseball's saddest moment.

[1984]

You Can Hear It *All* in the Batter's Box

BY BRUCE KEIDAN

The social center of a baseball diamond is an area only a few feet square from which home plate juts like a peninsula.

The outfield is a place of pastoral solitude, and infielders post themselves at intervals, like soldiers on guard duty. You have to call time out just to visit the pitcher's mound. Ah, but those few square feet around home plate are Friday night at a singles bar. A little crowded, maybe, but a good place to be if you are looking for action.

Upon that tiny plot of ground, the catcher, the batter and the plate umpire all must ply their trades. The rules of the game place the three of them at cross-purposes. Being mature and civilized men, they work out their differences. And from their salt-encrusted exchanges is the stuff of legends made.

Catchers talk to batters: Says the Pirates' Bill Madlock: "The worst I ever heard was Manny Sanguillen. He never let up. He'd say, 'How ya doin', Madlock? How's your family?' And I'd say, 'Shut the [expletive] up, Sangy. I'm trying to hit.' He'd say, 'Oh, yeah? Where you goin' tonight?'

"There are other guys who do it. But Sangy, with his broken English, you'd have to struggle to understand what he was saying. And then you'd catch yourself trying to make sense of it, and you'd have to

"I JUST LOVE THROWING MILLIONAIRES OUT OF A GAME !"

step out and call time, because you were laughing so hard."

The Pirates' Tony Pena seldom talks directly to a batter because he is busy scolding his pitcher almost all of the time. But batters have a tendency to get caught up in the monologue. "I don't do anything intentionally to try to bother the hitter's concentration," Pena says. "Except one time. . . ."

"It was in 1982," Pena remembers. "Rick Rhoden was pitching for us against Cincinnati, and David Concepcion was hitting."

Chuck Tanner, the Pirates' manager, called Pena to the dugout. "This guy's wearing us out anyway," he told his catcher. "Let's try throwing the fastball right down the middle every darn pitch this time. And tell him it's coming."

Concepcion, perhaps confused, promptly struck out. He walked away from the plate muttering, "I just can no hit this guy."

Sometimes the message is ominous. Says Pirates shortstop Tim Foli: "I've had catchers tell me when I stepped in, 'Be alive.' Meaning somebody on their bench has decided it's time for one of our hitters to get knocked down."

Catchers talk to umpires: "The catcher has an advantage over the hitter because he's back there with him the whole inning, every pitch," Foli says. "A good catcher works the umpire over the course of the game. As long as he doesn't turn around to complain, the crowd isn't aware of it, and the umpire usually doesn't mind."

"You hear the catcher all the time telling the umpire he missed a call," Madlock says. "It doesn't really bother me, except once in a while when you hear an umpire say, 'You might be right.' That's when it might become a three-way conversation."

Batters talk to umpires: Charlie Hough was pitching for the Los Angeles Dodgers. He threw a knuckleball a foot outside. The plate umpire, Art Williams, called it a strike. Madlock turned and looked at Williams, then silently handed him the bat.

"What's this for?" Williams demanded. "*You* hit it out there; I can't," Madlock said.

Williams dropped the bat as though it were ticking. "You're out of the game," he shouted.

"What for?" Madlock demanded.

"You embarrassed me, handing me that bat," Williams said.

"Well, you embarrassed me, calling that pitch a strike," Madlock reasoned.

To no avail.

"But umpires now are a lot better than they used to be," Madlock says. "Most of them now, if they miss a call, they'll admit they missed it. And then there's nothing you can say. So you just go back to work."

Umpire Tom Gorman once called a strike against Madlock on a ball that bounced in the dirt a foot in front of home plate. Madlock asked the hitter's eternal question: "Where was that pitch?" Explained Gorman: "Hell, I don't know."

Batters talk to catchers: It has been told many times. It may even be true:

A catcher pointed out to Henry Aaron that he was gripping the bat with the label facing away from him. "What difference does it make?" Aaron retorted. "I'm up here to hit, not to read."

Sal Yvars was a catcher with the New York Giants and St. Louis Cardinals. When Earl Torgeson of the Boston Braves stepped into the batter's box and Yvars was catching, the result was often a brawl between the two of them before the first pitch was thrown. It all started one day when Torgeson broke out of an 0-for-21 slump with a line-drive single—and happened to glance back in time to see Yvars break his bat over home plate.

Umpires talk to catchers: "The batter comes up there concentrating so hard, he won't even say hello," says John Hirschbeck, a third-year umpire in the American League. "You're back there with the catcher for nine innings, so you try to get along with him."

Grady Hatton, now a San Francisco Giants scout, recalls a game from his playing days at Cincinnati in which Beans Reardon was umpiring behind the plate. "There was two out in the ninth inning, and the pitcher got strike two on me," Hatton says. "Beans says to the catcher: 'Let's get this thing over with. Give this boy a good low fastball and let's all get out of here.' And damned if they didn't strike me out on a good low fastball the next pitch."

Umpires talk to batters: Hatton's manager with the Reds was Rogers Hornsby, who believed that a hitter should force the pitcher to throw a strike before hitting away. Hornsby insisted on flashing the "take" sign to each hitter to start his at-bat. As word of that tactic flashed around the league, opposing pitchers began lobbing their first pitch over the heart of the plate for called strikes. And the Reds' batters fumed helplessly.

One day, after watching the Giants' Sal Maglie toss strike one past him, Hatton was startled to hear umpire Dusty Boggess call the next pitch—a low, outside fastball—strike two.

"What the hell was that?!" Hatton demanded.

"Now wait a minute, Grady," Boggess said. "If you took one for that no-good son of a gun Hornsby, you can take one for old Dusty."

Mired in a batting slump, the New York Yankees' Lou Piniella complained irritably when he thought umpire Ken Kaiser was too slow in signaling a called strike. Kaiser nodded.

An instant before the next pitch was released, Kaiser screamed: "Strike three!" Piniella froze. And as the ball sailed past him into the catcher's mitt, Kaiser inquired:

"That one fast enough for you, Lou?"

[1985]

When New York Was the Hub of the Baseball World

BY JOE DONNELLY

It was a glorious time in New York's baseball history. Late September thrived with pennant fever, and if there wasn't one New York team involved, there were two. And in one dazzling finish, the Yankees had to wait on a three-game playoff between the Giants and Dodgers to see which one of those National League teams they would play in the World Series. The year was 1951, and Bobby Thomson hit the shot heard 'round the world.

From 1949 through 1957, the three New York teams filled 15 of the 18 berths in the World Series. It started out as the time of the Duke and was soon to be the time of Willie and Mickey as well. The Yankees would win again in 1958, their seventh World Series won in nine tries in 10 years, but it wasn't quite the same; the Dodgers and Giants had started calling Los Angeles and San Francisco home that year.

New York managed to become a two-team town soon enough. But when the Bronx was up, the Mets were down. And vice versa. Then came last September and the poignant memories of a time gone by were stirred. Could it happen again? Could a World Series belong to New York? Baseball junkies were savoring a matchup between Dwight Gooden of the Mets and Don Mattingly of the Yankees at a game-deciding juncture.

The Yankees and Mets failed to make the dream come true in '85. Still, for a time last September rekindled memories of a beautiful past—the time of Willie, Mickey and the Duke and others. They remember it well, and when called upon to share their memories of baseball glory gone by and of the fans and the New York scene as they saw it in late September and early October, they were delighted to do so.

Things were a bit different then. Baseball didn't offer its first night World Series game until 1971. And a seventh game was over by October 10 or sooner, while the 1985 World Series didn't *start* until October 19. Their playground was the bright clearness of an early autumn day with the fall foliage right around peak time. It was a beautiful time when New Yorkers almost came to count on a Subway Series.

WILLIE MAYS

"I had just turned 20 years old when the Giants called me up in 1951. I had been to New York before, when I was 15 and playing for the Birmingham Black Barons. Our bus burned up in the Lincoln Tunnel. That was my introduction to New York. We played the New York Cubans in the Polo Grounds and we had to use their extra uniforms the next day. I was just a wide-eyed kid then.

"I was still really young in 1951, but what a year for memories that was. I broke in going 0-for-12 in three games in Philadelphia, and when we got back to New York I was in the clubhouse crying. Leo [Durocher, the Giants' manager] relaxed me by telling me I was his center fielder no matter what. I was able to relax even more when, right after that, I hit my first big-league homer. It was off Warren Spahn in the Polo Grounds.

"I lived in a lady named Anne Goosby's house. That was a house the Giants arranged for me when I came up to make sure I was taken care of. The fans who lived near where I lived on 155th Street and St. Nicholas would make sure I was in bed by 10 o'clock at night. Every night about five or six would come by and make sure I was in or they would wait until I got home. They were that intent we should catch the Dodgers. The strain of that pennant race got so great I wouldn't dare be out later than that.

"In New York they know about baseball. You can't fool them. They knew when you were dogging it and they knew who could play and who couldn't. You had your favorite team and you pulled only for those people. And you pulled for those people every year because the players didn't jump around like they can now. So you knew what to expect when you played in Brooklyn or in Yankee Stadium where we played in the World Series my first year. Especially Brooklyn.

"I don't think I was hated in Brooklyn. But when you played good ball against their team, I don't think they liked it. I think my second series there I hit two home runs in a game, and when I came out of the park to the garage, all four of my tires were slashed. It wasn't anything they had against me. It was just they were Dodger fans and that was it. I had to go home on the subway with Monte Irvin. I called Leo and said, 'If you want me to come back, you better get my car back.'

"After the pennant race, you relax if you're in the World Series. You know you're there. The real pressure is getting to the World Series. And my rookie year it all came down to the final playoff game against the Dodgers in the Polo Grounds. Now that was pressure.

"I was in the on-deck circle when Bobby Thomson batted in the ninth inning. I thought Dressen [Charlie Dressen, the Dodgers' manager] would walk Thomson, and I would come up and Leo would pinch hit for me. That was what was going through my mind. Leo said he wouldn't have, but I'm still not convinced. But it doesn't really matter.

"If you look back, those years with three outstanding center fielders in New York are very special. I don't think you have another period that can come close to that type of environment. Each team's fans would talk about their center fielder as if he was the greatest. I'm talking three teams, three center fielders, three Hall of Famers."

MICKEY MANTLE

"It seemed like every World Series we played the Dodgers. Not always, but often enough. My first year in the big leagues we played the Giants in the '51 Series. But I don't have memories of that one, not good ones anyway. My dad died and I got hurt. So I want to forget that year. But 1952 and the rest of the years when the Dodgers were in Brooklyn were special. The fans helped make it that way, and so did the players.

"Pee Wee Reese, Duke Snider, Jackie Robinson and Roy Campanella, all those guys were like my heroes. And all of a sudden I'm playing against them. It was probably the most fun time I ever had in my life. I remember that first time against the Dodgers I broke up a double play, I hit Pee Wee and almost knocked him out into center field. I got a kick out of it because he says, 'God damn, kid, take it easy. This ain't the last game.'

"Casey had told me about throwing behind the runners at first base. I used to try that from time to time if they come around first too fast. He told me if you try that with Robinson, he'll go to second on you. So I faked it to first, he went to second and I threw him out by about 10 feet. He kind of gave me one of those I'll-get-you-next-time looks.

"I didn't feel the same toward the Giants as I did toward the Dodgers. I didn't even know Willie Mays then [in '51] with both of us being rookies. Whenever I played against the Dodgers, it was a big deal. I'm not kidding. It was like playing against my idols all of a sudden.

"I was a Cardinals fan growing up. We were able to get Harry Caray on the radio in Oklahoma. Stan Musial was my first idol. Then I came to New York and it was Joe DiMaggio. Then I saw Ted Williams hit and he became my idol. But the Dodgers, it was like the whole team was my idols. I knew every one of them from reading about them. And to play in Brooklyn was different. The ballpark was different—379 to dead center compared to 461 in ours—and so were the fans.

"There was this postgame show on TV where they'd bring on a star of the game. But they didn't have a TV room in the ballpark. So the star of the game had to go to a bar about a block or two away and go into the back of the bar. I did it one time and I said, 'I'm never going to do that again.' You had to go in there in your uniform. You had to walk by everybody and they're cursing you up and down. I was scared to death.

"Pee Wee was special. He used to come by and holler into our clubhouse after we won the Series: 'Screw the Yankees!' He would have disappointed Billy [Martin] and me if he didn't come by, and I think he knew that. They finally beat us the one time [in 1955] and he comes by and hollers in: 'Har, har!'

"You know what used to be fun. Get on the bus and ride to Brooklyn. People used to be waiting on you to come by. And they'd either love you or hate you. That was fun. I'd give anything to see another Subway Series. I think it would be great."

DUKE SNIDER

"Ever since I was a little kid I always dreamed of playing a World Series game in New York. I was playing against grown men since I was 14 years old. I saw the movie *Pride of the Yankees* several times and cried more each time I saw it. I became a Lou Gehrig fan, not necessarily a Yankee fan. I was from southern California. All the major league baseball we could connect with then was in the newsreels or the movie itself.

Duke Snider, smiling broadly, comes home to a welcome from Dodger teammates Pee Wee Reese (1) and Junior Gilliam (19) after belting a three-run homer over the right-center field screen in Game 2 of the 1956 World Series at Ebbets Field. Yogi Berra is the Yankee catcher. The Dodgers, Yankees, and Giants helped make New York a focal point for baseball fans in the 1950s.

"When I eventually came up to the Dodgers, they offered me several selections of a uniform number. That was in 1947 and I asked if number 4 was available. That had been Gehrig's number. It was available and [clubhouse man] John Griffin said, 'Well, you're a power hitter. The last guy to wear this number was Dolph Camilli. Sure, you can have number 4.'

"So I had my number and all of a sudden, in 1949, the World Series game I had dreamed about was there. I hadn't been eligible in 1947. We opened in Yankee Stadium, Allie Reynolds to pitch against Don Newcombe. They announced the starting lineups. I was to bat third, and I went out to the third base foul line when I was introduced. My knees were shaking. I couldn't swallow. And I looked around and thought to myself, well, here I am.

"My first Series wasn't all that good. I struck out eight times and tied a World Series record set by Rogers Hornsby. Reynolds got me three times that day. The harder he threw the ball, the harder I swung. I was a complete failure my first World Series. I was really down about that. But I managed to make up for it later on. In 1952 I hit a home run against Reynolds and I had four in that World Series.

"We had great fans. The stands were so close to home plate, it was like they were standing in the batter's box with you. You made friends. We had block parties where I lived in Bay Ridge during the season. Many of them have passed away or moved away. It's amazing where some of them pop up.

"I went to Ebbets Field once maybe a year after the team moved away. I know it was prior to my coming to the Mets. A friend of mine drove me by. There were broken windows in the front. I just told him, 'I don't want to go by there again. I want to remember the way it was.' Barney Stein, a photographer, sent me a picture of them knocking down the right field fence with a big steel ball. I never went back again until it was an apartment building. I guess I've been by about three times for ceremonies or whatever, but I don't really care to go by there.

"Still, it doesn't jar the memories of the team. We were a very special and talented team who became the sentimental favorite in the baseball world after all those World Series lost to the Yankees. When we finally did win it in Yankee Stadium in 1955, we got into two buses and headed back to Brooklyn with our wives, mothers, dads, what have you.

"It was like a ticker-tape parade. Everybody knew our route. I don't know why or how. There were people hanging off light standards, out windows and off roofs. There were thousands and thousands. All the way across the Brooklyn Bridge and all the way to the Mobil station behind right field where we parked our cars. It was like everybody in the world was a Brooklyn Dodger fan."

[1986]

The True Story of Babe Ruth's Visit to an Ailing Youth

BY BRIAN SOBEL

The story of Babe Ruth visiting a critically ill child, and with a bombastic promise helping him to recover, has been told innumerable times over the past many years. As with all such stories, the facts seem to change each time the tale is recounted. In various articles and books, one finds a different version of Ruth's visit in almost every case. The true story, as it turns out, is even more interesting than any published account because it has several elements that have never been reported.

In 1926 the New York Yankees fought off late-season challenges posed by the Cleveland Indians, Philadelphia Athletics and Washington Senators to win the American League pennant. Finishing with a 91-63 record, the Yankees were led by the man they called the Babe, or Bambino, the Sultan or King of Swat. By whatever nickname, George Herman Ruth had indeed established himself as the champion of the long ball, and perhaps in retrospect is the most charismatic player ever to grace the baseball diamond. By way of comparison, in 1926 Ruth hit 47 regular season home runs, which easily placed him first in the majors. The second leading home run hitter that year was Chicago's Hack Wilson, whose 21 National League round-trippers paled alongside Ruth's accomplishment.

Meanwhile, as baseball dominated the scene, a drama was unfolding which would, in the space of several weeks, be the basis for one of the all-time human interest stories. It was the chronicle of a child and the kindness of baseball's most famous player. It involved the Babe and a youngster named Johnny Sylvester.

Sylvester at that time was an 11-year-old living in Essex Fells, New Jersey, about 20 miles west of New York City. Now, 59 years later he calls Garden City, New York, his home. Today, at 70 years old, Sylvester is president of a small packaging machinery business where he has worked for nearly 45 years. Though decades have passed since the visit of Babe Ruth to his bedside, Sylvester still remembers the incident as if it happened yesterday.

It all started after Sylvester was hurt while riding horseback in New Jersey. "The horse stepped in a hole along the path," recalls Sylvester. "We both went down and the horse got up before I did and stepped on my head. I then developed osteomyelitis [an inflammatory disease of the bones resulting from an infection]. The accident happened during the summer, and by fall I was very sick."

Johnny Sylvester's father was a well-known executive of the National City Company of New York, a company engaged in underwriting securities. When a staff member of National heard the young boy was gravely ill, he promptly went to work. Through his connections, he was put in touch with both the Cardinals and Yankees who were getting ready to open the World Series. Each team sent an autographed baseball, however the one sent by the Yankees contained a special message. "On the ball, Ruth wrote me a short note," recalls Sylvester. "It said, 'I'll hit a home run for you in Wednesday's game.' Well, as it turned out he actually hit three home runs that day which stood as a World Series record for years and years until it was tied by Reggie Jackson in 1977."

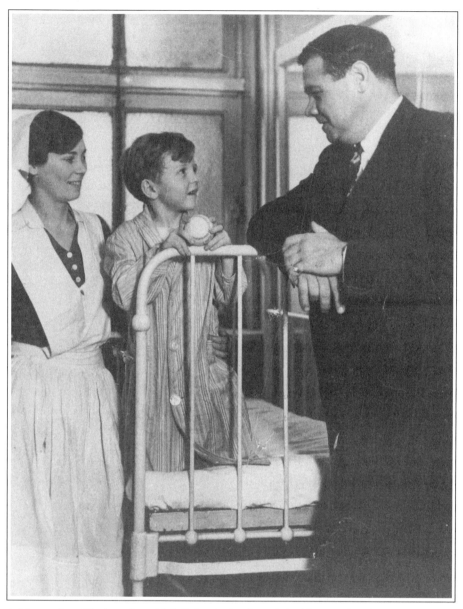

A bigger-than-life American idol, Babe Ruth often visited hospitalized kids to bring them a little cheer and, perhaps, an autographed baseball. Here, he is seen during just such a visit in 1933 at Presbyterian Hospital in New York City.

In subsequent years, through constant retelling, the story became twisted. Articles are reprinted even today which tell of Babe Ruth coming to the hospital a day before the World Series and giving Sylvester a ball, bat and glove. The stories usually describe the grieving parents crying at the doorway of the hospital room as Ruth brings a smile to the child's face with a promise to hit a home run in the opening game. Then too, the story of Sylvester's illness has also been reported incorrectly. However, like all stories which grow up to be legends, this one had some basis in fact.

Though not promising to hit a home run in Game One of the World Series, Ruth did promise to hit a home run for Johnny in Wednesday's game, which was actually Game Four held in St. Louis. One of the home runs Ruth hit that day was later described as, "one of the most prodigious homers ever hit in Sportsman's Park." The famous visit, about which so much has been written, came nearly two weeks after the conclusion of the World Series.

On his way to a baseball game for handicapped children, Ruth stopped off to visit Sylvester. "I'll never forget the moment he walked through the door of my bedroom," says Johnny. "Remember, I had been lying there for several weeks, and I had followed the Series and especially that day when Ruth had hit the three home runs. I had no idea Ruth was going to come out to my house. I can remember his face most of all as he stooped to get his tremendous body through the door of my bedroom. The really amusing part of the story is at that time we had a maid and she and my mother were in my room when we heard a knock on the front door. She went down to answer and came back up to say a man named Babe Ruth wanted to see me. She had no idea who Ruth was, and of course you can imagine my reaction!"

Babe Ruth's visit to Sylvester's home seemed to stir the emotions of nearly everyone. "I've kept a scrapbook, put together at that time, which contains clippings of stories about the visit. Accounts ran in papers all over the United States, and in London, Paris and elsewhere," says Sylvester. "At the time, I was still pretty sick, but certainly over the critical stage. Ruth stayed with me for nearly a half-hour that day and we talked about all sorts of things, but mainly baseball. I remember him to be very compassionate and friendly. I've always felt his visit, though probably suggested by others, was sincere. As many people know, quite a few of Ruth's similar visits to sick children went unreported. Mine was probably unique because of the timing and his promise which he wrote on the baseball."

Also unreported were the other personages who wrote or stopped by Sylvester's house in the weeks following the glut of publicity. First came the great Red Grange, who brought Johnny an autographed football. Then, arriving by mail was a letter and tennis racket from Bill Tilden. The racket, Tilden noted, was used to win a Wimbledon championship. Also, about this time another package came to the doorstep containing yet another baseball from a Yankee. "This one from Lou Gehrig," says Sylvester. "Without telling anyone, including the press, he simply took a baseball, one that was the last out in a World Series game, and sent it to me with a note saying he had saved it and thought I might like to have it. I guess everything you read about his quiet elegance is true."

In the following months Sylvester recovered and in time to be invited to opening day of the 1927 season at Yankee Stadium. There he had his picture taken with Ruth, Gehrig, and the other Yankees, which generated yet another round of publicity.

Following the opening-day ceremonies, life returned to normal for the youngster and the years began to slip by until the outbreak of World War II. Sylvester became a naval officer and went to serve in the Pacific. At that point he would have hardly expected his path ever again to cross that of Babe Ruth's. However in 1947, with Ruth dying of cancer, the *New York Daily News* arranged a visit by Sylvester to the home of the Bambino.

"Claire, the Babe's wife, met me at the door and we went in," recalls Sylvester. "Ruth was obviously a very sick man who had lost a lot of weight, and he looked very gaunt sitting in his pajamas and bathrobe. But the visit was unforgettable and I had a chance to thank him again for coming to see me when I was sick. Now, with him everyone was, 'Hi, Kid,' so I don't know how well he remembered his original visit to me. But we chatted about various things and then I said goodbye for the final time and unfortunately never spoke with him again."

Sylvester feels he benefited greatly by that famous visit in 1926 and says in some ways it helped him live up to his potential. He became a graduate of Princeton, father of one son, and still has all the keepsakes from those days many years ago. "I'm also still a Yankee fan," says Sylvester, "and I've been out to the ballpark many times over the years, though of course the Yankees' management probably wouldn't know who I am today." As for reflection, he says, "I just look back on the events as a rare experience for a kid. Also, it proved most clearly to me that professional athletes, even one as great as Babe Ruth, are human, too."

[1986]

Ted Williams Talks About the Art of Hitting

BY RON MENTUS

During the 1920s, a skinny youngster practiced swinging a baseball bat in the backyard of his San Diego home. Grasping a Bill Terry model, the aspiring big leaguer assumed the lefty stance of his hero. Imitating the legendary New York Giants' star, he swatted baseball after baseball, all home runs soaring out of the Polo Grounds.

When he was 23, in only his third season in the American League, he batted .406 in 1941, the last major leaguer to attain that lofty figure.

His 19-year career with the Boston Red Sox propelled him to a Hall of Fame election in 1966, so when Ted Williams speaks about hitting, people listen.

Now living in Florida, far removed from the days of madding crowds, autograph hounds, photo seekers and media attention, baseball's "Splendid Splinter" spends his leisure time soaking up the sun and deep-sea fishing. Talk about baseball? Even at 67, he still bats .400 in that department.

"When I grew up in San Diego, I played baseball every day," he said. "I hit day and night. People used to say about me, 'Look—he's a natural.' It wasn't that—you've got to practice!

"Hitting a baseball is the hardest thing to do in sports. It's even harder today; there are so many distractions for kids, there's just not as much opportunity for them."

His lifetime average of .344 establishes him as an authority on the art of hitting. Known for his strict adherence to the strike zone, stories abound that unless Williams swung, umpires would automatically call the pitch a ball, respecting his judgment. Williams chuckles.

"I used to be criticized because I wouldn't go after a pitch 'this much' out of the strike zone," he said, indicating a minute space between his thumb and forefinger. "Now that I'm retired, they say I was 'disciplined' as a hitter."

An astute practitioner of fundamentals, Williams is not in agreement with the now-popular Charlie Lau theories of hitting which many coaches and major leaguers advocate.

"I don't agree with Lau," he says emphatically. "His 'hit down' and 'top hand' theories are wrong. The main thing is: hips ahead of hands. You've got to strive to be quick. Most of today's hitters hold their hands too high and there's no point to it.

"Lower the hands and keep them in the strike zone. The stance should be comfortable and balanced; swing slightly upward. Bend the knees and crouch—but don't bend your head. Keep the head still.

"I laugh when I hear coaches emphasizing 'Keep your eye on the ball.' Sure, you've got to keep your eye on the ball—you have to for self-preservation. But you don't have to be told to do that.

"I don't like to see batters stand too far away from the plate. It leads to poor hip action. The farther back and away you stand, the less chance there is that you'll hit the ball hard. Then you hear about rolling your hands. Do that and you'll be hitting nice grounders to the third baseman and the shortstop. Hit the ball and follow through . . . but you've got to get those hips out ahead of the hands.

"As much as I tried to hit the ball in the air, most of my outs came on ground balls. I don't think there are too many good-looking hitters around today because there are too many hitting theories. A lot of ill-advised coaching retards kids' progress. The good swingers don't make enough contact with the ball because they don't know enough about the mental part of the game."

The mental aspect of the game—thinking—is one which Williams feels is too often ignored. The count, pitch location, game situations, and an idea what the batter should be looking for from the pitcher, are qualities that Williams feels contribute to the making of a good hitter.

He recalled attending a dinner with Hall of Famer Sam Rice, who asked Williams if he was a "guess" hitter. "I told him, 'Sure, I was a guess hitter. If the count's in your favor, there's no reason in the world why you shouldn't guess what the pitcher's going to throw.' He says he'd talked to a lot of modern hitters and that they were all afraid to guess. 'And they're all hitting .250,' he said."

While with Minneapolis during his minor league days, Williams remembers a situation occurring during a game at Columbus that was instrumental in his hitting success.

"It was a night game and the pitcher had two strikes on me. I was determined not to strike out, so I choked up on the bat—and hit one out of the park. Not many people knew that about me, but on certain occasions I would choke up on the bat.

"Using a lighter bat also helps. I used one that was 32 ounces, one of the lighter bats in the league. You don't need a heavy bat for power. Bat speed is important; the faster you get the weight out front, that equals the speed of the pitch.

"A lighter bat makes you quicker. Near the end of his career, even Jimmie Foxx went to a lighter bat. And with two strikes on you, you've got to make adjustments. I think the most important thing is to try and hit the ball up the middle—hard.

"They used to say I could count the stitches on the ball. Bill Dickey would try and soft-talk me by asking, 'How big does the ball look today?' Well, it looked pretty small, so I always tried to pick it up [as the pitcher threw] as soon as possible."

Players' observations of the same individual often differ. Williams recalled an instance of a game against Detroit when Don Mossi, a left-hander, was inserted as a reliever. Williams and teammate Billy Klaus huddled near the on-deck circle, observing Mossi's warmup tosses.

"He had a good fastball," Williams recalls of Mossi. "As he warmed up, he looked like he was throwing pretty hard. I thought, 'Wow, this guy looks tough.' After another pitch, 'Boy, he really threw that one.' Then another and I'm saying, 'Geez, he's throwing aspirin tablets today.' He looked real sharp to me.

"So Klaus, who's also watching, turns to me and says, 'I hope he doesn't think he's gonna get away with throwing crap like that!'" Mossi proceeded to retire them both.

At an All-Star game in Baltimore, Williams once batted behind Mickey Mantle. Although his memory is a bit hazy regarding the opposing pitcher, Williams thought it was a hard-throwing righty from Philadelphia (probably Turk Farrell).

"Well, he throws three fast ones right by Mickey. As we trotted to the outfield, I asked Mickey, 'How fast is he?' And Mickey says, 'He'll be just right for you.' Next inning I get up there, get a foul tip off him and he strikes me out, too."

During his career, Williams cited Hoyt Wilhelm, Eddie Lopat, Whitey Ford ("Never gave you a good pitch") and Bob Lemon as hurlers he found difficult to hit against. Of Yogi Berra, he stated, "Yogi had a great ability to

Ted Williams shows off his classic, left-handed swing in his early days with the Red Sox. He finished his Hall of Fame career by hitting a home run in his last major league at-bat in 1960. He had a .344 lifetime batting average.

get the bat on the ball and he was strong. He was a lot smarter than people gave him credit for."

Of his .406 in 1941, he says, "It was my third year in the league. I had the American League pitchers down cold. They didn't know where to pitch me. I think it was just all my experience coming together for me that season."

Sixteen years later Williams again flirted with .400, belting .388 at the age of 39 to win the A.L. batting crown.

"I almost did it," he recalled. "Because it was later in my career and they didn't think I could pull the ball that much any longer, the defenses opened up; I had a lot more holes to hit at.

"I think the slider is the most effective pitch in baseball. Astroturf has changed the game and yes, I think someone will hit .400 again. Rod Carew almost did it (.388 in 1977) and George Brett (.390 in 1980). Somebody will come along and put it all together and do it."

His career average of .344 and 521 homers are impressive figures, ones that today's mound mainstays are probably glad not to be challenged by.

The menacing presence of No. 9 in a batter's box was not looked forward to by many pitchers.

Out of baseball for more than 25 years, Ted Williams is still capable of talking a good game.

In his heyday, Williams' bat did most of the talking.

[1986]

Here's the Quickest Way
to Be Ejected from a Game

BY BOB HERTZEL

There are two words in major league baseball that will create a situation with an umpire that will end a player's day in a hurry.

No, not those two words.

Show up.

That is, "show up" as in embarrass, as in the day when John Kibler was working home plate and Bruce Froemming first base in Dodger Stadium. The Pirates and Dodgers were embroiled in a hotly contested battle when a hitter took a half-swing.

"Soon as he did everyone on the bench was shouting for Kibler to ask Froemming for help," said Pirates' pitcher-turned-broadcaster Jim Rooker. "He did. Froemming looked right into the dugout and shouted 'No.'"

That was all Goose Gossage needed. He was on the bench, and when Froemming refused to grant the strike, Gossage jumped to the top step and flamboyantly pinched his nose in the traditional P.U. pose.

A *People Magazine* photographer caught the pose and so did Froemming, who sent Gossage to the showers.

That was in 1977.

Move ahead nine years. It is 1986, Chicago, and Froemming is working the plate. He calls strike three on Cincinnati's Dave Parker, who dislikes the call enough to take the end of his bat and draw a line in the dirt to show Froemming where the pitch was.

You do not show up Bruce Froemming.

Froemming came from behind the plate and drew a line himself, this one dissecting the middle of the plate.

"OK, we're even," he said.

Parker returned to the bench but, as he did, he shouted at Froemming.

"He cussed me. He had to leave," said the umpire.

Which brings us to the ultimate question in umpiring and, fittingly enough after the aforementioned spats involving Froemming: Where does the umpire draw the line when he is being shown up?

Bruce Froemming is one of the more flamboyant, recognizable umpires in the National League. He is short and round, a veteran of 15 seasons and a man who is known to be quick on the trigger.

He says the reputation may be an exaggeration.

"So the fans don't get the wrong idea, I've got one ejection this year," Froemming said late last August. "It's not to say tonight I won't get three or four. You never know where trouble is going to come from. It can come from any direction.

"I had maybe three or four last year. People think I throw a lot of guys out, but I'm not out there to throw guys out. The thing is, the players know you. They know who and who not to push.

"I'm consistent," he continued. "I treat everyone the same. I love a laugh. I love to have fun. But when I walk between the lines I'm all business to a point where I'm not going to show you up, you don't show me up.

"Each umpire has his own way. Some are quick, others take more," Froemming concluded. "And then, there's a guy who does nothing, who sees or hears nothing, never calls a balk or obstruction, just calls safes and outs, balls and strikes . . . that's a crime.

"Those are the guys who get crapped on on the field."

Which brings us back to what is showing up an umpire.

"What is showing up an umpire?" Froemming asks. "A pitcher comes off the mound, glaring at you. We call it surveying. If you have a good catcher, he'll say, 'Leave it alone, I got it.' He'll take care of matters for you, but sometimes he can't get there quick enough." The case comes to mind . . .

Don Sutton was pitching a shutout in Chicago when Froemming saw him scuff the ball on the pitching rubber.

"We caught him," Froemming said. "Dick Stello asked for the ball at third base, and Sutton threw the ball so hard that Stello had to move and the ball hit into the brick wall. Now we can't catch the scuff."

When Froemming went to ask him what was going on, Sutton screamed at Froemming.

"He was gone and there was nothing that could save him," Froemming recalled. Or . . .

"A player gets a called strike, gets out of the box, and says, 'That bleeping pitch was outside.' That's OK. He's just talking to me.

"Now, here's the other side of it. 'Where's the bleeping pitch?' Now he's turned and his head's bobbing and he's waving his arms. Now he's got 15 guys in the dugout on my tail, he's got me teed off and he's got the fans on my tail.

"So, you say to him, 'Hey, you want to play tough with me, the bleeping game is over.'"

Ejections end it for the moment, but always there is a new incident. Sometimes the players bring it on themselves. The umpires know who the troublemakers are.

In the 1970s there was an outfielder named Alex Johnson who, when called out on strikes, would walk between the catcher and umpire and drop his bat . . . on the umpire's feet.

"I had Johnson at Tulsa," Froemming said. "He was a pain in the butt, but Tim Foli was the worst I've ever seen. I think [Harry] Wendelstedt and I got him four times each one year and that was just in our crew. That didn't happen by accident."

Foli, said Froemming, would go out of his way to put the umpire in a compromising position. Froemming admits that on questionable calls, some players would be allowed a little more leeway in making their point than others.

"I never blew a call," he said, smiling. "Let's just say I've made several questionable calls. If a guy's got a beef, you listen. If it's a decent guy, you let him go longer. A guy like Foli, he didn't get any time. You couldn't wait for him to get to you so you could run him, and that's the truth."

"Foli and Frank Taveras would cost us [Pirates] five games a year," said Rooker. "You can't tell me the umpires were going to give us the close calls with those two guys there just waiting to be thrown out."

The most celebrated ejection in the '86 season came when Charlie Williams ejected San Diego's Steve Garvey, who had gone 17 years without being ejected. Garvey, who rarely argues with an umpire, objected to a call at the plate, a call replays showed the umpire had missed.

Williams was quoted as saying Garvey had shown him up.

The league office, through Blake Cullen, the director of umpires, has a slightly different story.

"The argument had gone on and on," said Cullen. "The umpire finally said it had gone far enough and he didn't want to hear another word. He [Garvey] said it and he was gone."

No cursing, no theatrics. And Garvey was gone.

"Every case is different," said Cullen. "Not everyone ends up in an ejection." Consider a couple:

Al Hrabosky, the Mad Hungarian, walks halfway to the plate after a call he doesn't like and asks for a new ball. He's given it, returns to the mound, than shakes the new ball off and asks for another.

New ball, same routine. Hrabosky says it's no good. Do it again. Same thing.

Now Dick Stello, the umpire, is mad. He meets Hrabosky halfway to the plate, pulls out all his baseballs and says, "Pick one."

Hrabosky does, returns to the mound, feels the ball and says, "Not this one, either."

He has now had his fun but Stello does not run him. Instead he takes yet another ball from his bag, stands in front of the plate and rolls it to the mound. Hrabosky laughs and play continues.

Or:

In Phoenix, where Rocky Bridges is managing and Billy Lawson is umpiring. Johnnie LeMaster claims he has been hit on the hand by a pitch. Lawson says no. Unknown to Lawson, however, is the knowledge that LeMaster, as a youth, had lost the top portion of his pinky.

During the argument, Bridges turns to LeMaster and says, "Go ahead, show him your hand."

LeMaster holds up the pinky with the top half missing.

Lawson doesn't even blink. "Tell you what, Rocky," he says. "You find the rest of that finger, I'll give him first base."

The rule of thumb is to keep things from getting violent.

"You don't want the crowds to start in," said Cullen. "You can't let the player do something to incite the crowd."

If there is a complaint you hear, it is that the umpires today are tougher than ever on players and take less and less lip.

"If that's true, you can thank—or blame—instant replay for it," said Cullen. "The umpire knows that while the argument is going on the play is being shown from seven different angles. He doesn't know if it shows he's right or wrong, but he's thinking 'I can't stand here for five minutes while they're showing it [the replay].'"

However, Barney Deary, who heads the major league baseball umpire development program, says, "We have changed some of the procedures" in instructing umpires.

"We teach them to cope and to outwit the players," said Deary. "The idea is we are trying to keep them around."

Froemming says the umpire development program is to blame for a number of young umpires who are being pushed around by the players.

"The umpires today, through the development program, are taught to be a lot more tolerant than umpires in the past. Therefore you see in many cases ball players getting away with things with certain umpires that they'd never get away with with others.

"When they get here it takes a Lee Weyer or a John Kibler to tell them, 'Hey, you can't take that crap.'

"What you're doing is teaching them twice. When they were in the minor leagues—with exceptions—they were taught they had to take a lot of stuff from the players."

[1986]

Tom Seaver Picks His Ten Most Memorable Games

BY JACK LANG

Tom Seaver pitched 656 games in the majors, and even now he can tell you something about each and every one of them.

But when you've pitched a no-hitter, five one-hitters, a World Series victory and 61 shutouts on the way to a 311-205 record, certain games stand out.

Last July Seaver's No. 41 jersey was retired and he was inducted into the Mets' Hall of Fame. Before that emotional afternoon, he was asked to recall the ten games that stand out most in his 20-year career.

Get ready for some surprises. Not all ten games were pitched in a Met uniform. Here, in his words, are Tom Terrific's recollections.

1. August 4, 1985—"My 300th victory with the White Sox at Yankee Stadium. I never was statistically oriented when I was pitching. Consistency was what I strove for. But as you get closer to a magical number, you begin to feel and understand the importance. For a single personal game, that one was the highlight of my career."

2. April 22, 1970—"The day I struck out 19 San Diego Padres at Shea, the last ten in succession. I happened to be throwing the ball extremely well. I had it all, power and precision. I used just fastballs and sliders. The circumstances were right for me. It was an overcast day and it was difficult for the batters to see. Plus it was a close game (2-1), so the pressure was on all the way."

3. July 9, 1969—"That was the one-hitter against the Cubs. I took a no-hitter into the ninth and had one out when Jimmy Qualls broke it up. Conceivably it might be the best game I ever pitched, considering the pennant race, the 54,000 fans in the stands. The hitters were doing everything I wanted. I think I made two mistakes in the game. One of them was to Qualls. I didn't know much about him as a hitter. I had never seen him before that night."

4. July 11, 1967—"The All-Star game in Anaheim. My idol growing up was Hank Aaron. Here I am in the clubhouse before the game dressing next to him. A year and a half before, I was pitching college ball at USC. Now I am surrounded by Aaron, Willie Mays and people like that. As I walked in from the bullpen in the 15th inning, I looked around at all the stars on the field and was awed. But the moment I got on the mound, I felt I belonged. I deserved to be there. I pitched a scoreless inning to get the save. I walked Carl Yastrzemski on four pitches—all of them on purpose.

He was the only one they had left who could hurt me, and I wasn't going to let him."

5. *October 15, 1969*—"The fourth game of the World Series. I went ten innings to beat Baltimore, 2-1. It was great to win a 10-inning game, but the difference was the next day when Kooz [Jerry Koosman] pitched and won the fifth and clinching game. The Koosman game was much more important from a team-winning effort. When you're pitching, there is a continual flow of emotions. My game was important to me only because it made what happened the next day possible."

6. *May 1, 1974*—"It was a game in Los Angeles in which I got a no-decision. I left after 12 innings with the score tied, 1-1. Steve Garvey's homer was the only run I allowed. I struck out 16, walked only two and allowed only three hits. From a pitching stand-point, strictly as a purist, it was one of the best games I ever pitched. We lost in the 14th."

They called him "Tom Terrific," and Tom Seaver lived up to the billing, pitching the Mets to a pennant in 1969 and 1973, throwing a no-hitter for the Reds in 1978, and gaining his 300th victory with the White Sox in 1985. He was elected to the Hall of Fame in 1992, receiving 98.8 percent of the writers' vote total.

7. *July 9, 1985*—"My 298th win. It came with the White Sox against Cleveland in Chicago against Bert Blyleven. I won, 1-0, on a home run by Carlton Fisk. I have the ball in my trophy room. The significance of that game to me was that I was still pitching so well late in my career."

8. *April 25, 1967*—"My third start in the big leagues. I had a shutout going into the ninth, but a routine grounder went through the legs of my roomie, Buddy Harrelson, and the Cubs tied the score. We won, 2-1, in the 10th on Al Luplow's single. After the game I'm ecstatic, but Buddy Harrelson is sitting in front of his locker in tears. 'I cost you your shutout,' he was crying. Those are beautiful memories you don't forget. Buddy was like a brother to me. We went out for dinner that night. And we didn't come right home. We were just a couple of puppies."

9. *August 16, 1968*—"We were playing Houston at Shea and I took a 1-0 lead into the ninth. With two out and two strikes on Jimmy Wynn, I

hung a slider and Jimmy put it into the parking lot. I wound up with a no-decision. I made just one bad pitch. But it showed me early in my career the significance of one pitch. Twenty years later, I'm still kicking myself for that pitch."

10. September 30, 1971—"Last game of the season at Shea. I thought it was the best year of my career. I had an earned run average of 1.76, I led the league with 289 strikeouts, only 61 walks and threw four shutouts. In 28 starts I allowed two earned runs or less. In 32 starts I allowed less than three. Despite everything else I accomplished that year, I still had to win on the last day of the season for 20 wins. I got it with a seven-hitter against the Cardinals, striking out 13. I've always felt it was my best season."

Former teammates and opponents were recently asked for their views of Tom Seaver as a pitcher and friend. Here is how they responded:

Tim McCarver: "Seaver was the consummate professional. He always figured out some way to beat you. When you were quick enough to catch up to his fastball, he used his intelligence. He figured out when to challenge you and when to finesse you. He had overwhelming confidence on the mound. He was in charge out there. I caught him in the 1967 All-Star game. I caught four pitchers in that game—Chris Short, Don Drysdale, Mike Cuellar and Seaver. I had faced Tom, but I never realized his ball exploded the way it did until I caught him. He threw so hard, my hand hurt."

Steve Garvey: "He was the consummate competitor. Hitting against him was the ultimate challenge. He's a man who understands and appreciates the tradition and history of the game. That's why he's so willing to give back to the game off the field what he took from the game on the field."

Johnny Bench: "Tom was not only a great pitcher, he's a great person. A good man. He's considerate. He's kind. He likes to have fun. And he can laugh at himself. He's very real. He's the kind of guy you can play cards with, do crossword puzzles with, go to dinner with or walk into the White House with. He's the kind of guy you'd want for a brother."

Tommy Hutton, who, in six seasons with the Phillies, batted .450 against Seaver, more than 200 points above his lifetime average: "I can't explain why I had success hitting against Seaver. I just seemed to be able to guess right with him. If I guessed fastball, I got it. If I guessed changeup, I got that. It was just luck, and I feel honored to have had such good luck hitting against such a great pitcher. He was a class guy who mastered his position."

Pete Rose: "He was your ultimate professional. Very intelligent, hard working, mechanically sound and a great competitor. He's one of the few pitchers who didn't lose velocity when he threw down in the strike zone. It was a pleasure to play against him because he was a great competitor and a Hall of Famer."

Bud Harrelson: "Tom always had a lot of class. He's a thinking person on the field and off the field. He always was well organized, thinking things out. He's very special. I always looked upon him as a big brother, even though we're the same age. I roomed with him for eight years, and I have a brother's love for him. The first time I saw him, I thought, 'A guy that age shouldn't be that smart.' He had a maturity and a confidence beyond his years. As a pitcher he was the best I ever played with. It was a thrill to be behind him and watch him work. If he walked a hitter, you never said, 'Oh, bleep.' He usually had a reason. On the mound and off, Tom always had a direction."

[1990]

1939 Was a Vintage Year in Major League History

BY GEORGE VASS

Few years have marked as clear a division between eras as does 1939, a watershed year in history when Hitler's Nazi armies marched into Poland to begin the cataclysm of World War II.

In another sphere, far more pleasant to recollect for those younger in spirit than in body, 1939 also stands out, but in a haze of nostalgia rather than in a dark cloud of dismay because it is a borderline between different ages of baseball.

Even now, 50 years later, the great players of 1939 come into focus crisp and clear in reputation and memory: Joe DiMaggio, Ted Williams, Bob Feller, Johnny Mize, Mel Ott, Bucky Walters, Ernie Lombardi, Ducky Medwick, Luke Appling, Enos Slaughter, Hank Greenberg, Lefty Grove, to name a few.

It is a year to celebrate with a Golden Anniversary in 1989, and with good reason because it has a special significance for baseball as well as history in general, both in retrospect and at the time.

Consider a few of the events of 1939, a year in which a spectacular World's Fair was held in New York, near the site of the current Shea Stadium, home of the Mets:

• Commissioner Kenesaw Mountain Landis dedicated the new Baseball Hall of Fame at Cooperstown as part of the celebration of the game's alleged 100th anniversary. In conjunction with this, the U.S. Postal Dept. issued a commemorative stamp honoring the "centenary" of the game.

• On May 17, sports and television joined forces for the first time in the United States as NBC Television broadcast a game between Columbia

University and Princeton. On August 26, NBC followed this up with its first major league game, the Brooklyn Dodgers vs. the Cincinnati Reds at Ebbets Field, foreshadowing a future alliance with enormous impact on the way baseball would be structured and financed.

• On May 2, Lou Gehrig, the "Iron Horse" of the New York Yankees, was forced by what would turn out to be a fatal illness to end his playing streak at 2,130 games. On July 4, Gehrig gave his famous farewell speech at Yankee Stadium: "I consider myself the luckiest man on the face of the earth."

• On July 11, an American League team with six Yankees—DiMaggio (cf), Red Rolfe (3b), Bill Dickey (c), George Selkirk (lf), Joe Gordon (2b), Red Ruffing (p)—in the starting lineup defeated the National League 3-1 in the All-Star game at Yankee Stadium.

• In early October the Yankees swept the Reds in four games in a World Series whose most notable moment, maliciously labeled "Schnozz's snooze," came when Cincinnati catcher Ernie Lombardi, who had a big nose, lay stunned by a collision at the plate as DiMaggio scored from first base.

Those were among the memorable events of 1939, and some remain ever fresh in the recollections of those who were boys or young men at the time. And especially so in a sports world in which baseball was king, still unchallenged in any meaningful way by professional football, basketball or hockey.

But to the generations that have embraced baseball in the 50 years since, which comprises the vast majority of today's fans, those events have taken on the trappings of history, legend or myth. It is not likely their conception of baseball, as it was played in 1939, is as near to the mark as is that of their elders who took to it in their formative years.

Time is a stealthy deceiver, and while 50 years may seem a half step to a historian, it is a long mile in the narrower scope of baseball. A sharp reminder of this may be the fact that 1939 is as far removed from us as the days of King Kelly, Charles Comiskey, John Montgomery Ward, Cap Anson and other legendary players of 1889 were from those who were in their prime 50 years later.

It is a misconception cherished by those blinded by nostalgia that baseball is an unchanging game, that from one generation to the next there is little alteration.

Not so. There is a world of difference in baseball and its trappings as it existed in 1939 and as it flourishes today. A few of those differences:

• The major leagues were confined to 16 teams, ten less than today, and none was located farther west than St. Louis. Only ten cities had major league teams, because New York had three, Chicago, St. Louis, Philadelphia and Boston two apiece.

• Most games were played in the daytime. Night games had come in four years earlier and were limited in number, which may partly account for the superb hitting feats of that time.

• The ballparks in general were smaller, dingier, and relatively ill kept by today's standards, with the playing fields covered with grass, artificial turf not having made its appearance. The amenities by today's standards would be considered primitive, and that includes the locker rooms.

• The Designated Hitter rule did not exist, and the batting abilities of some pitchers—such as Ruffing, Wes Ferrell and Ted Lyons—were duly appreciated.

• Pitchers were expected to finish games they started, and the concept of the "stopper" had not been born, although relief pitching was accepted as a necessary evil. As an illustration, the N.L.'s leading pitcher, Bucky Walters (27-11), completed 31 of 36 starts. His teammate, Paul Derringer (25-7), completed 28 of 35.

• The equipment, particularly the fielder's gloves, was rudimentary compared to that of the 1980s. The batters wore neither plastic helmets nor gloves. A guy wearing gold chains around his neck would have been laughed out of the game.

• In contrast to the attendance figures of today, when teams often top the two million mark for a season and occasionally reach three million-plus, crowds were much smaller on the average, with few teams drawing more than one million.

• Teams traveled by train rather than by plane as they do now, and that made for long trips, which may have built up greater camaraderie among players than is the case today.

And even the approach to the game, that of the managers and coaches, and that of the players, was subtly different from what it is today.

Take the brush-back pitch, that intimidator which currently often sets off a charge to the mound such as Oakland's Mark McGwire made during a game in the '88 season. In 1939, batters accepted it as part of the game.

John Mize, the Cardinals' slugger of '39 who led the N.L. in batting and home runs (.349 and 28), testified to that in the book *Baseball When the Grass Was Real,* by Donald Honig.

". . . When I broke in, throwing at hitters was part of the game, it was expected," Mize said. "If you couldn't take it, you were better off going home, because once they found out you couldn't take it then they would really let you have it. It never worried me. I figured any guy that threw at me knew I could hit him, because the only reason you throw at a guy is to try and scare him."

Clearly, Mize and his contemporaries saw things differently than do the players of 50 years later.

And when it came to financial rewards, what a world of change from 1939 to 1989.

DiMaggio's salary for 1938 was $25,000, after a season in which he had batted .346 with 46 home runs and 167 RBI. In '38 he came up with .324, 32 HR and 140 RBI. And during the '39 season he was paid $35,000, less than the superstars of '89 such as Don Mattingly and Andre Dawson are paid each week.

The negotiations in 1938 between DiMaggio, who was asking for $40,000, and Yankee general manager Ed Barrow illustrate the approach of that day when the nation had not yet fully emerged from the Great Depression.

"Young man," Barrow said, "do you realize Lou Gehrig only makes $43,000 after 13 years?"

So there's the background of 1939, baseball with a difference, yet baseball as a game that superficially, even when played in the baggy flannel hot uniforms that contrast so strongly with the trim, cooler outfits of today, seems much like that of 1989.

And perhaps, after all, it is a game that has changed less than any other team sport in the last half-century, certainly less than football or basketball, whose rules and style of play have fluctuated far more sharply.

What is certain is that we can identify with the major events and players of the '39 season without the least hint of difficulty.

Sure, there was a slight difference in the way the pennant races were conducted. There were only eight teams in each league and no divisions, so it was a clear-cut path to the World Series, with no League Championship Series intervening. The pennant winners went to the World Series. It was that simple.

And in '39 things were particularly simple in the American League where the Yankees continued to dominate as they had in the previous three seasons.

It was an age of dynasties, and the Yankees epitomized it and seemingly were still in their prime in '39 with outfielders DiMaggio, Charlie Keller, Tommy Henrich and George Selkirk, catcher Bill Dickey, second baseman Joe Gordon, third baseman Red Rolfe, shortstop Frank Crosetti and with Red Ruffing and Lefty Gomez leading the pitching staff.

Even the early-season loss of Gehrig did not slow down this team, which had won three straight World Series, and the Yankees were in first place from May 11 to the end. They stumbled only once, incredibly being swept five straight by the Red Sox in early July, but recovered to finish 17 games ahead of Boston.

In spite of finishing a poor second, however, the Red Sox had something to be grateful for—a rookie sensation who was to become baseball's finest hitter for the next two decades.

For 1939 was the year Ted Williams broke in at the age of 20, and did it with a flourish, batting .327, hitting 31 home runs and setting a rookie record with 145 RBI.

He was raw in the field, but as a hitter there was never a question. A 1939 teammate, Doc Cramer, a fine hitter and outfielder himself, testified to that. Red Sox manager Joe Cronin asked Cramer to help Williams with his fielding.

"So I had him out there with somebody hitting them to him," Cramer said. "He'd miss one, catch one, then miss a couple more.

"Finally he said, 'Ah, Doc, the hell with this. They don't pay off on me catching these balls. They're gonna pay me to hit. That's what they're going to do.'

"And I said, 'Well, I can see that, Ted. They're gonna pay you to hit.' There was no trouble seeing that. He had the swing."

That he did, a swing that was to produce a lifetime batting average of .344 and 521 home runs before his career ended in 1960, though he missed almost five full seasons with military service in World War II and the Korean War.

Clearly, his coming was one of the highlights of the 1939 season in the A.L.

Another was the emergence into full-fledged stardom of Cleveland's Feller, not yet 21 and only in his fourth season, as he became the league's premier pitcher with a 24-9 record and 246 strikeouts in 297 innings.

Among the other hitters, DiMaggio sparkled, leading the league in batting with .381, with 30 HR and 126 RBI, while Boston's Jimmie Foxx came up with .360, a league-leading 35 HR and 105 RBI. Detroit's Hank Greenberg, having an average season, batted .312, with 33 HR and 112 RBI.

These statistics, in a time of giants, while insufficient to capture the spirit of the age, are yet an indication of the way the game was played in that day as a glance at the N.L. of '39 will confirm.

While the Yankees continued to dominate the A.L., a new power arose in the N.L. with the Cincinnati Reds brushing aside the New York Giants, St. Louis Cardinals and Chicago Cubs, who had won most of the pennants in the previous decade.

The Reds, who had finished last two years earlier, rose on the wings of Walters and Derringer and the hitting of first baseman Frank McCormick, who batted .332 with 18 HR and a league-leading 128 RBI. They brushed off a late challenge by the Cardinals to finish five games in front, winning their first pennant in 20 years.

Walters, the 27-game winner, was chosen the N.L.'s MVP and rewarded with a contract for $22,000.

As for the second-place Cardinals, traveling the bridge from the Gas House Gang of the earlier '30s to the dynasty that was to dominate the

N.L. during the World War II years and beyond, their most notable attribute next to Mize was a legendary outfield—Enos Slaughter, Terry Moore and Ducky Medwick.

Still, above all, 1939 was the culmination of one of the many great periods of the Yankees, who won 106 games that season and swept the World Series from the Reds, as they had swept it the previous year from the Cubs. It was their fourth straight World Series title, and in the four years they had a 16-3 record in Series play.

But by the time the '39 World Series was played, the shadows were closing in on the end of an age.

The German armies had conquered Poland in a three-week campaign and were already massing in the West in the preliminaries to the conquest of France, Belgium and the Netherlands the following spring.

And even if Pearl Harbor was two years away, the future cast its shadow, and many of the great stars of '39, such as Williams, DiMaggio, Feller, Greenberg, would eventually spend years in military service.

In America's world at large, millions flocked to see that most popular of movies, *Gone with the Wind*, while President Franklin Delano Roosevelt sought to warn a reluctant and disbelieving nation of a storm to come, more destructive and far more extensive than the Civil War.

The most popular singers of the day, Kate Smith and Bing Crosby, warbled of love and hope in a time that knew nothing of rock and roll while Bob Hope, Fibber McGee and Molly, Fred Allen and Jack Benny brought laughter to millions of families huddled around radios who were barely aware of the imminence of the approach of the even more hypnotizing media of television.

It was 1939, a year worth recalling 50 years later because it was the end of one age and the beginning of another in baseball as well as in history.

[1989]

Memories of My Opening Day No-Hitter

BY BOB FELLER

Here's a trivia question that pops up on quiz shows and sports talk shows every now and then:

Q. Name the only time that every player on a team had the same batting average before a particular game, and had the same average after the game.

A. April 16, 1940, when the Chicago White Sox lost a no-hit game on the Opening Day of the season. Every Chicago player had a batting average of .000 before and after the game.

After three near-misses, I finally made it onto the roster of those who have pitched a no-hit game, fewer than 200 in the game's history since 1901, when the American League was established and organized baseball was formed with two leagues.

No one could have been expecting it on the basis of my previous game. Against the Giants in my final exhibition game before the season opened, I was shellacked for ten runs and 15 hits in five innings. But that goes back to the question of a pitcher pacing himself. I knew it was only a tuneup. I wasn't going to beat my brains out in that game and then have the White Sox beat them out on Opening Day, when the game counted.

It was a cold, damp day in Chicago, and a raw wind was blowing in off Lake Michigan.

Bob Feller, pictured early in his Hall of Fame career. Despite the fact he spent more than three years in the navy as a gun-crew chief on the *USS Alabama* during World War II, he won 266 games, led the American League in strikeouts seven times and in six seasons had 20 or more victories.

Mom, Dad and Marguerite [Feller's sister] were there. So were the Commissioner, Judge Landis, and American League president Will Harridge.

Mom had reason to keep her fingers crossed that day, and the possibility that her son would pitch a no-hitter had nothing to do with it. The family sat in that same ballpark the year before when I beat the White Sox on a six-hitter for my sixth win against only one loss by mid-May. I got them the best seats in the house, between home plate and first base.

I went the full nine innings that day, but Mom didn't. Chicago's third baseman, Marv Owen, sliced a line drive foul that shot straight in my family's direction like a guided missile on target and hit Mom in the face. She had to be helped from the ballpark and was hospitalized for two days with two black eyes and an ugly collection of cuts and bruises.

The whole experience was upsetting enough as it was, but one more thing made it even worse—it was Mother's Day.

So when Mom tested her luck on the following Opening Day, she was rewarded by seeing her son pitch a no-hitter, with no foul balls hit her way. The combination of low temperatures and the Chicago wind made for an extremely uncomfortable afternoon to watch a baseball game, or to play one. The only people in the whole ballpark who were warm were the pitchers and catchers.

It looked like anything but a budding no-hitter when the White Sox loaded the bases in the second inning, but that was from my walks, not their hits. I worked my way out of that jam and then settled into a routine that held the Sox quiet into the ninth inning. Meanwhile, in the fourth, we took the lead, with a little help from my friends. My roommate, Jeff Heath, singled, and my friend behind the plate, Rollie Hemsley, tripled to the wall in right-center field. It turned out to be the only run of the game.

The suspense grew in the late innings. The crowd knew I was making another strong bid for my first no-hitter. The team knew it and was going out of its way to avoid any mention of the subject, in keeping with one of baseball's many superstitions. I never felt that way, though, about that one or any of the game's other superstitions. My teammates didn't have to bother avoiding the subject. I knew full well I had a no-hitter going, and so does every other pitcher in that situation. If he tells the reporters after the game that he wasn't aware of it, don't you believe him.

In the ninth, the tension was compounded by the presence at the plate of Luke Appling, the White Sox Hall of Fame shortstop. Luke was "Ol' Aches and Pains" because he was always complaining of various hurts, but it never seemed to bother him when it came to playing some of the best defense of any shortstop in the majors or hitting .388 to lead the league, which he did four years before.

There was one other thing that Luke did better than anyone else in the sport—hit foul balls. He was a master, the best I've ever seen, at flicking his bat to foul off a pitch while he waited for the one he wanted. It didn't make any difference if he had two strikes either. He was so good at it and so confident in doing it that he just stood up there and took a poke at every pitch, with no concern that he might miss it and strike out.

He came up to bat with two outs and the bases empty in the ninth inning, determined to break up my no-hitter. Then he went into his act. The same guy who once fouled off 18 straight pitches just to use up a lot of baseballs because he was mad at management about his contract started doing the same thing to me. He knew what inning it was, that I had to be running out of gas soon. I was a hard thrower, and by the ninth inning, hard throwers sometimes are tiring.

Appling worked the count to two balls and two strikes and then started waving that magic wand. He fouled off the next four or five pitches. We might still be there if a counter-strategy hadn't occurred to me. I wasn't going to keep throwing and play into his hand, so I threw the next two pitches outside the strike zone. That got rid of Appling with a walk. I already had issued four walks, so another one wasn't going to make any difference anyhow.

That brought up Taft Wright, one of the good hitters in the league and one I had trouble with from time to time because he was such a good contact hitter. Wright hit a sharp ground ball to the left side of our second baseman, Ray Mack, who was able to knock it down before it got through to right field. He picked it up quickly with his bare hand, regained his feet and threw to first for the last out of the game. I had my no-hitter.

That game produced the wildest welcome home you ever saw for just our first win of the season. Seven thousand fans greeted our train when we rolled into Union Terminal in Cleveland, which exceeded the station's biggest crowd by 2,000 people. There was a public address announcer and a uniformed band under the direction of one of the city's best-known conductors, Manny Landers. The mayor, Harold Burton, was there, and so was Cleveland's baseball immortal, Tris Speaker. When the team left the train station, we had a motorcycle escort.

[1990]

Remembering the Tree
That Played Center Field

BY FURMAN BISHER

In the days of the Atlanta Crackers Southern Association baseball club, a large magnolia tree stood in center field, on a terrace rising just above the playing level of their home park. Until the latter seasons at Ponce de Leon Park, when a scoreboard blocked it out, the tree was in play. Only Eddie Mathews, then a kid of 19, ever hit a ball into the tree, the story goes. I can confirm that, but I can't deny there may have been others.

In the season of 1956, the Crackers had a center fielder named Jack Daniels—his real name—who was for one season the best center fielder I've ever seen. Anywhere. He was the only one I ever remember running up a bank to make a catch under a magnolia tree.

Ponce de Leon Park is gone, the ground auctioned off 25 years ago. Down the left field line is a place called the Great Mall of China. In right field, where billboards rose in rows, is a catering service. In center field, the old magnolia tree still stands, maybe a little larger, maybe not.

The other day I went out to see the tree. Litterbugs had left Snickers wrappers, Kentucky Fried Chicken bags, McDonald's cartons, styrofoam

The tree that once graced the center field terrace at Ponce de Leon Park in Atlanta can be seen in this photo taken from the grandstand area behind home plate. The site of the park, once home of the Atlanta Crackers of the Southern Association, was auctioned off in 1965.

cups beneath it, the stuff you see where America displays its bad manners. But we had a visit, the tree and I.

Well, Tree, long time no see, or something like that. You still look the same, haven't changed a leaf. I know how us old guys like to hear that, but I mean it. You look like you could still go nine if they transplanted you to center field downtown in the stadium. And you might cover more ground than some we've had.

I tell people about you being the only tree I ever saw play center field in pro baseball, and they don't believe me. They should have been here when you were in your prime and the Crackers were winning all those pennants. Don't be modest, you did your part. You were their 10th man long before anybody ever thought of the wretched DH.

(Don't ask me what that means. I can't even talk about the DH without getting sick at my stomach.)

I wonder, Tree, if you ever miss the old gang. Some of them are still around town. Bob Montag, the home run king; Buck Riddle, who hit a few himself; Dick Grabowski, Bob Sadowski. Don't see anything of Whitlow Wyatt anymore. He never leaves his county.

Mathews came through and managed the Braves and went, and Chuck Tanner, too. Both asked about you. I lied. I told them you were doing great. I didn't tell them I hadn't seen you in 20 years. Clyde King was through town the other day and I told him I'd just visited you. This time I wasn't lying.

I always guessed that if any of the old guys came to town and asked about you, it would be Jack Daniels. "Sour Mash," they called him. I always thought he was your closest friend, much time as you spent together around that terrace. Nobody could go up that rise and pull in a drive like he could. Then make the throw. Then come to the plate and give you as much action.

The season he played center field for Clyde King, Jack Daniels had the most curious set of stats I ever saw. He'd spent a season with the Braves, mostly doing defensive gigs and caddying for the big hitters. When he got to Atlanta in '56 he was only 29 years old, but he was on his way down. The season he had, Tree, was like one last shot of a Roman candle.

He led off and was the most unusual leadoff hitter I ever saw. His time at bat was either a home run, a walk or a strikeout, it seemed. He hit 34 home runs, walked 143 times and struck out 113 times. Scored 126 runs, led the club in everything. In his 669 times at bat he reached base 320 times, counting walks and hits, and that's nearly a .500 average.

Tree, you just didn't see that being done in those days. You should have appreciated him. You had the best view of any of us.

The last news I had of him wasn't good. While he consumed a good deal of the product whose name he bore, that wasn't his problem. He'd had part of a leg amputated because of a diabetic condition, and that's secondhand news. Tell you one thing, you could have Mantle or Mays or Reiser or any of those guys, but for one season with the glove, I'd take Jack Daniels.

I haven't asked you about your memories, but then I forget that trees don't talk, except in movie cartoons or Disneyland. If you could, you would tell me if Mathews was really the only guy who reached you with a drive.

Oh, there's a lot you could tell. Do the railroad men still wave when the train passes on the bank? Did the guys in the left field bleachers really make bets on balls and strikes? Have you found happiness without the Crackers?

I don't want any answers, Tree. Just let me get away from here before I get any sillier.

[1990]

I Can Always Go Back

BY JON BEATTY FISH

Baseball, as I know it, started on the blacktop of old highway 91, running through our small Utah farming community of Toquerville. My father would gather the 20 boys in town each night after work for a game of "500."

At age three it was my responsibility to place my ear on the ground, before each pitch, to ensure that no cars were coming over the bridge, north of town. I was faithful to that calling during the four long summers of 1953–56. Dad made certain that he stayed after the game to hit me some fly balls and grounders. He also let me hit a few with that gigantic 34-ounce homemade bat, milled from the hardwoods of Pine Valley Mountain to the west.

"Choke up, son," he would holler, "and give it a rip!"

A few weeks after his untimely death in 1956, Mother moved the seven of us to St. George. I turned eight that hot July and promptly became involved in a "little league" for eight-year-olds.

Our diamond was George Miles' cow pasture. George was 89 and often sat on a T-shaped milk stool to call balls and strikes.

I was fortunate to pitch. That meant I did not have to chase grounders and fly balls through cow manure, the ditch behind second base, or the pigpen in shallow right center.

Uncle Lewis, my mother's youngest brother, gave me a mitt. It was a four-fingered Al Kaline model, and it was the best mitt on the team.

After Dad's demise, my older brother became my surrogate baseball father. He hit about 10,000 fly balls to me that summer. He caught my pitching, and let me hit his pitching, until it was so dark that baseball became risky to both of us.

By the summer of 1958, with my brand new orange-colored, fake leather Roberto Clemente–model glove, I had made the official Little League All-Star team; complete with hatpins that were shaped like the state of Utah. We played teams from as far away as Golden, Colorado and Ely, Nevada.

My grandfather took me to old Cashman Field in Las Vegas that summer to watch the Phillies play the Cardinals. It was a classic match-up between Richie Ashburn and Stan Musial. By that time in my life, all there was for me was baseball. I could find no other reason for living, though I was deeply loved by my family and friends.

In the hot Nevada sun that spring, Musial hit a towering shot to deep left center. Mr. Ashburn got to it as it bounced for extra bases.

Then one of those weird plays in baseball happened.

The Ashburn throw to the cutoff man, in shallow center, hit something—perhaps a rock or a hard spot—and it bounded back toward the great Philadelphia outfielder. Musial picked up the third base coach's signal and kept right on coming around the bases.

Mr. Ashburn raced forward toward the ball. Ruben Amaro was also racing outward toward it. On the dead run Ashburn scooped it up and threw a strike to home plate, where Musial was dashing toward the end of an inside-the-park home run.

Dad had told me about Stan Musial a thousand times.

"The best pure hitter who ever lived!" he'd say.

As I jumped to my feet from my seat halfway between home plate and the first base dugout, I could see Mr. Musial panting and gasping for breath as he made his way toward home.

The ball was flying swiftly toward the target given by the spread-legged catcher.

At that one moment in time, when Musial went down into his slide, in my mind, my father was dressed in the Cardinals gray and he slid toward home plate where the umpire called him safe.

Stan Musial jumped to his feet in elation and jubilation!

I cheered wildly.

The summers went by. It was now 1962. I was 14 years old and a freshman in a tiny high school with a four-class enrollment of 167.

I made the varsity baseball team!

Now I had a Wilson autographed Phil Linz glove that was state-of-the-art, as far as I was concerned. It was the top of the line at Coleman's hardware store.

I paid $27.50 for that mitt. That was a lot of hay hauling and irrigating that summer.

We had a particularly cold spring. The Wasps baseball team had spent the previous afternoon scattering sand on the wet spots at the fairgrounds. We wanted desperately to complete that first game against our archrivals, the Morgan High School Trojans.

I wanted it most of all because I was going to start the game. Our senior "star" had pulled a muscle a day or two earlier in the week. As the number two pitcher, I was now promoted to the top spot.

My older brother, Ash, who had spent all those hours helping me immerse myself in the game, was our clean-up hitter and the first baseman. I had practiced throwing to him a thousand times that spring—though it had been in the gymnasium with tennis balls. My pickoff move was a dandy. I intended to use it that day.

When the bottom of the seventh, and final, inning came, the Trojan hitters had barely gotten out of the batter's box. I had thrown a perfect game for six innings, and now I intended to close it out in similar fashion.

The first batter waved clumsily at a third strike.

One down and only two to go.

Batter number two popped to short left field and Davey J. took it easily. He whipped it around the horn as if we were already in the "dog days of August." I felt as confident as he appeared.

Two down and one to go. All of those Little League and Pony League starts had never produced a no-hitter, let alone a perfect game.

I thought about Don Larsen, Whitey Ford, Herb Score, Warren Spahn, and Don Newcombe. My mind raced wildly over the past three or four years since the Dodgers had moved to Los Angeles.

All of those night games on "50,000 watt, clear channel KFI in Los Angeles" were clearly vivid in my mind. That little black RCA radio had tuned in the Dodgers with a clarity that will never be equaled again, for me.

In my mind I could see Johnny Podres shaking the rosin bag. I could see young Don Drysdale sidearming opponents with his whip.

I only had one out to go. His name was Paul Giacovinni. He was the opposing pitcher. Paul was a tall, mighty senior. I was a tiny, little freshman. Could I do it? Could I do what only a few others had ever accomplished on any level of competition?

I turned a fastball over and pegged the first pitch in the ground about three feet in front of home plate. It bounced all the way to the screen, even though Richard Remund tried to block it.

Giacovinni stepped out and slapped his cleats with his bat, a la Mickey Mantle. I started to worry.

"Don't get in a hole with this guy," I thought. "We're only leading 1-0 on Ash's 4th inning solo home run. If he gets hold of one it'll go 500 feet and we'll be tied."

Paul leaned backward on the second pitch, but Doug Johnson—the hometown umpire and regional agriculture agent—called out "Strike one!"

Now I was regaining my confidence.

The third pitch was an off-speed curveball. One of those high school roundhouse pitches that takes ten minutes to get to the plate.

Paul Giacovinni hit it 450 feet down the right field foul line. It landed on the race track, clearly foul. Umpire Johnson ran all the way past first base to get a clear look. The huge stadium crowd of approximately 25 parents sighed a collective gasp of relief.

Now I had him right where I wanted him. He thought he could hit anything I would throw up to him, and I thought differently.

He was down to me one and two. I thought he would become defensive, so I shook Richard off three straight times.

"He's going to have to hit my best pitch," I remember thinking. "I can hit the outside black of the plate with my fastball any day of the week."

And I did.

Paul extended those long arms, turned on that freshman fastball and hit a low liner toward the gap between Ash and Rex Winterton. Though it was hit hard, I watched it leave the bat in slow motion.

As it passed my position on the mound, I realized that it was just like those low liners I had hit against Ash all of my life in George Miles' cow pasture. Sometimes we had even practiced knocking over the milking stool.

"He's got a chance at getting it," I realized, instinctively starting toward the bag, to cover.

Older brothers are the real "boys of summer."

Ash backed off a step and threw his body to the right. That old, raggy softball glove of his trapped the screaming hardball.

From his side, he threw a perfect strike to the bag—as we had practiced a thousand times. I took it in stride, my right foot and the ball arriving at the base and glove in perfect unison. Paul Giacovinni was out!

I had pitched a perfect game. My teammates had played a perfect game. Paul Giacovinni had thrown a three-hitter, and lost.

As I raced to help Ash to his feet, the first snowflake of that 5th day of April, 1962, hit my eye. Before our team could get loaded on the old International school bus, it was snowing in blizzard fashion. Soon the old ball diamond at the county fairgrounds was obliterated with six inches of a late spring snowstorm.

That evening we celebrated my mother's 39th birthday. No one was happier than I. I felt perfect. I was certain that the game of baseball was.

There would be other summers. The later ones could never equal the earlier ones. I fully intended to tell Roberto Clemente about my old glove at a later date, when I got to the majors.

Vietnam stopped that.

However, even in the jungles of Southeast Asia, baseball, played by those boys of summer, ruled supreme. It kept many from going bonkers. I relived those earlier summers a million times in my mind.

The memories of baseball. How wonderful they are. I can always go back.

[1991]

Rickey Henderson . . . There He Goes!

BY KIRK KENNEY

Oakland left fielder Rickey Henderson is on first base. How did he get there? A hit. A walk. It doesn't matter. He won't be there long.

Henderson gets his lead, cautiously measuring three strides from the bag. He crouches forward. His hands dangle loosely between his legs. He stares out at the mound. And he smiles.

"I think you have to be cocky," said Henderson. "It's essential if you want to do something."

What Rickey Henderson is going to do is steal second base. If he has a mind to, he'll also steal third. And there's very little anybody can do about it.

There he goes. . . .

Henderson glances once toward the catcher as he races to second base. He dives in head first. His gloved hands grab the base without leaving any fingerprints. The perfect crime. A base hit by a teammate and Henderson scores.

"People didn't realize what stolen bases meant to the game until recently," said Henderson, who returned to his native Oakland midway through the 1989 season after spending four and a half years with the New York Yankees. "In the time I've been playing and stealing bases it's been catching people's eyes, but I don't think stolen bases were eye-catching before that."

Henderson's numbers are eye-catching. All those stolen bases add up. In 1982 they added up to 130, giving Henderson a single-season major league record. Lou Brock had held the record with 118.

Early in the 1991 season, Henderson will steal another record from Brock, who finished his career in 1979 with a major league record 938 stolen bases. Henderson began his career in '79 and had 936 stolen bases going into the '91 campaign.

As the '91 season opened, the Rickey Watch was winding down. Oakland A's officials have done exhaustive research charting Henderson's progress. They know how many times he's stolen second (717), third (215) and home (4). They know every pitcher he's stolen from (Floyd Bannister has allowed the most with 16).

"I thought I would be a stolen base guy," said Henderson. "I was stealing 80 or 90 bases a year in the minor leagues, so I thought I could have success in the major leagues.

"When I first started I was a straight-out runner. You blink your eyes and I was gone. It didn't matter. But now pitchers are blinking and twinkling and coming over and trying to get me. You have to be able to read that. Now there's more strategy and skill."

Amazingly, Henderson believes the best is yet to come.

"I think I'm just starting to peak," said Henderson, a 5-10, 195-pounder who turned 32 last December. "Nolan Ryan's pitching and he's 40-something. Pete Rose and Reggie Jackson were playing in their 40s. I could last as long as they did.

"I'm looking to take it [the stolen base record] to 1,500 or 1,600. All I have to do is get 50 a year over the next 10 years, and when I get 70 or 80 that just puts me further along. Anything can happen. But if I get it over 1,500, I think it would be very tough for somebody to come along and beat it."

Henderson is proud of his stolen-base accomplishments, although he doesn't want them to overshadow his all-around performance. He is annually among the league leaders in most offensive categories. Last year was no different, except that his performance finally led to MVP honors.

"When I'm done," Henderson said, "I want people to think, 'He was a great ballplayer. He was an all-around player.'"

First, he had to sell management on the idea.

"When I used to go in and talk about my value is to the club, I always heard about the home run hitters and RBI guys," said Henderson. "I said, 'I score as many runs as that guy has RBIs. What's the difference? He couldn't knock the run in if I wasn't out there to score.'

"Once I went to arbitration and they said, 'You can't hit home runs.' That's when I started to hit home runs. It wasn't that I couldn't hit them. It was that I didn't try. My job was to get on base and score runs and make things

Rickey Henderson holds up the base after setting a new record for thefts in 1982. He finished the season with 130 steals, and by the end of 2003 he had collected 1,406 stolen bases.

happen. Now they were saying that I had to hit home runs to be a big guy. Let me go work on that."

Henderson's 45 homers to lead off games is a major league record.

"People should have been paying closer attention, because for the past 10 years he's been a multi-dimensional threat," said Oakland manager Tony La Russa. "There are a lot of ways he wins games."

Never was Henderson's impact more obvious than during the 1989 American League Championship Series between Oakland and Toronto.

It seemed Henderson was always on base, causing problems for the Blue Jays. He batted .400 (6-for-15) with seven walks. That gave him the opportunity to set a playoff record with eight stolen bases. He also had two homers in the series, which the A's won in five games.

It wasn't just how Henderson did it but the way he did it that bothered the Blue Jays.

In the seventh inning of Game 2 of the series, he stole second and third on consecutive pitches. It was his steal of second that infuriated Toronto. Henderson tiptoed the last few steps into the base when he saw there would be no throw from Blue Jays catcher Ernie Whitt.

"He tried to show us up when he came up short," said Whitt. "I don't care what the score is or what the situation is, when you have the base stolen you don't do what he did to us."

Said Henderson: "I don't really try to show up the other team. If I've got the base stolen and I look at the catcher and he's not going to throw the ball, I'm not going to slide and break my neck. If I've got the base stolen and I stand up, so what?"

Toronto third baseman Kelly Gruber has a word for it.

"Hotdogging," said Gruber.

Henderson has a different word for his style of play.

"Showmanship," said Henderson. "To me, baseball is entertainment. People say hotdogging. What's that mean? It's entertainment."

La Russa, who managed the Chicago White Sox from 1979 to '86 before going to Oakland, recalls plenty of times his teams were "entertained" by Henderson.

"You always look at every game how you got beat," said La Russa, "and there were too many times where it was Rickey's defense or single or extra-base hit. It went beyond Rickey's effect on our defense and pitcher.

"There are a number of guys who do the same things. Some are great base stealers. Others hit the home runs. But who has the whole package?"

Still, it's Henderson's base-stealing that draws the most attention. A recent television commercial drives this point home.

A baseball manager and his catcher are in a room with a movie projector. They're watching film of Henderson stealing base after base against the team. The manager says they should make the bases farther apart for Henderson. The catcher just hangs his head.

Oakland catcher Terry Steinbach recalls what it was like trying to stop Henderson when he played for the Yankees.

"If we had a lead, we didn't worry about him too much," said Steinbach. "If it was later in the game and he was the important run, then it was really tough. We had to try things to break his concentration, try to keep him from getting a good jump and stealing that base."

Did it work?

"Nope," said Steinbach. "He pretty much did what he wanted. He's definitely the best leadoff hitter in baseball. There's no doubt about it."

Perhaps Toronto manager Cito Gaston came up with the best plan to stop Henderson after watching him during the 1989 championship series.

"I guess the best thing to do when Rickey goes for second is throw the ball to third," said Gaston. "Maybe we can get him on his way over there."

[1991]

The Persuasive Healing Powers of Baseball Trivia

BY STEPHEN D. BOREN, M.D.

When I was a surgical resident at Tufts New England Medical Center in Boston, Massachusetts, I quickly learned that I could use my baseball trivia knowledge to help treat my patients. Bob was a 39-year-old patient with a broken neck who had paralysis and numbness similar to that suffered by Roy Campanella after his tragic auto accident in 1958. He had a surgical incision on his buttocks that was not healing properly, and he spent his entire days lying on his belly, thinking about his young wife, his three children, and his non-healing wound. On my first day on this surgical service, I walked into his room and was immediately greeted with "How is my wound looking?"

I glanced around the room and noted several Boston Red Sox posters. I briefly commented to Bob about the memorabilia and immediately realized he was a loyal Red Sox fan. I suddenly asked him, "Who did the Red Sox trade to get Jackie Jensen?"

As Bob lay there thinking about that question, my intern, senior resident, and I removed his dressing, cleaned the wound, and applied sterile gauze. Since he had a broken neck, he could not feel our work. He was facing forward and could not see what we were doing. Finally he said, "All right, who was it?"

"Tom Umphlett and Mickey McDermott," I replied.

"Gosh, you're right," Bob responded.

We started to leave the room. "Wait," said Bob. "How does the wound look?"

"It is getting better," I truthfully answered.

Later that day, our surgical service returned. Bob again asked, "How is my wound looking?"

Quickly I asked, "Who was the Red Sox regular first baseman in 1953?"

"That's a good question," said Bob. As he pondered about it, we again worked on his wound.

"Harry Agganis," he answered.

"No, Agganis was their first baseman in 1954." We cleaned the wound and changed the dressing as he kept thinking.

"All right, who was it?"

"Dick Gernert," I replied.

"I cannot believe I forgot him," said Bob. "Hey, how does my wound look?"

"It is getting better," I replied.

Twice a day for two months this ritual was repeated as I tossed trivia questions at him to take his mind off his physical problems. Bob's wound was gradually healing. His spirits were also improving. One day Bob said, "I hope you know as much medicine as you know baseball!"

After I left the surgical service, I became an Emergency Medicine physician. I remembered Bob's case and the good results I had with using baseball trivia, so I continued to use my baseball knowledge in the various emergency rooms that I worked.

One five-year-old child poured PineSol Cleaner in the family's beef stew. I had to pump his mother's stomach while a pediatrician pumped his brother's stomach. The mother was upset by her young son's crying, and I wanted to distract her. I asked her, "Do you have any hobbies or interests?"

"I am a Cleveland Indians baseball fan" was her startling answer.

So I asked, "Name the eight regular position players for the 1954 pennant-winning Indians."

She lay there thinking about Jim Hegan, Vic Wertz, Bobby Avila, George Strickland, Al Rosen, Al Smith and Larry Doby. Like almost everyone, she missed Dave Philley. I also explained that Bill Glynn actually played more games at first base that year than did Wertz. She told me that concentrating on my questions rather than on her son's condition kept her "from going crazy."

Every patient who has a cut that I will sew up, gets asked, "What do you want to talk about?" I do not want them worried about their cuts. I want them to be as relaxed as possible. I have talked to patients about politics, art, football, basketball, automobiles, archaeology, anthropology, history, and other subjects. I must admit that I prefer it when they want to talk baseball. I find out what their level of knowledge is and what interests they have. If a patient is a Chicago Cubs fan, I always ask, "What three Cubs hit home runs their first official time at bat?" So far, no one has responded, "Frank Ernaga, Cuno Barragan, and Carmelo Martinez." [Editor's note: Paul Gillespie of the Cubs also hit a home run in his first at-bat on September 11, 1942.]

One Detroit Tiger fan was surprised to discover I knew that George Vico had hit a home run his first time at bat. "How did you know that?" he asked me.

"I told you I know baseball" was my answer.

Once I was examining a pleasant, elderly patient with dementia. Oddly enough, when people lose their memory they forget recent events but retain their past memories. Thus he was talking quite intelligently about the 1920 Chicago White Sox and knew that Byrd Lynn was their second-string catcher. Yet he could not tell me his own address!

I have used baseball trivia to give medical lectures to both medical audiences and the general public. Before I gave a talk to the local chapter of the American Heart Association, I had slides made of baseball cards. When I talked about various types of heart disease, I showed them cards of Tony Conigliaro, Frank Hiller, Hal Smith, Mayo Smith, Joe Sparma, Bill Sarni, Carl Morton and other players with heart disease. Smith's and Hiller's cards reflected that one can return to sports after a heart attack. Conigliaro's card sadly reflected the need to have prompt cardio-pulmonary resuscitation (CPR) after a cardiac arrest. All showed that young, healthy people can be stricken by heart disease.

I have used these same baseball card slides for giving lectures to physicians when I teach advance cardiac life support (ACLS). These colorful and interesting slides are a welcome change from the many boring standard teaching slides.

When I teach medical students and interns about eye diseases, I use my slides of baseball players with vision problems. Thus they see slides of George Sisler, Ryne Duren, Dennis Higgins, Herb Score, Bill Sudakis, Whammy Douglas, and other baseball players who were plagued by visual disturbances.

I had one elderly gentleman who kept coming into my Emergency Room by ambulance with multiple vague complaints. I could never find anything wrong with him. All his tests were always normal. I discovered he was a lonely widower who liked baseball. He told me he had a tryout with the Chicago Cubs in the early 1930s.

After that I would quickly examine my lonely friend to make sure he was not "crying wolf" too often, and then talk about Phil Cavarretta, Augie Galan, Billy Herman, and Gabby Hartnett. I would get him some coffee and a donut, and go about seeing the medically ill patients. I would stop back in his room, talk a little about the other Cubs players such as Stan Hack, and then contact his son. His son, a local police officer, would come immediately and apologize profusely because "Dad should not be bothering you all the time."

I explained that I did not mind. I told him I did not spend time with his father when there were truly ill patients who needed immediate care, but I felt he was a pleasant, lonely man who also needed attention.

Once I took care of a ten-year-old boy who was cut in a minor car accident. He had just returned from a baseball card show and had his card album with him.

I immediately noticed the carefully guarded treasure. He talked to me about his real old cards—cards from the early 1980s! He reluctantly gave the album to his mother so I could examine him and suture his wounds. Several years later I worked with his mother who was a nurse. I did not remember her at all. She remembered me. She said, "My son was so relaxed and happy talking to you about the baseball cards. He had been so scared about getting stitches. I want to thank you for what you did for him."

Early one morning I saw an elderly man with severe shortness of breath. He was in heart failure. Part of my standard patient evaluation is always to ask what sort of work they do. Frequently this gives me an idea of what might cause their medical problems. For example, a patient with lung problems might be breathing harmful chemicals at work. This patient told me that he had driven a shuttle bus for a local hotel for the past twenty years. "What did you do before that?" I asked him.

"I was a pitcher in the Negro League" was his surprise answer. He told me about pitching to Sam Jethroe in Chicago around the time of the Negro All-Star Game in 1942 or 1943. I asked if he was right-handed or left-handed. He said left-handed.

Thus I started his chart with "This 72-year-old former Negro League left-handed pitcher presents with sudden onset of shortness of breath."

Later on I noticed both my intern's and my resident's evaluations of my patient. Each started off "This 72-year-old former Negro League left-handed pitcher presents with sudden onset of shortness of breath." Considering that these "Third World" physicians did not have even a basic idea about baseball, I found this plagiarism a sincere form of flattery!

[1991]

The Game I'll Never Forget

BY RYNE SANDBERG AS TOLD TO GEORGE VASS

I was in shock. I really was, right after the game that day in June 1984. I just couldn't believe it. You dream of having games like that, but you never really expect to have one.

I'm not all that comfortable talking about myself. Still, I have to admit that game against the Cardinals at Wrigley Field in June [23] 1984, when we were a game or two out of first place, is the one that comes first to mind when anybody asks me about the most memorable game I've played in.

A lot of people saw that game because it was a Saturday "Game of the Week," so it was on television all over the country. People still remind me about it and often ask me whether it is one of my outstanding memories, and I'd have to say it is.

Maybe more than that one game itself, what happened later was what makes it stand out for me even now. We went on to win the division championship that season, and a lot of people seem to think that game was a turning point for us. I believe it just might have been.

At the time we were in a three-way battle for first place with the Mets and Phillies, and we'd just gotten Rick Sutcliffe in a trade from Cleveland. We all knew Sutcliffe was a big-game pitcher, and that trade convinced us management was going all out to win that year. That gave us an added boost of confidence, the feeling that we could do it.

The game didn't start out like anything special. I got a single in the first inning to drive in a run and tie the game at 1-1, but then the Cardinals scored six runs in the second inning to take a 7-1 lead.

When we went into the bottom of the fifth inning we were still down 7-1, and it looked like it might not be our day. Somewhere in there I got another single, but it went to waste.

We scored a couple of runs in the fifth and I drove in one of them with a ground-out, but the Cardinals got the two runs back in the sixth so we were down 9-3, still trailing by six runs.

We really stirred it up in the bottom of

Ryne Sandberg blossomed into the National League's MVP in 1984, leading the Cubs with his bat and glove. He topped all league second basemen in fielding, committing only six errors in 870 chances. He hit .314 with 36 doubles, 19 triples and 19 homers to go with 32 stolen bases.

the sixth when we finally got to the Cardinals starter, Ralph Citarella.

We had three runs across and men on second and third when I came to bat for the fourth time in the game. Neil Allen, another right-hander, was pitching for the Cardinals, and I got a single off him that knocked in two more runs.

So it was 9-8 and it was a ballgame again, the kind of game you get so often in Wrigley Field when the wind is blowing out. You're never really out of a game there in a situation like that. I've been in a lot of big-scoring games in Wrigley, some really wild games.

I led off the ninth inning against Bruce Sutter, who was one of the best relievers at that time with that split-finger forkball. He'd been with the Cubs before I was, so him pitching against us meant something extra to the fans.

I'd never hit Sutter particularly well—not too many people did at that point in his career—but this time I hit a home run to tie the game at 9-9.

What a lot of people may not remember is that after that we loaded the bases but Sutter got out of the jam to send the game into extra innings.

We just couldn't seem to hold the Cardinals. Willie McGee had a great game that day (he hit for the cycle) and he was in the middle of a Cardinal rally in which they scored two runs in the 10th to take an 11-9 lead.

It looked pretty bleak for us, especially with Sutter pitching. You just don't get too many chances against a pitcher like that.

We were down to our last out in the 10th, down two runs, when Bob Dernier drew a walk. I was the next batter and I can't say I was thinking home run. Not against Sutter, not against anybody. You just hope to get the ball in play, to keep things going, that's what you try to do most of the time.

But Sutter threw me a pitch I could drive, and I hit another home run to tie the game at 11-11. Hitting two home runs off Sutter? It was just one of those things that happened. And it happened at the right time.

We went into the 11th inning all tied up again, and Lee Smith shut down the Cardinals.

Then Leon Durham won the game for us. He singled, stole second and took third when the throw went into center field. After the Cardinals walked the bases loaded, Dave Owen hit a single to score Durham and we'd won the game 12–11.

Like I said, I was in shock after the kind of day I'd had, five hits, seven runs batted in and two home runs—and those off Sutter.

Later, somebody told me Whitey Herzog, the Cardinals manager, had said something about me being the greatest player he'd ever seen. Well, I took that as a compliment, what else could I say.

But I know that was my best game, if I had to pick and choose. It was my biggest day in baseball.

More than that, the game was important to us as a team. It kind of amazed us, being able to come back like that, and we just began to roll and won the division title.

[1993]

Pursuit of Home Run Record
Exacted a Big Toll on Aaron

BY BRUCE LOWITT

The ballpark won't be there in a few years—not the mound from which Al Downing threw the ball nor the bullpen where Tom House caught it. The place that became the shrine to Henry Aaron's 715th home run, the Babe

Ruth record-breaker he hit 20 years ago last April 8, will be more parking lot than park.

And Aaron will miss it. Atlanta–Fulton County Stadium was more than just foul lines and fences to him. It was home. It was the place where all the sweet suffering came to an end, where he could finally begin to enjoy the game again.

"I have an attachment to it," he said. "I realize Atlanta needs a new stadium (the team will move into a new one after the 1996 Olympics), but I love the place. I had a lot of great moments there, not just the home run. . . . I lived in that ballpark, slept there many nights."

He was going through a divorce then, living at the Landmark Apartments. When fans and the media found out where he was, they laid siege on him. The ballpark became his refuge.

There was a trainer's room off the Atlanta clubhouse. After a night game, after all the interviews, he would repair to that room to sleep. "The trainer's table was like a big bed, comfortable," Aaron said.

On the road he would stay apart from the team, often registered under an alias. "I should have been able to enjoy that time," he said. "All I wanted to do was play baseball, and I couldn't enjoy that at all. . . . I wouldn't have wished that year on anyone."

The 1973 season ended with Aaron one home run shy of Ruth's hallowed 714. The Braves opened 1974 in Cincinnati. Aaron wanted to sit out the series against the Reds, "to make sure I'd break the record in front of people who came out to see me every day."

Commissioner Bowie Kuhn ordered Aaron into the lineup on Opening Day against the Reds. "I thought since I was the principal character in this, he should've talked to me, gotten my feelings," Aaron said. "If I had to do it over again, I'd say, 'Forget it. I open the season in Atlanta.'"

Instead he played Game 1 in Cincinnati, and in his first at bat, his first *swing* of the season, he crushed a Jack Billingham 3-and-1 fastball for a three-run homer to tie Ruth. He sat out the next two games and, against the Dodgers on a Monday night on national television and in front of 53,775 fans (still an Atlanta stadium record), he faced Downing.

"When the game started, I wanted to hit the homer, just to get it over with," Aaron said. "Not so much because of the controversy. It's that my teammates were having to put up with so much."

It was 9:07 p.m., the fourth inning, the Dodgers leading 3-1 and Darrell Evans on first. "Downing got caught in a situation where he couldn't walk me. He had to throw something I could hit."

Downing's first pitch was a changeup in the dirt. The second one was a low slider. Then it was gone.

"It wasn't hit as hard as the one off Billingham," Aaron said. "The one off Downing was a typical Atlanta homer [the stadium is still known as the

Hank Aaron being greeted by Atlanta Braves teammates at home plate after he had hit his 715th career homer on April 8, 1974, breaking Babe Ruth's record. He connected against Al Downing of the Dodgers. Aaron finished his career with 755 home runs after playing 23 years in the majors. In 1982 he was elected to the Hall of Fame.

Launching Pad]. I had hit enough of them there that I knew it had a chance of going out."

In the Braves' bullpen in left-center field, relief pitcher Tom House positioned himself under the ball, in front of a huge bank-card billboard that read: *Think of it as money.*

"If I didn't catch it, I'd still have the stitches stamped on my forehead," House said.

The ball and bat Aaron used are in a bank vault in Atlanta. "I'm going to give them to Cooperstown eventually. One guy offered me close to $200,000 for the ball, but it's not for sale at any price," said Aaron, who finished with 755 career home runs with the Braves and Milwaukee Brewers.

Half an hour after *the* home run, after the celebration and the speeches and the turmoil had ended (and after half the ballpark had emptied) the game resumed. The Braves won 7-4.

"The home run was more relief than anything," Aaron said. "It was ironic that people enjoyed it more than I did. I was just looking forward to going back to playing baseball the way I'd played it before."

He had spoken the previous year with former Yankee Roger Maris, who had broken Ruth's record of 60 home runs in a season (Maris hit 61 in 1961). Maris had been vilified, not only because he was chasing Ruth's ghost but because he wasn't Mickey Mantle, the far more popular Yankee slugger. "He told me what he went through," Aaron said. "I was prepared not to let the same things happen to me."

Aaron survived that pressure, the hate mail and death threats, not only because he was chasing Ruth's ghost but because he was a black man doing it. "I used to tell people, 'I'm not trying to make people forget Babe Ruth; I'm trying to make them remember Henry Aaron. I think I did that.

"I've never thought I was in his shadow. That was other people. The Babe hit majestic home runs. People say if he hadn't been a pitcher he might've hit another 700. I didn't make the rules. When I hit 715, the record was mine. I believe eventually—and it's gradually being shown—that people are going to think, 'Hey, this man hit a lot of home runs.' No matter how you slice it, 755 is a lot of home runs.

"My career was fulfilled. I don't have any regrets. I got just about everything I could have gotten out of it. I played in two World Series, 24 All-Star Games, finished with a batting average over .300 (.305). I have nothing to be ashamed of."

[1994]

Aging Baseball Glove Leaves a Touching Legacy

BY GARY SCHWAB

The person who usually handles questions about baseball gloves, the "Glove Man" they call him, is not in when I call Rawlings Sporting Goods in St. Louis. Instead I'm transferred to Ruth in public relations.

I try to explain what I'm looking for, without really knowing, and Ruth says, "I understand about fathers."

Twenty seconds later, she's back on the phone. "Maybe this will help in your story," she says, and starts to read:

"A baseball glove is a beginning and an ending . . ."

You get only so many baseball gloves in a lifetime.

I have a home movie where, in short pants on an Easter Sunday, I unwrap my first baseball glove. My second glove took me through Little League. My third was stolen from my high school locker. My parents gave me my fourth glove as a present when I was 26.

I won't get another. I'm 42 now and will use the glove I have for the rest of my life.

My father had only one glove in my time with him. It's a Rawlings T-70, the George McQuinn Claw.

McQuinn was an All-Star first baseman for the St. Louis Browns in the late '30s and early '40s. He's remembered in baseball history books as a "solid-hitting, excellent-fielding first baseman."

My dad would have preferred a Lou Gehrig model, his hero, but that year Rawlings didn't offer a glove named after the great Yankee player.

In 1943, when a five-piece maple dinette set sold for $29.85 and kids under 12 got in the local Broadway Theatre for nine cents, the Claw was a top-of-the-line model at $15.35.

It's listed as "the hit of '41 and '42" in an ad on page 345 of the 1943 *Baseball Guide and Record Book,* next to a Pacific Coast League schedule that includes the notation "Buy War Bonds to Speed Victory."

In 1943 the country was in the heart of World War II. My dad was 15, a left-handed first baseman, then and always. In baseball you become your position if you play it long enough, and I never imagined him anywhere other than at first.

By the time I was old enough to field ground balls and throw out imaginary runners in our games of catch after dinner in the '50s, I saw my father's glove as an extension of his hand. When he put it on and we played, he took on a physical grace he didn't possess in the rest of his life.

He was 6-foot-4, a dream of a first baseman for a kid trying to learn to play shortstop. His reach allowed him to get the balls I threw too high or too wide; his skills allowed him to shuffle his feet, keeping one on the base, and short-hop the throws that were too low.

He taught me how to throw, how to hit and, during a camping vacation in Michigan in the sand dunes one summer, how to hook slide.

And when I got my first baseball glove, he taught me how to break it in.

First work oil into the glove, especially the pocket area. Take a few throws to fit your hand into the glove, put a ball in the pocket and tie the glove closed with heavy rubber bands for a few days.

Do that and the glove becomes yours. It starts off on the rack and can belong to anyone for a price, but once you've shaped it and marinated it, it's yours.

My father's glove is more than 50 years old now. The leather is dark, some strings are missing and you can barely make out George McQuinn's name.

My father died suddenly in December [1993] at 65 of a heart attack. He was at home in Cleveland after watching on television the Charlotte Hornets beat the Cleveland Cavaliers. Watching a good ball game is not a bad way to go out, we joked in the fragile days after, when you find yourself crying or laughing at times you never expect.

And almost immediately, I knew there was one possession of his that I wanted—his baseball glove.

My mother looked for months, reporting regularly that she couldn't find it anywhere. I found it last June on his workbench, sitting out in plain sight.

It wasn't there when I went home for his funeral, and although I would like to believe it just appeared, more likely my mother found it and passed it over as worn, folded leather instead of the magical glove I had described.

We who care about baseball sometimes make too much of the game, but really it is no different than anything you love and try to hold onto.

No different than a pair of dancing shoes saved in a box in the attic, or a dog-eared copy of *Charlotte's Web* that your mother used to read at bedtime.

At first we talked of framing my dad's glove. But I wanted it where I could get at it—to feel the imprint of his hand, to smell the leather, to remember.

So I keep it on a shelf next to mine. When I sit up late at night sometimes and I reach for a glove, it's his I get down. Even though it's the wrong hand for me, I put it on and it feels just right.

I put on his glove and it could be 1961 again, when we sat at Municipal Stadium in Cleveland on a Sunday afternoon and watched Roger Maris chase Babe Ruth's home run record.

It could be any afternoon in the park. He would hit me high, high fly balls and I would chase them down, laughing, thinking I could catch every one.

Or it could be the last game I watched with him, the two of us sitting with my daughter, Jesse, two summers ago, watching the Knights play in Charlotte on a brilliant summer night.

During those times we talked baseball, not philosophy. But if you care about the game, you learn from its rhythms.

You learn there is always a beginning, a spring when anything's possible.

You learn there is always an ending that never changes once it's played out.

The ball always goes through Bill Buckner's legs and the Red Sox always lose the Series. Mitch Williams always throws the same pitch, Joe Carter always hits it into the left-field seats and the Blue Jays always win.

We never spoke of it, but I think we both knew what was at stake.

We celebrated in life, and now I celebrate him in death.

When I sit and throw a baseball into the deep pocket of his glove, I have no regrets. I just miss him.

"A baseball glove is a beginning and an ending," Ruth of the Rawlings public relations department is reading over the telephone. "A child's first sure step toward adulthood; an adult's final, lingering hold on youth.

"It is promise, and memory."

She skips further down on the essay on company stationery that is entitled "What Is a Baseball Glove?" and continues:

"Above all, a baseball glove is the union of family recreation and togetherness; a union beyond language. . . ."

She continues reading, but I don't hear the rest.

[1995]

Hall of Fame Batters and Pitchers Name Their Toughest Opponents

BY WILLIAM J. GUILFOILE

Hall of Fame members were surveyed over recent years with the question, "Who was the toughest pitcher or batter you faced during your career, and why was he a special problem?"

Here is how they responded:

Billy Williams: "Ray Sadecki. When Ray first came into the league with the Cardinals, I would get my hits off him when he threw hard stuff because I was an aggressive hitter; but when he started to learn how to pitch it was tough, because he threw a lot of off-speed pitches and I just couldn't wait. It was a case of him knowing he could get me out."

Ted Williams: "Any pitcher throwing sinkers and hard sliders."

Ralph Kiner: "Ewell Blackwell. Toughest right-handed pitcher for right-handed batters. With his sidearm delivery, gangly physique and the velocity of his fastball, it was most difficult to find the ball. It was on top of you before you knew it. He also would knock you down at the drop of a hat. He was lean and mean."

Stan Musial: "Curt Simmons. Curt's herky-jerky delivery was very hard to time. He threw hard with a tailing fastball."

Roy Campanella: "Ewell Blackwell. He was so tough because he threw sidearm and had good stuff."

Luke Appling: "Lefty Grove. His fastball had great speed and movement."

Pee Wee Reese: "Ewell Blackwell. He was not only a problem for me but for anyone that ever faced him! He was 6-6, had long arms, came from third base, good curve, sinker ball and a little nasty on the mound. I bunted on him one time, it went foul; when he picked it up he said 'Pee Wee, I don't like people to bunt on me.' Needless to say, I didn't anymore. Didn't want to wake him up. His best year was 1947 (22-8) I believe. If he had stayed healthy he would have been one of the greatest of all time. As Walker Cooper once said, 'If all the pitchers were like Ewell, we would be back on the farm plowing the fields and planting corn.'"

George Kell: "Bob Feller and Bob Lemon. These two were the very toughest for me—Bob Lemon because everything he threw broke in the same direction. It might be down and out or down and in or straight down, but always down. He never pitched above the waist. Bob Feller threw harder than any man I ever faced and that alone was tough enough, but he also had one of the best curveballs I've ever seen. Plus he had a herky-jerky motion that hid his pitches well, and he was just wild enough so you did not dare dig in."

Enos Slaughter: "Walter (Jumbo) Brown. I just did not hit him."

Al Lopez: "Hal Schumacher. He had a hard, fast sinker."

Lou Boudreau: "Hal Newhouser. He never threw a straight ball—the pitch was either moving up, down, sinking or rising. P.S. I was fortunate not to have to bat against my pitching staff of Lemon, Feller, Garcia, Gromek, Bearden, Smith and Paige!"

Buck Leonard: "Satchel Paige. Because of his great speed."

Yogi Berra: "Alex Kellner. I couldn't pick up his delivery because of his strange herky-jerky style."

Brooks Robinson: "Frank Lary. Sinking fastball. He liked to pitch inside a lot and then throw a little quick breaking ball away. I just could never hit him. He was very intimidating. I always felt when he pitched inside, he didn't care if he hit you or not."

Willie McCovey: "Bob Veale. He was about 6-6, a left-hander and very wild. Being a left-hander didn't pose a problem because I actually enjoyed hitting against left-handers since they made me concentrate more at the plate. But in the case of Bob, he wasn't just wild low, or high, or inside but wild in all directions, which is a problem for any hitter. The fact that he was so tall made it a little tough for me to pick up his pitches, and being wild besides is the reason he gave me so much trouble."

Ernie Banks: "Sandy Koufax. Sandy was a special problem for me because he possessed exceptional control, speed, and a great curve ball. He was highly disciplined, extremely committed and a very private person. These qualities enabled him to concentrate on his profession without a lot of unnecessary distractions."

Willie Stargell: "Juan Marichal. Juan had a fastball, curveball, slider and screwball—each pitch he threw at any time, in any situation, and at various speeds. On any day that could be a combination of 9 to 11 different pitches. The key to hitting is timing. When facing Juan sometimes there was no such thing as you getting your timing down. A note: Sandy, Gibson, Drysdale, Carlton, Seaver, Ryan, Sutton, Niekro, Jenkins, and many others need to know they were not a piece of cake either."

Eddie Mathews: "Juan Marichal."

Bobby Doerr: "Bob Feller. Had an overpowering fastball and a very good curveball. A tough motion made it harder to pick up his pitches."

Red Schoendienst: "Carl Erskine and Sandy Koufax. Both had deceptive deliveries; it was hard to pick up the ball upon its release. They could also mix up their pitches with great control. They seemed to have command of their fastball, change and curve and could use any pitch and put it anywhere over the plate when necessary. They were smart pitchers, and it was a great challenge to face them."

Al Kaline: "Nolan Ryan. I was 38 years old, and he could throw hard and he was wild."

Mickey Mantle: "Too many to pick one out, but Dick Radatz supposedly K'd me 44 out of 66 times, or some crazy amount. He could throw pretty hard and he kept the ball up and in."

Johnny Mize: "Claude Passeau. He had a bad finger on the glove hand, and they allowed him to rub the ball in the glove. He would throw the ball to the left-handed batter, and the ball would break inside on your fist. Players call it a sailer. I never used my favorite bat, because I would break it."

Cool Papa Bell: "When my timing was off, they were all a problem."

Rick Ferrell: "Bob Feller. I remember Feller when he first came into the American League and pitched at Old League Park in Cleveland—I think he was about 18 at the time. He used a big motion in his delivery and was very fast with a good curveball. I have been told his fastball was once clocked at 105 mph. I didn't see it, but I don't doubt it. The four years he spent in the service prevented him from setting records they would still be shooting at."

Billy Herman: "Bucky Walters. He was a right-handed sinkerball pitcher, and I didn't like the ball breaking inside to me."

Bill Dickey: "Dazzy Vance had a terrific fastball and a curve that was hard to follow. He wore a shirt with long floppy sleeves that distracted the hitter when trying to follow the ball."

Charlie Gehringer: "We did not have speed clocks during my playing days. In my baseball career, I never hit against anyone who threw the ball with more speed than Lefty Grove, plus the fact that he rarely threw curves or changes of pace especially in his early years."

Monte Irvin: "Ewell Blackwell. He was a right-hander, threw very hard, was mean and came at you from the side. Need I say more?"

Duke Snider: "Juan Marichal. His control and deceptive windup and delivery of his pitches were a problem. His fastball and curve were both high-quality pitches. He later came up with a screwball, but I was his teammate then and was able to see him confuse the other hitters instead of me! He and Koufax were the best I have seen."

Although he wasn't much better than a .500 career pitcher with an 82-78 lifetime record, Ewell "The Whip" Blackwell was regarded by many National League batters as their most unwelcome adversary on the mound. He missed three years in the army, 1943–1945, earning most of his wins with the Reds from 1946 to 1952.

Harmon Killebrew: "Stu Miller. I faced a lot of tough pitchers in my career, but Stu Miller gave me more trouble than anyone else because of his great motion. The ball never seemed to get to home plate; it was as if it was on a string and he was pulling it back. I believe I had only two hits off him in my career (one a home run). If I'd had to face him every day I'd have been back in Payette, Idaho, real fast!"

Some Hall of Fame pitchers were asked, "What hitter gave you the most trouble during your career, and why was he a special problem for you?" Here's how they responded:

Whitey Ford: "Nellie Fox. He never seemed to strike out and he had a good eye. He never overswung, just tried to hit singles and doubles. Nellie had no trouble against left-handers—he hung in very good against them. He was a great competitor."

Hal Newhouser: "Ted Williams. The problem pitching to Ted was, he made you throw strikes in the zone he wanted, not the strike zone I wanted. And on top of that, he wouldn't chase any bad balls outside of the strike zone if you got two strikes on him."

Don Drysdale: "Way too many to name, but Willie McCovey comes to mind! I tried to throw him overhand, deep-cutting curves, but my only problem was that I didn't have one!"

Early Wynn: "Ted Williams. He was a great hitter every time he came to bat, day in and day out. He didn't chase bad pitches in the dirt or above the letters. He had great eyesight and knew where the strike zone was. He also knew what pitches every pitcher had and which was his best pitch."

Rollie Fingers: "Harmon Killebrew. It didn't make any difference what I threw—he hit it; and it just wasn't that he hit it—it was where he hit it. If he had accumulated frequent-flyer miles on fly balls off me, he could have gone to Europe and back at least four times."

Bob Feller: "Tom Henrich. He never overswung. He made a ball be a strike, and he would swing at a low overhand curve now and then. Tom would go for the single and cut down on his swing with two strikes. He was a good clutch hitter and hard to strike out—it seemed as if he was always looking for the pitch I was delivering."

Ferguson Jenkins: "Roberto Clemente. He was an awesome hitter, a great talent, a super human being. Without him in Pittsburgh, in the '60s and '70s, the team would have just been another ball club. Roberto was the backbone of the team."

Jim Palmer: "Rod Carew. He had a .328 lifetime average as a major leaguer."

Catfish Hunter: "Tony Oliva of the Twins, because he could hit any pitch anywhere. He did not have a weakness."

Bob Lemon: "Minnie Minoso. He'd stand right on top of the plate. You could hit him any time you wanted. I didn't want to hit him, though, because he was a friend."

Robin Roberts: "Ernie Banks."

Tom Seaver: "Willie McCovey. He was a very aggressive hitter who looked for my best pitch—the low fastball. Since McCovey was essentially a low ball hitter, he had a high number of pitches in his 'wheelhouse' each time we faced each other."

[1995]

Farewell to Mickey Mantle, One of Baseball's Greatest

BY DAVE VAN DYCK

Mickey Mantle was, to an entire generation, more than perhaps the greatest baseball player of all time.

He was a genuine god, an all-American hero who graduated from the area of zinc mines in rural Oklahoma to the gold mines of glittering New York.

He was idolized by adults and emulated by kids, from both the smallest of towns and the biggest city.

He was more than just a baseball player: he was blond, talented, famous, rich and lived life to its fullest. And he played for the Yankees. He was the Babe Ruth and Joe DiMaggio of the 1950s and 1960s.

And so, when he died last August 13, not only the baseball world grieved but a generation of men and women who felt like he belonged to them.

For Mantle, so seemingly indestructible as a Yankee, succumbed at age 63 to a rapidly spreading cancer that progressed from his liver to all his vital organs.

Mantle received a liver transplant June 8, but on August 1 it was announced the cancer had spread to his right lung. Then, doctors said it had spread through his body. He died at Baylor University Medical Center in Dallas, with his wife, Merlyn, and son David at his bedside.

Bobby Murcer, a teammate of Mantle's late in his career, a fellow Oklahoman and now a Yankees announcer, said, "Mantle was an idol of mine. He was the greatest player I ever saw play baseball. I don't think to this day Mickey realized how much he touched the hearts of fans. We truly lost not only a major league hero but a person who portrayed the innocence and honesty that we'd all like to have."

In the end, videotapes showed a weak and frail Mantle. But old black-and-white newsclips will forever keep alive memories of Mantle as an unsurpassed baseball player who three times won the Most Valuable Player award and hit a record 18 World Series home runs.

There probably will never be another Mickey Mantle in sports, so athletic on the field and admired off it. He came along at a time when people exalted in the good and excused the bad in their hero's personal life.

Mantle was a product of the times, playing hard during work hours and living hard after hours. Although he later came to regret those days, the late-night exploits of Mantle and teammates Whitey Ford and Billy Martin became legendary.

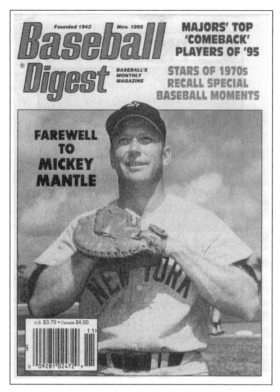

The cover of the November 1995 issue of *Baseball Digest*, with an accompanying article, paid tribute to one of the Yankees' all-time greats.

In truth, Mantle lived much longer than he ever expected. The son of a poor miner, Mantle watched family and friends succumb at young ages.

"My dad died at 39," Mantle said in Tony Kubek's book *Sixty-One.* "My uncle, both his brothers and my grandfather all died young. I'm the first male in my family to make it to 45 since I don't know when.

"They all had Hodgkin's disease, and that came from working in the zinc mines."

Mantle even had a son named Billy who developed the same disease and died last year of a heart attack at age 36.

Kubek, a Yankee teammate, writes, "Mickey talked a lot about death. The thought of dying scared him, and that's part of the reason he lived the wild life so long. He was trying to squeeze the most out of every second, yet trying to forget the prospect of dying at the same time. He was an interesting contradiction."

And yet there was no contradiction to the way he played baseball, even with battered legs that nearly crippled him from pre-adulthood. In fact, baseball scouts passed on the amazing high schooler, thinking his legs would give out before his heart.

But Mantle played 18 big league seasons, replacing DiMaggio in center field for good in 1952—at the age of 20. By the time he was 26, he had won back-to-back MVP awards. By the time he retired after 1968, he had hit 536 home runs, played in 12 World Series and 17 All-Star Games and had led the league at least once in every major offensive category, except hits, doubles and stolen bases.

And he probably could have done that, had his legs allowed him to. Still considered maybe the fastest player ever, Mantle suffered from osteomyelitis in his left leg at a young age and multiple knee operations in the prime of his career.

"When I had knee surgery in 1951," Mantle said later, "I never did the exercises. Maybe if I had, my legs would have lasted longer. I don't know. I was young. I figured it was never going to end."

Mantle rarely took batting practice for fear of injury, but in 1962, at the age of 30, he won his third MVP award. That season, despite making only 117 starts, he still led the league in walks.

"Best one-legged player I ever saw," longtime Yankees manager Casey Stengel said.

"By 1961 . . . it wasn't unusual for him to need help getting out of a cab," Kubek wrote. "He'd sort of brace himself and put out his hand. One of us would grab him by the wrist and literally pull him out of the cab."

And yet Mantle made up for his physical problems with superhuman upper-body strength, even though he never lifted weights. Once, a Mantle home run was measured at 620 feet.

A natural right-handed hitter, Mantle nonetheless made his fame for hitting left-handed home runs over the short right-field wall at Yankee Stadium. That he was a switch-hitter was a lasting testament to his father, Mutt, who named his son after 1934 World Series hero Mickey Cochrane and who started coaching his son in baseball when Mickey was only two years old.

Mutt Mantle's never-ending dream to have his son play baseball came true in 1949, when the Yankees signed him to a Class D contract for $1,150 bonus and $400 a month. Two years later he was in the same outfield as DiMaggio.

"When I was young and 'healthy,' I believe I was the best," Mantle said later in life. And an entire generation agreed.

Mantle was not the greatest baseball player ever, although many say he could have been were it not for injuries.

Mantle was not even the greatest Yankee ever. Babe Ruth was.

There are those who say Mantle was not even the greatest outfielder of his time in New York. Giants fans say it was Willie Mays; Dodgers fans say it was Duke Snider.

And there are those who will argue that Mickey Mantle wasn't even the best Yankee of his time. They say that Yogi Berra was.

But statistics don't always tell the story of superstardom. For Mantle could do things better than any of the others, when his legs would allow. He was faster than any of them, he could hit a ball farther than any of them, his arm was as good.

No, Mantle statistically wasn't the best baseball player ever.

But he was the most recognizable.

You see, Mantle and national television joined the major leagues together. They became instant hits together.

Mantle's Yankees played in 12 World Series and won seven of them. In the 1950s and early 1960s, the World Series meant the Yankees vs.

somebody. And television was there to record it all, when the World Series was still the world's biggest sporting event.

The World Series became Mantle's stage for the entire United States. His fame grew with each fall, with each Mel Allen New Yorkese description of his heroics.

So it is little wonder many fans remember Mantle as the greatest ever, because he was—at least in the World Series. He still holds records—probably unreachable—for home runs (18), RBI (40), runs scored (42) and walks (43).

Mantle may have been the Golden Boy of the Golden Era, but it is impossible to put a ranking on the greatest players of all time, although most historians agree Ruth was unparalleled.

The book *Total Baseball* has devised a ranking of baseball players called "Total Player Rating." It lists Mantle as 11th, behind such players as Ruth, Willie Mays, Ty Cobb, Hank Aaron, Ted Williams and Mike Schmidt.

Mays, Snider and Stan Musial may have been better—at some things at some times. Mays hit more home runs, Musial more doubles and Snider was the only one with five straight 40-homer seasons.

All had fewer strikeouts than Mantle. But no one—including Williams—hit more home runs from 1942 to 1960. And yet Mantle should be remembered as more than a home run hitter.

Ten times he hit better than .300, six times he led the league in runs scored, five times he led the league in walks, four times in home runs and three times in slugging percentage.

He also won a Triple Crown in 1956, when he hit .353, slammed 52 homers and drove in 130 runs while leading the league in runs scored and slugging.

[1995]

High School Coach Recalls Nolan Ryan as a Young Pitcher

BY JIM KREUZ

Nolan Ryan's high school baseball coach Jim Watson recalls the day he witnessed a feat that has yet to be repeated before his eyes, one that foreshadowed what Ryan would accomplish in the future. "Back in those days [fall of 1960] they had the President's Physical Fitness test," recalled Watson, "and one of the three events was the softball throw. I was helping out the

8th-grade physical education coaches because the junior high and high school at Alvin [Texas] back then were both on the same campus.

"The coaches and I were sitting up in the stands, having just lined up about two hundred 8th-grade kids at one end of the football field, and were watching as they were throwing a softball from the goal line, one at a time. Most would throw it to the 30- or 40-yard line, about 60 to 70 yards. That was about average.

"Then this skinny kid steps up and throws it *over the goal posts on the other end of the field. In the air!* We made him throw it again, and the second toss went through the goal posts just like the first! Remember, this is the 8th grade. I asked his PE coach who he was, and he replied, 'Nolan Ryan.' He threw that softball at least 50 yards farther than any other kid that day.

"I had seen a few of his Little League games, but I wasn't that impressed, and wasn't eagerly awaiting him. In fact, to show you just how smart I was, I figured he'd be a shortstop or third baseman, because he could hit well and could throw hard. Because of his velocity as a 12-year-old, I thought he might make us a starting pitcher one day, but he was just one of the kids; he didn't stand out."

Watson was asked if the story about Ryan throwing newspapers while he was growing up helped contribute to his arm strength, and this was his reply: "I even asked him that question. He told me, 'Actually Coach, I threw papers with my left hand. I would throw them out the driver's side window, and would throw them over the car with my left hand. That was just newspaper hype. It was started by the *Houston Post*'s Mickey Herskowitz.'"

"Prior to the game during Easter break of Nolan's sophomore year, I had pitched him in a few spots, but I played him at shortstop quite a bit. He was a really good high school hitter, and he liked playing shortstop. Over the Easter holidays we were scheduled to play South Houston, one of the top teams in the Houston area that year. Quite a few of the guys went to the beach for the weekend, and the game was on a Saturday night. So I told them before they left to be back here by 4 o'clock, and 'If you're not back by then, you don't play.'

"So, naturally because Ryan was a sophomore, he was there on time. But some of my seniors didn't make it back in time, so I sat them on the bench. I told Nolan, 'You get to pitch tonight.' Well, he pitched a no-hitter, and remember, it was against one of the top Houston teams. He just blew the ball by them. I think he struck out 15 or 16 (in a seven-inning game). From that point on, I knew I had someone special. Oh, I think he walked about six or seven, which was all right because we beat them by one or two runs. I'd never seen a ball move like that. He could throw a ball as hard his sophomore year as he could his senior year. He was a natural.

"In 1964, Nolan's junior year, we had a really good team. That year Deer Park won our district and went on to the State 4A [largest-school classification] finals, finishing No. 2 in the state. We beat them four times that year, in tournaments and district play, and Nolan beat them every time. But we couldn't beat Clear Creek. We lost out to Deer Park by one game, and the only games they lost were to us, in over 20 games.

"The high school games were spaced out enough so that he could pitch probably 70 percent of the games. With Nolan, I could pitch him on two days' rest. Those high school games only went seven innings, and in most cases he could throw half-speed and win. He always felt good.

"Our first district game during his senior year, Nolan beat Deer Park, the team to beat in our district, and he beat them pretty handily. The next two games we played Dickinson and Clear Creek, both good, solid clubs. Dickinson beat us 1-0, with Ryan pitching, and Clear Creek beat us 2-1, also with him pitching. So we had just completed two bad games, and really, that was our season, it was over. Or so I thought. The day after the second loss, at practice, they were just doggin' it. In their own minds they were thinking, 'We will never win the state championship now.' I don't mind telling you that I was down too, but I couldn't let them see it. They were lollygagging around, and I told 'em they'd better hustle up or we would stop practice and run. They just kept it up. Well, I stopped practice and took them over to the track, which was adjacent to the ballpark, and we ran and we ran and we ran. Everyone ran until they were puking. Looking back now, it was anger on my part. Nolan threw his guts out also. After that, I sent them in for their shower. My B team was playing in Texas City, so I went over there to see them play.

"I wasn't planning on pitching Nolan the following day, by the way. Red Murff was sitting up in the stands with a group of scouts, and he said, 'Hey, Jim, Bing Devine is coming down tomorrow to watch Nolan pitch. Bing is the GM of the Mets.' I said, 'Well, Red, he's not pitching tomorrow.' Red said, 'Oh, he's got to, he's got to!' I told him there was no way he could pitch, and told him about how I ran him until he couldn't see.

"Red was on the phone to me the next day, pleading with me. On the bus that was taking us to the game against Channelview High, I called Nolan over to ask him how he was doing. He said, 'No way, I've had it.' I said, 'Well, Bing Devine of the Mets is coming down to see you pitch. Do you think you can gut it up for a few innings?' He said, 'I don't know, but I can try.' I felt really bad. Then I had to go tell Pat Wagner, the scheduled starter, that Nolan was going to start. Pat understood.

"I've never seen such an atrocious game! By the third inning, Devine was gone. He was long gone. I told Red Murff before the game started that Ryan was hurting, but Red said he'd be OK because it was only Channelview, one of the weaker teams in the district. They had us down 5-0 after one or two innings. We brought Pat Wagner in and won the game. In fact, we didn't lose another game until the state title game. This game woke 'em up. Several months later, after Nolan signed with the Mets, I told him I cost him $30,000 or $40,000 in his bonus. I think they gave him a $30,000 bonus for signing.

"We beat Snyder 5-3 in the semi-final game during Nolan's senior year, and they were the top-rated team in the state. Nolan threw a one-hitter. If I had known then what I know now, after we'd gotten a three-run lead, I would have pulled Nolan and put Pat Wagner in. That would have enabled Nolan to be somewhat rested for the state championship game the following day. Before the final game, Nolan said he felt fine, so I played him. He would have done OK if we'd gotten out of that first inning. Unfortunately we made three errors and got behind 3-0 real quick. Ryan was upset, so I pulled him. We ended up losing 6-3. But we had an outstanding season, and Nolan went 19-3.

"During Ryan's sophomore year, one day during practice I got into the batter's box and told Nolan to give me all he had.

A power pitcher throughout his career, Nolan Ryan toiled 27 years in the majors, completing his journey with 324 wins and a monumental record of 5,714 strikeouts. When he was inducted into the Hall of Fame in 1999, he was accompanied by George W. Bush, a former executive of the Texas Rangers, who pleaded with attending writers not to ask any political questions.

"*I couldn't see the ball*, and it was in broad daylight. I wasn't a trained batter, and was half scared because at times they'd try to hit me. You see, we had a rule that if you got hit by a ball or a bat, and you rubbed it, you had to run a lap around the track. It was mental toughness. One day Nolan hit me right square in the back with a pitch, and I got up and everyone looked at me. I didn't rub it though. I couldn't. [While Coach Watson was telling this story, he was grimacing with pain and rubbing his back.]

"I used to scream at Nolan when he'd throw a curve ball. His curve ball would break maybe a couple of inches, and they'd knock it out of the ballpark. His fastball might at times only break a couple of inches, but they couldn't see it. They all wanted to throw that curve ball. I let him call his own game. But for every curveball, I wanted him to throw four or five fastballs. And I didn't want him to throw a curveball with two strikes on the batter. He was happy with that. He didn't have a changeup; it was his curve. I can't remember him ever striking out a batter with the curve.

"Nolan was a leader, but not a loud-mouthed leader. Everyone looked up to him."

[1996]

Hack Wilson Belted Homers, Hecklers with Equal Gusto

BY JOHN B. HOLWAY

Burly, barrel-shaped Hack Wilson loved to hit, drink, and fight, though not necessarily in any particular order.

"With apologies to Ernie Banks," Chicago newsman Eddie Gold writes, "Hack Wilson was probably the Cubs' most exciting player on and off the field." From 1926 to 1931 "no Cub belted more homers, took more belts, or belted more people in barroom brawls."

How could he hit so well with a hangover? "I see three balls," Hack once shrugged, "and swing at the middle one."

Cubs manager Joe McCarthy once gave Hack a temperance lecture, dropping a worm into a glass of alcohol. The worm promptly died. "What does that prove?" Joe asked.

"If you drink, you won't get worms?" Hack asked helpfully.

In 1930, Wilson enjoyed perhaps the greatest season of any batter in history. He slugged 56 home runs, still the National League record, and drove in 191 runs, still the all-time major league mark. The home run mark will fall some day, but the RBI record may last as long as baseball is played as we know it.

Wilson has been dead for almost half a century, but he's still batting them in.

According to biographers Robert S. Boone and Gerald Grunska, Reds catcher Clyde Sukeforth was sitting in the bullpen when Wilson konked the ball "high up into the seats." It bounced back into the field, however, and umpires, thinking it had hit the wall, wouldn't give him a home run. "Of course we weren't going to say anything," Sukeforth said, "but Hack really had 57 homers that year."

Later, Chicago researcher Bob Sutterman discovered that Wilson was short-changed another RBI. The official scorer gave the credit to Cubs first baseman Charlie Grimm, although Wilson clearly drove the run in.

Wilson's original record was 190 RBI, later adjusted to 191 after research on the matter was officially accepted.

For two wonderful years, 1929–30, Hack was one of Chicago's two most famous citizens. The other, of course, was gangster Al Capone.

Wilson's best buddy was his roommate, pitcher Pat Malone. One of their favorite pranks was to set fire to customers' newspapers in hotel lobbies.

Standing only 5-6 and weighing 190 pounds, Wilson was "built like a Hungarian wrestler," as writer Westbrook Pegler put it. In fact, the nickname "Hack" came from a popular wrestler of that day, George Hackenschmidt. Hack's broad shoulders tapered into size six baseball shoes. Columnist (and later TV host) Ed Sullivan called him baseball's "mightiest dwarf" and "the world's heaviest midget."

Wilson "was a colorful, colorful ball player," says ex-shortstop Elwood "Woody" English, the last surviving member of the great Cubs team of 1929. "He was a great friend and a great fellow."

"He used an awfully long bat with a thin handle," remembers English, now 89 and living in Newark, Ohio. "If he'd strike out, he'd hit the little end of the bat on home plate, and the handle would fly up in the air. He was strong. He was a long-fly-ball hitter, wasn't a line-drive hitter. He never pulled the ball too much down the left field line."

One of Wilson's drives slammed into the center field scoreboard in Wrigley Field. "There was a dent in there for a long time," English smiles. The scoreboard was then at field level, not atop the bleachers as it is now, but the blow is still considered the longest ever hit in that yard. (Dave Kingman may have hit one farther, but it went out of the park.)

That night Wilson went out to a wild party, drinking Prohibition booze. He was thrown in the hoosegow and ordered to pay a fine of one dollar.

Bill Veeck, later the owner of the Indians, Browns, and White Sox, was then the son of the Cubs' general manager. In 1930, he said, he walked into the locker room in Chicago to find trainer Andy Lotshaw trying to sober Wilson up before a game. Lotshaw put a 50-pound cake of ice in a huge tub and wrestled Hack into it. Wilson fought to climb out, but Lotshaw pushed him back in. Every time Hack's head went down, the ice bobbed up. "It was a fascinating sight," Veeck wrote, "watching them bob in perfect rhythm. First Hack's head, then the ice, then Hack's head, then the ice."

Veeck wasn't sure just what day it was but, Stengel-style, said, "You could look it up—it was the only day in Hack's life that he hit three home runs in one game."

A great story, and probably true. But it must have happened on another day. Hack hit the three homers in Philadelphia, showing no signs of the effects of John Barleycorn. Before the game he was marching impishly up and down the foul line with a bat on his shoulder to the quick-step tune of a Moose Lodge band and to the merriment of the crowd.

Hack loved to clown.

The only thing quicker than his laugh were his fists.

After one catcher called him Fatso, Hack reached into the mask, twisted the receiver's nose, and pushed him backwards.

When Cincinnati bench jockeys called Hack a bastard (he was illegitimate), he plunged into the whole bench and had to be pulled away by cops, ushers, and players.

As Gold says, Hack often hit the bottle, and one day he hit the bottler: he charged into the stands to pummel a loudmouth milkman. The judge called it self-defense.

Lewis Wilson was called "Stouts" by the kids in Ellwood City, Pennsylvania, where he was born in 1900. He quit school in the sixth grade to swing a sledgehammer in a locomotive factory at $4 a week.

In 1921, Hack hopped a freight to Martinsburg, West Virginia, to land a job as catcher in the Blue Ridge League. He once played nine innings in agony after a teammate smeared hot liniment oil in his jock strap.

New York Giants manager John McGraw came for a look and protested that "he ain't got no neck." Nevertheless, McGraw concentrated on Hack's biceps, not his neck, and dug down for $11,500 for him.

Wilson reported to the Giants at the end of 1923 with almost no money. He almost starved for four days before someone told him he could just sign the checks in the hotel restaurant. In his first full season, 1924, Hack batted .295.

The next year he smashed a 500-foot home run in the New York Polo Grounds. In 1926 he was with the last-place Cubs. In spring training manager Joe McCarthy was driving to Mass on Sunday morning when he swerved to avoid a car speeding toward him with several men hanging out the window, bottles in their hands. Behind the wheel was Wilson.

Joe made Hack play the game that afternoon, and Wilson responded with three home runs, one of them the longest ever hit in Los Angeles' Angels Stadium. McCarthy gave him the rest of the afternoon off. "Otherwise," he sighed, "you won't have the strength left to go out tonight."

Wilson led the league with 21 home runs as the Cubs rose to fourth.

In 1927, Hack led the league in homers again, with 30. His stumpy legs raced all over center field as he led the league in putouts too.

The next year, Malone joined the team. In Boston, Wilson and Malone got so drunk they wrecked their hotel room, and the manager evicted the entire team.

However, Hack led the league in homers again, with 31, Malone won 18 games, and the Cubs rose to third.

The great Rogers Hornsby joined the Cubs in '29, batting third ahead of Wilson. Hornsby batted .387 with 39 home runs. Wilson also slammed 39 over the fence and drove in 159 runs, breaking Hornsby's National League mark. Malone led the league with 22 wins, and the Cubs won the pennant.

The World Series, however, would end in disaster for Hack.

Connie Mack's A's won two of the first three games. In Game 4, Chicago opened an 8-0 lead until the A's began rattling hits all over the outfield. In the outfield, Wilson was struggling with a new pair of sunglasses. He lost one fly ball in the sun. Then with two men on, Mule Haas (.323) lifted an outfield fly. Hack lost it in the sun too, for an inside-the-park three-run home run as the A's went on to win 10-8.

McCarthy, however, defended Hack, saying gently, "He didn't put the sun out there."

The next day the A's rallied to beat Malone, 3-2.

"We got a big share of the World Series pot," English recalled, "something like $2,800 or $3,000 apiece for our split. Isn't that awful? Now the average player makes a million dollars a year. Isn't that ridiculous?"

That winter Art "The Great" Shires of the White Sox challenged Wilson to a bout in the ring, but stipulated that "I'll only fight him on a sunny day."

Wilson made fun of himself. He asked waiters to turn the lights down "so I won't misjudge my soup."

Then came Wilson's record-setting year of 1930, one of the greatest seasons any hitter has ever had. It was the hit-happiest season in this century, thanks to a lively ball wound with a special Australian wool. A batter who hit .302 that year was below average.

In the first five games of the season, Hack knocked in only one run.

As late as July 15, Hack had only 24 home runs officially and 82 runs batted in. Then he got hot. July 26 was his three-home-run day.

In a blistering August pace, Hack hammered 13 homers and drove in 53 runs.

Back then fans and reporters weren't as record-happy as they are today. Box scores didn't report RBI, and some papers didn't keep a running count of them.

Also, the lively-ball era had been born only ten years earlier, so the batting records that seem so hallowed today were brand-new then. The major league RBI record, 175 by Lou Gehrig, had been set only three years earlier. The National League home run mark, Chuck Klein's 43, was only one year old.

Hack tied Klein's mark on August 26. The next day he cost his team a run by dropping a fly ball in the field, so, the story goes, he promised the

A short, 5-6 right-handed batter who wore only a size six shoe, Hack Wilson set National League records in 1930 when he hit 56 home runs and drove in 191 runs for the Cubs.

pitcher "a legit homer, and in this very inning" to make up for it. Then he delivered the record-breaker.

By August 31 Hack had 46 home runs and 156 RBI, and the Cubs had opened up a five-game lead.

At Pittsburgh September 6, the Cubs won by a typical 1930 score of 19-14. Hack slugged two singles and a homer to knock in four runs, thereby setting a new National League record.

Only one man remained ahead of him in the record book—Gehrig—although Chicago's lead had shrunk to a half-game over St. Louis. Within a week, they had fallen to third.

On Sunday the 15th, Hack swatted two singles and a homer to pull himself up to 172 RBI, only three behind Gehrig's mark.

Two days later in New York, Wilson busted two home runs, Nos. 51 and 52, good for four RBI, to move ahead of Lou to a height no man had ever reached before. And he was within sight of Ruth's home run record of 60 as well. Hack needed eight homers in the nine remaining games.

Yet when Hack hit No. 53 on the 22nd, the headline writers ignored the feat. Wilson hit No. 54 two days later, but the headline writers thought Bobby Jones' golf grand slam was bigger news.

Meantime *The Sporting News* had been studiously ignoring the greatest RBI assault in history. At year's end the paper didn't even name him to its all-star team.

Hack went into the next-to-last day of the season with 54 homers and 184 RBI. Malone, seeking his 20th victory, faced Ray Kolp (7-12) of the Reds. Hack won the game for his pal with two home runs to bring his official total to 56—only Ruth had ever hit more. The homers knocked in four runs for 188 for the season.

On the final day 20,000 people came out to Wrigley to watch an other-wise meaningless game against the seventh-place Reds. Most of them were there because of Hack's small chance of slugging four home runs to tie Ruth's record. He failed to reach home run range, but he did hit two sin-gles good for two more RBI and a subsequently revised total of 191. The second and last came in on a scratch infield hit in his final at bat.

The afternoon *Daily News* didn't even bother to tell its readers about the total. Hack also batted .356.

Wilson was voted the N.L.'s Most Valuable Player, which was worth an extra thousand dollars in his pay envelope.

That winter he sat down with Cubs owner William Wrigley to negoti-ate a new contract, ticking off all his batting records. "And," he added proudly, "I've also led the league in strikeouts for four straight years." If Babe Ruth could make $80,000, Wilson reasoned, he ought to make $50,000. He settled for $33,000.

"I was at the top of my career," Hack recalled many years later.

It was a steep slide downhill after that.

"I started to drink heavily," he said. He spent the winter in bar rooms, and "when spring training rolled around, I was 20 pounds overweight."

Hack complained that new manager Hornsby wouldn't let him swing on the fat 3-1 and 2-0 pitches as McCarthy had. In addition, the new ball was stitched with raised seams, which made curves snap and fastballs hop. Everyone's hitting went down, especially Hack's.

He didn't hit a homer until May 2, and the Cubs drifted to fourth place. The crowds razzed Hack, "and I kept on getting the old razzberries all year."

Meanwhile, "I couldn't stop drinking." Caught in a police raid on an il-legal speakeasy, Wilson dove through the men's room window. The cops found him wedged tightly in the frame, kicking furiously. He finished the year with 13 homers.

In '32 Wilson was dealt to the Brooklyn Dodgers, taking a pay cut to $7,500. He worked hard to get in shape and hit 23 home runs in bandbox Ebbets Field to help the Bums finish third. His old teammates, the Cubs, won the pennant without him.

Wilson fell to .267 and nine home runs in 1933. He was resting in right field one day while the manager made a pitching change. When the out-going hurler angrily threw the ball against the fence, Hack, startled out of a daydream, played it smartly off the wall and threw a strike to second base.

His hitting fell to .245 and six homers the next year, his last year in the majors. Back in Martinsburg, Hack opened a combination bar and pool hall. His wife divorced him, and he contracted a venereal disease.

He moved back to Brooklyn as a greeter in a bar near Ebbets Field, singing "Take Me Out to the Ball Game" for drinks.

In 1932, Gehrig had knocked in 184 runs. In 1937 Hank Greenberg ended with 183. Jimmie Foxx had 175 the next year, but no one has seriously challenged the mark since then. The closest were Ted Williams and Vern Stephens, who reached 159 in 1949.

Meanwhile Hack worked at a public swimming pool in Baltimore, handing out towels. In 1943 he was living on welfare in a run-down hotel when his old buddy, Malone, came to visit him. After two straight days of drinking, Pat stumbled home in a rainstorm. He was dead of pneumonia a week later.

In 1948, Wilson's landlady found Hack unconscious on the floor with his head bleeding badly. On November 23, three months after Babe Ruth's mammoth funeral in New York, Hack Wilson died in obscurity. The National League sent $350 to cover his funeral.

Only one week earlier, in a gravelly whiskey voice, he had given a nationwide NBC radio audience what might be considered his own epitaph:

"There are kids, in and out of baseball," he warned, "who think because they have talent, they have the world by the tail. It isn't so. In life you need things like good advice and common sense. Kids, don't be too big to take advice. Be considerate of others. That's the way to live."

[1996]

How Outfielder Pete Gray Met the Big League Challenge

BY JOHN STEADMAN

That a one-armed man could play in baseball's major leagues stands as one of the most astonishing achievements in all the history of sports. It was more than a half-century ago, with World War II coming to an end, that Pete Gray played for the St. Louis Browns and, since then, has preferred to fade into the background, resisting most attempts to talk about the experience.

He's reclusive and gives the impression that even the smallest interest in him must be based on some kind of one-man "freak show" curiosity. His days in his native Nanticoke, Pennsylvania, are almost all the same, visiting a restaurant for morning coffee, sitting a spell in Patriot's Square, stopping by the Town Tavern operated by a cousin, Bertha Vedor, and picking up his mail.

Pete is 81 but doesn't look it. He's as slender as a fungo bat, walks with a fast-paced, almost nervous stride, as if at all times he's in a hurry to get some place for an important appointment. He never married, lives in the same house where he was born and doesn't have a telephone.

When sportswriters call friends to intercede for interviews, he says, "Tell them I'm out of town." Or he might explain he isn't available in summer or during the winter, depending upon the season of the year. It's all an excuse.

Obviously, celebrity status has made him uncomfortable. He protects his privacy by being elusive. No doubt he has been wounded by previous meetings with reporters so, as personal policy, prefers to reject all requests.

Not too long ago we sat on a bench in Patriot's Square with Gray and mayor Wasil Kobella and, once Gray began to reminisce, the stories of his boyhood and entrance into professional baseball came with a rapidity that belied an earlier reluctance to talk about himself. Nanticoke, with close proximity to Wilkes-Barre, had a population of 38,000 in the mid-1930s, when Pete was growing into manhood.

Now, with the coal mines, cigar factory and silk mill all memories of the past, Nanticoke has lost many of its once basic employment opportunities. The last census showed a total of 12,267 residents, predominantly Ukrainian and Russian, according to the mayor, and the community is 70 percent Catholic. Gray is of Lithuanian ancestry; his real name is Peter Wyshner.

The city has a cleanliness and order to it that makes it immediately attractive. It was here that Pete Gray grew up in the rolling greenery of Luzerne County, where men going underground to work in the mines always faced the inherent danger of losing their lives.

Nanticoke is where at age six Pete jumped off the running board of a vegetable truck, owned by a huckster who was allowing him to make deliveries for pocket change, and an accident occurred that changed his life.

When he fell to the ground, his right arm was caught in the spokes of the wheel and almost torn from his body. Amputation was necessary. "I don't remember," he said, "but my brother Tony always said I was a natural right-hander, that I held a pencil and fork that way. So I had to become a left-handed ball-player."

This makes what Pete was to achieve later even more remarkable. By necessity, he changed over to bat and throw with his left hand, the only one he had. With one arm he had to devise a system to play the outfield.

He caught the ball in his glove, pushed the glove under the stump of his right arm, let the ball roll across his body, grasped it in his bare hand and made the throw—all in a split-second motion.

The glove, now on display at the Baseball Hall of Fame in Cooperstown, New York, was given to him by an undertaker who lived in nearby

Pete Gray was 30 years old when he played in 77 games for the St. Louis Browns in 1945. He collected 51 hits in 234 at-bats, including six doubles and two triples. After catching a ball in the outfield, he deftly maneuvered his glove so he could get the ball to his left hand and make a throw to the infield cutoff man.

Hanover. "I took out all the padding," he explained. "I went to a shoemaker who put a piece of stiff leather on one side of the glove that gave it firmness. When the ball hit the glove, it kind of closed."

At the plate he batted from the left side and held the bat in his left hand. His reputation as a young player became established in the Wilkes-Barre area and in 1942 led to his joining Three-Rivers of the Canadian-American League where he batted .381 in 42 games. The surprised owner didn't know he was getting a one-armed player but, because Pete had made the trip, decided to give him a chance.

"You could hear a pin drop when I came up the first time," recalls Gray. "They announced my name in French and English. The bases were loaded in the ninth inning, a tie game. I hit a line drive on a 1-1 count and we won, 2-1. The fans took up a collection. They gave me $850."

He once had what he thought was an opportunity to go to Philadelphia for a tryout with the A's. He entered the club office at Shibe Park but, while waiting to see owner-manager Connie Mack, he met his son, Roy.

"Where's the kid we are supposed to look at?" asked Roy. He was stunned to learn that the prospect was standing there in front of him, a one-armed man. "I was told then that Connie was busy and couldn't waste his time seeing me," remembers Gray.

Mack was quoted as saying he had enough trouble finding capable players with two arms and didn't see any future for a one-armed candidate. In 1944, Mack finally met Gray when the Philadelphia Sportswriters Association honored him as the "most courageous athlete of the year."

Mack, talking to Gray, said, "There was a one-armed fellow one time who wanted a tryout. Are you the same boy?" Gray, of course, answered in the affirmative. The next year, Gray particularly enjoyed dominating a series when the Browns beat the A's in St. Louis and Connie, the rival manager, was there to watch him do it.

Another similar incident happened in Miami, where the Philadelphia Phillies were in training camp in 1940: "All I wanted was for manager Doc Prothro to look at me. I went down to the field and asked him to let me work out. He said, 'Get off the field, Wingy, or I'll have the police come get you.'"

That scenario had a similar postscript, too. In 1944 he played for the same Prothro when they were together at Memphis in the Southern Association, where this one-armed marvel batted .333 and led in stolen bases with 68.

He won the league's most valuable player award, and his contract was sold to the St. Louis Browns.

Gray, by his performance, made Prothro revise his opinion. The Memphis manager, after seeing what he could do, said, "The majors are in for a big surprise. They'll be amazed to find out a fellow with just a left arm can do things better than a lot of two-armed guys around. I'm sure he'll stick." Remember, a war was on and baseball rosters had been depleted.

Gray batted only .218 with the Browns in 1945. The most impressive thing was that in 234 at-bats he struck out only 11 times. "Fastball pitchers never bothered me," he said. "I was weaker on change-ups."

The reason is that once he began to offer at a pitch he couldn't "stop the bat" because he didn't have two hands to use as a brake. With only one hand, off-speed deliveries had him out in front and vulnerable with little to hit with.

The 1945 Browns were defending American League champions and had a chance to win again. Some teammates were critical, saying that rival clubs were taking an extra base on balls hit to Gray in center field.

"That's the way I remember it," said Irv Hall, who played for the A's. "But let me tell you, it was amazing what he could do. Infielders knew they couldn't make a mistake on any ball he hit because we all found out how fast he could run."

Another surprising thing is that Pete used a 36-ounce bat, heavier than most players were swinging then and now. He was doing it all with one hand. About the only thing he couldn't do was tie his baseball shoes, so a coach or another player had to assist him.

His reputation was of a tough competitor who could fight effectively with one arm if he had to, and that he was distant in personal relationships. We once asked a Browns coach, Zack Taylor, if it was true that Pete was a "mean SOB."

Taylor answered, "Let me put it this way. To play in the big leagues with one arm you better be a mean SOB."

Bob Feller, Hall of Fame pitcher, says Gray provided "an enormous emotional lift for wounded veterans coming home from World War II who saw what honest-to-God determination could do."

Gray made $5,500 with the Browns but remembers that Bill DeWitt, a team official, gave him a bonus of $1,500.

The saga of Pete Gray, even 51 years from his emergence in the majors, is intriguing and exciting. He's an everlasting credit to the human spirit, a man who sits on a park bench with his memories and only rarely shares them with others.

[1996]

A Belated Salute to Four Old Ballparks

BY RAYMOND MILLER

The warm feeling many Americans harbor for baseball parks goes way beyond mere affection. It intermingles with the more mysterious emotions usually associated with religion, and thus has more to do with Native American ancestor worship than with the architecture unit in Art Appreciation 101. It might also be noted that the ballpark calendar offered for sale this year by the Hall of Fame is called "Hallowed Ground," or that one of the many fine recent books on the subject bears the title *Green Cathedrals*!

The classic ballparks built between 1909 and 1923 are regarded as shrines, as, well, hallowed ground. Wrigley Field and Fenway Park generate feelings of reverence in people who've never set foot in Chicago or Boston. And the horror of possibly losing Tiger Stadium to "progress" once compelled hundreds of Detroit fans to encircle the old yard and give it a big, loving hug.

Yet among the classic parks that were built—or rebuilt—in steel and concrete as baseball entered its glory years, there are four that have, alas, been sadly forgotten. No one wipes away a tear when their names come up. No one writes in funereal prose about how much the game has lost since they shut down. Why, there are even some—oh, blasphemy!—who actually laugh at their memory. I am writing, of course, of the Phillies' Baker Bowl, League Park in Cleveland, Griffith Stadium in Washington, D.C., and Boston's other park, Braves Field. Now, wipe that smirk off your face, and let's give them their due!

What, you may ask, did Ebbets Field in Brooklyn have that these parks didn't? A classic park is supposed to have odd dimensions, right? Well, here you have your Little League fences (right field in Baker Bowl and League Park) as well as outfield expanses you'd have trouble clearing with a howitzer (left field in Griffith Stadium, center field in League Park, and all of Braves Field). You like odd architectural details? What about the medieval clubhouse in dead center at Baker Bowl? Or League Park's perverse right field wall? And how can you forget that right-angle projection which made the center fielder's life interesting in Washington? Although some people might laugh, there's nothing in any of these parks a devotee of the Polo Grounds should get smug about.

Some people would say that this is the problem—location. Put Griffith Stadium in New York, and all those talking heads in Ken Burns' baseball film would have been singing its praises. But let's be honest—the most salient difference between the revered classics and our sad-sack foursome was the talent in the home-team locker room. You can't win with stiffs, and winning is what sanctifies a ballyard, old or new. And Baker Bowl, League Park, Griffith Stadium, and Braves Field knew precious little of that. Together these four parks hosted a grand total of eight World Series—that's only two more than were played in Ebbets Field alone between 1947 and 1956. (Baker and League combined saw a mere seven World Series *games*.)

Meanwhile the Braves or Phillies occupied the National League cellar 14 times between 1919 and 1938, and the Senators . . . well, we all know what they did, and where they finished doing it, too. If the forgotten four are remembered at all, it's usually for what the other guys did: Braves Field was where the Giants won to force the fateful playoff in 1951. When people mention Griffith Stadium nowadays, it's almost always when talking about the mammoth shot that Mickey Mantle drove over the left field bleachers in 1953.

These grounds had a lot of other things in common. Those in Philly, Cleveland, and Washington were all built on the site of a wooden 19th-century National League field. They all had "monster" walls in right, similar to Ebbets Field and Shibe Park. They were tiny—capacity at Griffith rarely cracked 30,000; at League Park it was under 23,000; and Baker Bowl was lucky to seat 20,000. And they all at one time or another bore the name of the league their team represented (a common practice in the old days).

By contrast, Braves Field was the first of the modern "super stadiums"—newer than all the classic parks except Yankee Stadium, and holder of baseball's attendance records before the latter facility opened in 1923. Like League Park and Griffith Stadium, it was designed by Osborne Engineering of Cleveland (so was Yankee Stadium, for that matter). It shares one other, more dubious, distinction with League and Griffith—and Baker, too: along with Ebbets Field, these were the first of the original steel-and-concrete parks to be closed to baseball.

Baker Bowl, Philadelphia

Long before Candlestick Park and the Kingdome, Baker Bowl was the most despised baseball stadium in the nation. By the time the Phillies abandoned it in 1938, hard-hearted Philadelphians were calling it the "Dump on the Hump"—"the Hump" being a railroad tunnel that passed under the outfield—and other unflattering names. One baseball writer sarcastically characterized off-season renovations in the visitors' locker room as consisting of new nails on which the players could hang their clothes. And once it was gone, it was most definitely forgotten—my whole family is from Philadelphia, but I wasn't sure Baker Bowl ever really existed until I saw some old photographs in a book. The only thing my father had to say about the ancient pile was, "It had a tin wall in right field that clanged like a garbage can lid whenever the ball hit it (cackle, cackle)!"

Ah, but it wasn't always like this. When it opened on May 2, 1895, National League Park was the glory of the baseball world, the first modern ballyard. It replaced a wooden facility that had burned during the previous season. Owner Al Reach was bound and determined that fire would never inconvenience his club again (not to mention threaten the lives of its fans), so the new park was built with brick and steel. It took your breath away to look at it, a veritable castle that summoned images of Camelot. It featured a newfangled upper deck, cantilevered to eliminate obstructing pillars and supported by quasi-medieval turrets. A wedge-shaped, two-story clubhouse dominated straightaway center, and a 40-foot wall loomed over right field, 279-plus feet from home plate. (In fact, it was tin on brick.) By 1910 the second deck was extended to the pole in right and halfway down the line in left. These were the only major renovations to Baker Bowl, which, incidentally, looked from the air more like a footbath than a bowl.

From the beginning, that right field wall made an inviting target for left-handed power hitters. It's no coincidence the Phils won the first game in their Taj Mahal by the football-like score of 19-10, or that two of their lefty sluggers finished first and third in homers in the park's first year. Scores regularly reached double figures throughout its long service life, and bashers from Gavvy Cravath (1912–1920) to Chuck Klein in the 1930s kept that tin wall rattling. The 1930 Philly lineup plated 543 runs at home (more than the 1927 or 1961 Yankees could manage) and batted a collective .315.

But we all know that power can take you only so far. The Phillies regularly led the league in most offensive categories in the mid-1890s but never finished any higher than third. Then, after spotty success in the first two decades of this century—a pennant in 1915 and a few second-place finishes—they nosedived into the second division. In the 1920s and '30s, they ended the season as high as fourth exactly once. That fearsome 1930 unit might have scored all those runs at home, but their pitching staff gave up 100 more, and they finished dead last.

Meanwhile, Baker Bowl was going to seed. With an average attendance of less than 3,000 souls per game, the owners didn't have the capital for basic maintenance, much less the expansion and modernization that was so desperately needed to compete in the modern era. By the mid-'30s, fans in the lower deck preferred to watch the game standing up in order to avoid being showered by rust and other debris when the folks in that once-innovative upper deck stomped their feet. The Phillies' owners fell victim to the deadly Catch-22 of sports: they had to renovate the park in order to attract fans, but since fans weren't coming in the first place, they couldn't afford to.

So in the end, the park that once took the fans' breath away left them holding their noses. The Phillies finally grew tired of all the mean jokes and moved into Shibe Park as tenants of the A's in mid-season, 1938. Their shabby little jewel box was ignominiously relegated to midget auto races, donkey baseball, and other indignities before being mercifully torn down in 1950.

To my knowledge, nobody uttered a peep of protest, much less went out to hug the decaying relic. Today, shabby storefronts extend the length of the old tin monster in right; a gas station stands where that signature clubhouse once stood; and a dour '50s-era glass and steel office building occupies the site of the majestic main entrance at 15th and Huntingdon. Unless you've read some baseball history, you'd never know that a major league ballpark once occupied the site.

League Park, Cleveland

No, it only seems like the Indians played forever in Cleveland Stadium (nee Lakefront Stadium), the infamous Mistake by the Lake. For the better part of their first 46 years, their home was winsome League Park, at the corner of 66th and Lexington. This ballpark isn't so much despised as forgotten. But in any case, it certainly deserves better than history has given it.

The original League Park was built of wood and served as the home of the N.L. Spiders throughout the 1890s. The Cleveland Spiders were a fine club, winning the second half of a split-season pennant in '92 and finishing second in 1895 and '96. But their owner, Frank Robison, wasn't satisfied with the way they drew. Unable to find the right price for this franchise, he went and bought another, the future St. Louis Cardinals, and transferred all his best ballplayers, including pitcher Cy Young, from the shores of Lake Erie to the banks of the Mississippi. The disemboweled Cleveland team finished the 1899 season with an all-time worst record of 20-134. The luckless arachnids were dropped by the league for 1900, and League Park sat abandoned.

But not for long. The upstart American League transferred one of its franchises there in 1901, and big league baseball once again flourished on

Lexington Street. By the end of the century's first decade, the owners were faced with more fans than the rickety plant could safely hold, and League Park was redone in steel and concrete for the 1910 season.

The result was a ballpark as eccentric as any the game has known. Like many urban yards, League Park's dimensions were schizophrenic—both cramped and spacious at the same time. It took a healthy 375-foot poke to clear the left field wall at the pole, and both power alleys were over 400 feet away from home. The deepest point (in left-center) was originally a cavernous 550 feet, and it never got shorter than 450 feet. The right field wall, however, beckoned to the batter a scant 290 feet away, and the club had to replace up to 30 windows a year in the Andrews Storage building just beyond it.

Now, a word about that right field wall—because it was a beaut. It stood 45 feet high (counting the screen in play at the top) and was so constructed that, according to author Michael Gershman, "balls could hit three different surfaces, with five different outcomes." When the batter lined a ball to right, even the left fielder had to stay alert, for if it hit one of the steel supports in that wall just right, *he* would be the one to chase it down.

For my money, that alone would have been reason enough to hold on to League Park but, alas, the city got ambitious, and the club got greedy. In a misguided attempt to land the 1932 Olympics, Cleveland hired Osborne Engineering to build an athletic Shangri-La on the shores of Lake Erie. By 1931 the Olympics were headed for L.A., and Lakefront Stadium was all dressed up with nothing to do. Until the Indians were finally lured there the following year.

Now, sure, Lakefront could hold nearly four times as many people as League Park, but it didn't take long to find out that a lot of those 80,000 couldn't see what was going on on the field, and that they were liable to freeze when the wind blew in off the lake. The players discovered that the stadium felt empty with anything less than capacity, and they were daunted by its vast dimensions (Babe Ruth once claimed he couldn't play the outfield there without a horse).

And so, common sense entered into a pitched battle with wounded community pride and plain avarice. The Tribe decided to move back to League Park, but only on weekdays and Saturdays. Lakefront Stadium would be saved for Sundays and holidays, when they had a better chance of drawing a huge crowd. But greed finally won out for good in 1946 when the otherwise saintly Bill Veeck succumbed to visions of yearly attendance records and abandoned the little ballpark for good. League Park was demolished in 1951, although the old ticket office and part of the outfield bleachers still stand in the community playground that bears its name.

We all know the rest of this sad story. After an all-too-brief flirtation with glory in the '40s and '50s, the Cleveland Indians degenerated into one of the majors' sorriest franchises. You always had the feeling, though, that that miserable stadium was dragging them down like a gigantic albatross around their necks. I mean, how would *you* feel playing in a fog-enshrouded mausoleum night after night, in front of friends, moths, and the lunatic with the tom-tom? There are a number of morals in all this: Big isn't always Better, Money isn't Everything, "Modern" does not always mean "Superior." I wonder: How many people close to the Indians secretly wish that Veeck had stayed in League Park?

And is it my imagination, or does shiny new Jacobs Field bear a passing resemblance?

Griffith Stadium, Washington

No baseball team has garnered less respect than the Washington Senators. In their own lifetime they became a literary symbol for futility (the play *Damn Yankees*). Today they are the Team That Time Forgot. Everybody knows the Dodgers started in Brooklyn; I'd wager that 50 percent of knowledgeable fans are aware the Orioles began life in St. Louis as the Browns. But most fans probably think the Twins sprung full-grown from Ford Frick's forehead in 1961. And those darned expansion Senators just make matters worse—not even seasoned baseball writers know whether to assign the legacy of Walter Johnson to Minnesota or Texas. All that's left of the Senators is the old, dumb line, "First in war, first in peace, last in the American League".

Wilting contempt has also been the lot of the Senators' old home, Griffith Stadium. No other classic ballpark has been so actively dissed by contemporary writers: Michael Gershman calls it "unremarkable" and "the Rodney Dangerfield of ballparks." David Nemec once described it as "decrepit, archaic." And Robert Creamer admits in his introduction to *Lost Ballparks* that he never liked the place (and this in a work that celebrates the very concept of classic ballparks!).

But fans of the Griff should come out of that closet. If old ballyards are indeed hallowed ground, the lot off of 7th St. N.W. is as sacred as any. This was the baseball home of Walter Johnson and Josh Gibson, for gosh sakes, not to mention a whole slew of underappreciated players like Hall of Famers Sam Rice and Heinie Manush. Harmon Killebrew, number five on the all-time homer list, got his start here. And historians generally regard the 1924 World Series—the Senators' only championship—the best in the decade.

Washington fans have had a tough row to hoe over the years. On two separate occasions in the 19th century, they had National League teams go belly-up on them. Their entry in the fledgling American League was also a stinker, and their first owner gave up on them after only three years. The new owner saw fit to move their makeshift park on Brandenburg Road to the site of old National Park (or Boundary Park) in north-central D.C., which had been the home of the defunct N.L. Senators. Set in from 7th St. and Florida Ave., on a green trapezoid where an oak grove had once flourished, Washington's new/old American League Park was typical for the wooden stadia of the time, with its modest covered grandstand and small foul-line pavilions, its very short foul lines and the veritable prairie in center.

When the era of classic ballparks started in earnest, the Senators seemed unlikely to jump on the bandwagon. After all, they were still an aesthetic and economic failure. But then fate intervened—in 1911 a plumber's torch ignited the combustible structure at the worst possible time, only weeks before opening day. Insurance provided a measly $20,000 settlement, but they still managed to rebuild enough of the park to start the season on time.

True to the times, the stands were recast in steel and concrete and expanded. In order to make room for the new, larger left-field pavilion, the diamond had to be tilted 45 degrees to the right, and thus were born the future Griffith Stadium's two most distinctive characteristics. The once-miniscule left-field line now extended the length of the lot, and, even after the subsequent addition of a massive bleacher section, exceeded 400 feet. Meanwhile, in order to provide big-league dimensions in right and center, the club was forced to buy property that once stood outside the fence. Unfortunately, the people who owned the flats by the old right field corner refused to sell, and so the new center field wall had to make a detour around them. This became a right-angle projection into the outfield, and the big tree on the lot just outside the wall became a local landmark. (Babe Ruth once launched a drive into this tree.) The unusual combination of prodigious left field line and center field bulge gives Griffith Stadium the appearance in some old photos of a gigantic, broken-backed washtub.

Over the years, major renovations to Griffith Stadium were few and far between. The foul-line pavilions were double-decked in 1920, and because these were graded more steeply than the home-plate grandstand, the new second-deck roofs were fifteen feet higher than the grandstand roof. This odd touch makes it look like the stadium is tipping its hat, or perhaps waving. The bleachers were added in 1924. In 1956 the club erected a six-foot screen some 50 feet in front of them in a desperate attempt to make the Griff more hospitable to their right-handed power hitters.

With bombers like Killebrew, Roy Sievers and Jim Lemon, and good young pitchers like Camilo Pascual, the Senators were actually inching toward respectability by the end of the decade. They didn't gel, though, until after Cal Griffith moved them to Minnesota for the start of the 1961 season. Meanwhile, the A.L. perversely foisted another loser on the nation's capital, and Griffith Stadium was home address to a new group of baseball Senators in 1961. That team moved the following year to what is now called RFK Stadium, the first of those donut-shaped multi-purpose stadia that now blight the North American sports landscape.

Griffith Stadium was torn down in 1965 to make room for the new Howard University Hospital. Like the equally unlamented Baker Bowl, there is no indication that major league baseball had ever been played—sometimes quite well, thank you—on the site.

Braves Field, Boston

I date my passion for old ballparks not to my first visits to Wrigley or Fenway but to a professional soccer game. In the summer of '74 I caught the Boston Minutemen of the old North American Soccer League at Nickerson Field, home of the Boston University Terriers. Several of the little plant's features caught my eye right away. First was the quaint building that squatted by the entrance to the grandstand. It was of another era, and not the sort of structure one associates with an urban college football stadium. It looked more like a quaint old suburban train station. Then I was struck by the near-side grandstand. It was an imposing mountain of concrete, with row after row of benches. It looked nothing at all like the spindly metal-framed bleachers on the other side of the field, which were more like standard issue for a low-budget football facility. Then I happened to glance to my right. The space beyond the end zone did not look like it belonged in a football stadium. The far wall seemed to be curved, and the ground between it and the end line was irregularly shaped.

This was the clincher: "That belongs in a baseball park!" I thought. Suddenly, historical vistas opened before me: Of course! There *had* to have been two ballparks in Boston. After all, the Braves had been the first team in town. . . . My suspicion was soon confirmed, and I subsequently learned my attention had been drawn to the only remnants of old Braves Field— the ticket office on Gaffney Street, the right field pavilion, and the original wall in right and center.

The Boston Reds (later, the Beaneaters) had been the juggernaut of the 19th-century National League, winning eight pennants between 1877 and 1898, and finishing in the running on many other occasions. However, as the 20th century dawned, their fortunes took a decided turn for the worse—they were so badly clobbered by the upstart American League's player raids that even their erstwhile "Royal Rooters" abandoned them for the new Pilgrims (now Red Sox). Depleted of many of their stars, they finished last five times between 1906 and 1912.

In those sorry days, they played in the equally sorry South End Grounds, the site of National League ball in Boston since 1876. Once opulent, with a lovely many-towered grandstand, it was now but a decrepit shell of its former self. To make matters worse, it was wedged between railroad tracks, a roundhouse, and a busy street. There was no space for expansion and no way to escape the noxious locomotive fumes. And if that wasn't enough, the hated Red Sox were *nouveau riche* neighbors, playing in the Huntington Avenue Grounds just across the tracks to the north.

The man who purchased the team in 1911, contractor James Gaffney, was determined to move, especially after the Sox opened modern Fenway Park the following year. To this end, he purchased an old golf course on Commonwealth Avenue.

Then the Braves' fortunes turned again. They stunned the baseball world in 1914 by winning 62 of their last 78 games to steal a pennant, before trouncing Connie Mack's lordly A's in the World Series in four straight. Suddenly the time seemed right to build that new park on the old Allston Golf Club links. And, by God, it would not be just any ballpark, either—Gaffney said he intended to build "the greatest ballpark in the world!"

If the fate of Baker Bowl teaches us that earthly grandeur is fleeting, and if the history of League Park illustrates the truism that big isn't always better, Braves Field is an object lesson on the evils of overweening vanity and self-interest. Gaffney started out by selling the more attractive Commonwealth Avenue frontage for a nice profit. This meant putting Braves Field on the back of the lot, hard by the Charles River—and another stretch of railroad tracks. Fans who thought they had left soot and stench behind when the South End Grounds were abandoned were in for a sorry shock.

Gaffney also insisted on having the biggest park in the majors. Why not? He owned the world champions, after all. What better opportunity to sell bushels of tickets? So Braves Field had more seats than any other park in the majors. The papers reported that over 50,000 people came to its grand opening, and the Red Sox set then-astounding attendance records when they borrowed it for their World Series appearances in 1915 and 1916.

Finally, the bumptious owner loved the inside-the-park homer more than any other play, and decreed that batters be able to pop one in any direction. Therefore Braves Field was big in the other sense—its outfield dimensions were gargantuan: 402 feet down both lines, and a whopping 550 feet to straightaway center.

But this vanity plant soon foundered on Gaffney's myriad miscalculations. Whenever the wind blew in from the Charles, fans found themselves not only chilled but befouled by locomotive grit. And because of its great size, too many of those 40,000-plus seats were far, far away from the action.

Most important, however, the game itself changed shortly after Braves Field opened. Thrilled by Babe Ruth's exploits, baseball fans wanted to see baseballs flying *over* the fence, not bouncing toward it across a green pasture. It took five years to hit the first ball out of Braves Field, and no one succeeded in clearing the left field wall until 1924. And so the "greatest ballpark in the world" was passé before it had reached its 10th birthday.

The stadium hung on the team like an ill-fitting suit. With something approaching frenzy, the owners had it altered literally every year: bleachers were added in left and center, then removed; home plate was moved up, back, right, and left; all manner of inner walls were tried in the outfield. Braves Field never looks the same in any two photos from the '30s and '40s.

Nothing helped, of course, and since the Braves' dynasty was so short-lived—they were back into the basement by 1922—who cared anyway? As we saw in the case of the Phillies and Baker Bowl, a bad team simply isn't going to have enough capital to make major stadium improvements.

Those once-impressive steel-and-concrete stands couldn't be moved closer to the action without being completely rebuilt. And without the means to develop first-rate talent, it's going to be the opposition feasting on new, cozier dimensions every time!

Braves Field had one last hurrah in the mid- to late 1940s. Dynamic new owners jazzed up the team's dowdy image. They introduced the still-popular "tomahawk" uniforms, spent money on good players, and fixed up the old park. Trees were planted in center field to obscure the offensive train smoke, the stands were painted, and lights were installed for the first time. The Braves finally got to play a World Series there in 1948. But these latter-day glory years were just as fleeting as those in the teens, and by 1952 the team could attract only a pitiful 280,000 fans a year. The Braves headed west to Milwaukee in '53, and their erstwhile "super-stadium" lay fallow for a few years before being purchased by Boston University and converted into Nickerson Field.

Could anything have redeemed these neglected ballparks in our collective memory? A few more pennants, perhaps. Richer owners, making more timely renovations. Space for more fans. The stands in League Park and Griffith Stadium could probably have been expanded; Lord knows, Braves Field sat on enough real estate to be completely redone. Baker Bowl was probably beyond the pale, but who knows? Where there's a will—and some extra scratch—there's always a way.

The game has flourished since they've been torn down. But I'd still say we've lost something. After all, baseball needs more eccentric outfield walls, not less. So the next time you celebrate the old ballparks, save a kind word for Baker Bowl, League Park, Griffith Stadium, and Braves Field. Reputations to the contrary, they deserve it.

[1996]

The Day I Collected Babe Ruth's Autograph

BY JOHN DEEDY

When I was growing up in the 1930s in central Massachusetts, baseball cards were for play. We pitched them against walls or a flight of stairs until the corners were rounded and the cards so bent that they fluttered instead of sailing crisply toward their target.

Autographs of the stars? We collected them, sure, but we pinned them to the bedroom wall, where they stayed until the paper yellowed and rolled up on itself or, if in an autograph book, we stuck them in a drawer and as often as not forgot about them. Certainly we didn't run around the corner, as many kids do now, and hawk them with some dealer in sports memorabilia. Anyway, those dealers didn't exist in our Worcester neighborhood.

Which is to say the collecting of sports memorabilia wasn't the passion for us that it is for kids today. We had our stacks of baseball cards, sure, but they weren't any more precious than Indian cards. I'd have swapped a Lou Gehrig for a Geronimo or a Sitting Bull anytime. Autographs? You couldn't pitch them like baseball cards and you didn't swap them around. They were of secondary interest.

Thus when Lefty Grove stopped by the house one day after pitching for East Douglas in a Blackstone Valley League game, neither I nor any of my pals asked him for an autograph. My brother, Ed, was even disdainful. "Just because he can throw a ball better than me . . ." he said.

Ed was 8, maybe 9. The rest of us, a little older and naturally a lot wiser, were awed by Grove—his size (when you're 10 or 11, 6-feet-3 is mountainous), his huge hands, his rural Maryland accent. We had never heard anything like that in our land of the broad a's. We posed for a snapshot with him by the copper beech tree in the back yard, and it was like standing alongside the biblical Moses. To have solicited an autograph would have been unseemly. Besides, he was a guest.

In fact, I don't even remember Grove being approached for an autograph at the park in East Douglas, though it's likely he was. If so, there was no circus. In those days it was satisfaction enough to behold one of baseball's luminaries in the flesh, even if as a ball player on that particular day he wasn't breaking a sweat. At batting-practice speed, Lefty Grove could zip it by most any Blackstone Valley batter.

Again, we're talking about the 1930s. Grove was a member of the Boston Red Sox, but the Red Sox weren't scheduled to play that day, and on days off a player's time pretty much was his own. If there were a few bucks to be picked up in a semi-pro game, why not? Major league salaries were not that great. Besides, there was the Depression. Fifty, 75 or 100 bucks wasn't small change when 35 bucks was a week's pay—if you were lucky enough to have a job.

New England towns took their baseball rivalries seriously in those days and, Depression or not, money could be found for a ringer if it was to prove a town's superiority over, say, Uxbridge or Mendon or Woonsocket. Bragging rights, as they say. East Douglas wasn't the only team that shopped for outside talent. I recall Bo Bo Newsom of the Washington Senators pitching for one town team or another. Newsom wasn't the sure-bet Hall of Famer Grove was. Still, he spent 20 years in the majors, and journeyman or not, he wasn't traveling to the Blackstone Valley for the scenery. There's precious little of it there, if truth be told.

Anyway, Lefty Grove was at our house—I should say our flat, for home was the third floor of a three-decker at 12 Wabash Avenue on Worcester's Vernon Hill. He was there because East Douglas' coach, Jack Barry, was dropping me off en route back to Boston with his prize for the day. Barry was my uncle, and I had traveled to the game with him. It was late afternoon, hospitality was in order, and my father was ever the good host. Lefty Grove was in no rush to get back to a hotel room in Boston.

My uncle, be it said, had the contacts necessary to get a Lefty Grove to East Douglas. A former big leaguer himself—11 years with the Philadelphia Athletics and the Boston Red Sox—he had ties to the Red Sox still as a scout and friend of general manager Eddie Collins. Twenty years before, the two had comprised half of Connie Mack's famous Philadelphia A's $100,000 infield—Eddie Collins being at second base and Jack Barry at shortstop. I have a picture of myself sitting smack-dab between the two of them. Come to think of it, I never asked either of them for an autograph. From a half-century's distance, there was a mass of autographs I could have collected as a kid had it occurred to me. This was mostly because Jack Barry was also the baseball coach at Holy Cross, and for years I was the team's batboy. The signatures were mine for the asking. One didn't even need an eye for the sure-fire prospect. Ex–major leaguers were all over the place, it seemed, when Holy Cross was playing. Jesse Burkett, a Hall of Famer, living in Worcester, would be in the stands. When Harvard came to town, it was with Stuffy McInnis as coach; McInnis was the first baseman on that Philadelphia A's infield. One year a radio network sent Frankie Frisch, the

Fordham Flash, to broadcast a Holy Cross game. Frisch, another Hall of Famer, was just out of baseball and testing a new career as a sportscaster.

In fact, there were scores of sports celebrities I could have asked for autographs. I never did. It seemed tacky, a bit gauche. A person's privacy was not to be intruded upon, his fame not to be exploited. It was a rule that followed me through life.

Thus, years later, when I spotted Joe DiMaggio in the gallery at a Westchester Golf Classic, I forgot all about Arnold Palmer, Johnny Miller, Paul Harney and the likes of them. I followed DiMaggio for several holes and never approached him about signing my program book. Another year, Joe Garagiola was in the gallery, and I didn't approach him either, although I suspect he would have welcomed the move. That Joe was from a different mold than DiMaggio, much more extroverted.

All of which is preliminary to a confession. One memorable day, I did break my code of respect for the privacy of the famous. I not only got Babe Ruth's autograph but, "Bless me, Father, . . ." went to shameless lengths to do so.

It was back in 1935—April 15, 1935, to be exact. Babe Ruth had signed on with the Boston Braves after 21 glorious years with the Red Sox and the New York Yankees, and was embarking on what would prove to be his last season in baseball. In those days the Braves traveled to Worcester each spring for an exhibition game with Holy Cross. So, too, did the Red Sox, and being an American League partisan, ordinarily that visit would have interested me more. But this was Babe Ruth who would be in town, The Bambino, Mr. Baseball himself. I bought myself an autograph book, determined to get his signature.

I knew I'd be in a position to do so. A crowd of 10,000—huge for Fitton Field—was expected, but as the Holy Cross batboy I'd be right there on the same field as the god of the diamond. I was a 12-year-old, and I plotted my strategy.

Obviously I could ask my uncle to get the autograph for me. After all, he and Ruth were teammates on the Red Sox before that infamous trade that sent Ruth to the Yankees for 30 pieces of silver. In 1917—the year Ruth, a pitcher then, won 24 games—my uncle had actually been Ruth's manager. A winter or two before, Ruth and his first wife, Helen, had stopped by the Barrys' second-floor flat in my grandmother's house at 1 View St. in Worcester, ostensibly for a short visit; they stayed until it was time to leave for spring training. Yet I felt that to ask my uncle to solicit an autograph would have been like asking Muhammad to go to the mountain. I couldn't do that. People asked him for his autograph.

So maybe I should approach Ruth myself, invoking my mother's name. She was a child, at home still with her mother on the first floor when the

Ruths were staying upstairs. Babe Ruth would ruffle her blond hair when they passed one another. Indeed, my mother's first pair of ice skates was given to her by Helen Ruth. Mrs. Ruth was off to Florida with the Babe—and the Barrys—and certainly she wasn't going to need ice skates there. Problem was, there was no guaranteeing I'd be able to get close to Ruth, given the anticipated crowd and the police security.

Replica of Babe Ruth's signature.

Ah, but what about the Holy Cross first baseman? Babe Ruth would be at first for the Braves and at that position for Holy Cross would be Nick Morris, a classy fielder and strong hitter out of Medford and an idol, too, of mine. He and Ruth would be exchanging positions each inning, and one would expect there would be opportunities for him to pick up an autograph. I talked to Nick and he was agreeable. "Just wait for the right moment, Jackie, OK?" he said.

That moment didn't come in the first inning, which had drama enough of the diversionary kind. Ruth stepped up to bat, third in the batting order, when a man bolted from the stands and headed toward the batter's box. People startled, and the police detail of more than 20 officers tensed. But the "intruder" was only Mayor John C. Mahoney making an impromptu presentation of the key to the city to Ruth. Ruth accepted it graciously, stood to the plate and, in the *Worcester Telegram*'s phrase, "rolled weakly" to Morris at first.

The second inning came and went. Nick Morris still hadn't made an approach and I was becoming a trifle nervous. It was a chilly afternoon with occasional clouds appearing, carrying the threat of rain. Surely a valuable property like Babe Ruth wouldn't be playing the whole game. "Don't worry, Jackie," Morris told me. "I haven't forgotten. I'll get your autograph."

Third inning. Ruth walked on a three-and-two pitch and trotted to first. He and Morris chatted, and an arrangement was agreed upon. The inning over, Morris returned to the bench, took my autograph book, tucked it in his hip pocket. As the teams exchanged sides in the fourth inning, Ruth paused, signed the book—and all hell broke loose.

Thousands of people poured out of the stands, overwhelming the police, and converged on Ruth for autographs of their own. Players on both sides took cover. Jack Barry was livid and directed at Morris a barrage of purple prose he probably hadn't used since being spiked by Ty Cobb in 1912; he was mad that day, too, I understand. Morris said, simply, "I only did it for your nephew," and handed me the autograph book.

I got a dark look, no chastisement. The volcano gradually subsided.

The police cleared the field, but the fans weren't to see much more of the Babe. Ruth had promised at a press conference in Boston the day before the game, "I'll do my level best to bust one on the nose for the home folks." It wasn't to be.

He came to bat in the fifth inning and walked again, whereupon he was lifted for a pinch runner and whisked away. He left waving good-byes and calling out to the bleachers, "Hope to see you again."

That was all the baseball for Babe Ruth on April 15, 1935, but no one felt cheated. From the moment he had entered the ballpark, a motorcycle escort shooing away the advance guard of autograph seekers, he had put on a grand show, accommodating pre-game demands for his signature, horsing around with the fans, even taking a seat with the Holy Cross College band and tooting on a trombone.

However, though Ruth was gone, the fourth-inning autograph incident had set the tone for the rest of the afternoon. It seemed all a Boston Braves player had to do was glance toward the stands and eye contact would set off another stampede, the targets now Wally Berger, Billy Urbanski, Randy Moore, Pinky Whitney and other stars, albeit of a lesser kind. The game was played to the last out, but as sports editor Roy Mumpton observed in the *Worcester Telegram*, "interruptions were many, and long."

The Braves won the game with three runs in the ninth, 5-2, but the outcome was anticlimactic. The real winner had been Ruth. The day had belonged to him.

Twenty-eight games later, the Braves now into their regular season, Babe Ruth retired from baseball. The years had caught up with the greatest hitter in the history of the game. Ruth realized it as well as the rest of the world; he was batting only .181, some 160 points below his career average.

That was a sad day for baseball—and for me—although there was the consolation of having been present at one of Ruth's last games, even if it was only an exhibition contest. And, of course, there was that autograph.

I had tucked the autograph away, and though decades were to pass I never forgot it. I moved on from Vernon Hill—to the army, a stretch in Ireland, journalism jobs in several cities. But in my mind's eye I could still see that 3-by-5-inch autograph book with the black cover in the top right-hand drawer of a desk in the bedroom, just waiting to be picked up.

By 1985 that 1935 autograph had solid value. Only a few years before, I had seen an autograph of Babe Ruth at B. Altman's in New York City with a price tag of more than $2,000. Indeed, the autograph was probably the most valuable single item in my parents' house. But it wasn't value I was looking to recoup. I was after a piece of my youth.

My parents died within a few months of one another in 1985, and my brothers and I closed the flat out. I had only one thing in mind: finding that autograph. I went to the bedroom desk. There was no autograph book. I hunted room by room, fearing the worst the more I looked. I picked among a stack of old football and baseball programs in the shed out back, relics in their own way but not what I was after.

The autograph of Babe Ruth wasn't there. It had vanished, and I was left with a sorrow, one that lingers yet. Except there is the memory, a memory that disappointment cannot dislodge and which $2,000, or whatever the current value of a Babe Ruth signature is, cannot buy. I had stood on the same diamond as the greatest player in all of history. I had gazed on immortality.

And six decades later, I still had my own field of dreams. Who needed an autograph?

[1997]

Larry Doby: An Overlooked Black Pioneer in the American League

BY IRA BERKOW

Larry Doby remembers clearly his first day in the major leagues, that day 50 years ago when he broke the color barrier in the American League. It was 11 weeks after Jackie Robinson had played his first game for the Brooklyn Dodgers in the National League. Doby remembers the excitement of that day when he became only the second black player in the major leagues—he had hardly slept in four nights leading up to it—and he remembers the dismay.

Saturday, July 5, 1947, a sunny morning in Chicago: Lou Boudreau, the manager of the Cleveland Indians, took the 22-year-old second baseman into the visiting team's locker room in Comiskey Park and introduced him to the players. Each of Doby's new teammates stood at his locker and looked over the young black man who had just been purchased by the Indians' owner, Bill Veeck, from the Newark Eagles of the Negro National League. Doby and the manager went from player to player.

"Some of the players shook my hand," Doby recalled recently, "but most of them didn't. It was one of the most embarrassing moments of my life."

When the 6-foot-1-inch, 185-pound newcomer, born in South Carolina but raised in Paterson, New Jersey, stepped onto the field before the game with the White Sox, he stood on the sideline in Cleveland uniform No. 14, glove in hand, for what he recalled as five or ten minutes. "No one offered to play catch," he said. Then he heard Joe "Flash" Gordon, the All-Star second baseman, call to him: "'Hey, kid, let's go.'" And they warmed up.

Doby, a left-handed batter, was called in to pinch-hit in the seventh inning and after "hitting a scorching drive foul," he struck out.

But he was officially a big leaguer, one who the following year would help the Indians win the pennant and the World Series. He became the first black player to hit a home run in a World Series, made six straight American League All-Star teams and, at one time or another over a 13-year big-league career, led the American League in homers, runs batted in, runs scored and slugging average, as well as strikeouts. When he retired in 1959, he did so with a .283 career average and 253 home runs.

As baseball this season celebrates the 50th anniversary of breaking of the color barrier in the big leagues, virtually all of the attention has been centered on Jackie Robinson, which is understandable since he was the first.

"And that's the way it should be," said Doby. "But Jack and I had very similar experiences. And I wouldn't be human if I didn't want people to remember my participation."

Doby went through much the same kind of discrimination and abuse that Robinson suffered—not being allowed to stay in the same hotels and eat in the same restaurants as the white players, hearing the racial insults of fans and opposing bench jockeys, experiencing the reprehension of some teammates. But while Doby will be honored at the All-Star Game—which, coincidentally, will be played in Cleveland on July 8—he in some ways seems the forgotten man.

"Jackie Robinson, of course, deserves all the credit he gets," Boudreau said. "But I really don't think that Larry gets the credit he deserves for being the pioneer in the situation he was in."

About Robinson, Doby said: "I had the greatest respect for Jack. He was tough and smart and brave. I once told him, 'If not for you, then probably not for me.'"

Lou Brissie, who pitched for the Philadelphia A's beginning in 1947, recalled: "I was on the bench and heard some of my teammates shouting things at Larry, like, 'Porter, carry my bags,' or 'Shoeshine boy, shine my shoes,' and, well, the N-word, too. It was terrible."

Brissic, who was from South Carolina, had been shot and left for dead in Italy during World War II. He pitched with a large steel brace on his left leg and instinctively felt an identity with the young black player. "He was a kind of underdog, like me," Brissie said.

Doby has not forgotten the abuse: the "N-word" being used every day, the calls of "coon" and "jigaboo," the times when he slid into second base and the opposing infielder spit in his face.

"I never sought sympathy or felt sorry for myself," Doby said. "And all that stuff just made me try harder, made me more aggressive. Sometimes I'd get too aggressive, and swing too hard, and miss the pitch."

But he cannot forget the sense of loneliness, particularly after games. "It's then you'd really like to be with your teammates, win or lose, and go over the game," he said. "But I'd go off to my hotel in the black part of town, and they'd go off to their hotel."

Doby is now 72, his hair sprinkled lightly with gray. He is huskier than in the old photos of him breaking in with the Indians. He works for

Debut Dates of First Major League African-American Players

	(Since 1900)	
Player	Debut Date	Team
Jackie Robinson	April 15, 1947	Dodgers
Larry Doby	July 5, 1947	Indians
Hank Thompson	July 17, 1947	Browns
Willard Brown	July 19, 1947	Browns
Dan Bankhead	August 26, 1947	Dodgers
Roy Campanella	April 20, 1948	Dodgers
Satchel Paige	July 8, 1948	Indians
Don Newcombe	May 20, 1949	Dodgers
Monte Irvin	July 8, 1949	Giants
Luke Easter	August 11, 1949	Indians
Sam Jethroe	April 18, 1950	Braves
Ray Noble	April 18, 1951	Giants
Artie Wilson	April 18, 1951	Giants
Harry Simpson	April 21, 1951	Indians
Willie Mays	May 25, 1951	Giants
Sam Hairston	July 21, 1951	White Sox
Bob Boyd	September 8, 1951	White Sox
Sam Jones	September 22, 1951	Indians
George Crowe	April 17, 1952	Braves
Buzz Clarkson	April 30, 1952	Braves

Major League Baseball, handling the licensing of former players. Wearing a tie and suspenders and an easy smile and forthright manner, this father of five, grandfather of six and great-grandfather of three reflected on his years as a ballplayer as he sat recently in a sunny 29th-floor room at the Baseball Commissioner's office in Manhattan.

"When Mr. Veeck signed me," Doby said, "he sat me down and told me some of the do's and don'ts. He said, 'Lawrence'—he's the only person who called me Lawrence—'you are going to be part of history.' Part of history? I had no notions about that. I just wanted to play baseball. I mean, I was young. I didn't quite realize then what all this meant. I saw it simply as an opportunity to get ahead.

"Mr. Veeck told me: 'No arguing with umpires, don't even turn around at a bad call at the plate, and no dissertations with opposing players—either of those might start a race riot; no associating with female Caucasians—not that I was going to. And he said remember to act in a way that you know people are watching you. And this was something that both Jack and I took seriously. We knew that if we didn't succeed, it might hinder opportunities for other Afro Americans."

Doby had been leading the Negro National League in batting average at .415 and home runs with 14, when he was signed by the Indians. He began as a second baseman but was switched to the outfield, where he would be assured of starting. But he was unaccustomed to playing there, and in an early game in center field and with the bases loaded, he misjudged a fly ball in the sun and the ball hit him on the head. It caused his team to lose.

After the game, Bill McKechnie, an Indian coach who had befriended Doby, said to him, "We'll find out what kind of ballplayer you are tomorrow." Doby recalled that McKechnie smiled. "It was a challenge and a kind of vote of confidence," Doby said. "The next day I hit a home run to win the game."

Doby appreciated Gordon and McKechnie and the catcher, Jim Hegan, in particular, who would seek to salve his disappointments and perhaps take a seat next to him after he had struck out or made an error. "They were tremendous," Doby said. "But there were others who don't remember, or don't want to remember, some of their actions. And sometimes I'd see them later and they'd say, 'Hey, Larry, let's go have a beer.' I thought, 'When I needed you, where were you?' I forgive but I can't forget. I politely decline their invitations."

Doby spent his grammar school years in Camden, South Carolina. He recalls seeing the white people riding in fringed, horse-drawn buggies through the black neighborhood, and tossing dimes and nickels at the small black children. And then they would rub the children's heads for good luck.

"My grandmother warned me never to pick up the money," Doby said. "She thought it was undignified. And then I always tried to act in a dignified manner. When I was in the major leagues, some people thought I was a loner. But, well, when Joe DiMaggio was off by himself, they said he just wanted his privacy. And midway through the 1948 season the Indians signed Satchel Paige, and they made him my roommate. Well, he was almost never in the room. I'm not sure where he went. But he was a character and he enjoyed being perceived that way. He'd come into the clubhouse and clown around, and did some Amos 'n' Andy stuff. I didn't think it was right—at least, it wasn't right for me."

Eddie Robinson, the Indians' first baseman when Doby broke in, said: "I thought it took a lot of courage for Larry to go through what he did. He handled himself quite well."

Larry Doby broke in with the Cleveland Indians as the first black player in the American League on July 5, 1947, less than three months after Jackie Robinson made his debut with the Dodgers.

But when Boudreau put Doby at first base to start the second half of a double-header on Doby's second day in the major leagues, Robinson wouldn't let him use his glove. "I didn't want anyone else playing my position—and it had nothing to do with black or white," Robinson said. As Doby recalls, the Indians were able to borrow a first baseman's glove for him from the White Sox.

Doby had been the only black player on the East Side High School baseball, football and basketball teams in Paterson. He went briefly to Long Island University and Virginia Union before being drafted into the navy.

He first learned of Jackie Robinson's signing with the Dodgers organization when he was on a Pacific Island in 1945. "I wondered if I might have a chance to play in the big leagues, too," Doby said. "Until then, I thought I would just go back to Paterson and become a high school coach."

Robinson and Doby were followed into the big leagues in 1947 by three other blacks: Henry Thompson and Willard Brown, who joined the St. Louis Browns in late July, and Dan Bankhead, who came up to the Dodgers in August. Thompson and Brown lasted for only a few weeks (though Thompson returned in 1949 to play several years with the New York Giants) while Bankhead pitched the rest of the season for the Dodgers.

Roy Campanella joined the Dodgers in 1948, and Don Newcombe made it in 1949. But by 1950 only five major league teams had been integrated. By 1953 there were 20 blacks on seven of the 16 teams. And it wasn't until 1959, when the Boston Red Sox played Pumpsie Green, that every major league club had a black player.

Doby gives talks at schools and discusses the changes in American life. "I know people are critical and say that not enough progress has been made in baseball, or sports in general, particularly in the coaching or administrative levels," he said. "And I believe there has not been enough progress made either. But when you look at other elements of American society, sports stacks up pretty good. If Jack and I have left a legacy, it is to show that teamwork—the ability to associate and communicate—makes all of us stronger."

In 1978, Doby was named manager of the White Sox, taking over for Bob Lemon midway through the year. He held the position for just 87 games, posting a record of 37-50.

"I was the second black manager in major league history," said Doby, "after Frank Robinson."

Frank Robinson became the first African-American to manage in the majors, when he took over the helm of the Cleveland Indians starting in 1975. "Funny thing," Doby said, with a smile, "I followed another Robinson."

[1997]

Life in the Bullpen

BY JERRY CRASNICK

Anyone who thinks the bullpen is always a nice, serene place to kick back and watch a baseball game never took a gander at Goose Gossage when he was in his prime.

For most closers, the adrenaline rush begins in the seventh or eighth inning. Gossage was different. He began to feel a churning sensation in his gut somewhere between "the Land of the Free" and "the Home of the Brave."

When Gossage got that Ninja warrior look in his eyes, he was better left alone.

His teammates knew enough not to bother him. Fans and birdbrains weren't always so intuitive.

Once or twice during Gossage's tenure with the Padres, the San Diego Chicken thought he might make an entertaining foil. Gossage told him in no uncertain terms to take a hike back to mascot school.

"The Chicken would come down and want us to play in his little skits, and I'd tell him, 'Get your butt out of here. Go bother the guys in the other bullpen,'" Gossage said.

"I was so intense, I didn't want anything to get in my way. I never wanted to look back and say, 'Damn, I took the edge off.' To me, entering a game was like going into battle."

Every reliever prepares for battle in his own way. Lee Smith steeled himself for competition by taking marathon naps in the trainer's room. Gossage spent hours feeding off his intensity and working himself into an emotional frenzy.

While relievers come in all sizes, shapes and mind-sets, they share a common sanctuary. The bullpen is part frat house and part waiting room. The players and coaches who inhabit it are an integral part of the team, and a completely separate entity. "You know what it's like?" former big league reliever Larry Andersen said. "If the dugout is the earth, the bullpen is the moon. You know you're part of the team. But if a guy hits a home run or a pitcher works out of a tough inning, you can't take part in the celebration. You're kind of isolated down there. You feel like you're Gilligan at times."

Said Padres closer Trevor Hoffman: "We're by ourselves. Most of the time, they stick us in the farthest part of the park they can find in a little cubbyhole. And they leave us down there."

During a blowout or the early innings of a game, the bullpen can be a monument to juvenile behavior. But in the late innings of a close game it's as tense as a space capsule before liftoff. As the various roles kick in, long men, setup men and closers all experience a sense of anxiety. Hoffman refers to the phenomenon as "gaming up."

"I'm OK when I step on the mound and start getting loose," Detroit closer Todd Jones said. "For me, the hardest part is sitting around and pulling for my teammates. It's hard on your stomach, your heart and your head. I could do a Rolaids commercial out there."

The bullpen is as much a part of baseball lore as high socks or tape-measure homers, but the origin of the term is vague. The first documented use of the word "bullpen" appeared in the December 1915 issue of *Baseball Magazine.*

In the *Dickson Baseball Encyclopedia*, some baseball mainstays take a crack at explaining the term.

"You could look it up and get 80 different answers," Casey Stengel said. "But we used to have pitchers who could pitch 50-60 games a year, and the extra pitchers would just sit around shooting the bull, and no manager wanted all that gabbing on the bench. So he put them in this kind of pen in the outfield to warm up. It looked like a kind of place to keep cows or bulls."

Longtime Yankees pitcher Johnny Murphy said the term evolved from the Bull Durham tobacco signs that dotted the outfield fences where relief pitchers warmed up. And Paul Dickson writes of relievers, "One other theory likens them to reserve bulls in bullfighting who are penned near the arena should the starting bull be found lacking."

Over the years the baseball bullpen has become a community unto itself. As any reliever will attest, several factors go into making the bullpen experience a positive or negative one.

Relievers spend a lot of time interacting with fans. Depending on the ballpark and the city, this can be a good or bad thing.

"The best fans are probably in the Midwest," Giants closer Rod Beck said. "St. Louis. Cincinnati. Chicago. Sure, they'll get on you because they're rooting for their team, but for the most part they know who you are and what you've done. They know their baseball."

The worst fans? Everybody has an opinion.

Former Cincinnati reliever Rob Dibble once observed that fans in San Francisco behaved as if they were raised near a nuclear plant. Hoffman confirms that 3Com Park crowds are not the most forgiving.

"San Francisco was tough for me after I hit Robby Thompson in the face [with a pitch]," Hoffman said. "The people there wanted my head. But at least I knew why they were yelling at me."

That's rarely the case in Philadelphia, where fans heckle players on general principle.

"The people in Philly have a hard time liking their own players, so you can imagine what it's like for visitors," Hoffman said. "They throw things at you, and their vocabulary is filled with obscenities. They seem a little bitter. Hey, it's not my fault they have to live there."

When Gossage pitched for the Yankees, a Boston fan once spit in his face in the bullpen. The Fenway Park security crew made up of Boston University football players dragged the offender beneath the stands.

"If the guy had a gun, I think he would have killed me," Gossage said. "I think the boys from B.U. pummeled him. They came back and said, 'Goose, we took care of him.'"

Colorado Rockies reliever Jerry Dipoto, who spent two years in New York, saw rowdy fans at Shea Stadium pelt players with batteries, coins and ice in the bullpen. If that weren't bad enough, children sometimes took part in the abuse.

"One time John Franco was standing on the bullpen mound and this kid leaned over the edge," Dipoto said. "He couldn't have been 7 or 8 years old, and he yelled, 'Hey Franco, you suck!'

"Johnny looked up at the father and said, 'Nice way to raise your kid.' And the father yelled back, 'Well, you do suck.'"

Beck has seen the same phenomenon on display at other parks.

"A little kid will tell you that you're horse(bleep), and the parent is standing right there laughing at him," said Beck, shaking his head. "That's a product of society right there."

How do six or seven relief pitchers, a bullpen coach and a bullpen catcher pass the time on a typical summer evening? They watch a major league baseball game for free.

But when the action drags, they have a variety of time-killing mechanisms at their disposal.

Rockies relievers typically spend an inning or two playing trivia, with Dipoto, a walking baseball encyclopedia, providing the questions and answers.

Word-association games are popular. And in the San Francisco bullpen, relievers like to listen to games on the radio, catch the broadcasters' mistakes and poke fun at them.

"I've heard stories where guys play this thing called 'the pain game,' where they pull hairs out of each other's nose and try to see whose eyes water the most," Beck said. "I haven't really been a part of fun stuff like that."

Sunflower seeds are at the core of bullpen activity. Relievers will typically set up a cup and flick seeds at it. If an umpire or ball boy is standing nearby, he might serve as the designated target.

Andersen took the sunflower seed-craze to a new level. When he got bored, he liked to crack open the tips and pinch seeds onto his eyelids and face.

"The most I ever had was 86 or 87," Andersen said. "It looked like a hive of bees had attached themselves to my face. Some of the little kids would laugh, and some would get scared."

For those who might characterize Andersen's behavior as immature, he replies, "It goes back to the old saying: 'You can only be young once, but you can be immature forever.'"

Now and then, a reliever rises above the mundane and conceives a stunt that's truly inspired. Twice last season, Toronto pitcher Dan Plesac slipped out of the pen, pulled a grounds-crew outfit over his uniform and helped drag the infield.

When Andersen played for Philadelphia in the mid-1980s, the bullpen phone rang, and backup catcher John Wockenfuss responded by sprinting up the stadium ramp to the parking lot. A few minutes later, the gate opened and Wockenfuss drove pitcher Kevin Gross to the mound on the back of his Harley-Davidson.

No bullpen is complete without a jokester, the guy who can keep everybody loose or silence a boozed-up heckler with his rapier wit.

Andersen loved watching former Philadelphia teammate Mitch "Wild Thing" Williams in action.

"He had the greatest comeback lines for people," Andersen said. "One time a guy got on him real bad and Mitch said, 'Hey, I don't get on you when you're picking up my garbage at six in the morning.'"

In the Colorado bullpen, Steve Reed qualifies as quip-master general. Reed has a knack for cutting down an obnoxious heckler, even turning the crowd in the players' favor without resorting to profanity.

"We'll all look at each other and say, 'Reeder is going to get this guy. It's just a matter of time,'" Curtis Leskanic said.

"He'll slowly but surely put his sunglasses on and it's like Sylvester Stallone when he turns his hat around in that movie *Over the Top*."

Some players are fortunate enough to rate jokester status without trying. Dipoto's all-time favorite is an obscure lefty named Don Florence, who spent two months with the Mets in 1995.

"We used to call him Cliff Clavin," Dipoto said. "He was from New Hampshire, and he talked just like the guy on 'Cheers.' He wore his hat real crooked and walked sideways. He was goofy, and he knew he was goofy. He was like free entertainment out there."

Sunflower seeds, gum, candy bars and Gatorade are staples in any bullpen. It's not unheard of for a famished reliever to swap a baseball for a bag of peanuts or, every now and then, a hot dog.

Former Houston reliever Charlie Kerfeld crossed the line when he visited Rusty Staub's barbecue stand at Shea Stadium during a game. Kerfeld might have gotten away with the stunt if the game wasn't televised.

"I remember walking through the players' lounge and seeing Tim McCarver do the replay," Andersen said. "He'd say, 'Every time Charlie's head goes down, you can tell he's taking a bite.' Hal Lanier was our manager that year. It didn't go over real big with him."

In 17 big league seasons, Andersen never saw anyone drink a cold beer in the bullpen. But he admits he was tempted. "If it was 95 degrees and 120 on the turf and the guy behind me was drinking a beer, I'd probably turn around and give him a little grief," Andersen said.

On the list of relief no-nos, taking a nap in the bullpen probably ranks somewhere between eating a slice of pizza and drinking a beer.

"I've never seen anyone fall asleep in our bullpen," Leskanic said. "We have some tired arms, but not tired bodies."

Said Andersen: "Most guys who need sleep make sure to wear sunglasses. But if you wear them when it's cloudy and overcast, that's a dead giveaway."

Along with a solid mound and plenty of elbow room, each reliever looks for something different in a bullpen.

Gossage was big on proper ventilation. He recalls that the bullpen in Kansas City was "hotter than hell."

Hoffman likes a good view of the replay scoreboard, because it might give him some pointers for the later innings.

Beck has mixed feelings about the visiting bullpen at Coors Field. "Architecturally it's beautiful," he said. "The only thing I don't like is that it's way out in center field. It's a long jog when you get into the game."

Dipoto, who has pitched in both leagues, ranks the bullpen at Sky-Dome in Toronto as the most comfortable in baseball.

"They have the big, tall, cushioned seat above the wall," Dipoto said. "It's just the right length from the wall that you can put your feet up. The only bad thing is, you have to walk down the stairs to warm up. You can bite it and break a leg."

Several relievers mentioned the importance of a good "echo." If a pitcher can hear the catcher's mitt pop in the bullpen, he's bound to enter the game with a spring in his step.

"A good echo gives you that nice false sense of security," Dipoto said. "It's all about acoustics."

Dodger Stadium and Kauffman Stadium in Kansas City are renowned for their echo effect.

"When I warmed up in Kansas City, it was unbelievable," Gossage said. "It was deafening. I'd hit the catcher's mitt and it sounded like an M-80. It was a loud crack—like a gun going off."

The longer relievers are together, the more they tend to bond. Through several years of triumphs and shared suffering, Reed, Leskanic, Darren Holmes, Mike Munoz and Bruce Ruffin have become extremely close in Denver. Literally and figuratively.

"You're like a family within a family," Leskanic said. "We're in a 20-foot radius of each other for four hours a day."

Bullpen buddies look out for one another. When a San Diego fan tossed a beer at Dipoto this season, Leskanic summoned security to have the offender ejected. Andersen once restrained Danny Darwin from climbing into the stands after a beer thrower.

And when Detroit's Jones was playing winter ball in Venezuela, he climbed into the stands and tackled a teenager who poured beer on his pitching coach. "If I did that in the big leagues, I'd get a lawsuit," Jones said. "I thought to myself, 'What am I doing in the stands? And why am I grabbing this guy I don't even know?'"

By the nature of their jobs, relievers adopt an all-for-one, one-for-all mentality. The bullpen might be a monument to inactivity. Then the phone will ring, and it's as frantic as an ant farm. With a bad pitch or poor decision, each reliever knows he can undermine what his teammates have spent several innings trying to accomplish.

Colorado pitching coach Frank Funk gave his share of hot feet as a reliever with Cleveland and Milwaukee in the '60s. Any prank that defused tension made sense.

"More often than not, a reliever comes into a game in a pressure situation," Funk said. "The game is usually on the line. If you stayed serious all the time, you'd go nuts."

[1997]

Veteran Umpire Says Managers Were More Defiant Years Ago

BY JOHN KUENSTER

"In my early years in the majors," said veteran American League umpire Dale Ford, "I think we all should've gotten combat pay.

"At that time we had a lot of confrontational managers in our league, guys like Earl Weaver, Billy Martin, Del Crandall, Dick Williams, Ralph Houk, Frank Robinson, Gene Mauch.

"I think in my career, I must've tossed Weaver a million times. We used to call him 'Rooney' after the actor Mickey Rooney because he was short. It was easy to pick out his voice if he was yelling from the dugout. I remember one time he was giving it to me, and [Mark] Belanger and Brooks Robinson told me, 'Run that little b———, we're tired of hearing him, too.'

"One of the funniest things I ever saw on the field happened in a game between the Yankees and Orioles. It had been raining and the ground was wet. I had run 'Rooney' but he came back to the plate to argue some more and tried to kick dirt on me, but he forgot the ground was wet. When he started to kick, he slipped and fell on his fanny. You should've seen the expression on his face when he went down. I couldn't keep from laughing.

"Billy Martin was another one. Will Rogers [old-time humorist] once said he never met a man he didn't like, but he never met Martin."

Like Weaver, Martin was noted for his volatile temper and often took out his anger in demonstrations against the umpires. Ford recalled a comical incident that involved Martin years ago.

"I was at second base during a game in Oakland when Martin managed the A's. Steve McCatty was on the mound. The bases were loaded. Out comes Art Fowler from the A's dugout. He was Martin's pitching coach but he didn't do much coaching. He was really Martin's drinking partner.

"I could hear what McCatty and Fowler were saying.

"McCatty says to Fowler, 'What's wrong? I know they got the bases loaded, but I'm throwing good. What am I doing wrong?'

"'I don't know what the hell you're doing wrong,' says Fowler, 'but I do know one thing: Billy's pissed off at you.'

"With that, Fowler marches back to the dugout. McCatty then pitches to the next batter who hits a bases-loaded home run, and at that point you know what hit the fan. Martin went absolutely nuts.

"Most of the managers didn't carry a grudge in those days if your call went against them," Ford added. "I admired Ralph Houk, because if we had a difference, it was all over the next day. But Martin and Weaver, they'd carry on a grudge for five years!"

Despite being a thorn in the side of umpires and holding the lifetime record among managers for most ejections (97) from a game, Weaver was elected to the Hall of Fame in 1996. However, his fiery counterpart in defiance of baseball law and order, Billy Martin, did not have a happy ending to his career, dying in a traffic accident at age 61 on Christmas Day, 1989, a year after he had been bounced as manager of the Yankees.

This spring, Ford begins his 24th season of umpiring in the American League, and since 1975 has officiated in two World Series, one All-Star Game, and "a handful" of League Championship Series.

While he doesn't downgrade the baseball wisdom and game tactics of the old-time managers, he thinks the current field bosses rank a notch above their predecessors.

"The managers today are younger, smarter, and not as confrontational," he said. "They are good communicators. Phil Garner, Johnny Oates, Mike Hargrove—they're great guys. They let you do your job, but that doesn't mean I won't run them if I have to."

Asked how managers and players might view him, Ford said, "They know I work hard, and they know I won't stand for any prolonged arguments."

One of 13 children, born in Jonesboro, Tennessee, Ford, 55, would like to see some steps taken to speed up games. When he's working behind the plate, he doesn't like to see batters wandering away from the box after taking a strike they don't like. It's a ploy that extends games unnecessarily. "When they do that, I tell 'em, 'Get back in there. Let's go. You're putting me to sleep back here.'"

He also believes the majors should enforce the 20-second rule on pitchers to prevent needless delays in the game. Rule 8.04 states, "When the bases are unoccupied, the pitcher shall deliver the ball to the batter within 20 seconds after he receives the ball. Each time the pitcher delays the game by violating this rule, the umpire shall call 'Ball.'"

Managers Earl Weaver, left, and Billy Martin, pictured in a jovial mood in 1985, gave umpire Dale Ford all sorts of trouble on disputed calls.

"They ought to put the clock on the pitchers," Ford said. "It's a good rule, and would help keep a nice rhythm to the game."

Ford has umpired in a number of memorable games. What was his most memorable one?

"I was behind the plate in Game 6 of the 1986 World Series," he recalled. "The Red Sox were ahead by two runs, 5-3, in the bottom of the tenth. The Mets had two runners on base with two outs, and Ray Knight at the plate. Calvin Schiraldi had him down, no balls and two strikes, and he throws a fastball right down the middle. Knight singled. That made it 5-4. Then (Bob) Stanley comes in and lets the tying run in from third on what was called a wild pitch to Mookie Wilson. But it wasn't a wild pitch in my mind. The ball almost hit me in the head. I think it should've been a passed ball. Rich Gedman didn't get his glove up. Then Wilson hit the ball that went through Bill Buckner's legs at first to win the game for the Mets, 6-5.

"I think the fans criticized Buckner too much for losing the game. Schiraldi should've taken some blame for throwing that pitch right down the middle to Knight when he was so far ahead on the count."

Another game that lingers with Ford took place in April 1976. "It was my first game behind the plate that season. The Orioles against the Yankees in Baltimore. Ross Grimsley against Catfish Hunter. Catfish won, 3-0, and he took only two hours and one minute to do it. That's the way games should be played."

Before breaking into the majors, Ford umpired in the Florida State League, Carolina League, Southern League, and American Association. When he attended an umpire development school in Florida, his tutor was Bill Kinnamon.

Kinnamon once told Ford that when he (Kinnamon) joined the American League umpiring staff in 1960, veteran arbiter Johnny Rice warned him that the "toughest call is throwing a guy out of a game after you blew the hell out of a play."

How about Ford. What does he consider the toughest call?

"The checked swing is one," he said. "Sometimes it's hard for the plate umpire to determine whether the batter went around. If the pitch is called a strike on a checked swing, the strike stands. If it's called a ball, the catcher or pitcher may ask for confirmation from the first or third base umpire who might have a better angle on the swing.

"Another tough call involves balls that are touched by fans. In the American League you have parks—in Baltimore, Cleveland and New York—where fans can reach out and touch a ball that's in play, and it can cause nightmares. Like that case in Yankee Stadium in 1996 when a kid reached over the right field wall to catch a ball hit by Derek Jeter against the Orioles in the League Championship Series. Rich Garcia—he's one of our best umpires—called it a home run. On that hit he was running toward the right field wall and didn't have time to get back far enough so he'd have a good angle on the ball. To do that, he would have had to be almost against the wall to see if the ball would have fallen short if the kid had not reached out to glove it.

"Sooner or later," Ford added, "every umpire gets a play like that, and sooner or later he will make the wrong call—but not that often. These are judgment calls, and we stand by them."

A grandfather four times over, Ford during the off-season works out two hours a day to keep his six-foot, 203-pound frame in good shape.

In his school days he was a catcher, "a pretty good country player, but I knew I wasn't good enough to make it some day to the majors," he said. "I wanted to stay close to the game, so I started umpiring high school and college games. Then I went to umpiring school."

He's traveled a long way since then, but he still has a passion for baseball, and a down-to-earth, common sense way of talking about his profession. He smiled when someone reminded him that "umpiring is the only occupation where a man has to be perfect on Opening Day and improve as the season goes on."

In keeping with that impossible scenario, he admitted he listens to critical advice about his work on the field.

And who provides that advice?

"My wife, Joyce," he said. "She knows the game. She's my best critic."

Who said umpires couldn't be diplomatic?

[1998]

I Never Turned the Other Cheek

BY BILL ROGELL AS TOLD TO NICK C. WILSON

I was born in Springfield, Illinois, on November 24, 1904, but spent most of my time in Chicago because my father died when I was seven and my mother died when I was eleven.

I was an orphan. So I lived with one of my sisters and was eventually kicked from pillar to post.

I was the fifth of eight brothers and sisters so I lived any place I could find a bed to sleep in. There was a time when I had bread and water for breakfast and bread and water for dinner.

I was 14 when I quit school to go to work, but while I was in high school I played semi-pro baseball on Sundays and I was paid $10 per game. I had to play under fictitious names so I could still play on the high school baseball and football teams. At 14, I had two kid brothers that I supported, and I sent them through school. Both of them became successes.

When we were young, we used to cover the old balls with tape and we could only afford one ball and bat. In fact, we only had one glove for four or five of us. Between innings the guy on the other team used your glove.

My boyhood idol was "Shoeless Joe" Jackson. When I was a kid in Chicago, I used to work my butt off just to save a dollar, and I used to go to the White Sox ballpark and sit in the left field bleachers because he played left field. Everyone said Jackson couldn't read or write, and later I learned that he would wake up at dawn and just lie in bed waiting for his roommate to wake up. He did this so he could follow him down to breakfast and order whatever the roommate ordered. He couldn't read the menu.

I played on the sandlots and one day in 1921 a group of ex–big league ball players came along and told me I was a good prospect. So they recommended me to a team in Buffalo, which was the equivalent of AA baseball. I was an amateur, but they saw something in me.

A couple of years later, I ended up with a team in the Southwestern League in Kansas. One day in 1923, I was in the bank in Coffeyville, Kansas, and I saw the great Walter Johnson standing there. He lived in the area. Well, we got to talking. I was puffed up like a balloon. So proud. I finally said, "Mr. Johnson, I'll be seeing you in the major leagues. Just look for me 'cause I'll be there."

Just two years later I finally broke into the majors with the Red Sox and one day we were playing the Washington Senators. Walter Johnson was pitching and he was beating us 8 to 0. I didn't get called into the game until the 5th inning, and I eventually came up to the plate to bat. Well I'll be damned if he didn't walk halfway in off the pitching mound and he said to me, "Young man, you made it!"

He remembered. That's amazing! I was so surprised and shocked. So he threw a fastball in there and I just stood there still in shock, and he threw the second one right down the middle. These pitches were soft, like batting-practice balls. I didn't realize he wanted me to hit one. He came down off the mound again and said to me, "Get over the shock and hit one!" I was just standing there with my mouth open.

The next one he threw I hit off the left-center field wall, and when I pulled up at second base he turned around and said, "Nice hitting! Hope you stay for a long time." I was just a kid. I could have dropped dead.

So let's get back to 1924 when I went to Salina, Kansas, in a class "D" league. In the Southeastern League in 1924, we used to go from town to town in several passenger cars, traveling at night.

We would travel across desolate, wild country, so I used to sit up at the front of the car with a .22 pistol shooting at rabbits.

I hit .317 that year, and the Red Sox scouts noticed me and offered to buy me from this Kansas team. I found out when someone from the Sox called me on the telephone and I nearly fell through the floor.

I had no particular batting style, but I used to move around the plate quite a bit. Depending on the pitcher's style, I'd either be up on top of the plate or I'd be way back. If he was a curveball pitcher, I'd be even with the plate.

When I first started in the big leagues I made $300 per month, and during the off-season I'd take any job I could get. I peddled milk. I sold for a tool and die business. That $300 didn't go too damned far, it was chicken feed.

I was a switch-hitter, which I picked up from just playing around, but the Red Sox tried to make me hit right-handed all the time and it screwed me up. I learned a lot playing with the Red Sox, but I sat on the bench too much. I would watch and learn, so when I got to Detroit I thought I was ready.

I met my wife in 1925 when I was with the Red Sox. She was a fan and she used to go to the ball games. One day she asked me for an autograph and we started talking. I was single, she was single, so we got together. We were married in 1930, so this year is our 68th anniversary

Back in the 1920s equipment was much different. They don't have gloves today. They have nets. Our gloves were flat with very little padding. I used to take the glove apart and then I'd soak it in water and let it dry out again. Then I would rub it thoroughly with Vaseline to make the glove soft, and then it would dry.

Even the balls were different. In the 1920s the seams on the ball were higher and it was wound looser. Today's ball is too tight; that's why it travels so far.

In 1930 I was traded to Detroit and I stayed there for ten years.

I remember one day I was playing with the Tigers in Fenway Park and they had a little incline in left field. Robert "Fatty" Fothergill was playing for us in left when a pop fly came out to him. He chased that ball and tripped and fell flat on his face on the incline, and the ball hit him right in the back. I should have run out to get the ball, but I couldn't. I just stood there laughing, I couldn't help it. He was a big guy and he could drink more beer than anyone I knew.

I played ten years with Charlie Gehringer, and I think he was the greatest second baseman in baseball, but very little is ever said about him. He didn't have a big mouth or show off. Charlie Gehringer and I were more than just friends, we were like brothers. The Lord gave us our skills. Believe me, few are chosen and given the ability to play major league baseball.

If you want to know why the 1920s and 1930s were the Golden Age of Baseball, just look at the Hall of Fame. There are more men in there from that era than from any other time.

Take Babe Ruth. Babe was a nice guy and I liked him. In Detroit the clubhouses were right next to each other. Both teams had to go through our dugout and down a flight of stairs to get to the clubhouses. I don't know why, but every time we played the Yankees, Babe would come out early and he would sit in our dugout and start talking. He would call me "The Little Guy" and tell me I was the captain of the infield.

One day I asked Babe who was pitching today and he said Lefty Gomez. Well, I told him to watch me because I would hit a home run over the left field fence onto Cherry Street, and sure enough I did. In fact the ball landed in the back of a truck.

Babe wanted to be friends with everybody. He had a certain charisma, a closeness, a desire to be your friend. One thousand years from now Babe Ruth's name will still be magic. I've played against Ted Williams, Joe DiMaggio, Cobb, Ruth and Gehrig, but if you ask me who was the best in terms of raw natural talent, I would have to say that left fielder for the White Sox, Joe Jackson. My boyhood hero.

Only one time I got in trouble with the press. I was just starting with Detroit and a certain sportswriter with the *Detroit Free Press* didn't think I was playing hard enough. He wrote, "Rogell is afraid to step on a crack in the sidewalk for fear he would go into a slump."

Well, I was really quick-tempered back then, and that comment made me so dang mad. One day I saw him on the street, I grabbed him and shook the hell out of him.

That was the only way I could fight him back. After that day, not another negative word was written about me.

Our manager, Mickey Cochrane, wouldn't stand for any joking or laughing on the bench. It was serious baseball and you had to watch the game. He had a reputation as a man who was hard to get along with. "Black Mike" they called him. We had to report every morning at ten o'clock, but Mickey canceled that on Sunday so we could go to church.

We had our tricks to win games and get the edge. I chewed tobacco ever since I was four years old, so when our pitchers got in trouble, they'd throw the ball to me and I spit tobacco in the glove and rub dirt on the ball so it would dye black.

Well, that ball became so tough to see we'd get the next hitter out.

I'll never forget the day Tommy Bridges was pitching against the Yankees in New York. Tony Lazzeri was hitting and suddenly I heard their third base coach yell something. Well I knew he was stealing our catcher's signs and telling Lazzeri what pitch was coming next.

I called for time and called Mickey Cochrane out to tell him what was happening. Well, we came up with a plan.

On the next pitch, our catcher signaled for a curveball and sure enough the third base coach made a certain sound.

Bridges wound up and threw a fastball that missed Lazzeri's ears by four inches. When Lazzeri got up off the ground he yelled at the third base coach, "No more signs, no more signs!"

We never had helmets to protect us at the plate. I've been beaned several times, including once by Lefty Grove, and I think three times by Bob Feller.

Lefty Grove had an incredible fastball that would rise, but one day I got three hits off him and I heard him say, "That little S.O.B. isn't going to hit off me again!"

So the next time I came up, he threw at my head. It's a good thing I threw my hand up first because the ball hit me in the hand and bounced up into the seats. He was lucky I couldn't get up, because if I had I would have broken both of his knees.

I had to be tough and aggressive. Those were tough times. I had to stand up for myself. Once I hit an opposing catcher in the jaw for throwing a ball at me after I slid into home plate, and once I jumped on Ben Chapman of the Yankees with my spikes after he spiked Charlie Gehringer.

I believe everything in the Bible except turn the other cheek. I sure as hell never turned the other cheek.

Gehrig spiked me one time and I even have a picture of it. He hit a double to right center and the outfielder threw me the ball as Gehrig came into second. He could see the ball, and he knew he didn't have to slide but he did and knocked me flat.

That day I had to have seven stitches put in on my knee. I immediately grabbed him by the hair and stuck his nose in the dirt. I was ready to fight, and 40,000 people booed me. Look, I was 155 pounds and he was 210 pounds.

Then I warned him that he had better watch his foot the next time.

"When I come down to first base I'll step right on it," I said. But you know he was the nicest guy. I'll never understand why he slid. That was my livelihood. If they're out to get me I'm going to get them.

I remember playing with a couple broken fingers. I just taped them up because we had to play. If you didn't, somebody else got your job.

I played in the 1934 and 1935 World Series and we won in 1935 against the Cubs. In the 1934 Series against the Cardinals, I accidentally hit Dizzy Dean in the head on a double-play ball. He didn't duck. Just as I crossed the bag and threw the ball, he got in the line of fire. I never did see him. I had so much time that I threw it softly. He was lucky because I could have fractured his skull.

The most money I ever made in baseball was $15,000 in 1935, but I had three families to support, my own, my wife's and my brother's. It was the Depression, so I had to work at anything I could find. I even sold cars. I was lucky though because nobody was working back then.

I left the Cubs after my only season with them in 1940. I entered politics and stayed there for 40 years in Wayne County.

During the 1940s I participated in the war bond drive and I gave away most of my mementos to raise money. I gave away a uniform, some bats, balls and my World Series ring, and I don't regret it.

To tell you the truth, I watch baseball on TV, but I enjoy watching kids play more.

[1998]

Trickery Has Always Been Part of Big League Baseball

BY WAYNE LOCKWOOD

Unlike golf, baseball has never pretended to be a gentleman's game. The rule of thumb, from the sport's earliest days, has been pretty much that whatever you can get away with is acceptable.

"A baseball purist," Tony Gwynn says, "will tell you that it's only cheating if you get caught."

Gwynn doesn't necessarily agree with that, as it happens, but he is a realist. He knows that this is a game that has always winked at subterfuge, skullduggery and downright underhanded tactics. Kind of admired them, as a matter of fact.

A golfer will call a penalty on himself for accidentally double-hitting a chip, but a baseball player will swear on his mother's grave that he caught a line drive that television replays clearly demonstrate he trapped.

Nobody thinks much about it. That's just the way it is. You do what you have to do.

If that includes stealing signs and doctoring baseballs and corking bats and generally treating the rules of the game as if they were a challenge rather than a guideline, well, catch me if you can.

It's a tradition, dating back to baseball's roots and some of its greatest early players. Before John McGraw was a storied manager, he was a third baseman who, among other things, had this little trick of holding a baserunner's belt as he tagged up to score on a fly ball. In the days of only one umpire, it was sometimes possible to get away with things like that.

Pete Browning, a previous victim of the tactic, unbuckled his belt the next time around and trotted home while holding his pants up while Mc-Graw was left at third with Browning's belt in his hand.

The man who probably did more than any other to set an early code of conduct for the game was Michael Joseph "King" Kelly, one of baseball's first superstars and probably its most popular player before the turn of the century.

As it happens, Kelly was one of the shrewdest, too, then or now. A keen student of the rules, he didn't so much violate them as he did force changes to cover loopholes only he seemed to see.

While the game's only umpire followed the flight of a base hit, Kelly frequently would dart directly home from second base without bothering to touch third, or proceed directly from first to third across the pitcher's mound. Soon there was more than one umpire.

Perhaps Kelly's most celebrated moment, outside of his induction into the Hall of Fame in 1945, came during a game in which he was not playing. As a foul pop-up headed toward the dugout and it became obvious that his catcher, Dimples Tate, could not reach it, Kelly stepped off the bench, announced, "Tate, you're out of the game," and caught the ball.

Under the rules of the day, Kelly, as his team's captain, had the right to make a substitution any time he chose. An argument ensued, but Kelly's action stood. The rule was soon changed.

In Kelly's day, any caught foul tip was an out. Kelly, a catcher, would keep birdshot in his mouth and snap them between his teeth whenever a hitter swung and missed, reproducing the sound of a foul tip. His ruse eventually was discovered when Kelly choked on the shot one day and spewed it on the ground in front of an umpire.

"Calm down, kid—only one more hit and we're out of the pennant and you're back in the minors—everything's on your shoulders—calm down!"

Set against such a tradition, is it any wonder that even today, a century later, pitchers continue to scuff and cut baseballs so as to make them act erratically, hitters continue to be busted for illegal bats and arguments continue to flare about teams attempting to steal each other's signs?

There is a code of conduct. You just have to understand the code. Some cheating is acceptable and some is not, depending on who's doing the evaluating.

"Cleveland, the White Sox and the Giants in the Polo Grounds used to have guys in the scoreboard stealing signs," says Padres broadcaster Jerry Coleman, who played for the New York Yankees from 1949 through 1957. "That, I think, is underhanded cheating, just like Alvin Dark when he was managing the Giants, watering the basepaths at Candlestick to make it a swamp to slow down Maury Wills, or the third base line in Cleveland being slanted so that everything rolled foul because Al Rosen couldn't move a lick.

"Then there's the other kind of cheating, like when you look at the [foul] balls when Nolan Ryan is pitching and find seven that look like somebody took a razor to them. That's kind of like, 'If you can get away with it, it's OK cheating.'"

Coleman freely admits that Hall of Fame left-hander Whitey Ford cheated for his Yankees. So did Whitey, for that matter.

"[Catcher Elston] Howard might scrape a ball before he threw it back to Whitey, or put some mud on it," Coleman said. "Whitey could use that very effectively."

After his playing days, Ford acknowledged that "I threw mostly cut balls and mud balls the whole game" during the fourth game of the 1963 World Series. "I had pretty good luck, too, because the Dodgers only got two hits off me."

Unfortunately for Ford, one was a home run by Frank Howard and the other was Howard's run-scoring single, giving the Dodgers a 2-1 victory. Cheaters don't always prosper.

"I guess I didn't cut the ball enough," Ford said.

Whitey didn't always need Elston Howard's help, either.

"I'd wear this ring on my right hand, my glove hand," he said. "During games I'd stand behind the mound rubbing up the ball and take my glove off. The rasp would do some job on the ball. When I needed a ground ball, I'd cut it good. It was as though I had my own tool bench out there with me."

Is it any wonder that people don't become overly exercised when Joe Niekro is caught with an emery board, or Gaylord Perry fidgets with his cap and uniform continually (and later writes a book entitled *The Spitter and Me*), or Rick Honeycutt is apprehended with a tack taped to his finger? Hey, Hall of Famers have done it. Why not me?

Honeycutt's bust, which came in 1980 when he was pitching in Seattle, may have been one of the most embarrassing. Not only was he caught red handed, er, fingered, but after he was ejected from the game Rick forgot about the tack and wiped his hand across his brow, leaving a bright red scratch.

"I haven't been in trouble like that since the last time I was sent to the principal's office," Honeycutt said. "What an ordeal. Crime never pays."

Except that often it does.

"I'd say that about 5 to 10 percent (of pitchers) doctor the ball and probably the same for bats, although you don't really know until something happens there," Gwynn guessed.

"If you can get away with it, more power to you. If you get caught, then there's retribution. You've got to know that going in."

Former Kansas City Royals outfielder Amos Otis freely admitted to using a corked bat during his playing career without ever being caught.

"If we were losing late in a game and needed a home run, or if I was going up against a pitcher who threw particularly hard, I used one," Otis said in 1994.

At the completely unacceptable end of the cheating scale stands Hal Chase, a graceful athlete regarded by many as perhaps the best fielding first baseman ever. He also holds the all-time American League record for errors by a first baseman (285), a fact attributed to the belief that Chase was involved in gambling on and throwing games as early as 1909 until he was shunned from the game after the 1919 season.

He was believed to help recruit the Black Sox group of eight, including Joe Jackson, who were banned for allegedly throwing the 1919 World Series to Cincinnati.

"He has a corkscrew for a brain," the *New York Press'* Jim Price once said of Chase.

That kind of cheating, no one condones.

When it comes to picking off the other team's hit-and-run sign, however, let the user beware.

"That's part of the game," said Padres bench coach Rob Picciolo. "That's why you change signs.

"If the other team picks them up, you change them again. If you don't, that's your fault. It's not their fault for being observant and watching the game and picking up on what we're doing. That's part of baseball.

"You're always trying to get the edge. But there's a certain etiquette to it, too."

Even when you cheat, in other words, you have to play by the rules.

[1998]

Hall of Famers Recount Lasting Memories of Major League Debuts

BY JOHN KUENSTER

During a pleasant weekend in late July, a distinguished array of Hall of Fame members gathered at baseball's major league shrine in Coopers-town, New York. The time and place were conducive to reminiscing about special moments of the game that have lingered in the minds of some of the assembled former hitters and pitchers who were all asked this question:

"What is the lasting memory you have of your first major league game?"

Here is how 18 Hall of Famers answered the question (debut date in parentheses):

Bob Feller, 80, pitcher (July 19, 1936)—"I joined the Indians when I was 17, about July 7 or 8, 1936. In my first game [July 19] I wound up pitching the eighth inning in relief, mopping up against the Washington Senators in Griffith Stadium. I had one strikeout, against Buddy Lewis, but somehow the official scorer failed to mark it down in his scorebook. But Buddy always told me he was my first official strikeout.

"In my first start that year [on August 23], I beat the St. Louis Browns and struck out 15. Charlie George was my catcher. They had some good players—Lyn Lary, Beau Bell, Harlond Clift. I remember Rogers Hornsby, their manager, pinch-hit against me, but I don't remember what he did.

"I won that game, 4-1, and I was very happy. There was a big fuss in the clubhouse after the game. We had some wonderful guys on that team— Mel Harder, Hal Trosky, Denny Galehouse. Steve O'Neill was the manager. He was like a father to me.

"I had extra good stuff that day. I threw everything high and inside to both left and right-handed batters. But I finished the season 5-and-3, mostly because I was wild all the time."

Ted Williams, 81, left fielder (April 20, 1939)—"It was Opening Day at Yankee Stadium. Lefty Grove against Red Ruffing. I was hitting sixth and struck out against Ruffing in my first two at-bats. Ruffing had a pretty good fastball, and a hard slider.

"In my first at-bat, I fouled off two pitches, and then struck out on a high fastball. My second time, he gets me on another high fastball.

"After I struck out the second time, Jack Wilson, one of our pitchers, comes over to me in the dugout and says, 'What do you think of the big leagues now, kid?'

"Well, I'm really ticked off, and tell him, 'Screw you. I know I can hit this guy.'

"Next time up I doubled off the wall in right-center, and when I pulled into second, Joe Gordon came over to me and says, 'Are you nervous?' I told him I was scared to death."

Lou Brock, 60, left fielder (September 10, 1961)—"I broke in with the Cubs at Wrigley Field late in '61, and when I saw my name on the lineup card and heard Pat Peiper announce my name over the loud speaker as the starting center fielder, I had a joyful feeling. It was a joy that knows no age. And when I crossed the line to go out to center, it was fantasy meeting reality.

"We played the Phillies that day, and Robin Roberts pitched against us. I got a single to center field my first time up and struck out my second time at bat. But, frankly, I don't remember anything else about that game."

Yogi Berra, 74, catcher (September 22, 1946)—"I came up in the last two weeks of the season in '46. We played the A's, and I remember hitting a homer off Phil Marchildon.

"Spud Chandler was our starting pitcher, and before the game I said to him, 'Don't be afraid to shake me off if I don't call the right pitch.'

"He said to me, 'Don't be afraid to call anything you want, because I can get all my pitches over the plate.'

"Was I nervous? Yeah, a little bit, but I always got that way when it was the first game of the year, or before a World Series game."

Don Sutton, 54, pitcher (April 14, 1966)—"We were playing Houston, and I was ahead, 2-1, at Dodger Stadium when they sent Ron Perranoski in to relieve me. It was the seventh or eighth inning. I left two runners on base, so when Perranoski gave up a three-run homer to Rusty Staub, I lost my first start.

"My feeling when I first went out to the mound? I was wondering what took me so long. I had been in the minors all of five months, and remembered what my managers, Norm Sherry at Santa Barbara and Roy Harts-field at Albuquerque, told me: 'Throw strikes, change speeds, and back up third if you have to.'

"I figured pitching in the majors would be no different from what they told me. Actually, my greatest fear was failure.

"But I grew up listening to baseball all my life. I played in Little League, Pony and Colt leagues, and I had already played certain game situations a thousand times in my mind. So, mentally, I was ready."

Bob Gibson, 64, pitcher (April 15, 1959)—"I swear to God, I don't remember my first game. Our manager was Solly Hemus. In spring training I thought I had earned a spot as a starter, but I made my debut as a reliever, in a game that had gotten completely out of hand for the Cardinals.

"I was aggravated to no end, and don't even remember what team we played [it was the Dodgers in L.A.]. I was supposed to start in L.A., then in St. Louis. Instead they sent me to the minors, Omaha. I was angry as hell.

"When I came back, in my first start, I pitched a shutout against Jim O'Toole and the Reds. But I have to say I didn't have a wonderful experience in my first major league game."

Brooks Robinson, 62, third baseman (September 15, 1955)—"I got two hits and drove in a run for the Orioles against the Washington Senators in Baltimore. Chuck Stobbs was their pitcher.

"I was so excited at going 2-for-4, after the game I went to the Southern Hotel and called my mom and dad in Little Rock [Arkansas] to tell them about it. I didn't know why I had been playing in Class B ball [Piedmont League] before. I knew I could play in the big leagues.

"Well, I learned. In my next 18 at-bats, I went 0-for-18 and struck out ten times to finish the season. I went back to the minors with San Antonio in the Texas League a couple of times before rejoining the Orioles for good in 1957."

Harmon Killebrew, 63, first baseman (June 23, 1954)—"I was 17 when I joined the Senators at Comiskey Park in Chicago in 1954. Bucky Harris was our manager. I started out as a second baseman.

"Bucky put me in to pinch-run in my first game. I weighed about 195 then, but I could run. When I was at first base, Walt Dropo [Sox first baseman] seemed like he was nine feet tall.

"Somehow I made it to second base, and there I got close to [shortstop] Chico Carrasquel and [second baseman] Nellie Fox. And I thought, 'Oh my God, what am I doing here with these guys?'

"We then went to Philadelphia where I started my first game at second base. We had a good infield— Eddie Yost at third, Pete Runnels at short, and Mickey Vernon at first. I got my first hit off Alex Kellner, a single. I wound up with two singles and a double, and we won, 9-2. I thought, 'This is going to be easy.' Boy, was I wrong!"

Harmon Killebrew was 17 years old in 1954 when he first joined the Washington Senators for a game against the White Sox. He recalled thinking at the time, "Oh my God, what am I doing here with these guys?"

Jim Palmer, 54, pitcher (April 17, 1965)—"In my first year with the Orioles in '65, my roommate was Robin Roberts. I was 18, and he was 38. I guess they figured if I roomed with him on the road, I'd learn something.

"My first game was at Fenway Park, and Hank Bauer calls me in from the bullpen to relieve Roberts with the bases full.

"I get to the mound, and Bauer asks me, 'Are you nervous?'

"I say, 'No.'

"'Then what are you doing with the extra ball in your glove?'

"I already had one ball in hand but had forgotten to get rid of the warmup ball that was in my glove.

"The batter was Tony Conigliaro. I never threw a grand slam in all the years I pitched. And I wasn't about to give Tony anything good to hit. I got two strikes on him with high fastballs, and then got strike three with a pitch at his knees."

Nolan Ryan, 52, pitcher (September 11, 1966)—"We [the Mets] were playing the Braves at Shea Stadium. The thing that sticks with me is the first time I faced Hank Aaron. I got him to pop up to first base, to foul out.

"The other memory from my first game is that Joe Torre hit a home run off me. I thought I made a decent pitch to him, but he hit it out."

Fergie Jenkins, 55, pitcher (September 10, 1965)—"The Phillies had a lot of good starters when I came up in 1965—Chris Short, Jim Bunning, Ray Culp. My first game was in relief of Bunning against the Cardinals at Connie Mack Stadium. I struck out Dick Groat, the first batter I faced, on four pitches.

"I threw fastballs and sliders. It was the eighth inning with runners on second and third when I relieved Bunning and struck out Groat. I pitched four and a third innings to get the win."

Tom Lasorda, 72, manager who also pitched briefly in the majors (August 5, 1954)—"The first game I pitched for the Dodgers was against Cincinnati at Ebbets Field. I came on in relief. I set down the first batter, Johnny Temple, and the second, Roy McMillan.

"Up comes Gus Bell, and I figure if I can get him out, I won't have to face Ted Kluszewski who was in the on-deck circle. Klu had already hit a couple of home runs, and I didn't want to face him. Who would? He had trimmed the sleeves off his jersey to show those bulging muscles of his. He was frightening.

"Anyhow, I get Bell to hit a grounder to Gil Hodges at first. Hodges was one of the best-fielding first basemen in the league. Know what? He booted the ball, and Bell was on first.

"Now, here comes Kluszewski. No way was I gonna let him hit his third homer. I threw him a hellacious curve and got him to bounce the ball right back to me, and I threw him out."

George Brett, 46, third baseman (August 2, 1973)—"My first game was at Comiskey Park against the White Sox in 1973. Stan Bahnsen was pitching for the Sox. On his first pitch to me, I hit the ball back to him, and he caught it. My second time up, I got a broken-bat single.

"We won the game [3-1] and it was great flying to Minneapolis for our next series against the Twins. I was only 20 and had to sneak a drink on the plane."

Robin Roberts, 73, pitcher (June 18, 1948)—"I had been pitching for Wilmington, Delaware, in the Interstate League for a couple of months when the Phillies called me up in June 1948. I was 20 years old, and when I got to Connie Mack Stadium I was struck by how beautiful the ballpark was.

"Our manager was Ben Chapman. I made my first start against the Pirates in Philadelphia. They had some good hitters—Stan Rojek, Frank Gustine, Ralph Kiner, Wally Westlake and Danny Murtaugh.

"I was excited, but I felt like I was prepared to pitch in the big leagues. I had a great fastball and a curveball. The Pirates spoiled my debut, though. I lost the game, 2-0."

Warren Spahn, 78, pitcher (April 19, 1942)—"In April 1942, I relieved in two games, but I don't remember much about them. The [Boston] Braves were managed by Casey Stengel, and they sent me down to the minors, to Hartford in the Eastern League where I won 17 games before they brought me back up in September.

"I was so thrilled to be in the big leagues. When I first came up I had a fastball, curve and changeup. My father, he was an amateur ballplayer, taught me to use all the momentum I could muster when I pitched.

"The game I remember most that year was one played at the Polo Grounds in September. I was pitching and we were losing to the Giants, 5-2, when the game was forfeited because kids had swarmed onto the field in the eighth inning. The kids had been admitted free for bringing scrap metal to the park to aid the war effort. They got restless and invaded the field. So we took the game by forfeit, 9-0, and statistically all I got out of it was a start and complete game, no win or loss."

Orlando Cepeda, 62, first baseman (April 15, 1958)—"I've always felt my first game was the biggest game of my career. It was a dream come true.

"We [the San Francisco Giants] were playing the Dodgers at Seals Stadium. My first base hit was a home run off Don Bessent.

"He threw me a changeup and I hit it into right center for a home run. We won the game, 8-0."

Steve Carlton, 55, pitcher (April 12, 1965)—"My first game memory? [Bob] Beetle Bailey of the Pirates hitting a home run off me on my first pitch at the old ballpark in St. Louis."

Stan Musial, 79, left fielder (September 17, 1941)—"I started the '41 season in the Western Association [Springfield] and then went to Rochester in the International League before the Cardinals brought me up.

"In my first game, we were playing the Braves in St. Louis. Our manager was Billy Southworth, and he put me in the lineup for the second game of a double-header.

"The first pitch thrown to me by Jim Tobin was one I had never seen before. It was a knuckleball. In my first at-bat I hit a popup to third base. The next time I doubled to score two runners. I got another hit, and we won the game."

[1999]

Dowd Report Details Extensive Gambling on Baseball by Pete Rose

BY JOHN KUENSTER

It measures 8½ inches wide, 11 inches in length, and contains 228 pages between soft, green covers. It is the John Dowd report to then-Commissioner Bart Giamatti, detailing incriminating evidence of Pete Rose's gambling on baseball when Rose was manager of the Cincinnati Reds. The report is dated May 9, 1989.

In his introduction, Dowd, a Washington, D.C., attorney who formerly worked for the Justice Department, explains the purpose of the report, based on a thorough, four-month investigation of Rose.

Dowd and his investigative staff had been retained by the commissioner's office to look into reports that Rose, in violation of Major League Rule 21, had bet on major league games, including Reds games.

Rule 21(d) warns: "Any player, umpire, or club or league official or employee, who shall bet any sum whatsoever upon any baseball game in connection with which the bettor has a duty to perform shall be declared permanently ineligible."

Dowd further states, "Betting on baseball by a participant of the game is corrupt because it erodes and destroys the integrity of the game. Betting on one's own team gives rise to the ultimate conflict of interest in which the individual player/bettor places his personal financial interest above the interest of the team.

"Gambling is conducted in secret by its participants. Normally, little is recorded and what is written down is destroyed shortly after payment of the wager.

"Payments are often made in cash by runners between the bookmaker and the gambler because cash is fungible [exchangeable] and difficult to trace. The runners provide insulation and, thus, deniability to the gambler and bookmaker.

"The telephone is used to conduct the wagering business by the participants. It is often difficult to determine who is wagering with whom because many phones are used by the bookmakers, runners and gamblers.

"The product of gambling, particularly sports action, is debt, (sometimes) enormous debt which leads to obligations, which leads to corruption.

"The secret gambling enterprise is typically exposed only when a participant is apprehended and begins to cooperate with the authorities. The gambling enterprise is designed to leave few tracks and, upon exposure, to provide alibis to the participants."

Dowd, in effect, was describing the modus operandi of Rose and his associates, and proceeded to substantiate his critical findings in page after page of his report, naming bookmakers and go-betweens who testified Rose bet on baseball in 1985, 1986 and 1987.

The only reason this information is being resurrected here so long after it was originally revealed is that last November Rose began a push to get himself reinstated in baseball, once again denying he ever bet on the game.

Enough is enough!

Rose thumbed his nose at the one rule that must be strictly observed if the game is to survive at the professional level.

So many baseball fans believe in him and sympathize with him because they never read the damning evidence against him in the Dowd report.

The major leagues' all-time leader in hits, Pete Rose stained the game and his reputation by gambling on baseball.

Perhaps Rose's plaintive cries of innocence are merely a reflection of our permissive times wherein lying by people in high places (Bill Clinton) and denial by celebrities (O. J. Simpson) have helped warp the conscience of society and erode our sense of right and wrong.

So Pete Rose holds the major league record for most hits (4,256), games played (3,562), at-bats (14,053), singles (3,215), and seasons (10) with 200 or more hits than any player in history.

So he was one of the most popular major leaguers ever, whose competitive drive earned him the sobriquet of "Charlie Hustle."

"So what?" a cynical antagonist might say, pointing out that Rose was also a compulsive gambler who crossed the line and betrayed the game he says he loves.

Perhaps if Rose had admitted betting on baseball and expressed his remorse and apologies during the last ten years of his banishment, his lifetime expulsion might have received some serious reconsideration.

But at this writing he hasn't taken those steps, and late last year was even threatening to sue major league baseball for his long exile, which, he claimed, was impairing his livelihood.

He even said he had a fingerprint and handwriting expert who would dispute the disclosures in the Dowd report that his fingerprints and handwriting were found on baseball betting slips. However, as might be expected, Rose didn't say how he would counteract the overwhelming number of telephone calls made on his behalf or by himself to bookies, recording his baseball bets from April 8 through July 3, 1987. In April alone that year, there were 278 calls, indicating heavy gambling activity.

During that three-month period in 1987, while managing the Reds, Rose made 385 bets on baseball, according to the commissioner's office.

The ledger indicates that on certain days, Rose bet on as many as 11 teams (May 2), also on as many as 10 teams (May 9, June 9, 10, and 29, and July 3), and wagered on an average of six teams a day.

On May 9, for example, he lost $3,400 on the Reds, $2,800 on Houston, $3,000 on Boston, $2,800 on Milwaukee, $2,000 on San Diego, $2,800 on Detroit, $2,000 on the White Sox and $4,000 on the Yankees, while winning $2,200 on the Braves and $2,000 on the Dodgers.

On May 10 he won $2,400 on San Diego, $2,000 on Los Angeles, $2,000 on Boston, $2,000 on the Yankees and $2,000 on Detroit, while losing $3,400 on the Reds, $3,200 on Milwaukee, $2,800 on Houston and $2,800 on the Mets.

On May 11 he won $2,000 on the Reds, $2,000 on the Yankees and $2,000 on Toronto, while losing $4,000 on the Red Sox, $2,000 on Atlanta, $3,800 on Houston, $3,400 on Los Angeles and $2,000 on Detroit.

These wagers, recorded by both his Cincinnati go-between Paul Janszen and Franklin, Ohio, bookmaker Ron Peters, were documented by the commissioner's office. Janszen relayed Rose's bets to Steve Chevashore, a Rose acquaintance, who in turn placed the bets with a Staten Island, New York, bookie known only as "Val" but later identified as Richard Troy.

Rose would wager anywhere from $2,000 to $4,000 a team, with the total amount gambled sometimes topping $20,000 on a particular day of activity. There was no evidence uncovered that Rose bet against the Reds.

Nonetheless the enormity of his gambling could easily have placed him in a position of compromise, tempting him to "fix" a game somewhere along the line for his own financial gain.

It should be noted that between 1985 and 1987, Rose ran up a rash of gambling debts. It was noted in the Dowd report that "within a three-month period of time, Rose was in debt over $400,000 to the bookie in New York via Mike Bertolini (a New York friend of Rose) in baseball betting alone."

In March 1998, *Baseball Digest* published the results of a poll among its readers, asking them for their opinions as to whether Pete Rose should be reinstated in baseball. Eighty-two percent of responding readers favored the readmission of Rose.

Be that as it may, it should never be forgotten that gambling by players almost destroyed major league baseball years ago, with the most famous case involving the 1919 World Series which was "tossed" by a small group of White Sox headed by pitcher Eddie Cicotte and first baseman Chick Gandil.

Although acquitted in court, eight White Sox players were banished forever from baseball for their alleged participation in the scandal. The outcasts, besides Cicotte and Gandil, included third baseman Buck Weaver, whose only guilt was that he knew about the "fix" but never informed on his miscreant teammates, and illiterate outfielder Joe Jackson who batted a resounding .375 in the Series against the Cincinnati Reds.

Commissioner Kenesaw Landis probably could have given a pass to Weaver and maybe even to the unsophisticated Jackson who tried to return his share of bribe money.

But Landis never changed the terms of lifetime punishment, and what might have become one of baseball's great dynasties was erased from the major league scene.

Before they died, both Cicotte and Jackson expressed their sorrow for what they did to hurt baseball.

Rose stained baseball, but not by trying to fix games. He did, however, hurt himself terribly by violating its most sacred rule.

John Dowd, as well as many baseball figures, high and low, think the biggest barrier on the road to reinstatement for Rose is Rose's refusal to admit and apologize for his gambling actions more than ten years ago.

There is no stigma attached to legal gambling. Baseball managers, coaches and players can toss their money away on horse races or dog races. They can buy all the state lottery tickets they want. They can gamble on the stock market.

But they can't bet on baseball games.

A copy of Rule 21 is posted on bulletin boards in every major league and minor league clubhouse.

Pete Rose has known all about the rule since he was a rookie in 1963. He ignored it in the 1980s and has only himself to blame for the severe personal price he has paid for his indiscretion.

[2000]

Why Left-Handers Are Different

BY GERRY FRALEY

The wisdom has been passed on from generation to generation: You win in baseball with left-handed pitchers.

Clyde King, a New York Yankees special assistant who has been in the game for 57 years, says he learned the lesson from Hall of Famer Branch

Rickey. Gene "The Little General" Mauch, who managed 26 seasons in the majors, picked up the teaching from Hall of Famer Clark Griffith.

"Clark, one of the wisest men in baseball, once told me, 'Give me all the left-handed pitchers, and I'll beat you to death,'" Mauch says. "This search has gone on since the first big league manager."

The Rangers are the latest club to join the trend. General manager Doug Melvin said the club needed to have more of a left-handed bent, and he kept his word by adding three left-handers for the rotation: Darren Oliver, Kenny Rogers and Justin Thompson.

Left-handers toil in a world made for right-handers. School desks, car ignitions and voting booths are built for right-handers. Nothing is built for left-handers.

To be right-handed is to be normal. The Latin word for right is dexter, meaning skill.

To be left-handed is to be different. The Latin word for left is sinister. It all changes in baseball.

Most team sports look to fill positions. In baseball, handedness matters most. The game values left-handers overall and left-handed pitchers in particular.

"The good Lord smiled on me when he gave me left-handed genes," says left-hander Tommy John, who won 288 games in a 27-year career.

What makes left-handers so special, or so different?

The more left-handed pitching, the better a team's chances.

Says who?

The standings.

Left-handed starters win more often than right-handed starters. In the American League over the past three seasons (1997–1999), left-handed starters had a winning record (608-581) and a 4.49 ERA. In that same span, right-handed starters had a losing record (1,773-1,893) and a 4.98 ERA.

"After a certain point in the draft, I'd tell our people, 'Take all the left-handed pitchers you can get,'" former New York Mets general manager Frank Cashen says. "We'd corner the market if we could. A southpaw is a commodity."

Left-handers became known as "southpaws" in the sporting press of the 1890s. To keep the sun from blinding spectators in the most expensive seats, teams positioned their parks so that pitchers faced west. The left-handers' elbows pointed south.

There are practical reasons for left-handers' success.

The left-hander holds runners at first more effectively than right-handers because he faces the base from the stretch. The shorter lead decreases the possibility of a runner going from first to third on a hit.

The left-hander usually faces right-handed hitters. Those batters are less likely to take advantage of the hole on the right side, caused by the first baseman holding the runner, than left-handed hitters.

There is also the neutralization factor.

Left-handed hitters have advantages equal to what left-handed pitchers enjoy. The best way to stop left-handed hitters is with left-handed pitchers. Through the last generation, left-handed hitters annually hit about 25 points lower against left-handed pitchers than against right-handed pitchers.

The word left carries a negative connotation in many languages.

In German, *linkisch* translates to left and clumsy, awkward or socially inferior. In Spanish, the word for left-handed, *zurdas*, also means wrong way. The Italian word *mancino* means both left—and dishonest.

True or false: Left-handers cannot throw a ball straight.

False, says former major league left-hander Tug McGraw. It is all an optical illusion, McGraw says. Left-handers look different because they are the minority, McGraw says. Their pitches seem to move more than they really do.

Most baseball people agree with McGraw, with the reasons ranging from the force of the Earth's movement in the Northern Hemisphere to the styles of deliveries.

Some of the best left-handers of the last 50 years—Sandy Koufax, Sam McDowell, Warren Spahn—used an overhand delivery. Most left-handers have a low three-quarters delivery, releasing the ball from a lower point than right-handers.

Former major league manager and pitching coach Ray Miller says left-handers probably gain a "body lean" as they cope with a right-handed world. That gives left-handed pitchers the lower release point and allows left-handed batters to handle low pitches.

The lower release point gives the pitches more movement, making the left-hander more effective.

"A left-handed pitcher has an advantage because his ball moves," King says. "You don't know why, but it does. There's no answer. I've asked Mr. Rickey that question, and he could not answer it. It's the only question I asked him that he didn't answer."

The extra movement often leads to control problems for left-handers. Tommy Byrne, a left-hander, is the career leader for walks-per-nine-innings at 6.9.

Left-handers make up about 9 percent of the general population. They appear at more than double that rate on major league staffs.

Excluding position players given mop-up duty, a total of 571 pitchers appeared in the majors last season. There were 162 left-handers in that group, giving them 28.4 percent of the staffs' spots.

In baseball jargon, left-hander means to be goofy, spacey, odd.

The designation probably began with left-hander Rube Waddell. He had four consecutive 20-win seasons (1902–1905) with the Philadelphia Athletics and a then-record 349 strikeouts in 1904. He led the A.L. in strikeouts from 1902–1907 with the A's and the N.L. in 1900 with the Pirates.

But Waddell's erratic behavior overshadowed his pitching. He liked to chase fire engines, lead parades and play marbles under the stands between innings of games. He was a man-child who probably was mentally deficient, but in baseball he became a "flake."

Other left-handed pitchers perpetuated the image: Nick Altrock, who became a baseball clown; Hall of Famer Lefty Gomez; Bill "Spaceman" Lee; and McGraw.

There have also been rational left-handers and erratic right-handers such as Dizzy Dean and Bobo Newsom, but the lasting image of left-handers is one of "flakes."

There is something different about left-handers, traits that affect their character and their pitching.

Dr. Martin Samuels, chief of neurology at Boston's Brigham and Women's Hospital, says a left-hander's brain "is wired differently." Left-handers' brains are more symmetrical, which leads to more communication between the two sides. That makes the left-hander more flexible and more able to deal with visual and spatial problems.

For baseball, that means a left-hander should be better than a right-hander for determining where a pitch should go and how the body should function in the delivery.

Because there are no brain surgeons in dugouts, baseball people accept what they see. There is something special about left-handed pitchers.

[2000]

Cal Ripken: More Than Baseball's Iron Man
BY PHIL ROGERS

Holding court on the dugout steps, Cal Ripken Jr. seemed very much a man at peace with his place and time. Another game would begin in about an hour, but Ripken was in no hurry to go screw on his game face.

His inexorable march on 3,000 hits reached its conclusion last April 14 when he lined a single to center field off Minnesota's Hector Carrasco in the seventh inning of Baltimore's 6-4 victory over the Twins at the Metrodome, his third hit of the game. Since the historic mark, there was time for reflection about baseball and life.

Ripken once considered them one and the same, but that has changed in recent years. The death of his father and a new understanding of his mortality have given the 39-year-old Maryland native a new appreciation of every day he wears a Baltimore Orioles uniform.

"So many good things have happened to me in the game of baseball," Ripken said. "When I do allow myself a chance to think about it, it's almost like a storybook career. You feel so blessed to have been able to compete this long."

Ripken is baseball's iron man. And then some.

There is so much more to Ripken, it's almost a shame that his career will be defined by his tireless pursuit of the late Lou Gehrig. Long before Ripken's victory lap around Camden Yards, the dozens of handshakes and stops to chat with fans he knew by name, Ripken was one of those rare guys who could do it all, and his 3,000-hit achievement underscores that. He became the 24th player to reach 3,000 hits.

Ripken always has been among baseball's smartest, most dedicated players. Some believe he is the best shortstop ever. But the one distinction nobody can question is the streak of 2,632 consecutive games.

Now he has another that says at least as much about him as a ballplayer.

"I was relieved," Ripken said after reaching the plateau. "I felt a weight was lifted from my shoulders."

He's only the seventh member of the ultra-select 3,000-hit club also to have 400-plus home runs. The others are Hank Aaron, Willie Mays, Eddie Murray, Stan Musial, Dave Winfield and Carl Yastrzemski.

Think about those names a moment.

Baltimore natives will talk all day long about Ripken as a complete player. But those who don't remember baseball before the Clinton presidency may think of him only as the guy whose ego wouldn't allow him to take a day off even if he was hurting and the Orioles were out of contention.

The latter perspective overlooks the achievements that got Ripken started on his road to the Hall of Fame. Among them:

• He led the A.L. with 211 hits, 47 doubles and 121 runs scored when he was only 23, leading the Orioles to the world championship.

• He hit between 21 and 34 homers a year from 1982 to '91, when the Orioles were based at Memorial Stadium, not their current bandbox. Although never regarded as a power hitter, he outslugged Cecil Fielder and Ken Griffey Jr. to win a home run contest at the '91 All-Star Game in Toronto.

• He committed only three errors in 161 games at shortstop in '90. Ripken handled 428 consecutive chances without an error at one point in '90. Ripken led A.L. shortstops in double plays eight times, another record.

One of the best all-around shortstops of modern times, Cal Ripken not only set a major league record for playing in the most consecutive games but epitomized class in everything he did on and off the field.

• His first stolen base was a steal of home, executed during a double steal.

If not for these kinds of contributions, Ripken would not have had the chance to become baseball's greatest fixture. But the consecutive-games streak that began innocently enough in 1982 reached such epic proportions that his spot in the lineup became a daily subplot that often overshadowed everything else with the Orioles. It left him open for criticism, including direct or subtle accusations of selfishness.

While the Dow Jones Industrial Average rose more than 7,000 points during Ripken's 17-year streak, stock in him seemed to rise and fall according to the fate of the Orioles. They won the World Series in '83, his second full season, but haven't been back.

"In the past, I considered the emphasis on the streak to be an assault on him," younger brother Billy Ripken, a Baltimore teammate for seven seasons, told the *Baltimore Sun*. "There was an awful lot of blame pointed his way whenever something went wrong with the Birds. Usually, it was because he was tired and wasn't helping the team. It was venomous, I thought."

Ripken played every day for more than three years after breaking Gehrig's record of 2,130 consecutive games. He took himself out of the lineup on September 20, 1998, which lessened the shock when he went on the disabled list in April and August last year.

Ripken's transformation from the realm of the infinite to the finite was completed in September, when he underwent back surgery.

When Ripken arrived at the Orioles' camp last spring, no one knew how he would hold up. But longtime teammates immediately noticed changes both in Ripken and in the way he is perceived.

"It seems like ever since '95 there has been a question following him," Orioles right-hander Mike Mussina said. "There always seemed to be a question about his motivation for playing every day, then afterward the question about how long he would keep doing it, then the questions about his back. But I guess since Cal sat down, the questions haven't seemed quite as loaded."

Ripken probably would have joined Tony Gwynn and Wade Boggs in reaching the 3,000-hit milestone last season if not for back surgery. But he might not have appreciated it as much as he will now that the chance to play the game he loves was almost taken away.

"The big picture is I love doing what I do," Ripken said. "I love being a baseball player. I want to be a baseball player as long as I can."

Ripken is signed only through this season, but the Orioles surely will resign him if he wants to come back. He says he's at the point where "you evaluate year to year," but he clearly believes he still can contribute to a winning team.

Ripken has won two American League Most Valuable Player awards and has been in 17 All-Star games. But he has hit .340 only once in his career. He did it last year.

"I've had a few seasons where everything seems to go right swinging the bat," Ripken said. "I feel like I'm right on the ball all year. It was like that in '83 and in '91. I got it going and stayed in a groove all year. Last year I felt totally good in the batter's box. Selfishly, you wish you could have applied that to 350 at-bats instead of just over 300."

Ripken not only stemmed the ebbing tide of his career batting average but also did it while mourning the death of his father, with whom he was extremely close.

Longtime Baltimore Orioles coach Cal Ripken Sr. lost his battle with cancer about a week before Opening Day in 1998.

"It was devastating losing a father," Ripken said. "It was a horrific experience. I know everybody has to go through it, but that doesn't make it any easier."

Ripken once grimaced when anyone raised the subject of retirement. Recent photo shoots have been agreed to with the provision that there would be no pictures taken from the rear. Ripken has no interest in helping illustrate the passing of his career.

But there's no stopping the question, and he has prepared himself to answer it patiently. He took a philosophical stance on it earlier in the season.

"It doesn't worry me," Ripken said. "I don't think of retirement as sad. Nobody ever has played at this level forever. Some people defy the odds. Nolan Ryan played until he was 46 or 47. I could play recreationally forever, but at this level it is tough."

Ripken batted only .143 in spring training. He concedes that his back remains a source of concern.

"I approached some things very cautiously, because the finish line for me was to leave spring training healthy," Ripken said. "Coming off back surgery, you don't know what to expect. Even at crunch time, you probably feel like you let it all hang out, but you can't."

Ripken was batting only .257 with 13 homers and 42 RBI through June 20, playing in 57 of Baltimore's first 68 games.

When he went 3-for-5 against the Twins last April 14, when he got his 3,000th hit, he became the third player to do so at the Metrodome.

It would have meant a lot for Ripken to get his 3,000th hit at Camden Yards.

"Obviously, if you could plan it out to be perfect, you'd plan it to happen at home, which also happens to be my hometown," he said. "But you'd be doing a dishonor to the game if you tried to fudge it."

[2000]

Jimmy Piersall's Antics Overshadowed His Talent

BY BOB DOLGAN

Jimmy Piersall was the noisiest ballplayer the Indians ever had. He was always talking, often at the top of his voice, on the team bus, in the clubhouse and on the field.

In three tumultuous years in Cleveland, from 1959 to 1961, he was a riotous package of fun, trouble and skill. The center fielder battled with pitchers, umpires, sportswriters, scorers and fans. He also was a great guy to interview.

Most fans loved him. "They knew I wasn't two-faced," he said. He recorded two songs, "Please, Jimmy Piersall," and "Rookie of the Year," and talked/sang them in shows at the Hippodrome, Olympia, Elysium and Berea theaters.

It is good to see Piersall has lost none of his spirit at age 71. "I feel great," the old rascal said from his home in Illinois. "I had a triple bypass in 1976 and a quadruple bypass in 1984. I asked my doctor how many more years I have left and he said, 'You're too ornery to die.'"

He had nine children by the time he was 31 and playing for the Indians, and now has 25 grandchildren.

Piersall, who used to broadcast Chicago baseball games and still does three radio shows a week, said he is set financially. He and his second

A gifted center fielder, Jimmy Piersall was noted for offbeat antics during his 17-year career, including a caper in which he ran the bases backwards after hitting his 100th lifetime home run when he was with the Mets.

wife, Jan, to whom he has been married for 20 years, own two houses, one in Arizona.

"I'm the gooney bird that walked to the bank," he said. "I'm doing better than most of those guys who said I was crazy."

He had detailed his emotional and mental breakdown as a Boston Red Sox rookie in his best-selling book *Fear Strikes Out*.

After his retirement as a player, Piersall wrote another book, *The Truth Hurts*, in which he said in the first line: "Probably the best thing that happened to me was going nuts. Nobody knew who I was until that happened." He had been institutionalized.

After his recovery, most baseball people thought Piersall was deliberately putting on a show with his antics. Others thought he was still suffering from the effects of his illness. Maybe a little of both was true.

Bob Hale, 67, a former pinch-hitter with the Indians and now a retired school principal, said, "When there were 40,000 in the stands or the game was on TV, you could expect Jimmy to make something happen. I think it was calculated. But he was a fine player and a lot of fun."

Former outfielder Tito Francona, 67, agreed. "Jimmy was smart as a fox," he said. "Every time he got kicked out of a game, he made more money. People sent him money to pay his fines. I remember a game in Yankee Stadium where he ran to second base and did jumping jacks. Then he ran behind the monuments and sat down."

Rocky Colavito, 67, recalled the time he was playing next to Piersall in the Indians outfield in Detroit. "He was in center and I was in right," said Colavito. "All of a sudden, I saw him running to the 395-foot sign in center where two guys were sitting by themselves. He came back laughing. I asked him what happened and he said, 'Those two guys have been yelling at me through the whole game. I just spit in their face.'"

In Cleveland's Municipal Stadium, Piersall would sit on top of the fence. Bleacher fans would yell, "Hey, Jimmy, the men in the white coats are coming." The quick-witted Piersall would answer back.

"I didn't mind if they yelled at me," Piersall said. "But when they came on the field, it was a different story."

That happened twice within three weeks in 1961, both in Sunday doubleheaders against the Yankees. A crowd of 56,307 at the Stadium saw a burly fan run at Piersall in center. He wanted to shake his hand. "You touch me and I'll kick you in the rear," Piersall said, reasoning the man could have a knife. The fan squared off at Piersall, and then ran. Piersall punted him. Then, in front of 57,824 at Yankee Stadium, two fans, 17 and 18, charged him, calling him a nut and throwing punches. He had shouted at the populace in defense of teammate Vic Power, who was being booed. Piersall defended himself well, landing punches and another field goal as teammate Johnny Temple and police helped out.

The skirmish took the play away from Roger Maris and Mickey Mantle, who were waging their epic duel for the home run title.

Piersall refused to press charges after the melee. "I've had 117 fights and that's the first time I've ever won," he said.

Aside from the escapades, Piersall had talent. When he came up with Boston in 1952, Yankees manager Casey Stengel said he was the best right fielder he had ever seen. He had a great arm then, but injured it after a throwing contest with Willie Mays. "I didn't get hurt in the contest," Piersall said. "I hurt it the next day."

Piersall became a brilliant center fielder, a quick man who always got a good jump on the ball. He was smart and canny, knowing exactly where to play hitters.

When Francona replaced Piersall in center for Cleveland in 1959, Jimmy would stand in the bullpen and position him. Once, with Elston Howard of the Yankees up, Piersall told Francona to move toward right center. Francona, figuring the right-handed Howard would pull the ball against the pitcher, who did not have much speed, shifted toward left center instead.

But Howard hit the ball to right center. "That's the last time I didn't listen to Piersall," Francona said.

Piersall was a good hitter, too, averaging .272 in 17 seasons. He led the league in doubles once and hit as many as 18 homers. His best season came with Cleveland in 1961, when he hit .322.

He had trouble with manager Joe Gordon as the Indians almost won the 1959 pennant. "Joe didn't like me," Piersall said. "We should have won the pennant that year. It was the best club I was ever on."

The late Gordon was quoted as saying: "So help me, before I'm through I'm going to belt Piersall."

"You couldn't dislike Jimmy," Colavito said. "He was fun. He had a commercial deal with Neptune Sardines and would always bring some to the clubhouse."

"He said the sardines were the reason I hit .363 in 1959," Francona said. Piersall would answer almost any question an interviewer asked. He was friendly with uncritical writers, but he always seemed to be feuding with somebody in the press. In Minnesota he ordered two Twins writers out of the clubhouse. On at least one occasion he threw a baseball at a sportswriter from center field during warmups, missing by 10 feet. He circled writers who were smoking cigarettes like a caged lion. "If you want to talk to me, you'll have to put out that cigarette," he said.

He frequently argued with official scorers and umpires. He regrets the power umpires have assumed today. "You can't even look at an umpire anymore," he said. "Baseball can be a very dull game. People don't come to see the umpires."

He prided himself on getting opposing players angry, hoping to distract them. "Now the players pat each other on the ass," he said.

Piersall burst on the scene as a rookie with the Red Sox in 1952. He suffered a breakdown from the pressure of trying to make the team and began doing things never before seen on baseball fields.

He ran up the screen behind home plate; spread his arms in imitation of an airplane when running to first base; dropped his bat and imitated the pitcher's motion; left the plate and ran to first to give a stage whisper to a runner. When an umpire called him out on strikes in the minors, he pulled a water pistol and sprayed the plate, saying, "Maybe now you can see it."

All this was told in *Fear Strikes Out*. It was later made into a movie starring Anthony Perkins. Piersall hated Perkins' portrayal because the actor was so unathletic. His father, played by tall, domineering Karl Malden in the movie, was actually a small, friendly man, judging from a visit he once made to the Cleveland dugout.

"The book was the truth," Piersall said. "The movie was not my story."

When the Indians traded Piersall to Washington for Dick Donovan and Gene Green, he expressed happiness to a Cleveland baseball writer. "I don't have to read your stuff anymore," he said. "You and those two columnists. You guys are killing baseball in that town. But I like you anyway. We're pals, right, even though I think you're a (expletive)."

Piersall went on to play with the New York Mets, where he ran himself into everlasting legend by trotting around the bases backward after hitting his 100th home run.

"Yeah, but don't forget I was a good ballplayer, too," he said. That he was.

[2001]

Tony Gwynn Strived for Perfection as a Hitter

BY CHRIS JENKINS

His vision was extraordinary in the beginning, testing out in spring training every year at 20-10. But then it was 20-15, a decrease alarming enough to Tony Gwynn that he laughingly admits to cheating on eye exams by memorizing the bottom line of the chart. Very resourceful fellow.

Actually, he tried eyeglasses during batting practices around 1994 or so. Somewhere out there, he suspects, he fears, are baseball cards with him in spectacles.

"I couldn't stand wearing them," Gwynn says. "I looked like a dork."

His hands are smallish, tiny really, considering the feats they've produced and awards they've held. One of them alone couldn't grip a basketball, though Gwynn could dribble behind his back and between his legs and whip a blind pass so fine he was named point guard on the same All-WAC backcourt as Danny Ainge.

Gwynn could dunk, too, once upon a time in the Western Athletic Conference. The same legs, while never overly muscled, carried him 60 yards in 6.7 seconds. On the court, on the bases, in the batter's box, his first step was his best one.

Still, while his athleticism always was grossly underrated, Gwynn never was the prototypical physical specimen like Andre Dawson or Eric Davis or Vladimir Guerrero.

Gwynn didn't beat you with his body.

Well, from the neck up, yes. Beat your brains out, he did, with his brains.

The power of Gwynn's vision wasn't nearly as strong as his powers of observation. If his hands were as small as cat's paws, they were also as fast, but not as quick as his thought processes. The way others honed their abs and arms, Gwynn conditioned his instincts.

When his knees grew scarred and heels grew sore and legs grew slower, Gwynn could tell leading off first when a pitcher was looking at him or just pretending to look at him, the way that maddening Greg Maddux does it. Gwynn sometimes stole bases by breaking for second before the pitcher turned back toward the plate.

Likewise, although his peripheral vision enabled him to stare straight at the pitcher and see the entire defensive set-up, Gwynn sometimes got opposing infielders to suddenly shift to his desire. Awaiting a pitch, he'd give a certain glance at a spot between first and second, then chuckle inside while Bret Boone hurriedly moved over to the spot to create an opening for Gwynn's next hit.

Start to finish, from his rookie season of 1982 to his retirement year of 2001, the one thing Gwynn could do better than any man in the game was put wood to ball. Neither time nor surgery could take away his most basic, most pure skill.

"Get a good pitch to hit," he says, "and hit it."

So simple.

"When it's going good, yeah, it is," says Gwynn. "Hands and hips, hands and hips. And eyes."

Always, the eyes. He used them to study the videotape of himself and the videotape of the other guy, the pitcher du jour. Out on the field, he watched the opposing pitchers as they warmed up, noting how they set up on the mound, toeing the left or right side or middle of the rubber.

Attention to detail. Mental data processing.

How many times have pitchers seen those brown eyes peering out at them? Doing the Gwynn Squint. A sniper looking through the scope.

"If the guy came over the top, my eyes were focused on the logo of his cap," Gwynn says. "I'm looking at the cap, looking at the cap. Then as he's winding up or coming from the stretch, my eyes shifted to the release point. Once you get to the release point, you're looking for the ball in his hand. You might see the hand turn. Might see the finger up.

"Whatever it is that allows you to recognize what it is and where it's going."

The great pitchers, recognizing Gwynn's greatness, resorted to what makes them great. Not that Greg Maddux had much luck with it—Gwynn hit .429 against him—but the four-time Cy Young Award winner mixed up his motion and movements and locations on Gwynn more than anybody else.

Tony Gwynn won eight National League batting titles with the Padres, matching the National League record held by Honus Wagner.

You'd swear there were tacks sticking out from the mound when Tom Glavine was pitching against Gwynn, so often did the lefty change the places he toed the rubber and revised his delivery, yet Gwynn is the only one who seemed to notice. The professorial Orel Hershiser used to try to outthink Gwynn by never releasing a pitch from the same place twice.

"With those guys, I never tried to get too aggressive," Gwynn says. "I just took what they gave me." As the ball approaches at anywhere between 75 and 101 mph, Gwynn's mind took the pitch into slow motion, like the many times he'd hit the freeze-frame button on his VCR in the little room directly behind his locker at Qualcomm Stadium. Indeed, the video study prepared Gwynn for the trajectory of the ball as it spins in various ways.

Whatever the pitch, though, Gwynn wanted his body to wind up in the same well-balanced stance to hit it.

"When the front foot lands, the body stops," he says. "It's like a forward anchor. I don't stride forward. I just pick up the front foot and put it down. If I do that right, I'm in position to hit, and I'm taking the knob of the bat to the ball. My hands are going to lead the way, and the body is going to rotate and follow the knob of the bat.

"The pitch that throws that all out of whack is the splitter, because it comes out of the hand looking like a fastball. Then the bottom falls out of it. As you set that foot down and begin to pull the knob through, you recognize that ball's going down, you have to adjust midstream."

Whereas sluggers like to meet the ball out in front of the plate, Gwynn's perfect point of contact is directly over its heart. He recognized early in his career that whenever he got to a fastball too soon, he usually rolled over on it, grounding out harmlessly.

Once the Padres had lost leadoff batter extraordinaire Alan Wiggins, pitchers began giving Gwynn regular dosages of curveballs, and he remembers the anguish of those two months of the 1985 season before he got the hang of the breaking ball.

Seven more years passed, too, before Gwynn would heed Ted Williams' advice to stop finessing inside pitches and start driving them. Only then did Gwynn become the complete hitter. He made it look so automatic, and so often it was.

"When it's all good, man, it just happens like that," Gwynn says. "You don't think about it. You don't feel it. You don't concern yourself with it."

Gwynn, on the other hand, wasn't the type to let a 5-for-5 night relax him from his routine. A single hitless night would get him back to the ballpark even earlier than usual the next day, plopping down baseballs on the tee, a tedious process that most players eschew as irrelevant to facing live pitching.

"He'd go through 100 baseballs a day on that tee," says former teammate Steve Finley, now with the Arizona Diamondbacks. "Then he'd put 50 more balls on the tee just to make sure it was ingrained in him."

Gwynn would go back to the tapes, too. More than any television producer, Gwynn became identified with the implementation of videotape in baseball.

In fact, well before Gwynn was a professional ballplayer or even a college athlete, he was a videographer of sorts. As a teen, he'd hoist one of those cumbersome first-edition cameras to tape the play of his father's Pop Warner football teams, although the family didn't have a VCR at home.

The use of video early in his major league career, Gwynn says, "turned around my career." Alicia Gwynn would tape Padres road games, and while most husbands drive their spouses nuts with the remote control, Alicia would watch along with Gwynn as he replayed and replayed his at-bats. In the process, too, she became a pretty good hitting coach.

"We'd be sitting there and Alicia'd be holding [first-born son] Anthony on her lap," Gwynn says. "I'd be talking to myself and they'd be listening. I'd show her something I'd done—play it, rewind it, play it, slow-motion it—and she got really good at recognizing the things I saw.

"She was a basketball fan but became a very astute baseball fan. Now she tells me all the same kinds of things I used to tell her back in those days. 'That pitch there? You've got to swing at that pitch. [Voice rises in mock disgust.] What're you doing? You're ahead in the count and you tried to get greedy!'

"It's funny now, but . . . believe me, I know I was lucky."

Alicia aside, the person who grew more familiar with Gwynn's swing than anybody was Merv Rettenmund, the Padres' hitting coach for nine years before leaving to join the Atlanta Braves.

"Greatest hitter I've ever seen," says Rettenmund. "Tony taught me more about hitting than I ever taught him." Before he came to the Padres,

Rettenmund says he had already gotten a primer on Gwynn from Doug Rader, who as a Class-AAA manager had been the one to inform Gwynn he was going to the majors in '82.

"Rader called Tony 'the guy with the little hands,'" Rettenmund says. "I just call him the greatest hitter I've ever seen."

Ironically, the most interesting appraisal that Rettenmund ever heard about Gwynn had nothing to do with stroke or pitch recognition or focus. It was a team psychologist who told Rettenmund that one overriding trait you usually find in great players is consistency. As people, not just athletes.

"That's Tony," Rettenmund says. "Tony never was one of those up-and-down guys. At the end of the day, you couldn't tell if he'd gone 3-for-3 or 0-for-3. If Tony's been anything over his career, it was consistent. Incredibly consistent."

Twenty big league seasons. Only his first (1982) ending below the .300 mark—55 hits, 190 at-bats, .289. Whatever the outside interferences—the injuries, financial setbacks, questions about whether he'd be resigned, the rare squabbles with teammates and jealousies in the clubhouse, the millions of media obligations over the years—he kept his eye on the ball.

That should be the bottom line on Tony Gwynn. Memorize that.

Highest Career Batting Averages for Players With 3,000 Hits

Player	ABs	Hits	BA
Ty Cobb	11,434	4,189	.366
Tris Speaker	10,195	3,514	.345
Nap Lajoie	9,589	3,242	.338
Tony Gwynn	9,288	3,141	.338
Eddie Collins	9,949	3,315	.333
Paul Waner	9,459	3,152	.333
Stan Musial	10,972	3,630	.331
Cap Anson	9,104	3,012	.331
Wade Boggs	9,180	3,010	.328
Rod Carew	9,315	3,053	.328
Honus Wagner	10,439	3,420	.328
Roberto Clemente	9,454	3,000	.317
Paul Molitor	10,835	3,319	.306
Hank Aaron	12,364	3,771	.305
George Brett	10,349	3,154	.305
Pete Rose	14,053	4,256	.303
Willie Mays	10,881	3,283	.302

[2002]

First Base, the Game's Social Hub

BY DAVID ANDRIESEN

Early last season, Ichiro Suzuki singled and cruised into first base, a location he would frequent throughout the summer.

Standing beside him during the next at-bat was Kansas City Royals first baseman Mike Sweeney, who doesn't speak Japanese but knew what to say.

"I went to Japan the previous year on a tour of major league players, and when someone would get a hit, they'd have this booming voice in English on the public-address system that would say, 'Nice batting!' Sweeney said.

"So the first time Ichiro got on against us I just said in a deep voice, 'Nice batting,' and he started laughing."

First base is the social hub of the baseball diamond, where for a few pitches the base runner and defender act as if they're at a cocktail party instead of embroiled in athletic competition.

"It's usually not much, just small talk," said Anaheim first baseman Scott Spiezio. "How's the family? How many kids you got now? Where you guys going to dinner? If it's somebody you don't know, it's generic stuff. How ya doin'? Nice day."

It's the same kind of dialogue fostered by elevators and post office lines.

"You're this close to the guy," Mariners second baseman Bret Boone said, holding his hands two feet apart. "It would be uncomfortable if nothing was said."

"As the first baseman, you're definitely the ambassador of the team," said Tony Clark, who manned first in Detroit for seven years before moving to Boston this season.

"If you were lucky enough to get to first base on the road, you got a chance to ask the guy where everyone was going after the game," said Steve Lyons, who played from 1985 to 1993. "I'd be like, 'OK, we got three or four guys on the team that are cowboys, so we need a cowboy bar.' And we need a jazz bar and we need a metal bar. Next time I get here you need to have three or four ideas for where to go tonight."

Some of the nicest players in the majors are first basemen, including Seattle's John Olerud. But the Bellevue, Washington, native does all his chattering on the field—he's the quietest Mariner off the field.

"I probably do more talking on the field than anybody else, which is pretty ironic," he said.

"Tony Muser, our former manager, would get mad at me sometimes because I talk too much to guys at first base," Sweeney said. "He says, 'You can get their autographs after the game or take them to dinner after the game,' but that's just my personality. If someone says hello to me, I'm going to say hello to them."

Not that the conversations are always smooth—particularly if a base runner isn't aware of Sweeney's devout Christian lifestyle.

"Sometimes the guy will come over and you don't know him or don't have anything in common with him. He'll start talking about going to the booby bar or something, and I'm like, 'Uh, you got the wrong guy, man.'

"Sometimes the conversations are pleasant, but sometimes you're saying, come on, I hope the batter gets a hit so this guy can go to second."

You might even get stuck standing next to someone you recently tried to beat up, as happened to Spiezio during spring training.

"I got in a fight this spring with the Padres, and when we played them again later in the spring I got to first and [Phil] Nevin was there," he said. "We were sort of wrestling around during the fight, but you know, baseball is baseball. We know that stuff is part of the game."

With baseball's increasing international diversity, there are more occasions in which the first baseman and the base runner don't speak the same language. It is generally the responsibility of the non-English speaker to know enough to exchange pleasantries in English.

"I just assume that it's going to be in English," Olerud said, "and if he doesn't respond, we're kind of at a stalemate."

Ichiro, the first Japanese position player in the majors, presented a unique situation for most first basemen. The Rangers' Rafael Palmeiro last season had members of the Japanese media teach him how to say, "You're the man" in Japanese.

Most have been surprised to see how much English Ichiro knows.

"Ichiro got hit by a pitch from [former teammate Aaron] Sele, and I was going to ask him what he did to piss Sele off," Spiezio said. "He beat me to the punch. He said, 'Does he hate me?' I said, 'Yeah, what did you do to him last year?' It was a slider, obviously he didn't hit him on purpose, but we had some fun with it."

Spiezio likes to have fun with players he knows, like Frank Menechino, Oakland's vertically challenged, smack-talking second baseman.

"Menechino got hit in the foot by [Angels pitcher Scott] Schoeneweis two times in a game, and he was all huffing and puffing the second time he came to first," Spiezio said. "I said, 'I'd be pissed too, if a guy was throwing at my head like that.' He thought that was pretty funny. It kind of lightened the mood."

[2002]

Sign Language, Baseball's Hidden Communication

BY LARRY STONE

It all looks so innocent, at times even comical. Yet all the exaggerated gyrations, the clandestine touches and subtle movements that make up baseball's secret language of signs open a door into a fascinating and complex culture (and controversial subculture) of the sport.

Except for the ball itself, the surreptitious communication from catcher to pitcher, from manager to base coach, from base coach to base runner, from infielder to outfielder (and various other combinations and permutations of transmitted sign language that take place in the roughly 20 seconds between pitches) might be the most essential element for completion of a coherent ballgame.

"I don't think you could play without signs," said baseball historian Paul Dickson, author of the forthcoming book on signs, *The Hidden Language of Baseball*.

"It would be chaotic. The manager would have no way to communicate. The pitcher would be doing anything he wanted. There would be no coordination, no battery as we know it."

That's not to say that signs are always conveyed smoothly. Mariners announcer Ron Fairly recalls one Dodgers teammate who, upon being flashed the squeeze-bunt sign while batting with a runner on third, gave third base coach Preston Gomez a puzzled look and called out, "This pitch?" Suffice it to say, the squeeze was hastily taken off.

Former first baseman Dick Stuart was so inept at picking up signs that Gomez once got his attention, moved his arms in a running motion, and pointed to second. "That was his steal sign," Fairly said.

The Dodgers once had a squeeze call that required the third base coach, Leo Durocher, calling the base runner by his last name. One day, Frank Howard reached third, and the play was on. Durocher edged over and said:

"OK, stay awake, Howard."

Howard looked at him quizzically and said, "Aw, Leo, you know you can call me Frank."

Nor does it mean signs are always happily received, or conveyed. Rangers designated hitter Cliff Johnson once got a take sign on 3-0 and was so peeved he shot the middle finger at third base coach Art Howe.

Mariners manager Jim Lefebvre felt compelled to replace third base coach Bob Didier in 1990, reportedly because Didier would sometimes ignore Lefebvre's signs and put down his own. Such subversion is anathema to the team unity fostered by signals, the importance of which can be measured by the lengths managers have gone to get their message across.

Billy Martin once called plays by phone, from his hospital bed, while convalescing from a punctured lung. Jack McKeon, ejected from a minor league game, returned in a mascot's uniform to relay signs to his team. (At least, that's the oft-told legend. McKeon denied the story, attributing it instead to another longtime baseball man, Steve Boros.)

Upon being ejected from a minor league game while managing Key West in the Florida State League, Don Zimmer climbed a light pole and flashed his signs from there. Giants manager Roger Craig recalled peeking out through a hole behind the dugout after an ejection, and noticing a tipoff by the opposing base runner that he was going to steal. Craig got the attention of the acting manager, told him to call a pitchout, and they nailed the runner.

Dickson estimates that more than 1,000 silent instructions are given during the course of a nine-inning game.

Those can range from the most rudimentary of signs between catcher and pitcher—one finger for a fastball, two for a curve, three for a changeup, a system unchanged since Little League—to a series of complicated motions from the third base coach that can be more difficult to decipher than spy code.

Some coaches, such as Gomez, had different signs for every player on the team. Gene Mauch was notorious for his complicated signs. Some teams change the signs every series, or even use a different set every three innings. And some employ arcane systems that befuddle their own team as much as the opponents.

The Red Sox in the 1970s had a system based on numerical values, requiring players to add and subtract the number of touches by a coach to determine the play. After outfielder Bernie Carbo was caught stealing one night, manager Darrell Johnson angrily confronted him, asking Carbo what he had seen to make him run.

"Two plus two," Carbo replied. "That's four—the take sign," said Johnson. "The steal is five."

"Damn!" said Carbo. "I added wrong."

Yankees bench coach Zimmer, considered one of the greatest third base coaches ever, said his goal was to keep his signs as simple as possible.

"I don't care what the manager gave to me," he said. "They could be tough. My objective was to give them to the players with the easiest set of signs I could have. It's hard enough to hit off a 95 mph fastball without having to think, 'What was that?'"

Mariners second baseman Bret Boone admits, however, that no matter how attentive you are at the plate, "Everyone misses them now and then. You get caught up in the game, and sometimes you're vegging out and you don't get them."

Bobby Murcer, former All-Star outfielder, played for the Giants in 1975 under manager Wes Westrum, who was renowned for stealing signs. At the end of spring training, Westrum's third base coach, Joey Amalfitano, gathered the team to unveil their signs for the season.

"He says, 'We're doing this, doing that, adding this, subtracting that, multiplying these two,'" Murcer recalled. "I said, 'Wait a minute, we're not going to be able to get those signs. They're way too complicated.'

"It was typical of Wes. He was so paranoid everyone was stealing his signs, because he could always steal everyone else's."

Mere moments after the first sign was relayed (most likely in the 1800s), rest assured that a new pastime cropped up—the obsessive efforts of the opposing team to steal those signs.

Those efforts, in turn, have spurred great moral debates, innumerable brush-back pitches, frequent accusations of unfair play, and the development of a code of ethics that has stood the test of time.

Most baseball people will tell you that sign stealing accomplished through good old-fashioned observation is perfectly acceptable. Sign stealing that requires the use of blatant espionage and electronic gadgetry (and baseball has a long, sordid history of such attempts) is not.

"Some people think when you steal signs, you're cheating," said Zimmer, who has more than 50 years in professional baseball. "If I'm on second base, and the other team is dumb enough to let me steal the signs and I relay that to the hitter, that's just baseball.

"Now, if you're doing something illegal—someone sitting in the stands with binoculars or something—to me, that's not right."

And a corollary to the ethical code: Even the acceptable mode of sign stealing must be pursued with extreme caution by the practitioner.

"It's like swimming in the water hole down by the creek," former Mariners pitcher Norm Charlton said. "There's a sign that says 'Swim at your own risk.' It would be dangerous to stick up a sign out there on the pitcher's mound that says 'Steal signs at your own risk,' but that's pretty much the way it is."

Just ask Mike Scioscia. In 1991, while with Cincinnati, Charlton suspected the Dodgers' Scioscia was stealing the signs of the Reds' catcher while baserunning at second base, then relaying them to Dodgers hitters. Charlton hit Scioscia on the arm with a pitch and was suspended for a week and fined heavily when he unabashedly told reporters why he had plunked Scioscia—and that he might do it again.

Twelve years later, Charlton's only regret is his public honesty that led to the suspension, not his actions.

"There's all kinds of elaborate things you can do to conceal your signs," he said. "[Jamie] Moyer's great at it. He's got first sign, second sign, third sign, a sign on odd days, even months, odd years, when it rains outside, when he drove his truck to the park. You're basically not going to steal his signs.

"I'm pretty much completely opposite. I'd rather my infielders know them. If the runner on second base knows them, that's fine. If he wants to relay them to the guy hitting, there was an easy way to take care of that. One conversation with the catcher: You call for a slider away, I'll throw a fastball up and in. That pretty much cures the sign stealing."

The practice of "peeking" by a hitter—glancing back while at the plate to look at a catcher's signs or location—is regarded as an even stronger breach of etiquette, almost certain to be remedied by the pitcher, if caught.

"First of all, there's no one that can tell me I can't look back," Zimmer said. "But then that pitcher has the right to throw at me, if he wants."

Some hitters use wraparound sunglasses to hide their "peeking." Others are so subtle as to look not at the sign but at the catcher's shadow for an indication if he's setting up inside or outside.

"If you look at Ken Griffey Jr., every time he calls time after the pitcher comes set, it's one of two things," a major league coach said. "He either didn't get the sign from the guy on second correctly, or when he steps out he looks back to see where the catcher was set up on that pitch."

It can be a costly endeavor. The late Al Cowens had his jaw shattered by White Sox pitcher Ed Farmer in 1980 after peeking back at the catcher. Cowens was looking for a breaking ball away, and got a fastball up and in.

"Peeking is just too blatant," said Dave Valle, a Mariners broadcaster and former catcher. "That's when you want to tell a guy, 'Hey, you're doing something that could be dangerous to your own health.'"

Said Charlton, "If I think they're stealing signs, and we go slider away, and throw a fastball in, and the guy gets hit in the wrist—of course, I'd never hit anyone on purpose—but if he has a broken wrist and misses three months, that could cost you several million dollars. It's a team game, but you're paid on individual stats. The question is: Is it worth it?"

Sign stealing, however, has proven to be a universal yearning, without regard to age, culture, or potential consequences. Former major leaguer Jeff Burroughs stole signs in the championship game of the 1993 Little League World Series, helping his son's Long Beach team to victory (the son, Sean, is now the San Diego Padres' third baseman).

The Cuban team was suspected of stealing signs from Team USA in the gold medal game at the 2000 Olympics. Japanese great Sadaharu Oh was accused (and exonerated) of a sign-stealing scandal while managing the

Daiei Hawks in 1998 that allegedly involved a television camera, a walkie-talkie and a megaphone.

Among those accused of stealing or relaying signs have been Bernie Brewer, the Milwaukee mascot who would slide into a giant beer stein after home runs at old County Stadium, and the guy who maintained the fountains at Kansas City's Kauffman Stadium.

Sign stealing can involve incredible minutiae. In his book *Oh, Baby, I Love It!* Tim McCarver insists that Gene Mauch, his 1972 Montreal manager, could tell who was covering second base on steal attempts by watching the interaction of the shortstop and second baseman, who communicated behind the shield of their gloves.

"Mauch couldn't actually see the open or closed mouth—he'd watch the vein in the infielder's neck," McCarver wrote. "If the vein contracted, his mouth was open, and that meant he was saying, 'You!' So Mauch knew the other guy would cover. He was never wrong."

McCarver figures he got a half-dozen extra hits that year by guiding the ball to the area vacated by the covering fielder.

Sometimes the scope and magnitude of sign stealing is vast. In a 2001 *Wall Street Journal* article that electrified the baseball world, it was revealed that the 1951 New York Giants, who overcame a 13½ game deficit to win the National League pennant, were aided by a telescope in their center field clubhouse that picked up signs, which were then signaled by buzzer to the bullpen and relayed to the batter.

(Dickson, who did exhaustive research on the '51 Giants for his book, concludes that while the sign stealing was absolutely real, Bobby Thomson was not given the sign that resulted in his legendary "Shot Heard 'Round The World," a pennant-winning homer off Brooklyn Dodgers pitcher Ralph Branca.)

The era from 1940 through the 1960s was filled with such spy-novel espionage. In 1948, Cleveland Indians rookie Al Rosen, just called up from the minors, was pulled aside by one of the team's veterans before one of his first big league at-bats at old Cleveland Stadium.

Rosen was advised to check the center field scoreboard while at the plate—specifically, where the innings were listed. If he saw an arm hanging out of one of the vacant slots it meant a curveball was coming.

"Bob Porterfield's pitching for the Yankees," recalled Rosen, now 79 and semi-retired in Palm Springs, California. "I look up and see an arm hanging out of the scoreboard. Sure enough, he threw a curve, and I got a base hit.

"I thought, 'No wonder they're so good here in the big leagues.'"

What Rosen later learned—to his moral distress—was that the Indians had devised an elaborate sign-stealing scheme that year, masterminded by their star pitcher, Bob Feller.

Feller later admitted the Indians used the telescopic sight he had employed in World War II as a gunnery mate on the *USS Alabama*. Feller kept the device when he was discharged, and the Indians put it to use in their scoreboard, trained on the opposing catcher.

"I didn't like it at all," Rosen said. "I realized it was just the wrong thing. It's one thing if base runners pick up the sign, or if you steal them from the bench. But when you started doing all the other stuff, that's out-and-out cheating, I don't like that. None of my clubs [he later became general manager of the Yankees, Astros and Giants] would ever do anything like that."

Rosen gritted his teeth and went along with it. But in 1960 a Chicago White Sox pitcher named Al Worthington took a moral stand that nearly cost him his career.

That year the White Sox devised a sign-stealing system that involved hiding an employee in the Comiskey Park scoreboard, outfitted with a pair of binoculars.

He used the binoculars to pick up the signs from the opposing catcher, then relayed them to the White Sox hitters by virtue of various lights rigged into the scoreboard, each one indicating a certain pitch.

Worthington—a devout Christian who had pitched for seven years for the Giants and Red Sox before joining the White Sox—was so offended that he actually quit baseball after the season and went home to college, missing the next two years. He resumed his major league career in 1963 with the Reds.

"It was the right thing for me to do," said Worthington, now 73 and retired near Birmingham, Alabama. "We had a man hidden in the scoreboard. There were hundreds of lights in there. When a certain light came in, that meant one pitch. If it wasn't cheating, then it would be out in front."

Worthington said he expressed his disapproval to Sox manager Al Lopez but was told that he was expected to abide by the sign-stealing system—"and I wouldn't." Club Owner Bill Veeck told him he should listen to the manager.

"At the end of the season, I left his office, went to the airport, and I already knew what I had to do," said Worthington. "January came, and I had to make a decision: Go to college, or go back [to the White Sox]. I chose to go to college."

In detailing the incident in his classic autobiography *Veeck as in Wreck*, Veeck defends his team's scoreboard manipulation as common practice.

"I doubt if there is one club that hasn't tried it at one time or another in recent years," he wrote. "There is absolutely nothing in the rules against it."

That latter statement is still true, according to Ralph Nelson, the major leagues' vice president of umpiring. The only official sanction he knows is a league-wide bulletin filed in the late 1980s that prohibits of the use of walkie-talkies and other electronic devices in the dugouts.

"There's some unwritten rules about it, a little code of honor," Nelson said. "In the past, there have been complaints, and the league presidents used to investigate that stuff. Everyone understands it's illegal, but there's nothing I've seen written."

By all accounts, the blatant spying from scoreboards and stands isn't done much anymore, though the sophistication of video and television equipment has opened a potent new avenue for stealing signs.

"With the technology of the centerfield camera, zoomed in all the time on the catcher, you can steal those signs like nothing," Mariners coach Rene Lachemann said. "But the thing is, I've had players who didn't even want to know what was coming, unless they were 100 percent sure. And even then, there were guys who still didn't want any part of it."

Clearly, the efforts of teams to gain an edge by stealing opponents' signs will never cease. Even Worthington has no problems with that, if it's done in an open and clean manner—honor among thieves, in other words.

"If the coach can pick it up," he said, "it's part of the game."

[2003]

Secret to My Perfect Game
Was Good Control

BY DON LARSEN AS TOLD TO AL DOYLE

I didn't know I was going to pitch that game [Game 5 of the 1956 World Series] until I came to the park.

In those days I started and relieved. I had 20 starts and 18 relief appearances in '56. We were always available, even when we were starting. Casey [Stengel] would use you for an out or two sometimes if you were a starter. We all did what Casey wanted us to do.

I started Game 2 against the Dodgers, and I was wild. I gave up four runs in one and two-thirds innings, and Casey didn't like that. We lost 13-8 to the Dodgers in that game.

Everyone asks how I felt before the perfect game. You never feel bad when you're in the World Series. You've got all winter to rest.

Many times Casey and pitching coach Jim Turner announced the starting pitcher for the next day's game the day or night before. If the starter

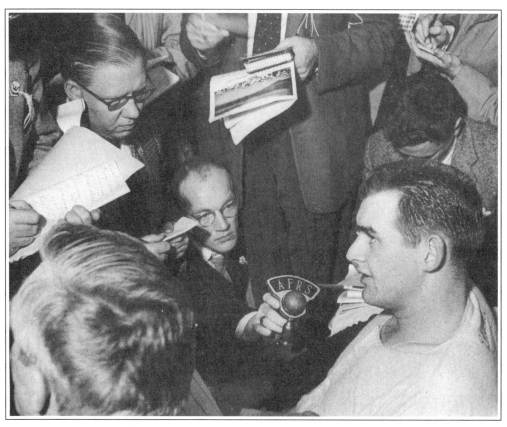

Don Larsen being interviewed in 1956 after pitching the first perfect no-hitter in World Series history. He threw only 97 pitches in stifling the Brooklyn Dodgers, 2-0.

was undetermined, then Frank Crosetti, our third base coach, performed a Yankee ritual of placing the warm-up ball for that day's game in the starting pitcher's spikes prior to game time.

When I came to the ballpark for Game 5, I entered the clubhouse to find the ball and learn I was to be the starting pitcher.

I felt confident as I prepared to face the Dodgers because we were in Yankee Stadium and had won eight of our last nine games there.

I threw mostly fastballs, with some sliders and a few curves. I never had such good control in all my life as I had in that game. That was the secret to my success. A walk is the worst thing in the world for a pitcher. I'd almost rather give up a home run than a walk. Five of my seven strikeouts were called third strikes. I was throwing the ball right on the black of the plate.

I opened the game by striking out the first two batters—Junior Gilliam and Pee Wee Reese—on called third strikes. Then Duke Snider hit a soft fly to right fielder Hank Bauer.

Retiring the Dodgers in order helped build my confidence, and I was more relaxed on the mound.

The Dodgers had a tough lineup from top to bottom. After Gilliam, Reese and Snider, they had solid hitters in Jackie Robinson, Gil Hodges, Sandy Amoros, Carl Furillo, Roy Campanella and the pitcher. Campanella was batting eighth in the Dodgers lineup, so that gives you an indication of the quality hitters they had.

I retired the first 11 batters before Snider came up for his second at-bat and hit a ball deep to right field that would have been a home run, but it went foul. I then caught him looking at a slider for my fifth strikeout.

Mickey Mantle saved the no-hitter when he made a great catch on a ball Hodges hit to the deepest part of left-center field in the fifth inning. Mickey also got our first hit—a homer off Sal Maglie in the bottom of the fourth inning. Mick's homer proved to be all the Yankees would need, but at the time it gave us a one-run lead in a tight pitching duel.

People forget that Maglie pitched a hell of a ballgame that day, giving up only five hits and two runs, but it was enough for us to win the game.

I knew I was pitching a no-hitter, since every pitcher knows when he's throwing one. I tried to engage in conversation with some of our players on the bench during the game, but they all avoided me like the plague. That doesn't happen only in the World Series; it's a baseball superstition for players to talk to a pitcher working on a no-hitter.

Going into the bottom of the ninth, I was three outs from a perfect game and, more important, giving the Yankees a three-games-to-two lead in the World Series.

Furillo led off the inning with a fly ball to Bauer in right. One out. Campanella followed with a ground ball to second baseman Billy Martin. Two outs. Then Dale Mitchell entered the game to pinch-hit for Maglie, and on a 1-2 count I struck out Mitchell for the final out.

Yogi Berra jumped into my arms after the last out, and he gave me the ball. I had my hat, glove and ball from that game silvered. They were sold in an auction a few years ago, and the money went towards my grandson's college fund.

I didn't know it was a perfect game until someone told me in the clubhouse. The Yankees never gave me a penny for that game.

I got a few endorsements that winter, but nothing like what would have happened today. Just one of the endorsements was in New York. I went on *The Bob Hope Show,* but I never appeared on *The Ed Sullivan Show.*

The biggest surprise came when I got my contract for 1957. Even though I was 11-5 and threw the perfect game, George Weiss [then the Yankees general manager] offered only $13,000, which wasn't much of a raise from $12,000.

Arthur Richman [then a New York baseball writer and now a Yankees senior adviser] has been a good friend for a long time, and he wrote a letter on my behalf to Weiss. Weiss replied with a letter that read, "If you forget you wrote this letter, I'll forget I received it." Weiss could be a cold person.

The game has changed a lot since those days. There were only eight clubs in each league, and the winner's share was only $8,700 for the '56 World Series.

The people in New York were sort of spoiled. They had three teams, and the World Series was played there almost every year.

But Game 5 of the 1956 Series is the one I'll never forget.

[2003]

In '52, Virgil Trucks Won Only Five Games, But Two Were No-Hitters

BY BILL DOW

He's one of four pitchers to throw two no-hitters in a single season, and at age 86, Virgil Trucks still receives stacks of fan mail requesting autographed photos and baseballs.

The letters often evoke bittersweet memories of a strange season more than 50 years ago, when Trucks accomplished a rare feat in one of the Tigers' worst seasons ever.

"I don't charge for my autograph," Trucks said, "and I answer every request I receive."

And if folks ask him about the no-hitters, he will modestly oblige and tell them what he remembers, and what he would like to forget.

"When I was called up to the Tigers at the end of the 1941 season, it was the first time I had crossed the Mason-Dixon line or even seen a major league game," said Trucks, a native Alabaman who now lives in Pelham, Alabama. "Just to walk into the locker room and see players like Hank Greenberg, Charlie Gehringer and Rudy York was quite a thrill."

Virgil Oliver "Fire" Trucks might have been starstruck, but the stocky right-hander knew how to throw heat and already had thrown four no-hitters in the minors.

Although his major league no-hitters didn't come for another 11 years, Trucks rapidly became one of the league's premier pitchers. He went 14-8 in 1942 and 16-10 in '43, then served two years in the navy. Remarkably, within a week of being discharged he won Game 2 of the 1945 World Series against the Chicago Cubs, pitching all nine innings in a 4-1 victory in Detroit.

"My no-hitters were special, but without question that was my greatest baseball thrill ever," Trucks said.

Sportswriters quickly dubbed the powerful pitching staff of Dizzy Trout, Hal Newhouser and Trucks as "TNT."

In 1949, Trucks led the American League in strikeouts with 153 and in shutouts with six, and he finished with a 19-11 record. He also was selected to the All-Star Game.

But by 1952 the Tigers had taken a mighty fall. On May 15 the team was mired in the basement when a crowd of only 2,215 showed up at Briggs Stadium to see 35-year-old Trucks face the Washington Senators.

"It seems like hundreds of people have told me they were there, but I know better because the park was nearly empty," Trucks said. "We were playing so badly that nobody wanted to see us play."

When Virgil Trucks pitched his two no-hitters in 1952, the Tigers were a woeful, last-place team, finishing with 104 losses, 45 games behind the pennant-winning Yankees. After he was traded at the end of the season, Trucks became a 20-game winner in 1953, pitching for the Browns and White Sox.

That day, though, fans were treated to one of the most dramatic no-hit games in history. Trucks was locked in a pitcher's duel with right-hander Bob Porterfield.

"Virgil was throwing absolute bullets," recalled George Kell, the Tigers' Hall of Fame third baseman. "But as a fielder, protecting a no-hitter was absolutely nerve-racking. You make up your mind that you're going to get a glove on any ball if you can. And of course, it's an unspoken word that you never talk about it."

With two outs in the bottom of the ninth, and no score, Tigers slugger Vic Wertz stepped up to the plate. On the first pitch, Wertz belted the ball into the far reaches of Briggs Stadium's right field upper deck to win the game.

"I immediately jumped up in that small dugout and bumped my head on the ceiling," Trucks said. "I didn't draw blood, but I sure saw some stars."

The dazed pitcher ran onto the field and was the first to greet Wertz at home plate.

"Believe me, it was a great relief to see Victor hit that one out," Kell said. "After the way Virgil pitched, you just wanted to get it over with."

Besides Wertz, Trucks was especially grateful to another teammate.

Before the game, Trucks noticed that his spikes had shrunk and were pinching his feet. Pitcher Art Houtteman told Trucks he could borrow a pair of his spikes, the same ones Houtteman wore earlier that year when he lost a no-hit bid with two out in the ninth.

"They fit perfectly for me the rest of the year," Trucks said. "Art kept trying to get 'em back, but I wouldn't do it."

Two months later, Trucks threw another magnificent game against the Senators. After yielding a single to the first batter, Eddie Yost, Trucks retired 27 in a row for another 1-0 victory.

Then came August 25 at Yankee Stadium, where Trucks once again threw a no-hitter. But unlike the dramatic game in May, this one would be controversial.

In the third inning on a bang-bang play, Phil Rizzuto was ruled safe at first after hitting a one-hopper to Tigers shortstop Johnny Pesky, who had trouble getting the ball out of his glove. Official scorer John Drebinger of the *New York Times* immediately ruled it an error, then changed his mind and called it a hit.

Other writers in the press box pestered Drebinger and told him it should have remained an error. Drebinger finally called Pesky in the dugout, and Pesky told him he had juggled the ball and should have made the play.

For the second time, Drebinger changed his mind, and when it was announced to the crowd in the seventh inning that the play was ruled an error, fans roared their approval.

"The thing that really bothered me about that play is that Rizzuto was really out at first," Trucks said. "We were all arguing with the first-base umpire, and I nearly got tossed from the game."

In the bottom of the ninth, after Mickey Mantle struck out and Johnny Groth made an outstanding catch in center, Trucks secured his second no-hitter when Hank Bauer hit a one-hop bullet to second baseman Al Federoff, who easily threw him out.

The New York fans gave Trucks a standing ovation as he was mobbed by his teammates.

"I still think a lot of those New York fans were die-hard Giant and Dodger supporters who loved to root against the Yankees," Trucks said.

Though he always will be remembered for the no-hitters, Trucks said he probably pitched better games in his career.

"I pitched the same way every game, with mostly a 95- to 100-mile-per-hour fastball," he said. "With the same motion I also threw an 85-mile-per-hour slider and a 75-mile-per-hour changeup. That really threw the hitters off."

But even in the year of the no-hitters, Trucks finished with a 5-19 record, due in large part to the team's anemic hitting. In his five victories, Trucks yielded only nine hits.

The Tigers finished in last place for the first time, with a 50-104 record. Their winning percentage of .325 was the lowest team record for futility until the 2003 Tigers finished with a .265 mark (43-119).

"The '52 season was bittersweet for me," Trucks said. "The sweet part was the no-hitters, but the rest of the season left a very bitter taste. We just went out there and tried to win, but we just didn't jell. If it had been a better season, we would have celebrated the no-hitters much more."

That December, while he recovered from gallbladder surgery at Henry Ford Hospital, his wife dropped a newspaper on his lap with headlines that declared he had been traded to the St. Louis Browns.

"I was very unhappy about that and the way I found out," Trucks said.

But he won 20 games in 1953 while pitching for the Browns and Chicago White Sox, and he won 19 the next season at Chicago. Before ending his 17-year career with the Yankees in 1958, Trucks also pitched for the Athletics and, in 1956, the Tigers again. He later barnstormed one year out West with Satchel Paige and a team of Cuban ballplayers, coached in the early 1960s with the Pirates and worked as a scout for the Tigers until 1990.

[2004]

Fielders List Most Difficult Defensive Plays by Position

BY JACK ETKIN

During the baseball season, defensive highlights are a nightly television staple, a handful of plays that range from the extremely athletic on up to just jaw-dropping amazing.

An outfielder will leap against a wall to catch a ball headed for the seats or make an all-out dive, catching a ball headed toward a gap. An infielder will charge a slowly hit ball and make a strong, accurate throw off balance. Players will spear hard grounders with backhanded finesse, make over-the-shoulder catches or turn double plays by leaping over oncoming base runners.

When asked about the toughest play for him to make, Greg Maddux said, "The slow roller down the third base line." An agile fielder, Maddux won 14 Gold Gloves for defensive excellence through 2004.

Pitchers and catchers will pounce on bunts, spin and throw and just barely get fast runners.

Defense makes for wonderful theater. It also contributes mightily to winning baseball and in ways that have more to do with consistency and steadiness than acrobatics.

In a game replete with statistics, defense is difficult to measure. Errors are the most obvious indicator but hardly telling, because a good defender will make more errors simply by virtue of having superior range. Fielding percentage, putouts, assists and the more arcane gauges such as range factor are obscure, if not altogether out of sight.

Mention .406 and Ted Williams' batting average in 1941 comes to mind. None of baseball's magical numbers deals with defense. For example, does .996 conjure the fielding percentage in the 2000 season for Andruw Jones, the superb center fielder of the Atlanta Braves, who made two errors that year and has won six consecutive National League Gold Glove awards?

A Gold Glove is the highest defensive honor. It is voted on by managers and coaches—one player at each position in each league—and also is highly subjective. And because there's no mandate that the Gold Glove team include a left fielder, center fielder and right fielder, the outfields are skewed toward center fielders.

For example, in 2000, the N.L. Gold Glove outfield included three center fielders—Jones, Jim Edmonds of St. Louis and Steve Finley of Arizona. The same situation occurred in the American League in 1997 and 1998 when center fielders Edmonds, then playing with Anaheim, Seattle's Ken Griffey Jr. and Bernie Williams of the New York Yankees comprised the A.L. Gold Glove outfield. It also happened in the A.L. in 1992 (Devon White, Griffey and Kirby Puckett) and 1993 (Griffey, White and Kenny Lofton).

That's not surprising, given the baseball adage about the need for strong defense up the middle. The New York Mets attempted to remedy their defense up the middle by acquiring for the 2004 season shortstop Kaz Matsui and center fielder Mike Cameron. Those moves came after the

Mets finished tied for 14th in the league in fielding percentage last year and committed 118 errors, a figure exceeded by three N.L. teams.

Not that anyone needed to look at numbers to know the Mets' defense was horrid in 2003. It still was not good in 2004 when the Mets made 116 errors through games of August 29, more than any other N.L. club. Errors are the flip side of the nightly highlights reel, just as obvious as the great plays but completely uninspiring.

Outstanding defense is not just a matter of doing something stunning, although that's certainly part of it. There are subtleties involved, particularly on plays that occur almost routinely but bring inherent difficulties.

A host of players who have won Gold Gloves were asked to cite the hardest plays they have to make at their positions. The question was simple: What's the toughest play you have to make? As the following answers—in the players' words—show, very good defenders know the demands of their position involve nuances to make challenging plays that come with the territory but don't necessarily make the nightly highlights package.

First Base—Todd Helton (Colorado Rockies—Two Gold Gloves)
"For me, there's a couple plays that I'd say are tough. On a bunt play running in—toward the ball—and you're going to throw it to second and try to get the lead runner. It's not that the throw is that hard. The tough part is knowing whether you should go to second or not, because you can't even see the runner. Sometimes you have to rely on the second baseman and the shortstop yelling at you—telling you whether to try for a force play at second.

"That's a tough play, the other one is when you're holding a runner and coming off the bag and a guy hits it back toward the line and you're going to your right. You have to have it timed right so your feet are on the ground when the pitch is going across the plate, if you're going to have any shot at catching it."

Second Base—Roberto Alomar (Chicago White Sox—10 Gold Gloves)
"Turning the double play. I don't worry that much about the throw from the shortstop. I worry more about the runner. You know your partner, and you tell him where to throw the ball and things like that. I think the key at second base is to know who's running toward you. It's always in your mind that the guy's going to slide hard.

"If the guy throws the ball right toward the runner, then you've got to catch it and throw it. If you throw the ball right to my chest, I can do whatever I want around the bag with my feet. I can trick him with my feet. He doesn't know if I'm going to go to the front or the back of the bag or the side.

"If the throw is toward the runner, I have to go to where the ball is. If you really have to reach, he's going to slide right on top of you."

Shortstop—Barry Larkin (Cincinnati Reds—Three Gold Gloves)
"The toughest play is the slow backhand between short and third with a fast runner. Tony Womack slapping a slow ball between short and third base, and you go over, don't have time to get in front of it and you got to catch it on the run and make the play.

"Your momentum's taking you to the right, toward third base, so your throw's obviously going to sail to the right, up the first base line toward the runner. So I try to throw it past the first baseman and kind of fade it to him. With your momentum the ball's going to sail a little bit to the right, so you throw it a bit to the left. For me, that's the toughest play to make, hands down."

Third Base—Scott Rolen (St. Louis Cardinals—Five Gold Gloves)
"The toughest play for me is the ball hit right at you. You have no depth perception on the ball hit right at you. You can't tell how hard the ball's hit sometimes. You get a big right-handed hitter up there, a pull hitter, big swing—you can't always tell how hard that ball's hit when it comes right at you. By the time you figure it out, it's that in-between hop that you either come back on or go forward on. You're either aggressive or passive-aggressive, whichever way you want to look at it.

"It's kind of the changeup off the bat; you're not sure how hard it's hit. Then it's right at you, and you have no depth perception. You don't know how close it is to tell you where that hop's going to be. When you come in and barehand balls or have to dive toward the line, you see the ball right there. On this play, you don't. When you barehand a ball, if the ball doesn't go in your hand just right, the guy's safe. It's a do-or-die play, so it's hard to say that's a tough play. If the slow roller you pick up bare-handed is hit hard enough, it's an easy play. If it's not hit hard enough, you just pick it up and throw it. There's a knack to doing it, but you don't really go out and work on it. You either make that play or you don't."

Center Field—Mike Cameron (New York Mets—Two Gold Gloves)
"The ball hit straight over my head. There's no angles. You can't tell depth or the speed of the ball or anything. What I try to do is kind of freeze a little bit and stay low, to have a better opportunity of reading it.

"I'll just kind of take like a small drop step back—kind of like a stutter, starter step, or something like that—so I can at least kind of gauge and see what I can do if I need to go in, go back or whatever.

"But it's tough. Why it's tough is because it freezes you, period. But if you go in, you're done.

"If I stay low in an athletic position, and I'm in a momentary freeze, if I have to jump I can do that, or if I have to go sideways I can do that. But if I'm standing up, I have to go down first. If I have to go in, I first have to go down."

Center Field—Ken Griffey Jr. (Cincinnati Reds—10 Gold Gloves)
"The toughest play is going to the wall. You have two objects that are moving, and one that isn't. And the one that isn't is harder than the two that are. You're just trying to find out where you are on the field as you approach the wall. Usually the wall is high enough that you can see it with your peripheral vision. Other than that, you just try to time your jump, if you have to jump.

"The main thing is getting to the wall. If you can get to the wall, you have a chance to catch it. You don't think about crashing into the wall. You can get hurt, but that's just part of being an outfielder—the fact that at all costs, you want to catch the ball. And that's what separates good outfielders from bad outfielders. The good outfielders try to make that play for you.

"If I've got to go against the wall, I'm going to go. I don't have a problem with it. I can't think about if I'm going to get hurt or not, because then you're not going to give 100 percent."

Right Field—Larry Walker (St. Louis Cardinals—Seven Gold Gloves)
"Now, at my age [37], probably the toughest play I have to make is running laterally, either to my left or my right to the gap or the corner to cut off a ball. That's the toughest thing I have to do right now, because it requires me to have a quick jump at a backward angle, then be able to bend down and get the ball. And if I do go down [on the ground], to get back up.

"There's a lot of things right there that really affect me. I used to be able to do that play, grab that ball, pounce on my feet and throw a strike to second.

"Now, every motion is more pronounced, where everything used to flow altogether—the lateral movement, trying to catch a ball on the ground, reaching down to get it, bending over. On that play a lot of times, you see an outfielder—the ball's three feet away from them and they let it go.

"A lot of people say, 'Why didn't he just reach down and pick it up?' Well, the smart thing to do is let it go hit the wall, pick it up, keep the guy at second. You reach down and pick it up, make one mistake and the ball's there and you're going that way hard. By the time you stop or fall down and get back up and get the ball, now it's a triple. That's why so often that ball close to an outfielder, they let go."

Catcher—Brad Ausmus (Houston Astros—Two Gold Gloves)
"The toughest play is a bunt down the third base line with a fast runner, because the way people are taught to field the ball, you have your back to the first baseman and you kind of come up with the ball, pick up first base and throw all in one motion. And it's very easy to get your sights out of whack, not to mention the ball could easily sail on you because of the way you're spinning as you're throwing. You don't have sight of your target when you come up to make a throw. With a fast runner, you have to do this quickly. If you overthrow, there's a chance of him being on third."

Pitcher—Greg Maddux (Chicago Cubs—13 Gold Gloves)
"The slow roller down the third base line. It's your longest throw. You have the least amount of time. And you have to do it off balance. If someone very fast like Tom Goodwin hits it, you've got to get on it earlier to throw it. But if a slow guy hits it, you might get there later. You might be able to cover more of the third base line off a slow guy. But you have to make the play the same way.

"It's all footwork. You've got to make sure you get your feet under you when you throw, or you can launch it down the right field line somewhere. You stay under control, and you either beat it or you don't. If you want to try to make the play while sprawled, you run the risk of having the guy on second or third.

"They don't hit you too many balls like this in PFP [pitchers' fielding practice]. You throw balls against a wall to practice this play. I've always practiced it."

[2004]

Ichiro Suzuki: Hitting Sensation

BY DAVE van DYCK

For those who remember Ozzie Guillen as a White Sox player, they know he never saw a pitch he wouldn't swing at, from eyelashes to shoelaces, from outer space to his inner reach.

Therefore, Guillen last season should have felt like he was watching an old tape when Seattle's Ichiro Suzuki stepped into the batter's box.

"Hah," Guillen said. "Ichiro has a better swing than me and he's fast.

"He gets 200-some hits every year, I got 200 every three years."

Guillen may exaggerate, but he is right, of course. The comparison between the two definitely ends at style.

As for substance, the most hits Guillen ever had in a season were 156, the highest average .288. Suzuki hit .350 as a rookie and this year broke the all-time hits record for a season, which the St. Louis Browns' George Sisler set in 1920 with 257.

But what kept Guillen in the big leagues for 15 seasons is the same thing that makes Suzuki so good—they will nibble at any bait a pitcher casts; heck, they'll bite on a bare hook if they think it will get them on base.

"It's a joke," Oakland's Mark Mulder said. "I've thrown some great pitches on him and he still gets hits.

"When I throw a sinker in to any other lefty, they pull it foul or hit it off their foot. When I throw it to him, he hits a line drive down the third base line. You just go, 'What is that? How did he do that?'

"I throw the guy well and he probably has six or seven infield hits. It's just that he gets hits in so many ways others don't. He gets more hits of a different variety than anybody else."

Actually, he just gets more hits, period, than anybody else.

He ended August 2004 with three hits, which meant he needed only 46 in September and the final three games of the season in October to pass Sisler.

He went into the month of September with 212 hits after collecting 56 safeties and batting .463 in August to become the first player with back-to-back 50-hit months since Joe Medwick of the Cardinals accomplished the feat in 1936.

"Ichi gets three hits," teammate Bret Boone says, "like the rest of us get one."

Suzuki, who came to the United States after winning seven consecutive batting titles in Japan, was on the verge in the closing weeks of the '04 campaign of breaking one of baseball's longest-held and least-known records, one that was overlooked in these days of the Big Boom. Singles just aren't sexy anymore.

But make no mistake, Sisler's mark was overlooked only because it has been covered by dust for so long.

The top ten, all-time hit producers for one season have been joined by only one batter since 1930.

And that one is Ichiro Suzuki in 2001 and this year. Not Pete Rose or George Brett, not Barry Bonds or Ted Williams, not Wade Boggs or Tony Gwynn.

In fact, in 2004, Suzuki joined Sisler, Rogers Hornsby and Fred Lindstrom as the only players to have two 230-hit seasons during their careers.

How good a season did Suzuki have in 2004?

In 161 games played, he batted .336 at home and .405 on the road; .401 against left-handed pitching and .359 versus right-handed throwers; .382

Ichiro Suzuki of the Mariners established a new one-season major league record in 2004, collecting 262 hits over 161 games. He broke the former record of 257 hits set by George Sisler of the St. Louis Browns in 154 games in 1920.

in day games and .370 under the lights; .321 before the All-Star break and .429 since the mid-summer classic; .385 when leading off an inning, .376 with runners in scoring position, .481 with runners in scoring position and two outs, .375 with the bases empty, .372 with runners on base and .583 with the bases loaded.

He also led the majors during the season with 262 hits and a .373 batting average while ranking second in the A.L. with 36 steals. The left-handed batter had 80 multi-hit games, became the first player to have three 50-hit months in one season and reached 200 hits in each of his first four years in the majors.

Missing only one game in the 2004 campaign, he averaged 1.6 hits per contest.

It's sort of a ballet with a bat.

"He does things you don't think are possible," says former Seattle teammate Ben Davis, now a catcher with the Chicago White Sox. "He's unbelievable.

"But you watch him take batting practice and he hits balls farther than anybody. I would put my money on him in a home run contest."

"My second year in Japan," White Sox announcer Darrin Jackson says, "he hit 25 home runs and the league leader had only 28. When we were going to the All-Star series in Yokohama, he hit a ball out of the stadium in batting practice."

That's quite an accomplishment for a five-foot, nine-inch, 170-pound hitter who pokes the ball.

"Whoa, whoa, time out," interrupts Mark McLemore, who played with Suzuki in his first three U.S. seasons: "First and foremost, he does not 'poke' the ball. People think he slaps the ball. I challenge anybody to get on the other end of the ball and try to catch it. He drives the ball as hard as anybody.

"You have to use your talent. That's what a home run hitter does. Why mock a guy because he can outrun them? It's not his fault he's the Japanese Jet."

So how do pitchers get Suzuki out? "Soft and away, maybe," a scout said. But wouldn't Suzuki slam that pitch into left field?

"I'm not saying it's going to work," the scout replied. "I'm saying that's where you might pitch him to minimize the damage."

"I just throw it and let him hit it and hope it lands in the right spot," Oakland's Tim Hudson says.

"He's one of those guys," McLemore says, "who not only takes advantage of pitchers' mistakes but hits a good pitch too."

"If you look at his past," White Sox pitcher Shingo Takatsu said through an interpreter, "it's not really surprising."

Takatsu faced Suzuki only once in the majors—Ichiro grounded out—and because they were in separate leagues, rarely faced him in Japan.

Takatsu said the way to pitch to him "depends on the situation," but you can guarantee something soft and away may be the best way to approach him.

As Suzuki neared the record, there was the question of whether he would be pitched around—if that is possible—or walked intentionally. Of course, Suzuki is so fast and such a base-stealing threat, walking him could create the same situation as a double.

"No way you want to walk him," Mulder said. "Maybe, if we were tied for the division lead and there's a runner on third."

Another question raised prior to Suzuki's breaking of Sisler's record was whether Ichiro would be walked or pitched around just to keep a Japanese player from breaking an American record.

That happened in the past when Americans approached Japanese records in Japan.

At the time Jackson didn't think that would happen.

"Heck, I don't think our players even know what the record was and who held it," he said.

Maybe it's because Suzuki plays in relative obscurity in Seattle instead of New York, and in the Pacific Time Zone instead of the Eastern, but as the 2004 regular season came to a close, the news about Ichiro's skill as a hitter had pretty much been absorbed by baseball fans nationwide.

Since 1900, there have only been seven players who have recorded 250 or more hits in a season, and Seattle's Ichiro Suzuki became the first to join this elite group in 74 years. Among these batters, Chuck Klein is the only one not to have two 50-hit months during his season of 250-plus safeties, and Suzuki is the only one to compile 50 or more hits in a month three times. Klein and Al Simmons are the only members to accomplish the feat without leading their league in hitting. In 1925, Simmons collected 253 hits and batted .384 but lost the A.L. batting race to Harry Heilmann who finished with a .393 mark. Klein batted .386 with 250 hits in 1930 for the Phillies, but finished behind Bill Terry of the Giants, who totaled 254 hits and a .401 BA, and Babe Herman (.393) of the Dodgers.

[2004]

The Home Run, Baseball's Glamour Event

BY LARRY STONE

Through the 2004 season, there had been more than 225,000 home runs hit in major league history, starting May 2, 1876, with Ross Barnes of the Chicago White Stockings ("straight down the left field to the carriages, for a clean home run," according to the *Chicago Tribune*) and ending with homers hit on October 3, 2004.

That doesn't count the 766 in the World Series, the 534 in the League Championship Series, the 308 in the Division Series—through 2003—or the 164 in the All-Star Game.

It also doesn't count, of course, all the soaring drives that curved just to the wrong side of the misnamed foul pole (or to the right side, except the umpire didn't see it that way). It doesn't count the ones robbed by leaping, tumbling outfielders, or the ones that died at the warning track, the victims of stiff winds or heavy air or mighty swings that were just a tick off kilter.

Nor does it include the three hit by Michael Jordan in the minor leagues, nor the 868 hit by Sadaharu Oh in Japan, nor the one that 75-year-old Luke Appling hit in an old-timer's game in Washington, D.C., in 1982.

It does, however, include one homer temporarily nullified because of a bat with too much pine tar, and one off a transformer in Detroit. It includes one by a portly left-hander that he may or may not have called (we like to think he did). There was that one that bounced off the head of an outfielder, right over the fence. And one in the gathering twilight of Coogan's Bluff.

Home runs have always been baseball's glamour event, the one that inspires both poets and statisticians. Most ballplayers are loath to admit they swing for the fences, but they're lying if they say they don't savor the moment when it happens.

"I remember Billy Williams hitting a homer one day at Wrigley, and when he got back to the dugout he said, 'I felt that one all the way down to my toes,'" remarked Hall of Famer Ernie Banks. "When you catch it right, it's a perfectly wonderful feeling. It's one you continuously want to have. You practice, you change hats, change stances, get a little more history on the opposing pitcher, all in search of that feeling. It's a feeling that's unbelievable when you hit the ball right and it goes out of the park."

Banks, who hit 512, putting him in the exclusive (but getting less so by the year) 500-homer club, is just getting started.

"When you round the bases, the feeling is still there, the memory of it. When you touch home plate, it's still there. When you get to the dugout, it's still there. It lingers throughout the game, throughout your ride home. I'm telling you, it's amazing."

Mr. Cub would get no argument from another 500 HR–club member, Reggie Jackson, who said famously that hitting a home run was better than sex—prompting Roberto Alomar (not a prolific home run hitter, it should be noted) to say, "I think Reggie is lying."

Mike Cameron, a member of the even rarer four-homer-in-a-game club (just 15 players belong), was also skeptical of Jackson's claim.

"I doubt *that*—but it's a sexy feeling," he said with a laugh. "Reggie's right about that."

Jackson once put the lure of the long ball a slightly different way: "God, do I love to hit that little, round sum-bitch out of the park and make 'em say, 'Wow!'"

They have been hit over the Green Monster, onto Waveland Avenue (and promptly thrown back, if hit by the enemy) and into McCovey Cove.

Home run balls have been fought over in the bleachers (and in court), sold for huge profit and treasured for life in bureau drawers. Announcers have forged careers over clever or bombastic home run calls, and some of the most famous—"It could be, it might be, it is!"—are part of the national lexicon. Others, like "Fly, fly away," are regional catchphrases.

Home runs have saved baseball more than once, and probably will again. After the Black Sox scandal of 1919, it was Babe Ruth. After the new deadball era of the 1960s, it was Hank Aaron and Carlton Fisk. And after the strike of 1994, it was Mark McGwire and Sammy Sosa, in their frantic battle for the season record in 1998.

Oh, there are detractors, people who think homers are sound and fury, signifying nothing.

George Foster, who hit 52 for the Reds back in 1977, when 50 homers really meant something, once said, "I don't know why people like the home run so much. A home run is over as soon as it starts . . . the triple is the most exciting play of the game."

Mark Armour, president of the Northwest chapter of the Society of American Baseball Research, notes that home runs, strikeouts and walks are all on an inexorable rise, a troika of activities that condenses the action to the pitcher, catcher and batter.

"My personal thought is that in comparison to other events in baseball, the home run is the one that involves the least number of people," said Armour. "I think it's somewhat less interesting than things like the double and triple. I realize it's a minority viewpoint, however."

Indeed, the home run has seared itself into the national consciousness, the very phrase becoming a symbol of ultimate achievement. Its name brings to mind the epic journeys of Homer, author of the *Odyssey* and the *Iliad*—and also of Bart Simpson's father, which just goes to show that the homer can appeal to both the literati and the common man.

Mighty Casey struck out, but that Bucky Jacobsen precursor no doubt jacked a few out of the yard, too. Who can forget Roy Hobbs, using a bat cut from a tree split by lightning (Wonderboy) to hit a blast off the stadium lights, starting a fiery storm of sparks? Or mythical Washington Senators manager Robert Shafer, desperate to catch the Yankees, vowing: "I'd sell my soul for one long-ball hitter—hey, where did you come from?"

Richard Ben Cramer, the Pulitzer Prize–winning biographer of Joe DiMaggio, wrote of Americans, "We love power. It's about how we see ourselves. It's how we're good when we're very good—with overwhelming force."

That is why Babe Ruth, emerging from the powerless days of the early 20th century (when the ball wasn't just dead but dirty—so soiled by the end of the game it could scarcely be seen), was such a revelation.

He embodied (or more likely created) the larger-than-life spirit of the Roaring '20s, and when he socked 29 home runs in 1919, aided by the advent of springier baseballs, he was a national sensation. The sport needed it, too, as the magnitude of a crooked World Series began to resonate.

Ruth (who died, appropriately and astonishingly on the same date as his kindred spirit in wretched excess, Elvis Presley—August 16), hit a mind-boggling 54 homers in 1920, 59 in '21, 60 in '27—totals so completely beyond his peers as to be almost unimaginable.

But not for long. Bill James, the noted baseball researcher and author, argues that Ruth's biggest contribution was to change the mind-set of his peers by making the home run, derided by influential pioneers like Ty Cobb and John McGraw, not just fashionable but desirable.

Yale physicist Robert Adair, in his book *The Physics of Baseball,* tried to quantify the lyrical act of hitting a baseball out of the park.

"It's a climactic thing, just from the human side," he said. "There's a drama to it, whether it's 'Casey at the Bat' in the 1890s, to today. Also, tactically, it's really an important thing, in that a home run is worth about 1.4 runs on the average."

Adair crunched the numbers and concluded that, under standard conditions and using an 85-mph fastball as the gauge, "450 feet is about the maximum that ballplayers can hit the ball."

Of course, baseball isn't played under standard conditions, and any number of variations—a pitcher throwing 90-plus mph, the altitude of Coors Field, a doctored bat, a livelier ball, a smaller ballpark, a steroids-enhanced ballplayer—can change the dynamics.

All those factors have been cited as causes of the latest homer explosion that began in 1996 and continues unabated.

Home run sluggers are certainly the gladiators of the baseball diamond. They do it bigger than anyone else.

Few get to experience that sensation. Banks has done so more times than anyone but 15 men in history. He says, "I've forgotten what it feels like.

"You work so hard in spring training, in batting practice, to get that feeling again, to hit that ball solid," Banks said. "Sammy Sosa has a hop when he hits it, he gets that feeling, and he knows it, and hops in the air. Those who watch it know it's gone, and they rise up. Everyone has a feeling.

"I've had Mickey Mantle say to me, when he hit a home run, the feeling he had and the thought he had behind it, that someone might have driven 75, 100 miles to see him play, and to see him hit a home run, and it's so satisfying to him that it was worth people's time to come that distance and see him play and hit a home run.

"I still get it all the time from people who remember seeing me hit a home run and how much it meant to them. It's a major, major part of baseball. When I see kids playing Little League, boy, I like to see them hit a home run just one time, to get that feeling of it."

[2004]

When Red Sox Terminated
"The Curse of the Bambino"

BY DAN SHAUGHNESSY

They did it for the old folks in Presque Isle, Maine, and White River Junction, Vermont. They did it for the baby boomers in North Conway, New Hampshire, and Groton, Massachusetts. They did it for the kids in Central Falls, Rhode Island, and Putnam, Connecticut.

While church bells rang in small New England towns and horns honked on the crowded streets of the Hub, the 2004 Red Sox won the 100th World Series last October 27, completing a four-game sweep of the St. Louis Cardinals with a 3-0 victory on the strength of seven innings of three-hit pitching by Derek Lowe. Playing 1,042 miles from Fenway Park, the Sox won it all for the first time in 86 long and frustrating seasons.

"This is like an alternate reality," said Sox owner John W. Henry, soaked in champagne. "All of our fans waited their entire lives for this."

True. New England and a sprawling Nation of Sox fans can finally exhale. The Red Sox are world champs. No more Curse of the Bambino. No more taunts of "1918." The suffering souls of Bill Buckner, Grady Little, Mike Torrez, Johnny Pesky, and Denny Galehouse are released from Boston Baseball's Hall of Pain. The Red Sox are champions because they engineered the greatest comeback in baseball history when they won four straight games against the hated Yankees in the American League Championship Series. It was a baseball epic, an event for the ages putting the Sox into a World Series that was profoundly anticlimactic.

En route to eight consecutive postseason wins, the Sons of Tito Francona simply destroyed a Cardinal team that won a major-league-high 105 games in 2004. The Sox did not trail for a single inning of the four-game sweep. No Cardinal pitcher lasted more than six innings, and St. Louis's vaunted row of sluggers was smothered by the likes of Curt Schilling, Pedro Martinez, closer Keith Foulke, and Lowe. The Cards batted .190 in the Series with cleanup man Scott Rolen going 0-for-15.

In the finale, a game played under a full moon/lunar eclipse on the date of Boston's Game 7 loss in the excruciating 1986 World Series, Johnny Damon led off with a home run and the Sox were never threatened. Trot Nixon added a pair of runs with a bases-loaded double in the third. Lowe mowed down St Louis for seven innings, then let relievers Bronson Arroyo, Alan Embree, and Foulke finish the job.

It ended when Edgar Renteria went out on an easy grounder to Foulke. Foulke ran toward first and underhanded the ball to first baseman Doug

Mientkiewicz. A half-hour later, the historic ball was locked in the grasp of Mientkiewicz's right hand.

Manny Ramirez, who hit .412 with a homer and four RBI against the Cardinals, was named World Series MVP, almost exactly one year after the Sox put him on waivers. The Boston brass spent most of last winter trying to trade Ramirez for Alex Rodriguez. Now they are world champs and Manny is the MVP. Alternate reality, indeed.

"I think we learned a lot when we played against the Yankees," said Ramirez, "because we lost the first three games. And today I was talking to some of the guys and I said, 'Hey, let's go. Don't let these guys breathe.' We know what happened against New York. We came back. . . . So we came back and won."

And now it's time to toast to Ted Williams, Tom Yawkey, Sherm Feller, Dick O'Connell, Haywood Sullivan, Joe Cronin, Eddie Collins, Tony Conigliaro, Ned Martin, Helen Robinson, Jack Rogers, and thousands of others who toiled for the team but died before seeing their Sox win a World Series.

It's time for smiles on the faces of Carl Yastrzemski, Bobby Doerr, Dominic DiMaggio, Charlie Wagner, Gene Conley, Bill Monbouquette, Chuck Schilling, John McNamara, Joe Morgan, Earl Wilson, Mike Andrews, Reggie Smith, and hundreds of other men who wore the Red Sox uniform but never won in October. And don't forget Curt Gowdy, Lou Gorman, Dick Bresciani, Joe Mooney, and all the ushers and Sox employees who are as much a part of Fenway Park as the Green Monster and Pesky's Pole.

Time for the Nation to rejoice. Time to dance. Time to go to your window, open it wide, stick your head out and scream, "The Red Sox won the World Series." No one's been able to do that in Boston since Woodrow Wilson was president.

There was an air of inevitability about the Sox' prospects before the final game of the Fall Classic. The Sox knew they had the Cardinals on the mat and they knew that no team in hardball history ever came back from a 3-0 World Series deficit.

Busch Stadium was a friendly venue for swelling ranks of road-tripping Sox fans. Cardinal loyalists love their team but hold no hatred for the Bostonians, and one got the feeling that some St. Louis fans might have bailed and sold their tickets after the disheartening loss to the Sox in Game 3. There were a lot of Sox fans in the stands who lingered long after the final out.

Veteran Tim Wakefield was given the honor of carrying the World Series trophy out of the clubhouse and onto the field where the Sox celebrated with their families and acknowledged fans who remained in the stands cheering well over an hour after Foulke fielded the last grounder.

For the record, it took precisely six minutes for the first "Yankees Suck" chant to break out after the Red Sox finally won the World Series.

Lowe gave up a leadoff single in the first, then retired the next 13 Cardinals in order.

St. Louis sluggers took a lot of ugly swings. The Cardinals did not put up much of a fight. After just three innings, it felt like it was already over.

This is what it must have felt like in 1918.

"I thought we had a great scouting report," said Terry Francona, the first man to manage the Red Sox to a World Series win since Ed Barrow. "But what it comes down to is having really, really good pitchers."

Schilling, Martinez and Lowe had a composite ERA of 0.00 over the 20 innings they pitched, allowing only 14 base runners.

While Lowe mowed down the Cards, fans back home in New England chilled champagne, slipped tapes into VCRs, and prepared to wake infants so they could someday tell them they'd witnessed a historic event.

After celebrating on the field and in the visitors' clubhouse, the world champion Red Sox went back to their hotel, packed, and bused to the airport for a charter back to Boston.

If form holds, the Red Sox' gaudy, well-earned rings will be handed out in a ceremony April 11 when the 2004 World Series championship flag is raised above Fenway Park for the home opener.

The team in the third-base dugout for that historic event? The New York Yankees.

Sweet.

[2005]

Teamwork Keyed the White Sox Title Run

BY JOHN KUENSTER

In 2005 the Chicago White Sox relied on an impressive collaboration of talent that brought them their first World Series title in 88 years. Their brand of teamwork paid big dividends during a run that saw them win 11 of 12 postseason games, eliminating such challengers as the Red Sox, Angels, and Astros as they rose to the top of the baseball world.

"We ground it out from Day One," said left fielder Scott Podsednik after the White Sox beat the Astros, 1-0, in Game 4 of the Fall Classic. "No one cared about stats or themselves."

"Everybody was a part of this," added pitching coach Don Cooper. "We're a team without superstars, without big egos."

"They're special," said manager Ozzie Guillen, "because of the unity they have."

That unity was due in large measure to Guillen himself, described by some writers as a Hispanic Casey Stengel whose rapid, nonstop recitations mesmerized media ensembles throughout the playoffs.

"He keeps everybody happy and loose," said Jermaine Dye after receiving the World Series Most Valuable Player Award during the champagne-soaked celebration in the White Sox clubhouse in Houston following the sweep of the Astros. It was Dye's ground-hugging single up the middle that scored Willie Harris from third base with the winning run in the eighth inning of Game 4.

That particular turning point in a nail-biting, scoreless battle between starting pitchers Freddy Garcia and Brandon Backe reflected the way the White Sox gained an upper edge in

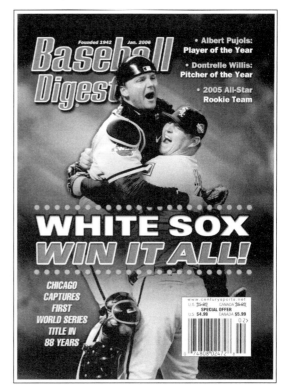

The January 2006 cover of *Baseball Digest* celebrated the improbable: the World Series-winning Chicago White Sox, champions again after 88 years.

many games last season by playing "small ball." Following that style, Guillen instinctively made the right move in sending the little-used Harris to pinch-hit for Garcia as the leadoff batter against the hard-throwing, right-hand relief pitcher Brad Lidge.

Harris bats left-handed and has speed. He slapped an opposite-field single to left. Next came Podsednik, and he sacrificed Harris to second. With two outs, Dye applied the coup de grace.

Earlier Guillen had made an adroit call in Game 3 when he sent pinch-hitter Geoff Blum to the plate in the 14th inning. With the score tied, 5-5, Blum—who ironically once played for the Astros—belted a home run to right field at Minute Maid Park off reliever Ezequiel Astacio. The Sox added another run and went on to win the marathon, 7-5.

While Chicago displayed strong starting and relief pitching, as well as clutch situational hitting and sound defense at critical junctures in the World Series, the team also applied power on offense to stymie the Astros. In Game 1, Dye homered in the first inning off Roger Clemens to give the Sox an early lead that moved on to a 5-3 victory.

Then in Game 2, Paul Konerko hit a grand slam and Podsednik delivered a ninth-inning blast to the right-center-field bleachers to close out a 7-6 triumph that turned the U.S. Cellular Field crowd into a state of mass frenzy on a chilly, rainy Sunday night.

Small ball, long ball, defense (third baseman Joe Crede, shortstop Juan Uribe) and pitching (Jose Contreras, Mark Buehrle, Jon Garland, Freddy Garcia, Neal Cotts, Bobby Jenks)—the White Sox had it all in 2005.

They were a diverse lot, with players who originated from the Dominican Republic, Venezuela, Japan, and Cuba, as well as from such states as Missouri, Georgia, California, Texas, Florida, Oregon, Illinois, New York, and even Rhode Island (Konerko). They showed the world Chicago doesn't always deserve its "second city" epithet. They carried through a class performance that involved all 25 members of their roster, even though Guillen shouted "Viva Venezuela! Viva los latinos!" at the end of an in-game interview during the World Series.

How good was this White Sox team? Konerko put that question in perspective after Game 4 had gone into the record books.

"We're different than a lot of teams that win the World Series," he said. "We've got a bunch of low-key guys. We're not a team that was a lock to win.

"We could start the playoffs tomorrow and get knocked off in three games because we aren't some unbelievably great team. We're just a team that played our best baseball when we had to."

They were able to do that because they reflected a unity based on the principle that the sum is greater than its individual parts.

"We had 25 guys pulling on the same rope," concluded Podsednik. "You can't get to where we are with just a couple of guys performing."

Last season the White Sox took the field accompanied by a team motto which read, "Win or die trying."

In the end, they won all their crucial games without showing any signs of cardiac arrest or even enduring a hiccup.

[2006]

Credits

Grateful acknowledgment is made to the following publications and individuals for permission to reprint articles that appeared in *Baseball Digest* in the years noted at the end of the articles in the text.

"Baseball's Best Batters" by Billy Evans, condensed from *Esquire* magazine. "Ty Cobb Thrived on Fierce Opposition" by Bob French, *Toledo Blade*. "Baseball in Paris, 1918" by Heywood Broun, from the book *The A.E.F., with General Pershing and the American Forces*. "How Connie Mack Passed Up Babe Ruth" by Red Smith, *Philadelphia Record*. "'34 Series Win, 'A Big Day in My Life'" by Dizzy Dean, as told to John P. Carmichael, *Chicago Daily News*. "When Goslin Edged Me Out for the Batting Title" by Heinie Manush, as told to John P. Carmichael, *Chicago Daily News*. "You Can't Kill the Umpire" by George Barr, condensed from *American* Magazine. "Pitchers Are Sissies Now" by Kid Nichols, as told to Sam Molen, condensed from *Pic* magazine. "Joe Jackson, Finest Natural Hitter of Them All" by Arthur Daley, *New York Times*. "The Messiest No-Hitter" by Red Smith, *New York Herald Tribune*.

"My Greatest Thrill as a Player" by Casey Stengel, as told to John P. Carmichael, *Chicago Daily News*. "Grover Alexander Shatters a Myth About '26 World Series" by Gerry Hern, *Boston Post*. "Ed Walsh Fanned the 'Big Three' on Nine Pitches" by Jimmy Cannon, *New York Post*. "Fighting Billy Martin" and "Roy Campanella's Tricks Behind the Plate" by Charles Dexter, courtesy of the author. "Jocko Conlan: 'Umpires Must Have Command and Respect'" by Robert Cromie, *Chicago Tribune*. "How the Braves Lost Out in Signing Willie Mays" by Sam Levy, *Milwaukee Journal*. "For All-Around Skill, 'You Should Have Seen Old Hans'" by Francis Stann, *Washington Star*. "How to Stay Alive on Second Base" by Nellie Fox, as told to Milton Richman, *This Week* magazine. "Did Buck Weaver Get a Raw Deal?" by James T. Farrell, courtesy of the author.

"That Called Homer? It Never Happened!" by Herbert Simons, courtesy of the author. "The Mickey Mantle I Know" by Merlyn Mantle, as told to Christy Munro, *Look Magazine*. "The Most Exciting Team Ever" by Jimmy Cannon, North American Newspaper Alliance. "What It Takes to Be a Winning Pitcher" by Roger Kahn, *New York Times Magazine*. "What Players Thought When Under Pressure" by John Kuenster, *Chicago Daily News*. "The Spitter That Lost the World Series" by Herbert Simons, courtesy of the author. "The Case of the Nervous Batter" by Leonard Koppett, *New York Post*. "Hornsby's Five Fabulous Years" by Tom Meany, from the book *Baseball's Greatest Hitters*, copyright 1950 by A. S. Barnes and Co. "How Early Wynn Made DiMaggio Quit" by Art Rosenbaum, *San Francisco Chronicle*. "The Lingering Shadow of the Iron Man" by Al Hirshberg, *Pageant* magazine.

"The First Baseman Who Outpitched Walter Johnson" by George Sisler, as told to Lyall Smith, *Chicago Daily News*. "Eddie Cicotte: 'I Did Wrong But I Paid for It'" by Joe Falls, *Detroit Free Press*. "My Double No-Hit Game" by Jim Vaughn, *Chicago Daily News*. "Jim Gilliam Recalls Tough Times in Negro Leagues" by John Wiebusch, *Los Angeles Times*. "How Casey Stengel Got His Nickname" by John Kuenster, *Baseball Digest*. "Don Drysdale Put His Brand on the Hitters and the Game" by Jim Murray, *Los Angeles Times*. "Rudy York's Letter to his Son" by Furman Bisher, *Atlanta Journal*. "What Baseball Needs Is a Little More Hostility" by Joe McGuff, *Kansas City Star*. "Home Run Record a Bitter Memory for Roger Maris" by Ira Berkow, *New York Times*. "Tragic Pitch Recalled by Carl Mays" by Jack Murphy, *San Diego Union*.

"Baseball—A Bridge Between Two Silences" by Frank L. Ryan, courtesy of the author. "Mental Blunders Are Part of the Game" by Edward Prell, courtesy of the author. "When the Cardinals Ended the Yankee Dynasty" by Tim McCarver, as told to Allen Lewis, courtesy of the author. "When a Midget Batted as a Major Leaguer" by Bob Broeg, *St. Louis Post-Dispatch*. "The Making of a Baseball Fanatic" by

Sister Mary Barbara Browne, C.S.C., courtesy of the author. "The Jackie Robinson I Knew" by Wendell Smith, *Chicago Sun-Times*. "Roberto Clemente Was a Sensitive Superstar" by Milton Richman, United Press International. "The Day I Got My 3,000th Hit" by Stan Musial, as told to George Vass, courtesy of the author. "The Day Cleveland Went Wild" by Lou Boudreau, as told to Irv Haag, courtesy of the author. "Andy Seminick Once Decimated the Giants' Infield" by Richie Ashburn, *Philadelphia Bulletin*.

"I Remember the Polo Grounds" by Jack Lang, courtesy of the author. "And Their Catchers Weren't Too Good, Either!" by Harold Rosenthal, courtesy of the author. "The Love Story of a Baseball Legend" by Brad Willson, *Daytona Beach News Journal*. "Ernie Banks, Baseball's Ambassador of Goodwill" by John Kuenster, *Baseball Digest*. "Curt Flood: Baseball's Forgotten Pioneer" by Murray Chass, *New York Times*. "Luck Had a Role in My Perfect No-Hitter" by Sandy Koufax, as told to George Vass, courtesy of the author. "Why the Red Sox Hate the Yankees" by Ray Fitzgerald, *Boston Globe*. "Stealing Home Is Not for the Faint of Heart" by Melvin Durslag, *Los Angeles Herald-Examiner*. "Lefty Gomez Enlivened the Game with Comedy" by Jerry D. Lewis, courtesy of the author. "Reggie's Moment Arrived in the '77 World Series" by Joe McGuff, *Kansas City Star*.

"Ted Williams Goes Back to Where It All Began" by Charles Maher, *Los Angeles Times*. "When Gabby Hartnett Hit His Homer in the Gloamin'" by John P. Carmichael, courtesy of the author. "The Bat: A Hitter's Most Prized, Pampered Possession" by Thomas Boswell, *Washington Post*. "Bob Uecker, Baseball's 'Rodney Dangerfield'" by Bob Verdi, *Chicago Tribune*. "How It Was in the Old Days of Class 'D' Baseball" by Ben Fanton, courtesy of the author. "Dad, How Come We Never Played Catch?" by Andy Lindstrom, courtesy of the author. "Warren Spahn Names His Toughest Batting Foes" by George White, *Houston Chronicle*. "The Mellowing of Leo 'The Lip' Durocher" by Richard Dozer, *Phoenix Gazette*. "Where Have All the Bench Jockeys Gone?" by Mark Kram, *Detroit Free Press*. "Pennant Fever Revives Cub Trivia Quiz" by Mike Royko, *Chicago Sun-Times*.

"Mental Discipline, Key to Defensive Excellence" by Peter Gammons, *Boston Globe*. "Memories of a Tryout with the New York Yankees" by Frank J. Vespe, courtesy of the author. "Hall of Famer Who Almost Didn't Make the Majors" and "The Mighty Mite Who Rarely Struck Out" by Walter M. Langford, courtesy of the author. "You Can Hear It *All* in the Batter's Box" by Bruce Keidan, *Pittsburgh Post-Gazette*. "When New York Was the Hub of the Baseball World" by Joe Donnelly, *Newsday*. "The True Story of Babe Ruth's Visit to an Ailing Youth" by Brian Sobel, courtesy of the author. "Ted Williams Talks About the Art of Hitting" by Ron Mentus, courtesy of the author. "Here's the Quickest Way to be Ejected from a Game" by Bob Hertzel, *Pittsburgh Press*. "Tom Seaver Picks His Ten Most Memorable Games" by Jack Lang, *New York Daily News*.

"1939 Was a Vintage Year in Major League History" by George Vass, courtesy of the author. "Memories of My Opening Day No-Hitter" by Bob Feller, from the book *Now Pitching: Bob Feller*, courtesy of the Carol Publishing Group. "Remembering the Tree That Played Center Field" by Furman Bisher, *Atlanta Journal and Constitution*. "I Can Always Go Back" by Jon Beatty Fish, courtesy of the author. "Rickey Henderson . . . There He Goes!" by Kirk Kenney, *San Diego Tribune*. "The Persuasive Healing Powers of Baseball Trivia" by Stephen D. Boren, M.D., courtesy of the author. "The Game I'll Never Forget" by Ryne Sandberg, as told to George Vass, courtesy of the author. "Pursuit of Home Run Record Extracted a Big Toll on Aaron" by Bruce Lowitt, *St. Petersburg Times*. "Aging Baseball Glove Leaves a Touching Legacy" by Gary Schwab, *Charlotte Observer*. "Hall of Fame Batters and Pitchers Name Their Toughest Opponents" by William J. Guilfoile, courtesy of the author.

"Farewell to Mickey Mantle, One of Baseball's Greatest" by Dave van Dyck, *Chicago Sun-Times*. "High School Coach Recalls Nolan Ryan as Young Pitcher" by Jim Kreuz, courtesy of the author. "Hack Wilson Belted Homers, Hecklers with Equal Gusto" by John B. Holway, courtesy of the author. "How Outfielder Pete Gray Met Big League Challenge" by John Steadman, *Baltimore Sun*. "A Belated Salute to Four Old Ballparks" by Raymond Miller, courtesy of the author. "The Day I Collected Babe Ruth's Autograph" by John Deedy, *Worcester Magazine*. "Larry Doby: An Overlooked Black Pioneer in the American League" by Ira Berkow, *New York Times*. "Life in the Bullpen" by Jerry Crasnick, *Denver Post*. "Veteran Umpire Says Managers Were More Defiant Years Ago" by John Kuenster, *Baseball Digest*. "I Never Turned the Other Cheek" by Bill Rogell, as told to Nick C. Wilson, courtesy of the author.

"Trickery Has Always Been Part of Big League Baseball" by Wayne Lockwood, *San Diego Union-Tribune*. "Hall of Famers Recount Lasting Memories of Major League Debuts" by John Kuenster, *Baseball Digest*. "Dowd Report Details Extensive Gambling on Baseball by Pete Rose" by John Kuenster, *Baseball Digest*. "Why Left-Handers are Different" by Gerry Fraley, *Dallas Morning News*. "Cal Ripken: More Than Baseball's Iron Man" by Phil Rogers, *Chicago Tribune*. "Jimmy Piersall's Antics Overshadowed His Talent" by Bob Dolgan, *Cleveland Plain Dealer*. "Tony Gwynn Strived for Perfection as a Hitter" by Chris Jenkins, *San Diego Union-Tribune*. "First Base, the Game's Social Hub" by David Andriesen, *Seattle Post-Intelligencer*. "Sign Language, Baseball's Hidden Communication" by Larry Stone, *Seattle Times*. "Secret to My Perfect Game Was Good Control" by Don Larsen, as told to Al Doyle, courtesy of the author.

"In '52, Virgil Trucks Won Only Five Games, But Two Were No-Hitters" by Bill Dow, *Detroit Free Press*. "Fielders List Most Difficult Defensive Plays by Position" by Jack Etkin, *Rocky Mountain News*. "Ichiro Suzuki: Hitting Sensation" by Dave van Dyck, courtesy of the author. "The Home Run, Baseball's Glamour Event" by Larry Stone, *Seattle Times*. "When Red Sox Terminated 'The Curse of the Bambino'" by Dan Shaughnessy, *Boston Globe*.

Index

A NOTE ON THE EDITOR

John Kuenster has been editor of *Baseball Digest* and executive editor of Century Publishing Company in Evanston, Illinois, since 1969. A former staff writer and columnist for the *Chicago Daily News*, he has spent his life in journalism and has written extensively for newspapers and magazines. He is a former president of the Chicago Chapter of the Baseball Writers Association of America and has also edited *From Cobb to Catfish*, a baseball anthology. With David Cowan he wrote *To Sleep with the Angels*, a widely praised account of the Our Lady of the Angels school fire in Chicago. Mr. Kuenster lives with his wife Sue in Evergreen Park, Illinois, while the rest of the family, including eight children, twenty grandchildren, and eight great grandchildren, reside in the Chicago area.